From Roosevelt to Truman

Potsdam, Hiroshima, and the Cold War

On April 12, 1945, Franklin Roosevelt died and Harry Truman took his place in the White House. Historians have been arguing ever since about the implications of this transition for American foreign policy in general and relations with the Soviet Union in particular. Was there essential continuity in policy, or did Truman's arrival in the Oval Office prompt a sharp reversal away from the approach of his illustrious predecessor? This study explores this controversial issue and in the process casts important light on the outbreak of the Cold War. *From Roosevelt to Truman* investigates Truman's foreign policy background and examines the legacy that FDR bequeathed to him. After Potsdam and the American use of the atomic bomb, both occurring during Truman's presidency, the United States floundered between collaboration and confrontation with the Soviets. The resolution of this debate represents a turning point in the transformation of American foreign policy. This work reveals that the real departure in American policy came only after the Truman administration had exhausted the legitimate possibilities of the Rooseveltian approach of collaboration with the Soviet Union.

Wilson D. (Bill) Miscamble, C.S.C., was born in Roma, Australia, and educated at the University of Queensland. He pursued graduate studies in history at the University of Notre Dame, where he received his doctorate in 1980. He then served for two years as North American Analyst in the Office of National Assessments, Department of Prime Minister and Cabinet, Canberra, Australia. In August 1982, he returned to Notre Dame and entered the priesthood formation program of the Congregation of Holy Cross of which he is now a member. He was ordained a priest in 1988 and has taught at Notre Dame since then. He chaired the History Department from 1993 to 1998. His book *George F. Kennan and the Making of American Foreign Policy, 1947–1950* (1992), received the Harry S. Truman Book Award. He also authored *Keeping the Faith, Making a Difference* (2000) and edited *American Political History: Essays on the State of the Discipline* (with John Marszalek, 1997). He has published a number of articles, essays, and reviews and has received a number of awards for his teaching at Notre Dame.

From Roosevelt to Truman

Potsdam, Hiroshima, and the Cold War

WILSON D. MISCAMBLE, C.S.C.

University of Notre Dame

CAMBRIDGE
UNIVERSITY PRESS

CAMBRIDGE UNIVERSITY PRESS
Cambridge, New York, Melbourne, Madrid, Cape Town, Singapore, São Paulo

Cambridge University Press
32 Avenue of the Americas, New York, NY 10013-2473, USA

www.cambridge.org
Information on this title: www.cambridge.org/9780521862448

First published 2007

Printed in the United States of America

A catalog record for this publication is available from the British Library.

Library of Congress Cataloging in Publication Data

Miscamble, Wilson D., 1954–
From Roosevelt to Truman : Potsdam, Hiroshima, and
the Cold War / Wilson D. Miscamble.
    p.   cm.
Includes bibliographical references.
ISBN-13: 978-0-521-86244-8 (hardback)
ISBN-10: 0-521-86244-2 (hardback)
1. United States – Foreign relations – 1945–1953.   2. Truman, Harry S., 1884–1972.
3. World War, 1939–1945 – Diplomatic history.   4. World War, 1939–1945 – United States.
5. Nuclear warfare – United States.
327.73009′044–dc22   2005036290

ISBN-13   978-0-521-86244-8 hardback
ISBN-10   0-521-86244-2 hardback

To
my sister and brother
Jenny & Phillip ofm

Contents

Preface

On April 12, 1945, the United States Senate recessed around five o'clock, and its presiding officer, Vice President Harry S. Truman, walked leisurely to the office of House Speaker Sam Rayburn for end-of-day drinks and conversation. As soon as he arrived, Rayburn told Truman to call presidential press secretary Steve Early, who immediately summoned him to the White House. Expecting to see President Franklin Roosevelt, he was ushered instead into the study of Eleanor Roosevelt. "Harry," she informed him, "the President is dead." Momentarily stunned, Truman eventually spoke and asked with genuine concern, "Is there anything I can do for you?" Mrs. Roosevelt replied insightfully: "Is there anything we can do for you for you are the one in trouble now."[1] Within two hours, Truman recited the oath of office, becoming the thirty-third president of the United States. Immediately after his swearing-in ceremony, the new president addressed the hastily convened cabinet. "It was my intention," Truman recalled saying, "to continue both the foreign and domestic policies of the Roosevelt Administration."[2] How effectively he fulfilled this promise has been the subject of intense discussion ever since.[3]

Over the last four decades, historians of various stripes waged a serious debate over how well – if at all – Truman fulfilled his commitment to continue Roosevelt's foreign policy, particularly his policy toward the Soviet Union. Some historians framed the question rather pejoratively as in the case of Thomas G. Paterson who asked, "How much of a difference did it make that a parochial, ill-informed, impatient man like Harry S. Truman replaced a cosmopolitan, knowledgeable Roosevelt just when the international system was undergoing

---

[1] This account is taken mainly from Truman's memoir. See Harry S. Truman, *Memoirs*, Vol. I, *Year of Decisions* (New York, 1955), p. 15.

[2] Truman, *Year of Decisions*, p. 19.

[3] Among some of the early critics of Truman for failing to follow FDR's lead were Roosevelt's one-time advisers, Joseph E. Davies and Henry Morgenthau, Jr., and Roosevelt's son Elliott who made his charges in his 1946 memoir *As He Saw It*. See the discussion of these in Thomas G. Paterson, *Meeting the Communist Threat: Truman to Reagan* (New York, 1988), p. 100.

tremendous change?"[4] However slanted this particular formulation may be, the key issue remains clear. What difference did the transition in American leadership from FDR to Harry Truman exert on U.S. foreign policy in general and on relations with the Soviets in particular?

Beginning especially in the 1960s, some historians discerned a sharp break between the policies of the two presidents such that they assigned a large measure of responsibility for the onset of the Cold War to Truman and his supposedly hard-line advisers.[5] In this view, Truman reversed a relatively successful policy of cooperation with the Soviet Union and, in so doing, provoked the dissolution of the Grand Alliance. In effect, the death of Franklin Delano Roosevelt brought on the Cold War. Historians of both orthodox and revisionist persuasions vigorously disputed this thesis.[6] Most orthodox historians denied a reversal in policy, although disagreements existed within the group over the nature of the policy that Roosevelt left Truman to continue. Herbert Feis, the undisputed dean of the orthodox school, argued that Truman pursued FDR's firm but conciliatory policy, while Arthur Schlesinger, Jr., argued that the basis for continuity rested in Roosevelt's prior conversion to a relatively tough policy toward the Soviets.[7] On the revisionist side, historians like Gabriel Kolko, who emphasized the causal force of America's expansionist, capitalist political-economic system, largely dismissed the role of personalities and downplayed the impact of Truman's accession to power on American policy toward the Soviet Union.[8] These various (and rather contradictory) responses failed to stem the tide of arguments that portrayed Truman's arrival in the Oval Office as a crucial way-station on the road to the Cold War.

In substantiating their thesis of a reversal in policy toward the Soviet Union, its proponents focused especially upon Truman's meeting with Soviet Foreign

---

[4] Thomas G. Paterson quoted in Mark J. White, "Harry Truman, the Polish Question, and the Significance of FDR's Death for American Diplomacy," *Maryland Historian*, 23 (Fall/Winter 1992), p. 29. Paterson concedes that "postwar conflict would have been present no matter which man was present," but he argues that "Roosevelt was more patient with the Russians, more willing to settle issues at the conference table, more tame and less abusive in his language, less abrupt in his decisions, and more solicitous of Soviet opinion and fears than was Truman." Noting the significance of these differences in "tactics and the mechanics of policymaking," he declares them as contributing to the onset of the Cold War. See Thomas G. Paterson, *On Every Front: The Making of the Cold War* (New York, 1992), p 112.

[5] For early versions of this interpretation, see Denna F. Fleming, *The Cold War and Its Origins, 1917–1960*, 2 vols. (Garden City, NY, 1961), I, pp. 265–89; Gar Alperovitz, *Atomic Diplomacy: Hiroshima and Potsdam* (New York, 1965); and Diane Shaver Clemens, *Yalta* (New York, 1970), pp. 267–91.

[6] For a good survey of the early literature on the Cold War that clarifies the various schools of interpretation, see J. Samuel Walker, "Historians and Cold War Origins: The New Consensus," in Gerald K. Haines and J. Samuel Walker, eds., *American Foreign Relations: A Historiographical Review* (Westport, CT, 1981), pp. 207–36.

[7] Herbert Feis, *Churchill Roosevelt Stalin: The War They Waged and the Peace They Sought*, 2nd ed. (Princeton, NJ, 1967), pp. 596–600; Arthur M. Schlesinger, Jr., "Origins of the Cold War," *Foreign Affairs*, 46 (October 1967), p. 24.

[8] Gabriel Kolko, *The Politics of War: The World and United States Foreign Policy, 1943–1945* (New York, 1968), pp. 381–82.

Minister Molotov on April 23, a meeting at which, according to columnist Drew Pearson's colorful description, Molotov "heard Missouri mule driver's language."[9] At this celebrated clash, Truman reprimanded Molotov for the Soviet failure to carry out the Yalta accord on Poland, sharply curtailed the Soviet minister's attempt at an explanation, and stated bluntly "that he desired the friendship of the Soviet government but that it could only be on the basis of mutual observation of agreements and not on the basis of a one way street."[10] Although Charles Bohlen's official minutes do not record the incident, Truman claimed that in an acrimonious final exchange Molotov exclaimed that "I have never been talked to like that in my life," to which he retorted: "Carry out your agreements and you won't get talked to like that."[11]

The April 23 meeting with Molotov and the discussions Truman had with his advisers prior to it served as the keystone of arguments for a reversal of policy. Daniel Yergin in his influential *Shattered Peace*, published in 1977, argued that what was said at the meeting "signified a major shift in American attitudes towards the Russians" and that the exchange "symbolized the beginning of the postwar divergence that led to confrontation."[12] This essential position has been argued more recently by historians like Warren Kimball and Diane S. Clemens. The former argued that "there was a sharp reversal in presidential policy once Harry S. Truman took over that office" and that "it seems that Roosevelt's death provided an opportunity for what came to be called Cold War ideology to set the broad strategy for American diplomacy."[13] The latter contended that "beginning in March and culminating in late April 1945, a political battle was fought in the highest echelons of the government of the United States, the objective of which was to overturn the wartime policy of cooperation with the Soviet Union. As long as Franklin D. Roosevelt remained president, the attempt failed; but in the aftermath of his death, it was successful."[14] More notably, this reversal thesis has trickled down, so to speak, into influential textbooks and found an eager expression in more popular histories of the Cold War and is now widely held.[15]

---

[9] Drew Pearson quoted in Fleming, *The Cold War and Its Origins*, I, p. 268.

[10] Memorandum of conversation by Charles E. Bohlen, April 23, 1945, *FRUS*, 1945, V, pp. 256–58.

[11] Truman, *Year of Decisions*, p. 82.

[12] Daniel Yergin, *Shattered Peace: The Origins of the Cold War and the National Security State* (Boston, 1977), pp. 73, 83.

[13] See Warren F. Kimball, *The Juggler: Franklin Roosevelt as Wartime Statesman* (Princeton, NJ, 1991), p. 180.

[14] Diane S. Clemens, "Averell Harriman, John Deane, the Joint Chiefs of Staff, and the 'Reversal of Co-operation' with the Soviet Union in April of 1945," *International History Review*, 14 (May 1992), p. 277.

[15] On textbooks, see for example Paul S. Boyer, *Promises to Keep: The United States Since World War II* (Lexington, MA, 1995), pp. 42–43; and William Chafe, *The Unfinished Journey: America Since World War II*, 3rd ed. (New York, 1995), pp. 56–57. On popular histories, see Martin Walker, *The Cold War and the Making of the Modern World* (London, 1993), p. 19, which presents April 23 as the moment "when the balance in American policy began to shift, away from Roosevelt's wartime trust, to Truman's post-war suspicion."

The lively plot line of the new president sharply reversing his predecessor's conciliatory policy and violently berating the foreign minister of an Allied nation possesses a certain dramatic quality. It surely satisfies those who like their stories of the past served up simplistically and in the stark colors of black and white. But for those who seek a fuller understanding of the past, a more nuanced and careful approach is required – one that sets the Truman–Molotov meeting in its proper context and appreciates that it was but a single episode in a sustained series of actions during Truman's early months in office. One must resist the temptation to use a single incident as emblematic of his whole approach to the Soviets. More exploration is needed to understand how successfully – if at all – Harry Truman fulfilled his commitment to continue his vaunted predecessor's policies. This study undertakes such an exploration and seeks to resolve the matter as to whether Roosevelt's death should be portrayed as representing "a turning-point in American foreign policy."[16]

This study unashamedly is Washington-centered and, to a significant extent, White House–centered, although it records the influences upon and the constraints applied to American policy by other powers and their representatives. In this regard, it avoids a tendency in some American studies to present the emergence of the Cold War as a drama with only two principals, the United States and the Soviet Union.[17] Here the British role is not ignored, and the significant contributions of the British policy makers Winston Churchill, Anthony Eden, Clement Attlee, and Ernest Bevin are duly noted. It rests upon a firm conviction that the existing and substantial literature on the Truman administration's foreign policy neither has discerned correctly the full meaning of the presidential transition from Franklin Roosevelt nor has understood adequately and explained the development of the policies his successor pursued after April 12, 1945.[18]

Although a quite separate study, this work's conceptual approach builds upon and borrows from my earlier effort to understand the development of policies in the State Department during a later period of Truman's presidency.[19]

---

[16] The issue is framed this way in Mark J. White, "Harry Truman, the Polish Question, and the Significance of FDR's Death for American Diplomacy," p. 29.

[17] This tendency is evident in Melvyn P. Leffler's *A Preponderance of Power: National Security, the Truman Administration and the Cold War* (Stanford, CA, 1992).

[18] Some recent studies have addressed related aspects of this book's subject. See Michael Beschloss's *The Conquerors: Roosevelt, Truman and the Destruction of Hitler's Germany, 1941–1945* (New York, 2002), which focused on policy toward Germany, and J. Robert Moskin, *Mr. Truman's War: The Final Victories of World War II and the Birth of the Postwar World* (New York, 1996), which mainly discussed the military defeats of Germany and Japan. The best study of American policy making during the period considered by this book remains John Lewis Gaddis, *The United States and the Origins of the Cold War, 1941–1947* (New York, 1972). Also insightful are Randall B. Woods and Howard Jones, *Dawning of the Cold War: The United States' Quest for Order* (Athens, GA, 1991), and Robert James Maddox, *From War to Cold War: The Education of Harry S. Truman* (Boulder, CO, 1988).

[19] Wilson D. Miscamble, *George F. Kennan and the Making of American Foreign Policy, 1947–1950* (Princeton, NJ, 1992).

The present study likewise adopts what Barry Rubin has termed "a middle ground between two extremes: the dry diplomatic history that presents decisions as clear-cut and inevitable by omitting the clash and blend of motives, personalities, abilities, and even accidents that occur in the policy process, and the journalistic account focusing on gossip and personalities to the exclusion of fundamental issues and options."[20] It seeks to capture something of the world of the policy makers, especially Truman, with its inevitable compromises, ultimate objectives only dimly perceived, and constantly competing pressures that confused and obscured policy vision.[21] It accepts the complexity, the uncertainty, the sheer messiness of policy making and tries to convey the tense atmosphere in which policy makers usually worked, the heavy pressures they endured, and the complex of influences that weighed upon them.

My approach is much influenced by the insight of the British historian C. V. Wedgwood that "history is lived forward but it is written in retrospect. We know the end before we consider the beginning and we can never wholly recapture what it was like to know the beginning only."[22] This study attempts to avoid simply reading history backwards and writing of Truman's foreign policy in light of subsequent Cold War events. My effort has been to provide some sense of the evolution and development of policy from the perspective of Truman as a maker of it and to avoid the unrealistic and rather mechanical quality that characterizes many studies of American diplomatic history. I accept the premise that individuals can and do make a difference in foreign policy as one can appreciate readily by imagining the course of events if Henry Wallace had won the vice-presidential nomination in 1944 rather than Truman. Events then might easily have turned out quite differently, to state the obvious.

In pursuing this study of the development of the Truman administration's foreign policy, a genuine effort has been made to treat the president as more than a one-dimensional figure. Truman has often been misunderstood by both his defenders and his critics and presented in an overly simplistic manner as a plain-spoken, straightforward, decisive figure best captured by the motto proudly displayed on his desk – "the buck stops here."[23] In reality, he was a more complex man blessed with certain strengths and beset with notable limitations who was occasionally given to uncertainty and indecision on matters of foreign policy. Understanding this more complicated figure allows for a deeper appreciation of his foreign policy as I trust this study well clarifies. It is indebted to Truman's recent biographers, especially to Robert H. Ferrell for clarifying so

---

[20] Barry Rubin, *Secrets of State: The State Department and the Struggle Over U.S. Foreign Policy* (New York, 1985), p. xi.

[21] This relies on Lisle Rose's discussion of the gulf between "the writing of history and the effective making of it" in his "The Trenches and the Towers: Differing Perspectives on the Writing and Making of American Diplomatic History," *Pacific Historical Review*, 55 (February 1986), p. 99.

[22] C. V. Wedgwood, *William the Silent* (New York, 1967), p. 35.

[23] This point is well made in Alonzo L. Hamby, "An American Democrat: A Reevaluation of the Personality of Harry S. Truman," *Political Science Quarterly*, 106 (Spring 1991), p. 35–37.

well Truman's talents and toughness as a politician and to Alonzo Hamby for revealing the more complex Truman personality in such compelling fashion.[24]

The overly simplified view of Truman usually portrays him as a veritable blank sheet with regard to foreign policy when he became president. This view neglects his range of involvements and experiences in the foreign policy domain prior to taking office and the deep convictions he brought to it. This study initially investigates Truman's foreign policy background because an appreciation of it is essential to understanding his early actions as president. Any assessment of these actions depends upon a clear grasp of the legacy that FDR bequeathed to Truman. Clarifying Roosevelt's hopes and plans for the postwar world is an obvious prerequisite for determining if Truman continued or reversed his policies. Had the Teheran and Yalta conferences settled divisive issues within the Grand Alliance such that a steady and cooperative course had been charted? Are there grounds for conjecture about what Herbert Mitgang has termed "the great might-have-been," which resides in "whether post-war Soviet-American relations would have been different had Roosevelt lived."[25] Was the postwar peace lost because of FDR's death? Or is such conjecture mere wishful thinking? Was President Roosevelt in reality in the process of reversing his own policy of cooperation by April 1945 and already moving along the road to becoming the "Cold Warrior" that Truman later became?[26]

Upon locating Truman in the Oval Office, this work looks in detail at his first challenging days in office culminating with his controversial meeting with Molotov on April 23. It identifies the pressures and influences upon him and indicates those advisers – including a notable foreigner – who guided his actions. It then proceeds to track Truman's policy making in the months prior to the Potsdam Conference. The effort is to discern not only what Truman did but also *why* he did it. In doing so, I seek to borrow from the biographer's approach of

---

[24] Ferrell presents Truman as a political professional who possessed "extraordinary talents." See Robert H. Ferrell, *Harry S. Truman: A Life* (Columbia, MO, 1994), p. 92. For Hamby's effort to "demythologize [Truman] but not to debunk him," see his *Man of the People: A Life of Harry S. Truman* (New York, 1995), p. 641. His work has been especially important for this study. I also have benefited from David McCullough's eminently readable *Truman* (New York, 1992), which, while presenting an overly "heroic" Truman, captures something of the drama and importance of the events in which Truman was involved. Let me also note the influence upon me of a brilliant (and highly favorable) essay on Truman by Max Lerner – "Harry S Truman: The Plutarchian President," in Max Lerner, *Wounded Titans: American Presidents and the Perils of Power*, ed. Robert Schmuhl (New York, 1996), pp. 187–217.

[25] Herbert Mitgang, "Of Three Unlikely Allies and Their Conflicts," *New York Times*, July 23, 1991, p. C16.

[26] On this point, note Robert Dallek's observations regarding FDR that "in the last weeks of his life he was already moving towards an accommodation with the likelihood of a postwar U.S.-Soviet clash," and furthermore that "the inevitable collapse of the wartime friendship would have turned FDR into a tough-minded Cold Warrior as determined to defend America's national interest against Soviet Communism as he had been to protect it from the Nazi-fascist threat." Robert Dallek, *Franklin D. Roosevelt and American Foreign Policy, 1932–1945* (New York, 1995), p. 551. These observations are included in an "Afterword" added in 1995.

"retrieving a set of mental processes" that the new president applied.[27] Which advisers did he find most trustworthy? Did they change during these months, and, if so, why? How did Truman as a neophyte leader deal with the other principal members of the Grand Alliance – the Soviet Union and Great Britain – and their erstwhile leaders Joseph Stalin and Winston Churchill?

As the reader will assuredly note, Truman's policy making can't be understood in a static manner. It must be discerned while appreciating the dynamic of constantly changing circumstances. One of the most significant of these was the movement toward the successful testing of the atomic bomb, which raised crucial questions about how the new and powerful weapon should be used both in war and in diplomacy. Did the likely possession of the atomic bomb transform American military calculations as the war came to an end and alter U.S. intentions toward its Soviet ally?[28] Should the bombing of Hiroshima be seen as the opening salvo in the Cold War as Gar Alperovitz suggested so provocatively more than forty years ago?[29] How is the Potsdam conference, Truman's one and only exercise in Big Three summitry, related to America's possession of the A-bomb? Would FDR have used the atomic weapons in the manner that Truman authorized? Would his approach have been similar at the concluding summit of the Second World War?

In the aftermath of the Potsdam meeting, Truman entrusted much of the responsibility for the execution of American foreign policy to his new secretary of state, James F. Byrnes, who served in this capacity until George C. Marshall succeeded him at the beginning of 1947. American endeavors during Byrnes's secretaryship are not susceptible to easy categorization. There are obvious attempts at cooperation and instances of confrontation with the Soviets, and at times the United States edged somewhat to the sidelines as the British clashed more directly with the Soviets. Clarifying the main developments over the period and their causes is the object here. Clearly after 1947, Truman led a major transformation of American foreign policy. The United States assumed sweeping new international obligations motivated in large part by a desire to preserve the security of the noncommunist world from perceived Soviet expansionism. As is well known, for example, the United States worked to secure the political and economic recovery of the European democracies devastated by a brutal war, and it joined them in forging a military alliance committed to the defense of Western Europe. A new conceptual worldview of America's

---

[27] This borrows from John Lewis Gaddis's discussion of the biographer's task in Gaddis, *The Landscape of History: How Historians Map the Past* (New York, 2002), p. 114.

[28] Richard B. Frank raises the issue of a transformation of military calculations in the final months of the war in his *Downfall: The End of the Imperial Japanese Empire* (New York, 1999), p. xviii.

[29] Alperovitz first published *Atomic Diplomacy* in 1965 and a revised and expanded edition in 1985. For the revised edition, see Gar Alperovitz, *Atomic Diplomacy: Hiroshima and Potsdam – The Use of the Atomic Bomb and the American Confrontation with Soviet Power*, rev. ed. (New York, 1985). See also Alperovitz's later effort *The Decision to Use the Atomic Bomb and the Architecture of an American Myth* (New York, 1995).

international role surely was framed during Truman's tenure as president. When the Missourian consigned his office to Dwight D. Eisenhower on January 20, 1953, the United States stood unmistakably as a global power with global interests committed to playing a central and abiding role in international affairs and locked in a deep and protracted conflict with the Soviet Union. One might ask if such a result could be seen as consistent with the directions that Franklin Roosevelt had consigned to his successor in April 1945.

Perhaps as the foregoing suggests, this work is mainly one of a "splitter" as opposed to a "lumper" (to borrow yet again J. H. Hexter's terminology which John Gaddis has made so familiar to American diplomatic historians). It at least partly resists the lumper's temptation "to systematize complexity [and] to reduce the chaos, disorder and sheer untidiness of history to neat patterns."[30] But this is not to suggest that this work does not have implications for lumpers and splitters alike, and I seek in the concluding chapter to draw these out and to clarify their meaning for the debate over America's participation in the Cold War and its responsibility for it. Now that the Cold War is over, one strain of thinking suggests that there is no longer any need for historians to go on fighting it, as it were.[31] In this time of transition from one discernible era in international relations to another, this sense might be seen as an understandable desire to move beyond the Cold War and to avoid undue celebration of the American triumph in it. Yet the central importance of the Cold War to the twentieth century cannot be disputed. To avoid seeking to understand it more fully is to engage in a most curious scholarly denial. Given the moral and political stakes involved in the Cold War, its enormous impact on the postwar world, and its implications for the present, the historian is obliged to continue the work of comprehending better its origins and course. This study aims to further that endeavor.

---

[30] John Lewis Gaddis, *Strategies of Containment: A Critical Appraisal of Postwar American National Security Policy* (New York, 1982), pp. vii–viii.

[31] Michael Hogan exhibits something of this in his uncharacteristically vituperative review essay, "The Vice Men of Foreign Policy," *Reviews in American History*, 21 (June 1993), pp. 320–28.

Acknowledgments

I can say without fear of any contradiction that this book has been some years in the making. In fact, its origins lie in work I did as a graduate student at the University of Queensland thirty years ago. I renewed my serious engagement with the topic in the early 1990s after completing my book on George F. Kennan and the Policy Planning Staff. However, my appointment in 1994 as chair of the History Department at the University of Notre Dame pushed my research and writing of this book to the "back burner." My subsequent appointment as Rector of Moreau Seminary at Notre Dame removed it from the metaphorical stove altogether. With the completion of my service as Rector in 2004 and with the benefit of a sabbatical year at Yale University, I finished the research and writing of the book the reader presently holds. I am very glad to have done so because I now have an acceptable answer to the many people who inquired over the past years as to the progress of my "Truman book." That answer is, of course, that it is now available for purchase!

In the course of completing this study, in rather episodic fashion over this lengthy period, I have acquired debts to both people and institutions. I wish to acknowledge them here, although, of course, the responsibility for the study's contents belongs solely to me. In identifying those to whom I am grateful, I fear that I might have forgotten someone. If so, let me apologize for that in advance.

My initial work on this topic took form as a M.A. thesis at the University of Queensland under the direction of Joseph M. Siracusa. He introduced me to the study of American diplomatic history and to serious historical research. I value his continued friendship and support. My doctoral mentor at Notre Dame, Vincent P. DeSantis, has been a constant source of encouragement for me to remain committed to my work as a historian, especially when other responsibilities seemed to be leading me down a different path. I am glad that we now do some co-teaching, and I look forward to addressing the subjects raised in this book in his courses in the future.

I owe my greatest debt for their work on this book to my colleagues Thomas Blantz, C.S.C., and Steven J. Brady. Each has read every word of the manuscript and commented upon it at length. They are true friends. Others who read parts of the manuscript and offered helpful comments include John Lewis Gaddis, Robert Jervis, Diane B. Kunz, Bruce H. Smith, and John Young, C.S.C. Stephen M. Koeth, C.S.C., took time away from his own studies to give the next-to-final draft of the manuscript a careful reading and made helpful corrections. My two readers from Cambridge University Press made valuable suggestions that ultimately led to improvements in the book. Robert Beisner graciously shared his forthcoming study of Dean Acheson, which helped me clarify significant matters of interpretation. Marc Tractenberg generously shared his thoughts regarding the Potsdam settlement and made available source materials from his *A Constructed Peace.*

In addition to the work of Beisner and Trachtenberg, I am indebted to the historians of American foreign policy whose studies I have drawn from in completing this book. Readers of the footnotes will note the large number of scholars from whose labors I benefited, but I must make special note of Robert H. Ferrell, Richard B. Frank, John Lewis Gaddis, Alonzo L. Hamby, Fraser J. Harbutt, Warren F. Kimball, Deborah Welch Larson, Elizabeth Kimball MacLean, Eduard M. Mark, David Robertson, Gaddis Smith, and Randall Bennett Woods. I especially want to express my debt to Robert H. Ferrell for his fine example of scholarly integrity and for his great editing work, which has made so many primary source materials easily available to other historians. On a more personal level, I want to express my gratitude to Thomas Alan Schwartz and Diane Kunz for their continued friendship, which, in ways they probably don't appreciate, has helped sustain my scholarly work. My friend Jim McAdams, director of the Nanovic Institute for European Studies at Notre Dame, gave me sound advice on publishing this book and on other matters.

Over the years I have had a number of student research assistants aid me in various endeavors. Some may have helped in researching this book, while others might only have been forced to listen to me whine about how I wasn't working on the book. I dubbed each of these able folk as "chief of staff," and I am glad to thank here: Lina Ona Balciunas, Emily Todd Bastedo, Carolyn D'Amore, Laura Holland Hoey, Laura Keane Sanderson, Carol Dominguez Shay, and Paul Wasinger. In the History Department at Notre Dame, Myrtle Doaks and Jackie Wyatt have provided me with administrative support and with friendship as have Judy Kuzmich and Diane Welihan at Moreau Seminary. I trust they know how I appreciate both.

In a very basic way, archivists and librarians have made my work possible and I readily acknowledge my debt to the staffs of all the libraries and archives listed in the bibliography. I want to specifically thank my friends at the Harry S. Truman Library, especially Liz Safly and Randy Sowell for their willingness to assist me – even at long distance! The staff of the National Archives Photographic Branch, from where I obtained the photos used in this book, also proved most cooperative and efficient. I was able to test out certain of the arguments offered in this book on various audiences at the National War College, Old Dominion University, the Cold War History Group at the University of California at Santa Barbara, and Sacred Heart University and with my colleagues in the History Department at Notre Dame. I'm grateful to those who organized for me to speak and to those who offered their response to my work.

Institutional debts which I must note are to the History Department of the University of Notre Dame; to the Institute for Scholarship in the Liberal Arts at Notre Dame, which awarded me two research grants; to Dean Mark Roche of the College of Arts and Letters at Notre Dame; to the Harry S. Truman Institute for National and International Affairs; to the Congregation of Holy Cross who "carried" me for a year; and to the International Security Studies Center at Yale University, where I was a visiting Fellow in 2004–5. I also must thank all the fine people at Cambridge University Press who contributed to the preparation and production of this book. Lewis Bateman gave support from the outset. I trust I might have the chance to work with him again. I also thank Ciara E. McLaughlin, Camilla T. Knapp, and Sara Black for their assistance. It has been a pleasure to work with them. Cynthia Landeen prepared the index with competence and dispatch.

George Kennan once pointed out "that the studying and writing of history is a relatively lonely occupation." In retrospect, I might have finished this book sooner if I had experienced more such "loneliness," but, however that may be, I know I could not have finished it without the interest of good friends who encouraged me along the way. I thank my *confreres* in Holy Cross, especially the men of Moreau Seminary, whose brotherhood I treasure. I owe a special debt to John Young, C.S.C., and the Maple Street community in New Haven where I resided during my sabbatical year. I am also grateful to Daniel, Mary Ann, and Alice Rogers for their wonderful generosity in support of my scholarly efforts. My time in New Haven was blessed by the friendship and kindness of Sun-Joo Shin and Henry Smith (thanks for all the meals!); Fr. Dan Sullivan and the people of Our Lady of Mt. Carmel Parish in Hamden; and John Gaddis and Toni Dorfman. I went to Yale with the express purpose of completing my book, but, as all true students of history know, things never turn out quite the way one expects. Quite surprisingly, I gained at Yale a renewed commitment to my teaching ministry, which I hope to apply to my students' benefit at Notre Dame in the coming years. This came through observing devoted teachers like Toni Dorfmann, John Gaddis, Paul Kennedy, and Charles Hill in action. I am grateful to the latter three for allowing me to participate in their year-long Grand Strategy seminar and to the excellent students who constituted it.

Lastly, I must thank my family members who have supported me over a long period on this and all else I have undertaken. My parents and my sister and brother, Jenny and Phillip, maintained an interest in the book and never doubted that I would complete it. Neither my sister nor my brother worked their way through much of my book on George Kennan, and I don't really expect them to read much more of this work. Yet, each has been a fount of support for me since our days growing up in Roma, and the dedication here is but a token of my love and gratitude.

Preparation

The Making of an [American] Internationalist

American and Wilsonian Roots

International affairs held little interest for the vast majority of Americans when Harry S. Truman was born in Lamar, Missouri, in 1884, during the pedestrian presidency of Chester Arthur.[1] This was especially so for the future president's hardworking relatives and neighbors who made their living for the most part by tilling the fertile soil of the great Missouri–Mississippi Valley. Neither the nation's principal concerns at the time nor his particular circumstances connected Harry Truman to developments beyond the nation's shores, and little happened during his childhood in Independence to alter this situation. Unlike his privileged presidential predecessor, Truman had neither youthful experiences of foreign travel nor of living abroad. Unlike Franklin Roosevelt and John Foster Dulles, he had no relatives who participated in the evolving foreign policy establishment at the dawn of the twentieth century. He received no special education or training that sharpened his interest in the diplomacy of his nation. Instead his small-town boyhood is most distinguished by its sheer and parochial ordinariness – his glasses and piano lessons aside – and it hardly constitutes an auspicious start for this son of the midwest who would assume the vast responsibility of leading his nation through the final months of World War II and into the postwar era.

One should not assume, however, that the seasoned if unsophisticated politician whom Chief Justice Harlan Fiske Stone swore into office on April 12, 1945, maintained the same essentially blank slate on foreign policy matters as, say, the young man who graduated from Independence High School in 1901. Much

---

[1] This section relies heavily on the marvelous research of the three major Truman biographies. Specific quotations are noted, but this general acknowledgment is essential. See David McCullough, *Truman*; Robert H. Ferrell, *Harry S. Truman*; and Alonzo L. Hamby, *Man of the People*. The observant reader will note quickly a sharp difference in interpretation in this chapter from that offered by Arnold Offner's *Another Such Victory: President Truman and the Cold War, 1945–1953* (Stanford, CA, 2002).

happened in the intervening decades, although it did not happen dramatically or quickly in Truman's case. For much of the early part of the twentieth century, he was quite unconcerned with matters of international relations and of America's role in the world. America's and his own participation in World War I significantly broke the drought of his disinterest, but his return home soon led him to focus anew on more provincial matters. Only his arrival in the U.S. Senate in 1935 forced him to devote some sustained – if, at times, naïve – attention to defense and foreign policy questions. But as he gained confidence within that deliberative body, he eventually emerged as a forthright advocate of military preparedness in response to fascist aggression in Europe and Asia and then, during the war, as an active proponent of American involvement in a postwar international organization specifically and in world affairs generally. Far from being some sort of human tabula rasa on the subject, he carried with him into the Oval Office deeply held views on foreign policy as well as various attitudes and certain elemental convictions about the United States. These influenced his actions there considerably.

Little in Truman's early life indicated that he would become a politician, let alone a major world leader; nevertheless, it was during this time that his character, convictions, and outlook on life were formed. His parents raised him in an environment that emphasized such virtues as honesty, modesty, loyalty, patriotism, responsibility, and moral purpose, which Truman, with little evidence of any rebellion, took to heart. His religious formation in a Presbyterian Sunday School and as a member of Grandview Baptist Church further confirmed such qualities in and for him. His education gave him the standard fare for the beginning of the century, which probably meant a stronger knowledge of geography and better writing skills than many high school graduates at the beginning of the twentieth-first century. What Truman's education did not provide, as Alonzo Hamby astutely has noted, "was a sense of complexity and relativity [because] standards were clear, fixed, and simple." This had important consequences for the man Truman would become. "Harry's schooling conspired with his moral and religious upbringing to leave him with the conviction that personal behavior, and by extension that of societies and nations, should be guided by universally understandable Victorian maxims, that distinctions between good and evil were unambiguous, that there were few gray areas in life."[2]

Truman's high school years bridged the turn into the new century when the United States put behind it memories of the depression of the 1890s and burned brightly with new confidence. Truman and his classmates assuredly sensed this national confidence if only indirectly, and they shared a deep faith in the American project. While some Truman relatives had sympathized with the South during the Civil War, and while he held Robert E. Lee among his heroes, there was no doubt about his devotion to his country, one and indivisible. It was simply a part of him that required no articulation. Undoubtedly he shared something of the common American view that Providence had smiled especially

[2] Hamby, *Man of the People*, p. 13.

kindly on the United States. He would not have contested the notion that this nation had some divine commission to witness its virtues to other nations and that its democratic system was superior to any others. During his senior year and moved by the poetry of Tennyson, Truman copied some verses from "Locksley Hall." The poem held forth a vision of the future that concluded:

> Till the war-drum throbbed no longer, and the battle-flags were furl'd
> In the Parliament of Man, the Federation of the World.
> There the common sense of most shall hold a fretful realm in awe,
> And the kindly earth shall slumber, lapt in universal law.[3]

Even though Truman carried these verses in his wallet right through to his presidency, there is no evidence that the one-world philosophy that underlay them exercised real influence on him or his thinking at the time. This high school senior was hardly a Wilsonian before Wilson.

In school and to a lesser extent afterward Truman read voraciously, as is well known, favoring Mark Twain and Charles Dickens and, most passionately, works of history. "Reading history, to me," he later recalled, "was far more than a romantic adventure. It was a solid instruction and wise teaching which I somehow felt that I wanted and needed."[4] In encyclopedic fashion, he paid some attention to all the major civilizations, but his real focus was on the lives and actions of great men and women. Late in his presidency he recalled reading "about the World's Great" as a teenager and listed over sixty individuals – among them Moses and Joshua, Darius I and Cyrus the Great, Hannibal and Caesar, Charlemagne and Jenghis Khan, Elizabeth of England and Frederick the Great – who attracted his interest.[5] His approach to history, however, remained rather simpleminded. Jonathan Daniels, one of his early (and friendly) biographers who knew Truman in the White House, observed that the president "imagined himself a great historian but actually...knew the kind of history that McGuffey would have put in his readers, and he liked the historical anecdote that expressed a moral."[6] He eventually developed what one of his biographers generously describes as "a rough philosophy of history" which "emphasized personalities and assumed patterns." In Truman's thinking, men made history rather than history the man. In order to move the world forward, he assumed, the men who make history would draw on the lessons of the past and avoid the mistakes of those who preceded them.[7] He certainly would apply this approach to history as he contemplated the proper course

---

[3] For the full poem and discussion of its significance, see Hamby, *Man of the People*, p. 13, and Ferrell, *Harry S. Truman*, p. 21.

[4] Truman quoted in David McCullough, *Truman*, p. 58.

[5] Diary entry January 1–2, 1952, in Robert H. Ferrell, ed., *Off the Record: The Private Papers of Harry S. Truman* (New York, 1980), pp. 224–25. In a letter to journalist Edward Harris, July 19, 1950, Truman opined "that real history consists of the life and actions of great men who occupied the stage at the time." Ferrell, ed., *Off the Record*, p. 187.

[6] Jonathan Daniels quoted in Ferrell, *Harry S. Truman*, p. 20.

[7] The argument here and the direct quotations are from Hamby, *Man of the People*, p. 14.

for the United States as his nation struggled to defeat the Axis powers and to fashion a lasting peace.

Truman's reading of history did not draw him into any serious engagement with contemporary issues and events, especially issues of foreign policy. The Spanish-American War, the debate over Empire, Theodore Roosevelt's more activist diplomacy including the taking of the Panama Canal Zone, appear to have troubled him little if at all.[8] Perhaps his decision to join the Missouri National Guard in 1905 owed something to the nationalist fervor of the time and reflected his patriotism, but his desire for camaraderie and some adventure seems to have been just as important.[9] Nonetheless his membership in the Guard sustained an interest in military affairs first demonstrated by his unsuccessful effort to gain admission to the U.S. Military Academy at West Point prior to his high school graduation. His Guard membership in time played a key part in his story, but his training with the Guard from 1906 to 1911 seemed of little consequence at the time, aside from giving him a break (of sorts) from farming when his artillery battery spent a week in camp each summer.

Truman never suffered any doubts concerning his political outlook. His family provided him with an identity as a Democrat, which he adopted as inheritance and retained as conviction. The little boy who went to first grade with Grover Cleveland's name on his cap became the teenager who personally heard William Jennings Bryan's oratory at the 1900 Democratic Convention in Kansas City, who in turn became the young man who thrilled to the news of Woodrow Wilson's election in 1912 and held Andrew Jackson as his great hero. But his engagement in political affairs even at the local level was minimal, and his family hardly pushed him to it. Instead, after his brief experience as a bank clerk in Kansas City, his family recalled him to run its farm in Grandview. He responded dutifully, demonstrating during his long, hard, and unexciting years as a farmer a notable capacity for work and a deep sense of responsibility. His long courtship of Bess Wallace perhaps leavened his toil, but in the years prior to World War I his life seemed lodged in a rut deeper than any furrow he plowed. The sheer drudgery of farm life and the never-ending holding pattern quality of his relationship with the woman he adored might have soured a man on life. Truman, it seems, was not such a man. Perhaps he was engaged in an interior struggle to "become the sort of man who would win the respect of his peers and, above all, of his father" and could not dare relent or question his own life.[10] But there seemed also to be an inner toughness, a determination to keep doing one's duty come what may or, at least, until there came a higher call.

Although Truman openly admitted little unease with his own lot, he expressed more concern over the broad direction of his nation during the years prior to the outbreak of war in Europe. In 1911, before he left on a trip to South

[8] Ferrell makes essentially this point in his *Harry S. Truman*, pp. 20, 35.

[9] On Truman's experience in the National Guard, see Ferrell, *Harry S. Truman*, pp. 35–36.

[10] Hamby, *Man of the People*, p. 3.

Dakota, Harry wrote Bess that "I bet there'll be more bohunks and 'Rooshans' up there than white men" and went on to describe it as "a disgrace to the country for those fellows to be in it." Adopting the yeoman-farmer stance of a "purist" Jeffersonian democrat he went on to explain that "if they had only stopped immigration about twenty or thirty years ago, the good Americans could all have had plenty of land and we'd have been an agricultural country forever. You know as long as a country is one of that kind, people are more independent and make better citizens. When it is made up of factories and large cities it soon becomes depressed and makes classes among people. Every farmer thinks he's as good as the President or perhaps a little better."[11]

Truman presumably considered himself a superior American to the various late-arrivals who apparently threatened his pure vision of the republican experiment. Truman's correspondence to Bess Wallace contained a number of insulting references to other races and ethnic groups. He described Mexico as "Greaserdom" and also wrote Bess in 1911 that "I think one man is as good as another so long as he's honest and decent and not a nigger or a Chinaman. Uncle Will says that the Lord made a white man from dust, a nigger from mud, then threw up what was left and it came down a Chinaman. He does hate Chinese and Japs [sic]. So do I. It is race prejudice I guess. But I am strongly of the opinion that negroes ought to be in Africa, yellow men in Asia, and white men in Europe and America."[12] Such racial and ethnic prejudices occasionally burst forth in Truman's private remarks throughout his political career, but they were hardly determinative. The man who would enter a business partnership with his Jewish friend, who worked as part of the urban, ethnic machine of an Irish Catholic political boss, and who spoke out more forcefully for civil rights for African Americans than any president since Lincoln proved that he was not dominated by his racist views and could move some distance beyond those he held as a young man.[13]

The Great War in Europe that brutally decimated a generation of that bloody continent's young men initially did not have much noticeable impact on Truman. As Robert Ferrell observed, Truman rarely commented either on the

[11] Truman to Bess Wallace, October 16, 1911, in Robert H. Ferrell, ed., *Dear Bess: The Letters from Harry to Bess Truman, 1910–1959* (New York, 1983), pp. 52–53.

[12] See Ferrell, ed., *Dear Bess*, pp. 34, 39.

[13] This view differs considerably from that of Offner's *Another Such Victory*, p. 5, which presents Truman as entrapped by his "parochial nationalism." One should also note the rather sad reality that racist and discriminatory comments were hardly the preserve of farmers from Missouri during the early decades of the twentieth century. For example, note the observations by Ellen Feldman regarding Eleanor and Franklin Roosevelt's ethnic slurs and racism during the same decade that Truman made his most egregious comments. According to Feldman, "during the early days of their marriage ER wrote her mother-in-law that the 'Jew party' at Bernard Baruch's was 'appalling. I never wish to hear money, jewels, or labels mentioned again.'" Furthermore, "in 1917, on an official trip to Haiti, FDR's behavior to his hosts was as unfailingly courteous as his enjoyment of his colleagues' racist jokes was hearty." See Ellen Feldman, "FDR and His Women," *American Heritage*, 54 (February/March 2003), p. 59. Note also that evidence of Woodrow Wilson's racism and bigotry is substantial.

carnage at the front or even on the submarine issue which so divided the United States and Imperial Germany from 1914 through 1916. Instead, "like millions of other Americans, he . . . felt as remote from Europe as if Jackson County were somewhere in China surrounded by the Great Wall."[14] This changed quickly when on April 6, 1917, President Woodrow Wilson signed a declaration of war against Germany. "Stirred," as he later put it, "in heart and soul by the war messages of Woodrow Wilson, and since I'd joined the National guard at twenty-one I thought I ought to go." He remembered feeling like "a Galahad after the Grail."[15] He easily could have avoided military service on any of several grounds, including his age (now thirty-three), his miserable eyesight and his occupation as a farmer. But he signed up immediately. It was truly "the turning point in his life" and a liberation of sorts.[16]

Truman left the definition of war aims and the articulation of the conflict's meaning to the president, but he undoubtedly thrilled to the high-minded purpose that Wilson established for his nation. For the United States, this could not be a struggle motivated by something so base as national interest or designed merely to restore the balance of power in Europe. In Wilson's brilliant oratory, the war became a crusade to make the world safe for democracy and to establish a new international order based on self-determination for all people. Wilson put it best: "we shall fight for the things which we have always carried nearest our hearts – for democracy, for the right of those who submit to authority to have a voice in their own government, for the rights and liberties of small nations, for a universal dominion of right by such a concert of free peoples as shall bring peace and safety to all nations and make the world itself at last free."[17] Truman gladly assented, filled with admiration for the president and a genuine "democratic idealism," which Wilson so effectively tapped.[18]

While Wilson defined the war, Truman prepared to fight it, and after a year of training, he left the United States for the first time as Captain Harry Truman commanding Battery D of the 129th Field Artillery attached to the 35th Division. In France, he saw some fierce and bloody action and participated in the Meuse-Argonne offensive of 1918. Across the Atlantic and far from home, he discovered that he possessed courage under fire and that he could lead men. The latter discovery redirected his life for leading men in war suggested to him the possibility of leading them in peace. Furthermore, his wartime friends gave him a core group of political supporters. "My whole political career," he once said with only slight exaggeration, "is based upon my war service and war associates."[19]

The guns in Truman's battery stopped firing as scheduled at eleven o' clock, November 11, 1918. Later that month, he and some fellow officers obtained

[14] Ferrell, *Harry S. Truman*, p. 56.
[15] Robert H. Ferrell, ed., *The Autobiography of Harry S. Truman* (Boulder, CO, 1980), p. 41.
[16] McCullough, *Truman*, p. 102.
[17] Ferrell quotes Wilson in *Harry S. Truman*, p. 56.
[18] Hamby, *Man of the People*, p. 57.
[19] Truman quoted in Ferrell, *Harry S. Truman*, p. 57.

leaves and spent some time in Paris – where he caught a brief glimpse of Wilson – before heading south to Marseilles, Nice, and Monte Carlo with a brief side-trip into Italy. It was his first real travel in a foreign country, and one is struck by the conventional sightseeing quality of his touring – everything from Notre Dame cathedral to the *Folies Bergere*. After two weeks, Captain Harry rejoined his men and waited impatiently to go home. Their job was done he thought. The Paris peace conference meant little to him. "For my part," he observed, "and every A. E. F. man feels the same way, I don't give a whoop (to put it mildly) whether there's a League of Nations or whether Russia has a Red government or a Purple one, and if the President of the Czecho-Slovaks wants to pry the throne from under the King of Bohemia, let him pry but send us home."[20] The stirring appeal of Wilson's war message seemed long forgotten as he wrote his cousins of his anxiety "that Woodie [sic] cease his gallavantin' around and send us home at once and quickly." His regiment finally left Brest on April 9, 1919, and reached New York eleven days later. Truman resolved "that if old lady Liberty in New York harbor wanted to see me again she'd have to turn around."[21]

Truman rushed home to the welcoming arms of Bess Wallace whom he soon married at long last. Perhaps understandably given his lengthy wait to wed his childhood sweetheart, he doesn't appear to have spared much time to sympathize with Woodrow Wilson in his unsuccessful attempts to gain Senate ratification for the Versailles treaty and American participation in the League of Nations for which it provided. Yet Truman's wartime experience provided him with an intellectual and emotional rapport with past American foreign policy. Under the pressure of world events during the late 1930s, the fact of his participation in the war and his recognition that he had in some sense fought for Wilson and his Fourteen Points became significant formative influences on his thinking.[22] History sometimes does play a part in making the man.

Politician

Truman's stint in the army freed him from the farm for other possibilities. The pure Jeffersonian democrat readily succumbed to the lure of Kansas City. The newly married war veteran turned his attention first to a business venture as America entered the roaring twenties. His famous haberdashery partnership with Eddie Jacobsen soon foundered on the twin shoals of excessive debt and meager sales.[23] Truman refused to declare bankruptcy and insisted on paying

[20] Truman quoted in Ferrell, *Harry S. Truman*, p. 69.
[21] Ferrell, ed., *The Autobiography of Harry S. Truman*, p. 51.
[22] For later evidence of this, see Oral History Interview with Dr. Walter H. Judd, April 13, 1970, by Jerry Hess, Harry S. Truman Library (hereafter HSTL). Judd, a sometime congressional colleague of Truman, recalled that "I had been a young soldier in World War I, and he had been a captain in the field artillery, and when we got to know each other better we talked about our various military experiences. He felt, as I did, that we had made a mistake in 1918 and '19 when we imagined that we could pull back from the world, not recognizing our own situation in the world had changed."
[23] On "Truman and Jacobsen," see Hamby, *Man of the People*, pp. 94–100.

off all his creditors – an obligation he proudly met. The failed businessman's rescue from his embarrassing commercial foray came from an unlikely source. Boss Tom Pendergast enlisted Truman to run with the backing of his corrupt political machine for eastern county judge of the Jackson County Court in 1924, and so a political career began.[24] Although defeated in 1926 Truman came back two years later to win election as his county's presiding judge, an office rather like a county executive which he held until he left for the Senate. He energetically pursued his responsibilities of building and maintaining county roads, buildings, and facilities.

Those who tend toward Truman hagiography argue that the future president was a beneficiary of the Pendergast machine's political power but remained unsullied in any way by its corrupt practices. No doubt Truman appears as a moral giant compared to some of his machine associates whose principal aim in life centered on lining their own pockets. He had a positive vision for the future, genuinely sought to use government to improve the lives of citizens, occasionally tried to limit the corruption involved in the letting of contracts, and, most notably, never profited personally from the illegal activities of the machine. The rosy view of Truman as the epitome of moral rectitude and pure as driven snow stretches the truth however. It ignores Truman's own troubled conscience, which forced him to wrestle privately with the question of whether the good ends he sought justified the suspect means he used. "I wonder if I did right to put a lot of no account sons of bitches on the payroll," he pointedly mused in the early 1930s, "and pay other sons of bitches more money for supplies than they were worth in order to satisfy the political powers and save some $3,500,000 [this figure was part of a bond issue and represented the amount he estimated the "crooks" would have taken if he had not fended them off with small compromises]." He concluded somewhat tentatively that "I believe I did do right," although to add reassuring weight to this side of his own internal debate he noted that "anyway, I'm not a partner of any of them and I'll go out poorer in every way than when I came into office."[25]

Truman's qualms about financial corruption do not seem to have extended to deep concerns about the vote fraud which undergirded Boss Tom's remarkable ability to deliver tremendously lopsided victories for his candidates, such as Judge Harry Truman, in districts under his control. Truman the politician knew he needed the Pendergast organization's votes if he wanted to obtain office, and he welcomed everyone of them. His moral outlook on life made what William Lee Miller rightly has called a "rather stark compromise with realities" in pursuit of political victory.[26] His political compromise with the Pendergast machine helped carry him to victory in the U.S. Senate race of 1934.

[24] For a critical view of "Boss Tom" and the Pendergast machine, see Lawrence H. Larsen and Nancy J. Hulston, *Pendergast!* (Columbia, MO, 1997). Also see Lyle W. Dorsett, *The Pendergast Machine* (New York, 1968), and on Truman's relationship with Tom Pendergast, see Robert H. Ferrell, *Truman and Pendergast* (Columbia, MO, 1999).

[25] Truman is quoted in and this paragraph relies upon the fine essay by William Lee Miller, "Two Moralities," *Miller Center Journal*, 2 (Spring 1995), pp. 22–23.

[26] Miller, "Two Moralities," p. 24.

Even when the Pendergast machine collapsed under attack from federal investigations and its aging leader found himself dispatched to Leavenworth for tax fraud, Truman did not jump ship and disassociate himself from the organization. He might easily have done so, as Miller insightfully has suggested, rationalizing that his obligation was minimal because the Pendergasts after all had initially needed "a well-respected veteran, a farmer and a Baptist, to provide their reach out into the rural part of the county" and later "needed his accomplishments as an honest, efficient, road-building, courthouse-building county judge to provide a deodorant for their doings of other kinds."[27] Political opportunism perhaps called for a break with his backers of old. His enduring association with the Pendergasts hurt his national reputation especially after Boss Tom's imprisonment. It severely threatened his chances for reelection to the Senate in 1940. Whatever the weight of these pressures, Truman stayed steadfastly loyal to his first political sponsor even, while vice president, attending Tom Pendergast's funeral. Loyalty was a prime political virtue for him. He would give it and, at times more tellingly, turn on those whom he believed had not extended it to him.

Truman learned other key and lasting lessons during his training in the political school of Jackson County in addition to overseeing projects and winning close elections. He learned how to cooperate and how to compromise in the interest of gaining agreements and completing tasks. One keen historian rightly has commented that "conciliation and adjustment, Truman believed, were the lifeblood of politics; although he had principles they did not lead . . . to inflexible policies."[28] Truman was not rigid and certainly not averse to accommodation for a worthy political end. His Protestant and rural background hardly prevented him from collaborating with the urban Catholics who staffed much of the Pendergast organization. His lack of a well-developed public philosophy made it easier for him to be pragmatic. He was as far from being an ideologue as possible, scraping by with a vague and worthy sense that government should be utilized for the good of the people. He considered politics to be an honorable calling and in pursuing his work he placed high value on the importance of keeping one's word.[29] He "judged men by their reliability in keeping agreements, and it was the standard by which he, in turn, wanted to be judged."[30] It proved to be a standard that he thought also should apply to nations in their behavior.

---

[27] Miller, "Two Moralities," pp. 24–25.

[28] John Lewis Gaddis, "Harry S. Truman and the Origins of Containment," in Frank J. Merli and Theodore A. Wilson, eds., *Makers of American Diplomacy: From Theodore Roosevelt to Henry Kissinger* (New York, 1974), p. 192.

[29] In an undated handwritten manuscript, circa late 1940s or early 1950s, Truman defined a politician as "a man [sic] who is interested in good government." He counseled that "more young men and young women should fit themselves for politics and government," and notably commented that "I would risk my reputation and my fortune with a professional politician sooner than I would with the banker or the businessman or the publisher of a daily paper!" Raymond H. Geselbracht, compiler, "Harry Truman Speaks," *Whistlestop: Harry S. Truman Library Institute Newsletter* (Fall 2002), p. 2.

[30] Gaddis, "Harry S. Truman and the Origins of Containment," p. 192.

The world of Kansas City politics notably failed to provide Truman with any sustained instruction in international relations. Boss Tom was not the type selected for charter membership of the Council on Foreign Relations, and his machine cared little for matters beyond its purview. Pendergast eventually supported Franklin Roosevelt at the 1932 Democratic convention in Chicago, which Truman attended as a delegate, primarily because he hoped the New York governor would win and would assist in tackling the Depression.[31] Truman's political circle contained few individuals who thought conscientiously about foreign policy questions. Truman's own intellectual curiosity appears never to have led him to read seriously anything on crucial international matters such as the Kellogg–Briand Pact or the London Economic Conference. Even after his election to the Senate, he managed to pursue his career without regularly reading journals like *Foreign Affairs*, without paying much attention to columnists like Walter Lippmann, without cultivating foreign contacts, and without consulting either formal or informal advisers on international relations. His membership in organizations like the American Legion and the Masons proved valuable for personal friendship and political support but contributed little to enlarging his worldview.

Truman's mind was neither inquisitive nor especially wide-ranging. In the Senate, he diligently applied himself to the careful study of a few issues such as transportation and interstate commerce. His efforts reflected earnest and hard work but not a superior intellect at work. In comparing Truman to Lyndon Johnson, Dean Acheson (who loved Truman) suggested that "they were cut from the same cloth. They both come from border states, they are both profound patriots, good politicians and genuine progressives in policy. But Johnson has an A mind and Truman a B mind."[32] Now a superb intellect is hardly an essential requirement for a politician, and the failures of "brilliant" politicians litter the historical landscape, including those of the president to whom Acheson compared Truman unfavorably. Similarly, high intellect is no strong predictor of success in pursuing the affairs of state. In Truman's case, however, it must be noted that he demonstrated minimal facility for creative or conceptual thinking and no eagerness to rush into unfamiliar areas. He never claimed either the ability to be a "quick-study" on issues or the capacity to reformulate policy hastily and to chart a new direction.[33] This was not his style and, his reputation for decisiveness notwithstanding, he rarely moved precipitously.[34] As president,

---

[31] On Pendergast and Truman at the 1932 convention, see McCullough, *Truman*, p. 195.

[32] Acheson quoted in Eugene V. Rostow, "The Apotheosis of Harry," *Times Literary Supplement*, November 27, 1992, p. 4.

[33] In this context, one might also note Jonathan Daniels' comment that "Roosevelt's mind, intellectually, was far less stereotyped than Truman's, and maybe that explains why Roosevelt was not as simple and direct as Truman." Daniels quoted in Ferrell, *Harry S. Truman*, p. 404.

[34] Alonzo Hamby has made this point in considering Truman's decision making as president concluding that "every major decision of his presidency...was the product of careful political or diplomatic planning and group consensus, not individual whim. The man who liked to present himself as a quick decision maker was actually slow and cautious on the big things." See

as we shall see, he very rarely moved on his own, probably held back by a curious combination of good sense and a lack of intellectual confidence.

"The Senator from Pendergast" kept a low profile during his early years in Washington, D.C., attending primarily to his domestically oriented committee work and suffering the snubs of many, including the White House, which took his solid support for the New Deal for granted.[35] A poor public speaker, he rarely spoke from the Senate floor characteristically intent on becoming a workhorse not a show-pony. He did enter the Senate chamber to vote, however, and supinely supported the neutrality legislation of 1935, 1936, and 1937, which denied the president authority to discriminate between aggressors and their victims and which plunged the United States to the extremes of its interwar isolationism. He later characterized such support as "a mistake," explaining his support for the neutrality laws as a result of being "misled by the report of the munitions investigation . . . headed by Gerald Nye." He described Nye as "a demagogue senator from North Dakota" and as "an America Firster," although in a quite revealing admission he claimed not to have known of Nye's outlook at the time.[36] His votes resulted from sharing in the naïve and widespread hope to prevent American involvement in the seemingly endless and complex conflicts of Europe, but the Missouri senator never succumbed to the more virulent strains of the isolationist virus. He never needed some dramatic conversion experience brought on by the Japanese attack on Pearl Harbor to break free from isolationists restraints. Indeed, as Nazi Germany and Imperial Japan pursued their aggression in the late 1930s, Senator Truman began to express concern regarding the implications of their ugly actions for American security.[37]

Apostle of Preparedness

On March 7, 1938, Truman spoke to an American Legion meeting in Washington, D.C., and outlined his views on "national defense and its relationship to peace." This speech represented his first major effort to enunciate an interpretation of the past and a prescription for the future. It also foreshadowed many of the points he developed over the next three years. After admitting his desire for peace, he warned his audience that "we must not close our eyes to the possibility of another war, because conditions in Europe have developed to a point likely to cause an explosion at any time." He then reviewed the

Hamby's insightful essay, "An American Democrat: A Reevaluation of the Personality of Harry S. Truman," *Political Science Quarterly*, 106 (Spring 1991), p. 52.

[35] On Truman's Senate work, see the discussion in Eugene F. Schmidtlein, "Truman the Senator," Ph.D. diss., University of Missouri, 1962. See especially pp. 135–49 for discussion of Truman's work on transportation issues, which helped produce the Civil Aeronautics Act of 1938.

[36] Truman, *Year of Decisions*, p. 175.

[37] Early evidence that Truman at least was examining American foreign policy issues more seriously by late 1937 was his reading into the *Congressional Record* of a *Washington Post* editorial of November 24, 1937, entitled "No Peace through Passivity." See *Appendix to the Congressional Record* 82, part 3 (Washington, DC, 1937), p. 185.

foreign policy pursued by the United States and revealed a developing conviction that the United States erred in not signing the Versailles Treaty and in not
joining the League of Nations. "We refused to sign the Treaty of Versailles,"
and, in consequence, he argued, "did not accept our responsibility as a world
power." Borrowing from the free-trade gospel of Secretary of State Cordell
Hull, he claimed that the United States "tried by tariff walls to reap the benefits of world trade without giving anything in return," but this did not work.
Demonstrating his ambivalence toward the neutrality laws he had supported,
he continued,

so in the last Congress we adopted a new policy of neutrality. We virtually abandoned
our century-old "freedom of the seas" and authorized the President, in his discretion,
to declare embargoes against warring nations and to warn our citizens to stay off the
vessels of belligerents: All this has been brought about by present world conditions. The
intent of this activity is very laudable, and I hope it will keep us at peace.

Significantly, however, Truman cautioned his Legion audience that "we are
living in a world of realities." The United States was the richest nation on
earth and would need to defend its wealth. "In the coming struggle between
democracy and dictatorship," he prophetically argued, "democracy must be
prepared to defend its principles and its wealth." The best way to keep from
fighting again, he told his fellow veterans, was "to be adequately prepared for
all contingencies."[38]

Truman's broad and essential recommendation for the future was military
preparedness, and he became increasingly preoccupied with defense issues
during 1939, an interest facilitated by his membership on the Senate's military appropriations subcommittee. When the congressional session ended in
November 1939, he set out with some Senate colleagues on a one-month tour
of army bases and defense facilities in Central America and the West Coast
designed to assess the requirements for hemispheric defense. Hitler's invasion
of Poland in September 1939 and the declarations of war in Europe provided
the backdrop for this inspection and fact-finding exercise. It also seems to have
been an opportunity for Truman to escape from his political burdens following
Boss Tom's conviction and from a "profound weariness and demoralization"
at his political prospects in the upcoming 1940 Democratic primary where
Missouri Governor Lloyd Stark planned to challenge him.[39]

Truman enjoyed this long trip immensely as his letters and postcards to
his wife and daughter Margaret indicate. Departing from Ft. Knox, Kentucky,
the senators traveled by air to Ft. Sill, Oklahoma, and on to San Antonio,
Brownsville, and Vera Cruz and then to Guatemala, Nicaragua, Panama, El
Salvador, and back through Mexico City to San Diego, Seattle, and Denver.[40]
Truman met a significant number of Latin American leaders and officials along

---

[38] Truman speech at George Washington Post, No. 1, American Legion, Washington, DC, March
7, 1938, in *Appendix to the Congressional Record 83*, part 9, p. 945.

[39] On this point see Hamby, *Man of the People*, p. 234.

[40] Truman's visit can be tracked through his letters to Bess and Margaret gathered in Monte M.
Poen, ed., *Letters Home by Harry Truman* (New York, 1984), pp. 124–36.

the way including a young Anastasio Somoza in Nicaragua, whom he described as "a regular fellow" and the Guatemalan dictator, Jorge Ubico, whom he praised in a letter to Bess "for eliminating graft in [his] country."[41] This trip, however, led to no lasting contacts or to any special interest on Truman's part in the Central American region. It served simply to confirm his interest in defense questions, and apparently it also recharged his political energies for the contest with Stark.

Truman's international views were not limited to his realist interest in improving his nation's defense capabilities. During 1939, in what has to be one of the more bizarre associations of his career, he found himself attracted to Dr. Frank N. D. Buchman's Moral Rearmament movement.[42] Buchman's organization originated in the Protestant minister's evangelical labors in Cambridge, England, but in the late 1930s Buchman eagerly spread his message across the Atlantic, beyond the college student audience. One close student of Truman's rise to power has argued that Moral Rearmament was "permeated with nonsectarian religiosity that Truman found appealing" and suggested that its very name grabbed his interest "as he felt a sick world would soon be cleansed by fire unless people awakened to their moral responsibilities."[43] However that may be, Truman appeared on stage at the June 1939 meeting at Constitution Hall in Washington when Moral Rearmament officially was launched in the United States, and he read a greeting from President Roosevelt to the large and enthusiastic audience. A few days later, he reported on this meeting to the Senate and described Buchman's movement as "something which will unite men and nations on a plane above conflict of party, class, or political philosophy" (a vision that bore significant similarity to the brotherhood of man ideal of his treasured Freemasons.) He then proceeded in an uncharacteristically grandiloquent outburst and with evangelical fervor to express his "confidence that America will play her full part in this cause [Moral Rearmament] on whose fortunes the future of civilization must largely depend."[44]

Truman's engagement with Moral Rearmament continued throughout the year. In October, he taped a speech that Buchman included in a worldwide broadcast promoting Moral Rearmament and proffered the view that "the future of civilization must largely depend upon the success of moral rearmament." Not surprisingly, Buchman expressed his gratitude for the senator's "statesmanlike words." In November, he acted as intermediary to recruit Roosevelt to participate in a Moral Rearmament world broadcast with the queen of Holland, the king of Belgium, and other European royalty. The president declined and also refused to meet with Buchman.[45] Roosevelt's caution

---

[41] Truman letter, November 22, 1939, in Ferrell, ed., *Dear Bess*, p. 431.
[42] On this movement, see Tom Driberg, *The Mystery of Moral Rearmament* (London, 1964).
[43] Richard Lawrence Miller, *Truman: The Rise to Power* (New York, 1986), p. 364.
[44] Truman speech, June 8, 1939, *Congressional Record* 84, part 6, p. 6830.
[45] See the summary memorandum, November 8, 1939, Franklin D. Roosevelt Papers: President's Personal File, Franklin D. Roosevelt Library (hereafter FDRL), Folder 6337.

sent up no warning signals for Truman, and he maintained his association with Buchman's movement and used his influence where possible in support of the organization.[46]

The significance of Moral Rearmament for Truman does not mean that he was integral to the movement or that he understood its true nature and shared its real objectives. Richard Lawrence Miller has presented the Buchmanites as a proto-fascist group aimed at controlling individual liberties, which is hardly how Truman saw them. During the 1944 campaign, when the journalist George Seldes warned Truman of the authoritarian and anti-Semitic tendencies of the group, the Democratic candidate for vice president distanced himself from it.[47] Truman avoided speaking about the group after that point, presumably hoping that no antagonistic journalist would probe the depth of his one-time commitment. If one had, it is likely that Truman would have explained his involvement in terms of his efforts to strengthen his country for the challenges that lay ahead of it. He had seen no dichotomy between his practical commitment to military preparedness and his moralistic desire to reform the hearts and minds of men and nations through Moral Rearmament. Indeed moral and military rearmament complemented each other in his mind. A morally and spiritually bankrupt nation would be incapable of mounting a successful defense of its territory and principles.

Truman gave voice to his dual rearmament hopes in a rambling speech in October 1939 in Caruthersville, Missouri, where he justified his support for the proposed amendments to the existing Neutrality Act containing the cash and carry provision for arms, which clearly would benefit Britain and France. Just a month after the German and Soviet ravaging of Poland, he denounced Hitler, Stalin, and Mussolini as having "gone back to a code little short of cave-man savagery" and warned "if there isn't a moral reawakening in high places in this old world, we'll go into another and darker age than the tenth century ever was." In rather messianic fashion, he declared "the role of this great Republic is to save civilization," although he assured his audience that the United States should keep out of the war. Truman then turned to the past and focused on Woodrow Wilson and World War I. He portrayed Wilson as destroyed by a combination of "European power politics...and the United States Senate" and assured his audience that Wilson's Fourteen Points "are just as good today as ever." He lambasted the "professional pacifists and professional neutrality preachers" who had tried to make Americans believe that World War I was fought for profits. In contrast, he clearly stated his belief that "we went in because more than 500 American lives had been ruthlessly taken by the same savage policy now being pursued by the German Government." With all this as preface, he addressed the neutrality revisions and presented them as a means "to strengthen our position as a neutral." When referring to the sale of munitions,

---

[46] Miller, *Truman*, p. 367.

[47] For Miller's intriguing discussion and his report on Seldes's warnings to Truman, see *Truman*, pp. 367–68.

however, he rather contradicted himself and admitted his view that "we should not help the thugs among nations by refusing to sell arms to our friends." He bluntly explained to his fellow Missourians that "it is in our interest, our very selfish interests to lift the embargo." With all that said, he finally emphasized the need for military preparedness arguing with acuity that Americans should not "sit idly by and let a catastrophe come upon us as England and France have done."[48]

The reaction of the residents of Caruthersville to this speech remains unknown, but it certainly revealed significant themes in Truman's emerging views on foreign policy. Most obvious in the context of the times was his recognition of the dictators and his clear-headed appreciation of the danger they represented. Truman's prescription of military preparation as the means to nullify the danger also stood out. Less obvious, although a precursor of his later views was his championing of Woodrow Wilson and his Fourteen Points. His reading of history, which portrayed Wilson and World War I in a favorable light, gave some hint of his later internationalist sentiments. His unquestioned faith in American moral superiority, displayed in his attribution to the United States of the role of savior of world civilization, suggested further that he expected the United States to play a central role in the maintenance of a moral world order. But as Truman moved into the decade that would see him propelled to the leadership of his country, such themes and ideas were still in a process of refinement.

National defense provided the focus for Truman's foreign policy views during 1940. Within and outside the Senate, he emphasized the importance of the whole western hemisphere to the defense of the United States. In June he supported a resolution managed by Sen. Tom Connally of Texas, which provided for the maintenance of the Monroe Doctrine.[49] In a radio address later that same month, Truman gave the ritual assurance demanded of everyone from FDR down that the United States should not get involved in "the European brawl," but then he asserted that it should defend the western hemisphere and "sell all the planes and materials possible to the British Empire."[50] Truman shared with Roosevelt the view that the United States could serve as the arsenal of democracy.

Running parallel to and closely linked with Truman's emphasis on defense was an ever deeper dissatisfaction with neutrality. In April 1940, he included in the *Congressional Record* an article by the journalist Barnet Nover concerning the fate of the Scandinavian countries. His introductory comment that "the experience of the Scandinavian countr[ies] should be a warning to us" suggested his substantial agreement with Nover who wrote that Americans could

---

[48] Truman speech at Caruthersville, Missouri, October 8, 1939, *Appendix to the Congressional Record*, 85 part 2, pp. 202–03.

[49] *Congressional Record* 83, part 2, p. 1963.

[50] Truman radio address on national defense, June 30, 1940, *Appendix to the Congressional Record* 86, part 16, p. 4192.

not view developments in Scandinavia "with any measure of complacence. Quite the contrary. These developments have a lesson for us which cannot be disregarded with impunity. For there are loud voices raised in this land which repeatedly insist that peace is something you can achieve by wishing, by legislation, by oratorical legerdemain. The struggle in Norway shows how dangerous an illusion that can be."[51] The shameful and disastrous consequences of appeasement diplomacy and neutrality were deeply etched in Truman's mind. The appetites of totalitarian regimes could not be satiated by concessions. This experience eventually would be of notable importance to his decision making as president.[52]

While brutal war quickly encompassed more and more of the world, Truman was caught up in a tough battle at home in the Missouri Democratic primary, which he fought with a tenacity rather comparable to Churchill's Britain as it stood alone against Hitler's victorious armies. With no help at all from Franklin Roosevelt and with meager campaign funds, Truman refused to concede to the better financed Governor Stark.[53] Calling for a strong national defense and reaching out for the support of farmers, blacks, and organized labor in classic New Deal fashion, he crisscrossed the state relentlessly and proved himself a tough and capable politician. He astutely drew a third candidate into the race thereby dividing the anti-Truman/Pendergast vote, and with late support from a rising St. Louis politico named Robert Hannegan he secured a narrow victory. After an easier victory in the general election, a more confident Senator Truman returned to Washington intent on making his mark in the area of greatest concern to him – national defense.

In a thoughtful speech in the Senate early in 1941, Truman outlined areas in the national defense program, especially in the letting of defense contracts, that demanded investigation. As the United States moved to rebuild its defense forces after allowing them to waste away to a mere skeletal operation during the 1930s, Truman, having unsuccessfully volunteered for military service, wanted to ensure that expenditures were wisely spent.[54] He secured the establishment of a special investigating committee to undertake the task and chaired it, and his energetic leadership of what became known as the Truman Committee in time

---

[51] Barnet Nover, "Peace as a Policy: A Lesson from Scandinavia," *Washington Post*, April 29, 1940, read into *Appendix to the Congressional Record 86*, part 15, p. 2518. Truman's comments introduce the piece.

[52] On this point, note Ernest R. May, *"Lessons" of the Past: The Use and Misuse of History in American Foreign Policy* (New York, 1973), pp. 19–86.

[53] For evidence of the failed efforts of the Truman campaign to secure some backing or endorsement from Franklin Roosevelt, see the material in Franklin D. Roosevelt Papers: President's Personal File, FDRL, Folder 6337.

[54] According to Truman's own account, he went down to see Chief of Staff, General George C. Marshall, "and told him I'd like to quit the Senate and go into service as a field artillery colonel and an instructor in F.A. tactics. He asked how old I was and I told him I was fifty-six years old. He pulled his reading glasses down on his nose, grinned at me and said, 'We don't need old stiffs like you – this will be a young man's war.' He was right, of course, but it hurt my feelings and I decided to do something for the war effort on a constructive basis." Ferrell, ed., *The Autobiography of Harry S. Truman*, pp. 74–75.

"reconstructed his image from that of a machine politician to a statesman of democracy."[55] The terms of reference of Truman's committee limited the sphere of its investigation to the defense production program.[56] It did not impinge on defense policy or strategy or on foreign policy, and Truman consciously attempted to avoid any moves that might leave his committee open to the charge of trying to "run defense."[57] Truman attended primarily to the area where his Jackson County expertise could be easily applied – matters of contracts and construction of defense infrastructure – aiming to make the United States more effective in the war he knew was coming for it.[58]

Even though Truman left the details of foreign policy formulation to others, he continued in broad terms to be a strong supporter of efforts to deter the Axis powers and to assist the outgunned British. He never played a role in the Committee to Aid the Allies, but his views were consonant with its. He strongly supported the Lend–Lease legislation and notably voted against the many amendments aimed at restricting Roosevelt's execution of the bill's provisions. He favored the arming of American merchant ships for convoy duty to England and backed FDR's interventionist efforts. He stopped short of advocating war against Hitler because "like Roosevelt and most other interventionists, he understood that the country would not yet accept so stark a prospect, that the message of preparedness and limited aid was far more acceptable, whatever its illogic."[59]

Truman immersed himself in the work of his investigating committee throughout 1941 as the onset of war moved closer for his nation. He offered one rather flippant comment on a foreign policy question in June 1941, however, which lodged in people's memories and was used by some to characterize his pre-presidential foreign policy views. When Hitler betrayed Stalin and launched the massive Nazi attack on the Soviet Union, Truman told reporters that "if we see that Germany is winning we ought to help Russia and if Russia is winning we ought to help Germany and that way let them kill as many as possible, although I don't want to see Hitler victorious under any circumstances. Neither of them think anything of their pledged word."[60] The remark has been seen as evidence of Truman's inherent and consistent anti-Soviet feelings, although it should be noted that Arthur Krock of the *New York Times* observed that Truman offered it "though not too seriously."[61]

---

[55] Hamby, *Man of the People*, p. 260.

[56] *Congressional Record* 89, part II, p. 1615.

[57] Truman, *Year of Decisions*, pp. 190–91. For a good contemporary outline by Truman of his committee's function and purpose, see his speech delivered in Des Moines, Iowa, July 30, 1943, in Harry S. Truman Papers: Senatorial and Vice-Presidential Speeches File, HSTL, Box 2.

[58] Truman wrote to Luther Ely Smith, February 6, 1941, that "we are facing a bunch of thugs, and the only theory a thug understands is a gun and a bayonet." Quoted in Hamby, *Man of the People*, p. 268.

[59] Hamby, *Man of the People*, pp. 267–68.

[60] Truman quoted in *New York Times*, June 24, 1941, p. 7.

[61] Arthur Krock, "In the Nation," *New York Times*, June 24, 1941, p. 18.

Seen in context, Truman's offhand remark is less significant. Of course, it was not far from the foreign policy mainstream at the time. "Even the supporters of the Administration's foreign policy were uncertain and divided on the issue of aid to the Soviet Union," William Langer and S. Everett Gleason later noted. "Not a few expressed the hope that the two hated dictatorships would bleed each other white and thus relieve the world of the totalitarian threat. Others held that Stalin, having concluded his nefarious pact with Hitler was now getting nothing more than his just deserts."[62] Truman bore none of the illusions regarding the Soviet Union favored by sympathetic liberals willing to dismiss lightly the tragic consequences of Stalin's horrendous rule.[63] He had no detailed knowledge of the horrors of collectivization nor the terror and the purges, but he knew a little. This knowledge, when joined to the Nazi–Soviet pact and Stalin's aggression in 1939–40 against Finland and Poland, sufficed to make him hostile to the Soviet regime, which he saw in dramatic contrast to his treasured democratic republic. He never developed any woolly-headed and morally obtuse sympathy for the Soviet experiment – if that is the term for that sad tyranny – but what is striking is the total lack of consequence on Truman's actions from his remark and the views that lay behind it. He dutifully supported the extension of massive amounts of Lend–Lease aid to Russia. He raised not the slightest qualm as Roosevelt forged an alliance with Stalin after Pearl Harbor. Obviously, he appreciated that America's own security interests were entwined with aiding the Soviets against Hitler's Germany and eventually he looked to them as partners in a new postwar world order.[64]

Fighting the War and Planning for the Peace

The Japanese attack on Pearl Harbor finally brought the United States into the vast conflagration known as World War II. It was barely two decades since Truman and his men had crossed the Atlantic to defeat the Kaiser. Now an even stronger and more brutal German foe confronted them in Europe in alliance with a Japanese Empire that quickly dominated all of Asia. With the nation at war and committing its tremendous energies and resources to build a massive military force, the Missouri senator pursued his demanding work so vigorously that at times he suffered physical exhaustion. He toured defense plants regularly and issued reports that identified incompetence, bottlenecks, and wasteful spending. He worked well with both Republican and Democratic committee members and gained valuable experience in bipartisan cooperation. His labors

---

[62] William L. Langer and S. Everett Gleason, *The Undeclared War, 1940–1941* (London, 1953), p. 543.

[63] On Stalin's rule, see Robert C. Tucker, *Stalin in Power: The Revolution from Above, 1928–1941* (New York, 1990). On efforts during the late 1930s to counter the views of pro-Soviet front organizations that attracted sympathetic liberals, see Richard Gid Powers, *Not Without Honor: The History of American Anticommunism* (New York, 1995), pp. 144–45.

[64] Hamby's analysis of Truman's views of the Soviet Union is insightful. See *Man of the People*, pp. 270–71.

attracted national attention. A *Look* survey of Washington journalists in 1944 voted him as one of the ten most valuable officials in Washington. In short, he truly emerged as a significant Washington politician.

Truman's success with his investigating committee, and his increasing prominence appeared to give him enhanced confidence to reflect on the war and its meaning for the future. He marched in close step with the broad policies of the Roosevelt administration and shared its emphasis on winning the war and supporting its allies. Occasionally, he made his own views known on more specific issues. In July 1942, he included in the Senate record an editorial that called for the urgent establishment of a second front in Europe to relieve the Russians. He introduced it by noting that "the editorial very adequately expressed the thinking and the attitude of the people of the Middle West on this subject."[65] The exigencies of war rather than any special concern for Stalin's nation undoubtedly prompted his comment, but he obviously had moved well beyond his thinking of June 1941.

During 1942, the first year of America's formal involvement in the war, Truman sought to interpret its meaning and its causes. In his rather simple formulation, the war was a massive struggle between good and evil. Where the Soviet allies fit into this moral calculus remained unexplored. Instead, Truman moved to elucidate the cause of it. In a speech delivered in November 1942, he asserted that "the war we are fighting is a continuation of the one we fought in 1917 and 1918." As he presented it, "the victors of that war had the opportunity to compel a peace that would protect us from war for many generations. But they missed the opportunity." Unfortunately, isolationism reared its ugly head and "a Republican Senate jettisoned the League of Nations and kept the most powerful nation in the world out of an international effort to prevent future wars."[66] In the classic American fashion, which unerringly sees the United States as the center of the story, whether it be for praise or for blame, Truman clarified that the American failure to join the League of Nations and the consequent failure to compel peace lay at the root of the present conflict. This historical analysis greatly influenced his deliberations on prescriptions for the postwar world.

Truman hardly stood alone in holding these sentiments. The memory of what befell Wilson also haunted Franklin Roosevelt and many in his administration. They feared that peace would again bring the resurgence of isolationism.[67] In order to counter isolationism, the United States would need to commit itself to

[65] "A Second Front – Now or Never," *St. Louis Star Times*, July 14, 1942, read into *Appendix to the Congressional Record* 89, part 9, p. A2918.

[66] Truman speech, Jackson County, MO, November 2, 1942, Harry S. Truman Papers: Senatorial and Vice-Presidential Speeches File, HSTL, Box 2.

[67] On this point, see Arthur M. Schlesinger, Jr., "Back to the Womb: Isolationism's Renewed Threat," *Foreign Affairs* 74 (July/August 1995), pp. 4–5. Note especially Schlesinger's observation that "for Roosevelt, the critical task in 1943–45, beyond winning the war, was to commit the United States to postwar international structures before peace could return the nation to its old [isolationist] habits."

a new international order and to membership in new international structures. During 1943 as battles raged in every theater of the war, a number of individuals turned their attention to such postwar structures. Early in February, Vice President Henry A. Wallace approached FDR with his ideas on a possible postwar organization. According to Wallace, the politically astute president replied that "he didn't think either he or I should take the lead in asking for the authorization [of a United Nations organization to consider specific problems] and suggested that I get somebody like Senator Truman, Senator Maybank or Senator Hatch to work on the problem."[68] For the most part, Roosevelt opposed detailed discussion of how the Allies should organize the peace out of fear that airing the issue might provoke the isolationists, disrupt the war effort, and, of course, tie his own hands.[69] In this instance, perhaps he aimed to enlist a stalking horse to gauge the strength of isolationist firepower, but more likely he hoped to attract a figure who might build a broader base of congressional support for the internationalist cause than could his unpopular vice president.

Roosevelt's suggestion of Truman hints that he knew that the energetic chair of the Special Committee to Investigate the National Defense Program already was involved in discussions concerning the problems of the postwar world. Along with other members of his Senate committee, Republicans Joseph H. Ball of Minnesota and Harold H. Burton of Ohio and his fellow Democrat, Carl A. Hatch of New Mexico, Truman directed attention to the need to establish a new international organization. One congressional contemporary recalled that it was "their working together [on the Truman Committee and] seeing the awful costs in men and materials and money of a war like this" which convinced them of "the absolute necessity to find some other way of resolving international difficulties than by having wars every generation."[70] The senators concluded that the United States should act before the war's end to establish a new world body, and they resolved to sponsor a Senate resolution to this end. Since his investigating committee so occupied Truman, the other senators asked Lister Hill of Alabama to join them and so maintain a bipartisan balance. Truman played only a background role in the drafting of what became know as the B2H2 resolution.[71]

Although not a major drafter of the final resolution, the Missouri senator was recognized as one of the driving forces behind it. Senator Arthur Vandenberg inferred that Truman was ultimately responsible for the resolution

68 John Morton Blum, ed., *The Price of Vision: The Diary of Henry A. Wallace, 1942–1946* (Boston, 1973), p. 182.

69 See Dallek, *Franklin D. Roosevelt and American Foreign Policy*, p. 419.

70 Oral History Interview with Dr. Walter H. Judd, HSTL.

71 This relies on Robert A. Divine, *Second Chance: The Triumph of Internationalism in America During World War II* (New York, 1967), p. 92. Robert Divine was able to interview Senator Ball during his research. For further details of the resolution, see Potomacus, "The Senator from Minnesota," *New Republic*, May 31, 1943, pp. 727–29. Potomacus reported that "the [B2H2] resolution was enthusiastically endorsed by [Wendell] Wilkie, by Senator Truman, who had helped to prepare it, and by Senator Thomas."

when he confided to his diary that Senator Ball "said that the four authors had been 'delegated' by Senator Truman at a previous luncheon where a number of Senators had discussed the matter."[72] In submitting his resolution, Ball made no direct reference to Truman, but careful observers both in the Senate and outside it closely identified him with the resolution.[73] Truman made this transparently clear. When Ball foreshadowed the submission of his resolution, Truman expressed his belief that the United States "could not possibly avoid the assumption of world leadership after this war ended," and added "that it was well to get Congress's view on the record now."[74] After its submission, he issued a statement declaring himself "100 percent for" the B2H2 resolution, which he claimed "would simply state in clear and definitive terms that effective collaboration with the United Nations to maintain world peace and stability after the war is the foreign policy which the people of the United States would prefer if the other nations will go along with us."[75]

Ball submitted his resolution on March 16 and offered it as "a sound starting point for Senate action." His resolution asked the United States to bring the members of the United Nations coalition against the Axis powers together to form an international body with specific areas of authority – among them, the establishment of "procedures and machinery for peaceful settlement of disputes and disagreements between nations," and the provision of a United Nations military force that might "suppress by immediate use of such force any future attempt at military aggression by any nation."[76] The latter provision struck some senators as radical and caused consternation. Certainly Ball's resolution possessed more specificity and force than the rather general resolution introduced some weeks later for consideration in the House of Representatives by a young congressman from Arkansas named J. William Fulbright.[77] Whatever the initial reactions, Ball found his measure referred to the cautious Senate Foreign Relations Committee chaired by Senator Tom Connally.

Truman's support of the B2H2 resolution reflected the refocus of his primary foreign policy concerns from defense preparedness in 1941 to concern for the postwar world in 1943. His major foreign policy assumptions were readily apparent and essentially twofold. First, an international organization would be essential to maintain peace and stability after the war, and second, the

[72] Arthur H. Vandenberg, Jr., ed., *The Private Papers of Senator Vandenberg* (Boston, 1952), p. 39.

[73] Writing immediately upon Truman's accession to the presidency, TRB asserted that "Truman was primarily responsible for the Ball–Burton–Hatch–Hill resolution; he planned the dinner of a dozen Senators that launched it and picked the four who signed it." TRB, "Washington Notes: The New President," *New Republic*, 23 (April 1954), p. 39. Also note I. F. Stone's claim that "I can authoritatively report that the famous B2H2 resolution originated in Mr. Truman's office." I. F. Stone, "Farewell to FDR," *Nation* 160 (April 21, 1945), p. 437.

[74] Truman quoted in *New York Times*, March 14, 1943, p. 1.

[75] Truman quoted in *New York Times*, March 20, 1943, p. 5.

[76] *Congressional Record* 89, part 2, pp. 2030–31.

[77] On Fulbright and his resolution, see Randall B. Woods, *Fulbright: A Biography* (Cambridge and New York, 1995), pp. 80–85.

United States could not refrain from major engagement in world affairs. The Ball resolution recognized these assumptions providing as it did for American leadership in a postwar world body. Many Americans shared these basic views intent, like Truman, on avoiding the mistakes of the past.[78] These assumptions guided the Missouri senator and convinced him that American participation in a new world body was the essential foreign policy objective. His assumptions, however, rested on a shaky foundation that made them strangely naïve in retrospect, although they hardly appeared so at the time. He largely ignored the reality that the Allies, especially the "Big Three," would need to collaborate well to maintain real peace. The interests and outlooks of these other countries remained unexamined. Without submitting the issue to any extensive analysis, Truman accepted that Great Britain, the Soviet Union, and the United States would continue their cooperation after the defeat of their common foe. For him, the real danger to postwar peace lay within America.

American isolationism in Truman's view represented the main threat to American participation in a world organization and to its world leadership and the danger needed to be routed from the field. Truman played his part to this end. He participated in the scheme conceived by Senator Ball and Representative Fulbright and sponsored by the United Nations Association, which sent bipartisan congressional teams on speaking tours to promote the internationalist cause.[79] He joined Republican Walter Judd of Minnesota on an arduous two-week tour – twenty-seven meetings in nineteen different cities – in July–August of 1943 through the midwest states of Iowa, Nebraska, and Kansas, traditional hotbeds of isolationist sentiment.[80] Truman was no eloquent orator like Judd, a former evangelical missionary to China, and he stuck to a familiar script at every meeting at which he spoke.[81] But his words were his own and deeply felt. He called for a "lasting and just peace" and argued that military victory would be futile "unless we lay a foundation in our postwar world that will secure for all men everywhere their basic rights." Reflecting the resurgence of Wilsonianism, which so gripped him and his colleagues, he explained that "we are fighting now that the Four Freedoms shall be not only freedoms for the United Nations but a heritage for all the peoples of the world." American political ideals and values, it seems, were to be given universal application. With evangelical fervor, Truman asserted that "History has bestowed on us a solemn responsibility." The United States must "be a mighty force at the peace

[78] See Divine's *Second Chance*. Also see John Lewis Gaddis, *The United States and the Origins of the Cold War*, pp. 23–31.

[79] For greater detail, see Divine, *Second Chance*, pp. 127–28.

[80] Details of this tour are provided in Oral History Interview with Dr. Walter Judd, HSTL. At their meetings, according to Judd's recollection, he would "speak first on *why* we had to have a world organization and then the Senator would follow with *how* to achieve it." Also see Lee Edwards, *Missionary for Freedom: The Life and Times of Walter Judd* (New York, 1990), pp. 88–89.

[81] Truman delivered the same speech in Des Moines, Iowa; Hastings, Nebraska; Grand Island, Nebraska; Omaha, Nebraska; and Lincoln, Nebraska. Harry S. Truman Papers: Senatorial and Vice-Presidential Speeches File, HSTL, Box 2.

conference. We failed before to give a genuine peace – we dare not fail this time." Truman went on to outline the Ball resolution before concluding with a forceful call to avoid repeating "the blunders of the past."[82]

Truman derived some hope from his midwest tour. He found that "the people are awake to the situation and are no longer the strong isolationists they were in the past."[83] Despite growing public support, getting the Senate on record in support of the internationalist agenda remained a challenge. Secretary of State Cordell Hull, himself an ardent internationalist, wanted to ensure a decisive vote in support of any proposal for participation in a world body so as to deny encouragement to the heirs of William Borah and Henry Cabot Lodge.[84] This and the administration's own desire to preserve maximum freedom of action encouraged a lowest common denominator approach. In late October of 1943, the Senate moved to consider a more general resolution than Ball's measure which simply provided "that the United States, acting through its constitutional processes join with free sovereign nations in the establishment and maintenance of international authority with power to prevent aggression and to preserve the peace."[85] This measure, soon named the Connally resolution for its principal sponsor, represented a cautious response to the more strongly worded message of the internationalists within and outside the Senate.[86]

The ardent Senate internationalists opposed the generality of Connally's proposal and Florida's Claude Pepper submitted an amendment that included within it a call for the United States to join an international organization "with authority to settle international disputes peacefully, and with power, including military force, to suppress military aggression and to preserve the peace of the world."[87] Truman joined Pepper and twelve other senators, soon dubbed the "willful fourteen" in an ironic play on Wilson's epithet against his senate foes, in cosponsoring the amendment. On November 2, he came to the Senate floor and argued that "the Connally resolution is not specific, that it does not specify

---

[82] Truman speech, Des Moines, Iowa, July 30, 1943, Harry S. Truman Papers: Senatorial and Vice-Presidential Speeches File, HSTL, Box 2. On the enduring impact of "Wilsonianism," both in the 1940s and beyond, and for some attempt to define it, see John A. Thompson, *Woodrow Wilson* (London, 2002), pp. 250–51.

[83] Truman to Leonard Williams, August 23, 1943, Harry S. Truman Papers: Senatorial Files, HSTL, Box 150.

[84] Cordell Hull, *The Memoirs of Cordell Hull*, 2 vols. (New York, 1948), II, p. 1261.

[85] *Congressional Record* 89, part 7, p. 8663.

[86] For a good overview of the Connally resolution, see Philip J. Briggs, *Making American Foreign Policy: President–Congress Relations from the Second World War to the Post–Cold War Era*, 2nd ed. (Lanham, MD, 1994), pp. 15–29. The *Nation* editorialized regarding the Connally resolution: "Expected to be thinner than the Ball–Burton–Hatch–Hill proposal, the sub-committee's resolution is even weaker than the unexciting Fulbright measure." *Nation*, October 23, 1943, p. 458. For a contemporary discussion of the origins of the Connally resolution see Blair Bolles, "Senators and the Peace," *Nation*, 157 (October 16, 1943), pp. 426–28. Bolles described Truman as one of the senators who could be "counted on not only to prod the Foreign Relations Committee to bring on its resolution but to put up a hard fight on the floor to strengthen that resolution if it turns out to be weak."

[87] *Congressional Record* 89, part 7, pp. 8684–85.

the establishment of an organization with power to act in order to prevent aggression of such outlaw nations as Germany, Fascist Italy and Japan, and that it does not authorize the grant of power necessary to enforce decisions." Turning to his major and familiar theme, Truman declared that "isolationism cannot end and will not end unless the Senate is willing to end it." He warned again that "a small group of willful men kept us from assuming our obligations in 1919–1920, and the same thing can happen again." Looking from the past to the future, he revealed his fear "that another and worse war will follow this one unless the United Nations and their allies and all the other sovereign nations decide to work together for peace as they are working together for victory."[88] These ardent convictions had become a fundamental part of Truman's political outlook.

The persuasive power of Truman's words on his colleagues was never tested because the Pepper amendment never came to a vote. In a compromise measure, Connally included section four of the Moscow Declaration, which had just been signed by Cordell Hull, as section four of his own resolution, which prompted Pepper to withdraw his amendment. On November 5, 1943, Truman joined eighty-four other senators in passing the revised Connally resolution. Only five senators cast negative votes. The internationalists appeared triumphant, and Truman shared the general satisfaction. According to his daughter, the future president considered his work on the B2H2 resolution and on the Connally resolution to be among his most important Senate achievements.[89] His support for the Ball resolution and for the Pepper amendment certainly placed him in the forefront of Senate internationalists. His deeply felt views would influence his actions as president as he struggled to reconcile his rosy hopes and plans with the challenging international realities he confronted.

Truman's work for the internationalist cause proved his major foreign policy concern in 1943, but he also took time to make clear his outrage at the Nazi treatment of Europe's Jews. Truman shared the general Zionist sympathies of many of his fellow Democrats, despite the occasionally insensitive references to Jews in his private remarks and correspondence. In April 1943, he spoke at a large rally in Chicago aimed at highlighting the danger Hitler posed to Jews in lands under his control. He denounced a "mad Hitler" for his herding of Jews into concentration camps and – at a time when some were still disputing the atrocious reality of what we know as the Holocaust – he warned that no one could "doubt the horrible intentions of the Nazi beasts. We know that they plan the systematic slaughter throughout all of Europe, not only of the Jews but of vast numbers of other innocent peoples." What to do? Naturally, the war should be fought vigorously in order to bring Hitler's monstrous rule to an end. But he added that "today – not tomorrow – we must do all that is humanly possible to provide a haven and a place of safety for all those who can be grasped from the hands of the Nazi butchers," and he advocated that "free lands must

[88] *Congressional Record* 89, part 7, p. 8993.
[89] Margaret Truman, *Harry S. Truman* (New York, 1973), p. 157.

be opened to them."[90] Truman refrained at this point from endorsing a Jewish homeland in Palestine knowing well the serious implications of such a measure on relations with Great Britain and the Arab peoples. He explained privately to a constituent that the issue should be "very circumspectly handled" but promised with more prescience than he could have imagined that "when the right time comes I am willing to help make the fight for a Jewish homeland in Palestine."[91]

Abolishing Power Politics and Creating the United Nations

As the war entered its final years, an increasingly utopian quality afflicted American policy making and public expectations regarding the postwar world. Cordell Hull, upon returning from the Moscow Conference in late 1943, declared that soon "there will no longer be need for spheres of influence, for alliances, for balance of power, or any of the other special arrangements through which, in the unhappy past, the nations strove to safeguard their security or to promote their interests."[92] International relations, it seemed, were to be transformed. A new world organization with the United States at its center would surely create Tennyson's parliament of man. Harry Truman thoroughly warmed to such visions and continued his efforts to bring them to fruition.

In January 1944, he spoke to the United Nations Forum in Washington, D.C., and concentrated his remarks on "power politics," which he claimed would be "the major problem to overcome in building the foundation of a decent and sane postwar world." In order to construct "a lasting peace," the world needed "a new improved league of nations made up of the United Nations and controlled by Britain, China, Russia and the United States in the name of all and for the welfare of all." In words that might have amused practitioners of *realpolitik*, he sought to avoid a "postwar scramble for the spoils of war, for more power at the expense of other nations." Now was the time to "adopt some adequate substitute for power politics." The answer lay in outlawing war "by creating a new machine of peace more powerful than any machine of war," with a powerful international police force as its means of enforcement.[93]

Truman's conception of his proposed world body being controlled by the "Big Four" powers bore some similarity to Franklin's Roosevelt's four policemen concept, which the president had outlined to Soviet foreign minister Molotov in May of 1942.[94] Such a conception in both instances relied upon

[90] For the rally and Truman's remarks at it, see McCullough, *Truman*, pp. 286–87.

[91] For Truman's correspondence with his constituents and further discussion of his views on a Jewish homeland in Palestine, see Hamby, *Man of the People*, pp. 269–70.

[92] Cordell Hull, Address before Congress regarding the Moscow Conference, November 18, 1943, *Department of State Bulletin* 9 (November 20, 1943), p. 343.

[93] Truman speech at the United Nations Forum, January 17, 1944, *Appendix to the Congressional Record*, 90, part 8, p. A266.

[94] See memorandum of Roosevelt–Molotov conversation, May 29, 1942, *Foreign Relations of the United States*, 1942 (Washington, DC, 1961), III, pp. 568–69.

continued cooperation between the major Allied powers. In Truman's case, this was further emphasized by his call for an international police force. He surely saw the Soviets as worthy allies and as acceptable partners in shaping the postwar world. There were no qualifications in his public or private remarks that suggest fears that the Soviets might endanger the conception of the post-war peace he supported. Instead, Truman extolled the unity of purpose and the achievements of the Allies. In February, he told an audience in Jacksonville, Florida, that "when you fabricate a rifle for our Army or a shell for our Navy or when you produce a bushel of wheat for our brave Chinese, British or Russian Allies, you must take grim delight in seeing the definite product that is tipping the scales in favor of the democracies."[95] How the Chinese or the Russians war-ranted inclusion among the democracies went unexplored and unexplained.

Truman's vision for the future included not only political cooperation between nations but also economic collaboration among them. In March 1944, he joined his fellow Democratic Senators Elbert Thomas of Utah and Harley Kilgore of West Virginia in sponsoring a resolution calling for continued economic collaboration among the wartime allies in order to maintain an "enduring peace." It called on the president to convene a meeting of Allied representatives "for the purpose of considering the joint measures and inter-national organization by which the resources of member nations can be most effectively developed in friendly collaboration with one another."[96] In their spe-cific analysis, the three sponsors argued that a prosperous economic future on which real peace depended required "an economically healthy United States." But this, in turn, was contingent upon "a volume of foreign trade above and beyond anything we have had before." They warned that "the future peace depends on the abandonment of political nationalism and economic imperial-ism and autarchy."[97]

Such views were consistent with and assuredly derived from the free trade doctrine that Cordell Hull had pushed since the 1930s. Truman and his col-leagues now looked for means to implement it. The future president later recalled conversations with colleagues in which he "would point to a map of Europe and trace its breadbasket, with Hungary a cattle country and Rumania and Ukraine as the wheat area. Up to the northeast lay western Germany, northern France, Belgium, and Britain with their coal, iron and big industries." The task, as the senators saw it, was "to help unify Europe by linking up the breadbasket with the industrial centers through a free flow of trade."[98] These raw thoughts favoring free trade and European economic integration would prompt Truman's pet free-waterways proposal at the Potsdam Confer-ence. They also reflected in their unrefined and rather down-home formulation

[95] Truman speech, Jacksonville, Florida, February 14, 1944, Harry S. Truman Papers: Senatorial and Vice-Presidential Speeches File, HSTL.
[96] *Congressional Record* 90, part 2, p. 2299.
[97] *Congressional Record* 90, part 2, pp. 2299–3000.
[98] Truman, *Year of Decisions*, p. 263.

the very same intellectual commitments in favor of economic and political lib-
eralization that underlay the Wilsonian vision of a democratic and capitalist
world order. And, again in a rather similar manner to Wilson, the ideas were
sincerely offered based on an untested assumption that the world's peoples
readily would embrace the liberal American vision that would redound to their
benefit. The applicability or acceptablility of these ideas for other nations, such
as the Soviet Union or Britain and its empire, simply remained unexamined.

The promotion of American entry into a new international organization
and the defeat of isolationism continued to attract Truman's energies and concerns throughout 1944. The overblown rhetoric of this plain man suggests the
depth of his convictions on the issue. "Do we not owe it to our children, to
all mankind," he asked of an audience in Toledo in June 1944, "to be sure
that these catastrophes do not engulf the world a third time. This is America's
destiny."[99] Later in the year, he wrapped the United States in a divine mantle
and asserted that "Almighty God intends this nation to assume leadership in
world affairs to preserve the peace."[100] Truman went to his party's 1944 convention intent on securing "a strong, plainly worded foreign policy plank to let
the world know that America will take a hand in international affairs after the
war." He suggested that if his Democratic Party couldn't write a better platform
than the Republicans, "without an ambiguous foreign policy plank," then they
ought not hold a convention.[101]

The 1944 Democratic convention in Chicago produced a satisfactory platform. It also nominated Truman as its vice-presidential candidate to run with
Franklin Roosevelt in the November election. A group of party insiders led by
national chairman Robert Hannegan and national treasurer Ed Pauley joined
forces to convince Roosevelt to drop Henry Wallace and to put Truman in
his place. The party officials worried about the president's health and wanted
"a reliable man as his running mate" rather than the personally erratic and
politically liberal Wallace.[102] "There was," as Max Lerner put it, "a dying king
and no accepted heir at a time of danger when a war was not yet settled and
a peace not yet framed."[103] There were a number of pretenders to the throne
eager to displace Wallace as heir apparent. Truman arrived in Chicago intent
on nominating one of them, his former Senate colleague James F. Byrnes. Only
reluctantly did he agree to be nominated, after getting definite clarification that
he had the support of the cagey Roosevelt, who had dallied with at least four
candidates at one point or another. When FDR instructed Hannegan to tell
the hesitant Truman that "if he wants to break up the Democratic Party in
the middle of a war that's his responsibility," the issue was sealed. The dutiful

---

[99] Truman speech, Toledo, Ohio, June 14, 1944, Harry S. Truman Papers: Senatorial and Vice-
  Presidential Speeches File, HSTL.
[100] *New York Times*, October 25, 1944, p. 12.
[101] *New York Times*, July 10, 1944, p. 16.
[102] Ferrell, *Harry S. Truman*, pp. 162–64.
[103] Lerner, "Harry Truman: The Plutarchian President," p. 200.

Truman gained release from his commitment to Byrnes and allowed his name
to be placed in nomination against Wallace. He won decisively on the second
ballot.[104]

Truman's nomination certainly owed much to the political skills of the party
leaders who massaged FDR into considering him the best running mate even
though the president had no close relationship with the Missouri senator.
Truman's essential quality was his broad appeal to all interest groups and
geographic regions in the party, which set him apart from both Wallace and
Byrnes. A unified party was deemed essential to win a fourth term for Franklin
Roosevelt, and that made all the difference. Truman's internationalist perspective and his good reputation and contacts within the Senate also played a
part. Roosevelt's confidante Harry Hopkins recalled that the president "wanted
somebody that would help him when he went up there [to the Senate] and asked
them to ratify the peace."[105] Roosevelt envisaged that his new running mate
would play a key role in obtaining Senate approval for this postwar proposals,
especially American participation in a new world organization. In his acceptance speech, Truman confirmed his readiness "to help the commander in chief
to win the war and save the peace. I have always been a supporter of Franklin
D. Roosevelt in domestic and foreign policy and I shall continue to do just
that with everything I have as V.P."[106] His sincere ambition was to serve the
president.

After his nomination, Truman toured the country extensively hammering
home a partisan message that equated support for the Republicans with isolationism. He warned against a "Congress of Nyes and Tafts," compared Thomas
Dewey to Warren G. Harding, and challenged the Republican nominee to disassociate himself from eight isolationist senators in his party.[107] He met with
Roosevelt infrequently during the campaign and received no specific briefings
on policy matters, although he probably received very broad details of the
Manhattan Project to develop the atomic bomb.[108] Soon after the convention,
he met with FDR and lunched with him on the lawn behind the White House.
Roosevelt's haggard appearance and trembling hands shocked him, but political professional that he was, he played his part in maintaining the deception
regarding Roosevelt's health and pronounced the president as "fine" and still

---

[104] Ferrell is excellent on all the details. See his *Harry S. Truman*, pp. 165–71, and his more detailed
study *Choosing Truman: The Democratic Convention of 1944* (Columbia, MO, 1994). Also
note David M. Kennedy's interpretation that "the senator [Truman] was the man who would
hurt the ticket the least." Truman was "a one-man 'Missouri Compromise' who might not add
much but was unobjectionable to Roosevelt and would do no political harm." See his *Freedom
from Fear: The American People in Depression and War, 1929–1945* (New York, 1999),
p. 792.

[105] Robert E. Sherwood, *Roosevelt and Hopkins: An Intimate History* (New York, 1948), p. 882.

[106] Truman quoted in Ferrell, *Harry S. Truman*, p. 171.

[107] *New York Times*, October 24, 1944, p. 1.

[108] On this matter, see Ferrell, *Harry S. Truman*, p. 172.

PHOTO 1. President Franklin D. Roosevelt and Senator Harry S. Truman, his running mate in the 1944 election, at a lunch on the lawn of the White House, August 18, 1944. (Courtesy National Archives)

"the leader he's always been."[109] Despite Republican efforts to raise doubts about his health, Roosevelt again emerged victorious in the election. "I am very happy over the overwhelming endorsement which you have received," Truman telegrammed him. "Isolationism is dead."[110]

On January 20, the presidential inauguration took place on the south portico of the White House. Henry Wallace administered the oath to Truman, and then Roosevelt struggled to his feet and took the presidential oath for the fourth time. Just two days later the president left for Yalta in the Crimea to meet with

---

[109] Truman quoted in Hamby, *Man of the People*, p. 285. In private, Truman confided to his friend Harry Vaughan that he was shocked by FDR's feeble appearance. "[H]e's just going to pieces," he explained. "I'm very much concerned about him." Truman quoted from Ferrell, *Harry S. Truman*, p. 172. Also note that Robert Ferrell, the dean of Truman scholars, suggests that FDR briefed Truman on the atomic bomb at this August 18 lunch. If so, the briefing must have been in very general terms and was never followed up in any significant way. For further details on FDR's disturbing health condition at this time, see Robert H. Ferrell, *The Dying President: Franklin D. Roosevelt, 1944–1945* (Columbia, MO, 1998), pp. 83–91.

[110] Truman, *Year of Decisions*, p. 219.

PHOTO 2. President Franklin D. Roosevelt waves to the people who attended his inauguration at the White House on January 20, 1945. On his right is Vice President Harry S. Truman and on his left, his son, Colonel James Roosevelt. (Courtesy National Archives)

Josef Stalin and Winston Churchill. He charged Truman with the difficult task of securing Wallace's confirmation as secretary of commerce, but shared little of his plans for his pending summit meeting. Truman knew his place and did not presume to make any inquiries in the domain of diplomacy. Even upon his return from Yalta, Roosevelt gave Truman no serious briefings. Of course, it was hardly his way to share information freely and so, he feared, to weaken his control over policy making. Truman made no special effort to compensate for the presidential reticence even though he early on had recognized that Roosevelt might die in office and despite one nerve-wracking episode when rumors of the president's death circulated through the Senate.[111] He assembled no policy-oriented staff as vice president and certainly had no influential foreign policy adviser whose counsel he considered. He sought neither briefings from the state or war departments nor consultations with American officials who had accompanied FDR to Yalta. A denial that the great leader could be struck down

---

[111] For Truman's recognition, see Ferrell, *Harry S. Truman*, p. 175. On the rumors in the Senate, see Truman interview, January 23, 1954, Harry S. Truman Papers: Post-Presidential Files, HSTL, Box 643. (The Senate "rumor" confused FDR's death with that of his loyal military aide General Watson.)

on the eve of victory beset Truman as it did everyone else in the administration. All around the president "continued to play their private game of pushing mortality into the indefinite future."[112]

Roosevelt's disgraceful failure to brief his vice president fully only served to confirm Truman in his own foreign policy views, which he found confirmed by the president's public statements. On his return from Yalta, FDR assured a joint session of the Congress of the prospects for "a peace based on the sound and just principles of the Atlantic Charter, on the conception of the dignity of the human being, and on the guarantees of tolerance and freedom of religious worship." With Truman seated behind him, Roosevelt explained that "the Crimean Conference was a successful effort by the three leading nations to find a common ground for peace . . . it spells – and it ought to spell – the end of the system of unilateral action, exclusive alliances, and spheres of influence, and balances of power and all the other expedients which have been tried for centuries and failed."[113] A new day was dawning. Power politics would be dispatched to the dustbin of history. Truman joined the legislators on their feet applauding the president and the future peace he promised.

After a month in Washington upon his return from Yalta, Roosevelt left for his retreat in Warm Springs, intent on regaining his strength under the warm Georgia sun. Truman had little opportunity to deepen his relationship with the president during this time. He recalled that he saw Roosevelt only twice aside from at cabinet meetings where "Roosevelt never discussed anything important."[114] He troubled him little and only on matters of domestic politics. When he did approach him, as with a suggestion that Hannegan be named postmaster-general, he did so with great deference and respect.[115] Regardless of his occasional past criticisms of the president, especially at the time of his 1940 primary fight, he held Roosevelt in some awe and admired the courage of the president as he sacrificed his health, his very self, in order to win both the war and the peace.

On April 12, 1945, with victory over Hitler less than a month away, Franklin Roosevelt died. Within hours, Harry Truman was sworn in as president and assumed the great responsibility for leading his nation through to victory in war and to success in formulating a lasting peace – a responsibility that he neither sought nor expected and that he had hoped would be FDR's. He brought to the presidency a firm belief that a peaceful postwar world depended upon the adoption by the United States of world leadership in both the political and economic spheres. He saw the establishment and operation of a new world organization

---

[112] Henry Morgenthau 3rd, "The Last Night at Warm Springs," *New York Times*, April 12, 1995, p. 25.

[113] *Congressional Record* 91, part 2, pp. 1621–22.

[114] Truman mentioned this to Jonathan Daniels. See Jonathan Daniels, *The Man of Independence* (Philadelphia, 1950), p. 259. See also Truman, *Year of Decisions*, pp. 34–35.

[115] On the suggestion, see Truman to Roosevelt, April 5, 1945, Franklin D. Roosevelt Papers, President's Secretary's File, FDRL, Box 167. On this matter, also see Hamby, *Man of the People*, p. 288–89.

as crucial and viewed the meeting to design such a body, which was scheduled to
meet in San Francisco late in April, as tremendously important. Like his predecessor, he expected to work in collaboration with the wartime Allies in shaping
the postwar international structure. Truman brought a deep conviction that
America's role and vision in this effort must be central. The United States must
redeem the error of 1919. It could not retreat but must engage and embrace
the world and impose its stamp upon it. In retrospect, it is easy to label this
outlook as arrogant. But in light of both the disastrous course of the twentieth
century to that point, which was blamed on American disengagement, and also
of the renewed faith of Americans in their political and economic institutions
brought on by their triumph in the war, it is understandable and, in some ways,
deeply admirable.[116]

Truman did not bring to the presidency any significant reservations concerning the policies or goals of Franklin Roosevelt as he understood them. He had
taken on the vice presidency and left behind his beloved Senate in order to serve
with Roosevelt to secure the lasting peace he had labored for so vigorously over
the previous years. His service as vice president deepened his commitment to
continue along the course that FDR had publicly charted. He pledged himself to
bring to fulfillment the goals that Roosevelt had set and with which his internationalist commitments seemed in perfect alignment. Most crucial was to defeat
the isolationists and to enter a new world organization.

In light of the myriad failures of the United Nations organization over the
last sixty years, it might seem odd that Truman and, it should be added, so
many of his contemporaries placed such great faith in a new world body. Yet
one cannot understand his initial actions in office unless one appreciates just
this.[117] Truman, ever the American patriot for whom the United States was
the greatest country, believed the world required American leadership of a new
world organization. With this leadership in place, real peace might be realized

---

[116] I'm influenced here by the observations of Alan Brinkley, "For America, It Truly Was a Great
War," *New York Times Magazine* (May 7, 1995), pp. 54–57.

[117] In some sense, Truman's enduring devotion to the United Nations lasted throughout his administration. In his 1949 inaugural address, he declared that the first point of his four-point foreign
policy program would be "to give unfaltering support to the United Nations and related agencies" and to "continue to search for ways to strengthen their authority and increase their
effectiveness." Inaugural Address, January 20, 1949, Truman, *Public Papers of the Presidents
of the United States: Harry S. Truman, 1949* (Washington, DC, 1964), p. 114. After taking the
decision to intervene in the Korean War in June 1950, Truman told John [Jack] Hickerson of
the State Department over a drink that "I hoped and prayed that I would never have to make
a decision like the one I have just made today. But I saw nothing else that was possible for me
to do except that. Now, with this drink, that's out of my mind. Jack, there's something I want
you to know. In the final analysis I *did this* for the United Nations. I believed in the League
of Nations. It failed. Lots of people thought that it failed because we weren't in it to back it
up. Okay, now we started the United Nations. It was our idea, and in this first big test we
just couldn't let them down. If a collective system under the UN can work, it must be made
to work, and *now* is the time to call their bluff." Truman quoted in Ferrell, *Harry S. Truman*,
p. 323.

aided by the universal application of American political and economic ideals. Truman's internationalist views would come under assault from the earliest days of his presidency, and throughout his administration, he would struggle to reconcile his genuine idealist commitment to the United Nations with the realist demands of a world where interests and ideologies clashed and where power politics could not be avoided.

2

Inheritance

Franklin Roosevelt's Uncertain Legacy

Titan and Fox

Two days after the death of Franklin Roosevelt, the *New York Times* assured its readers that "there will prevail in Washington a continuity." Featuring the authoritative voice normally associated with its prolix opinions, the *Times* noted that this would be "particularly true in the field of foreign policy." This expansive editorial guarantee rested on an analysis recognizing that "from the repeal of the Neutrality Act and the adoption of the Hull trade program, through lend–lease and the Atlantic charter, to Dumbarton Oaks and Yalta and San Francisco the road is clearly charted."[1] Contrary to the *Times* editorial, however, the road for Harry Truman and American foreign policy was not so clearly mapped. By April of 1945, Franklin Roosevelt's public vision of the postwar world found itself increasingly at odds with hard diplomatic realities. His grand vision set the expectations of most Americans, including Truman, regarding the postwar future, but it neither captured the true state of the relationships among the major powers nor hinted at the issues over which they differed.

Roosevelt's public vision – rooted in the Atlantic Charter, nurtured by the soothing assurances of the president and Secretary of State Cordell Hull during the war, and, in its final flowering, proclaimed to be close at hand following the Yalta conference – failed to anticipate a sizable gap between diplomatic realities and lofty principles. That it did not was a significant element of Roosevelt's legacy for he bequeathed to Truman an American public thinking of foreign policy in rather idealistic and universal terms. Of course, in addition to extravagant public expectations, Truman also inherited the complex reality of Franklin Roosevelt's foreign policy. It was emphatically no simple inheritance, and its provisions defied easy description. Roosevelt, unable to admit his own mortality, refrained from preparing any testament that might serve as a genuine guide

[1] *New York Times*, April 14, 1945, p. 14.

34

for his successor. No single aide qualified to interpret his plans and designs authoritatively. Instead, Roosevelt's various aides and advisers gave the new president conflicting views of his predecessor's intentions.

In light of the considerable disagreements among the president's advisers, it is hardly surprising that historians have differed fiercely over the broad direction of Roosevelt's foreign policy and its sagacity and over his preferred course of action at the time of his death. The same policy maker warmly praised by some historians as the "ultimate realist" who worked well within the domestic and international limits placed upon him has been bitterly lambasted by others as a "naive and idealistic blunderer" who never understood either "the Soviet Union or international relations."[2] The intensity of the debate over Roosevelt's foreign policy shows little sign of abating as works continue to appear defending or criticizing his record.[3]

Much of the disagreement regarding the state of American foreign policy at the time of Roosevelt's death results from the fact that it was so integrally linked to and was indeed an expression of an elusive figure, namely Franklin Roosevelt himself. The squire of Hyde Park stands in many ways as a worthy rival to the master of Monticello for the title of "American Sphinx."[4] He is a "Protean figure," as William Leuchtenburg would have it, whose various forms make him all at once "the best loved, most hated, most influential, most enigmatic" of modern American presidents.[5] Yet Roosevelt's place in American history rests secure and unshakable as a great leader in peace and war, an indisputable titan, a brilliant political practitioner, and the measuring rod for all subsequent presidents. In the depths of depression, he helped restore to an almost despairing nation real hope and energy with his New Deal measures and his memorable assurance that the only thing to be feared was fear itself. He overcame the powerful forces of American isolationism and unilateralism in the years from 1939 to 1941, and supported Great Britain and the Soviet Union in their deathly struggle against Hitler's Germany. After Pearl Harbor, he convinced the American people that they faced a truly global challenge that required the defeat of both Germany and Japan.[6] He led a unified nation

---

[2] For a comprehensive review of the extensive literature on Franklin Roosevelt's diplomacy during the Second World War, see Mark A. Stoler, "A Half Century of Conflict: Interpretations of U.S. World War II Diplomacy," *Diplomatic History*, 18 (Summer 1994), pp. 375–403. Quotations from p. 394.

[3] Among the best recent "defenses" of FDR are Warren F. Kimball's *The Juggler*; and Kimball's *Forged in War: Roosevelt, Churchill, and the Second World War* (New York, 1997). A vigorous critical analysis of Roosevelt's diplomacy is Amos Perlmutter, *FDR & Stalin: A Not So Grand Alliance, 1943–1945* (Columbia, MO, 1993).

[4] See Joseph J. Ellis, *American Sphinx: The Character of Thomas Jefferson* (New York, 1996).

[5] William Leuchtenburg, *In the Shadow of FDR: From Harry Truman to Bill Clinton*, rev. ed. (Ithaca, NY, 1993), p. xi; Arthur M. Schlesinger's review of Patrick Maney's *The Roosevelt Presence* in *Political Science Quarterly*, 108 (Fall 1993), p. 543.

[6] John Lewis Gaddis points to FDR's significance as an American grand strategist and argues that under his leadership "the United States was able to move in a remarkably short period of time from a strategy that had limited itself to controlling the western hemisphere to one aimed at

through to the brink of ultimate victory in the greatest armed conflict in history and served in the words of his friend Felix Frankfurter as "a symbol of hope for liberty-loving people everywhere in resisting a seemingly invincible challenge to civilization."[7] His extraordinary confidence, optimism, and ebullience shone through like a beacon giving light to help lesser mortals find their way.

Yet, when examining Roosevelt's portrait more closely and beyond the broad-brush strokes formed by his buoyant leadership of his nation through the Depression and the Second World War, his picture becomes more blurred, the exact nature of his accomplishments more debatable, and his enigmatic features impossible to avoid. Roosevelt might best be thought of as a remarkable exemplar of the "political fox" in action.[8] He was never limited by any central conviction or purpose. Rather as a "magnificently resourceful improvisor" and "a virtuoso in the use of power," he displayed during the New Deal a willingness to shift directions and to vary his methods without inhibition as circumstances required.[9] FDR's refusal to decide among various competing and in part contradictory approaches during the New Deal, such as vigorous enforcement of the anti-trust laws, or suspension of those laws and encouragement of business–government cooperation, or the creation of devices for centralized economic planning and management, illustrates well his mercurial style.[10] He relied more heavily on the force of his personality than on the force or consistency of his ideas, and in this sense there resides some insight in the remark attributed to Justice Oliver Wendell Holmes that Roosevelt possessed a first-class temperament but only a second-class intellect. FDR avoided arduous study of complex issues and chose not to outline detailed plans. Instead, a keen intuition and reliance on his brilliant political instincts powered his pragmatism and helped him dominate the American domestic landscape for over a decade.

Even though FDR's policy commitments and purposes at times proved difficult to pin down, no observer ever doubted his mastery of the White House and his complete comfort with and confidence in his use of presidential power. His image of the presidential office, Richard Neustadt once astutely noted,

---

winning a global war and managing the peace that would follow." See his discussion in Gaddis, *Surprise, Security and the American Experience* (Cambridge, MA, 2004), pp. 47–48.

[7] Felix Frankfurter, *Franklin Delano Roosevelt* – booklet containing Frankfurter's article originally published in *Harvard Alumni Bulletin*, April 28, 1945.

[8] See Owen Harries, "The Day of the Fox" *National Interest*, 29 (Fall 1992), pp. 109–12. Harries's terms are inspired by Isaiah Berlin's famous essay on Tolstoy, "The Hedgehog and the Fox." Also note, of course, James MacGregor Burns's classic study *Roosevelt: The Lion and the Fox* (New York, 1956).

[9] Harries, "The Day of the Fox," p. 109.

[10] Ellis Hawley's classic *The New Deal and the Problem of Monopoly: A Study in Economic Ambivalence* (Princeton, NJ, 1966) demonstrates brilliantly the alternate courses for economic action represented in the New Deal and the debates among their supporters. For FDR's continuing refusal to commit himself to a particular course of action as late as 1937–38, see Wilson D. Miscamble, "Thurman Arnold Goes to Washington: A Look at Antitrust Policy in the Later New Deal," *Business History Review*, 56 (Spring 1982), pp. 1–15.

"was himself-in-office."[11] No setback, not even the court-packing fiasco in 1937, appears to have dimmed his faith in his own judgment.[12] His decision to run for third and fourth terms probably owed as much to his inability to conceive of another occupant of the Oval Office as it did to the dangerous circumstances that convinced him of his indispensability to guide the American ship-of-state through stormy seas.[13] He dominated and sought to manipulate all those who served in his administration utilizing the practices of dividing authority and assigning overlapping responsibilities so as to pit subordinates against one another and so make himself the locus for all major decisions.[14] He relished moving outside established channels, and in diplomacy he seemed especially to enjoy overlooking State Department officials and foreign service professionals in favor of confidantes and personal emissaries like Harry Hopkins, Joseph Davies, and Averell Harriman.

Roosevelt's keen desire to preserve his freedom of action led him often either to postpone decisions or to make them hastily without significant study regarding implications or consequences. Both approaches would be evident in his wartime diplomacy. His self-assurance fueled by his dual triumphs over personal affliction and political opposition allowed a style of decision making largely unburdened by notable coherence and coordination. Roosevelt admitted as much when in 1942 he described himself as "a juggler" who never let his right hand know what his left hand did. "I may have one policy for Europe," he explained, "and one diametrically opposite for North and South America." Conceding that "I may be entirely inconsistent," he also admitted that he would "mislead and tell untruths if it will help win the war."[15] His wiliness and use of deliberate deception certainly served him well in maintaining domestic support for his administration before and during the war. He proved perfectly willing to tolerate a sizable disjunction between his private plans and his public policy expressions.

Roosevelt's personalization of his office and of American foreign policy made his juggler's act an especially difficult one to follow. Truman possessed none of his predecessor's nimbleness, nor did he desire to be such a solo or dominating performer. Roosevelt's death therefore immediately and inevitably prompted a major change in the *way* in which foreign policy was formulated. Truman

---

[11] Richard E. Neustadt, *Presidential Power and the Modern Presidents: The Politics of Leadership from Roosevelt to Reagan* (New York, 1990), p. 136. A close observer, Robert H. Jackson, commented that "Roosevelt liked the Presidency better than any man I have known who has occupied it....I think he liked it better than Truman, Hoover, or Eisenhower." Robert H. Jackson, *That Man: An Insider's Portrait of Franklin D. Roosevelt*, ed. John Q. Barrett (New York, 2003), p. 42.

[12] Max Lerner made this point in *Wounded Titans*, p. 166.

[13] On Roosevelt's decision to run for a third term, see Bernard Donahoe, C.S.C., *Private Plans and Public Dangers: The Story of FDR's Third Nomination* (Notre Dame, IN, 1965).

[14] Patrick Maney makes this point in *The Roosevelt Presence: A Biography of Franklin Delano Roosevelt* (New York, 1992), p. 191.

[15] Roosevelt quoted in Kimball, *The Juggler*, p. 7.

understood well that he could not be Franklin Roosevelt and devise policy in the manner he did. But he publicly pledged to carry on the great fallen leader's policies and to do as he would have done. Understanding those policies is the initial step in determining how well he succeeded.

Postwar Vision

The complexity of Roosevelt's modus operandi, a method impossible to systematize or replicate, should not disguise the fact that the broad outlines of his foreign policy were not especially complicated. Historians attuned to his Gordian activities in the realms of domestic policies and politics might be tempted to look for hidden motives and intentions. What is more apparent, however, is Roosevelt's steady commitment to certain key policy elements that together formed a vague vision for the postwar world.[16] This vision began to take serious shape in 1942, although he never felt able to share it fully with his own people. Instead the American populace was spoon-fed assurances that satisfied their insatiable appetite for idealistic objectives. They might expect in their time, the president expounded, a world of the Four Freedoms – of speech, of religion, from want, and from fear – and one in which "the right of all peoples to choose the form of government under which they will live" would be respected.[17] Despite repeated public assurances regarding the aims of extending freedoms and promoting democracy, the Roosevelt administration gave little explicit attention to specific means to foster self-determination. This seemingly bedrock American goal took something of a backseat to other dimensions of the Rooseveltian program.[18]

FDR's vision for the future was much influenced by the lessons he drew from the past.[19] Having watched Germany plunge the world into war twice within a quarter century, Roosevelt wanted to remove all possibility of any third attempt. There could be no repetition of the "stab in the back" claims that had so damaged the Weimar Republic. Germany and its allies would need to be defeated totally. Above and beyond the German defeat, however, Roosevelt aimed "to bring about a radical reduction in the weight of Europe," in world

---

[16] Warren Kimball's argument that "Roosevelt did have a foreign policy – or at least a set of consistent assumptions that shaped his reactions and policies" is persuasive. See Kimball, *The Juggler*, p. 18.

[17] Roosevelt outlined his "four essential human freedoms" in his Annual Message to Congress, January 6, 1941. See Senate Committee on Foreign Relations, *A Decade of American Foreign Policy: Basic Documents, 1941–49* (Washington, DC, 1950), p. 1. For the Atlantic Charter, see Joint Statement by President Roosevelt and Prime Minister Churchill, *FRUS*, 1941, I, pp. 368–69.

[18] John Lewis Gaddis made essentially this point when he noted that "for all their wartime rhetoric about self determination, the Americans had no plans to promote that objective comparable to their blueprints for collective security and economic recovery." John Lewis Gaddis, *We Now Know: Rethinking Cold War History* (Oxford, 1997), p. 198.

[19] This point is made by Gordon A. Craig and Alexander L. George in *Force and Statecraft: Diplomatic Problems of Our Time*, 3rd ed. (New York, 1995), pp. 87–88.

affairs.[20] Not only Germany but the other nations of continental Europe would be disarmed and permanently so. When Soviet Foreign Minister Vyacheslav Molotov visited Washington in May of 1942, the president took the opportunity over cocktails and dinner to share details of his evolving design. He dismissed what he described as Churchill's idea for a "revived League of Nations" as too "impractical" and instead suggested that after the war the United States, the Soviet Union, Great Britain, and (improbably) China would serve as "the policemen of the world."[21] The four powers would cooperate in the broad policing responsibility but have special obligations to walk the beat in their own regional neighborhoods. In Roosevelt's conception, it seemed acceptable that the defeat of German militarism would permit the extension of Soviet power into Eastern and Central Europe.[22]

Roosevelt's main effort aimed to preserve the wartime alliance as the key instrument for postwar cooperation. His vision bears some similarity to the concert system established by the European powers in 1815 after defeating Napoleon.[23] The victorious allies would form a consortium to oversee the behavior of other states in a spirit of genuine collaboration. He distinguished this system from classic balance-of-power and sphere-of-influence arrangements, which inevitably involved significant competition among the major powers. In his formulation, the nations would not be rivals but would function like the directors of an international cartel working together for their mutual profit and well-being. Roosevelt even appears to have hoped that, under the benign general supervision of the four policemen, colonies might be brought forward to independence under enlightened trusteeship arrangements. Colonial empires and exclusive spheres of influence would be made redundant.

Roosevelt accorded the United States the central place in the postwar world order that he envisioned. It would be first among equals among the policemen and would accept fully its international responsibilities. He envisaged no American retreat as after World War I, although he firmly rejected as unfeasible any permanent American political or military commitments in Europe.[24] The United States would exercise real leadership, especially by reshaping the international system and economy more in its own image and likeness. He wanted to extend "Americanism," as Warren Kimball would have it – the combination of American social, economic, and political liberalism – throughout the world. The United States would call other nations forth to a higher standard

---

[20] John Lamberton Harper, *American Visions of Europe: Franklin D. Roosevelt, George F. Kennan and Dean G. Acheson* (Cambridge and New York, 1994), p. 79.

[21] *FRUS*, 1942, III, pp. 568–69.

[22] Harper makes this point at greater length in *American Visions of Europe*, p. 88.

[23] This similarity is noted in Craig and George, *Force and Statecraft*, p. 91. The following sentences rely on their analysis. Also note Gaddis, *Surprise, Security and the American Experience*, pp. 51–55.

[24] This point is well developed by James McAllister in his *No Exit: America and the German Problem, 1943–1954* (Ithaca, NY, 2002), pp. 42–49.

to which he optimistically assumed they would respond. "The retrograde, the reactionary, the unprogressive [like the European colonial empires] had to be brought into the present; the angry, the disenchanted, the revolutionary [such as the Soviet Union] had to be convinced that their interests lay in the creation of a stable world where change took place without destruction."[25]

The economic side of FDR's Americanism grew out of his reading of the past and conformed well to the assumptions of key figures in his own Democratic Party such as Cordell Hull. Intent on avoiding the economic autarchy and Hobbesian policies that had contributed to the devastating Depression, he aimed to establish a liberal international economic order based on free trade and stable currency-exchange rates. The United States would renounce its former high-tariff policy in order to promote constructive economic relations throughout the world and so facilitate world prosperity. Reducing trade barriers and reforming the international monetary system became important American objectives, the technical details of which FDR left to others. This dimension of his postwar vision readily attracted domestic support, but other aspects of his planning enjoyed no similar fortune.

Roosevelt's global design, dependent on cooperation among the major powers, bore more echoes of his cousin Theodore's geopolitical approach to international affairs than it did to universalist Wilsonian notions involving a world organization. But FDR could not escape the clutches of the man whom he had served as assistant secretary of the Navy. Although he initially vetoed any attempt to revivify a League of Nations, by 1943 he was forced to concede on the issue – at least in part. Warned by Cordell Hull that world and domestic opinion would not support a "cabal of the big powers," Roosevelt permitted his secretary of state at the Moscow Conference to garner British and Soviet support for a "general international organization based on the principle of sovereign equality."[26] FDR's floating of his four policemen strategy in April 1943, in an interview with Forrest Davis of the *Saturday Evening Post*, had drawn a negative public reaction.[27] Thereafter, in order to ensure broad support for an internationalist postwar foreign policy allowing for American world leadership, he blurred "the differences between his own plan and the desire of the idealists [like Hull and, for that matter, Harry Truman] for a system of collective security based upon another, stronger League of Nations."[28] Out of this blurring emerged proposals for the Security Council of major powers to

---

[25] Kimball, *The Juggler*, pp. 186–87, is excellent on Roosevelt's assumptions.

[26] Moscow Conference "Declaration of Four Nations on General Security," *FRUS*, 1943, I, p. 756. Harper is excellent on this matter in *American Visions of Europe*, pp. 96–97.

[27] Forrest Davis, "Roosevelt's World Blueprint," *Saturday Evening Post*, 115 (April 10, 1943), pp. 20–21, 109–11.

[28] Craig and George, *Diplomacy and Statecraft*, p. 92. Robert Dallek insightfully has suggested that Roosevelt's "desire for a new world league with peacekeeping powers rested less on a faith in the effectiveness of Wilsonian collective security than on a belief that it was a necessary vehicle for permanently involving the United States in world affairs." Robert Dallek, *Franklin D. Roosevelt and American Foreign Policy*, p. 536.

accompany the egalitarian General Assembly in a new world organization that American planners crafted through 1944.[29]

After the Moscow Conference, Roosevelt regularly genuflected in the direction of a new world organization in order to shore up congressional and public support for American leadership in the postwar world. But he did not abandon his essential goal of continued postwar collaboration among the major wartime allies. Continued cooperation among Britain, the Soviet Union, and the United States ultimately remained the key element of his postwar vision, and he placed special emphasis on continued Soviet–American accord. He twice traveled halfway around the globe to meet the Soviet and British leaders not only to oversee wartime strategy but also to lay the foundations for postwar collaboration and to cement their practice of cooperation. He hoped to wean his erstwhile colleagues away from their dependence on traditional geopolitical practices and to persuade them gradually to adopt his postwar vision as their own. Only someone with his amazing audacity and deep confidence that he could overcome any political or strategic obstacle could have framed and pursued such a postwar vision given the individual actors and the political and economic systems involved.

During 1944 and the early months of 1945, FDR's vision appeared well on the way to becoming reality. Important pillars for the postwar system were forged at conferences at Bretton Woods, New Hampshire (July 1–22, 1944), and in the Dumbarton Oaks mansion in Washington, D.C. (August 21–October 7, 1944).[30] At Bretton Woods, the world's economic powers, including the Soviet Union, signed agreements that aimed to resolve the chronic instability so evident in the previous decade. With John Maynard Keynes and Harry Dexter White leading the way, the conference reached agreements on means to facilitate trade and investment and designed two notable economic institutions that became the International Monetary Fund (IMF) and the World Bank. The IMF would serve as "the regulator of the international financial system," aiding countries to overcome short-term balance of payments problems, "promoting currency stability and ending the destructive devaluations that crippled the interwar financial order."[31] The United States placed itself at the center of the new financial system by backing an international gold-exchange standard that allowed other countries to link their currencies to gold or to the dollar.[32] In a situation where foreign currencies backed by dollar reserves would have an

---

[29] For more detail on this subject, see Georg Schild, "The Roosevelt Administration and the United Nations: Recreation or Rejection of the League Experiment?" *World Affairs*, 158 (Summer 1995), pp. 26–34.

[30] For a detailed account of these meetings, see Georg Schild, *Bretton Woods and Dumbarton Oaks: American Economic and Political Postwar Planning in the Summer of 1944* (New York, 1995). Also see Harley A. Notter, *Postwar Foreign Policy Preparation, 1939–1945* (Washington, DC, 1949).

[31] Diane B. Kunz, *Butter and Guns: America's Cold War Economic Diplomacy* (New York, 1997), p. 8.

[32] The rate was thirty-five dollars an ounce. Kunz, *Butter and Guns*, p. 9.

indirect gold backing, American dollars became world money, the key international currency. America's financial strength also was essential in the World
Bank whose aims focused on more long-term economic measures. It would lend
money to assist nations devastated by war in their reconstruction and might
also aid poorer countries on their road to development. The promise of "a
ready source of capital to rebuild their economies and infrastructure" appealed
to many war-torn nations and presumably served as the magnet that attracted
the Soviets to participate in this gathering.[33] American officials for the most
part glossed over the contradictions between the nature of the Soviet system
with its command economy and the Bretton Woods system they devised. Great
power cooperation seemed to be on track.

The Dumbarton Oaks meeting demonstrated further the seeming healthy
cooperation among the major powers. The conference participants reached
agreement on a tentative draft for an international security organization. It
proposed an eleven-member Security Council on which the Big Five, the four
policemen joined by France (which was added at Churchill's insistence), would
have a permanent veto. This Security Council would be the real force in the organization in FDR's mind. The General Assembly in which all sovereign nations
were represented would exercise a more modest role. Whatever his earlier reservations about a new international peacekeeping organization, Roosevelt seems
to have warmed to the proposed United Nations. Its structures could provide a domestically acceptable venue, a cover of sorts, for the necessary great
power collaboration as well as serving as the vehicle to guarantee American
engagement in the world. He looked forward to the San Francisco Conference scheduled for April 1945, which would officially launch the new world
body.

Other dimensions of the Rooseveltian vision remained more problematic. His
hopes for China's advance and colonialism's demise seemed far from fruition in
the early months of 1945. His cavalier elevation of China to major power status
had not been matched by any notable improvement in that nation's political
or military strength. Nonetheless, with a certain patronizing air FDR treated
Chiang Kai-shek as a significant leader and met with him at Cairo in 1943. He
still hoped that China would emerge after the war as the significant regional
power in Asia.

Roosevelt felt deeply his opposition to colonialism. Historian Warren
Kimball insightfully noted that he held the "consistent position that colonialism, not communism, was the -ism that most threatened postwar peace and
stability."[34] This put him at significant odds with Winston Churchill. The two
leaders most certainly "did not march to the same drumbeat" as Averell Harriman correctly recalled, for "Roosevelt enjoyed thinking aloud on the tremendous changes he saw ahead – the end of colonial empires and the rise of newly
independent nations across the sweep of Africa and Asia," a trend which he

[33] Kunz, *Butter and Guns*, p. 10.
[34] Kimball, *The Juggler*, p. 64.

hoped to promote.[35] Churchill had some success during the war in negating Roosevelt's designs to dissolve the European colonial empires including that of his own nation. The American leader conceded ground on the issue while still hoping that the Europeans would move their colonies to eventual independence just as he planned to do with the Philippines. But Roosevelt never altered his deep dislike for the reactionary character of European colonialism, and he especially maintained a deep animus against renewal of French control of Indochina.[36] Whatever his setbacks in pursuing his anti-colonialist course during the war, his instincts and hopes remained strong. The tides of history were flowing his way, and the European colonial powers, while probably kicking and screaming all the way, would need to recognize it.

The keystone of Roosevelt's postwar vision remained close collaboration with his major wartime allies, Britain and the Soviet Union. His crucial effort during the war was to build relationships with Winston Churchill and Joseph Stalin, which would allow him to persuade or nudge or encourage them to share in overseeing the grand world of peace and prosperity of his dreams. He pursued these relationships quite differently and with quite different results.

Working with Churchill and Stalin

The legend of the great democratic leaders, Roosevelt and Churchill, working together like true friends to vanquish the fascist forces is a powerfully appealing one.[37] No one did more to promote it than Britain's indomitable wartime prime minister both in his moving tribute at FDR's death and in his influential memoirs with their splendid evocations of Anglo-American unity and their heroic portrait of the American president who had aided him in the darkest hours of Hitler's onslaught. Roosevelt was "the greatest American friend we have ever known," who Churchill later deemed the "saviour of Europe."[38] The destroyer-for-bases deal, the Atlantic charter, Lend–Lease, the amazing Anglo-American military cooperation, and the unprecedented collaboration on the Manhattan Project revealed the substance behind the legend. The leaders' extraordinary wartime correspondence revealed the extent of their partnership.[39] The

[35] W. Averell Harriman and Elie Abel, *Special Envoy to Churchill and Stalin, 1941–1946* (New York, 1975), p. 191.

[36] Gary R. Hess, "Franklin Roosevelt and Indochina," *Journal of American History*, 59 (September 1982), pp. 359–68.

[37] For a recent example of the genre that celebrates the Roosevelt–Churchill friendship, see Jon Meacham, *Franklin and Winston: An Intimate Portrait of an Epic Friendship* (New York, 1993).

[38] For Churchill's tribute to Roosevelt, see Martin Gilbert, *Winston S. Churchill*, Vol. 7, *The Road to Victory, 1941–1945* (Boston, 1986), p. 1301. Churchill described FDR as "saviour" in a letter to Clement Attlee, June 22, 1946, Papers of Clement Attlee, Modern Papers Reading Room, Bodleian Library, University of Oxford, Oxford, England, dep. 38. For the memoirs, see Winston S. Churchill, *The Second World War*, 6 vols. (Boston, 1948–1953) – hereafter individual volume title is given.

[39] In addition to the partnership aspect, however, the correspondence also reveals the tension between the two men. On this point note the astute observation by the writer Christopher

marvelous anecdotes told of the Roosevelt–Churchill friendship give it an almost magical quality. Rare (I think) are the episodes among international statesmen that would bring one to the bedroom of the other to share an inspiration aimed at expressing the common purpose of the allies only to find the other emerging from his bath. Yet in Harry Hopkins's familiar story, Roosevelt came to Churchill's room to share his phrase "United Nations" only to discover the newly bathed and cherubic Englishman "stark naked and gleaming pink." He apologized and undertook to return later only to have Churchill assure him that there was no need to go because "the prime minister of Great Britain has nothing to conceal from the president of the United States."[40]

The real character and outlook of Britain's wartime leader is difficult to extract from the "historical aura" that surrounds him as one of the "greats" of the twentieth century and from the deeply ingrained image of the "the jowly face and cigar" defiantly exhorting his people to fight on.[41] Yet it is the Churchill of the war years rather than the "Churchill of history" that we must seek to understand here. His portrait in the 1940s hardly constitutes an unblemished picture. Egotistical, erratic, histrionic, truculent, impulsive, and profoundly wrong-headed are just some of adjectives used to describe him even by sympathetic historians who, of course, also note his humanity, his courage, and his great gift with words.[42] Burdened with his "Black Dog" of depression and given to fits of pessimism, he sought to revive his spirits (or deaden his pain) by consuming vast quantities of alcohol. The remedy appears to have worked at times! His career prior to the late 1930s reflected an ambitious desire to grasp for power and the capacity to invoke deep-rooted distrust in his political colleagues. Churchill was an inveterate defender of the British Empire – an old fashioned imperialist – who gave no ground to the Indian independence movement. The great opponent of Hitler's tyranny in Europe proved unable to see that Britain's colonial subjects also deserved democracy or, at least, self-rule. Throughout the war, Churchill vigorously defended the empire and defined vital British interests to include the Mediterranean, the Persian Gulf, and the Far East.

Whatever the complexities, contradictions, and limitations of Churchill's personality and positions, he recognized with profound clarity the danger that Hitler represented to Britain, to Western democracy, and to liberty. When circumstances led to his assuming the leadership of his nation in the dark hours

Hitchens who, after reading the complete correspondence, "was astonished to find how much the two men had disliked and distrusted each other. Astonished, too, by the clarity and candor of this mutual disaffection, and by the way official history, most notably Churchill's own volumes, downplayed the fact." Christopher Hitchens, "The Medals of His Defeats," *The Atlantic Monthly*, 289 (April 2002), p. 133.

[40] Robert E. Sherwood, *Roosevelt and Hopkins: An Intimate History* (New York, 1948), p. 442. According to Sherwood, Churchill denied the veracity of this report.

[41] On Churchill's "jowly face and cigar," see Simon Schama, "Rescuing Churchill," *New York Review of Books*, 49 (February 28, 2002), p. 15.

[42] For this, see Schama's very insightful essay "Rescuing Churchill," pp. 15–17.

of 1940, he rejected entreaties that he explore accommodation with the Nazis so as to obtain "peace" and preserve something of an empire.[43] To his "imperishable credit," as Simon Schama has noted, when "faced with the alternatives of hanging on to the scraps of empire, courtesy of Adolf Hitler, or fighting to the end, whatever long-term damage might accrue to British power, he unhesitatingly opted for the latter."[44] He knew, almost instinctively it seems, that he must rouse his people to resist Hitler. He also understood the painful reality that British power by itself would never be sufficient to defeat his great foe. He recognized early on that the strength and resources of the United States would be needed to that end, and he eagerly sought American assistance and ultimately American participation in the war effort. He readily welcomed the emissaries that Roosevelt sent to him, foremost among them, Harry L. Hopkins.[45]

As Roosevelt's closest wartime aide, Harry Hopkins played a crucial role in nurturing the Anglo-American partnership. A prominent New Dealer and one closely identified with the more liberal/progressive elements of Roosevelt's domestic administration, Hopkins underwent a striking evolution into foreign policy emissary and adviser in the early 1940s. His unquestioned influence came not from any formal position but, unsurprisingly, from his access to and intimacy with FDR. The descriptions of Hopkins as Roosevelt's "alter ego," his "Sancho Panza," his "deputy-president," and his "Colonel House," suggest his importance.[46] Churchill later recalled for Robert Sherwood, Hopkins's biographer, that his subject "was a vital spring in the whole machine" of the wartime operation. In carefully chosen and sincerely meant words, he observed that "no one can ever measure, and neither America nor England can ever repay, what he did to make things go well."[47] Hopkins journeyed to England in the midst of

[43] Churchill has come in for severe criticism from British historians like Corelli Barnett, John Grigg, and John Charmley for his failure to protect the empire and his failure to recognize American hostility to it. See the discussion in David Stafford, *Roosevelt and Churchill: Men of Secrets* (Woodstock, NY, 2000), pp. 298–99.

[44] Schama, "Rescuing Churchill," p. 16. My view of Churchill also is influenced by John Lukacs, *Churchill: Visionary. Statesman. Historian.* (New Haven, CT, 2002).

[45] On Churchill's eagerness to welcome American emissaries, see Klaus Larres, *Churchill's Cold War: The Politics of Personal Diplomacy* (New Haven, CT, 2002), p. 36.

[46] For "alter ego," see David Fromkin, "Churchill's Way: The Great Convergence of Britain and the United States," *World Policy Journal*, 15 (Spring 1998), p. 7. For "Sancho Panza," see Alex Danchev, *On Specialness: Essays in Anglo-American Relations* (New York, 1998), p. 82. For "deputy-president," see Ted Morgan, *FDR: A Biography* (New York, 1985), p. 578. British ambassador Edward Halifax referred to Hopkins operating as a "second Colonel House" in Halifax to Eden, December 5, 1944, Eden Foreign Secretary Papers – Foreign Office Collection (FO 954), Main Library Special Collections, University of Birmingham, Vol. 30, Folder 589.

[47] Churchill to Sherwood, August 17, 1946, The Papers of Winston S. Churchill, Churchill Archives Center, Post July 27, 1945, materials (hereafter Churchill Papers with file and folder number), File 2, Folder 155. At the moment of victory in Europe Churchill wrote to Hopkins: "Among all those in the Grand Alliance, warriors or statesmen, who struck deadly blows at the enemy and brought peace nearer, you will ever hold an honoured place." Foreign Office to Washington Embassy, enclosing Churchill to Hopkins, May 9, 1945, Churchill Papers, Char 20/218. When Hopkins resigned from government service in July of 1945, Churchill assured him that "when the

the Blitz and confirmed for Roosevelt that Churchill would fight on and must be supported, thus providing the green light for Lend–Lease. In January 1941, as his visit came to an end, he forged an unbreakable bond with the British leader when he quoted to him "one verse from the Book of Books... 'Whither thou goest, I will go; and where thou lodgest, I will lodge: thy people shall be my people, and thy God my God' – even to the end."[48]

Churchill appeared never to doubt nor to question Hopkins's friendship again and looked to him for support even when he was at odds with his chief. Joined by their common hatred of Hitler, the two men worked tirelessly to defeat that rapacious enemy as true brothers-in-arms.[49] But beyond the Nazi defeat, Hopkins's vision for the postwar world diverged considerably from Churchill's, although the blustering Englishman never fully appreciated this reality. For Hopkins, the struggle was not one to restore an old and rather corrupt order. Instead he wanted "the common people of the earth [to] share the fruits of victory."[50] He sought a much more "progressive" peace than did Churchill, overly mired – so Hopkins thought – in his desire to protect the interests of the British Empire and too eager to link postwar American power to British interests under the label of Anglo-American partnership.

Just as with Hopkins and Churchill, so it was with Roosevelt and the British prime minister. The legend about and the genuine affection between the two leaders should not disguise the reality of their substantial differences during the war and in their divergent conceptions of the postwar world order. Warren Kimball rightly maintains that "it is impossible to understand the Roosevelt foreign policy without appreciating the wartime tensions that existed between Great Britain and the United States – between Churchill and Roosevelt – for the President saw those tensions as one of the major formative forces in the postwar world."[51] Churchill represented the old order, and his commitment to

history of these times come to be written, you will stand out as the greatest of American statesmen who served President Roosevelt, and one of the best friends that Britain ever had." Foreign Office to Washington enclosing Churchill to Hopkins, July 7, 1945, Eden Foreign Secretary Papers, Main Library Special Collections, University of Birmingham, FO 954, Vol. 30, Folio 803.

48 Moran diary, January 1941, in Lord Moran, *Winston Churchill: The Struggle for Survival, 1940–1965: Taken from the Diaries of Lord Moran* (London, 1966), p. 6. Little wonder that Churchill cabled Roosevelt of his gratitude to him "for sending so remarkable an envoy who enjoys so high a measure of your intimacy and confidence." For President from Former Naval Person, January 13, 1941, Harry L. Hopkins Papers, Franklin D. Roosevelt Library, Box 136. (Hopkins quoted from the Book of Ruth 1: 16.)

49 A sense of their brotherhood is conveyed in a Christmas 1944 message in which Hopkins told Churchill "that I am well aware of the heavy burdens you carry. Since our first meeting I have tried to share them with you. I would share them with you now." Halifax to Foreign Office enclosing Hopkins to Churchill, December 23, 1944, Eden Foreign Secretary Papers, Main Library Special Collections, University of Birmingham, FO 954, Vol. 30, Folio 608.

50 Hopkins to Eden, May 8, 1945, Avon Papers, Main Library Special Collections, University of Birmingham, 20/42/53.

51 Kimball, *The Juggler*, p. 64. See also Kimball's *Forged in War*. FDR's son, Elliott, also gave full voice to this view in 1946. See the article drawn from his memoir, *As He Saw It*, published under the title "FDR vs. Churchill – The Inside Story," *Look*, 10 (September 3, 1946), pp. 21–26.

his nation's empire and to its system of preferential trade conflicted with key elements of Roosevelt's hopes. The British prime minister's concern to restore France as a factor in the European power equation and his willingness to cut classic sphere-of-influence deals revealed him in Roosevelt's eyes to be at heart just another European power politician. Roosevelt and his close coterie of advisers, Hopkins most prominent among them, held this species largely responsible for the terrible diplomatic travails of the century. They planned to limit its role in the new age to come and expected some resistance in that regard. Eleanor Roosevelt tellingly recalled in 1946 that her husband "always thought that when peace came he would be able to get along better with Stalin than with Churchill."[52] The British leader was far too conservative and backward in his thinking.

Roosevelt and Churchill differed on a number of major matters during the war.[53] Some of their disagreements centered on issues of military strategy, such as the timing of the Second Front and the conduct of military operations in the Mediterranean theater. Other disagreements had a more political cast and reflected their quite different worldviews. Their clear divergence on the relative importance of China and France in international affairs found replication eventually in disputes over the future of Eastern Europe and of Germany and in discord in their assessments of Stalin's trustworthiness and intentions. Churchill's vision for the future relied upon continued cooperation between the British Empire and the United States. Viewing the United States and Roosevelt through rose-colored glasses, he assured himself that a powerful Anglo-American partnership would be the bedrock for postwar stability.[54] But Roosevelt found such a close and monogamous relationship less than enticing. The prospect of serving as consort to British imperialism evoked sentiments of repugnance in him, and such was the power equation between the two countries that Roosevelt found himself under no pressure to do so. Britain's strength was in decline relative to that of the United States, and this became more evident as the war progressed.[55] Roosevelt felt free to pursue other relationships, most importantly with Stalin, and to disparage Churchill in the final months of the war for "becoming more and more mid-Victorian and [for] slipping farther and farther back into last century thinking."[56]

---

[52] Eleanor Roosevelt recalled this in conversation with former Postmaster General Frank Walker. See Walker's diary entry for December 10, 1946, in Papers of Frank C. Walker, University of Notre Dame Archives, Box 123, Folder 37.

[53] The analysis in the following paragraph relies upon Keith Sainsbury, *Churchill and Roosevelt at War: The War They Fought and the Peace They Hoped to Make* (New York, 1994).

[54] For clear-headed analysis of Churchill's evangelical hopes for a "special relationship" with the United States and Roosevelt's refusal to participate, see Alex Danchev, *On Specialness*, pp. 154–55, esp. p. 2.

[55] Kimball argues persuasively that Anglo-American cooperation peaked, as it were, at the Casablanca Conference in January 1943. See *The Juggler*, pp. 80–81.

[56] Roosevelt quoted in Journal entry, January 10, 1945, Joseph E. Davies Papers, Library of Congress, Box 16.

Roosevelt deemed the cooperation of the Soviet Union as essential in the construction of his brave new world, and he set about to win it by seeking to build a bond of friendship with Generalissimo Joseph Stalin. His approach has been astutely described as one of "trust the Russians and win their trust in return."[57] His opposition to Marxist ideology and to the Soviet experiment had never been visceral. In the first year of his presidency, he had ignored the opposition of fierce anticommunists and proceeded to grant diplomatic recognition to the regime in Moscow.[58] But little came of the new relationship during the 1930s as each nation focused on what might be termed, with some understatement, its internal affairs.[59] William Bullitt, the first American ambassador to the Soviet Union, moved from high hopes and enthusiasm to deep disillusionment in the space of a few years as he came to appreciate the stark horror of Stalin's rule. Joseph Davies, his successor, maintained a regard for Stalin's state and a commitment to work with it only by ignoring or dismissing its realities – the purges, the show trials, the tyranny and brutality. Laurence Steinhardt, who replaced Davies, had realist blood in his veins and took an accurate measure of such events as the Nazi-Soviet pact, the Soviet attack on Poland, the War against Finland, and the seizure of the Baltic states. He saw the Soviets, quite correctly, as "accomplices" of Nazi aggression from 1939 to 1941, and this insightful understanding led him to oppose unrestricted aid to the Soviet Union after June 22, 1941, when Hitler launched Operation Barbarossa. Steinhardt recommended reciprocity – aid only in exchange for Soviet cooperation on a range of matters – but he eventually found himself marginalized for this advice.[60]

Roosevelt had condemned Soviet aggression against Finland in 1940 and, in a well-known address to leftist delegates of the American Youth Congress, he branded Stalin's regime "as absolute as any dictatorship in the world."[61] But the perfidy of Soviet international behavior during 1939–41 never appears to have registered fully with him. He never gauged that the Soviet Union, in George Kennan's words, "moved into the wartime period on the basis of a series of calculations which could scarcely have been more hostile and dangerous to the Western powers."[62] Stalin's alliance with Hitler, as Adam Ulam later noted,

57 Lerner, *Wounded Titans*, p. 172.
58 On Roosevelt's proceeding ahead despite anticommunist opposition, see Richard Gid Powers, *Not Without Honor*, pp. 113–14.
59 On the Soviet Union during this period, see Robert C. Tucker, *Stalin in Power: The Revolution from Above, 1928–1941* (New York, 1990).
60 This discussion of the three ambassadors rests largely upon David Mayers, *The Ambassadors and America's Soviet Policy* (New York, 1995), pp. 108–35. See also Dennis J. Dunn, *Caught Between Roosevelt and Stalin: America's Ambassadors to Moscow* (Lexington, KY, 1998), pp. 13–144.
61 Roosevelt, Address to the Delegates of the American Youth Congress, Washington, DC, February 10, 1940, in Samuel I. Rosenman, ed., *The Public Papers and Addresses of Franklin D. Roosevelt 1940*, Vol. IX (New York, 1941), p. 93.
62 George F. Kennan, "An Historian of Potsdam and His Readers," *American Slavic and East European Review*, 20 (April 1961), p. 292.

was eventually "rationalized as a natural and desperate step in view of the [supposed] British and French intention in 1939 to 'push Hitler eastward'" – a stance completely at odds with the British guarantee to Poland, which aimed precisely to restrain Hitler in the East.[63]

Despite his occasional public criticisms, Franklin Roosevelt afforded a benign interpretation to Soviet actions prior to June of 1941. An unsentimental appreciation of these craven actions never served as a brake on or even a cautionary guide for American policy as he set about to work with Stalin. Nor did FDR find Stalin's record of ruthless violence and ferocious internal repression as cause for restraint. Apparently he shared the sympathy of certain left-wing and progressive members of his New Deal coalition for the Soviets once they moved into the antifascist camp. It must surely be said that he flirted at least with something of the romance of many Western intellectuals regarding the Soviet experiment. That dire reality was judged not so much on what it was but rather on what it might become, and excuses were readily proffered for repression, terror, fear, and the total control of social and personal life as regrettable means to a worthy end.[64] As the war progressed, the president even proved quite relaxed in the face of warnings of Soviet espionage efforts to penetrate his administration, which succeeded notably as is now known.[65] Roosevelt held tough-minded critics of the Soviet Union largely at arms length throughout the war. He preferred the counsel of those like former ambassador Davies and, most importantly, Harry Hopkins.

Harry Hopkins proved instrumental in forging the wartime Soviet–American relationship. In July 1941, soon after Hitler betrayed Stalin and unleashed the might of the Luftwaffe and the Wehrmacht against Soviet Russia, Hopkins traveled to Moscow and met with Stalin. The Soviet leader instilled in the American emissary "complete faith both in his own powers of leadership and in Russia's will to resist."[66] Hopkins concluded that the United States must support the

---

[63] Adam Ulam, *The Rivals: America and Russia Since World War II* (New York, 1971), p. 13.

[64] My thinking here is influenced by Andrzej Paczkowski's powerful essay "The Storm over *The Black Book*," *Wilson Quarterly*, 25 (Spring 2001), pp. 28–34.

[65] On the Soviet efforts, see Allen Weinstein and Alexander Vassiliev, *The Haunted Wood: Soviet Espionage in America – the Stalin Era* (New York, 1999) see esp. pp. 157–61. After surveying recent literature on the topic, John Earl Haynes concluded that "hundreds of Americans, mostly Communists, assisted Soviet espionage. The spies included dozens of mid-level government officials as well as some in higher-level posts: not only Alger Hiss [in the State Department] but also Lawrence Duggan, the long-time head of the Latin American division in the State Department; Lauchlin Currie, a senior White House aide to President Roosevelt; Duncan Lee, a senior officer in the Office of Strategic Services . . .; and, most significantly, Harry Dexter White, the assistant secretary of the Treasury." John Earl Haynes, "The Cold War Debate Continues: A Traditionalist View of Historical Writing on Domestic Communism and Anti-Communism," *Journal of Cold War Studies*, 2 (Winter 2000), p. 100. On Soviet espionage, also see Joseph E. Persico, *Roosevelt's Secret War: FDR and World War II Espionage* (New York, 2001), pp. 366–78.

[66] Christopher Andrew and Oleg Gordievsky, *KGB: The Inside Story of its Foreign Operations from Lenin to Gorbachev* (New York, 1990), p. 288.

Soviets against the German onslaught and without placing restrictions on its assistance or insisting on any postwar political guarantees as a condition of its help. He deemed Steinhardt's reciprocity approach as offensive and, so it seems, he worked to remove those officials who held to it.[67] The same deep commitment to defeat Hitler which drew him to Churchill linked him with Stalin.[68] Within FDR's administration, Hopkins emerged as "a sincere and even aggressive friend of Russia and an intense admirer of Russia's gigantic contribution to the winning of the war."[69] But Hopkins did more than merely back military assistance to and cooperation with the Soviet Union. He helped shape a vision of the Soviet Union as a country with whom the United States could rightly expect to cooperate once the enormous task of defeating the Nazis had been accomplished. And he influenced Franklin Roosevelt to adopt this vision as his own.[70]

As a result of Hopkins's counsel, Roosevelt rather quickly determined not only that the United States must fully support the Soviet Union in its desperate military struggle against Hitler but also that he should elicit Soviet cooperation in shaping the postwar world order and accord them a key role in it.[71] The former determination is surely understandable, but the latter is questionable

[67] Andrew and Gordievsky address this topic and pay particular attention to Hopkins's efforts to remove the American military attaché Major Ivan Yeaton who "tried to persuade Hopkins to demand the right to send military observers to the front as a quid pro quo." They also suggest that Hopkins influenced the removal of Ambassador Steinhardt and the tough-minded anti-Stalinist Loy W. Henderson, who headed the Soviet desk in the State Department. See Andrew and Gordievsky, *KGB*, pp. 289–90.

[68] Of course, in recent years, there have been accusations that Hopkins was more than a sympathetic supporter of Stalin's regime in the battle against Hitler. The fact that he had a close and lengthy wartime relationship with an NKVD agent in Washington, Iskhak Akhmerov, has led to the charge that he was in fact a Soviet agent. (Akhmerov also served as Alger Hiss's "handler.") Andrew and Gordievsky are persuasive in suggesting that Hopkins was "an unconscious rather than a conscious agent." They suggest that he was naïve about the NKVD agent and "probably regarded Akhmerov simply as an unofficial intermediary chosen by Stalin because of his distrust (shared by Hopkins) of the orthodox diplomatic establishment." Andrew and Gordievsky, *KGB*, p. 287. On this subject, also see Eduard Mark, "Venona's Source 19 and the 'Trident' Conference of May 1943: Diplomacy or Espionage?" *Intelligence and National Security*, 13 (Summer 1998), pp. 1–31. However this issue is resolved finally, it is clear that Hopkins maintained close contacts with the Soviet government during the war and cooperated closely with it.

[69] Sherwood, *Roosevelt and Hopkins*, p. 345. Note that Sherwood added "but he [Hopkins] could never reconcile himself to a system which seemingly concentrated such absolute power in one mortal man."

[70] Note the analysis of Dennis J. Dunn who argues that Roosevelt and his key aides "thought that Soviet Russia was a country evolving toward democratic socialism. It had some rough edges due to its history and mistreatment, by the Western Powers, including the United States, and so it had to be treated tenderly and much of its pathological behavior had to be overlooked or tolerated. The best and most logical policy for the United States to follow was patience, accommodation, friendship, and unilateral aid and appeasement during the war, until democracy took root in the Soviet Union and Stalin's suspicion of the West dissipated." Note that Dunn observes that "Roosevelt, Hopkins, Davies, and [Philip] Faymonville played leading roles in the development and implementation of this policy." Dunn, *Caught Between Roosevelt and Stalin*, p. 263.

[71] On Roosevelt's decision making at this point, see Edward M. Bennett, *Franklin D. Roosevelt and the Search for Victory: American–Soviet Relations, 1939–1945* (Wilmington, DE, 1990).

indeed and was pursued on the basis of limited policy analysis that did not involve those blessed with genuine and tough-minded expertise on the Soviet Union. By May of 1942, FDR blithely could tell Molotov that the Soviet Union would be one of the four policemen who would manage the postwar world. Less than a year earlier Stalin had maintained faithfully and proudly his nefarious pact with Hitler.

It is essential in understanding America's Soviet policy to grasp how Roosevelt differed from Churchill. The essence of the British leader's stance was encapsulated in his oft-quoted remark that "if Hitler invaded Hell I would make at least a favorable reference to the Devil in the House of Commons."[72] He willingly worked with Stalin to defeat the common foe and sought to establish a genuine relationship with the Soviet leader. He suffered certain illusions regarding this possibility and occasionally admitted of Stalin to his close circle: "I like this man."[73] In retrospect we can see that the very person "who fought bitterly and single-mindedly against the appeasement of Germany and Hitler, went a very long way to appease Stalin and Russia."[74] Yet, in the end, he knew well that when he dealt with the Soviet tyrant he dealt with the "devil" and that the Soviet system was vile. Here lay the crucial difference between Churchill and Franklin Roosevelt. Churchill proved willing throughout the war to negotiate geopolitical deals with the Soviets, but Roosevelt rejected this approach and ambitiously aimed higher. He hoped to domesticate and to civilize the Soviet "devil" to adopt the American way. "Churchill," as Patrick Glynn persuasively argued, "while hopeful that long-term relations between the Soviet Union and the West might be improved as a result of the war, understood the essential nature of the Soviet regime and of Stalin. Roosevelt, whatever his other virtues and abilities, never did."[75] Roosevelt's failure should neither be blamed upon domestic or international constraints of one sort or another nor mitigated because of a lack

---

[72] Winston S. Churchill, *The Grand Alliance*, pp. 370–71.

[73] On Churchill's illusions and on his liking Stalin, see John Lukacs analysis on "Churchill and Stalin" in his *Churchill*, pp. 19–33.

[74] Lukacs, *Churchill*, pp. 22–23. On Churchill's relationship with Stalin and the Soviet Union, also see David Carlton, *Churchill and the Soviet Union* (Manchester and New York, 2000). Carlton clarifies that British Foreign Secretary Eden sought Soviet cooperation more eagerly than Churchill. Carlton summarizes that "at first, being slow to realize how many resources Roosevelt would devote to the Pacific theatre, he [Churchill] was inclined to minimize the Soviets' importance and accordingly was even less disposed than before to make concessions to them. But he soon showed signs of wavering and then, during 1943 and 1944, moved very far towards accepting the unavoidable necessity of treating Stalin as an indispensable partner, whose every wish, however repugnant, had to be taken with extreme seriousness. This evolution in Churchill's approach to Moscow was also probably greatly influenced by Eden, who emerged much earlier than his chief as a powerful advocate of far-reaching appeasement of Moscow." See pp. 93–94. Also see Martin H. Folly, *Churchill, Whitehall and the Soviet Union, 1940–45* (New York, 2000).

[75] Patrick Glynn, *Closing Pandora's Box: Arms Races, Arms Control, and the History of the Cold War* (New York, 1992), p. 92. Churchill's recognition of the brutal nature of Stalin's rule led him to observe as early as 1942 when the outcome of the war still hung in the balance that it would be a "measureless disaster if Russian barbarism overlaid the culture and independence" of Europe. Churchill, *The Hinge of Fate*, p. 562.

of viable options. He does not appear to have seriously considered possible alternatives, and he rejected the reciprocity approach of Ambassador Steinhardt. Only his extraordinary confidence in his own instinctive judgment and in his capacity to influence Stalin when joined to his reliance on a very narrow circle of like-minded advisers, such as Joseph Davies and Harry Hopkins, and – sadly, it must be said – one of the more remarkable exercises in denial in the annals of diplomacy can explain his attitude and actions.[76]

In August of 1943, in response to William Bullitt's warning of the "domination of Europe by Stalin's Communist dictatorship," FDR told the former ambassador that "I just have a hunch that Stalin is not that kind of man. Harry [Hopkins] says he's not and that he doesn't want anything but security for his country, and I think that if I give him everything I possibly can and ask nothing from him in return, noblesse oblige, he won't try to annex anything and will work with me for a world of democracy and peace."[77] Roosevelt pursued his relations with Stalin throughout the war on this basic rationale. He sought to convince the Soviet leader of the friendship of both himself and his country and personally assumed the central role in managing America's relations with the Soviets. Characteristically, FDR exuded optimism regarding his ability to manage the part. "I think I can personally handle Stalin better than either your Foreign Office or my State Department," he wrote to Churchill in March of 1942 even before his first meeting with Stalin. "Stalin hates the guts of all your top people. He thinks he likes me better, and I hope he will continue to do so."[78]

Roosevelt's personal "handling" was directed toward the quite impossible task of dispelling the prejudices and suspicions in Stalin's mind. A man for whom "envy, suspicion, a very real tendency to sadism, and a truly unlimited and insane jealousy were, in addition to an equally unlimited ambition, his driving qualities" was not disposed to being massaged or manipulated by the president of a capitalist nation whose ultimate destruction he welcomed.[79] Stalin, whose "extraordinary cunning and duplicity" had been so well honed in eliminating supposed rivals during the terror of the thirties, easily gained the initiative in the relationship and deftly placed on Roosevelt the burden of proving Western friendship.[80]

[76] On Davies's role see Glynn, *Closing Pandora's Box*, pp. 93–100.

[77] For Bullitt's warning, see his memorandum to Roosevelt, August 10, 1943, in Orville H. Bullitt, ed., *For the President – Personal and Secret: Correspondence between Franklin D. Roosevelt and William C. Bullitt* (Boston, 1972), pp. 595–99. For Bullitt's recollection of Roosevelt's comments, see William C. Bullitt, "How We Won the War and Lost the Peace," *Life*, 25 (August 30, 1948), p. 94.

[78] Roosevelt to Churchill, March 18, 1942, in Warren Kimball, ed., *Churchill and Roosevelt: The Complete Correspondence*, 3 vols. (Princeton, NJ, 1984), I, p. 421.

[79] The description of Stalin's driving qualities is from George F. Kennan's letter to Robert Tucker, August 11, 1994, in Kennan, *At a Century's Ending: Reflections, 1982–1995* (New York, 1996), p. 244.

[80] Tucker, *Stalin in Power*, p. 446.

Roosevelt was unstinting in his efforts to meet this test, moving – it is crucial to appreciate – far beyond what might have been necessary to encourage the Soviet military effort. In reality, of course, Hitler had left Stalin few options but to fight to the death. Despite this, the American president expended his energies to attempt to establish a special personal relationship with the Soviet leader. He ensured that huge amounts of aid were delivered to the Russians to assist in defeating the Germans.[81] He worked directly, through soothing reassurances in his radio addresses, and indirectly, through promoting such propaganda as Joseph Davies's memoir and movie *Mission to Moscow*, to improve the image of the Soviet Union in the United States.[82] He either downplayed or simply failed to appreciate the ideological chasm that divided the democracies from Stalin's totalitarian regime.[83] He largely ignored the evidence of Soviet culpability for the appalling Katyn Massacre and, in general, he refrained from criticizing the Soviets and refused to retaliate to rude or provocative behavior. Indeed he perceived the Russian predilection for "spitting in his eye" to be an almost mechanical part of their diplomatic technique, something which "they invariably straightened out of their own accord."[84] Roosevelt's complaisance cannot be explained away simply by his recognition of the military necessities for defeating Germany. It rested upon the tragic misperception that he could build a bond of friendship with his Soviet opposite.

[81] During the Second World War, the United States furnished the Soviet Union with more than 17,000,000 tons of supplies valued at over $10 billion. For details, see George C. Herring, Jr., *Aid to Russia, 1941–1946: Strategy, Diplomacy and the Origins of the Cold War* (New York, 1946).

[82] For a representative reassurance, see his radio address after the Teheran Conference where FDR said: "To use an American and somewhat ungrammatical colloquialism, I may say that 'I got along fine' with Marshal Stalin. He is a man who combines a tremendous, relentless determination with a stalwart good humor. I believe he is truly representative of the heart and soul of Russia [sic]; and I believe that we are going to get along very well with him and the Russian people – very well indeed." Christmas Eve Fireside Chat on Teheran and Cairo Conferences, December 24, 1943, Samuel I. Rosenman, ed., *The Public Papers and Addresses of Franklin D. Roosevelt*, Vol. XII, *The Tide Turns 1943* (New York, 1950), pp. 553–63 (direct quotation from p. 558). On *Mission to Moscow*, see Todd Bennett, "Culture, Power, and *Mission to Moscow*: Film and Soviet–American Relations during World War II," *Journal of American History*, 88 (September 2001), pp. 489–518, esp. pp. 494–96. Also note Steven Casey, *Cautious Crusade: Franklin D. Roosevelt, American Public Opinion, and the War Against Nazi Germany* (New York, 2001), p. 62, which notes that "Roosevelt was instrumental in getting this [Davies's] book turned into a full-length movie."

[83] Charles Bohlen's recollections are especially telling here. The suave diplomat who translated for FDR at Yalta and bore him no animus whatsoever recalled that "as far as the Soviets were concerned, I do not think Roosevelt had any real comprehension of the great gulf that separated the thinking of a Bolshevik from a non-Bolshevik, and particularly from an American. He felt that Stalin viewed the world somewhat in the same light as he did, and that Stalin's hostility and distrust, which were evident in the wartime conferences, were due to the neglect that Soviet Russia had suffered at the hands of other countries for years after the Revolution. What he did not understand was that Stalin's enmity was based on profound ideological convictions." Charles E. Bohlen, *Witness to History, 1929–1969* (New York, 1973), p. 211.

[84] Roosevelt quoted in Blum, ed., *Price of Vision*, p. 245.

Roosevelt's effort to reassure Stalin dominated his diplomacy from 1943 onward. At Casablanca in January of that year, he called for the unconditional surrender of the Axis aiming not only to guarantee the annihilation of German militarism but also to soothe Soviet concerns at the delay in a cross-channel invasion. "Of course it's just the thing for the Russians," he explained with more accuracy than perhaps he appreciated. "They couldn't want anything better."[85] Indeed so! In addition to revealing his deep animosity toward Germany, this decision reflected a certain disinterest on the president's part for the geopolitical realities of Europe. There was no serious analysis of the geopolitical implications of the complete defeat of Central Europe's great power. FDR simply wanted Europe's regrettable role as the powder keg igniting world conflict ended once and for all. He seemed rather blasé to the prospect of Soviet influence in Eastern and Central Europe.[86]

As the Red Army in a tremendous military achievement halted the German advance in 1943 and began to repulse the Nazi armies from Soviet soil and as the Western Allies fought their way up the Italian peninsula and prepared deliberately for their cross-channel invasion, the military defeat of Germany became a difficult but certain formality.[87] In this circumstance, political issues flooded to the fore. Upon the surrender of Italy in September 1943, Stalin brazenly called for the establishment of a military-political commission to direct "on the spot the negotiations with Italy."[88] Roosevelt and Churchill agreed to his request but deflected it somewhat by locating it in Algiers and placing it under the direction of the Allied commander in the area.[89] They denied plenary powers to the Commission and retained such powers for the Anglo-American forces. Roosevelt saw that this exclusion of the Soviets from any but

---

[85] Elliott Roosevelt, *As He Saw It* (New York, 1946), p. 117.

[86] On this point see Harper, *American Visions of Europe*, pp. 88–89. Note also that Roosevelt told British Foreign Secretary Anthony Eden in March 1943 that "the Russian armies would be in the Baltic States at the time of the downfall of Germany and none of us can force them to get out." In the same conversation, in response to Eden's account of grandiose postwar Polish ambitions, Roosevelt explained "that the big powers would have to decide what Poland should have and that he … did not intend to go to the Peace Conference and bargain with Poland or the other small states; as far as Poland is concerned, the important thing is to set it up in a way that will help maintain the peace of the world." Hopkins's memorandum of Roosevelt–Eden conversation, March 15, 1943, *FRUS*, 1943, III, pp. 13–18. In September 1943, FDR explained to then Archbishop Francis Spellman that there would be no point in opposing Stalin's territorial demands because the Russian leader had the power to take these areas regardless of what the United States or Britain might do. Robert I. Gannon, S.J., *The Cardinal Spellman Story* (New York, 1962), p. 223.

[87] The Soviet army carried the brunt of the fighting against German combat divisions in the period from June 1941 to the Anglo–American invasion of France in June 1944. For example, in December 1942, the Western allies engaged some six German divisions, while the Soviets faced 183. Danchev, *On Specialness*, p. 65.

[88] Stalin to Roosevelt, August 24, 1943; September 8, 1943; and September 12, 1943, *FRUS*, 1943, I, pp. 783, 784–85.

[89] On the formation and role of the Allied Control Commission, see John Lewis Gaddis, *The United States and the Origins of the Cold War*, pp. 88–90.

nominal participation in Italian affairs prepared the way for the exclusion of the Americans and the British from any but marginal involvement in the affairs of Eastern Europe. He reminded Churchill on the eve of the Teheran conference that the occupation of Italy would "set the precedent for all such future activities in the war."[90] Presumably he had the Soviets and Eastern Europe in mind.

At the Teheran meeting in November 1943, which at last brought Stalin and Roosevelt together along with Churchill, the American leader conceded to Stalin on his absorption of the Baltic states and the redrawing of Poland's boundaries.[91] He gently coaxed Stalin on the need for referendums in these areas, but his main request involved the Soviets keeping quiet about these arrangements until after the 1944 election in which he would need Polish-American votes. He demonstrated that he "shared Stalin's ardor for shattering post-war German power," and agreed to some kind of dismemberment for the German nation.[92] He rehearsed his idea of the four great powers "policing the world in the post-war period" for the benefit of the Soviet leader.[93] His main priority centered on gaining Stalin's friendship, which he sought at Churchill's expense with all the good sense of an immature teenage male trying to impress a member of the opposite sex by poking fun at a friend.[94] As he later recalled to Labor Secretary Frances Perkins, for Stalin's benefit he teased Churchill "about his Britishness, about John Bull, about his cigars, about his habits. It began to register with Stalin. Winston got red and scowled, and the more he did so, the more Stalin smiled. Finally Stalin broke into a deep hearty guffaw, and for the first time in three days I saw light. I kept it up until Stalin was laughing with me, and it was then I called him 'Uncle Joe.' He would have thought me fresh the day before, but that day he laughed and came over and shook my hand. From that time on our relations were personal and Stalin himself indulged in an occasional

---

[90] Roosevelt to Churchill, October 4, 1943, *FRUS, 1943*, II, p. 383

[91] On the Teheran meeting, see Keith Eubank, *Summit at Teheran: The Untold Story* (New York, 1985), and Keith Sainsbury, *The Turning Point: Roosevelt, Stalin, Churchill and Chiang Kai-shek, 1943: The Moscow, Cairo and Teheran Conferences* (New York, 1985). As early as May of 1942, Roosevelt had revealed to Adolph Berle that "he would not particularly mind about the Russians taking quite a chunk of territory; they might have the Baltic republics, and Eastern Poland and perhaps the Bukovina, as well as Bessarabia." Berle apparently responded that "the Atlantic charter might have something to say about this," and cracked that he hoped Roosevelt "would not be getting generous with Scandinavia" as well. Adolph Berle quoted in Persico, *Roosevelt's Secret War*, pp. 195–96.

[92] Michael Beschloss discusses this in *The Conquerors*, pp. 18–28.

[93] Bohlen minutes, Roosevelt–Stalin conversation, December 1, 1943, *FRUS: The Conferences at Cairo and Teheran, 1943* (Washington, DC, 1961), pp. 594–95. During this awkward conversation, Roosevelt spent time explaining the important relationship between American foreign policy and domestic politics!

[94] Churchill felt his decline in status as an equal to Roosevelt and Stalin at Teheran. He realized, Klaus Larres notes, "that after Teheran the major decisions concerning the remainder of the war and the post-war world would effectively be taken by the much more powerful Americans and Russians." Larres, *Churchill's Cold War: The Politics of Personal Diplomacy* (New Haven, CT, 2002), p. 49.

witticism. The ice was broken and we talked like men and brothers."[95] Their
meeting at Teheran convinced FDR that "to use his own term, Stalin was 'get-
at-able,'" a view that Harry Hopkins readily endorsed.[96] The sad misjudgment
evident here should not diminish the force of both this incident and his assessment in revealing Roosevelt's approach based on concessions and personal relations rather than on a hard-headed political-military strategy.

Churchill found Roosevelt's approach worrying to put it mildly. He had come
to realize that the American president "did not intend to insist to breaking point
on self-determination for the nations of Eastern Europe."[97] At the same time his
concerns about the Soviets deepened. On his way to the Teheran conference, he
explained to British minister Harold Macmillan that "Germany is finished....
The real problem now is Russia," although he lamented, "I can't get the Americans to see it."[98] His cherished hope for an Anglo-American bloc withered.
He felt acutely the lack of American support and worried that possibilities
of exchanging geographic concessions to the Soviet Union – such as granting
Stalin the Curzon Line as a border – in return for political concessions –such
as political independence for Poland – were evaporating.[99] After Teheran, his
painful travail continued. He suffered as America's windy rhetoric about opposing spheres of influence continued, while the Soviet Union inexorably marched
westward obviously intent on establishing their power and influence. In May
1944, even as he continued his efforts to deal with the Soviets, he minuted to
Eden: "I fear that very great evil may come upon the world.... The Russians
are drunk with victory and there is no length they may not go."[100] Eden deepened his prime minister's apprehension by admitting his fear that "Russia has
vast aims and that these may include the domination of Eastern Europe and
even the Mediterranean and the 'communizing' of much that remains."[101]

Meanwhile, as 1944 progressed, the Americans largely accepted as inevitable
Soviet control of much of Eastern Europe, hoping that Stalin would show some
restraint and refrain from Sovietizing the region. "The Russians are perfectly
friendly," FDR explained in March. "They aren't trying to gobble up all the
rest of Europe or the world."[102] With the Italian surrender serving as a precedent the Americans left it to the Soviets to handle the surrenders of Rumania,

---

[95] Frances Perkins, *The Roosevelt I Knew* (New York, 1946) pp. 83–85.

[96] Sherwood, *Roosevelt and Hopkins*, pp. 798–99. Hopkins, of course, encouraged FDR in his
belief that he could establish a personal relationship with Stalin and emphasized to him that
"Soviet–American friendship held the key to the postwar world." Andrew and Gordievsky,
KGB, p. 332.

[97] Carlton, *Churchill and the Soviet Union*, p. 104.

[98] Quoted in Larres, *Churchill's Cold War*, p. 51.

[99] Lukacs, *Churchill*, p. 37.

[100] Carlton, *Churchill and the Soviet Union*, p. 214.

[101] Eden quoted in Remi Nadeau, *Stalin, Churchill, and Roosevelt Divide Europe* (New York,
1990), p. 109.

[102] Roosevelt's informal, extemporaneous remarks to Advertising War Council Conference,
March 8, 1944, in Rosenman, ed., *Public Papers and Addresses of Franklin D. Roosevelt*,
Vol. XIII, *Victory and the Threshold of Peace, 1944–1945* (New York, 1950), p. 99.

Bulgaria, and Hungary, which made obvious sense in light of the location of the powerful Red Army.[103] Roosevelt's compliance, however, also guided policy toward Poland, which held a qualitatively different position from any of the former satellites of Germany. Poland had fought the Germans with vigor and honor from the beginning of the war. Its symbolic importance rested on the reality that Britain had entered the war in defense of Polish sovereignty. Poland had a government resident in London recognized by the British and the Americans and at one point by the Soviet Union until the Poles had complained too vigorously about the massacre of their officer corps at Katyn.[104]

Roosevelt's main effort on Poland throughout 1943 and 1944 focused on attempting to influence the London Poles to moderate their anti-Soviet stance and to compromise on the territorial issue – which he already had done at Teheran. Understandably, the Poles demonstrated some hesitation in pursuing the recommended course of moderation and elicited irritation from Roosevelt as a result. In March 1944, he told Henry Wallace that "the Poles as usual were handling things very badly, [and] that he thought Stalin's ideas were sound with regard to Poland."[105] When Polish Prime Minister Stanislaw Mikolajcyzk visited Washington in June, the president warned him that there were five times as many Russians as Poles and that "the British and Americans have no intention of fighting Russia." Instead, he counseled that the Poles should get with his program and agree to territorial concessions and changes in the composition of their government. He made it plain that "in this political year I cannot approach Stalin with a new initiative about Poland."[106] Given his domestic political needs, FDR aimed to minimize problems and to postpone any unpopular decisions. Events in Poland denied him a completely trouble-free course, although he manipulated Polish-Americans effectively with rather misleading election-eve assurances.

By late June of 1944, the Red Army's progress into Poland brought the administration of the newly "liberated" territories to the fore. Upon Churchill's pleading, Stalin agreed to meet Mikolajcyzk to seek a settlement. The Polish leader met Stalin on July 27, just a day after the Soviets with exquisitely brutal timing had announced that their puppet Polish Committee of National Liberation with a seat of government in Lublin would oversee the administration of Polish territories. Mikolajcyzk now faced a rival government and demanding terms from Stalin. To the shifting of Poland's borders west, the Soviets now added the requirement that the rival Polish "governments" be integrated.

---

[103] On the use of the Italian surrender as a precedent, see Admiral Leahy to Cordell Hull, March 28, 1944, *FRUS*, 1944, IV, pp. 161–62.

[104] On Katyn, see Allen Paul, *Katyn: The Untold Story of Stalin's Polish Massacre* (New York, 1991).

[105] Blum, ed., *Price of Vision*, p. 308.

[106] Roosevelt quoted in John Lewis Gaddis, *The United States and the Origins of the Cold War*, p. 144. On Roosevelt's meeting with Mikolajczyk in particular and on his efforts to avoid the Polish dispute because of domestic political considerations, see Harriman and Abel, *Special Envoy to Churchill and Stalin*, pp. 311, 331, 366.

Mikolajcyzk refused these demands, despite his desperate desire to gain Soviet military support for the marvelously courageous and reckless Warsaw uprising mounted in August by Polish patriots who wanted the privilege of liberating their capital city. His refusal helped bring the Polish issue to a disastrous denouement. Stalin rested his forces short of Warsaw at the Vistula River and left the Germans to take a vicious revenge on the Poles. Until very late in the uprising, Stalin even refused the use of Russian airfields to the Americans and the British who attempted to supply the Poles.[107] When the remnants of the Polish Home Army surrendered to the Germans on October 3, 1944, Stalin must have been well satisfied. With the almost complete decimation of the Home Army, the Polish Government-in-Exile had lost its most significant base of tangible power within Poland. This had the complementary effect of removing a serious obstacle to the assertion of authority by the Lublin Committee, which Stalin proceeded to recognize on January 1, 1945, despite two requests from Roosevelt for delay on that action.[108]

Soviet behavior during the Warsaw uprising shook the faith of keen observers. British Air Marshall Sir John Slessor later noted: "How, after the fall of Warsaw, any responsible statesman could trust any Russian Communist further than he could kick him, passes the comprehension of ordinary men."[109] The U.S. chargé in Moscow, George F. Kennan, later asserted that "this was the moment when, if ever, there should have been a full-fledged and realistic political showdown with the Soviet leaders, when they should have been confronted with the choice between changing their policy completely and agreeing to collaborate in the establishment of truly independent countries in Eastern Europe or forfeiting Western Allied support and sponsorship for the remaining phases of their war effort."[110] For Kennan's immediate superior, American Ambassador Averell Harriman, the Warsaw uprising proved a true moment of revelation and led him to question "the possibility of co-operation with Stalin."[111] Churchill sputtered and fumed and considered "stopping the supplies

---

[107] This was done despite the personal requests of Roosevelt and Churchill. One must note however that Roosevelt demonstrated much more caution than Churchill and sought to avoid any harm to American–Soviet cooperation. In reply to Churchill's suggestion that they dispatch a joint message to Stalin indicating their intention to send planes unless he directly forbade it, Roosevelt wrote: "I do not consider it advantageous to the long range general war project for me to join with you in the proposed messages to U.J.[Uncle Joe Stalin]." For Churchill's letter of August 25, 1944, and Roosevelt's reply, August 26, 1944 see Kimball, ed., *Churchill and Roosevelt: The Complete Correspondence*, Vol. III, *Alliance Declining, February 1994–April 1945* (Princeton, NJ, 1984), pp. 295–96.

[108] For the recognition, see Stalin to Roosevelt, January 1, 1945 (enclosed in Roosevelt to Churchill), *FRUS: The Conferences at Malta and Yalta, 1945*, pp. 225–26. For Roosevelt's requests for delay see Roosevelt to Stalin, December 16, 1944 and December 30, 1944, ibid., pp. 217–18, 224–25.

[109] Slessor quoted in John Wheeler-Bennett and Anthony Nicholls, *The Semblance of Peace: The Political Settlement after the Second World War* (London, 1972), p. 191.

[110] George F. Kennan, *Memoirs, 1925–1950* (Boston, 1967), p. 211.

[111] Harriman and Abel, *Special Envoy to Churchill and Stalin*, pp. 342–43.

to Russia via the Arctic route" if the Soviets held British supply planes forced to land behind Russian lines.[112]

Soviet behavior concerning the Warsaw uprising, however, in no way dislodged FDR from his fervent hopes to work amicably with the Soviet leader. Harriman tried to influence FDR through Harry Hopkins to whom he explained that the Soviets "have misinterpreted our generous attitude towards them as a sign of weakness, and acceptance of their policies." For the ambassador, the time had come "when we must make clear what we expect of them as the price of our good will." He did not propose "any drastic action but a firm and friendly *quid pro quo* attitude."[113] Harriman's recommendations for a somewhat tougher stance in negotiations with the Soviet Union found no receptive audience in the White House. Instead, Roosevelt continued to emphasize great power collaboration. "In classic Roosevelt style," Warren Kimball observed, "he...evaded, avoided, and ignored specifics regarding Eastern Europe, hoping to insulate the more important objective – long-term collaboration."[114] Perhaps he hoped that his largesse regarding the right (or lack thereof) to self-determination of the Eastern Europeans would encourage the Soviet leader to moderate his behavior and establish what might be termed a "soft sphere" in the region where benign oversight rather than brutal subjugation might be applied.

Churchill's concerns deepened further as 1944 progressed, especially his fears about the extent of the Soviet thrust westward and southward. In May he asked Eden: "Are we going to acquiesce in the Communization of the Balkans and perhaps of Italy?" He sensed the approach of "a showdown with the Russians about their Communist intrigues in Italy, Yugoslavia and Greece." Eden agreed and suggested to Churchill that "the time has come for us to consider from the long-term view what is going to be the after-war effect of these developments instead of confining ourselves as hitherto to the short-term view of what will give the best dividends during the war and for the war."[115] Not only Eastern Europe but vital British interests in the Mediterranean were at stake. Given not only America's unwillingness to apply its superior power in opposition to Soviet actions in Eastern Europe but also the likelihood that American military strength would be quickly withdrawn from Europe after Germany's defeat, Churchill resorted to the classic methods of geopolitics familiar to generations of British diplomats. He aimed to deal with Stalin to apply some limits to the extension of Soviet power. It was a position that emerged from British weakness and a clear desire to salvage something from an increasingly bad situation. Such thinking provides the background and rationale for Churchill's meeting in Moscow in October 1944 for the Tolstoy conference.

Circumstances had changed drastically since 1941 when Churchill had promised British support to a Soviet Union reeling from the Nazi betrayal and

[112] Churchill quoted in Nadeau, *Stalin, Churchill, and Roosevelt Divide Europe*, p. 107.
[113] Harriman to Hopkins, September 10, 1944, Harry L. Hopkins Papers, FDRL, Box 157.
[114] Kimball, *The Juggler*, p. 100.
[115] Churchill and Eden quoted in Nadeau, *Stalin, Churchill and Roosevelt Divide Europe*, p. 109.

invasion. The correlation of forces (so to speak) in 1944 now decidedly favored Stalin. Churchill continued his effort to obtain some modicum of Polish political independence without much success, but he refrained from going to the mat over Poland at this time. He still hoped to engage the Americans on that issue, and he needed to deal with Stalin on other matters. This, of course, is what they did in reaching their famous "percentages" agreement. As is well known from his own account, Churchill pushed a piece of paper across the table to Stalin on which he had written these arrangements for influence: "Roumania: Russia 90%. Greece: Great Britain (in accord with USA) 90%. Yugoslavia: 50–50. Hungary: 50–50. Bulgaria: Russia 75%." Stalin ticked the paper and instructed that Churchill should keep it.[116] The deal was done. It hardly constituted one of the finest achievements of British diplomacy, and some scholars have sharply criticized the agreement and its geopolitical accommodation.[117] Churchill certainly did concede to Stalin a certain dominance in parts of Eastern Europe. Yet, as David Carlton persuasively has noted, "the truth seems to be that at a time of great national weakness Churchill, without a single decent card in his hand, effectively bluffed Stalin into giving him a free hand in Greece."[118] Churchill understood that he was dealing as John Lukacs has put it with "a monstrous Tsar writ large, a new Ivan the Terrible," and that it was "geography and territory" that mattered most.[119] He wanted to keep as much as possible of it out of Stalin's grasp while still preserving the possibility of the Anglo–Soviet postwar cooperation, which would be the necessary basis for European stability.

Churchill's logic and actions may be faulted in retrospect, but at least they rested upon a fairly clear sense of Stalin's nature and ambitions. Roosevelt declined to follow Churchill's lead or to share his assumptions. His objection to the deal that Churchill brokered with Stalin owed less to any concern for Eastern Europe than it did to fears "that it would be perceived by U.S. opinion as another example of how the cynical, immoral European powers periodically got together to make secret agreements to divide up the spoils at the expense of the weaker states." Such a development might "jeopardize his postwar plans right from the beginning."[120] Postponement and obfuscation became his chosen

---

[116] Churchill, *Triumph and Tragedy*, pp. 227–28.

[117] See for example Theodore Draper, *A Present of Things Past: Selected Essays* (New York, 1990), p. 251, who argued that "if Stalin had any reason to believe that he could take Eastern Europe with impunity, he owed it in the first place to Churchill."

[118] Carlton, *Churchill and the Soviet Union*, p. 115. My analysis is also influenced by John Lukacs, *Churchill*, pp. 38–42.

[119] Lukacs, *Churchill*, p. 42.

[120] Alexander L. George, "Domestic Constraints on Regime Change in U.S. Foreign Policy: The Need for Policy Legitimacy," in Ole R. Holsti, Randolph M. Siverson, and Alexander L. George, eds., *Change in the International System* (Boulder, CO, 1980), p. 246. On the Churchill–Stalin deal, see Churchill, *Triumph and Tragedy*, pp. 197–212; and the chapter "Franklin D. Roosevelt & the Night Stalin and Churchill Divided Europe," in Joseph M. Siracusa, *Into the Dark House: American Diplomacy and the Ideological Origins of the Cold War* (Claremont, CA, 1998), pp. 1–30. For records of the meetings at the Kremlin, October 9–17, see Prime Minister's Operational File (Premier 3), File 434, Folder 2, Public Record Office. For Harriman's

instruments as he successfully won reelection and moved toward his second meeting with Stalin where he hoped to cement further postwar arrangements.

Yalta and Beyond

The Yalta conference holds a notorious reputation for those who associate it with the West's "betrayal" or "sell-out" of Eastern Europe. But Yalta should not be viewed as a signal moment of surrender or betrayal that produced the indefensible partition of Europe.[121] It was but another way-station on the course that FDR had long charted where he might apply his strategy of building personal relations in the interests of drawing the Soviets into his plans for a new postwar world order. When he joined Stalin and Churchill in the former summer palace of the Czars in the Crimean resort city, the die was largely cast. Having invested so much of himself in his effort to woo Stalin, he seemed incapable of contemplating second thoughts or reconsiderations. Harriman might undergo a conversion experience regarding the Soviets, but Roosevelt held more firmly to his old beliefs. His exhaustion and ailing health hardly predisposed him to deal anew with the realities of Stalin's actions and intentions.[122] Instead he still hoped to make good on the assurances given in his final inaugural address that "we can gain no lasting peace if we approach it with suspicion and mistrust – or with fear."[123]

The team he brought with him to Yalta was similarly ill-equipped to question let alone adjust American policy. The new Secretary of State Edward Stettinius, who replaced the long-suffering Cordell Hull, was quite inexperienced and ineffective and selected by Roosevelt (in typical fashion) largely for his pliability.[124] While the State Department remained on the periphery for the most part, Harry

recollections of the discussions see Harriman and Abel, *Special Envoy to Churchill and Stalin*, p. 358.

[121] Vojtech Mastny makes this same point in his *The Cold War and Soviet Insecurity: The Stalin Years* (New York, 1996), p. 22. Also note Adam Ulam's commentary: "But was Yalta *the* place of the Great Betrayal (or Deception)? No. The division of Europe resulted from a whole series of events: Soviet usurpations, Western sins of omission and commission, as well as sheer accidents – all going back to 1943 and continuing through to 1947. Yalta was simply one stage." See Adam B. Ulam, "Forty Years after Yalta," *New Republic* (February 11, 1985), p. 20.

[122] On the sad state of Roosevelt's health, see Robert H. Ferrell, *The Dying President*. Ferrell concludes (p. 4) that FDR was "in no condition to govern the Republic."

[123] Roosevelt's inaugural address, January 20, 1945, in Rosenman, ed., *The Public Papers and Addresses of Franklin D. Roosevelt*, Vol. XIII, p. 524.

[124] Cordell Hull had recommended Jimmy Byrnes as his successor, but Roosevelt went with Stettinius and explained his choice to his new secretary of state this way: "Jimmy had always been on his own in the Senate and elsewhere. I am not sure that he and I could act harmoniously as a team." As Byrnes's biographer David Robertson notes, "Stettinius caught on quickly" and observed "in other words, Jimmy might question who was boss" to which FDR commented "that's exactly it." There was no room for someone who might challenge seriously Roosevelt's established line. On this incident, see David Robertson, *Sly and Able: A Political Biography of James F. Byrnes* (New York, 1994), p. 379. On Hull's "suffering," see Irwin F. Gellman, *Secret Affairs: Franklin Roosevelt, Cordell Hull, and Sumner Welles* (Baltimore, 1995).

PHOTO 3. The Big Three at the Yalta Conference – Winston Churchill, Franklin Roosevelt, and Josef Stalin – February 1945. (Courtesy National Archives)

Hopkins – now ailing and exhausted like his chief – remained the president's key confidante on political–diplomatic matters. Roosevelt's intimate friend stayed wedded to their treasured vision of big-power cooperation, despite Harriman's explicit efforts to warn him that "unless we take issue with the present policy, there is every indication the Soviet Union will become a world bully wherever their interests are involved."[125] Roosevelt persuaded Jimmy Byrnes to join him on the trip in part to assuage Byrnes's anger at being passed over for the vice-presidential nomination but also to use him subsequently as "messenger to Congress" to promote the conference agreements. He assigned him no role other than that of observer, although that sufficed to transform "Byrnes into a perceived expert on Yalta and other international affairs."[126]

Roosevelt's decision to bring Byrnes to Yalta reflected his anxiety that domestic political forces, especially in the Senate, might block or interfere with his grand international project as they had done to Woodrow Wilson's. Of course, the real barrier to the implementation of his vision sat across the table from him

[125] Harriman to Hopkins, September 10, 1944, Harry L. Hopkins Papers, FDRL, Box 157.
[126] On Byrnes at Yalta and his subsequent efforts to lobby congress and the public, see Robertson, *Sly and Able,* pp. 379–87.

in the Livadia Palace in the person of Stalin. Stalin read from a quite different script than the American president. Perhaps "the imperial tradition of Russia reinforced by Marxist globalism" would have pushed any leader of Soviet Russia to engage upon significant territorial expansion in light of his nation's military success. But this "symbiosis of imperial expansion and ideological proselytism" was magnified in Stalin's hands and represented an extraordinary danger for Western and democratic interests.[127] Such was his "insatiable craving" for security and his deep suspicion and animosity to all that he did not control, he simply couldn't act in the more restrained manner for which Roosevelt hoped.[128] This was not a "normal" statesman wanting to expand his influence in the manner of the old European empires he detested. His definition of security "required ultimate and undiluted control over territories and, *ipso facto*, control over the population, their households and minds."[129]

When Roosevelt looked across the conference table, however, he did not see a brutal and ambitious tyrant but his crucial, if sometimes difficult, wartime ally and the man he deemed his essential partner in the postwar world. At Yalta, he eagerly sought Stalin's help, which the Soviet leader, ever eager to exploit conciliation and demonstrations of friendship, gave in carefully calculated measure. The substance of their negotiations on a range of subjects – the United Nations, the Far East and the Pacific War, and the Declaration on Liberated Europe, Poland, and Germany – and the immediate post-Yalta developments on these matters constituted a major part of the diplomatic legacy which Roosevelt consigned to Truman.[130]

Consistent with his vision of great power collaboration, Roosevelt placed special importance on gaining full Soviet participation in the planned United Nations organization. In his mind, the organization had evolved into the vehicle through which the major powers would expend their efforts and also as the crucial means to prevent any American retreat to isolationism.[131] At Yalta, final arrangements were made for the meeting of the United Nations in San Francisco on April 25 to settle on the charter for the new international organization. Also the questions of voting procedure in the Security Council and of

[127] On the "symbiosis," see Vladislav Zubok and Constantine Pleshakov, *Inside the Kremlin's Cold War: From Stalin to Khrushchev* (Cambridge, MA, 1996), pp. 3–6.

[128] On Stalin's "insatiable craving," see Mastny, *The Cold War and Soviet Insecurity*, p. 23.

[129] Zubok and Pleshakov, *Inside the Kremlin's Cold War*, p. 17. John Gaddis makes the point that Stalin was not "a normal, everyday, run-of-the-mill, statesmanlike head of government" in "The Tragedy of Cold War History: Reflections on Revisionism," *Foreign Affairs*, 73 (January/February 1994), p. 146.

[130] For a solid overview of the Yalta Conference and its principal issues, see Russell D. Buhite's *Decisions at Yalta: An Appraisal of Summit Diplomacy* (Wilmington, DE, 1986).

[131] Charles Bohlen, who served as FDR's interpreter at Yalta, recalled that FDR saw the UN as "the only device that could keep the United States from slipping back into isolationism." Bohlen, *Witness to History, 1929–1969* (New York, 1963), p. 177. On the difficulty of determining FDR's true thinking on the UN, see William C. Widenor, "American Planning for the United Nations: Have We Been Asking the Right Questions?" *Diplomatic History*, 6 (Summer 1982), pp. 245–65.

PHOTO 4. The conference table at the Yalta conference with Stalin, Roosevelt, and Churchill (in foreground) flanked by their advisers. (Courtesy National Archives)

the number of votes for the USSR in the proposed General Assembly seemingly were resolved and the path cleared for the successful birth of the new world body.[132] This achievement caused Roosevelt and Hopkins to leave Yalta in a "mood of supreme exultation."[133] This was for them the crucial issue. They took Soviet willingness to enter the UN as a promising sign for postwar friendship and collaboration.[134] This understanding received a sharp jolt in March when Stalin refused to dispatch Foreign Minister Molotov to the San Francisco meeting.[135] Roosevelt plaintively cabled the Soviet leader on March 24 of his fear "that Mr. Molotov's absence will be construed all over the world as a lack of comparable interest on the part of the Soviet Government in the great objectives of this Conference."[136] Roosevelt's plea left Stalin unmoved. Only the president's death caused the Soviet leader to reverse his decision.

On leaving Yalta, Roosevelt also felt pleased with his success in obtaining a clear pledge from Stalin that the Soviet Union would enter the war against Japan "two or three months after Germany has surrendered and the war in Europe has terminated." Stalin laid out clear conditions for his entry into the Pacific war. He would gain outright the Kurile Islands and the southern part of Sakhalin, have the status quo in Soviet-controlled Outer Mongolia confirmed, and regain the lease on the naval base at Port Arthur. While agreeing that China should retain sovereignty in Manchuria, Stalin extracted endorsement for a proposal for the joint operation by a Sino-Soviet company of the Chinese Eastern Railroad and the South Manchurian Railroad. Roosevelt cavalierly undertook to gain the concurrence of Chiang Kai-shek for these terms, which effectively conceded to the Soviets a sphere of influence in the region. Stalin, no doubt eager to formalize these favorable arrangements, indicated a willingness to conclude "a pact of friendship and alliance between the U.S.S.R. and China."[137] Throughout his

---

[132] Section I – "World Organization" – of the Yalta Protocol, *FRUS: The Conferences at Malta and Yalta, 1945*, pp. 975–76. For further details, see Townsend Hoopes and Douglas Brinkley, *FDR and the Creation of the U.N.* (New Haven, CT, 1997), pp. 172–79.

[133] Sherwood, *Roosevelt and Hopkins*, p. 869. Lord Moran, Churchill's doctor and a careful British observer, confirms this view noting that the Americans "are leaving Yalta with a sense of achievement, they feel they are on top of the world." Lord Moran, *Winston Churchill*, pp. 231–32.

[134] Hopkins told Sherwood that "We really believed in our hearts that this was the dawn of the new day we had all been praying for and talking about for so many years. We were absolutely certain that we had won the first great victory of the peace.... The Russians had proved that they could be reasonable and farseeing and there wasn't any doubt in the minds of the President or any of us that we could live with them and get along with them peacefully for as far into the future as any of us could imagine." Sherwood, *Roosevelt and Hopkins*, p. 870.

[135] Ambassador Andrei Gromyko informed Undersecretary of State Joseph Grew of the Soviet delegation and hence of Molotov's inability to attend on March 23, 1945. Grew then advised President Roosevelt and made the obvious point that the Soviet delegation was not "high-ranking." *FRUS, 1945*, I, pp. 151–52.

[136] Roosevelt to Stalin, March 24, 1945, *FRUS, 1945*, I, p. 156.

[137] "Agreement Regarding Entry of the Soviet Union into the War against Japan," *FRUS: The Conferences at Malta and Yalta, 1945*, p. 984.

negotiations of this matter, FDR treated it primarily as a military concern and, according to one close student of the episode, "it was apparently on the advice of the Joint Chiefs who viewed the problem in purely military terms... that he made his decision to pay the price of Soviet intervention."[138] Believing that an invasion of its home islands would be necessary to unconditionally defeat Japan and always eager to minimize American casualties, Roosevelt saw the benefits of a Soviet attack on Japan's Kwantung Army in Manchuria. Perhaps, as Averell Harriman later suggested, Roosevelt also wanted to obtain a clear delineation of Soviet desires in the Far East and to assure Soviet support for Chiang's Nationalist government. Whatever the relative importance of these factors, the Yalta Far Eastern Accord constituted an important element of Roosevelt's legacy to Truman.

With his eye set firmly on the need to maintain domestic support for his foreign policy, Roosevelt accepted the counsel of his State Department and pushed Stalin and Churchill to sign a Declaration on Liberated Europe. The Declaration reaffirmed the Atlantic Charter and called for the formation of interim governments in Europe "broadly representative of all democratic elements in the population and pledged to the earliest possible establishment through free elections of governments responsive to the will of the people."[139] Roosevelt's full purposes in securing this noble declaration of the self-determination principle are not easily discerned. Perhaps he aimed to use it as an instrument to convey to Stalin the need for moderation regarding the extent of Soviet political control of Eastern Europe. Perhaps, as Fraser Harbutt has speculated, he used the Declaration not only to "inspire a favorable opinion of his diplomacy at home [and to] protect him[self] from the political censure to which he was now immediately and dangerously exposed by Stalin's increasingly aggressive conduct in Eastern Europe," but also, in the long run, to "set a clear standard by which future Soviet conduct would be monitored by an expectant, moralistic American and perhaps world opinion."[140] Yet, Roosevelt's refusal to accept the State Department's proposal to establish a High Commission for Liberated Europe to enforce the Declaration suggests the limits of his commitment to its provisions.[141]

The Soviets exhibited some suspicion regarding the Declaration. Molotov recalled that Stalin greeted it "warily." But he rejected his foreign minister's outright objections to it and instructed him to "work it out. We can deal with it in our way later." For Stalin the important point was "the correlation of

---

138 Louis Morton, "Soviet Intervention in the War with Japan," *Foreign Affairs*, 40 (July 1962), p. 662.

139 "Declaration on Liberated Europe," Section 2 of the Protocol of Proceedings of the Crimea Conference, *FRUS: The Conferences at Malta and Yalta, 1945*, pp. 977–78.

140 Fraser J. Harbutt, *The Iron Curtain: Churchill, America, and the Origins of the Cold War* (New York, 1986), p. 88

141 Charles G. Stefan makes this point in his "Yalta Revisited: An Update on the Diplomacy of FDR and His Wartime Summit Partners," *Presidential Studies Quarterly*, 23 (Fall 1993), p. 759.

forces."[142] Of course, the declaration exerted little restraint on his actions. His broad approach and his general contempt for the Declaration on Liberated Europe received ample demonstration two weeks after Yalta when Soviet deputy-commissar for foreign affairs Andrei Vyshinsky bludgeoned Rumania's King Michael into dismissing the noncommunist Radescu government and then into installing in its place a government fully compliant to Soviet wishes headed by Petru Groza.[143] In response, Churchill asked FDR to join him in writing Stalin to prevent a purge of noncommunists in Rumania.[144] The president sidestepped the request and declared in words that are beyond definitive exegesis that "Rumania is not a good place for a test case."[145] Roosevelt's hesitation to weigh in effectively on the Rumanian issue certainly lends support to Robert Dallek's argument that the president had "for all practical purposes conceded that Eastern Europe was a Soviet sphere of control."[146]

Events in Poland confirm further FDR's reluctance to challenge Soviet behavior in the region. At Yalta, the Western powers formally agreed to the cession of a significant part of prewar Poland to the Soviet Union but deferred the issue of Polish boundaries in the West until a future peace conference. More crucial was the issue of who would govern within Poland, whatever its ultimate boundaries. Roosevelt worked with Churchill to secure a more independent and democratic Poland and seemingly with some success. The Yalta protocol provided that Stalin's puppet Lublin regime should be "reorganized on a broader democratic basis with the inclusion of democratic leaders from Poland and Poles abroad." The new government would be pledged to early free elections, which, so Stalin had informed Roosevelt, could be held just a month after Yalta.[147] Presumably in another effort to telegraph to Stalin his hopes, Roosevelt spoke of his desire to have the election be "beyond question." He told his Soviet opposite, it "should be like Caesar's wife," who, he added, "they say...was pure." Stalin revealingly responded that "they said that about her but in fact she had her sins."[148]

Despite the Western efforts at the conference, the Americans recognized the limits of the Polish accord. Secretary Stettinius later claimed the agreement was "what the two countries could persuade the Soviet Union to accept."[149] After

---

[142] Albert Resis, ed., *Molotov Remembers: Inside Kremlin Politics* [Conversations with Felix Chuev] (Chicago, 1993), p. 51.

[143] For further details of this incident, see William H. McNeill, *America, Britain, and Russia: Their Cooperation and Conflict, 1941–1946* (London, 1953), p. 575.

[144] Churchill to Roosevelt, March 8, 1945, *FRUS, 1945*, V, pp. 505–06.

[145] Roosevelt to Churchill, March 11, 1945, *FRUS, 1945*, V, pp. 509–10.

[146] Dallek, *Franklin D. Roosevelt and American Foreign Policy*, p. 524.

[147] Section 7 – "Poland," Yalta Protocol, *FRUS: The Conferences at Malta and Yalta, 1945*, p. 980. For Roosevelt's discussions with Stalin on elections in Poland, see Bohlen minutes, Fifth plenary meeting, February 9, 1945, *FRUS: The Conferences at Malta and Yalta, 1945*, pp. 776–81.

[148] For this interesting exchange, see Matthews minutes, Sixth plenary meeting, February 9, 1945, *FRUS: The Conferences at Malta and Yalta, 1945*, p. 854.

[149] Edward R. Stettinius, Jr., *Roosevelt and the Russians: The Yalta Conference*, ed. Walter Johnson (Garden City, NY, 1949), p. 300.

seeing the Polish accord, Admiral William Leahy exclaimed, "Mr. President, this is so elastic that the Russians can stretch it all the way from Yalta to Washington without ever technically breaking it." Roosevelt replied, apparently with resignation: "I know Bill – I know. But it's the best I can do for Poland at this time."[150]

After Yalta, FDR proved far less interested than Churchill in restraining the Soviet capacity to exploit the elasticity of the agreement. When negotiations in Moscow to forge a new provisional government bogged down, Churchill requested that a forceful joint message be sent to Stalin. "This is the test case between us and the Russians," the prime minister wrote gravely, "of the meaning which is to be attached to such terms as Democracy, Sovereignty, Independence, Representative Government and free and unfettered elections."[151] In a similar manner to the Rumanian case, however, Roosevelt declined to join Churchill and preferred to pursue further the Moscow negotiations. Unlike Rumania, Churchill would not be placated on the Polish case. He quickly fired off a passionate reply to Roosevelt, which struck to the heart of the issue. "Poland has lost her frontier," he exclaimed. "Is she now to lose her freedom?" Confessing that he did not want to get out of step with the United States, the British leader, nonetheless, explained that he "would need to make clear that we are in the presence of a great failure and an utter breakdown of what was settled at Yalta, but that we British have not the necessary strength to carry the matter further and that the limits of our capacity to act have been reached."[152]

Roosevelt's cautious response to Churchill's entreaty suggests his enduring commitment to a supine cooperation with the Soviets. Around this time, he indicated to his Cabinet that he was having "considerable difficulty with British relations" and jokingly remarked that the British "were perfectly willing for the United States to have a war with Russia at any time."[153] His reluctance to allow the Polish issue to be elevated to such a central place that it might rupture U.S.-Soviet relations and threaten the progress he had made on arrangements for the United Nations meeting and for Soviet participation in the Pacific War was obvious. His general view that the overall significance of Europe in world affairs must be reduced perhaps weighed in here as well. FDR tried to placate the obviously upset British leader. He denied that a major divergence in their positions existed and argued that "we have been merely discussing the most effective tactics and I cannot agree that we are confronted with a breakdown

---

[150] William D. Leahy, *I Was There* (New York, 1950), pp. 315–16. When Assistant Secretary Adolf A. Berle recalled that when he visited FDR soon after the latter's return from Yalta, the president told him: "Adolf, I didn't say the result was good. I said that it was the best I could do." Berle claimed that Roosevelt explained that he "had got the Russians' word for the reconstitution of the countries under Russian occupation. There were to be free elections. They were to choose their own governments." Adolf A. Berle, speech at Kalamazoo College, May 26, 1965, in Beatrice Bishop Berle and Travis Beal Jacobs, eds., *Navigating the Rapids, 1918–1971: From the Papers of Adolf A. Berle* (New York, 1973), p. 477.

[151] Churchill to Roosevelt, March 8, 1945, *FRUS*, 1945, V, pp. 147–48.

[152] Churchill to Roosevelt, March 13, 1945, *FRUS*, 1945, V, pp. 158–59.

[153] Walter Millis, ed., *The Forrestal Diaries* (New York, 1951), pp. 36–37.

of the Yalta agreement until we have made the effort to overcome the obstacles incurred in the negotiations at Moscow."[154] Churchill acquiesced for a while but watched with dismay as the Moscow negotiations made little progress. By the month's end, he again cabled his discontent to Roosevelt and complained of Molotov's plan to simply add "a few other Poles to the existing administration of Russian puppets." The prime minister called anew for a strong joint appeal to Stalin.[155]

Roosevelt's more somber response just two weeks before his death gave the first very tentative indications of some hesitations regarding the strategy of cooperation, which had guided his policies toward the Soviet Union throughout the war. He admitted to "anxiety" regarding the Soviet attitude since the Crimea conference and declared his acute awareness of "the dangers inherent in the present course of events not only for the immediate issues involved ... but also for the San Francisco Conference and future world cooperation." But FDR still hesitated to take up Churchill's more blustering, confrontational approach. He reminded his British colleague not to evade the fact that they had placed "somewhat more emphasis on the Lublin Poles than on the other two groups from which the new Government is to be drawn." Whatever the extent of his developing concerns regarding Soviet attitudes, the president still hoped for a settlement of the matter. At this point, however, he decided to "take up directly with Stalin the broader aspects of the Soviet attitude."[156]

"I cannot conceal from you," Roosevelt wrote Stalin on April 1, 1945, "the concern with which I view the development of events of mutual interest since our fruitful meeting at Yalta." In words that State Department subordinates and Admiral Leahy drafted for him, the president pointed to the "discouraging lack of progress" in implementing the Yalta agreements, especially those concerning Poland. In words that were uncharacteristically pointed, the president made it plain to Stalin that any Polish solution "which would result in a thinly disguised continuance of the present Warsaw regime would be unacceptable and would cause the people of the United States to regard the Yalta agreement as having failed." Roosevelt emphasized to Stalin yet again the need for popular support for American foreign policies and concluded with a warning that if the Polish question were not amicably settled, "the difficulties and dangers to Allied unity which we had so much in mind in reaching our decision at the Crimea will face us in an even more acute form."[157] While historians like Warren Kimball rightly have raised questions as to how accurately these clear warnings reflected FDR's own views, the importance of this communication should not be understated.[158] When read by Harry Truman less than two weeks later, it surely conveyed to him Roosevelt's deep concern about the impasse on the Polish issue and the need

---

[154] Roosevelt to Churchill, March 15, 1945, *FRUS*, 1945, V, pp. 163–64.

[155] Churchill to Roosevelt, March 27, 1945, *FRUS*, 1945, V, pp. 185–87.

[156] Roosevelt to Churchill, March 29, 1945, *FRUS*, 1945, V, pp. 189–90. On the drafting of this somewhat stronger response by State Department officials and Admiral Leahy, see the reference to the action sheet relating to it in Kimball, ed., *Churchill & Roosevelt*, Vol. III, pp. 592–93.

[157] Roosevelt to Stalin, April 1, 1945, *FRUS*, 1945, V, pp. 194–96.

[158] Kimball, *The Juggler*, p. 179.

to break the logjam on the matter. Understanding this is crucial to appreciating Truman's actions on the matter in his first weeks in office.

Whatever the depth of FDR's commitment to the views expressed in his message to Stalin, the missive itself had no impact on the Soviet leader. In an uncompromising reply on April 7, which an exhausted FDR read at his retreat at Warm Springs, Stalin blamed the American and British ambassadors in Moscow for the breakdown in the talks on Poland and accused them of departing from the terms of the Crimean conference.[159] Three days later Roosevelt cabled Churchill that they would need "to consider most carefully the implications of Stalin's attitude and what is to be our next step."[160] The president died before taking this step. What it might have been he left to fevered discussion among the many advisers who hastened to counsel his successor – whom, of course, he had not kept briefed on the matter. One might speculate that the ailing president was somewhat unsure himself what he should do. Such was the uncertain nature of the legacy he left to Harry Truman.

Roosevelt's hopes to persuade Stalin to moderate the extent of his domination in Eastern Europe had relied on a reassurance that Germany would be completely defeated and disarmed and effectively controlled in the postwar period. This he hoped would meet legitimate Soviet security needs and obviate the need for "tight-fisted Soviet control" over the region.[161] Roosevelt's harsh attitude to Germany, demonstrated especially by the policy of unconditional surrender, aimed not only to cement Soviet-American relations during the war but also to ensure Soviet cooperation thereafter.[162] The importance of the destruction of German power to the Soviets had been amply revealed by Stalin at Teheran where, at one point, he proposed – with some seriousness it seems – the "liquidation" of between fifty thousand and one hundred thousand members of the German officer corps.[163] Stalin had eagerly endorsed FDR's vague proposal for the dismemberment of Germany, and the two supported each other in proposing severe treatment for the German nation.

Such was the power of the president's instinctive sentiment to rid the world of German power once and for all that he endorsed the extraordinary plans of Treasury Secretary Henry Morgenthau to destroy German industrial capacity. He held it of "the utmost importance," as he made clear to Secretary of War Henry L. Stimson "that every person in Germany should realize that this time Germany is a defeated nation."[164] In September 1944, he had signed on to the Morgenthau Plan, which called for the dismantling of German

[159] Stalin to Roosevelt, April 7, 1945, *FRUS*, 1945, V, pp. 201–04.
[160] Roosevelt to Churchill, April 10, 1945, *FRUS*, 1945, V, p. 209.
[161] This point is made by Craig and George in *Force and Statecraft*, p. 93.
[162] Roosevelt explained his strategy to Eisenhower's political adviser, Robert Murphy, in 1944. See Robert Murphy, *Diplomat Among Warriors* (New York, 1964), p. 227.
[163] See Bohlen minutes, Tripartite dinner meeting, November 29, 1943, *FRUS: The Conferences at Cairo and Teheran, 1943*, pp. 553–54.
[164] Roosevelt to Stimson, August 26, 1944, quoted in John Morton Blum, ed., *From the Morgenthau Diaries*, Vol. 3, *Years of War, 1941–1945* (Boston, 1967), pp. 348–49. For a thoughtful

industry and envisaged a Germany "primarily agricultural and pastoral in character."[165] As the disastrous implications of this course of action for overall European recovery from the chaos and destruction of the war became obvious, Roosevelt deftly distanced himself from it and confided to Stimson that "Henry Morgenthau pulled a boner."[166] While Roosevelt indirectly disavowed the Morgenthau Plan, he nevertheless remained determined to "be tough with Germany."[167]

At Yalta, Roosevelt proved somewhat cautious on German matters. Now apprised of the likely consequences of Morgenthau's draconian measures and eager to avoid any repetition of the experience after World War I when the United States ultimately had bankrolled German reparation payments, FDR preferred to delay final agreements on a number of German issues. His rebuke to Morgenthau became clear with his refusal to accept any reparations agreement that likely would cause economic havoc in Germany, although he genuflected in Stalin's direction by agreeing to the figure of $20 billion as a basis for subsequent discussion. He made clear, however, his unwillingness "to contemplate the necessity of helping the Germans to keep from starving."[168] The questions of reparations, dismemberment, war criminals, and the cession of German territories ultimately were shunted off for further discussion.[169] Only on the question of giving the French an occupation zone and a seat on the Allied Control Council to oversee occupied Germany did the three leaders reach definite agreement, and here largely because the French zone was fashioned only from those assigned to the British and Americans. Roosevelt maintained his tough rhetoric with regard to the treatment to be meted to postwar Germany but deciding on the details of that treatment was yet another difficult burden he unknowingly consigned to his successor. In fact, when the president died, his administration was still debating its own basic occupation policies and administrative practices for the American zone.[170] The feuding between the War, State, and Treasury Departments over the extent to which the United States should apply repression or rehabilitation in Germany was yet another part of the confusing puzzle of German policy that Truman faced after April 12.

treatment of FDR's developing views on the German question see McAllister, *No Exit*, pp. 49–55.

[165] For details of the Morgenthau Plan, see Blum, ed., *From the Morgenthau Diaries*, Vol. 3, *Years of War*, pp. 356–59; and Michael Beschloss, *The Conquerors*, pp. 121–49.

[166] Roosevelt quoted in the Henry Lewis Stimson diaries, Henry L. Stimson Papers, Sterling Memorial Library (hereafter cited as Stimson Diaries), September 27, 1944.

[167] Pasvolsky minutes, Roosevelt–Stettinius conversation, November 15, 1944, *FRUS: The Conferences at Malta and Yalta, 1945*, p. 172.

[168] Bohlen minutes, Second plenary meeting, February 5, 1945, *FRUS: The Conferences at Malta and Yalta, 1945*, p. 622.

[169] Section 3 – "Dismemberment of Germany"; Section 5 – "Reparations"; Section 6 – "Major War Criminals"; and Section 7 – "Poland"; Yalta Protocol, *FRUS: The Conferences at Malta and Yalta, 1945*, pp. 978–80.

[170] For a discussion of this point, see Gaddis, *The United States and the Origins of the Cold War*, pp. 131–32.

The limitations of the agreements which Roosevelt and Churchill negotiated with Stalin at the Czars' Crimean resort are, in retrospect, easy to discern. And yet, Yalta should not be quickly dismissed as only a "futile and fumbling gathering" to borrow the censorious words of George Kennan.[171] If Roosevelt had lived longer, it is at least conceivable that he might have pursued actions that imposed on Yalta a completely different cast. Had a Roosevelt administration in office after April 1945 begun to challenge the Soviet domination of Eastern Europe, Yalta now might be viewed as the occasion not only where the president made his final effort to assay Stalin's willingness to cooperate but also where he drew a line in the sand (the Declaration on Liberated Europe) regarding Soviet behavior. In fact, Charles Bohlen, who translated for FDR at Yalta, judged the conference as "a test as to whether or not it was possible in practice to cooperat[e] with the Soviet Union."[172] Judge Samuel Rosenman, who helped FDR prepare his report to the congress on the conference, saw it as revealing "the patient effort of President Roosevelt in leaving no stone unturned in the search for world peace."[173] The problem for them was the Soviet failure to live up to the agreements reached there.

In a sense, the most serious problem with Yalta was not the terms of any specific agreement reached there but the vast overselling of the agreements, which heightened public expectations unduly. Jimmy Byrnes hurried back from Yalta and served as FDR's advance man, portraying the conference as the fulfillment of the Atlantic Charter. The treasured principle of self-determination, he reported, remained intact. The publication of the Yalta accords generated much favorable publicity and praise for Roosevelt's accomplishment. On March 1, FDR addressed a joint session of congress on the Yalta meeting in words he knew the legislators wished to hear. He spoke movingly from the well of the House chamber sitting at a desk in what was not so much an admission of his disability but an indication of his physical weakness. With Vice President Truman perched behind him and listening intently, he advised that Yalta had laid the foundation for a lasting peace settlement. It might not be perfect, he explained, "but it can be a peace – and will be a peace – based on the sound and just principles of the Atlantic Charter."[174] Heartened by the ringing applause, he petitioned the American people and their representatives to extend their active support for his handiwork.

---

[171] Kennan made this observation in a diary entry during a visit to Yalta in 1976. See George F. Kennan, *Sketches from a Life* (New York, 1989), p. 255.

[172] Bohlen to Samuel I. Rosenman, August 23, 1949, Samuel I. Rosenman Papers, FDRL, Box 18. Note also Edward Stettinius's comment to Anthony Eden in 1949 that "at Yalta Mr. Churchill and Mr. Roosevelt made a supreme effort to find a basis of peaceful collaboration with the Soviet Union; that it was a courageous and a wise effort; and if the effort had not been made, the world would not now know where the blame properly belongs for the present world situation." Stettinius to Eden, May 9, 1949, Avon Papers, Main Library Special Collections, University of Birmingham, 19/1/39B.

[173] Rosenman to H. Freeman Matthews, October 20, 1949, Rosenman Papers, FDRL, Box 18.

[174] Rosenman, ed., *The Public Papers and Addresses of Franklin D. Roosevelt*, Vol. XIII, pp. 570–86.

Roosevelt sought to build strong domestic support for his postwar plans, but he did so by being less than open with his people. The stakes he thought were too high for that. With the ghosts of Henry Cabot Lodge and company haunting him, he feared obstructionism from the Senate and believed that any admission of the likely limitations of the postwar settlement would be grist for isolationist mills. Arguably, as John Harper has noted, this "was another case of 'useful deceit,'" a circumventing of painful realities in the interests of a supposedly higher good, especially at a time when he believed he needed Soviet support in the Pacific war in order to minimize American casualties.[175] However that may be, Truman inherited a public unable to see through the thin tissue that papered over Big Three divisions and holding firm expectations for continued unity and joint purpose among the major allies. Roosevelt had never truly attempted to educate the American people on the blunt realities of the postwar world order, which inevitably would differ significantly from their Wilsonian ideals. That education took place after his death.

Rooseveltian Reconsiderations?

While most historians describe Franklin Roosevelt's efforts at Yalta as a further step – for good or ill – in pursuit of his broad vision of great power cooperation, some detect that he began to reconsider this approach in the months after the conference.[176] In response to the difficulties involved in the implementation of the Yalta agreements, so this view goes, FDR began a reevaluation of his long-held plans. The legitimacy of Roosevelt's second thoughts on his approach to the Soviets seems supported by the fact that he had held back certain arrows in his diplomatic quiver in anticipation of a time when he would need to apply pressure on Stalin and adopt more of a quid pro quo approach. Among the most significant of these were information regarding the research on atomic weapons and a commitment for economic assistance for postwar reconstruction in Russia.

Was FDR in the process of reevaluating his policy toward the Soviet Union? Ever since the Warsaw uprising he had been subjected to a sustained barrage of forceful advice from Averell Harriman in Moscow that he adopt a more quid pro quo approach. The State Department increasingly adopted this line of thinking, and there are fragments that suggest that he was on the verge of being persuaded. On March 24, 1945, Anna Rosenberg Hoffman lunched with

---

[175] Harper, *American Visions of Europe*, p. 126. Randall B. Woods and Howard Jones are more critical. They argued: "As the outcome of the Yalta meeting indicated, Roosevelt's foreign policy was paralyzed if not bankrupt by the opening weeks of 1945. Intimidated by isolationists and internationalists, FDR refused to educate the people of his country on the need to pursue a balance-of-power strategy in Europe. He clung to the hope that personal diplomacy could work a miracle." Woods and Jones, *Dawning of the Cold War*, p. 31.

[176] Notable proponents of this thesis whose works have been cited previously include Arthur Schlesinger and Robert Dallek. Also see Robert J. Maddox, "Roosevelt and Stalin: The Final Days," *Continuity: A Journal of History*, 6 (Spring 1983), pp. 113–22.

the president. After their luncheon, he was handed a cable, and according to her, "he read it and became quite angry. He banged his fists on the arms of his wheelchair and said, 'Averell is right; we can't do business with Stalin. He has broken every one of the promises he made at Yalta.'" Hoffman further recalled that he was "very upset and continued in the same vein on the subject."[177] Similarly, the president told the journalist Anne O'Hare McCormick on the day he left Washington for Warm Springs that "he fully believed what he said in his report to the Congress on the Yalta Conference decisions. But he found that Stalin was not a man of his word; either that or Stalin was not in control of the Soviet Government."[178] Such comments receive further support from an exchange between the president and Senator Arthur Vandenberg, a leading Republican spokesman on foreign policy and a person known for his critical view of the Soviet Union. The Michigan senator feared that his presence in the U.S. delegation to the San Francisco conference might cause difficulties in dealing with the Russians, and he volunteered "to break a leg." "Just between us, Arthur," Roosevelt replied without hesitating, "I am coming to know the Russians better, and if I could name only one delegate to the San Francisco conference, you would be that delegate."[179] Gauging the significance of these remarks is not easy. One must recognize, however, that in the case of the latter two comments, FDR might have been manipulating his conversation partners for domestic political purposes. One might expect that if FDR had genuinely been engaged in a reconsideration, it might have been conveyed to his principal subordinates or reflected in his policies. There appears little evidence for either.

Roosevelt made no effort prior to his death to alter his approach to military planning and strategy, which largely separated military objectives from political goals beyond the defeat of his Axis enemies. He supported his supreme commander in Europe, General Dwight Eisenhower, against Churchill's attempts to introduce political considerations into the determination of military strategy. The British Prime Minister's call to the American general to "advance as far eastward as possible" met firm rejection.[180] Churchill's pleas for Allied forces to drive toward Berlin and Prague left Roosevelt unmoved. He consistently refused to conceive of Soviet-American relations in terms of a military balance in Europe. At Yalta, just as he had done at Teheran, he explicitly advised that American troops would not remain in Europe to enforce the peace. He did not see it as conceivable that congress or the public would support "an appreciable

---

[177] Schlesinger, "Origins of the Cold War," p. 24

[178] McCormick told Harriman of this conversation in January 1954, and it is recorded in Harriman and Abel, *Special Envoy to Churchill and Stalin*, p. 444.

[179] Arthur H. Vandenberg, Jr., ed., *Private Papers of Senator Vandenberg*, pp. 154–55.

[180] On the dispute over military strategy, see Eisenhower to Churchill, March 30, 1945, and Churchill to Eisenhower, March 31, 1945, in Alfred D. Chandler, Jr., ed., *The Papers of Dwight David Eisenhower*, Vol. 4, *The War Years* (Baltimore, 1970), pp. 2562–63.

American force in Europe."[181] Whatever his reservations regarding the Soviets in the months after Yalta, he made no effort to use his conventional forces to improve the American bargaining position.

Did Roosevelt appreciate, however, that he had a proverbial ace up his sleeve with a new weapon of such destructive power that it would redefine the military balance? Did he withhold information regarding the atomic bomb in order to utilize it in future negotiations with the Soviets? Certainly the British and the Americans decided against sharing information on the Manhattan Project with the Soviet Union. (The Soviets, of course, had other sources on it!) Churchill had pushed FDR to agree at a meeting at Hyde Park in September 1944 to treat the matter "as of the utmost secrecy." They also agreed in this discussion on the military use of the weapon. "When a 'bomb' is finally available," their aide-memoire read, "it might perhaps, after mature consideration, be used against the Japanese, who should be warned that this bombardment will be repeated until they surrender."[182] Interestingly, FDR had broached the idea of sharing atomic information with the Russians at his Hyde Park meeting with Churchill but had been dissuaded by the prime minister's vigorous objections.[183] Roosevelt occasionally thought again of advising the Soviets on the atomic secrets but never moved on the matter.[184] Secretary of War Stimson's recommendation for the exclusion of Russia on the grounds that "it was essential not to take them into our confidence until we were sure to get a real *quid pro quo* from our frankness" received tepid agreement rather than enthusiastic endorsement from his chief.[185]

Stimson clearly saw the future sharing of atomic information as a potential diplomatic tool, but it is striking to note that Roosevelt himself never spoke of it in this manner. FDR for the most part postponed decisions on the issue and held to the terms of the Hyde Park aide-memoire while awaiting the successful test of a weapon. In mid-March, Stimson "went over with him the two schools of thought that exist in respect to the future control after the war of this project

---

[181] Bohlen minutes, *FRUS: The Conferences at Malta and Yalta, 1945*, p. 617. Also note that at Teheran, Roosevelt told Stalin that "any land armies needed in the event of a future threat would have to be provided by Britain and the Soviet Union." Hopkins minutes quoted in Sherwood, *Roosevelt and Hopkins*, p. 786.

[182] For discussion of the Hyde Park agreement and Roosevelt's subsequent discussions on the development and control of the atomic bomb see Richard G. Hewlett and Oscar E. Anderson, *The New World, 1939–1946*, Vol. I, *A History of the United States Atomic Energy Commission* (University Park, PA, 1962), pp. 325–29. Also see Martin J. Sherwin, *A World Destroyed: The Atomic Bomb and the Grand Alliance* (New York, 1975), pp. 108–14.

[183] Glynn, *Closing Pandora's Box*, p. 105.

[184] On March 9, 1945, according to Canadian Prime Minister MacKenzie King, FDR said that "he thought the Russians had been experimenting and knew something about what was being done. He thought the time had come to tell them how far the developments had gone. [But] Churchill was opposed to this." J. W. Pickersgill and D. F. Forster, eds., *The MacKenzie King Record*, Vol. II, 1944–1945 (Toronto, 1968), pp. 326–27.

[185] Stimson Diaires, December 31, 1944.

in case it is successful, one of them being the secret close-in attempted control of the project by those who control it now, and the other being the international control based upon freedom both of science and of access."[186] Stimson advised that the president must settle these matters before the first use of a bomb, and FDR agreed; however, his death intervened before he made any firm decisions. In the end, it was Truman who presided over the birth of the atomic age. When he did so he had some guidance that Roosevelt meant the new weapon to be used in the war against the Japanese, but little specific direction as to if and how the weapon should be subjected to international control and little indication that his predecessor planned to use it, in one way or another, as a weapon in his diplomatic arsenal.

While Henry Stimson pushed the diplomatic potential of sharing atomic information, Ambassador Harriman served as the catalyst for American reconsideration of the diplomatic potential of military and economic assistance to the Soviet Union. Harriman recommended a "friendly *quid pro quo* attitude" from the fall of 1944 onward but garnered little positive response in Washington regarding the delivery of wartime aid.[187] But Roosevelt adopted a different line on the question of postwar assistance. This matter rose to the fore early in January as a result of proposals by Secretary Morgenthau and Foreign Minister Molotov for sizable postwar loans and credits to the Soviet Union.[188] On January 10, Roosevelt told Morgenthau and Stettinius that he thought it "very important [that] we hold back and don't give them any promises of finance until we get what we want."[189] At Yalta, FDR did not bring the matter forward for discussion, and he initiated no consideration of the Russian request on his return. Indeed, Leo Crowley, head of the Foreign Economic Administration, recalled a conversation on March 30, 1945, in which the president concurred "very definitely" with his view "that it would be a great mistake to give any consideration to a loan of that size until we knew something about what the peace objectives of Russia were going to be" and further confided that "he had yet to obtain any concession from Marshall Stalin."[190]

---

186 Stimson Diaries, March 15, 1945. Also see Hewlett and Anderson, *The New World*, pp. 333–40.
187 In January 1945, FDR directed Secretary Stettinius to ensure the delivery to Soviet ports of "the maximum amounts of supplies." See Roosevelt to Stettinius, January 5, 1945, *FRUS*, 1945, V, p. 944.
188 For Morgenthau's proposals, see his memorandums to FDR, January 1, 1945, and January 10, 1945, *FRUS*, 1945, pp. 937–38, 948–49. Morgenthau proposed $10 billion in credits for the purchase of reconstruction goods. On January 3, 1945, Molotov told Harriman that if the United States would extend a $6 billion loan to the Soviet Union, the Soviet government would place large orders for capital equipment in the United States. See Harriman to Secretary of State, January 4, 1945, *FRUS*, 1945, V, pp. 942–44. Also see Harriman and Abel, *Special Envoy to Churchill and Stalin*, pp. 384–87.
189 Roosevelt quoted in Blum, ed., *From the Morgenthau Diaries*, Vol. 3, *Years of War*, p. 305.
190 Leo T. Crowley to Harold Faber, October 4, 1955, James F. Byrnes Papers, Cooper Library, Folder 922, quoted in Thomas G. Paterson, *Soviet–American Confrontation: Postwar Reconstruction and the Origins of the Cold War* (Baltimore, 1973), pp. 33–40.

Clearly Roosevelt had laid some initial groundwork for the development of policies on the diplomatic use of postwar aid, but he had never explicitly used it against the Soviets. He had been much more blunt in using the economic weapon against the British, even to threatening their wartime Lend–Lease aid. In a message to Churchill concerning the aviation conference held in November 1944, he warned that "if the conference should end either in no agreement or in an agreement which the American people would regard as preventing the development and use of the great air routes, the repercussions would seriously affect many other things." Then in a veiled threat, the likes of which he never made to Stalin, he explained that "we are doing our best to meet your lend–lease needs. We will face Congress on that subject in a few weeks and it will not be in a generous mood if it and the people feel that the United Kingdom has not agreed to a generally beneficial air agreement."[191] The president clearly understood the utility of the economic power his nation commanded, but he never applied it against the Soviet Union. This possibility along with the challenging task of wrapping up wartime aid was yet another element of the complex burden he left to Truman.

The disagreements over the implementation of the Yalta agreements in Eastern Europe, the Soviet downgrading of the San Francisco meeting along with annoying discord on other matters, such as the treatment of American prisoners of war by their Russian liberators, all combined to indicate that by April 1945 Soviet–American relations had entered a difficult phase.[192] In fact, on April 2 Secretary Stettinius warned his cabinet colleagues that a serious deterioration in relations with the Soviet Union had taken place.[193] The secretary of state and his subordinates could no longer avoid the obvious. Yet their partial conversion to a more quid pro quo approach similar to Harriman's in no way indicated that the president had made the same step. Even outrageous Soviet accusations during the so-called Berne Incident failed to dislodge him from his plans for postwar cooperation.

The Berne Incident exploded dramatically in the already charged atmosphere of Soviet–American relations of early April 1945. The incident involved possible Russian participation in the military surrender of the German forces in northern Italy. The Western Allies denied a Soviet request to send observers to this surrender negotiation, which prompted scurrilous and unfounded charges of Anglo-American-German complicity. These ended in Stalin's charge on April 3 that the Anglo-American negotiations involved the German commander, the abrasive Field Marshall Albert von Kesselring, agreeing "to open up the front and permit

[191] Roosevelt to Winant, enclosing Roosevelt to Churchill, November 24, 1944, Kimball, ed., *Churchill and Roosevelt,* Vol. III, p. 407.

[192] On the difficulties with Russia over the treatment of prisoners of war, see Harriman and Abel, *Special Envoy to Churchill and Stalin,* pp. 419–22; and Russell D. Buhite, "Soviet–American Relations and the Repatriation of Prisoners of War, 1945," *The Historian,* 35 (May 1973), pp. 384–97.

[193] Stettinius quoted in Millis, ed., *Forrestal Diaries,* pp. 38–39.

Anglo-American troops to advance to the East," in return for which "the Anglo–
Americans promised...to ease for the Germans the peace terms."[194] Stalin's
extraordinary charges surely hit the president hard. Roosevelt replied the next
day in a message largely drafted for him by the irreproachable General George
Marshall, whose genuine sympathy for the Soviets was sorely tested. "Frankly,"
the president stated, "I cannot avoid a feeling of bitter resentment towards your
informers, whoever they are, for such vile misrepresentations of my actions or
those of my trusted subordinates."[195] But even this astounding episode, which
demonstrated so starkly the complete lack of trust which the Soviet Union
had for its Western allies, did not spark serious reconsideration on Roosevelt's
part.[196]

When the negotiations in northern Italy failed, Roosevelt meekly turned the
other cheek and allowed the Berne Incident and Stalin's disgraceful accusations about his contemplating a separate peace with the Nazis to fade into the
background. In his very last message to the Soviet leader, sent just days after
this episode, the president wrote reassuringly that "mutual mistrust and minor
misunderstandings," such as that surrounding the Berne Incident, should not
be allowed to happen in the future.[197] Ambassador Harriman had questioned
the use of "minor" to describe the Berne Incident, but Roosevelt let the note
stand as originally drafted.[198] In the end, FDR's position on relations with the
Soviet Union was best captured in one of his final cables to Churchill. As Warren
Kimball has noted, this was "one of the very few messages the President drafted
personally during his stay at Warm Springs."[199] In it he advised the British leader
that "I would minimize the general Soviet problem as much as possible because
these problems in one form or another, seem to arise every day and most of
them straighten out as in the case of the Berne meeting. We must be firm, however, and our course thus far is correct."[200] That course for Roosevelt seems

---

[194] Stalin to Roosevelt, April 3, 1945, *FRUS*, 1945, III, pp. 742–43.

[195] Roosevelt to Stalin, April 4, 1945, *FRUS*, 1945, III, pp. 745–46.

[196] Robert Dallek has argued that Roosevelt's message to Churchill of April 6, 1945, regarding the
Berne Incident, testifies to his plans to limit the expansion of Soviet power. The president wrote:
"Our Armies will in a very few days be in a position that will permit us to become 'tougher'
than has heretofore appeared advantageous to the war effort." But much more persuasive is
Warren Kimball's analysis, which notes that "so cryptic a message as this does not mean that the
President had finally accepted the idea of a postwar Soviet threat and was advocating an early
form of military containment. This message merely endorsed the strong British protests over
Soviet accusations stemming from the German surrender talks in Berne; it did not refer to the
broader issue of Eastern Europe and Soviet actions there." See Dallek, *Franklin D. Roosevelt
and American Foreign Policy,* p. 534; and Kimball, *The Juggler,* p. 179. For Roosevelt's message
see Kimball, ed., *Churchill and Roosevelt,* Vol. III, p. 617.

[197] Roosevelt to Stalin, April 12, 1945, *FRUS*, 1945, III, pp. 756–57.

[198] Harriman to Roosevelt, April 12, 1945; and Roosevelt to Harriman, April 12, 1945, *FRUS*,
1945, III, pp. 756–57. Roosevelt wrote: "I do not wish to delete the word 'minor' as it is my
desire to consider the Berne misunderstanding a minor incident." Also see Harriman and Abel,
Special Envoy to Churchill and Stalin, pp. 439–40.

[199] Kimball, *The Juggler,* p. 179.

[200] Roosevelt to Churchill, April 11, 1945, *FRUS*, 1945, V, p. 210.

to have been the same one to which he had committed himself throughout the war. His death did not interrupt a major reconsideration of policy toward the Soviet Union.

Of course it is possible, as Robert Dallek has posited, that "had he lived, Roosevelt would probably have moved more quickly than Truman to confront the Russians."[201] But there is little indication that he was contemplating such a move, even following upon the imminent defeat of the Germans. FDR had preserved some diplomatic instruments for future use, but in the case of both the sharing of atomic information and the granting of a postwar loan, these instruments were designed to elicit Soviet cooperation. They were designed as carrots to coax the Soviets to share his broad vision not as sticks to compel Soviet compliance with agreements like the Declaration on Liberated Europe. To the end, he remained trapped by the same hopes and, sadly it must be said, illusions regarding the possibility for genuine cooperation with Stalin that had guided his actions from 1941 onward.

To criticize Franklin Roosevelt in this way is not easy – at least for this historian who readily acknowledges his tremendous accomplishments not only during the New Deal but also both in overcoming the powerful forces of isolationism and in leading the United States in the great coalition that defeated Hitler – and one does so hesitantly. There still exists a shield of sorts that seemingly protects the dominant president of the twentieth century and that encourages even the most capable of historians to assess Roosevelt's diplomacy toward the Soviets in favorable and forgiving ways.[202] Perhaps the desire to avoid any residual association with the extreme criticisms of those who, over a half century ago and for their own domestic political ends, falsely alleged that Roosevelt deliberately "sold out" half of Europe to Stalin at Yalta contributes to this tendency.[203] A sure awareness that Roosevelt's defenders will vigorously take up the cudgels against those who dare to criticize their champion might also play a part.[204] Maybe there is even more involved. Addressing FDR's violation of "the first principle of war-and-peace politics – the possession of turf,"

---

[201] Dallek, *Franklin D. Roosevelt and American Foreign Policy*, p. 534.

[202] See for example the broadly favorable portrayal of Roosevelt's strategy of "containment by integration" in John Lewis Gaddis, *Strategies of Containment*, pp. 9–13.

[203] See Athan G. Theoharis, *The Yalta Myths: An Issue in U.S. Politics, 1945–1955* (Columbia, MO, 1970), which identifies elements of the Republican Party who exploited Yalta for partisan advantage. Arthur Schlesinger, Jr., discusses the bitter criticism of Yalta that emerged in the late 1940s in his *A Life in the Twentieth Century: Innocent Beginnings, 1917–1950* (Boston, 2000), p. 453.

[204] For an example of a Roosevelt "defender" in action, see Warren F. Kimball, "Not Unwilling to Act," *Times Literary Supplement* (February 20, 1998), p. 24. Kimball has mocked the "new wave of Cold Warrior historians" and branded them the "new 'perfectionists' who, painting their passions on a canvas bereft of perspective, insisted that Churchill and Roosevelt 'sold out' eastern Europe to the Kremlin." See Warren F. Kimball, "The Incredible Shrinking War: The Second World War, Not (Just) the Origins of the Cold War," *Diplomatic History*, 25 (Summer 2001), p. 351. For another vigorous defense of Roosevelt, see Theodore Draper, *A Present of Things Past*, pp. 247–64.

Max Lerner cogently argued, that "if anyone else happened to be president – Wendell Willkie, Thomas Dewey, Henry Wallace – the historians and the political culture would have called it the idiocy it was. But it was Roosevelt, and it is a measure of the spell he casts over us that few even now dare condemn his actions and inactions outright."[205] The time has come finally to move beyond the Rooseveltian "spell" and to acknowledge honestly the limitations of FDR's efforts in preparing for the postwar world.

In response to criticism, Roosevelt's defenders ask bluntly for a better alternative that would have served American interests in the global war still being fought. In this regard, nothing can be definitively proved, but it seems clear that Roosevelt should have pursued a much more measured embrace of Stalin at the outset and to have allowed advisers genuinely knowledgeable about the Soviet Union to guide his outlook as to the possibilities of long-term cooperation with him. The effort should have been less to win Stalin's trust and more to win his respect. A politician as devious and deft as Roosevelt would have been able to apply quid pro quo tactics with rare skill if he had chosen and as his ambassadors like Steinhart and Harriman regularly recommended.[206] The policy options were not simply between efforts to cooperate on the one hand and adversarial actions on the other. Remi Nadeau has it right in noting that "Roosevelt did not begin to exercise the full octave of escalation that he commanded short of a final break. This unsophisticated approach to Big Three politics was his tragic shortcoming until he died at the moment of victory over the common enemy."[207] It is hardly exculpatory to suggest that FDR wanted to avoid the burden of responsibility for starting any conflict with Stalin or that his cooperative efforts put the burden for the Cold War firmly on Stalin.[208] Statesmen, in the end, must be judged not by their good intentions but by their real achievements.

---

[205] Max Lerner, *Wounded Titans*, p. 179. Of course the number of historians who have overcome the "spell" and now dare to criticize FDR has increased of late as the previously cited works of Remi Nadeau, Dennis Dunn, and Amos Perlmutter make clear. For a critique of Roosevelt's full diplomatic effort, see Frederick W. Marks III, *Wind Over Sand: The Diplomacy of Franklin D. Roosevelt* (Athens, GA, 1988). Also note that David M. Kennedy proved critical of Roosevelt's conduct of diplomacy, which he argued relied too heavily on the mistaken belief that goodwill and personal charm could resolve "conflicting interests of nations." See Kennedy, *Freedom from Fear*, p. 826.

[206] On the possible alternatives, note the incisive analysis of Henry Kissinger who explores options as of December 1941 and again after the battle of Stalingrad, at which point he suggests that "the issue of Eastern Europe's future could have been raised without risking either a Soviet collapse or a separate peace with Hitler. An effort should have been made to settle the political structure of territories beyond the Soviet frontiers and to achieve for these countries a status similar to that of Finland." See Henry Kissinger, *Diplomacy* (New York, 1994), pp. 406–22.

[207] Nadeau, *Stalin, Churchill, and Roosevelt Divide Europe*, p. 107.

[208] Robert Divine suggests that "at the very least, Roosevelt's attempt to seek a reasonable accommodation with the Russians threw the onus for the subsequent Cold War squarely upon Stalin," in his *Roosevelt and World War II* (Baltimore, 1969), p. 98.

Uncertain Legacy

In the early afternoon of April 12, 1945, Franklin Roosevelt rested in his Warm Springs cottage in the comforting presence of his old love Lucy Mercer Rutherford. Suddenly he looked up and said simply: "I have a terrific headache." He slumped forward, quickly lost consciousness, and died soon after. The doctors declared the cause of death a massive cerebral hemorrhage.[209] The tragic news spread quickly and set off a wave of mourning throughout the country. The great leader of the democratic cause had died on the very eve of military triumph and rightly won for himself a treasured place in the hearts of his people. Churchill described FDR's as "an enviable death" for he had "brought his country through the worst of its perils and the heaviest of its toils."[210] He led his country successfully in war and he died precisely at the right time, as the historian Patrick Maney has noted, to preserve his reputation.[211] Truman made essentially the same point some years later when he noted that "heroes know when to die." Truman was speaking of the greatness of Abraham Lincoln, but as William Leuchtenburg skillfully has shown he also was making an analogy between Lincoln's death and that of Franklin Roosevelt.[212] Given the enormously complex, ambiguous, and challenging nature of the inheritance he received from FDR, Truman's sentiment is surely understandable.

Truman's road ahead was not so clearly charted as the already quoted *New York Times* editorialist opined on April 13, 1945. In retrospect, it is easy to discern that by April 1945 the limitations of Roosevelt's grand vision were becoming apparent. As Robert Dallek, a historian very sympathetic to Roosevelt has noted, "his plans for a United States with substantial, but nevertheless limited, commitments abroad, an accommodation with the U.S.S.R., a stable, cooperative China, a passive France, and a smooth transition for dependent peoples from colonial to independent rule could not withstand the historical and contemporary forces ranged against them."[213] The limitations of the Rooseveltian vision were most obvious in Europe. Here FDR's "Palladian concept" to reduce Europe's role in world affairs had become in the harsh words of John Lamberton Harper, "less a serious political program than a personal conceit." In Roosevelt's design, the supervision of Europe had been assigned to Britain and Russia, but as Harper notes, these two nations "emerged from the war profoundly inimical and disproportionate in stature."[214] FDR largely avoided acknowledgment of this reality. He resisted British efforts to deepen the American commitment in Europe and left unanswered the question if Britain was to be left alone to face a new dominant continental power, and one that revealed

[209] Sherwood, *Roosevelt and Hopkins*, p. 880.
[210] Martin Gilbert, *Winston S. Churchill*, Vol. 7, p. 1301.
[211] Maney, *The Roosevelt Presence*, pp. 190–91.
[212] Leuchtenburg, *In the Shadow of FDR*, p. 40.
[213] Dallek, *Franklin D. Roosevelt and American Foreign Policy*, p. 537.
[214] Harper, *American Visions of Europe*, p. 129.

some willingness to establish its vile social system and political control wherever its armies marched. Facing the question honestly might have forced him to contemplate a transformation in American foreign policy, which he deemed unacceptable.

"What is striking in all this," Gordon Craig astutely observed, "is not merely the president's dogged belief that in the last analysis his personal influence with Stalin would overcome all differences, but his resolute refusal to think seriously about the European future."[215] His refusal lends credence to George Kennan's harsh accusation "that Franklin Roosevelt, for all his charm and skill as a political leader, was, when it came to foreign policy, a very superficial man, ignorant, dilettantish, with a severely limited intellectual horizon."[216] Roosevelt had made no contingency plans should his blueprint for an accommodation with the Soviets not come to fruition. Far from considering alternative approaches in a serious manner, he had never succeeded in effectively communicating his own central policy assumptions within his administration.[217] This was a crucial dimension of the legacy he left to Truman. By April 12, important sections of Roosevelt's administration exhibited restlessness with the behavior of the Soviet Union. They were increasingly perturbed by their wartime ally's obvious disregard for the hallowed Wilsonian principle of self-determination. Roosevelt might have remained committed until his death to his hopes for Soviet cooperation, but he left to Truman an administration that was far more skeptical of that approach.

Indeed, Truman became president in the midst of a debate over the means to deal with the Soviets. The disagreements over the Yalta accords, the potentially explosive Polish issue, the disputes over the composition of other Eastern European governments, the differences over German matters, and the suspicions from the Berne Incident combined to trouble many in the State Department. Even the malleable Stettinius entertained second thoughts. From his vantage point in Moscow, Ambassador Harriman had made the most strident case for a change of course from the fall of 1944 onward. Disgusted by Stalin's accusations regarding the Berne episode, Harriman put his thoughts on paper in a striking memo written on the eve of FDR's death. He rehearsed a long series both of Soviet refusals to live up to agreements and of direct insults to American officials and interests. He argued that the Soviets interpreted American magnanimity as "a sign of weakness" to be exploited. Then, he asked to "be

---

[215] Gordon A. Craig, "Diplomats and Diplomacy During the Second World War," in Gordon A. Craig and Francis L. Loewenheim, eds., *The Diplomats, 1939–1979* (Princeton, NJ, 1994), p. 30.

[216] George F. Kennan comment in symposium, "Allied Leadership during World War II," *Survey*, 21 (Winter–Spring 1975), p. 31. Kennan observed further that "Roosevelt knew nothing about Russia, and very little about Europe. This in itself would not have been so bad. What was worse was that he did not seek or value the advice of those who did know something about these places and could have told him something about them."

[217] J. Garry Clifford makes this point in "Juggling Balls of Dynamite," *Diplomatic History*, 17 (Fall 1993), p. 636.

given some concrete means of showing the Russian officials that their outrageous actions against us are affecting their vital interests" and explained that "the longer we wait the more difficult it will be and the more drastic the action on our part will have to be." He requested authority to inform Stalin directly "that if the Soviet Government continues its policies the friendly hand that we have offered them will be withdrawn and to point out in some detail what this will mean." Acknowledging FDR's concerns about the success of the San Francisco conference, he confessed his own fear "that the Soviets will take some position which is totally impossible for us to accept and which will doom the Conference to failure unless we have this situation out with them prior to the convening of the Conference." To avoid "a world dominated by Soviet policies," Harriman bluntly counseled, "we must abandon our conciliatory policies and put our reliance on a four square basis." The time to do this had arrived.[218]

Harriman's views, which FDR never read, testify to the turbulence in American policy toward the Soviet Union at the very moment President Roosevelt died. On this central issue, his administration resembled less a smooth sailing vessel where all the crew took direction from their captain than a poorly maneuvered sloop where the sailors were in grumbling dissent against the instructions of their skipper who they feared was guiding them badly. Their discontent was ready to rumble to the surface when events brought a new and inexperienced captain aboard. By April 1945, most of Roosevelt's subordinates did not support a reversal in the policy of cooperation with the Soviet Union, but they thought reconsideration regarding the means to better obtain such cooperation was in order. Harriman was the most vocal but not the only proponent of a more quid pro quo approach. A surprised Truman would learn all this in his first week in office.

Roosevelt is at fault for Truman's need to be subjected to a crash course in Soviet-American relations (and much else) during his early days as president. In the debate over whether or not Truman continued the policies of his predecessor, few historians bother to point out that Roosevelt failed to make any effort to advise his vice president as to his thinking, thereby leaving him largely in the dark as to what was to be continued. Nor had he selected and shared his thinking with a strong secretary of state who could guide the new president. Edward Stettinius, like Truman, would be buffeted about in the weeks after Roosevelt's death and could not speak authoritatively as to what "the president" would have done. Although Harry Hopkins and Joseph Davies remained sympathetic to his broad design, Roosevelt left no individual or group fully conversant with all aspects of his goals, intentions, and policies regarding the postwar settlement and relations with the Soviets. His extraordinary centralization of military and diplomatic policy making in his own hands and his consignment of the State Department to the periphery had this consequence. The absence of someone

---

[218] Draft memo to President and Secretary of State from Harriman, April 10, 1945, Averell Harriman Papers, Library of Congress, Box 178.

who could speak authoritatively of Roosevelt's plans meant that his written agreements, especially the Yalta accords, gained added importance. They surely reflected the Rooseveltian will, it was assumed. Those who pledged to continue his policies would place great emphasis on upholding the agreements made by the late president.

The lack of any effective briefing on foreign policy was but a part of Truman's weighty burden in following Roosevelt to the presidency. It was a daunting task. Roosevelt "so embodied everyone's notion of who 'the president' was that it seemed incomprehensible that anyone else could be president of the United States."[219] He was, to put it mildly, a hard act to follow. Truman would be regularly and unfavorably compared to his predecessor and condemned to live "in the long shadow of the dead President."[220] And that shadow wasn't all that Truman had to deal with. Coming into office in the way he did meant that Truman took over both Roosevelt's rather weak cabinet and his chaotic bureaucratic structure, the limitations of which soon became obvious.[221] He also received, as has been noted, a public and a congress conceiving of peace in the idealistic terms foreshadowed in Roosevelt's report on Yalta. Both the politicians and the people they represented looked eagerly toward the San Francisco Conference as the launching point for the brave new world FDR had promised.

Roosevelt could not pass on to Truman the personal relationships he had developed with Churchill and Stalin over the years of their wartime comradeship, although the consequences of this are questionable in their significance. FDR hardly seemed to rely on Churchill's friendship in the months after Yalta and worked mainly to restrain the British prime minister's publicizing of his disagreements with the Soviets. His power to restrain Churchill, however, came more from the reality of American power than from the strength of their personal relationship. Churchill most certainly would have acted differently had the power equation between the two been reversed. Conflicts of interest and judgment long had characterized the Roosevelt–Churchill relationship.[222] Such conflicts would continue after his death when Truman began to deal with the British leader.

Roosevelt had expended much effort to build a personal relationship with Stalin during the war but with little apparent result. Arthur Schlesinger's assertion that FDR's efforts to "work on and through Stalin" were not in vain and that he "retained a certain capacity to influence Stalin to the end" lacks supporting evidence.[223] Certainly such influence had not sufficed to persuade Stalin to send Molotov to the San Francisco meeting nor had it prevented him from

[219] Leuchtenburg, *In the Shadow of FDR*, p. 1.
[220] Leuchtenburg, *In the Shadow of FDR*, p. 2.
[221] On this point, see Ferrell, *Harry S. Truman: A Life*, p. 184.
[222] These are well recorded in Warren Kimball, *Forged in War*.
[223] Schlesinger, "Origins of the Cold War," pp. 48–49.

his scurrilous accusations of complicity with the Nazis at the time of the Berne Incident. And it certainly had not swayed Stalin to define his security interests more conservatively as the case of Poland displays so clearly. Nonetheless, as a recent study of Soviet foreign policy clarifies, Roosevelt "was the only president whom Stalin accepted as a partner."[224] His death was an important turning point for Stalin. Knowing little of Roosevelt's successor, the Soviet tyrant must have feared that never again would he find a capitalist leader so solicitous of his needs and interests. Truman's mere arrival in office and the uncertainty it involved must have hardened further Stalin's "deep suspicions of his Western allies."[225]

With some insight, Anthony Eden, Churchill's foreign secretary, once deemed Roosevelt "as too like a conjurer, skillfully juggling with balls of dynamite, whose nature he failed to understand."[226] It is an apt metaphor. In the end, Roosevelt passed those "balls of dynamite" along to Truman, who had none of his inclination and talent either to perform magician's tricks or to delude himself and his people. FDR's conjuring talent had led to a process of denial and avoidance, which found Western diplomacy at the war's end "perilously unprepared for the trials that awaited it." Endlessly clever but ultimately unwise, Roosevelt had "failed to anticipate the renewal of ideological conflict with Moscow."[227] He died, Micawber-like, still hoping for Soviet cooperation in the postwar world. Such was his conjurer's power that his successor "had to work," as Max Lerner insightfully noted, "not only in [his] shadow but also in the context of [his] illusions."[228] The power of those illusions was not inconsiderable.

Franklin Roosevelt deserves credit for bringing the American ship of state through to the edge of victory in the great world conflict. He did so in a manner that left the United States economically and militarily the most powerful nation in the world. This is, as Warren Kimball and Gaddis Smith have noted, legitimate reason to pay tribute to his accomplishment.[229] But with the exception of his economic planning, he had not effectively shaped realistic policies to guide his nation in the postwar era. The war had "irrevocably destroyed the [prewar] international system," leaving some fundamental questions: "What was to take

---

[224] Zubok and Pleshakov, *Inside the Kremlin's Cold War*, p. 39.

[225] Zubok and Pleshakov, *Inside the Kremlin's Cold War*, p. 37.

[226] Anthony Eden, *The Reckoning: The Eden Memoirs* (Boston, 1965), p. 433.

[227] Gordon A. Craig and Francis Loewenheim, "Afterword," in Craig and Loewenheim, eds., *The Diplomats*, p. 701.

[228] Lerner, *Wounded Titans*, p. 207.

[229] Kimball, *Forged in War*, p. 337; Gaddis Smith, "Forty Months: Franklin D. Roosevelt as War Leader, 1941–1945," *Prologue*, 26 (Fall 1994), pp. 131–39. The British historian A. J. P. Taylor has gone further, after assessing a balance sheet of losses and gains of the three major victorious powers, and argued that "of the three great men at the top, Roosevelt was the only one who knew what he was doing: he made the United States the greatest power in the world at virtually no cost." A. J. P. Taylor, *English History, 1914–1945* (New York and Oxford, 1965), p. 577.

its place? How was the readmission of the defeated powers to the society of
nations to be regulated? How was new aggression to be contained? How was
peace to be assured in an ideologically torn world?"[230] And, what should be
the role of the United States in fashioning viable responses to these challenges?
Ultimately, Franklin Roosevelt was not called to answer such questions. The
task fell to Harry S. Truman.

[230] Graig and Loewenheim, "Afterword," in Craig and Loewenheim, eds., *The Diplomats*, p. 702.

3

Initiation

Tactical Reversal, Strategic Continuity

Lightning Had Struck

Assuming the presidential office after the sudden death of one's predecessor has rarely been an easy undertaking. Andrew Johnson and Lyndon B. Johnson took office in more difficult circumstances than Harry Truman, especially because of the tragic assassinations of the men they served as vice presidents. Truman, luckily for him, had no serious questions raised about his legitimacy to hold the presidential office, unlike the successors to Abraham Lincoln and John F. Kennedy. This said, the burden set upon him on April 12, 1945, was a heavy one. Despite this obvious reality, diplomatic historians, as opposed to Truman's biographers, have extended little sympathy to the new president as he struggled to gain some hold on his enormous new responsibilities. His actions are reported routinely with little sense of either the pressures that weighed upon the man who made them or the personal turmoil that beset him. Yet, of course, the pressures were many, and the turmoil they provoked, significant. "The world fell in on me," Truman confided to his sister-in law on April 12, and he worried in his diary that night over the country's reaction to the death of a man "whom they all practically worshipped."[1] Truman later recalled that "lightning had struck, and events beyond anyone's control had taken command. America had lost a great leader, and I was faced with a terrible responsibility."[2]

The Truman who took up the responsibilities of the presidential office in April 1945 possessed many of the fine qualities that his admirers delight in noting. He was indeed "a person of tough fiber, plain, warm manners, direct approach, and earthy humor," who possessed both courage and the capacity to make a decision.[3] But he was more complex than this, and unless that reality

[1] Truman quoted in Lenore Bradley, "When the Lightning Struck," *Whistlestop: Harry S. Truman Library Institute Newsletter*, 23 (1995), p. 2.
[2] Truman, *Year of Decisions*, pp. 16–17.
[3] The quotation is from Robert J. Donovan, *Tumultuous Years: The Presidency of Harry S. Truman, 1949–1953* (New York, 1982), p. 395.

PHOTO 5. Chief Justice Harlan Fiske Stone administers the oath of office to President Harry S. Truman on April 12, 1945. Truman's wife, Bess, along with various cabinet members and White House aides look on, as does the portrait of President Woodrow Wilson. (Courtesy National Archives)

is grasped one cannot understand his early actions. Truman also was, as David McCullough has observed, "unprepared, bewildered and frightened" as he put on the mantle of office.[4] Not for nothing did he look "strained but grim" as he took the presidential oath.[5] As well as the virtues of honesty and loyalty that had characterized his personal and political life, Truman brought other traits to his new position, which set a context for how he exercised power. His distaste for complexity and his preference for clear and fixed standards along with his hesitation to engage in creative or conceptual thinking made him susceptible to a very straightforward approach to policy making. He also was a man, as Alonzo Hamby has identified so persuasively, who was disposed to both overwork and stress, and who was quite uncomfortable with personal confrontation. He constantly battled a deep insecurity that he masked with occasional demonstrations of bravado and decisiveness and for which, at times, he compensated with outbursts of anger.[6]

No doubt in his early days in office Truman must have been torn by inner doubts as to his own abilities to fill the gigantic shoes into which he had stepped. He also must have been aware in a general sense of the suspicions of many both within and outside the administration that he simply was not up to the job. He might not have read TVA director David Lilienthal's description of him as "Throttlebottom Truman," or heard Navy Secretary James Forrestal murmuring after his swearing-in ceremony, "Poor little fellow, poor little fellow," but the low estimates of Truman pervaded the atmosphere.[7] Fearing to appear "indecisive and ignorant" and manfully aware that the country needed him to rise to the occasion, he accentuated his forcefulness and decisiveness.[8] Some mixture – the exact ingredients of which are not subject to historical analysis – of courage and inner strength as well as of bravado regarding his capacity to make decisions drove him forward through pressure-filled days.

Whatever his desire to convey decisiveness and to present an image of himself as in full control of his position, Truman never acted precipitously or erratically on major matters of policy. "Every major decision of his presidency," Alonzo Hamby insightfully has noted, "was the product of careful political or diplomatic planning and group consensus, not individual whim." This decision-making approach was evident from Truman's earliest days. "The man who liked

[4] McCullough, *Truman*, p. 355.

[5] The description of Truman is that of Joseph Davies in "Death of Roosevelt," April 12, 1945, Davies diary, Joseph C. Davies Papers, Library of Congress, Box 16.

[6] On Hamby's analysis, see especially his "An American Democrat," pp. 33–55, and his *Man of the People*, pp. 482–87.

[7] David E. Lilienthal, *The Journals of David E. Lilienthal*, Vol. I, *The TVA Years, 1939–1945* (New York, 1964), p. 690; and Forrestal quoted in Townsend Hoopes and Douglas Brinkley, *Driven Patriot: The Life and Times of James Forrestal* (New York, 1992), pp. 204–05.

[8] My thinking here is influenced some by Ronald Steel, "Harry of Sunnybrook Farm," *New Republic*, 207 (August 10, 1992), p. 37. For an example of his exaggerating his decision-making ability, see his comments to British Foreign Secretary Anthony Eden: "I am here to make decisions and, whether they prove right or wrong, I am going to take them." Eden, *The Reckoning*, p. 621.

to present himself as a quick decision maker was actually slow and cautious on the big things."[9] From his first hours in office, Truman relied on advisers much more than did Roosevelt. And these advisers (and events themselves) tended to frame the issues for him to decide and to determine the timing of them.[10] Only rarely did Truman personally frame the issue or set the agenda, and he came to the presidency with no desire whatsoever to forge any major new direction.

Truman's temperamental instinct for a clear and uncomplicated approach to policy and his sincere support for what he understood to be Roosevelt's goals along with his concern to reassure the American populace pushed him quickly to assert that he would continue Roosevelt's policies and fulfill all the fallen leader's commitments. A quarter century of political life had convinced him of the importance of keeping one's word. He long had judged men by their reliability in keeping agreements, and this was a standard by which he wanted to be held accountable.[11] This outlook exercised a decisive hold on him in his early weeks in office as he aimed to uphold the agreements which his predecessor had negotiated.

Truman's instinctive commitment to continue FDR's policy was quickly displayed during the evening of April 12 when White House press secretary Steve Early relayed to him a press inquiry regarding the future of the San Francisco conference to form a new world organization scheduled to open on April 25. Secretary of State Stettinius already had briefed Truman on the matter, and he promptly instructed Early to announce that the conference would be held as President Roosevelt had directed. "There was no question in my mind," Truman recalled, "that the conference had to take place. It was of supreme importance that we build an organization to keep the future peace of the world."[12] Here his own deep internationalist sentiments firmly reinforced his dutiful obligation to follow Roosevelt's way. Thus he made his first significant policy decision as president.[13]

Other matters quickly claimed his attention on that traumatic evening. He requested that all Cabinet members remain in their posts, asked for their support, and promised, as Stettinius recalled, "that he would carry on to the best

---

[9] Hamby, "An American Democrat," p. 52.

[10] On Truman's approach to decision making, see the interesting discussion in Neustadt, *Presidential Power and the Modern Presidents*, pp. 144–45.

[11] This relies on Gaddis, "Harry S. Truman and the Origins of Containment," in Merli and Wilson, eds., *Makers of American Diplomacy*, p. 496.

[12] Truman, *Year of Decisions*, p. 19. For Stettinius's recollections, see his Record, April 12, 1945, Papers of Edward R. Stettinius, Jr., Alderman Library, Box 224. Stettinius told Truman that "we must win on world organization."

[13] Truman always claimed this as his first decision. Note his letter to John Foster Dulles responding to an invitation to join Dulles for a ceremony marking the tenth anniversary of the signing of the United Nations Charter where he wrote: "As you well know I have always attached the greatest importance to the establishment of international machinery for the prevention of war. My first act as president was to reaffirm this nation's desire for a world organization to keep the peace." Truman to Dulles, May 13, 1955, Papers of John Foster Dulles, Seeley G. Mudd Manuscript Library, Box 98.

of his ability."[14] At the close of Truman's first cabinet meeting, the venerable Secretary of War Henry L. Stimson claimed his attention and informed the new commander-in-chief of "an immense project that was underway – a project looking to the development of a new explosive of almost unbelievable power."[15] Such a cryptic summary constituted Truman's first serious briefing on the Manhattan Project, the program to develop the atomic bomb. The new president, presumably with his head spinning from the speed and weight of events, asked no questions of Stimson, and certainly he gained no full appreciation or understanding of the potential of this new weapon.[16]

Eventually Truman left the White House and headed for the relative tranquility of his apartment. His Washington residence, however, no longer served as a peaceful haven. Truman's life and circumstances had changed for good. Soon after his arrival home, the president received a call from Jonathan Daniels, Steve Early's assistant. There was a need, he explained, "for a statement for overseas consumption in order to meet enemy propaganda."[17] Truman gave Daniels the substance of a statement that the presidential aide then massaged into shape for release to the press and through it to friend and foe alike. "The world may be sure," it read, "that we will prosecute the war on both fronts, east and west, with all the vigor we possess to a successful conclusion."[18] Given his public statements, Truman left little doubt of his readiness to win the war and to win the peace just as Roosevelt had planned. A searing anxiety as to how to accomplish either one of these vast challenges might have been legitimate cause for a restless night, but Truman eventually put his worries aside and fell asleep. This was fortuitous for him. He had busy days ahead.

Knowing Nothing about Foreign Policy

On April 13, Truman executed his first official act as president by signing the formal proclamation providing arrangements for President Roosevelt's funeral and a day of national mourning.[19] His main task on his first full day in office focused on familiarizing himself with and advancing Roosevelt's objectives. While Truman firmly embraced the goals that his revered predecessor had set, by necessity he was forced to alter the manner of their implementation.[20] As he knew little of the details of American foreign and related military policy and had

---

[14] Record, April 12, 1945, Edward R. Stettinius, Jr., Papers, Alderman Library, Box 224.

[15] Truman, *Year of Decisions*, p. 20.

[16] Truman had engaged in some earlier vague conversations with Stimson about the Manhattan Project through his work on the Truman Committee. On this, see McCullough, *Truman*, pp. 289–91.

[17] Jonathan Daniels, *White House Witness, 1942–1945* (New York, 1975), pp. 284–85.

[18] Truman's statement, April 12, 1945, Truman, *Public Papers of the Presidents of the United States: Harry S. Truman, 1945*, p. 1.

[19] Truman outlined the activities of his day in a diary entry for April 13, 1945, included in Ferrell, ed., *Off the Record*, pp. 16–18.

[20] This point is made in Gaddis, "Harry S. Truman and the Origins of Containment," p. 194.

little familiarity with relations among the Big Three powers, he naturally turned to his diplomatic advisers for guidance. "With this seemingly logical decision," Irwin Gellman noted astutely, "the new president had instantaneously altered the course of how the United States had decided any major diplomatic issues since the start of the New Deal. Until Roosevelt died, the president had personally determined the direction of American diplomacy and then told the State Department how to react. Truman reversed the practice; he made policy after consultation with his foreign affairs experts."[21]

It was to his senior formal adviser on foreign policy, Secretary of State Edward R. Stettinius, Jr., that Truman first spoke officially on April 13. The secretary reported in general concerning current diplomatic matters and discussed some aspects of the coming United Nations conference at San Francisco. He advised his new superior of the State Department's advisory procedures and received from him a specific request that he prepare an outline of the "background and present status of the principal problems confronting the American government in its relations with other governments."[22] In essence, Truman requested elementary education in the issues he needed to address.

Truman next met with the military leaders of the United States – Secretaries Stimson and Forrestal, General George C. Marshall, and Admirals Ernest J. King and William D. Leahy. They provided him with a brief but pointed report on the success of the Allies on all fronts and gave estimates concerning the defeat of Germany and Japan. The Nazis, they cautiously predicted, would be defeated within six months, but a Japanese surrender could not be expected for at least eighteen months.[23] Soviet forces in the East and the Anglo-American forces in the West were rapidly closing their huge vise on Germany and were within two weeks of meeting each other at the Elbe River at Torgau. With air superiority established, the Western forces advanced on a broad front taking the surrender of hundreds of thousands of Germans as they marched forward. Yet, the chiefs of staff focused the new president's attention less on the likelihood of an imminent German collapse but on the possibility of Hitler's making a last stand in a mountain redoubt in the south of his battered nation. The situation in the Pacific War remained extremely challenging. Although the U.S. Navy now enforced a blockade on Japan, and American B-29s under the command of General Curtis LeMay pounded its cities, the Japanese continued their ferocious resistance and inflicted high casualties on the U.S. forces in a furious effort to defend the remaining outposts protecting their home islands. The battle for Okinawa, in the Ryukyu island chain and within easy flying distance of Kyushu, had begun just days before FDR's death and would grind on with appalling losses until mid-June. Extrapolating that the Japanese troops would defend their home islands with comparable ferocity, the chiefs' estimate of eighteen months seemed reasonable.

[21] Gellman, *Secret Affairs*, pp. 378–79.
[22] Truman, *Year of Decisions*, p. 24.
[23] On this meeting, see Truman, *Year of Decisions*, p. 29.

Truman accepted the reports of his military advisers without question. His expertise from the Truman Committee lay in budgeting matters and in the letting and fulfillment of military contracts. He made no pretense to being a military strategist. He did not probe his advisers about broad strategy or the tactics being applied in specific military theaters. He simply wanted them to continue moving forward to defeat the Nazis and the Japanese militarists as they had been doing for his predecessor. His only suggestion to them revolved around his sending a specific message to the armed forces after he had spoken directly to the congress. This brief meeting clarified that there would be essential continuity between Roosevelt and Truman in the military domain. Further confirming the point was Truman's seizing the opportunity as the meeting broke up to request Admiral Leahy to stay on in his position as chief of staff to the president. The tough-minded and flinty old sailor agreed, and he continued to be closely involved in American military and diplomatic decision making. Truman expected Leahy to advise him just as he had advised Roosevelt.

In a politically astute move, Truman traveled back up to Capitol Hill to join congressional leaders for an informal luncheon. Perhaps he sought solace and support in familiar surrounds and from men whose judgment and friendship he valued, but he also came with an agenda of sorts. He wanted to ensure continued bipartisan support for the conduct of the war and the making of the peace, cognizant of the crucial importance of full cooperation between the legislative and executive branches of government, especially in foreign policy. At the luncheon, he secured endorsement of his plan to address a joint session of the congress. He also informed Senator Arthur Vandenberg that he would not go to San Francisco personally to open the UN conference as FDR had planned to do. Vandenberg recorded Truman's expectation to "leave Frisco to our delegation," the delegation selected by Roosevelt.[24] Truman's decision meant no downgrading of his commitment to the San Francisco gathering but simply reflected his willingness to share with others the burdens of implementing foreign policy.

The new president's clear recognition of his limitations in the foreign policy domain prompted him to seek briefings and assistance from those whom he thought possessed greater knowledge of Roosevelt's plans. Foremost among those whose aid he sought stood the man he had planned to nominate for vice president in 1944, James F. Byrnes. Byrnes had hurried back to Washington from his home in Spartanburg, South Carolina, at Truman's request and came to see the president during the afternoon of April 13. "Understandably," Byrnes later wrote with just a hint of condescension, "he was overwhelmed by the task that had devolved so suddenly on him and was trying to familiarize himself with the more urgent problems confronting him."[25] Truman took the opportunity to question Byrnes about the Yalta conference and requested his one-time Senate leader to transcribe the shorthand notes he had taken

[24] Vandenberg, Jr., ed., *Private Papers of Senator Vandenberg*, p. 167.
[25] James F. Byrnes, *All in One Lifetime* (New York, 1958), p. 280.

of the conference proceedings. His approach was that of one determined to learn more of the agreements that Roosevelt had negotiated and the policies he intended to pursue. Byrnes used the occasion to brief Truman further on the Manhattan Project. He emphasized the vast investment of materials and funds in the project and the potential power of the weapon it aimed to produce.[26]

Other matters, however, were on Truman's mind. He introduced to Byrnes at this meeting his desire for him to play a prominent part in the new administration, indeed possibly for him to serve as secretary of state. Truman's awareness that the secretary of state was next in the line of succession convinced him that someone who had served in elective office should hold the job. Furthermore, he always had been "a great admirer of Byrnes" whom he had observed in the Senate and whom Roosevelt had seen fit to appoint to the Supreme Court and then to call to the White House to run the Office of War Mobilization where he earned the informal title of assistant president.[27] Truman's respect for the South Carolinian's ability and experience left him in no doubt that Byrnes was his man, and one senses in his eagerness to recruit his former Senate colleague a hidden assessment that his future secretary of state was more qualified than he to be president. Even deeper motivations were at play. Truman had been impressed that Byrnes had responded generously to his eventual nomination as vice president.[28] Their political friendship had not ruptured over the episode, which still weighed on Truman's mind. By his own later admission, Truman hoped that Byrnes's appointment as secretary of state "might help balance things up" for the events at their party's 1944 convention and soothe the pain of Byrnes's disappointment.[29]

Truman faced a problem in appointing Byrnes as secretary of state, namely that the current incumbent revealed no desire to resign and also played a central role in preparations for the American delegation's participation in the San Francisco meeting due to open in less than two weeks. Truman later dismissively judged Edward Stettinius, Jr., as "a fine man, good looking, amiable, cooperative, but never had an idea new or old," yet he depended on him heavily in

---

[26] On Byrnes briefing Truman on the A-bomb, see Robertson, *Sly and Able*, pp. 390–91.

[27] For Truman's recollection of his admiration for Byrnes see Interview with Truman, January 22, 1954, Harry S. Truman Papers: Post-Presidential Files, HSTL, Box 643.

[28] Byrnes apparently sent Truman a generous and witty congratulatory cable on July 22, 1944, to which Truman replied a few days later: "Dear Jim: Your telegram of the 22nd was certainly appreciated by me. Everybody got a kick out of your manner of wording it. I will be in Washington next week and you are the first person I want to see." Truman to Byrnes, July 27, 1944, James F. Byrnes Papers, Cooper Library, Folder 637.

[29] Truman, *Year of Decisions*, pp. 34–35. The observations of David Robertson, Byrnes's biographer, are of interest here. He suggests that Truman's offer and Byrnes's acceptance of it "reveal that each man acted under a political code of values that went beyond the simple demands of personality or ambition. Jimmy Byrnes was no sorehead, and he did not hold a grudge against Truman. Similarly, Harry Truman was no welsher. He paid his political debts, even when they had been incurred by the man [FDR] they had left behind at Hyde Park." Robertson, *Sly and Able*, p. 388.

his early days in office.[30] The president knew he could not upset the existing arrangements for the UN conference at which Stettinius would serve as chair and lead the American delegation. However, during the next two days, which were dominated by Roosevelt's funeral, he tried to persuade Byrnes to attend the San Francisco meeting as his "personal representative." Byrnes declined, thereby demonstrating his characteristic political acuity. The clever South Carolinian appreciated full well, and in a way that seemed to escape the man from Missouri, that dispatching him to San Francisco would upset the dynamics of the existing delegation. Leslie Biffle, the Senate secretary, even warned Byrnes at Hyde Park after FDR's burial that Senator Tom Connally, the volatile Texas Democrat who chaired the Foreign Relations Committee, "was having a fit" about the prospect of him joining the delegation.[31] Byrnes decided to avoid any brouhaha.

Truman (or Byrnes) obviously confided details of his hopes to bring Byrnes into the administration and for him to attend the San Francisco meeting to enough people so that, in the marvelous ways of the national capital, this became the subject for Washington gossip and press speculation. In such circumstances, an anxious Stettinius came to see Truman and asked for assurances about his future. Truman confirmed for him that he expected him to go to the conference as President Roosevelt had wished him to do.[32] With Stettinius at least temporarily secure in his position, Byrnes told Truman he planned to return to Spartanburg rather than stay on around the White House as a sort of gray eminence, "particularly in view of the newspaper publicity, because I would not think of being a Hopkins and I did not think he should have one around."[33] Before his departure Truman reaffirmed for Byrnes that he wanted him back in government service and implied again that he wanted him as secretary of state. Byrnes remained rather skeptical and he confided in a letter to his sister "that Truman is more than likely to change his views and I am not counting on his offering me the appointment of Secretary of State."[34] Byrnes,

---

[30] For Truman's later observations on Stettinius (and other cabinet members), see his unsent letter to Jonathan Daniels, February 26, 1950, in Ferrell, ed., *Off the Record*, p. 174. He also described Stettinius to Daniels in an interview as being "as dumb as they come." Truman quoted in Leuchtenburg, *In the Shadow of FDR*, p. 15.

[31] See Byrnes's expansive letter to his sister Leo [Fuller], April 28, 1945, James F. Byrnes Papers, Cooper Library, Folder 193. See also Byrnes letter to Leslie Biffle, April 26, 1945, James F. Byrnes Papers, Cooper Library, Folder 187. Senator Connally made his displeasure about the prospect of Byrnes going to the UN meeting known to Stettinius. According to Stettinius: "Senator Connally then hit the ceiling and said, 'Jimmy Byrnes has no business whatsoever in San Francisco. I'm for you anyway before him and if Byrnes goes out there like an FBI agent it will discredit you and me and the whole delegation. Don't let this get by you.'" Stettinius Calendar Notes, April 16, 1945, Edward R. Stettinus, Jr., Papers, Alderman Library, Box 224.

[32] For Stettinius's record of his conversation with Truman, see Calendar Notes, April 16, 1945, Edward R. Stettinius, Jr., Papers, Alderman Library, Box 224.

[33] Byrnes to Leo [Fuller], April 28, 1945, James F. Byrnes Papers, Cooper Library, Folder 193.

[34] Byrnes also told his sister: "I do not like the idea of being considered a candidate for a job. Particularly, when there is no vacancy in the job and I am placed in the position of planning to

nonetheless, transcribed his Yalta notes and dispatched them up to Washington and he held himself in waiting for a call to more serious responsibilities.[35]

Despite the persistent rumors regarding his own future, Edward Stettinius filled the role of principal foreign policy adviser to the new president during his first days in office. Perhaps more accurately, the secretary of state served as the conduit for foreign policy advice if not always as its source. Stettinius received praise for his enthusiasm, good nature, and gift for public relations, but few careful observers lauded his expertise on foreign policy. Dean Acheson, rather gently (at least for him!) later observed that "Stettinius had gone far with comparatively modest equipment." He portrayed him as the type of businessman-come-to-Washington who was "the product of a staff [and who was] lost without it."[36] Senator Vandenberg worried in his diary on the day after FDR's death about Stettinius's limitations: "Up to now he has been only the presidential messenger. He does *not* have the background and experience for such a job at such a critical time – altho[ugh] he is a *grand person* with every good intention and high honesty of purpose. Now we have *both* an inexperienced President *and* an inexperienced Secretary."[37] Stettinius's short tenure in office and the dismissive attitude toward him of many contemporaries has earned him "the dubious distinction of being the least-known secretary of state in the twentieth century."[38] Yet, understanding his role and his relationship with the new president in Truman's first weeks in office is essential if the means and ends of American foreign policy are to be correctly discerned.

In Truman's deliberations on replacing Stettinius with Byrnes, substantive policy issues played virtually no part. Truman hardly knew enough specific details to think in terms of implications of such a change for the content of policy. On the presidential train returning to Washington from Hyde Park, he confessed to postmaster general Frank Walker: "I know nothing of foreign affairs and I must acquaint myself with them at once."[39] In fact, however, he had been engaged in a crash course of instruction over the preceding two days with Stettinius serving as his primary tutor.

Learning on the Job

After Byrnes left Truman's office on April 13, Secretary Stettinius in the company of Charles E. Bohlen, the State Department liaison officer to the White House and an expert on Soviet affairs, took his place. The three men soon

oust a man." Byrnes to Leo [Fuller], April 28, 1945, James F. Byrnes Papers, Cooper Library, Folder 193.

[35] Byrnes to Truman, April 25, 1945, (forwarding Yalta Notes), James F. Byrnes Papers, Cooper Library, Folder 621.

[36] Dean G. Acheson, *Present at the Creation: My Years in the State Department* (New York, 1969), p. 88.

[37] Vandenberg, Jr., *Private Papers of Senator Vandenberg*, pp. 167–68.

[38] Gellman, *Secret Affairs*, p. 382.

[39] Diary entry, April 15, 1945, Frank C. Walker Papers, University of Notre Dame, Box 123.

moved to a full discussion of the difficulties in relations with the Soviet Union, especially regarding Poland. In brief moments during the day, Truman had glanced at the correspondence that had passed between Roosevelt, Churchill, and Stalin since Yalta, so when Stettinius informed him that "our relations with the Soviet Union since Yalta had deteriorated," he quickly replied that "he understood this but asked why." Stettinius, demonstrating quickly his notable limitations in foreign policy analysis, offered as an explanation that "Stalin had his own political problems within the Soviet Union and perhaps certain influences were being brought to bear on him from within his own country." Apparently Truman listened seriously to this variation on the laughable thesis that a more "moderate" Stalin was the victim of anti-Western forces within his own regime. Anxious to demonstrate that he would not be easily intimidated, Truman emphasized in response "that we must stand up to the Russians at this point and that we must not be too easy with them." The secretary of state gained the impression that the president thought the United States had been "too easy" on the Soviet Union.[40] Of course, any clearheaded reading of the post-Yalta Roosevelt–Stalin correspondence would have made such a conclusion hard to avoid. Nonetheless, Truman asked nothing of Stettinius in terms of any forceful actions and he endorsed the secretary's rather conciliatory recommendations to focus on the UN meeting.

Interestingly, Stettinius took the chance at this meeting to sing the praises of another person as a foreign policy adviser. He explained to Truman "that Mr. Hopkins had an extremely important and unique relationship as far as foreign relations were concerned, inasmuch as he was the one person who really thoroughly understood the various ramifications and the relations between Roosevelt and Churchill and Roosevelt and Stalin." He expressed his hope that Truman would capitalize on Hopkins's knowledge. The president quickly responded: "I have the greatest regard for Hopkins, he is a grand friend, and I plan to use Hopkins to the limits of his strength."[41] Truman's rapid response permitted little serious reflection on his part, but it suggests his eagerness to take up any suggestion that might confirm him as following Roosevelt's path in dealing with the British and the Soviets.

The pressing demands of relations with the major powers and their leaders weighed quickly on Truman. He turned first to deal with British Prime Minister Churchill and approved two telegrams to him, drafts of which the State Department had prepared. In the first, he thanked Churchill for his message of sympathy at Roosevelt's death and then addressed some of the pressing problems they faced, especially the "dangerous problem of Poland and the Soviet attitude towards the Moscow negotiations." Truman claimed familiarity with the exchanges between his predecessor and the other members of the Big Three

---

[40] Stettinius calendar notes, April 13, 1945, in Thomas M. Campbell and George C. Herring, eds., *The Diaries of Edward R. Stettinius, Jr., 1943–1946* (New York, 1975), pp. 318–19.

[41] Stettinius calendar notes, April 13, 1945, Campbell and Herring, eds., *Diaries of Edward R. Stettinius, Jr.*, p. 317.

and also told Churchill that he knew "in general what President Roosevelt had in mind as the next step."[42] Truman, of course, had no such knowledge and was dependent on his advisers for guidance. These men shaped the substance of his second message, which dealt with possible future steps on the Polish matter. The Americans feared that Churchill planned to make a statement in the House of Commons revealing the extent of his disagreement with the Soviets on the composition of the new Polish government.[43] Even someone as unprepared as Truman knew such a statement would be dynamite on the eve of the UN meeting. The Americans hoped to prevent it, so Truman wrote that "we should explore to the full every possibility before any public statement is made which could only be as matters now stand to announce the failure of our efforts due to Soviet intransigence." He cautioned Churchill by stating the rather obvious fact that "once a public announcement is made of a breakdown in the Polish negotiations it will carry with it the hopes of the Polish people for a just solution of the Polish problem to say nothing of the effect it will have on our political and military collaboration with the Soviet Union."[44] To secure such collaboration, Truman endorsed a more conciliatory approach. He wanted to continue working on Stalin in hopes of reaching a compromise on the Polish question, and he suggested that Churchill join him in a message to the Soviet leader.

The Soviets seemingly gave some grounds for hope on April 13. Stettinius informed Truman that Stalin, at the suggestion of Ambassador Harriman, had agreed to send Molotov to attend the San Francisco conference and had authorized his foreign minister to visit Washington, D.C., en route.[45] The Americans immediately confirmed the desirability of Molotov's proposed visit, and the following day Truman publicly welcomed it "as an expression of earnest cooperation in carrying forward plans for formulating the new international organization."[46] Privately Stettinius and his colleagues hoped that the Soviet minister's visit would be of benefit across a wider range of issues including Poland. Truman simply went along with this and moved on to other concerns. But Molotov's imminent arrival in Washington had important consequences. It heightened the debate within the administration over U.S. policy toward the Soviets that had been waged since Yalta, and it allowed for the

---

[42] Truman to Churchill, April 13, 1945, Harry S. Truman Papers: White House Map Room File, HSTL, Box 4.

[43] Churchill was under increasing pressure from both Labour and Conservative backbenchers who were "uneasy or even indignant about the treatment Poland had received at Yalta." He clearly had moved into a mode designed "to confront rather than conciliate Moscow." For his thinking at this time, see Carlton, *Churchill and the Soviet Union*, pp. 130–37.

[44] Truman to Churchill, April 13, 1945 (second message), Harry S. Truman Papers: White House Map Room File, HSTL, Box 4.

[45] Harriman to secretary of state, April 13, 1945, *FRUS*, 1945, I, pp. 289–90.

[46] White House press release, April 14, 1945, Harry S. Truman Papers: President's Official File, HSTL, Box 823.

return to Washington of Averell Harriman, who would play a key role in the debate.[47]

Late in the afternoon of April 13, Stettinius presented Truman with two lengthy memoranda that aimed to quickly enhance the new president's learning on foreign policy. The first focused on the conference to forge a new international organization and outlined for Truman the composition of the American delegation and its activities. It also alerted Truman to three important areas upon which there existed significant dispute or disagreement in the conference's preliminary discussions – the presidency of the conference, the question of trusteeships, and the controversial matter concerning the admission of White Russia and the Ukraine to initial membership in the proposed new world organization.[48] For each issue, the secretary provided FDR's most recent thinking on the matter and claimed the Rooseveltian imprimatur for the plans of his delegation to deal with them. With the perspective of over a half century, these questions concerning the UN might seem arcane or trivial, but they held an important place in the days leading up to the opening session in San Francisco. Fear that any one issue might torpedo the successful establishment of the new world body kept them to the fore of American concerns. The need to secure the foundation of what became the United Nations Organization was an absolutely critical objective, and Truman read the memorandum with that in mind. The new world body in his mind would be crucial in securing the peace after military victory was achieved. Its creation claimed a very high place among the Rooseveltian objectives that he needed to accomplish.[49]

The second memorandum Stettinius supplied responded to Truman's specific request earlier in the day for clarification as to the principal foreign policy problems confronting the United States. Truman took this document with him when he left the White House at day's end, and he read it at home in his apartment. It addressed a wide range of issues. Concerning the United Kingdom, it deemed Churchill's policy as "based fundamentally upon co-operation with the United States" and went on to assert that the British leader shared the American interpretation of "the Yalta Agreements on Eastern Europe and liberated areas." But, the report cautioned, Churchill was inclined "to press this position with the Russians with what we consider unnecessary rigidity as to detail." Turning to the Soviet Union, Stettinius's report alleged that, since Yalta, Stalin's

---

47 Stettinius initially had wanted Harriman "to stay on the job and not to return to the United States" but relented and gave his permission for the ambassador to return home once it was clarified that Molotov was coming to visit. See Stettinius's phone transcripts with Matthew Connelly (April 13) and James Dunn (April 14), Edward R. Stettinius, Jr., Papers, Alderman Library, Box 236.

48 Stettinius to Truman, April 13, 1945, *FRUS*, 1945, I, pp. 281–83.

49 For a study that provides a good sense of the significance that the U.S. administration and the American public accorded to the founding of the UN, see Stephen Schlesinger, *Act of Creation: The Founding of the United Nations: A Story of Superpowers, Secret Agents, Wartime Allies and Enemies, and Their Quest for a Peaceful World* (Boulder, CO, 2003).

government "has taken a firm and uncompromising position on nearly every major question that has arisen in our relations." It listed the most important of these as "the Polish question, the application of the Crimea agreement on liberated areas, the agreement on the exchange of liberated prisoners of war and civilians, and the San Francisco Conference." The report, furthermore, accused the Soviets of acting unilaterally in areas under their occupation and control and presented the Soviet refusal to agree to orderly procedures for the liquidation of Lend–Lease aid as a retaliation for the American failure thus far to agree to their request for a large postwar credit.[50]

Truman's private reactions to these alarming revelations remained unobserved. It hardly requires a leap of imagination, however, to assume that they made a deep impression on him, particularly when linked to his knowledge of the weighty difficulties in U.S.-Soviet relations derived from his earlier reading of FDR's correspondence. He would make policy toward the Soviet Union knowing well that American-Soviet relations were seriously strained, to put it mildly. No action or inclination of his had caused this situation but he would have to navigate his way forward in the midst of it. And in doing so, the State Department warned, he would need to be cautious in accepting Churchill's advice on strategy. Any normal mortal must have flinched somewhat at the difficult prospect that lay ahead.

Truman's troubles in the foreign policy domain hardly ended with Britain and the Soviet Union. Stettinius's report went on to focus on Poland, the Balkans, Germany, Austria, Italy, the question of supplies for liberated areas, and relations with the fascist-leaning government of Argentina. The report thereby introduced many of the issues that would strain Soviet-American relations in the upcoming weeks. The composition of the Polish government; the failure of the Allied Control Commissions in Bulgaria, Rumania, and Hungary; occupation policy for Germany; the surrender procedure and zones of occupation in Germany; policy for the occupation of Austria; the Yugoslav threat to Trieste; the possible admission of Argentina to the San Francisco meeting were all mentioned in the report. Truman surely must have staggered a little at the number and complexity of the problems that confronted him as the new occupant of the Oval Office. He gave no report of how well he slept that night.

On April 14, the day of Franklin Roosevelt's funeral, Truman rose early in his normal manner and worked further on the speech he planned to give to the congress two days later. Steve Early and Judge Samuel Rosenman, Roosevelt's able speechwriter, had already provided him with some early draft material. By nine o'clock, he was at work at his Oval Office desk. He asked a St. Louis banker and an old Missouri friend named John Snyder to serve as federal loan administrator and then received Secretary of the Treasury Henry Morgenthau, a man given to feverish fretting. The secretary pledged his cooperation

[50] "Special Information for the President," April 13, 1945, Harry S. Truman Papers: President's Secretary's File, HSTL, Box 186.

and volunteered his assistance, including on German matters. Truman later held the colorful view that FDR's Treasury secretary was a "blockhead [and a] nut" who "didn't know shit from apple butter," but for the moment he assured Morgenthau that he wanted him to stay on in his position. When Morgenthau observed that the financial capital had been moved from Wall Street and London to his desk at the Treasury, Truman quickly assured him, "That's where I want to keep it." When the obviously worried Treasury secretary responded that "the big boys will be after me, and I can't do what I have been doing unless I have the complete backing of the President," Truman promptly assured him that "you will have that from me." Reflecting on the meeting later, Morgenthau insightfully noted of Truman that "the man has a lot of nervous energy and seems to be inclined to make very quick decisions."[51] The president's quick assurances to the Treasury secretary certainly clarified his endorsement of Roosevelt's policies and indicated yet again Truman's intention to follow his predecessor's policies. But they also suggest an anxiety and the nervous insecurity of a person overcompensating in an effort to appear decisive.

Truman ended his meeting with Morgenthau to drive to Union Station to meet the train bearing Franklin Roosevelt's earthly remains back from Warm Springs. As his wife and daughter could not join him, Truman in a rather strange balancing exercise enlisted both James F. Byrnes and Henry Wallace, now secretary of commerce, to join him on this sad mission. Surely some what-might-have-been thoughts struck these former leading pretenders to Franklin Roosevelt's throne that day, but they soldiered on with Truman and together boarded the train on its arrival and met all the Roosevelt family. Then, cramped into the backseat of the presidential car, they followed FDR's body back to the White House along streets lined with grief-stricken men and women whose anguish touched Truman deeply.[52]

Roosevelt's simple funeral was scheduled for four o'clock so Truman returned to his West Wing office where Harry Hopkins soon joined him. Truman thought Roosevelt's closest aide looked even worse than his normal "pale and cadaverous" state, which was likely the case as he had left a hospital bed at the Mayo Clinic to journey to Washington.[53] Truman truly held Hopkins in high regard. He first had met him when still the presiding judge of Jackson County through Hopkins's work as New Deal relief czar. Once in Washington, Truman remembered Hopkins treating him with some respect when many had

---

[51] Blum, ed., *From the Morgenthau Diaries: Years of War*, p. 422–23. On Truman's later view of Morgenthau see Ferrell, ed., *Off the Record*, p. 174; and Leuchtenburg, *In the Shadow of FDR*, p. 15. For a more extended account of the Truman–Morgenthau meeting, see Beschloss, *The Conquerors*, pp. 220–21.

[52] McCullough, *Truman*, pp. 357–58, is very good on Truman and Roosevelt's funeral. The depth of the grief is suggested by Robert H. Jackson's observation that for his generation Roosevelt's death was "more like [that] of a father than of an official." Jackson, *That Man*, p. 165.

[53] Truman's recollections of Hopkins's appearance in an interview for his memoirs, February 12, 1954, Harry S. Truman Papers: Post-Presidential Files, HSTL, Box 643.

PHOTO 6. The new president, Harry S. Truman, waits for Franklin Roosevelt's funeral train to return to Washington, D.C., from Warm Springs, Georgia, April 14, 1945. He is flanked on his left by former vice president and now commerce secretary, Henry A. Wallace, and on his right by future Secretary of State James F. Byrnes. (Courtesy National Archives)

not, and this forever elevated Hopkins in his eyes.[54] He liked and respected Hopkins and anxiously waited the chance to speak with him.

"I need to know everything you can tell me," he implored Roosevelt's key lieutenant, "about Stalin and Churchill and the conferences at Cairo, Casablanca, Teheran and Yalta." The two men thereupon talked over lunch for almost two hours, and Truman later described Hopkins as a "storehouse of information," and one who "understood the leaders of the Soviet Union."

---

[54] Hopkins did not meet with Truman frequently during the New Deal but saw him officially on a few occasions. See the entry on Harry Truman in "Card File of Mr. Hopkins' Callers," Harry L. Hopkins Papers, FDRL, Container 341. On Hopkins' career, see George McJimsey, *Harry Hopkins: Ally of the Poor and Defender of Democracy* (Cambridge, MA, 1987).

Hopkins described Stalin as "a forthright, rough tough Russian." He was a "Russian partisan through and through, thinking always first of Russia," but one who could be "talked to frankly."[55] Through this benign portrayal, Hopkins lent weight to the notion that Stalin was merely some variation on the "tough political boss analogous to Tom Pendergast" with which Truman bore familiarity.[56] Speaking of Churchill, Hopkins emphasized the good relations between Roosevelt and the prime minister and urged Truman to continue them. Assuredly, Truman took Hopkins's counsel seriously and listened further as he outlined his view of Roosevelt's intentions and proffered his advice on the broad directions of foreign policy. The new president gained solace from Hopkins's expression of confidence that he would fulfill Roosevelt's policies.

Truman's eagerness to see Hopkins and his willingness to come before him like a dutiful student before a wise teacher reveals something of the president's sincerity in regard to continuing Roosevelt's approach. His open-ended questions to Hopkins and receptiveness to his views counter claims that Truman arrived in office unsympathetic to the Soviets and intent on effecting a change in policy toward them.[57] Also, Truman urged Hopkins to continue in government service, but the ailing New Dealer demurred and pointed to his troubled health. The offer stands as another marker of Truman's commitment to continuity for Hopkins was so closely identified with FDR. Never did Truman express concerns about Hopkins or about his conciliatory approach toward the Soviet Union. Even when ruminating privately on Hopkins as he drafted his memoirs in 1954, Truman gave no evidence of any reservations regarding the counsel Hopkins offered to him. On the contrary, he thought of Hopkins as "a very great asset" whose early death was "a great loss." He would have used Hopkins more had his health permitted, but so exhausted in the service of FDR had Hopkins become that his frail body permitted just one final mission in Truman's service.

After Hopkins's departure, Admiral Leahy brought Truman telegrams from Churchill, and the president worked on his speech to congress. One Churchill message directly replied to his own missive on the Polish question. With one exception, the prime minister expressed agreement with the joint message Truman proposed; he explained that Foreign Secretary Eden, who was en route to Washington, would present that objection for discussion. But the British leader could not stop there. Never one to err on the side of brevity in his communications, he took the chance to educate his American counterpart of the

[55] Truman, *Year of Decisions*, pp. 43–44. This material in Truman's memoir is drawn primarily from Truman's interview, February 12, 1954, Harry S. Truman Papers: Post-Presidential Files, HSTL, Box 643.

[56] This point and the quotation relies on Hamby, *Man of the People*, p. 314. Hamby notes thoughtfully that this notion "was among the most distinctive expressions of the innocence with which the United States began its assumption of world leadership."

[57] Truman later claimed – correctly – that he came into office with no "preconceived ideas" regarding Churchill and Stalin. See Truman interview, January 22, 1954, Harry S. Truman Papers: Post-Presidential Files, HSTL, Box 643.

realities, as he saw them, of Poland. "The Lublin Government," he explained, "are [sic] feeling the strong sentiment of the Polish nation, which though not unfriendly to Russia, is fiercely resolved on independence, and views with increasing disfavor a Polish Provisional Government which is, in the main, a Soviet puppet."[58] Truman had little time to reflect on this Churchill instruction on Poland, but it must have left some mark.

At four o'clock, he crossed to the East Room for Roosevelt's simple funeral service. No eulogies were delivered, just as Eleanor Roosevelt directed, and Truman spoke not a word but simply joined the other mourners at prayer. He never revealed what thoughts flashed through his mind during this service, but it is not unreasonable to suggest that he wondered why the God whom he and his predecessor believed in had seen fit to call Roosevelt at a time when so much seemed uncertain and in flux. That evening Truman joined the presidential train that traveled through the night and brought the mourners the next day to Hyde Park where they buried Roosevelt in a simple grave in the garden of his family estate. Flanked by his own wife and daughter, Truman stood still and with head bowed as Franklin Delano Roosevelt's body was lowered into the earth.

Yet Roosevelt continued to exert a power and exercise influence over Truman from the grave. As Truman later confessed to FDR's daughter Anna, her father was "always *The* President to me – and when I speak of the President I mean Franklin D. Roosevelt."[59] Truman knew well that he stood in FDR's shadow. Even his 1948 political triumph, for which he surely deserved to claim some personal credit, he attributed to the people's desire to continue "the policies which had been in effect for the last sixteen years."[60] During his early months in office, he reportedly would point to FDR's portrait and say, "I'm trying to do what he would like." William Leuchtenburg with some justification suggests that Truman saw himself "as nothing more than the executor of Roosevelt's estate."[61] Notwithstanding his occasional criticism of Roosevelt and his later snap judgment pronouncing General George C. Marshall and Winston Churchill as "the great men of World War II," which glaringly omitted FDR, Truman defined his task as carrying on as "the president" would have wished.[62] He might take

---

[58] Churchill to Truman, April 15, 1945, *FRUS*, 1945, V, p. 218.

[59] Truman to Anna Roosevelt Halsted, May 19, 1954, Anna Roosevelt Halsted Papers, FDRL, Box 76.

[60] Truman explained this to Churchill, November 23, 1948, Harry S. Truman Papers: President's Secretary's Files, HSTL, Box 115.

[61] Leuchtenburg, *In the Shadow of FDR*, pp. 7–8.

[62] For Truman's criticism of FDR for his "inability to pass on responsibility" and for wanting "personal aggrandizement," see his Diary entry, May 6, 1948, in Ferrell, ed., *Off the Record*, p. 134. For a recollection of Truman's judgment on Marshall and Churchill, see Interview with Edward T. Folliard, August 20, 1970, HSTL, transcript p. 46. This judgment should be weighed against Truman's view that Roosevelt was perhaps the greatest American president because of "the incredible number of things accomplished in his fruitful years in office." See Margaret Truman, ed., *Where the Buck Stops: The Personal and Private Writings of Harry S. Truman* (New York, 1989), p. 370. Late in his life, Truman was similarly critical of Roosevelt in interviews with Thomas Fleming. He judged him "the coldest man I ever met" but continued to assert that

actions that FDR would not have taken, such as allowing Herbert Hoover to again cross the portals of the White House and as replacing Stettinius with Byrnes, but he always saw such measures as means to secure the larger Rooseveltian ends.

Truman broadcast his commitment to continue Roosevelt's war and peace policies in the speech he delivered to Congress on April 16. "Today the entire world is looking to America for enlightened leadership to peace and progress," he assured his one-time colleagues of the legislative branch and his vast radio audience. Such leadership would emerge from a nation committed to the high ideals "eloquently proclaimed by Franklin Roosevelt." Truman affirmed that the United States would carry out its part of the strategy, which would bring the Allies victory and confirmed that under his leadership America would continue to demand unconditional surrender of its foes. The chamber greeted this firm commitment to total victory with a standing ovation. Turning to the problems of peace, Truman naturally focused on the San Francisco conference and the creation of a sound international organization. He invoked the memory of "our fallen leader" and went on to argue for the importance of this nascent body to the future peace of the world. He concluded with an appeal for support and ended his address with the words of King Solomon's prayer for an "understanding heart" to "discern between good and bad."[63] This prayer and its transparent recognition of his profound need for wisdom in discernment suggests he had learned something during his first days in office.

Making Ready for Molotov

Prior to his excursion to Capitol Hill on April 16 to address the congress, the president met Anthony Eden, the British foreign secretary, who had hurried across the Atlantic to attend Roosevelt's funeral and now eagerly took advantage of his presence in Washington to discuss matters of policy with his American allies. Eden stayed in close touch with Winston Churchill by cable, and together they labored deliberately to stiffen the American approach to the Soviets. Neither Churchill nor Eden possessed any first-hand knowledge of the new president or his intentions, and they worked to garner a proper assessment of his plans and capabilities.[64] In the meantime, the foreign secretary vigorously

he "was a great President [who] brought this country into the twentieth century." The elderly Bess Truman was less favorable to Franklin Roosevelt and "made it clear that she regarded Roosevelt's isolation of Truman, and his concealment of his own precarious health, a serious dereliction of duty." Thomas Fleming, "Eight Days with Harry Truman," *American Heritage*, 43 (July–August 1992), p. 56.

[63] Truman address to joint session of congress, April 16, 1945, Truman, *Public Papers of the Presidents of the United States: Harry S. Truman, 1945*, pp. 1–6.

[64] On April 13, Churchill wrote King George VI regarding Roosevelt's death and noted that "ties have been shorn asunder which years had woven. We have to begin again in many ways." Churchill Papers, Churchill Archives Center, Char 20/193B. On April 15, Eden and Ambassador Halifax met with Harry Hopkins in order to get his assessment of Truman. Halifax reported

lobbied his opposite number Stettinius and seized every chance to meet with Truman. The British hoped to use the Molotov visit as the occasion to break the logjam on Poland.

The British leaders had reacted more soberly than the Americans to the news of Molotov's impending visit to Washington. Eden, when reporting details of the visit to his chief in London, had observed that "this is all good news but we ought not to build too much on it for it yet remains to be seen what attitude Molotov adopts when he gets here." The foreign minister, nonetheless, found it "stimulating to have a chance to get to grips with the animal." He believed firmly that "steady pressure" must be kept on the Soviets and that "the best chance of success in any of the conversations here is that the Russians should understand to the full the seriousness for us all of the failure."[65] Of course, Churchill shared these views, which were essentially a replica of those that he had consistently advocated to Roosevelt during the post-Yalta period.

The British desire to work in harmony with the Americans in challenging the Soviet Union over Poland was in evidence in Eden's first meeting with Truman. They agreed easily upon a joint telegram to Stalin contesting the Soviet implementation of the Yalta agreement on Poland. The Truman–Churchill message objected to the Soviet-imposed Warsaw government's vetoing of other Polish representatives for inclusion in the proposed government of national unity. Interestingly, the joint message concluded with a request to Stalin to read again the American (and British) messages of April 1 "since they set forth the larger considerations which we still have very much in mind and to which we must adhere."[66] Truman must have seen himself rooted firmly in a path of continuity with Roosevelt since he reiterated the same grievance that FDR had raised earlier and called again for implementation of the Crimean decision.

The crucial Polish issue developed further during this time. In Moscow on April 16, Harriman met Stalin, who brassily suggested that a solution could be reached on Poland based on "the Yugoslav formula." Harriman rejected the proffered model in which the fervent Marxist Josip Tito had established firm control of the Yugoslav government and tolerated within it but a few members of the former Yugoslav government-in-exile as ineffectual window dressing. Stalin thereupon changed course and, despite an initial objection from Molotov, suggested that his foreign minister's presence in the United States "gave a splendid opportunity to attempt to reach an understanding since

---

to Churchill that Hopkins described Truman as "honest – capable – methodical – [who] would delegate work to those responsible." Truman had told Hopkins that "he felt equipped to handle domestic issues but completely ignorant of foreign" [although] "he had accepted F.D.R.'s general line without question." Hopkins did not "feel able to speak with confidence either of his courage or capacity to choose the right people." Halifax to Churchill, April 16, 1945, Churchill Papers, Churchill Archives Center, Char 20/214.

65 Eden to Churchill, April 15, 1945 (telegram no. 2557), Prime Minister's Operational File (Premier 3), Public Record Office, File 356, Folder 6, 350.

66 Truman to Harriman (enclosing Truman and Churchill to Stalin), April 16, 1945, *FRUS, 1945,* V, pp. 219–21.

not only could he discuss the question with President Truman but also with Mr. Eden and Mr. Stettinius."[67] Thus, at the Soviet leader's initiative, the Polish issue took its place on the list of items for discussion between Molotov and Truman.

Tension over the Polish issue mounted further when Harriman reported later that same day that Andrei Vyshinky, Molotov's deputy, had informed him that a Soviet-Polish treaty of mutual assistance was being prepared. Harriman, by now in no mood to color his views in diplomatic niceties and obviously angered by the Soviet action, bluntly gave his "personal opinion" to Stettinius that the "world would interpret the signing of such a treaty as an indication that the Soviet government did not intend to carry out the Crimea decision."[68] Truman read Harriman's report of his exchange the next day and claimed in retrospect that he was "disturbed" by what he described as "another Russian maneuver aimed at getting their own way in Poland." It was at this moment, he later recorded, that "I made up my mind that I would lay it on the line with Molotov."[69] Perhaps he did so, although the president's subsequent actions hardly bear out this recollection. Truman initiated no immediate protest designed to prevent the signing of the mutual assistance treaty. It was only at Eden's suggestion that Stettinius agreed to have the Americans "ask the Russians to postpone action until Mr. Molotov arrived and he [Eden] and the Secretary had a chance to talk with him."[70] Truman's attention necessarily was drawn from Poland to a host of other matters, although the Polish imbroglio never receded far from his attention in his early weeks in office.

The president's days continued in a flurry of activity. In the midst of everything, he and his family moved into Blair House, just across Pennsylvania Avenue from the White House, where they lived until Mrs. Roosevelt and her family vacated the East Wing early in May. On April 17, he met the American delegation to the San Francisco meeting, held his first press conference, conducted other meetings, and continued his study of a pile of reports that flooded into his office. The president spoke in generalities to the bipartisan UN delegation charging them with the establishment of an international organization that would not only prevent war but also obtain the support of the U.S. Senate. Given his long-standing commitment to the internationalist cause, he spoke with genuine feeling when he advised delegation members that he was "counting on them."[71] At his press conference Truman handled the straightforward questions in a brisk manner and took the opportunity to indicate his support for Roosevelt's foreign economic policies such as Bretton Woods and the Reciprocal

---

[67] Harriman to secretary of state, April 16, 1945, *FRUS, 1945*, V, pp. 223–24.

[68] Harriman to secretary of state, April 16, 1945, *FRUS, 1945*, V, p. 225.

[69] Truman, *Year of Decisions*, p. 50.

[70] Memorandum of conversation by Stettinius, April 17, 1945, *FRUS, 1945*, I, pp. 327–28. For the message sent on the same day to George F. Kennan, the American chargé in Moscow (Harriman had by this time departed for Washington), see *FRUS, 1945*, V, p. 227.

[71] Truman, *Year of Decisions*, pp. 59–60. Also see Notter, *Postwar Foreign Policy Preparation*, p. 438.

Trade Agreements program.[72] In spare moments through the day, he snatched glimpses at various reports including a "policy manual," which Stettinius had prepared for him outlining both "our general foreign policies" and "our policies toward each of the nations of the world."[73] From this lengthy compendium, Truman had confirmed for him that it was American policy "that, in complete cooperation with the other United Nations, we will not only carry through to final victory the war in which we are now engaged, but we will also continue constructing the framework of a secure and enduring peace." He also read here a revealing summary of the American stance on Poland, which pledged U.S. support for "a strong, free and independent Polish state," for the reorganization "on a broader democratic basis" of the existing Soviet-sponsored Polish regime, and for future free elections encompassing all democratic parties in Poland.[74] The disjuncture between pursuing the broad foreign goal of postwar cooperation and implementing more specific goals in places like Poland could not have escaped him.

Truman gave some attention to domestic matters the next day when he met with his budget director, Harold D. Smith, and gained from him a deeper appreciation for budgetary procedures and problems, but foreign policy issues constantly intruded on his time.[75] Secretaries Stettinius, Stimson, and Forrestal presented him with a joint recommendation on trusteeships, which outlined a trusteeship system allowing for the United States to maintain certain military and strategic rights in far-flung Pacific territories. Indicative of his developing modus operandi, Truman gave his approval without serious questioning to the policy proposed by his advisers.[76] Truman's evolving approach to policy making and his dependence on his advisers was clarified further when Prime Minister Churchill introduced the question of zonal arrangements in Germany. Churchill suggested that prior to the withdrawal of Anglo-American forces to their agreed-upon occupation zones – these forces had penetrated in places up to 100–150 miles into the occupation zone in Germany assigned to the Soviets – certain issues should be settled. He mentioned in particular "fair distribution of food produced in Germany," a matter then pending in the Allied Control Commission.[77] Thus the wily British statesman put before the new and inexperienced American president the proposition that the Anglo-American military withdrawal to their assigned zones should be used as a negotiating

---

[72] President's news conference, April 17, 1945, *Public Papers of the Presidents of the United States: Harry S. Truman, 1945*, pp. 8–13. On Truman's support for Bretton Woods, also note Blum, ed., *From the Morgenthau Diaries*, Vol. III, pp. 425, 433.

[73] Stettinius to Truman, April 16, 1945, Harry S. Truman Papers: President's Secretary's Files, HSTL, Box 159.

[74] Policy manual, "The Foreign Policy of the United States," April 1, 1945, Harry S. Truman Papers: President's Secretary's Files, HSTL, April 1, 1945, Box 159.

[75] Harold D. Smith diary, April 18, 1945, Harold D. Smith Papers, HSTL, Box 1.

[76] Memorandum of conversation by Stettinius, April 18, 1945 and "Recommended Policy on Trusteeships," *FRUS*, 1945, I, pp. 350–51.

[77] Churchill to Truman, April 18, 1945, *FRUS*, 1945, III, pp. 231–32.

tool with the Russians. He obviously wanted to pursue a more quid pro quo approach than FDR had permitted. Truman reacted cautiously to his proposal and referred the matter to the State Department and to the joint chiefs of staff. Whatever his other limitations at this time, making precipitous decisions on matters of consequence was not among them.

Truman seemed content to utter diplomatic platitudes and to approve the proposals of his advisers, but the impending visit of Commissar Molotov forced him to engage directly in the determination of policy.[78] Work had begun within the State Department for the Molotov visit as soon as it was announced but the return of Ambassador Harriman moved the American preparations into high gear. Harriman was a man on a mission intent on challenging what he saw as the unduly accommodating policy toward the Soviet Union then prevailing. The wealthy New Dealer brought all his energy and determination to the task. In a series of briefings, he reached not only the president but most of the senior American diplomatic and military officials. On April 20, he dominated a meeting of the secretary of state's staff committee, chaired by Undersecretary Joseph C. Grew, at which a substantial section of the high-ranking State Department officers were present. "Since the Crimea Conference," the ambassador explained, "the Russians have been greatly disturbed by the fact that for the first time they realized that we were determined to carry through what we said." Referring specifically to the Polish dispute, Harriman argued that "the time had come to eliminate fear in our dealings with the Soviet Union and to show we are determined to maintain our position." Indicative of his continued support for the reciprocity approach he had recommended to FDR, Harriman agreed with Grew that the United States possessed "great leverage in dealing with the Soviet Union."[79]

The ambassador shuttled from the State Department to the White House where he forcefully delineated his analysis of U.S.-Soviet relations for the president. He explained – and rather accurately it would seem in retrospect – that "the Soviet Union had two policies which they thought they could successfully pursue at the same time – one, the policy of co-operation with the United States

---

[78] For diplomatic platitudes, note that on April 19 Truman met a succession of foreign notables including Chinese foreign minister T. V. Soong who indicated that he would leave for Moscow after the San Francisco meeting to conclude a trade and mutual assistance treaty. Truman reassuringly affirmed his visit "so that relations between China and Russia could be established on a firmer basis in the interests of organizing the peace of the world." Truman, *Year of Decisions*, p. 81.

[79] Minutes of the secretary of state's staff committee, April 20, 1945, *FRUS*, 1945, V, pp. 839–42. Harriman expounded at much greater length and in a manner that revealed his clear-headed appreciation of Stalin's state and its purposes. He noted that "the basic and irreconcilable difference of objective between the Soviet Union and the United States, ... was its [the Soviet Union's] urge for its own security to see Soviet concepts extend to as large an area of the world as possible." In proposing a "course of action," Harriman recommended that "we must re-establish our respect in Moscow, and we must not tolerate Russian mistreatment of our people and disregard of our interests." He advocated "strong stands on minor points at first, to avoid giving the Russians the idea we had made a major change in policy."

and Great Britain, and the other, the extension of Soviet control over neighboring states through unilateral action." Harriman told his new chief, whom he did not know well, that American generosity had been "misinterpreted" and that the United States "had nothing to lose by standing firm on issues that were of real importance to us." Such counsel resonated perfectly with Truman's eagerness to defend American values and interests. He responded that he "intended to be firm with the Russians and [to make] no concessions from American principles or traditions for the fact of winning their favor. Only on a give and take basis could any relations be established."[80]

Harriman presumably gave an enthusiastic greeting to these presidential remarks seemingly endorsing a policy of greater firmness. He nonetheless continued his lessons for Truman by describing in blunt detail what Soviet control of a foreign country really meant, vividly suggesting in a manner similar to Churchill that the West confronted "a barbarian invasion of Europe." With the consequences of Soviet actions suitably exposed, the discussion refocused on the question of negotiation. The president and his ambassador agreed that some concessions might be made in negotiations, and Truman speculated that the Americans "should be able to get 85 percent" of what they wanted on important matters. Certainly two matters of real importance were the Polish issue and the formation of a new international organization, and Harriman probed Truman on his understanding of the relationship between them. Truman responded that "in his considered opinion unless the settlement of the Polish question was achieved along the lines of the Crimean decisions that the treaty of American adherence to a world organization would not get through the Senate." America's entry into a new world organization, it appeared, was dependent on a suitable resolution of the Polish issue. Such were the high stakes at play, and Truman resolved to tell Molotov "this in words of one syllable." The Missourian's feisty language, however, should not be interpreted as announcing his readiness to declare the Cold War open. Truman was simply emphasizing his readiness to push Molotov to uphold the Yalta agreements and so to settle the Polish issue. When Harriman queried him as to whether the United States would proceed with a world organization if the Soviets dropped out, Truman stated that "the truth of the matter was that without Russia there would not be much of a world organization."[81] The American dream, which Truman so thoroughly shared, to redeem the League failure and to establish a new international body to maintain the peace appeared in some danger of being shattered. Appreciating Truman's deeply felt commitment to bring that dream to fruition helps one understand his subsequent actions.

In concluding their interview, Truman honestly admitted to Harriman that he was "not up on all details of foreign affairs" but that he would rely on his advisers for help. As he left the room, the ambassador took Truman aside and, according to Truman's recollection, said, "frankly, one of the reasons that

[80] Memorandum of conversation by Bohlen, April 20, 1945, *FRUS*, 1945, V, pp. 231–32.
[81] Memorandum of conversation by Bohlen, April 20, 1945, *FRUS*, 1945, V, pp. 232–34.

made me rush back to Washington was the fear that you did not understand, as I had seen Roosevelt understand, that Stalin is breaking his agreements." Harriman explained his fear that Truman could not have kept up on recent cable traffic, and then, in a way designed to play to Truman's need for reassurance, he declared his great relief that Truman had "read them all and that we see eye to eye on the situation."[82] The ambassador skillfully reinforced Truman's intention to be firm with Molotov by confirming – inaccurately – that the president was on the same path as his predecessor, with whom Harriman had dealt extensively.

The meeting with Harriman played an important role in shaping Truman's plans for his meeting with Molotov. When Eden argued to Stettinius on April 21 that "some progress on this matter [Poland] was absolutely essential before San Francisco if the conference was to be a success," the secretary of state observed that "the President was prepared to tell Molotov that a failure to reach agreement on the Polish question in the near future would jeopardize the conference and would have such a reaction on public opinion in the country and the Congress that there would be little chance of a treaty carrying out the Dumbarton Oaks plan being approved by the Senate." Stettinius told his British opposite that Truman "felt that the continued failure to settle this matter satisfactorily endangered the entire position of the United States taking its place at the world table."[83]

Whatever the American concerns on the implications of a failure to resolve the Polish issue, Truman's administration continued to play it very straight in its dealings with the Soviet Union. The president's advisers and thus the president placed emphasis on holding to and carrying out agreements previously reached. Truman readily allowed that the U.S. delegation should agree to accord the Ukrainian and White Russian Republics initial membership in the new international body precisely because this fulfilled Roosevelt's previous commitment on the matter.[84] More significantly, the State Department objected vigorously to Churchill's suggestion to use troop withdrawals to German occupation zones as a bargaining chip in negotiation with the Soviets. Stettinius explained to Admiral Leahy, who coordinated responses for Truman on the issue, that "the formal acceptance by the three Governments of their zones of occupation was in no way contingent upon the conclusion of satisfactory arrangements for an equitable distribution of available food resources."[85] He warned of serious consequences for any attempt to make it so. This advice revealed the consensus view

[82] Truman, *Year of Decisions*, 88.

[83] Stettinius memorandum of conversation, April 21, 1945 in Campbell and Herring, eds., *Diaries of Edward R. Stettinius, Jr.*, pp. 327–28.

[84] Truman, *Year of Decisions*, p. 89; and Campbell and Herring, eds., *Diaries of Edward R. Stettinius, Jr.*, p. 326.

[85] Stettinius to Leahy, April 21, 1945, *FRUS*, 1945, III, pp. 235–36. The State Department's advice was replicated by the commander on the ground at this time. Dwight Eisenhower rejected a proposal from General George Patton on April 18 that "we had better take Berlin and quick!" See Beschloss, *The Conquerors*, pp. 222–23.

that the essential component of American policy toward the Soviets resided not in repudiating or modifying agreements for bargaining purposes but in carrying out such agreements and persuading their erstwhile Soviet allies to do the same. Truman accepted the State Department counsel, and on April 23, the very day he supposedly "laid it on the line" to Molotov, the president advised Churchill of his rejection of the suggestion that troop withdrawals in Germany be used as a negotiating tool against the Russians.[86] Truman held to this position, despite the blatant provocation provided by the signing of a Soviet-Polish treaty on April 21 in complete disregard of the American entreaties for delay.[87]

At a morning meeting on Sunday, April 22, the president discussed the Soviet-Polish treaty among other matters with his advisers in preparation for his meeting with Molotov scheduled for that evening. Although disturbed by the Soviet rejection of the American request to delay their signature of the treaty, Truman was a model of restraint. He said he preferred not to raise the treaty issue with Molotov but explained that if the Soviet minister chose to mention it, he would "tell him quite frankly that it had not been helpful in furthering a solution of the Polish question."[88] Truman hardly adopted the pose of a powerful leader anxious to give a visiting diplomat a good dressing down and eager to set a new policy direction. He had earlier told Stettinius that he thought it would be "good psychology" if he saw Molotov only briefly. Additionally, he revealed to his secretary of state that he was "very hazy about Yalta matters" and was amazed the Polish agreement wasn't "more clear cut."[89]

Initially, Truman had expected to meet Molotov once on Sunday evening after which the foreign ministers would move on to San Francisco to continue their discussions there.[90] When Stettinius had introduced this scenario to Eden, the British foreign secretary objected and argued that the Polish question should be discussed in Washington before the departure of the three ministers to San Francisco for the opening of the United Nations conference. "Americans were inclined to think that since Mr. Molotov was not arriving until tomorrow evening," the foreign secretary inelegantly reported to Churchill late on April 21, that "we should shift venue of talks at once to San Francisco. I opposed this however, for I felt that it is essential that we should have at least a day here with no other distractions to try to make progress with Polish affairs before we leave for San Francisco with the president's support."[91] Eden succeeded in

[86] Truman to Churchill, April 23, 1945, *FRUS*, 1945, III, p. 240.
[87] George Kennan reported the signing in Kennan to secretary of state, April 21, 1945, *FRUS*, 1945, V, p. 234.
[88] Truman, *Year of Decisions*, p. 75.
[89] See notes on meeting, April 21, 1945, in Campbell and Herring, eds., *Diaries of Edward R. Stettinius, Jr.*, pp. 324–25; and Stettinius calendar notes, April 15–23, 1945, Edward R. Stettinius, Jr., Papers, Alderman Library, Box 224.
[90] Stettinius mentioned Truman's initial expectation in conversation with Eden. See memorandum of conversation, April 21, 1945, Edward R. Stettinius, Jr., Papers, Alderman Library, Box 244.
[91] Eden to Churchill, April 21, 1945 (telegram no. 2773), Foreign Office Records, Public Records Office, Files of the Northern Department (hereafter N), 4495/6/G55. See also Stettinius's

persuading Stettinius and Truman for he reported to Churchill that his proposal had been accepted. When he later met with Truman on April 22, Eden accepted revised procedures, which entailed Stettinius giving the president a report on the foreign secretaries' discussions on April 23. Truman suggested that, if it should prove useful, "he should meet the three foreign secretaries together, though as to this he would be in a better position to judge tomorrow."[92] There is no evidence that Truman planned another separate meeting with Molotov.[93] All he contemplated was an initial meeting with the Soviet minister and the possibility the next day of a follow-up meeting with the three foreign secretaries; the latter possibility developed mainly out of the British foreign secretary's requests. In retrospect, Eden's desire to negotiate with Molotov in Washington, where the president's "support" was near at hand, influenced greatly the format of the discussions. His influence on the discussions did not end there.

Anthony Eden and the Truman-Molotov Conversations

Viacheslav Molotov arrived in Washington in the late afternoon of April 22. Stettinius met him at the airport and brought him to Blair–Lee house, which served as a residence for high-level diplomatic guests. Truman watched the simple reception for Molotov from his vantage point in his temporary residence next door in Blair House. He later learned from Stettinius that the two foreign ministers had spoken diplomatic niceties, recalled Franklin Roosevelt's memory, and shared a drink of orange juice together. Truman agreed to receive Molotov at 8:30 P.M., and Stettinius later noted in his diary that the president "seemed encouraged that Molotov was here and said he would receive him in a warm manner but would be very, very firm along the lines we discussed this morning."[94]

Molotov was not a man susceptible to warm greetings. He was a member of that "generation of professional revolutionaries, Bolsheviks, who stormed the skies to put an end to the old world and build the new," but a most unlikely member.[95] Far from "revolutionary" in appearance, he looked and acted the part of the natural bureaucrat for which even his fellow Bolsheviks held him in contempt. He "was generally called 'stoney-arse,' and Lenin once dubbed him

   memorandum of conversation with Eden, April 21, 1945, Edward R. Stettinius, Jr., Papers, Alderman Library, Box 244.

[92] Eden to Churchill, April 23, 1945, (telegram no. 2803 – drafted April 22), Foreign Office Records, Public Record Office, N 4549/6/G55.

[93] When Eben Ayers, an assistant in the press office, noticed that Molotov's name was not on the president's appointment list for April 23, he asked Truman about the Soviet minister's "coming in." Truman replied simply that "he would see the foreign minister if the latter wanted to see him." Ayers diary, April 23, 1945, Robert H. Ferrell, ed., *Truman in the White House: The Diary of Eben A. Ayers* (Columbia and London, 1991), p. 13.

[94] White House calendar notes dictated to V. N. Gallop by Stettinius, April 22, 1945, Edward R. Stettinius, Jr., Papers, Alderman Library, Box 244.

[95] Zubok and Pleshakov, *Inside the Kremlin's Cold War*, p. 8.

'comrade filing cabinet.'"[96] But this gray and colorless man became "Stalin's most loyal servitor." He accompanied him every step of the way loyally supporting the Soviet leader as he brutally established his domination of the party in the 1920s and then playing "a crucial and bloody role in the main domestic events" of the following decade – the "total collectivization of agriculture, with its attendant horrors of famine and mass 'de-kulakization,' and the Great Terror." Such events made Molotov a "party to the slaughter and exile of millions of peasants" and to the dispatch of many thousands of "enemies of the people" to the Gulag or their death.[97]

Molotov apparently suffered no disturbance in view of the mass suffering he witnessed and had few pangs of conscience – if any – as he labored with Stalin to build "socialism." This conscience-deficit must have benefited him considerably when he began his career as foreign minister by signing the Nazi-Soviet pact with Joachim Von Ribbentrop in 1939, thereby engaging, as George Kennan aptly has put it, in a cynical attempt "to buy off Hitler by sharing with him the booty of Eastern Europe."[98] According to his later recollections, Molotov saw his main task as foreign minister as being "to extend the frontier of the Fatherland to the maximum."[99] This was the aim he pursued unwaveringly throughout the war and especially toward its end as Soviet military success laid the basis for Red Army socialism – "the establishment and consolidation of communist regimes largely by Soviet military power in countries around the Soviet perimeter."[100] The all-important effort to win the battle for communism unquestionably justified any and all actions. "The depth of his convictions," Steven Merritt Miner has observed, "gave Molotov a rigid moral self-confidence that served to enhance his already brutal character."[101]

Poor Harry Truman! With a naiveté that is rather poignant in retrospect, he planned to greet Molotov warmly and then to encourage him firmly to hold to existing agreements. And this is exactly what he did when he met the Soviet minister after dinner on April 22. After the usual exchange of diplomatic pleasantries, he told his Russian visitor that "he stood squarely behind all commitments and agreements taken by our late great President and that he

96 Steven Merritt Miner, "His Master's Voice: Viacheslav Mikhailovich Molotov as Stalin's Foreign Commissar," in Craig and Loewenheim, eds., *The Diplomats*, pp. 65–100 (direct quotation from p. 66).

97 Albert Resis, "Introduction," in Resis, ed., *Molotov Remembers, Inside Kremlin Politics* (Chicago, 1993), pp. xvi–xvii.

98 Kennan, *At a Century's Ending* p. 232.

99 Resis, ed., *Molotov Remembers*, p. 8. A convinced Stalinist to his death, he would boast that he and his master "coped with this task quite well."

100 Resis, "Introduction," in Resis, ed., *Molotov Remembers*, p. xix. Poland received the harshest treatment of all the occupied Eastern European countries. See John Micgiel, "'Bandits and Reactionaries': The Suppression of the Opposition in Poland, 1944–1946," in Norman Naimark and Leonid Gibianskii, eds., *The Establishment of Communist Regimes in Eastern Europe, 1944–1949* (Boulder, CO, 1997), pp. 93–110.

101 Miner, "His Master's Voice," p. 66.

would do everything he could to follow along that path." He then introduced the "Polish matter" and described it as "the symbol of the future development of our international relations." He brought to Molotov's attention "a number of minor matters in respect to San Francisco," and expressed the hope that the foreign ministers would be able to settle them in Washington.[102] Truman's whole approach aimed at facilitating successful discussions between the three foreign secretaries and indicating the importance that the United States placed on the world organization and on an acceptable settlement of the Polish question. Molotov had his own concerns and asked for confirmation that Truman endorsed the "Crimea decisions on the Far East." He received an unambiguous assurance that the new president stood behind these decisions, which must have pleased him greatly given the favorable nature of them for the Soviet Union. The meeting ended on a friendly note with Truman proposing a toast to the leaders of the Big Three nations.[103]

The April 22 meeting, usually given only brief mention and, at times, ignored totally by historians, is of importance in understanding American policy toward the Soviet Union. It represented Truman's considered effort to deal with the Soviet Union in general and that nation's obdurate foreign minister in particular. At this meeting, Truman attempted to fulfill the undertakings and to implement the firm approach he had enunciated to Harriman, Eden, and Stettinius. That he implemented this approach rather ineffectively is largely immaterial. What is important is that he believed he had done so. At his staff meeting the following morning, "the president indicated he spoke plainly to the Russian."[104] If this had been the only occasion at which Truman engaged Molotov, such dramatically tempting hypotheses as "sudden reversal" and "immediate showdown" might never have seen the light of day and so not wrecked historiographical havoc for the past forty years.[105] That it was not the only encounter resulted from the failure of the meetings of the foreign secretaries to reach agreement on the Polish issue.

The first foreign ministers' session, held late in the evening of April 22, was useless. There was little agreement, although Eden and Stettinius conveyed forcefully to Molotov the essential need for a settlement of the Polish issue if

---

[102] Memorandum of conversation, April 22, 1945, *FRUS*, 1945, V, pp. 235–36. In this first conversation with Molotov, Truman obviously stayed extremely close to the advice of the State Department submitted in an April 22 memorandum on "points to be raised with Mr. Molotov." Memorandum for the president, April 22, 1945, Harry S. Truman Papers: President's Secretary's File, HSTL, Box 187.

[103] For the Soviet account of the conversation written by the Russian interpreter V. N. Pavlov, see Record of Conversation between V. M. Molotov and the President of the United States, Harry Truman, April 22, 1945, in Geoffrey Roberts, "Sexing up the Cold War: New Evidence on the Molotov–Truman Talks of April 1945," *Cold War History*, 4 (April 2004), pp. 115–18.

[104] Ferrell, ed., *Truman in the White House*, p. 13.

[105] For "sudden reversal" see Fleming, *The Cold War and Its Origins*, pp. 265–70. For "immediate showdown," see Alperovitz, *Atomic Diplomacy*, pp. 19–40.

the San Francisco conference was to be successful.[106] Sir Alexander Cadogan, British permanent undersecretary of state for foreign affairs, confided in a letter to his wife that the meeting "got us *nowhere* at all. M[olotov] appears to have no instructions from Stalin – or pretends to have none – and is simply mulish on every point."[107] Eden echoed his deputy's assessment in his report to Churchill. "We are just back from an hour and a quarter's discussion with Molotov over Poland," he cabled. "We made no progress whatever."[108]

Eden reacted quickly to the failure of the foreign secretaries to resolve the Polish dispute. In a telegram he reported to Churchill: "Since tonight's discussion I have spoken to Stettinius and told him that I took a very bad view of tonight's meeting with M. Molotov. I could see...[no] sign of any attention having been given to your joint message with the President." He saw no prospect for progress the next day. Noting that the Soviets were "quite unrepentant" over their treaty with the Lublin Poles, Eden expressed to Stettinius his feeling "that the fate of San Francisco Conference is at jeopardy." Importantly, Stettinius agreed and asked Eden for a suggested course of action. Eden seized the opportunity and proposed that if no progress was made at a second meeting of foreign ministers scheduled for the morning of April 23, then "the President should send for the three of us, receive our report and himself speak plainly to M. Molotov." The British minister later informed Churchill that Truman had agreed to this and "will be ready to receive the three of us at twelve thirty tomorrow."[109]

At his late-night meeting with Stettinius, Eden also suggested that to bring the Soviet government "up sharply against realities," the opening of the San Francisco conference be postponed while the secretaries continued to "hammer at the Polish issue in Washington." Eden reported that his American opposite "saw the force of the argument and said he would consider it."[110] Cadogan, also present at the meeting, more perceptively observed that Stettinius "professes to agree that we might have to postpone the Conference but the Americans are so dead set on the Conference that I doubt whether they'll really play along those lines." The astute British official appreciated the deep American commitment to a new international organization and the great desire to launch the organization with appropriate fanfare at San Francisco. This strong commitment, however,

---

[106] Minutes of the first meeting regarding the Polish question, April 22, 1945, *FRUS*, 1945, V, pp. 237–41. Eden had made this point clearly to Stettinius telling him that "the whole San Francisco Conference would be prejudiced if we were unable to show some step had been taken towards a settlement of the Polish question." He refers to his comments in Eden to Churchill, April 22, 1945 (telegram no. 2784), Avon Papers, Main Library Special Collections, University of Birmingham, 20/13/184.

[107] Alexander Cadogan to his wife, April 23, 1945, in David Dilks, ed., *The Diaries of Sir Alexander Cadogan, O.M., 1938–1945* (London, 1971), p. 732 (Cadogan's emphasis).

[108] Eden to Churchill, April 23, 1945 (telegram no. 2804), Prem 3, Public Record Office, 356/6/358.

[109] Eden to Churchill, April 23, 1945 (telegram no. 2805), Foreign Office Records, Public Record Office, N 4498/6/G55.

[110] Eden to Churchill, April 23, 1945 (telegram no. 2805), Foreign Office Records, Public Record Office, N 4498/6/G55.

only made the need to make progress on the Polish matter more urgent. Persuaded by Eden, Stettinius had come to the view that some forceful speaking by Truman to Molotov might break the impasse on Poland. "Ed undertook," Cadogan recorded, "that if we made no progress this morning [April 23] he wd [would] mobilize the President to talk like a Dutch Uncle to Molotov."[111] In Stettinius's undertaking lay the immediate origin of the more blunt treatment Molotov received at the meeting in the afternoon of April 23.

The foreign ministers convened again during the morning of April 23, but the meeting ended in stalemate shortly after midday.[112] "After two hours this morning," Eden reported in a now familiar lament, "we have made no progress whatever."[113] "Stoney-arse" Molotov remained immovable and could not be induced to give any ground on Poland so Stettinius left to report the disappointing outcome of the discussions to the president. Eden expected Truman to send for the three foreign secretaries, but Stettinius and Truman resolved on a different course which quickly gained the British foreign secretary's endorsement. "President will see Mr. Molotov this evening," Eden advised, "and explain to him in blunt terms the effect of his attitude on future co-operation between the great powers." The Americans hoped that this proposed conversation might, in Eden's words, "produce a more reasonable attitude by Russia." Whatever the outcome of this specific conversation the Americans determined that the Polish talks should continue out in San Francisco. They would neither delay the opening of the UN conference nor publicly admit an impasse in the Polish discussions. Eden went along with their procedure. "In all the circumstances," he told Churchill, "I think that we are right to fall in with this program for above all we must keep in step with the Americans."[114]

Eden's remark concerning the British falling in with the American program demonstrates that the Americans had not totally accepted all the proposals the British minister initially offered. Truman and Stettinius backed away from any suggestion to postpone the San Francisco conference and decided to continue discussion on Poland beyond Washington. Yet it seems likely that their rejection of options to highlight in a public way the differences on the Polish issue made them more willing to accept Eden's basic proposal to break the impasse in discussions. When Stettinius advised the president that an admonition to Molotov was called for, Truman found his course of action largely predetermined. Not for nothing did Churchill tell Eden that he was "in full accord with all you are doing to stiffen the Americans and back them up to the hilt."[115]

---

[111] Cadogan to his wife, April 23, 1945, in Dilks, ed., *Diaries of Sir Alexander Cadogan*, p. 732.

[112] Minutes of second meeting regarding the Polish question, April 23, 1945, *FRUS*, 1945, V, pp. 241–51.

[113] Eden to Churchill, April 23, 1945 (telegram no. 2809), Prem 3, Public Record Office, 356/6/360.

[114] Eden to Churchill, April 23, 1945 (telegram no. 2818), Foreign Office Records, Public Record Office, N 4511/6/G55.

[115] Churchill to Eden, April 24, 1945 (telegram no. 4098), Prem 3, Public Record Office, 356/6/361–2.

Presumably for reassurance for his planned course of action, Truman met with his senior diplomatic and military advisers. This meeting had not been previously scheduled, and it is not clear if Truman or Stettinius first suggested it. What is certain is that it resulted from the decision to meet Molotov a second time. "We were suddenly surprised by my getting a message to come to a meeting at two o'clock on an undisclosed subject," Secretary Stimson recorded in his diary.[116] Stettinius soon revealed the issue at hand when he opened the meeting by reporting on his discussions with Molotov and Eden. "A complete deadlock had been reached on the subject of the carrying out of the Yalta agreement on Poland," he informed the group of officials, all of whom Truman had inherited from FDR – Stimson, Forrestal, Harriman, General Marshall, Admirals Leahy and Ernest King, Charles Bohlen and James Dunn from the State Department, and General John R. Deane, who headed the American military mission in Moscow.[117] For the secretary of state, it was now clear "that the Soviet Government intended to try to enforce upon the United States and British Governments this [Lublin] puppet government of Poland and obtain its acceptance as the legal government of Poland."

Truman spoke immediately after his secretary of state, before hearing from any of his other advisers, and in a manner confirming he had been "mobilized" (to use Cadogan's term) by Stettinius during their talk after the second meeting of the foreign secretaries. The apparently exasperated president said that he had informed Molotov the previous evening "that he intended fully to carry out all the agreements reached by President Roosevelt at the Crimea." According to Bohlen's minutes, "he added that he felt our agreements with the Soviet Union so far had been a one way street and that could not continue: it was now or never." Upset by the threat that the failure of the Polish discussions exercised over the meeting to establish a world organization, Truman blurted out his intention "to go on with the plans for San Francisco and if the Russians did not wish to join us they could go to hell."[118] This comment obviously indicated Truman's agitated state, but it hardly represented his true position which recognized the necessity of Soviet participation in the San Francisco meeting. His decision, made earlier that very afternoon, to continue the Polish discussions in San Francisco during the conference revealed this.

Upon concluding his remarks, Truman requested his advisers to present their views. "The consensus of opinion among the group Truman had called

---

[116] Stimson diary, April 23, 1945, vol. 51, Henry Lewis Stimson Papers, Sterling Memorial Library, Stimson complained of the content of the meeting that "all this [was] fired at me like a shot out of a Gatling gun and before I had really time to crystalize my views at all on the situation about which I originally knew very little at all."

[117] One must note David McCullough's point that these were "all Roosevelt's people." As he notes, "there was no one from Truman's old senate staff, no new foreign policy adviser or Russian expert of Truman's own choice, no Missouri 'gang,' no one at all from Missouri but Truman." McCullough, *Truman*, p. 374.

[118] Memorandum by Bohlen, April 23, 1945, *FRUS*, 1945, V, pp. 252–55.

together," Leahy recalled, was that the time had arrived to take a strong American attitude toward the Soviet Union and that no particular harm could be done to our war prospects if Russia should slow down or even stop its war effort in Europe and Asia."[119] Only Stimson and General Marshall expressed reservations about a blunt treatment of Molotov. Truman closed the meeting with a telling comment provoked by the military assessment of General Deane that he "was satisfied that from a military point of view there was no reason why we should fail to stand up to our understanding of the Crimean agreements."[120] The president had obtained confirmation that there was no military need for America to acquiesce in the Soviet interpretation of agreements. His task was now straightforward – to put before Molotov the need for the Soviets to carry out agreements made with his predecessor just as he would uphold his side of those agreements. This simple and unnuanced position resonated perfectly with his deep convictions about the importance of keeping one's word and agreements in political life. It also cast him as standing up for the American understanding of the Crimea agreements. There was no question at all in his mind of a departure in any way from Roosevelt's policies. The issue was whether he could hold the Soviets to the agreements they had made with his predecessor.

At 5:30 P.M., Truman received Molotov for a second time. The foreign minister had Soviet ambassador Andrei Gromyko and his translator V. N. Pavlov to attend him. Stettinius, Harriman, and Admiral Leahy accompanied the president while Bohlen translated for him. Immediately, Truman zeroed in on the Polish matter, emphasizing that "the United States Government could not agree to be a party to the formation of a Polish Government which was not representative of all Polish democratic elements." Rather awkwardly, he shifted gears and informed the Soviet minister that the United States planned to go ahead with the world organization despite other differences that might arise. He warned that "the failure of the three principal allies who had borne the brunt of the war to carry out the Crimea decision with regard to Poland will cast serious doubt upon our unity of purpose in regard to postwar collaboration." American policy required public support, he reminded Molotov, and this was especially so in the case of economic collaboration.[121] These remarks were pointed but certainly not undiplomatic.

Molotov responded by speaking of the need for Allied cooperation and with vague murmurings of his hope for an agreement. He sought to justify Soviet actions with the charge that the Poles had worked against the Red Army. Truman primed for the encounter was in no mood to listen to obtuse verbiage. In quick succession, he interjected three times to the effect that all the Americans were asking "was that the Soviet Government carry out the Crimean

---

[119] Leahy, *I Was There*, p. 351.

[120] Memorandum by Bohlen, April 23, 1945, *FRUS*, 1945, V, p. 255.

[121] Memorandum of Truman–Molotov conversation, April 23, 1945, *FRUS*, 1945, V, pp. 256–57.

decision on Poland." According to Bohlen's minutes, Truman delivered the
second interjection with "great firmness," while he gave the third – which followed Molotov's rehash of the "Yugoslav formula" as a model for Poland –
"sharply." According to Bohlen's later recollections, Molotov "turned a little
ashy." However that may be, Truman went on to express his desire for the
friendship of the Soviet government and to warn that this "could only be on
the basis of mutual observation of agreements and not on the basis of a one way
street."[122]

In Truman's recollection, the meeting ended with the final acrimonious
exchange in which Molotov protested that "I have never been talked to like
that in my life, " to which he retorted: "Carry out your agreements and you
won't get talked to like that."[123] This episode seems to have been constructed
out of Truman's later exaggerated recollection of the ferocity of the meeting.[124]
Certainly it was neither recorded in the American minutes of the meeting kept
by Bohlen nor in the Soviet version kept by Pavlov.[125] Geoffrey Roberts recently
has argued that it was added by Truman to Bohlen's version at the time he wrote
his memoirs in the years immediately after he left office presumably to spice up
the exchange and to highlight his supposed firmness with the less than likeable
Soviet official. The difficulty, as Roberts skillfully notes, is that this imagined
exchange "played a central, iconic role" in many subsequent historical nar-
ratives, and it even influenced how later memoirists like both Harriman and
Gromyko came to portray the April 23 meeting. It is hard to dispute Roberts's
suggestion that "in the absence of Truman's highlighting and embellishment of
his encounter with Molotov it is doubtful that historians would have given his
'tough talking' such prominence." Furthermore, he is surely correct in asserting that "without the famous and fictional, angry exchange, the idea that the
Truman presidency inaugurated an immediate, decisive turn in Soviet-American
relations would have had much less purchase."[126] Whatever its colorful

---

[122] Bohlen minutes, April 23, 1945, *FRUS*, 1945, V, pp. 257–58. On Bohlen's later recollections,
see his *Witness to History*, p. 213.

[123] Truman, *Year of Decisions*, p. 82.

[124] On Truman's capacity to exaggerate conversations, see Hamby, *Man of the People*, p. 486.
Truman's embellishment of his role in certain conversations was noted by his naval aide,
Admiral Robert Denison, who recalled: "I have been with the president on occasions when
he had what appeared to me to be a perfectly normal and amiable conversation with a
caller. After the caller left, he would say to me, in effect, 'I certainly set him straight,' or 'I
let him have it.' The president's remarks seemed to me to have no conceivable relation to
the conversation I had just heard." Dennison quoted in Hamby, "An American Democrat,"
pp. 47–48.

[125] On the Soviet version, see record of conversation between V. M. Molotov and the president of
the USA, Harry Truman, April 23, 1945, in Roberts, "Sexing up the Cold War," pp. 118–21.

[126] Roberts explores this whole matter persuasively and at length in his "Sexing up the Cold War,"
pp. 105–15. Roberts also notes that "Truman's account of his first meetings with Molotov is an
instructive example of how a primary text by a key participant in events can direct and shape
the subsequent historiography." See p. 115.

qualities, the time has come to excise this episode as an emblem of Truman's early foreign policy.

Molotov hardly emerged from the meeting with his tail between his legs. Outside the Oval Office, he was entirely agreeable to having pictures taken with Truman, but Stettinius vetoed that possibility by declaring that Truman was far too busy.[127] He does not appear to have been perturbed in any way by Truman's genuine effort to speak firmly to him.[128] The Soviet minister proceeded on his way to further discussions with Eden and Stettinius. He remained singularly unimpressed by the new president and completely unmoved by his direct but diplomatic language.[129] In his own later recollections, he mocked Truman's effort to talk tough as "rather stupid" and dismissed Truman as "far from having Roosevelt's intellect." He thought the two presidents had but one thing in common – "Roosevelt had been an inveterate imperialist, too."[130]

Reactions to the second Truman–Molotov meeting varied on the American side. There was a recognition that the president had upped the ante in his level of firmness in addressing Molotov on the need for progress on the Polish question. The next day in his morning staff meeting Truman himself indicated that "he talked strongly to the foreign minister" and, notably, he seemed "hopeful of good effects from the meeting."[131] Stettinius informed Harry Hopkins that "the President did a magnificent job" and presumably reassured Truman in similar gushing terms.[132] Stettinius also reported on the meeting directly in a "thrilling message" to the influential Senator Vandenberg who worked up a lather of excitement and subsequently confided to his diary that "F.D.R.'s appeasement of Russia is over."[133] Not everyone was so thrilled as Vandenberg. Harriman, usually thought of as a major influence in Truman's supposedly tough approach, recalled later that he "was a little taken aback, frankly, when

---

[127] Ayers diary, April 23, 1945, in Ferrell, ed., *Truman in the White House*, pp. 13–14.

[128] Roberts argues that "it is doubtful that Truman's aggressive style even registered with Molotov, himself a bullying, abrasive personality (except in his dealings with Stalin)." Roberts, "Sexing up the Cold War," pp. 111–12. Based on the Soviet reports of the meetings, Roberts goes so far as to argue that "Molotov's meetings with Truman were significant for the Soviets, too, but not for the reasons traditionally cited. It seems that the main message Moscow took from the Molotov–Truman talks was a positive one – that the new American president was going to continue Roosevelt's policy of cooperation with the Soviet Union."

[129] Note Steven Merritt Miner's observation that "Molotov was not specially disturbed by Truman's anger; he expected hostility – open or veiled – from imperialist leaders." Miner, "His Master's Voice," p. 85.

[130] Resis, ed., *Molotov Remembers*, p. 55.

[131] Ayers diary, April 24, 1945, in Ferrell, ed., *Truman in the White House*, p. 14.

[132] On the report to Hopkins, see the memorandum on Mr. Stettinius's telephone conversations, April 23, 1945, Edward R. Stettinius, Jr., Papers, Alderman Library, Box 24.

[133] Vandenberg, Jr., ed., *Private Papers of Senator Vandenberg*, p. 176. The leading Republican internationalist echoed Truman's own position in declaring that "we will 'play-ball' gladly with the Russians and 'give and take' because we must have unity for the sake of peace but it is no longer going to be all 'give' and no 'take' so far as we are concerned."

the President attacked Molotov so vigorously." He regretted (albeit unnecessarily) that "Truman went at it so hard because his behavior gave Molotov an excuse to tell Stalin that the Roosevelt policy was being abandoned." He considered it "a mistake though not a decisive one."[134] Harriman's surprise is understandable for he had not been included in discussions between Eden and Stettinius, which resulted in the call for the president to admonish the Soviet minister so as to facilitate a diplomatic break-through on Poland.

The close collaboration between Eden and Stettinius had produced the tactical approach Truman adopted toward Molotov on April 23. After the meeting Stettinius hurried off a memorandum to Eden detailing the points Truman raised, and he sent a message "by word of mouth that the language used by the President had actually been stiffer than the memorandum suggested."[135] He seemed to be reassuring Eden that he had fulfilled his commitment regarding Truman's speaking firmly to Molotov, and indeed he had. The problem for both Eden and Stettinius was that their plan failed miserably. After a concluding discussion on the Polish question during the evening of April 23, Eden telegraphed London and admitted as much. "Molotov's attitude during this discussion," he observed with suitable British understatement, "does not encourage hope that he has been much influenced by his interview with the President."[136]

The April 23 meeting took place primarily because the British foreign secretary convinced his earnest and well-meaning American counterpart that the means to break through the impasse on the Polish question lay in a forceful approach to the Soviet foreign minister. The Americans, hoping thereby to guarantee a successful meeting at San Francisco, genuinely believed this course might be beneficial to their dealings with the Russians. Whatever Senator Vandenberg's private ejaculations, Truman saw himself working to uphold Roosevelt's agreements. His very concern to fulfill his predecessor's pledges set him up to follow the proffered course of action. Truman was hardly a wind-up toy set loose to perform in a programmed way by his advisers. But he moved carefully and in accord with the advice he received from the officials Roosevelt had chosen – in this instance especially Stettinius. It is unlikely that had he lived, the urbane Roosevelt would have approached Molotov in the same forceful manner as Truman.[137] In this sense, there was certainly a reversal of sorts in

---

[134] Harriman and Abel, *Special Envoy to Churchill and Stalin*, pp. 453–54.

[135] Eden to Churchill, April 23, 1945 (telegram no. 2842), Prem 3, Public Record Office, 356/6/363–4.

[136] Eden to Churchill, April 24, 1945 (telegram no. 2845), Prem 3, Public Record Office, 356/6/365. For minutes of the third meeting regarding the Polish question, see *FRUS*, 1945, V, pp. 359–62.

[137] On this point, one must note that Charles Bohlen thought that "Roosevelt's technique would have been different, his approach would have possibly been more diplomatic and somewhat smoother" but that "President Truman was merely saying what Roosevelt would have said had he been alive." Bohlen claimed that Roosevelt "was in no mood, the last time I saw him, only days before he died to take further violations of the Yalta accord lying down." Bohlen, *Witness to History*, p. 213.

the approach to the Soviets brought about by Roosevelt's death. But rather paradoxically, it emerged precisely because of the American effort to obtain Soviet compliance with what were perceived to be the terms of agreements FDR had negotiated. It occurred because of Truman's earnest desire to continue Roosevelt's policies, a desire that remained with him in the weeks and months ahead.

4

Instruction

Truman's Advisers and Their Conflicting Advice

So Many Things to Think About

As the Allied armies of the East and the West moved to deliver their final blows to Hitler's Germany, the differing goals and purposes of the major powers provoked disputes above and beyond the composition of the Polish government. The future of Central Europe was at stake during late April and May of 1945. The Americans and the Soviets disagreed over either the surrender/liberation or occupation arrangements for Austria, Czechoslovakia, Rumania, Bulgaria, Hungary, and, of course, Germany. Truman was swept along as these conflicts developed, forever struggling to gain some grasp on the situations. The maze of issues before him remained undiminished, and the pressure on him to make decisions, unrelenting. Issues involving the use of Anglo-American troops in Europe, the Yugoslav threat to seize Trieste, and the final surrender of Germany, along with matters to do with reparations and Lend–Lease, the atomic bomb, and the San Francisco conference all claimed his attention.

In dealing with the myriad of issues, Truman remained heavily dependent on his advisers, although initially there was no dominant voice among them. This did not constitute a problem for the president when there was a clear consensus among his counselors, but it caused him real difficulty when differences emerged in their recommendations. With Stettinius located on the west coast from April 24 onward and also heavily focused on matters pertaining to the UN meeting, leadership in the State Department devolved to his deputy, Joseph C. Grew, a serious and senior diplomat and former ambassador to Japan. Grew generated respect from government officials for his experience and competence, but he lacked the stature to impose any kind of coherent vision on the implementation of American foreign policy. He simply did not possess the political strength to bring the various officials who established military, economic, and diplomatic policy into anything approaching cohesive purpose. No one else in the administration stepped forward into this role, and the president proved quite incapable of undertaking it. Consequently, for much of the crucial month of May 1945, there existed a transparently ad hoc quality to American decision making.

Truman took advice from a number of different officials and tended to consider a variety of issues in quite discrete terms. No person or agency effectively considered how American military strategy, economic power, and atomic potential might serve the diplomacy of the nation. Truman merely muddled through like some struggling student learning in pressured circumstances from a group of rival professors who based their respective instruction on differing assumptions and assessments of the situation at hand. Surprisingly, in light of suggestions of his abandonment of FDR's cooperative approach, he increasingly accepted the views of those counselors who advocated a less confrontational approach toward the Soviet Union than the one he demonstrated in his meeting with Molotov.

The Polish issue continued to bedevil Soviet-American relations for much of this learning phase for Truman. On April 24, Stalin bluntly rejected the proposals put forth by Truman and Churchill in their joint message of April 18 and, for good measure, accused the Americans and the British of collusion and of trying to "dictate" to the Soviet Union.[1] Molotov voiced this party line in further meetings in San Francisco, warning that "if attempts were made using the Polish situation as an excuse to dictate to the Soviet Union no good would come out of it."[2] At the UN meeting, the Soviets attempted to obtain entry to the conference for the Polish regime they sponsored. The American delegation vigorously and successfully opposed this proposal.[3] Undeterred, the Soviets proceeded to cement their control in Poland and arrested a number of prominent underground leaders in early May, prompting an American protest. But the United States did little more than verbally object. Throughout May, Poland stood as a sign of the prevailing Soviet-American discord, but Truman backed away from forcing a further confrontation on the issue in face-to-face meetings with Stalin. Churchill lobbied hard for an early meeting of the three leaders, but Truman avoided this and let the Polish issue drift into a virtual limbo.[4] He had no eagerness to engage in summit diplomacy when his own endeavor to obtain a firm grasp of American policy was in such an early stage.

In addition to Poland, Truman confronted a range of other problems related to the extent of Soviet domination of Central European nations. He learned more fully in early May that the Soviet Union's control of the affairs of Rumania, Bulgaria, and Hungary was well advanced.[5] The influence of the Western allies in these nations promised to be minimal at best. The prospects for the Americans

[1] Stalin to Truman, April 24, 1945, *FRUS*, 1945, V, pp. 263–64.

[2] Bohlen memorandum of Stettinius–Molotov conversation, April 24, 1945, *FRUS*, 1945, I, p. 384.

[3] For Arthur Vandenberg's account of this episode, see Vandenberg, Jr., ed., *Private Papers of Senator Vandenberg*, p. 181.

[4] On Churchill's lobbying see his memo to Truman, May 6, 1945, *FRUS: The Conference of Berlin (The Potsdam Conference)*, 1945, I, pp. 3–4.

[5] Grew to Truman, May 1, 1945, *FRUS*, 1945, IV, pp. 201–03. See also Joseph C. Grew, *Turbulent Era: A Diplomatic Record of Forty Years, 1904–1945*, 2 vols. (Boston, 1952), II, pp. 1454–55.

and the British to exercise a more significant role were better in Austria and Czechoslovakia but in both countries the Soviets placed roadblocks in the way of the operation of joint control machinery involving the Western allies. Truman initially relied for counsel on Joseph Grew, who, like many of the State Department professionals, believed that the time had arrived to adopt a tough stance with the Soviets to ensure their compliance with existing agreements.[6] The president mainly followed Grew's lead on these matters, and he dutifully protested various Soviet actions emphasizing constantly the upholding of agreements already negotiated.

While differences over a range of issues simmered in Europe, diplomats from allied and associated countries labored in San Francisco to forge a new international peacekeeping body. Truman opened the conference with a radio address on April 25 when he put before the assembled delegates a choice between "the continuance of international chaos – or the establishment of a world organization for the enforcement of peace." He asked them to create the structure "which will make future peace, not only possible, but certain."[7] Creating any structure, let alone one with that utopian objective, proved easier said than done despite the foundation laid by the Dumbarton Oaks agreement. A series of disputes caused friction and division in the early weeks of the conference, and most of these saw the Soviet Union and the United States lined up in opposition. Public squabbling occurred over such matters as the conference presidency, representation for Poland, the seating of White Russia and the Ukraine, and the admission to the world organization of Argentina, which had spent the war openly sympathizing with the Nazi cause.[8]

Stettinius kept Truman in close touch with developments at the conference, but the president did not play an integral or determining role in developing the American position on the various matters raised.[9] He mainly authorized policies already determined and allowed the American delegation considerable autonomy. Even on the question of the admission of Argentina, which at one time he had opposed, Truman quickly succumbed to Stettinius's arguments that this pro-fascist power would need to be admitted in order to ensure the support of the Latin American republics for the admission of White Russia and the Ukraine.[10] Further illustrating Truman's malleability in the hands of his

---

[6] See Grew's letter of July 28, 1947 to Bohlen recalling his 1945 views, Department of State Records: Records of Charles E. Bohlen, 1941–1952 (Lot File 74D379), National Archives, Box 1.

[7] Truman address to the United Nations Conference, April 25, 1945, Truman, *Public Papers of the Presidents of the United States: Harry S. Truman, 1945* (Washington, DC, 1961), p. 21. For further details on the opening of the San Francisco meeting, see Schlesinger, *Act of Creation*, pp. 91–92.

[8] These matters are discussed in Hoopes and Brinkley, *FDR and the Creation of the U.N.*, pp. 184–91. See also Thomas M. Campbell, *Masquerade Peace: America's UN Policy, 1944–1945* (Tallahassee, FL, 1973).

[9] Stettinius's efforts are well revealed in Campbell and Herring, *Diaries of Edward R. Stettinius, Jr.*, pp. 333–73. Also see Schlesinger, *Act of Creation*, pp. 111–245.

[10] Minutes of 18th meeting, U.S. Delegation, April 26, 1945, *FRUS*, 1945, I, p. 416. Schlesinger, *Act of Creation*, pp. 131–32.

advisers, he later approved the delegation's proposal to include certain regional security arrangements – such as that provided for the western hemisphere under the Act of Chapultepec – within the UN framework, while at the very same time objecting in a different context to regional arrangements he thought "would tend to weaken the proposed world organization and would lead to a return to power politics."[11] The president hardly aimed to impose coherence and consistency on his nation's foreign policy. He simply reacted to proposals and to counsel as best he could.

Secretary of War Henry L. Stimson eagerly sought to instruct Truman on the implications of the potentially devastating new weapon being developed by the Manhattan Project. On April 25, Stimson and General Leslie Groves, the Project director, gave Truman a lengthy briefing on the weapon we know as the atomic bomb.[12] Here Groves reported on the genesis and current status of the atomic project while Stimson presented a memorandum explaining the implications of the bomb for international relations. Stimson addressed the terrifying power of the new weapon, advising that "within four months, we shall in all probability have completed the most terrible weapon ever known in human history, one bomb of which could destroy a whole city." He went on to allude to the dangers that its discovery and development foreshadowed and pointed to the difficulty in constructing a realistic system of controls. He then suggested that "the question of sharing it with other nations and, if so shared, upon what terms, becomes a primary question of our foreign relations."[13]

Stimson's briefing on April 25 alerted Truman to the relationship, or more accurately the potential relationship, between the atomic bomb and American policy toward the Soviet Union, but the president does not appear to have paid due attention to the lesson. Certainly he did not share Stimson's virtual obsession with the matter.[14] Truman focused less on the geopolitical implications of the possession of the atomic bomb and more on the personal burden of his

---

[11] On May 14, 1945, Truman rejected the proposal of Chinese foreign minister T. V. Soong for a regional security treaty for the Pacific. See Grew's memorandum of Truman–Soong conversation, May 14, 1945, *FRUS*, 1945, VII, p. 103. On May 12, Truman had approved Stettinius's "regionalism" proposal. "I don't see a thing wrong with it," he observed. "It sounds very good to me. It covers the world situation supreme and maintains our situation here as we want it." Truman–Stettinius phone conversation transcript, May 12, 1945, in Campbell and Herring, eds., *Diaries of Edward R. Stettinius, Jr.*, pp. 361–62.

[12] Truman, *Year of Decisions*, p. 104. See also Stimson Diaries, April 25, 1945, Henry Lewis Stimson Papers, Sterling Memorial Library. For a balanced history of the development of the atomic bomb see Hewlett and Anderson, *The New World*.

[13] Stimson Diaries, April 25, 1945, Henry Lewis Stimson Papers, Sterling Memorial Library, later claimed that "it was already apparent that the critical questions in American policy towards atomic energy would be directly connected with Soviet Russia." Henry L. Stimson and McGeorge Bundy, *On Active Service in Peace and War* (New York, 1947), p. 636.

[14] On Stimson, see Henry L. Stimson and McGeorge Bundy, *On Active Service in Peace and War*, (New York, 1947), pp. 612–33; Godfrey Hodgson, *The Colonel: The Life and Wars of Henry L. Stimson, 1867–1950* (New York, 1990), pp. 274–341; and McGeorge Bundy, *Danger and Survival: Choices about the Bomb in the First Fifty Years* (New York, 1988), pp. 54–129.

having to authorize the use of the awesome weapon. "I am going to have to make a decision which no man in history has ever had to make," he reportedly said to White House staffer Leonard Reinsch, the very next person he saw after Stimson and Groves left his office. "I'll make the decision, but it is terrifying to think about what I will have to decide."[15] Truman's sober contemplation of the possibility of authorizing the use of a weapon that might destroy a whole city, however, did not prompt his detailed reflection concerning the potential impact of the new weapon for international relations in general or his dealings with the Soviets in particular. Gar Alperovitz's elaborate and fanciful constructions to the contrary, he did not begin to design American diplomacy toward the Soviet Union in light of the impending possession of the atomic bomb.[16] Suggestions that he adopted some strategy of "delayed showdown" in which he deliberately chose to defer consideration of major issues with the Soviets until he held this weapon in the American arsenal impute a coherence to his foreign policy formulation that simply did not exist.

Following another meeting with Stimson on May 2, Truman appointed an advisory group, the Interim Committee, to consider the various questions raised by the imminent success in developing an atomic weapon.[17] He appointed Stimson as chair and designated James Byrnes to serve on it as his personal representative. Interestingly he named Byrnes only upon Stimson's recommendation and had seemed quite willing to allow this body to undertake its work without his appointing a specific delegate. The wily old war secretary, who undoubtedly had heard the rumors that Byrnes would replace Stettinius, presumably requested the South Carolinian to join the committee so as to gain him as an eventual conduit to the president, perhaps someone who might tutor the new chief executive on these matters. Certainly Byrnes and Truman engaged in no prolonged discussion about his service on the Interim Committee. On May 3,

---

15 J. Leonard Reinsch oral history interview quoted in S. David Broscious, "Longing for International Control, Banking on American Superiority: Harry S. Truman's Approach to Nuclear Weapons," in John Lewis Gaddis et al., eds., *Cold War Statesmen Confront the Bomb: Nuclear Diplomacy since 1945* (Oxford & New York, 1999), p. 16. Broscious observed that "this comment suggests that Truman fully understood the gravity of Stimson's briefing and was so startled by it that he felt compelled to unload its burden, however cryptically, upon the man who was neither a close adviser nor a personal friend." Also see Clark Clifford with Richard Holbrooke, *Counsel to the President: A Memoir* (New York, 1991), p. 58.

16 Gar Alperovitz titled a chapter in his *Atomic Diplomacy* "The Decision to Postpone a Confrontation with Stalin" and developed elaborate details of a supposed "strategy of delay." See *Atomic Diplomacy*, pp. 110–74. Note also that Truman received a skeptical report on the potential of the atomic bomb from Admiral William Leahy, who described it as "the biggest fool thing we have ever done. The bomb will never go off, and I speak as an expert in explosives." See Truman, *Year of Decisions*, p. 21.

17 The members of the Interim Committee were Henry L. Stimson, secretary of war (chairman); George L. Harrison; James F. Byrnes, personal representative of the president; Ralph A. Bard, undersecretary of the Navy; William L. Clayton, assistant secretary of state; Dr. Vannevar Bush, director, Office of Scientific Research and Development; Dr. Karl T. Compton, chief of the Office of Field Service, Office of Scientific Research and Development; and Dr. James B. Conant, chairman of the National Defense Research Committee.

Byrnes alerted his trusted friend Ben Cohen that he had been asked by Truman "to represent him on a Committee appointed by the Secretary of War to make an investigation of a matter so secret that he would not mention it over the telephone." Byrnes correctly suspected it had "to do with some of Vannevar Bush's work" and that it would involve his working with Stimson in the latter part of May.[18] As far as the written record reveals, Truman essentially left the committee to its own devices and the group focused during May on the primary question of the use of the atomic bomb against Japan rather than to its potential as a diplomatic lever for use against the Russians.[19] It is unlikely that Truman was much influenced in his policy making toward the Soviet Union during May 1945 by the prospect of his nation's solitary possession of atomic weapons. The redoubtable Stimson saw the two issues as crucially connected and spoke of the A-bomb as potentially a "master card" in diplomacy, but he certainly did not serve as Truman's close tutor in this area.[20] Truman did not track the deliberations of the Interim Committee with any care and simply waited for it to present conclusions to him. He had many more pressing matters to occupy his attention.

In the last days of the war in Europe, the American president was forced to engage in a pointed argument with the British prime minister over the use of military forces for political ends. Churchill objected to General Dwight D. Eisenhower's decision to stop his military advance at the Elbe. The British leader

[18] Byrnes to Cohen, May 3, 1945, James F. Byrnes Papers, Cooper Library, Folder 189.

[19] For details on the early meetings of the Interim Committee, see Hewlett and Anderson, *The New World*, pp. 353–54. Also note that Stimson later admitted that "the first and greatest problem was the decision on the use of the bomb." Stimson and Bundy, *On Active Service in Peace and War*, p. 617. Similarly, Byrnes remembered that the committee's "primary and immediate function was to make recommendations on the preparations of a test explosion in New Mexico and, if this proved successful, on the use of the bomb against Japan." Byrnes, *All in One Lifetime*, p. 283. Will Clayton, the State Department's representative on the Interim Committee, wrote to Richard G. Hewlett in 1958: "You say that a number of writers suggest that the target of the Bomb was not so much Japan as Russia. I know of no basis for this suggestion. There certainly was none in any of the discussions of the Committee at any meetings that I attended so far as I can recall." Clayton to Hewlett, December 16, 1958, in Frederick J. Dobney, ed., *Selected Papers of Will Clayton* (Baltimore, 1971), pp. 128–29. Also see Robertson, *Sly and Able*, pp. 390–413.

[20] On May 15, Stimson met Grew and Navy Secretary Forrestal at the regular State–War–Navy meeting and engaged in discussion regarding the possible involvement of the Russians in the Pacific war. In light of the matters discussed at this meeting, he confided to his diary later in the day: "The trouble is that the President has now promised apparently to meet Stalin and Churchill on the first of July and at that time these questions will become burning and it may be necessary to have it out with Russia on her relations to Manchuria and Port Arthur and various other parts of North China." He then continued that "over any such tangled wave of problems the S-1 secret would be dominant and yet we will not know until after that time probably, until after that meeting, whether this weapon is a weapon in our hand or not. We think it will be shortly afterwards, but it seems a terrible thing to gamble with such big stakes in diplomacy without having your master card in your hand." Stimson Diaries, May 15, 1945, Henry Lewis Stimson Papers, Sterling Memorial Library. Stimson diary reflections reveal that he was less than certain of the president's plans and perturbed that he was not conscientiously and clearly pursuing a strategy that saw the atomic bomb as a "master card."

wanted the Anglo-American forces to capture both Berlin and Prague if possible. He obviously saw the political value of such military successes. The prime minister tried to prod Eisenhower but without success. The supreme Allied commander, paying little attention to Carl Von Clausewitz's *On War*, refused "to intermingle political and military considerations."[21] Churchill thereupon tried an end-run around Eisenhower and appealed directly to Truman on April 30 arguing for the liberation of Prague and western Czechoslovakia. "If the western Allies play no significant part in Czechoslovakian liberation," he cautioned, "that country will go the way of Yugoslavia."[22] One might have expected that such a forceful entreaty might have some impact on a president who had decided to alter Roosevelt's accommodating policy. But Truman was not such a president. He did not seize this opportunity to use military forces for political ends. On the advice of General George Marshall, who bluntly noted that he "would be loath to hazard American lives for purely political purposes," Truman rejected Churchill's suggestion.[23] The president held the estimable Marshall in some kind of awe and hesitated to question his judgment on military matters.

Truman reacted similarly to the increasingly hard-line recommendations advanced by Undersecretary Grew as he did to Churchill's. Stettinius's stand-in warned Truman in early May that "hard bargaining" with the Soviets would be necessary, and he suggested that "the present military situation and its apparent possibilities offer some good material for such bargaining provided immediate action is taken."[24] Like the British leader, Grew wanted the American forces

---

[21] On Eisenhower's position, see his message to Marshall, April 23, 1945, in Chandler, ed., *The Papers of Dwight David Eisenhower*, Vol. 4, *The War Years*, p. 2583. For more detail on this whole matter, see Stephen Ambrose, *Eisenhower and Berlin, 1945: The Decision to Halt at the Elbe* (New York, 1967), pp. 88–98.

[22] Churchill to Truman, April 30, 1945, FRUS, 1945, IV, p. 446. For Churchill's views on Yugoslavia at this time, see his pointed comments to Stalin in a letter of April 29, 1945, where he complained that "the way things have worked out in Yugoslavia certainly does not give me the feeling of a fifty-fifty interest and influence as between our two countries. Marshal Tito has become a complete dictator. He has proclaimed that his prime loyalties are to Soviet Russia. Although he allowed the members of the Royal Yugoslav Government to enter his Government, they only number six as against 25 of his own nominees. We have the impression that they are not taken into consultation on matters of high policy and that it is becoming a one-party regime." Churchill to Stalin (telegram 2255), April 29, 1945, Churchill Papers, Char 20/216.

[23] Truman to Churchill, May 1, 1945, FRUS, 1945, IV, p. 446. Marshall quoted in Gaddis, *The United States and the Origins of the Cold War*, p. 209. General Omar Bradley, one of Eisenhower's top commanders, later expressed a certain regret at the American approach. He remarked of the Berlin possibility that "as soldiers we looked naively on this British inclination to complicate the war with political foresight and nonmilitary objectives." In his memoir written in 1951, he admitted that "at times during that war [World War II] we forgot that wars are fought for the resolution of political conflicts, and in the ground campaign for Europe we sometimes overlooked political considerations of vast importance." Omar N. Bradley, *A Soldier's Story* (New York, 1951), pp. 536, xi.

[24] Grew to Truman, May 5, 1945, FRUS, 1945, III, pp. 277–78. For an insight into Grew's "hard-line" views at this time see his memorandum of May 19, 1945, a copy of which is found in Bohlen Papers, Department of State Records: Records of Charles E. Bohlen, 1941–1952, National Archives, Box 1.

to make a run on Prague, but Truman again backed his military advisers and rejected this whole approach. With the final surrender of Germany on May 7, the question of maximizing territorial acquisitions quickly became redundant, although the related issue of the withdrawal of troops to their agreed zones simmered along close to the surface.

The Americans handled the process of the German surrender in a manner that fully confirmed their commitment to the terms FDR had propounded. When Heinrich Himmler, the Gestapo chief, proposed a surrender of German forces on the western front on April 25, Truman rejected it as an attempt at "piecemeal surrender." When informing Stalin of his rejection of the offer, Truman explicitly noted that in keeping with existing agreements "the only acceptable terms of surrender are unconditional surrender on all fronts to the Soviet Union, Great Britain and the United States."[25] Eisenhower carefully implemented this policy even to the point of threatening to "break off negotiations" with the Germans and to "seal the Western Front."[26] His actions clearly forced Admiral Karl Donitz, who headed what remained of a German government following upon Hitler's inglorious suicide on April 30, to surrender unconditionally to all three allies.

The announcement of the German surrender on May 8 understandably sparked great public jubilation in Washington, London, and Moscow. Churchill addressed a huge throng in Whitehall and conducted them in the singing of "Land of Hope and Glory." Less dramatically, Truman, on his sixty-first birthday no less, broadcast an address to his nation informing them that the "flags of freedom fly over all Europe" and calling on his fellow citizens to face the further great tasks of defeating Japan and winning the peace.[27] Not surprisingly, the president told his fellow Americans of his regret that Franklin D. Roosevelt had not lived to witness the Allied victory. Writing the next day to FDR's daughter Anna, Truman noted that it would have been "a most happy day if your father could have been present." He then went on to apologize for not thinking to invite Anna and her mother to come to the White House for the victory announcement. Rather plaintively but without exaggeration, Truman confided that "to tell you the honest truth, I have so many things to think about, I did not think of that."[28] Victory in Europe brought no let-up in the tremendous demands upon the fledgling president. This reality cannot be overstated in recapturing the policy-making experience of the Truman administration in these months before the Potsdam conference.

[25] For the Truman–Churchill discussion leading to the rejection of Himmler's offer, see transcript of Trans-Atlantic Telephone Conversation, April 25, 1945, *FRUS*, 1945, III, pp. 762–67. For Truman's message to Stalin of April 25, see Grew to Stettinius (which encloses the earlier message), April 25, 1945, *FRUS*, 1945, III, p. 768.

[26] Eisenhower to combined chiefs of staff, May 6, 1945, in Chandler, ed., *Papers of Dwight David Eisenhower*, Vol. 4, *The War Years*, p. 2649.

[27] Truman, *Year of Decisions*, pp. 232–33.

[28] Truman to Anna Boettiger, May 9, 1945, Anna Roosevelt Halsted Papers, FDRL, Box 76.

Occupation policy for and reparations from the now-defeated Germany remained important matters requiring presidential attention. The Yalta accord provided for such reparations but came to no specific agreements on their scope and size. Instead it allowed for the establishment of the Allied Reparations Commission to settle these issues, although at Soviet insistence FDR had accepted twenty billion dollars as the "basis for negotiation."[29] Both Harry Hopkins and Jimmy Byrnes alerted Truman to the importance of this matter during his first week in office. So alarmed, Truman had sought a more high-profile negotiator to handle the issue than the scholarly economist Isador Lubin whom FDR had named to represent the United States on the commission. Truman recalled wanting "a tough bargainer, someone who could be as tough as Molotov."[30] After initially asking former Postmaster General Frank Walker to take on the job, he settled upon Edwin Pauley, a wealthy California oil man and successful Democratic Party fund-raiser, who had the backing of Democratic National Committee Chairman Robert Hannegan.[31] Lubin stayed on as Pauley's deputy to supply appropriate continuity and technical support.

At the outset, Truman gave Pauley only vague instructions emphasizing the importance of his task and the need to avoid any repetition of the disastrous post–World War I reparations experience. Germany must not become a drain on the resources of the United States. A parallel notion also influenced British thinking on German reparations at exactly this time leading to the firm conclusion that Britain should not subsidize in any way German reparation payments.[32] The goal also guided the president's approval on May 18 of Pauley's instructions, prepared by the interdepartmental Informal Policy Committee on Germany, which explicitly noted that "this Government opposes any reparation plan based upon the assumption that the United States or any other country will finance directly or indirectly any reconstruction in Germany or reparation by Germany."[33] In what was becoming a characteristic pattern, Truman left Pauley to do his work after this point, although he knew that the questions of reparations and the German future would be major subjects in any meeting he might hold with Stalin and Churchill.

The objective of avoiding any extension of economic support to Germany also influenced Truman in approving on May 10 the revised occupation directive (JCS 1067), which tempered the harsh provisions of the Morgenthau Plan

[29] Yalta conference protocol, February 11, 1945, *FRUS: The Conferences at Malta and Yalta, 1945*, pp. 978–80.

[30] Truman, *Year of Decisions*, p. 342.

[31] Truman told Frank Walker on April 18 that both Hopkins and Byrnes agreed that reparations would be "his most difficult problem." Walker diary, entry for May 1, Frank C. Walker Papers, University of Notre Dame Archives, Box 123.

[32] On British thinking, see J. E. Farquharson, "Anglo-American Policy on German Reparations from Yalta to Potsdam," *English Historical Review*, 112 (September 1997), pp. 906–07.

[33] Instruction for the United States Representative on the Allied Commission on Reparations, May 18, 1945, *FRUS, 1945*, III, pp. 1222–27.

by permitting some German industry.[34] Incidentally, it also clarified that the State and War Departments had supplanted the Treasury as the main source for America's German policy. Treasury Secretary Morgenthau relentlessly offered to instruct Truman on German matters in late April and early May, hoping, no doubt, to convince the new president of the validity of his harsh approach to the defeated Germans. However, Truman, rather like Roosevelt in the last months of his administration, backed away from close identification with the Treasury Department's approach. He leaned more in the direction of Stimson and Assistant Secretary of War John J. McCloy who worried that "crippling German industry and therefore food production would penalize the other Europeans who had been Hitler's victims," set back chances for European economic and social rehabilitation, and make it more likely that the Americans might be forced to assist the Germans.[35] Yet, the new president hesitated to make this starkly clear to Morgenthau, and the treasury secretary unsuccessfully continued his lobbying on German matters until the very eve of the Potsdam conference.

The end of the war in Europe also placed before Truman a major issue regarding the future of Lend–Lease supplies to the Soviet Union. Congressional mandates held that Lend–Lease support for all its recipients should come to an end at the war's conclusion. But by late April 1945, as George C. Herring's careful analysis reveals, "two lines of argument had converged to create irresistible pressure for modifications in Russian Lend–lease policy. [Leo] Crowley's FEA [Foreign Economic Administration] and the army felt that adjustments had to be made to stick within the legal limits imposed by the Lend–Lease Act and to abide by the wishes of Congress. Harriman and the State Department desired changes in order to use Lend–Lease to influence the future direction of Soviet-American relations."[36] Harriman certainly served as a catalyst for an abrupt reduction of Lend–Lease aid to the Soviets. On May 9, he and Stettinius met in San Francisco and reviewed Soviet-American relations.[37] These deliberations led the secretary of state to instruct Grew to recommend to Truman that the "western Allies" should have priority over the Russians in future aid programs, that general Lend–Lease shipments to Russia should be curtailed while aid to Russia for eventual use in the Pacific war "should continue to be energetically pressed," and that the American attitude should be "firm while avoiding any implication of a threat or any indication of political bargaining."[38] On May 10, Harriman returned to Washington and raised this matter, among others, directly

---

[34] For the revised Directive to Commander in Chief of United States Forces of Occupation Regarding the Military Government of Germany, April 26, 1945, *FRUS*, 1945, III, pp. 484–503. (The directive was forwarded to Truman on April 26 but not approved until May 10.)

[35] Beschloss, *The Conquerors*, p. 231. For more details on the Truman–Morgenthau relationship and the contest to influence Truman on German occupation matters, see Beschloss, *The Conquerors*, pp. 230–37.

[36] George C. Herring, Jr., *Aid to Russia*, p. 200.

[37] Stettinius memorandum of conversation, May 9, 1945, Campbell and Herring, eds., *Diaries of Edward R. Stettinius, Jr.*, pp. 357–58.

[38] Stettinius to Grew, May 9, 1945, *FRUS*, 1945, V, p. 998.

with the president. Later that day, Truman spoke by phone with Stettinius about his conversation with Harriman. When asked if he liked the suggestion of "getting tough on Lend Lease shipments," the president hurriedly replied – and it would seem with a certain faux decisiveness – that "I agree with that entirely."[39]

Meanwhile Harriman joined in a discussion with officials from all departments and agencies concerned with Lend-Lease from which emerged a recommendation that Undersecretary Grew and Leo Crowley of FEA draft a memorandum for presidential approval providing for Lend–Lease cutbacks along the lines that Harriman had suggested.[40] Crowley and Grew for their different reasons relished this task. They presented their memorandum to Truman on May 11 and gained his approval of it that same day. On May 12, the Foreign Economic Administration executed Truman's order with a ferocity such that loading of supplies at docksides was halted and ships bound for Soviet ports were recalled. The Soviets naturally complained loudly and publicly about the American actions, although it was "the British who were hardest hit" as Truman later observed.[41] The episode added to the existing Soviet-American tensions and promised to further harm relations. Harriman, who had conceived of a more gradual reduction of Lend-Lease aid, quickly joined with Assistant Secretary of State Clayton in persuading the president to rescind his order. Truman did this immediately, and the loading of already-promised supplies resumed. Poor Clayton was left with the unenviable task of explaining to the Soviet embassy in Washington that it has all been a "mistake."[42]

Truman showed no interest either then or later in allowing the buck for this particular decision to stop anywhere near his desk. He remembered the incident as "clearly a case of policy-making on the part of Crowley and Grew," who in his reconstruction persuaded him on May 8 to sign a document that FDR supposedly had approved but not signed. This recollection simply does not comport with Grew's record of the May 11 conversation with Truman in which Crowley "wanted to be sure that the President thoroughly understands the situation and that he will back us up and will keep everyone else out of it. He [Crowley] stated that we would be having difficulty with the Russians and he did not want them running all over town looking for help."[43] When this briefing is joined to Harriman's conversation with Truman on May 10, there can be no doubt that the president misrepresented responsibility for the decision. Certainly he made no effort to reprimand either Grew or Crowley for exceeding his instructions, an action that would have been consistent with his later account of the Lend–Lease decision.[44]

---

[39] See Campbell and Herring, eds., *Diaries of Edward R. Stettinius, Jr.*, pp. 357–58.

[40] For more detail, see Herring, *Aid to Russia*, pp. 202–03.

[41] On Truman's observation, see *Year of Decisions*, p. 255.

[42] On Clayton's explanation, see Herring, *Aid to Russia*, p. 206.

[43] Memorandum of conversation, May 11, 1945, Papers of Joseph C. Grew, Houghton Library, Conversations V. 7, 1945.

[44] This essential point is made in Stuart L. Weiss, *The President's Man: Leo Crowley and Franklin Roosevelt in Peace and War* (Carbondale, IL, 1996), p. 227. Weiss's treatment of this whole episode and Crowley's part in it is instructive.

This episode is yet another case, and a telling one at that, that reveals Truman's significant, even if understandable, limitations in policy making during his early weeks in office. Here, Truman relied on the counsel of his relevant advisers. He did so rather quickly and in a manner that might superficially appear as "decisive" but without personally probing the implications and consequences of the action. When the recommended course was implemented in such a way that stirred protest and criticism, he quickly reversed himself when advised to do so by Clayton and Harriman. The Lend–Lease case demonstrates a president struggling to grapple with the myriad issues he confronted and thoroughly dependent on advisers to chart a path forward. And it clarifies that this president lacked the perception to distinguish between the differing emphases on this issue of Harriman on the one hand and Grew and Crowley on the other. One can rightly sympathize with Truman in this circumstance, but one cannot avoid acknowledging his limitations. Assuredly during the first two weeks of May, the American leader felt like a man pulled in many directions, and his decision making reflected just that. Despite the notorious inability of historians to resist the temptation to impose order and coherence on the past, one must admit that Truman's policy making at this time was not guided by some thoughtful analysis and well-developed strategy. Some of his actions might be branded harsh on the Soviets, but others reflect a genuine effort to guarantee postwar cooperation. If there was any guiding theme, it remained Truman's uncomplicated desire to have all sides carry out their agreements.

By mid-May, however, the negative reverberations for Soviet-American relations of the Lend–Lease fiasco and the broader tensions in the relationship with the Soviet Union increasingly troubled the new president. His reservations with the more confrontational approach toward the Soviet Union forcefully advocated by both Churchill and Grew became more apparent. He increasingly expressed notable circumspection at the hard-line advice he had received to that point. The necessary question is why, and a good part of the answer lies in the influence which Joseph Davies exerted on Harry Truman.

The Emergence of Joseph Davies

Joseph Davies was a wealthy Washington lawyer who had married the heiress of the Post fortune. A Democrat, he had served as chair of the Federal Trade Commission and as FDR's second ambassador to Moscow from 1936 to 1938. There his support for Stalin's regime knew few bounds and gained him the undying enmity of subordinates like George Kennan and Charles Bohlen who later presented him as "a dupe of Stalinist propaganda and a disgrace to U.S. diplomacy."[45] But during the war, Davies's reputation with Roosevelt and with the American public had remained high. His best-selling book *Mission to Moscow* published in 1941 and the Warner Brothers popular movie of the same name released two years later made him a key supporter of Soviet-American amity. And, as already noted, Roosevelt continued to utilize Davies as an informal

---

[45] David Mayers, *The Ambassadors and America's Soviet Policy* (New York, 1995), p. 119.

go-between with the Soviets throughout the war in which role he constantly advocated conciliation and cooperation with his friends in Moscow. With the onset of the Cold War, as Davies's biographer has noted, he became "a subject of scorn and abuse" for his perceived naiveté and misjudgments.[46] A tendency developed to denigrate or deny his role in postwar policy making. He has been treated rather like some disgraced Soviet figure airbrushed out of official photos for fear his presence might contaminate the reputation of the remaining subjects. But any full understanding of Truman's foreign policy in the months before the Potsdam conference must leave Davies very much in the picture.

Davies had dined with Harry and Bess Truman at a dinner in the vice president's honor hosted by the French ambassador and his wife in February of 1945. At it, Truman asked Davies to come and see him to discuss Russia and told the ambassador that he had been "much impressed with 'Mission to Moscow.'" He even invited Davies to sit in his box to hear Roosevelt's message on his return from Yalta.[47] Davies failed to take up Truman's offer due to health worries that soon hospitalized him, but he wrote Truman on April 15 eagerly offering to brief him on "this Russian situation upon which Peace and our own future so much depends." Davies claimed to have exclusive knowledge on certain points, and he volunteered to share them with the president at any time or place.[48] Truman replied, quickly inviting Davies to come to discuss the Russian situation as soon as his health permitted and assuring Davies that he would need the help of "men with your knowledge and experience."[49] His eagerness to meet Davies was genuine.

Truman patiently waited for Davies to visit him, but when Molotov came to town, he took the initiative and contacted the friendly former ambassador. Davies lunched at the Soviet embassy on April 23 and listened attentively to Molotov's concerns. Around the time that Stettinius must have been priming Truman to speak to him bluntly, the Soviet foreign minister shared his fears "that differences of interpretations and possible complications would arise which could not occur if Roosevelt lived." Davies sought to reassure Molotov. He described Truman as "a practical-minded, thoroughly honest, and strong man" who would be fair and give due regard to the Soviet point of view.[50] At the time, of course, Davies had no knowledge of the forceful presentation being prepared for Molotov, and he remained in the dark about Truman's second meeting with the Soviet foreign minister until April 30 when he finally

---

[46] On Davies, see the thoughtful biography by Elizabeth Kimball MacLean, *Joseph E. Davies: Envoy to the Soviets* (Westport, CT, 1992). For the quotation see p. 2.

[47] Davies diary, February 28, 1945, Joseph E. Davies Papers, Library of Congress, Box 16. Davies judged Truman to be "a modest, direct and fine type of American."

[48] Davies to Truman, April 15, 1945, Joseph E. Davies Papers, Library of Congress, Box 16. Davies noted that "there are things with which I alone am familiar, and which you are entitled to know. They would be of value to you in assessing the situation before Foreign Minister Molotov arrives."

[49] Truman to Davies, April 19, 1945, Joseph E. Davies Papers, Library of Congress, Box 16.

[50] Davies journal, April 23, 1945, Joseph E. Davies Papers, Library of Congress, Box 16.

visited the president and received a firsthand account. Truman replayed for Davies how he had asked Molotov to live up to agreements made at Yalta on Poland and other matters. "I gave it to him straight. I let him have it," Truman summarized with characteristic embellishment. "It was the straight one-two to the jaw. I wanted him to know that our cooperation had to be two sided; and not 'a one sided street.'" He was standing by his commitments, and the Soviets should do likewise. "Did I do right?" the president then asked, in the manner of a novice wanting reassurance from an experienced hand. Davies thought not.

"As tactfully as possible," Davies confided to his diary, he conveyed his alarm to Truman and then provided a lengthy tutorial for the president on Soviet-American relations. Stalin and Roosevelt had understood each other, and, with Roosevelt alive, the Soviets "felt secure that all agreements would be performed according to their spirit as well as the letter." Davies then gave a vigorous defense of the Soviet position on Poland. "As a matter of physical security for their armies in Germany they could not and would not permit Polish leaders who hated Russia to be in a Government of a 'Strong Independent Poland.'" The Soviets, he explained, "were sticklers for reciprocity as between allies." They had gone along with the Anglo-American dealings with such suspect groups as the Vichy government in North Africa and with the Badoglio government in Italy because they saw that such arrangements were vital to the Allies. "In return," he continued, "they expected reasonable cooperation as regards their vital security when dealing with Poland and a hostile Polish Émigré Government in London." And Davies did not stop there. He introduced a range of other topics including the hostility toward the Soviet Union that pervaded the lower levels of the State Department and the futility of trying to compel Soviet concessions.

Truman heard Davies out and reacted with all the earnest concern of a hardworking but slow-witted student trying to get his lessons straight. He agreed the future peace depended on cooperation among Great Britain, the Soviet Union, and the United States. It was, after all, precisely this cooperation he had hoped to obtain by pressing Molotov. Seemingly a little confused, he asked the man who would serve as an important adviser for him over the next few months: "Well, what should be done? What can I do?" Such questions could not have been uttered sincerely by anyone who had decided to reverse Roosevelt's policy toward the Soviet Union and had adopted a new and tougher approach to the Soviet Union. They came forth from the mouth of a man struggling to grasp the issues involved and to determine in what foreign policy direction he should travel.

Advice flowed forth from Davies. Truman needed to command Soviet confidence in American "good will and fairness." He needed to meet Stalin face to face and assure him that the United States and Russia were "natural friends." The new president, furthermore, should "maintain the position which Roosevelt had achieved as the balance holding the scales between Britain and the USSR for the purpose of keeping the Peace." Like FDR he must prove to the

Soviets that the Americans and British were not "in 'cohoots' against them." To all this, Truman listened patiently and did not challenge any of the points raised. The ambassador concluded by admitting that his analysis might be wrong, but he was certain that "without unity of the Big Three, there would not be a Chinaman's [sic] chance for a peaceful world." In light of that, he argued persuasively and in a way that reflected the Rooseveltian view: "it was just plain horse sense to exhaust every possible means . . . to preserve that unity." Truman and Davies parted in a cordial manner, and notably the president asked that Davies call him when he had concerns.[51] It was an invitation that Davies could not resist.

Davies worried about the deterioration in Soviet-American relations as manifested not only by the Truman–Molotov exchange but also by the more public squabbling between the wartime allies at the San Francisco meeting over matters like the conference presidency and the seating of White Russia and the Ukraine. He fretted especially about the "rough treatment" Molotov was receiving at the UN gathering. If it continued, he determined, "the situation will deteriorate even more swiftly and possibly disastrously." He decided to do all he could "to keep the situation 'fluid and sweet.'"[52] He dispatched off a soothing letter to Molotov assuring him of his confidence that Truman "will find, with you, a way to solve matters in difference in the common interest of both peoples and the Peace of the world."[53] Davies worked assiduously on Truman in the second half of May so as to justify his own confidence. His initial lesson to Truman did not effect any dramatic intellectual conversion but left the new president grappling with the complexity of discerning how to fulfill Roosevelt's goals. It does seem, however, to have made him more wary of accepting the confrontational counsel of Churchill and Grew regarding the use of American troops. This wariness deepened because Davies's words were reinforced by the cautious military advice offered by General Marshall and Secretary Stimson.

The new president's emphasis on fulfilling agreements certainly led him, with the firm backing of his military team, to reject Winston Churchill's continuing effort to have the American and British forces remain in the advanced military positions achieved at the time of the German surrender until political differences had been resolved. The Anglo-American forces held a significant swath of territory within the German occupation zone assigned to the Soviets, and Churchill viewed this land as a key negotiating tool. On May 11, the British prime minister reached a fever pitch of anxiety warning that the withdrawal of Allied forces to the previously agreed occupation zones, and the subsequent "tide of Russian domination sweeping forward 120 miles on a front of 300 or 400 miles" constituted "an event which if it occurred, would be one of the most melancholy in history." The Anglo-American forces should stay in place, he argued in the exasperated tone of a master trying to explain a simple but

[51] Davies journal, April 30, 1945, Joseph E. Davies Papers, Library of Congress, Box 16.
[52] Davies diary, May 2, 1945, Joseph E. Davies Papers, Library of Congress, Box 16.
[53] Davies to Molotov, May 2, 1945, Joseph E. Davies Papers, Library of Congress, Box 16.

fundamental point to a dense pupil, "until we are satisfied about Poland and also about the temporary character of the Russian occupation of Germany," as well as the political future of the rest of Eastern Europe.[54] Churchill confided his genuine anguish to Eden and fretted bitterly to him about the danger of their armies melting away while the Russians maintained their powerful presence in Europe.[55] His fearful concern was such that he even ordered some contingency planning for a military conflict with the Soviet Union and speculated about the possibility of a third world war.[56] On May 12, he fired off another impassioned telegram to Truman complaining of American air force and army transfers from Europe to the Pacific theater. Warning again of the Soviet danger, he dramatically avowed in words that would gain more public note the following year – "an iron curtain is drawn down upon their front." For him, it was "vital now to come to an understanding with Russia, or see where we are with her, before we weaken our armies mortally or retire to the zones of occupation."[57]

Churchill specifically encouraged Truman to take a strong military stand against the occupation by Josip Broz Tito's Yugoslav forces of the province of Venezia Giulia, which surrounded the port city of Trieste. Tensions over this matter had reached a boiling point by May 10, and a clash of arms between the Yugoslavs and the Allied forces commanded by British General Harold Alexander seemed imminent. Joseph Grew, like Churchill, had urged a tough response to what was seen as Tito's menacing grab for territory.[58] Truman eventually authorized protest messages to Tito and to the Soviet Union. He proved, however, very hesitant, especially in contrast to Churchill, about authorizing military force in order to compel Tito's acknowledgment of Alexander's authority in the region. On the advice of his own military staff, Truman told

---

[54] Churchill to Truman, May 11, 1945, enclosing text of telegram he had sent to Eden on May 4, 1945, *FRUS: The Conference of Berlin (The Potsdam Conference), 1945*, I, pp. 6–7.

[55] In response to the announcement of plans for American troop withdrawals, he wrote Eden: "What are we to do? Great pressure will soon be put on us to demobilize partially. In a very short time our armies will have melted, but the Russians may remain with hundreds of divisions in possession of Europe from Lubeck to Trieste, and to the Greek frontier on the Adriatic." Churchill to Eden, May 11, 1945 (T. 875.5), Churchill Papers, Churchill Archives Center, Char 20/218.

[56] Churchill complained to Eden that the troop withdrawal matter and Russian ambitions were "far more vital than the amendments to a world constitution which may well never come into being till it is superseded after a period of appeasement by a third world war." Churchill to Eden, May 11, 1945 (T. 875.5), Churchill Papers, Churchill Archives Center, Char 20/218. For a rather racy journalistic report on Churchill's contingency planning for war with the Soviet Union, see Ben Fenton, "Churchill's Plan for Third World War against Soviet Union," *Daily Telegraph* (electronic edition), October 1, 1998. For more sober analysis, see John Keegan, "The West Had to Protect Itself," *Daily Telegraph* (electronic edition), October 1, 1998.

[57] Churchill to Truman, May 12, 1945, *FRUS: The Conference of Berlin (The Potsdam Conference), 1945*, I, pp. 8–9. For a sympathetic summary of Churchill's thinking and policies as the war came to an end, see Martin Gilbert, *Winston S. Churchill*, Vol. 8, *'Never Despair,' 1945–1965* (Boston, 1988), pp. 3–19.

[58] Grew to Truman, May 10, 1945, *FRUS, 1945*, IV, pp. 1151–53. On the Trieste matter, see the various correspondence and memoranda in *FRUS, 1945*, IV, pp. 1125–71.

Churchill on May 20 that "I must not have any avoidable interference with the re-deployment of American forces to the Pacific."[59] A partial backdown on Tito's part on May 21 took much of the explosive force from this matter, and negotiations meandered on into June with the Americans and the Soviets eventually cooperating in a settlement.[60] Truman's caution and his refusal to be swept away by Churchill's provocative blandishments had prevented an outbreak of fighting between Tito's and Alexander's forces.

Joseph Davies proved a crucial influence on Truman's following the more cautious and even conciliatory approach eventually pursued over Trieste. On May 10, Davies had written to James F. Byrnes beseeching him to return to Washington because the "Russian situation" was "deteriorating so rapidly that it is frightening."[61] Byrnes's continued absence from the capital, however, prompted Davies to seek to rescue the situation himself. On May 12, the very day the FEA vehemently implemented the Lend–Lease cutback, the former ambassador wrote a long letter to Truman, which he read to the president at a meeting at the White House the next day. He pointed to "the rapid deterioration in allied relations" since their last talk and declared that "it threatens to destroy the unity which made victory possible and which only can preserve the Peace which was restored." Davies disparaged any "get-tough" approach with the Russians as counterproductive and warned that any attempt to isolate the Soviet Union would be "disastrous." He called instead for some understanding of the Soviet point of view and for "tolerance and a spirit of 'give and take.'" In such a disposition, he argued, lay the only hope for improved relations between the two wartime allies.[62]

---

59 Truman to Churchill, May 20, 1945, *FRUS*, 1945, IV, pp. 1169–70. One should note that in addition to protesting Tito's actions Truman proved willing to simultaneously challenge and thwart the efforts of Charles de Gaulle and the French to seize the disputed Val d'Aosta region from Italy. Truman told French Foreign Minister Georges Bidault that France was "doing very much what Marshal Tito is doing in Venezia Giulia and in Trieste," and he pressured him to rectify the situation. Further threats to cut off supplies of military equipment and munitions to the French Army brought the French into line. See Grew memorandum of Truman–Bidault conversation, May 21, 1945; Grew to Caffery, June 6, 1945, enclosing Truman to de Gaulle, June 6, 1945; and Grew to Caffery, June 5, 1945, *FRUS*, 1945, IV, pp. 698–99, 734–35.

60 See Richard S. Dinardo, "Glimpse of an Old World Order? Reconsidering the Trieste Crisis of 1945," *Diplomatic History*, 21 (Summer 1997), pp. 365–81. One should note Dinardo's persuasive argument that "the Truman administration's response to the Trieste crisis, then, was less a preview of Cold War containment than an attempt to enforce a peculiarly American vision of a cooperative new world order. Although Truman said he wanted to throw Tito out of Trieste after being provoked by Grew's warning of Soviet aggression, he delayed and asked for Stalin's help over British protests. The president only lost his extreme reluctance to face down the Yugoslavs once Stalin's cooperation made him confident that this would be a step toward, rather than away from, a new consensual international system more akin to FDR's Four Policemen than to a traditional balance of power among armed antagonists." Also see Roberto G. Rabel, *Between East and West: Trieste, the United States, and the Cold War, 1941–1954* (Durham, NC, 1988), pp. 52–73.

61 Davies to Byrnes, May 10, 1945, Joseph E. Davies Papers, Library of Congress, Box 16.

62 Davies to Truman, May 12, 1945, Joseph E. Davies Papers, Library of Congress, Box 16. Davies had been urged to contact Truman by Supreme Court Justice Felix Frankfurter, who like Davies

Davies's May 13 meeting with Truman was of decisive importance. Still reeling from the uproar and criticism over his Lend–Lease order, Truman was in a receptive mood both to receive Davies's phone call at 4:00 P.M. on a Sunday afternoon and his expression of concern at the deterioration in relations with the Soviets. He told Davies in almost chameleon fashion that he too was concerned at the deterioration and asked him to come over to discuss the matter. The president received Davies in the family quarters where evidence of the Trumans' recent move across Pennsylvania Avenue from Blair House was still much in evidence. Before getting down to business, Truman introduced him to his "mama," whom the ambassador deemed a "dear old lady – 93 – bright as a 'squirrel' and 'All American!'" It happened to be Mother's Day and Truman enlisted Davies to join them for "family supper." Only after sharing these more private moments – and in the process quickly deepening Truman's regard for him – did Davies retire with the president to the library to address the issue that had brought Davies to the White House. There the committed Sovietophile voiced his concerns only to have Truman repeat that he too was "greatly worried" by the deterioration in relations with the Soviet Union. Davies read his letter and then at Truman's request provided a long briefing on the wartime relations of the major allies.

Davies made no effort to disguise his sympathies for the Soviet Union. The interpretation of events that he provided would have been contested strenuously by other close observers of the U.S.-Soviet relationship such as Ambassador Harriman or State Department specialists like George Kennan and Charles Bohlen. But Davies had gained access and now had Truman's ear. He volunteered to cable Stalin to try to soothe matters, an offer that Truman readily accepted. The president, in an approach imitating that of FDR, asked Davies if he might take on a full-time job for him and perhaps serve as an emissary to Moscow to arrange a meeting with Stalin, but Davies declined because of his doctor's orders. Whatever the poor state of Davies's health, the two men talked until nearly midnight, and this conversation stands as the most sustained briefing Truman had yet received on U.S.-Soviet relations. Truman listened intently, and in an obvious mark of his trust and regard for Davies, he recommended a "libation" as they concluded their discussion and they thereupon shared some scotch.[63] Davies had made real progress in swaying the president to his more accommodating perspective regarding the Soviet Union and effectively established himself as a key instructor for the student-president. Churchill, Grew, and Harriman had in different ways tried out for the role, but Davies increasingly played the part.

Davies also succeeded here in undermining Truman's confidence in the "get-tough" advice that he had received from officials like Grew and Harriman

considered the Lend–Lease cutbacks both "untimely and unwise." Davies diary, May 13, 1945, Joseph E. Davies Papers, Library of Congress, Box 16.

[63] Davies diary, May 13, 1945, and Davies journal, May 13, 1945, Joseph E. Davies Papers, Library of Congress, Box 16.

and that had blown up on him in the Lend–Lease imbroglio. At their May 13 meeting, the former ambassador blamed "the anti-Soviet bias of American officials" for much of the tension that had erupted at the San Francisco meeting and notably drew from Truman both agreement that such hostility existed and a promise to correct the situation. The president alerted Davies that Byrnes would soon be appointed secretary of state and implied that this would mean a State Department more attentive to the concerns Davies had voiced.[64] Truman seemed eager to pass the buck for the deterioration of relations with the Soviets to the State Department and to wash his hands of responsibility.

In the days after the Davies visit, Truman shared his concerns about his hard-line advisers with other visitors. On May 16, FDR's daughter Anna met with her father's successor and, as she later reported to Henry Wallace, learned from Truman "that all his advisers had urged him to be hard with the Russians." In reply to the one-time vice president's inquiry as to how Truman felt "this has worked out," she recounted that "the President now feels that it was a mistake."[65] Two days later, Wallace himself met with the man who had succeeded him as vice president and heard Truman express concern about the Russian situation. Wallace seized this entree and expressed the hope that the president "would not accept the representations made to him by the State Department without looking at them twice." Truman responded quickly that "he had no confidence in the State Department whatsoever and that he was going to get new leadership as soon as possible."[66] The president went on to inform the secretary of commerce of his belief that the Russians had not kept to the Yalta agreements, but indicative of his desire for further cooperation he listed as a key priority getting Russia into the war against Japan.

Presidential reservations about the State Department appear quite genuine.[67] Truman's possession of what Alonzo Hamby described as "an intense distrust of Foreign Service professionals, whom he considered a pretentious, self-contained elite" – the "striped pants boys" etc. – presumably dates from this time. As Hamby also notes, although Truman would be heavily dependent on State Department professionals for the making of his foreign policy, he remained quite suspicious of them.[68] At this early stage of his presidency, Truman began to distance himself from the State Department officials upon whom he had leaned

[64] Davies diary, May 13, 1945, and Davies journal, May 13, 1945, Joseph E. Davies Papers, Library of Congress, Box 16.

[65] Anna Boettiger quoted in Blum, ed., *Price of Vision*, p. 448.

[66] Blum, ed., *Price of Vision*, pp. 450–51.

[67] Truman told James Forrestal on June 13 that "there wasn't much material in the State Department to work with," and on June 1, after describing to Henry Morgenthau his difficulties in completing arrangements for the Big Three Conference, he complained that "you don't know how difficult the thing has been for me. Everybody around here that should know something about foreign affairs is out." Millis, ed., *Forrestal Diaries*, p. 62; Blum, ed., *From the Morgenthau Diaries*, Vol. 3, *Years of War*, pp. 460–61.

[68] Hamby, *Man of the People*, pp. 314–15.

so heavily in his first weeks in office. In the privacy of his own diary, he listed Cordell Hull, Joseph Davies, and Harry Hopkins as "our three ablest foreign relations men" and lamented the fact that they were now "old and physically incapacitated."[69] Truman's assessment of the three men was genuinely held and stands itself as an interesting commentary on his grasp of international matters – or lack thereof. In the ensuing weeks, he relied even more heavily on Davies and turned to both the former ambassador and to Harry Hopkins to undertake crucial missions for him. It must have seemed to dispassionate observers as if Truman merely mediated Roosevelt's strategy and tactics.

Hopkins to Moscow and Davies to London

Even though Davies had declined Truman's invitation to trek to Moscow to visit Stalin to arrange a Big Three meeting, he readily assumed the challenge of working on this matter through written communication. The day after his important May 13 meeting with the president, he utilized the facilities of the Soviet embassy in Washington to cable Stalin (through Molotov who had returned to Moscow), assuring the Soviet leader that if only he and Truman "could have a frank, personal, heart-to-heart talk, many of these matters which threaten misunderstandings could be cleared up."[70] On May 20, Molotov replied and indicated not only Stalin's enthusiasm for such a meeting but his request that it be held somewhere in the vicinity of Berlin. Molotov added a personal touch for the man emerging as an important link between the Soviet and American sides by congratulating Ambassador Davies on his award of the Order of Lenin, which had been announced the previous day in recognition of Davies's untiring efforts to strengthen Soviet-American relations, and which, from a Soviet perspective at least, was richly deserved.[71]

The newly honored Davies conveyed copies of his correspondence with Molotov – which had been conducted completely outside official American channels – to President Truman on May 21. Also, he again expressed his concern at the deterioration in U.S.-Soviet relations and advised "that the situation be kept fluid, and that it requires patience, tolerance, respect, and a spirit of accommodation in the interests of peace."[72] Truman called Davies to the White House for another lengthy, late-night session that very day, and there Davies learned how influential his briefing on May 13 had been and how Truman had set the wheels in motion to send FDR's most trusted aide, Harry Hopkins, as an envoy to Stalin. The president explained how when Davies himself had declined his invitation to travel to meet Stalin because of his ill health, he decided to

[69] Truman diary, May 22, 1945, in Ferrell, ed., *Off the Record*, p. 35.
[70] Davies to Stalin (through Molotov), May 14, 1945, Joseph E. Davies Papers, Library of Congress, Box 17.
[71] Molotov to Davies, May 20, 1945, Joseph E. Davies Papers, Library of Congress, Box 16.
[72] Davies to Truman, May 21, 1945, Joseph E. Davies Papers, Library of Congress, Box 17.

accept a suggestion from Averell Harriman that Hopkins be dispatched to visit the Soviet leader.[73] Clearly the president intended to initiate efforts to solve some of the difficulties that bedeviled U.S.-Soviet relations. Breaking the logjam on the Polish issue held special importance as this troubling matter overshadowed the San Francisco deliberations on the new world organization.[74]

The proposal to send Hopkins to see Stalin had its origins in a conversation that Harriman had with Charles Bohlen as they flew back to Washington from the San Francisco meeting on May 10.[75] On their arrival in D.C., they visited Hopkins at his Georgetown home and presented this suggestion to him. Hopkins looked as sick as ever, but "the mere intimation of a flight to Moscow converted him into the traditional old fire horse at the sound of the alarm."[76] Hopkins despondently thought, however, that Truman would never agree to the proposal that Harriman presented to the president soon thereafter. Truman, in fact, initially proved hesitant and instead explored the possibility of sending Davies to Moscow. When Davies declined, he retrieved Harriman's suggestion and asked both Cordell Hull, whom he respected greatly, and Jimmy Byrnes for their views. Byrnes opposed the mission, but Hull assured Truman that Hopkins was an "excellent choice."[77] FDR's long-serving and much-ignored secretary of state also took the occasion provided by Truman's May 17 visit to his room at the Bethesda Naval Medical Center to express views that validated those offered by Davies. "Peace was impossible without Russia," he reportedly told the president, but "if the Russians trusted us, they would cooperate for world Peace." Displaying an admirable quotient of gullibility, he reassured the president that differences could be resolved "if handled with tolerance, patience and consideration." This after all "was what statecraft was for."[78]

Truman preferred Hull's advice over Byrnes's, but surprisingly he sought specific confirmation of Hopkins's integrity and loyalty. There is no evidence that the president already had received any briefings on Hopkins's wartime

---

[73] Truman diary, May 22, 1945, in Ferrell, ed., *Off the Record*, p. 35.

[74] For further details, see Schlesinger, *Act of Creation*, p. 170.

[75] Prior to producing the idea to approach Hopkins, Harriman had revived with Stettinius and Eden in a meeting on May 9 the possibility of his returning for discussions with the London Poles and then subsequently with Stalin in Moscow in hopes of making some progress on the Polish issue. According to Eden's report to Churchill on the meeting, "Mr. Harriman admitted that the prospects of any agreement being reached by this means were now slender, but he argued that Marshal Stalin was likely to be more open to argument than M. Molotov and that it might at any rate be possible to narrow down our differences to some extent preparatory to a meeting between Marshall Stalin, the President and yourself." Eden to Churchill, May 9, 1945 (No. 222), Avon Papers, Main Library Special Collections, University of Birmingham, 20/13/214.

[76] Sherwood, *Roosevelt and Hopkins*, pp. 885–87.

[77] Truman, *Year of Decisions*, p. 287. In his memoirs, Truman suggests that he first approached Hopkins on this mission on May 4, but his timing is quite incorrect here. Also see Ferrell, ed., *Off the Record*, p. 30.

[78] On the date of the visit, see Appointment Sheet, May 17, 1945, in Ferrell, ed., *Off the Record*, p. 27. For Davies recording of Hull's recollections of what he told Truman, see Davies journal, May 22, 1945, Joseph E. Davies Papers, Library of Congress, Box 17.

relationship with the NKVD agent Iskhak Akhmerov, which later led to the accusation that he served as "an unconscious rather than a conscious agent" for the Soviet Union, but perhaps he had been warned that Hopkins was too close to the Soviets.[79] However that may be, Truman sloughed off any concerns and assured himself in his irregularly kept diary that Hopkins was "perfectly loyal and his integrity was beyond question."[80] He requested that Hopkins take on the mission and gained a ready assent from FDR's closest confidante.

Truman informed Stalin on May 19 that Hopkins would join Ambassador Harriman on his return to Moscow in order to engage in broad-based discussions on U.S.-Soviet relations.[81] The same day, Truman met with Hopkins and briefed him on his mission. Returning to a familiar theme, Truman explained that he "was anxious to have a fair understanding with the Russian Government." This should be grounded in the carrying out of their existing commitments and agreements, although, indicative of Davies's influence, Truman seemed willing to accept some sort of face-saving arrangement rather than to hold out for any genuinely democratic settlement.[82] Truman provided Hopkins with real leeway on tactics suggesting that he "could use diplomatic language, or he could use a baseball bat" as he deemed proper. He indicated his willingness to meet Stalin and his preference to entertain him in the United States.[83] This hardly constituted a diplomatic briefing worthy of Metternich, but Hopkins appreciated well that Truman had tasked him with the responsibility to navigate U.S.-Soviet relations away from the turbulence that recently had rocked them and to move back onto a more even keel.[84]

---

[79] On this accusation (also mentioned in Chapter 2) and on the possible warning, see Andrew and Gordievsky, *KGB*, pp. 287, 349.

[80] Notes on Appointment Sheet, May 19, 1945, in Ferrell, ed., *Off the Record*, p. 31.

[81] Truman to Stalin, May 19, 1945, *FRUS: The Conference of Berlin (The Potsdam Conference), 1945*, I, pp. 21–22.

[82] Truman recalled his instruction to Hopkins in a note he wrote on May 23 where he recalled telling his delegate to "make it clear to Uncle Joe Stalin that I knew what I wanted – and that I intended to get it – peace for the world for at least 90 years. That Poland, Rumania, Bulgaria, Czeckoslovakia [sic], Austria, Yugo-Slavia, Latvia, Lithuania, Estonia, et al. made no difference to U.S. interests only so far as World Peace is concerned. That Poland ought to have 'free elections,' at least as free as [Frank] Hague, Tom Pendergast, Joe Martin or [Robert] Taft would allow in their respective bailiwicks. That Tito should be restrained at Trieste and Pela and Uncle Joe should make some sort of gesture – whether he means it or not to keep before our public that he intends to keep his word. Any smart political boss will do that." Memo, May 23, 1945, Truman Longhand Notes – Presidential File, Harry S. Truman Papers: President's Secretary's File, HSTL, Box 281. (Special thanks to Archivist Randy Sowell for assisting me to gain access to this document.) Also see the discussion of it in Robert L. Messer, *The End of the Alliance: James F. Byrnes, Roosevelt, Truman, and the Origins of the Cold War* (Chapel Hill, NC, 1982), p. 82. Clearly Truman thought of Stalin as a "political boss." Hamby, *Man of the People*, p. 320, addresses this matter.

[83] Notes on Appointment Sheet, May 19, 1945, in Ferrell, ed., *Off the Record*, p. 31.

[84] The British ambassador in Washington, Lord Halifax, caught something of Truman's purpose when he gave as "background reasons" for the Hopkins mission the "acute nervousness in responsible circles and amongst the public generally" in the United States over "the accumulating signs of difficulties with the Soviet Union." He explained that "the question was being asked

Truman quickly worked himself into a state of optimism regarding the prospects for the Hopkins mission. On May 23, he told Stettinius "that he had great confidence that Harry would be able to straighten things out with Stalin." In a manner suggesting that he considered that the issues dividing the United States and the Soviets were hardly intractable, he expressed his hopes to his lame-duck secretary of state "that the Hopkins mission was going to unravel a great many things and that by the time he met with the Big Three that most of our troubles would be out of the way."[85] Truman's optimism for improved Big Three relations was heightened by his companion decision to send Joseph Davies on a parallel mission to visit Winston Churchill.

The Davies mission grew out of Truman's discussion with the former ambassador on the evening of May 21, and it serves as a striking exemplar of both the influence that Davies exerted over Truman at this time and the ad hoc quality of Truman's decision making. According to Truman's own contemporary account, after he revealed his plan to send Hopkins to see the Soviet leader, he mentioned that he "was having as much difficulty with Prime Minister Churchill as he was with Stalin" but he "had no messenger" to send to him. Davies quickly overcame his health concerns and volunteered for the mission. He even went so far as to suggest "that if he could talk to Churchill he could make him see the light."[86] This light presumably meant adopting a more accommodating posture toward the Soviet Union. Certainly this is implied by Admiral Leahy's later observation that the Davies mission resulted from a fear that Churchill, deeply bitter at Soviet behavior, "might take some precipitate action that could seriously endanger the unity of the Big Three – which was so necessary to the achievement of any kind of permanent peace."[87] Davies aimed to prevent such an action.

Persuading Churchill to "see the light" as defined by Joseph Davies appears to have been the principal purpose of this mission. Truman hardly needed to dispatch another messenger to the British leader. Just days before, he authorized Ambassador Harriman to visit Churchill on his return trip to Moscow, but a Harriman briefing for the prime minister apparently sufficed no longer. Elizabeth Kimball MacLean rightly has noted that the experienced ambassador

whether Mr. Roosevelt's grand design is not in the process of evaporation from lack of initiative." Halifax continued that "this state of mind has even led so temperate a journalist as Walter Lippmann to argue that Britain is making too much running with the USSR and to advocate a return to the President's alleged role as mediator." See Halifax to Foreign Office, May 23, 1945 (No. 3602), Eden: Foreign Secretary Papers, Main Library Special Collections, University of Birmingham, FO 954, Vol. 30, Folio 771, US/45/119. For details of the concerns of elite liberal opinion at the deterioration in U.S.–Soviet relations, see Woods and Jones, *Dawning of the Cold War*, pp. 51–52.

85 Campbell and Herring, eds. *Diaries of Edward R. Stettinius*, p. 378.

86 Truman diary, May 22, 1945, in Ferrell, ed., *Off the Record*, p. 35. In Davies's recollection of the meeting, he reports that the president asked him "to secure agreement from Churchill that Truman and Stalin have an opportunity to size each other up before this [Big Three] meeting." Davies diary, May 21, 1945, Joseph E. Davies Papers, Library of Congress, Box 17.

87 Leahy, *I Was There*, pp. 369–70.

"understandably was insulted by Truman's decision to have Davies confer with Churchill immediately following his own visit."[88] Harriman's residual bitterness emerged forcefully in his later recollection that Truman's dispatching Davies to England "was one of the few gauche things Truman did during those first weeks in office."[89] Suggestions that Truman sent Davies to London simply to balance the Hopkins trip to Moscow or that he decided to send "a friend of Stalin's to see Churchill and a friend of Churchill's to see Stalin" impute too much deliberation to the genesis of the Davies mission.[90] These were subsequent glosses on the two missions. In deciding to send Davies to Churchill, Truman gave little apparent consideration to how the British prime minister might receive the recent recipient of a high Soviet honor. Nor did he worry much about the likely impact on U.S.-British relations, which suffered increasing strain and tension.[91] Truman lacked the sophistication and subtlety of thought to consider such matters. On May 22, he simply informed the prime minister of his plan to send Davies to London where he suggested his emissary would explore a number of matters he preferred not to handle by cable.[92] Churchill was left to ponder what these might be.

Insights into Harry Truman's amateurish thinking at this time can be gleaned from the observations he hurriedly entered on the pages of his appointment sheets and his diary. Some of his reflections seem confused to put it kindly. What should one make of his observation concerning Stalin and Churchill "that each of them was [trying to make me] THE PAW OF THE CAT to pull the chestnuts out of the fire and if there was going to be any cat's paw I was going to be the paw and not the cat."[93] Perhaps there is some glimpse here of his prepresidential view that the United States would be the decisive power in determining the direction of the international system and consequently that he could not take second place to either Churchill or Stalin but who could be sure? Truman's views are more readily discernible in his diary entry on May 22 written the day after he met with Davies and asked him to go to London. Here he deduced for his own benefit that "to have a reasonably lasting peace the three great powers must be able to trust each other and they must honestly want it." Demonstrating the deep commitment to postwar peace that had guided his internationalist efforts as a senator he confided to his diary: "I want peace and I'm willing to

---

[88] MacLean, *Joseph E. Davies*, p. 142.

[89] Harriman and Abel, *Special Envoy to Churchill and Stalin*, p. 459.

[90] This was Davies's subsequent explanation. See Davies journal, May 22, 1945, Joseph E. Davies Papers, Library of Congress, Box 17.

[91] On the increasingly strained relations, see Larres, *Churchill's Cold War*, pp. 96–99. Larres notes here (p. 97) that Truman did not do Churchill the courtesy of informing him in advance of Hopkins's mission to Stalin.

[92] Truman to Churchill, May 22, 1945, FRUS: *The Conference of Berlin (The Potsdam Conference)*, 1945, I, p. 63.

[93] Appointment Sheet, May 19, 1945, in Ferrell, ed., *Off the Record*, p. 32. (Emphasis in original.) The bracketed insertion in the quotation was suggested by Margaret Truman in her *Harry S. Truman* (New York, 1973), p. 253. It helps make some sense of her father's comment.

fight for it." Then, with his recent decisions to dispatch Hopkins and Davies as his envoys clearly in mind, he optimistically opined that "we'll get it."[94] The American president still deeply desired peace and hoped for good relations with both of the allies who had proved troublesome in his first months in office. He relied on Davies and Hopkins to restore them to a more harmonious state.

Truman's decision to send Davies to London caught the State Department completely by surprise. Certain State Department officials tried to delay the announcement of the Davies mission and to de-couple it in the public mind from that of Hopkins. But the White House press team of Steve Early and Charlie Ross rejected their entreaties in order, so Davies recalled, "to make it clear that the President was 'driving,' directing the job even-handedly, and sending envoys to both [Stalin and Churchill]."[95] Truman backed them up over the State Department's objection, and details of the two missions were announced publicly on May 23. The envoys left just days later. In the intervening time, Joseph Davies injected himself ever more deeply into what passed for a policy-making process. He received briefings from Admiral Leahy on highly classified Map Room correspondence. He consulted at length with Cordell Hull and Harry Hopkins and, in what was becoming a regular practice, had another lengthy session with Truman in the second-floor study of the White House on May 23.[96] Davies influence now reached its height, and it was by no means exhausted quickly.

Davies and Churchill

The Davies mission to London has for the most part received rather perfunctory treatment at the hands of historians. Eager to track the U.S.-Soviet relationship as a prelude to explaining the origins of the Cold War, they have skated quickly by the Davies–Churchill meeting and attended more closely to the Hopkins–Stalin exchange.[97] Davies's diplomatic exertions are treated essentially as a distraction away from the central story. But this is not how they appeared at the time, and a proper understanding of American foreign policy in mid-1945 requires an examination of this mission to London. It sheds light not only on how Truman viewed Churchill and the British but also suggests his broad foreign policy direction.

Davies flew to England on May 25 armed with a handwritten letter from Truman assuring Churchill that his emissary held his confidence and encouraging the prime minister to "talk freely and frankly to him, as you would to

---

94 Diary, May 22, 1945, in Ferrell, ed., *Off the Record*, p. 35.

95 Davies journal, May 22, 1945, Joseph E. Davies Papers, Library of Congress, Box 17.

96 Davies journal, May 22, 1945, Joseph E. Davies Papers, Library of Congress, Box 17; and diary entry, May 23, 1945, Joseph E. Davies Papers, Library of Congress, Box 17.

97 A notable exception is Elizabeth Kimball MacLean who provides a competent account of the Davies mission in her *Joseph E. Davies*, pp. 143–49.

me."[98] The garrulous British leader called Davies on the evening of his arrival and invited him to spend the weekend at Chequers, the prime minister's country residence. Davies gladly accepted with the proviso that he be allowed to retire by midnight in light of his doctor's orders. The prime minister, who had spent the day campaigning for the upcoming British elections, welcomed Davies to Chequers for dinner on May 26, but it was not until 11:00 P.M. that the two men began their serious conversation in Churchill's little sitting room. There, as Davies later reported in writing to Truman, he explained that the president "was gravely concerned over the serious deterioration in the relations of the Soviets with both Britain and the United States." In familiar mode, he instructed Churchill that without Big Three unity "there could be no reasonable prospects for peace." Truman's representative noted the American interest in a Big Three meeting and clarified that it "should be directed to securing a meeting of the minds." He also introduced the possibility of Truman's meeting Stalin prior to any tripartite conference to allow the American leader to develop a personal relationship with his Soviet opposite. Davies reported that Truman would support every agreement made by President Roosevelt, that he wanted "differences of opinion . . . cleared up," and that he desired "clear understandings" for such "new decisions" as were required. The United States would fulfill its obligations, and the American leader "would confidently expect the same from associated governments."[99]

The British leader, whose blood was no doubt warmed by both his earlier political campaigning and his uninhibited dinner drinking, had a quite different approach to matters. Like a volcano erupting, he launched into a "bitter denunciation of Russia," which he saw as a threat to the security and freedom of Europe. He revealed his basic policy as cooperation with the United States and repeated his warnings of the "grave dangers" that would result from the withdrawal of American troops. He saved his utmost ire for the suggestion from Davies of a separate meeting between the Soviet and American leaders from which he would be excluded.

Davies held his ground against the force and emotion of Churchill's criticism and in turn proceeded to lecture and challenge the British statesman on his implication that the Americans might deal behind his back and on his castigation of the Soviets. He even compared Churchill's viewpoint to the "old shred-bare arguments" of Goebbels and Hitler that "Europe had to be saved from the Bolsheviks and the communist menace; that they could not be trusted etc. etc." He tartly queried if Churchill felt he "had bet on the wrong horse" by

---

[98] Copy of Truman to Churchill, May 23, 1945, Joseph E. Davies Papers, Library of Congress, Box 17.

[99] For Davies's written report see Davies to Truman, June 12, 1945, *FRUS: The Conference of Berlin (The Potsdam Conference), 1945*, I, pp. 64–65. The substance of Davies comments are captured in the aide-memoire he prepared for Churchill, May 29, 1945, Joseph E. Davies Papers, Library of Congress, Box 17. See also "Topical Notes on Conferences with Prime Minister Churchill," June 3, 1945, Joseph E. Davies Papers, Library of Congress, Box 17.

allying with the Soviets against the Nazis. Davies later recalled that Churchill "pulled no punches – neither did I." That Britain's great war leader – the same one who had roused his nation to fight on against Germany when the situation seemed so hopeless and at the very time when Stalin had joined a pact with Hitler and the United States maintained its neutral stance – kept something approaching his calm through this exchange is testimony to a self-control rarely noted of him. But he did, and late in their exchange, he settled for a brandy and ordered a special nutritious soup for Davies. Around four in the morning he personally escorted Davies to his bedroom and patronizingly bid good night to "the great American Envoy." Davies, perhaps more sincerely, returned the greeting to "the greatest Englishman of all time."[100]

Despite the elaborate cordiality of their farewell, neither Churchill nor Davies had convinced the other, and each remained suspicious of the other's purpose. Davies feared that "the great architect for victory in the fighting will annihilate the Peace."[101] The prime minister, quite possibly wondering whether his conversation with Davies could have been as bad as he remembered, called the envoy to his bedroom at eleven o'clock on Sunday morning. Still in bed and wearing his dressing gown, Churchill began a second round of essentially the same conversation. Again Davies heard of Churchill's concern at the likely withdrawal of American troops from Europe and again he faced the Englishman's objection to any bilateral meeting that excluded him. Davies heard even more from Churchill throughout the day. His visit to Chequers ended with dinner at which he recalled that the talk consisted of a Churchillian "monologue berating the Russians."[102]

Churchill refused to limit himself to the spoken word. After consulting with Eden, who considered Davies a "vain amateur" and who recalled that Churchill "reacted violently" against Davies proposal of a separate Stalin–Truman meeting, the prime minister drafted a formal minute, which he gave to Truman's chosen messenger.[103] It emphasized that "the representatives of His Majesty's Government would not be able to attend any meeting except as equal partners from its opening." It also attempted some elementary instruction for Davies by noting that Britain and the United States were united by the common ideology of freedom while the "Soviet Government have a different philosophy, namely, Communism, and use to the full the methods of police government, which they are applying in every State which has fallen a victim to their liberating arms."

---

[100] Diary, May 26, 1945, Joseph E. Davies Papers, Library of Congress, Box 17. (This reworked entry is titled "Churchill reverts to Type.")

[101] Joseph E. Davies, "Weekend at Chequers," Joseph E. Davies Papers, Library of Congress, Box 17.

[102] Diary, May 27, 1945, Joseph E. Davies Papers, Library of Congress, Box 17.

[103] Eden, *The Reckoning*, p. 623. After his own meeting with Davies, Eden described him as "the born appeaser [who] would gladly give Russia all Europe, except perhaps us, so that America might not be embroiled." For good measure, he brutally but accurately added: "All the errors and illusions of Neville C[hamberlain], substituting Russia for Germany." *The Reckoning*, p. 624.

Churchill could not abide the equating of Britain and Russia as "just two for-eign Powers, six of one and half a dozen of the other, with whom the troubles of the late war have to be adjusted." Such talk savagely challenged his deeply held convictions concerning a special Anglo-American relationship. While express-ing his hope for "real friendship" with Russia, he outlined a long list of nations whose "independence and domestic liberties" were threatened by the advance of the Red Army. Such realities could not be ignored out of a "desire to placate the imperialistic demands of Soviet Communist Russia."[104] Davies remained unmoved by Churchill's acute insights which retain their force well over a half century later and contrast so starkly to the woolly-headed quality of much American thinking. Little wonder that Churchill developed a passionate dislike for Davies and confided to associates that "he needed a bath in order to get rid of the ooze and slime" accumulated from associating with this American.[105]

Churchill also attempted to communicate some of his concerns directly to Truman. On May 31, he cabled the president and stated emphatically that "I should not be prepared to attend a meeting which was a continuation of a con-ference between you and Marshall Stalin." He made clear that "at this Victory Meeting, at which subjects of the gravest consequence are to be discussed, we three should meet simultaneously and on equal terms."[106] At this time, as his biographer has noted "the Soviet threat was uppermost in Churchill's mind. As in the pre-war years, he was convinced that a weak policy would only encour-age the use and triumph of force."[107] He shared his concerns with associates like Eden and South African Prime Minister J. C. Smuts advising the latter on May 28 "that any sign that we can be bluffed and pushed about would have a deadly effect upon the future of Europe, which I regard with as much anxiety as I did before the outbreak of the war."[108] His intensive efforts to rouse American officialdom had produced little.

Truman recalled that Churchill's cable puzzled him so he waited for Davies to return to report on his mission before addressing it. His reliance on his adviser's counsel assuredly added to his hesitation. The president later claimed that Davies's suggestion that he preferred a separate meeting, with Stalin had been misunderstood. All he had sought was the chance to visit with both the Soviet and British leaders before the formal tripartite meetings began.[109] This

---

[104] "Note by the Prime Minister on Mr. Davies's Message," May 27, 1945, attached to Churchill to Eden, May 28, 1945 (M.529/5), Churchill Papers, Char 20/209. Davies maintains that Churchill did not give him this aide-memoire, although he must surely have conveyed its contents to the ambassador in their final meeting.

[105] For Churchill's remarks on Davies, see Kenneth Young, ed., *The Diaries of Sir Robert Bruce Lockhart, 1939–1965* (London, 1980), p. 443, quoted in David Carlton, *Churchill and the Soviet Union*, p. 140.

[106] Prime Minister to President, No. 60, Prime Minister's Personal Telegram, T.1027/5 Personal and Top Secret, May 31, 1945, Churchill Papers, Churchill Archive Center, Char 20/220.

[107] Martin Gilbert, *Winston S. Churchill*, Vol. 8, *'Never Despair,'* 1945–1965, p. 26.

[108] Prime Minister's Personal Telegram, T. 1008/5, No. 284 to San Francisco, "Top Secret and Personal," May 28, 1945, Churchill Papers, Churchill Archive Center, Char 20/220.

[109] Truman, *Year of Decisions*, pp. 289–91.

tends to put a very favorable gloss on his own involvement in Davies's attempt to arrange a separate meeting and it does not completely comport with the facts. It appears to be the fall-back position that the president seized on when Davies later reported to him that Churchill objected so strenuously to what he had proposed.[110]

In the meantime, as Truman waited for the return of his envoy, he seemed perfectly content to take a break from his intense focus on international affairs. He proved quite untroubled that Davies did not communicate with him during his mission in London and relished the chance to direct his efforts to the domestic scene where he felt much more comfortable. He gave some attention to budget matters and also made some changes to the Cabinet he inherited from FDR. He selected Tom C. Clark to replace Francis Biddle as attorney general, Lewis B. Schwellenbach to succeed Frances Perkins as secretary of labor, and Clinton Anderson to follow Claude W. Wickard as secretary of agriculture. He even found a little time to enjoy himself with games of poker, shots of bourbon, and rounds of wisecracking with cronies like George Allen, Ed McKim, John Snyder, Harry Vaughan, and J. K. Vardaman – men who placed few serious demands upon him.[111] His spirits rose and he even considered that his fledgling presidency was off to a good start, confiding to his diary that "no one was ever luckier than I've been since becoming the Chief Executive and Commander in Chief. Things have gone so well that I can't understand it – except to attribute it to God."[112] He certainly saw Davies and Hopkins who were calming his foreign policy and laying the groundwork for a Big Three meeting as answers to his prayers.

Davies returned from England on June 3 and reported to the White House the next day. Indicative of the high regard in which Truman held him, he joined the president for breakfast on the White House porch, spent the day catching up on the top secret cable traffic in the Map Room, dined with Truman and Admiral Leahy, and then met with the president alone until 10:15 P.M.[113] The next day he gave a full oral report on his mission to Truman and Admiral Leahy and unofficial secretary of state designate Byrnes.[114] Truman heartily endorsed Davies's efforts and later recalled that Davies "had represented my position and the policy of the United States with accuracy, carrying out instructions with exceptional skill." Truman, however, also fancifully claimed in his memoirs that he had interrupted Davies during his report when the envoy had recounted Churchill's warnings about the dire consequences of precipitous American troop withdrawals from Europe. He remembers telling Davies that he would not

---

[110] Elizabeth Kimball MacLean discussed this matter well in her *Joseph E. Davies*, p. 147.

[111] On his relaxation with his friends, see for example diary entry, May 30, 1945, in Ferrell, ed., *Off the Record*, pp. 38–39.

[112] Diary entry, May 27, 1945, in Ferrell, ed., *Off the Record*, pp. 37–38.

[113] Diary entry, June 4, 1945, Joseph E. Davies Papers, Library of Congress, Box 17.

[114] Concerning the oral report, see Truman, *Year of Decisions*, pp. 290–91; and Leahy, *I Was There*, pp. 378–80.

leave Europe at the mercy of the Red Army. Rather, "we would withdraw only the troops we could spare from Europe for our war in the Pacific. We were committed to the rehabilitation of Europe, and there was to be no abandonment this time."[115] Such a recollection in his memoirs, written in the midst of the Cold War, associated Truman more closely to the stance adopted in May–June of 1945 by Churchill. But at that time Truman, coached by Davies, and Churchill stood apart in their approach to the Soviet Union and their outlook as to the requirements to forge a lasting peace.

Churchill, the despiser of tyranny whether it be of a fascist or communist hue, wanted to stand up to the Soviet domination of Eastern Europe, already taking form in Poland and beyond. Truman, however, bore no desire to force or precipitate any conflict or confrontation with the Soviets. He wanted divisive issues settled, and he desired to obtain Soviet cooperation generally in the postwar world order and the specific assistance of Stalin and his armies in the Pacific War. Truman and his advisers like Davies and Leahy feared that Churchill's actions would endanger the unity of the Big Three and the prospects for permanent peace. Truman worked through May and June as a cautious brake on Churchill's seemingly provocative and confrontational proposals. And, the American leader conscientiously avoided appearing any closer to the British prime minister than he did to the Soviet dictator. There would be no suggestion of Anglo-American "ganging-up." In fact, Truman shared something of FDR's suspicions of Britain's desire to protect its imperial interests and he had nothing of the high personal regard for Churchill which he later developed following Churchill's visit to the United States in 1946.

Little wonder that Churchill later admitted to Truman that he held him "in very low regard" in the period up to the Potsdam conference. Churchill later lauded Truman as the one, who "more than any other man, [had] saved Western civilization" in the postwar period; nevertheless, he couldn't refrain from gently criticizing Truman's efforts in his first months in office.[116] In his memoirs, he excused Truman's performance on the basis of the limited information available to him and observed "that everything that we have learnt about him since shows him to be a resolute and fearless man, capable of taking the greatest decisions. In these early months his position was one of extreme difficulty, and did not enable him to bring his outstanding qualities into action."[117] Harry Truman later reveled in the praise bestowed on him and his actions by Winston Churchill, but in 1945 he exhibited no desire to garner it. He consciously pursued a quite different agenda from the British prime minister. Joseph Davies had made this clear in London, and Harry Hopkins simultaneously did the same in Moscow.

---

[115] Truman, *Year of Decisions*, pp. 291–92. There is no credible contemporary evidence for this.

[116] Churchill quoted in Robert H. Ferrell, *Harry S. Truman and the Modern Presidency* (Boston, 1983), p. 188.

[117] Churchill, *Triumph and Tragedy*, p. 480.

Hopkins and Stalin

Like Joseph Davies, Harry Hopkins left Washington on May 23. He traveled first to Paris, in the company of his wife Louise and Charles Bohlen of the State Department. Averell Harriman joined them there, and after lunching with General Eisenhower, the party flew straight across Germany and on to Moscow. Observing the ruins of Berlin from the air, Hopkins remarked: "It's another Carthage."[118] On arrival in the Russian capital, however, Truman's envoy focused his attention not on the defeated foe but on improving relations with the powerful wartime ally that had wrecked such devastation on the Nazi foe. Hopkins had visited Stalin in July of 1941 at the moment of greatest danger for the Soviets when their survival against the Nazi onslaught was seriously questioned. He had been at Roosevelt's side at both Teheran and Yalta, and he brought a reputation as a firm supporter of Soviet-American amity. He certainly would have included himself in the group he described to Stalin "as the friends of Roosevelt's policy and of the Soviet Union [who] were alarmed and worried at the present trend of events." When he first met the Soviet leader on the evening of May 26, he explained that this sympathetic group feared "that if present trends continued unchecked the entire structure of world co-operation and relations with the Soviet Union which President Roosevelt and the Marshal had labored so hard to build would be destroyed."[119] He had come to prevent this and to reverse the harmful trends in the U.S.-Soviet relationship. No other person was so well equipped to do so.

At their initial meeting, Hopkins sincerely assured the Soviet leader of the new American president's "desire to continue President Roosevelt's policy of working with the Soviet Union and his intention to carry out in fact as well as in spirit all the arrangements, both formal and informal that President Roosevelt and Marshal Stalin had worked out together."[120] Such assurances of continuity along with Hopkins's solicitous approach and his irreproachable reputation for friendship toward the Soviet Union guaranteed that his various exchanges with Stalin were conducted in what Harriman described as an atmosphere of "extraordinary candor and rare good feeling."[121] Hopkins led off with a survey of the various issues that he wanted to address – among them Truman's desire to meet Stalin, the establishment of a Control Council for Germany, matters related to the Pacific War and Russia's entry to it, and the future of relations between the United States and the Soviet Union with China. But he focused on the Polish question and explained to Stalin that "the deterioration in public

---

[118] Sherwood, *Roosevelt and Hopkins*, p. 887.

[119] Bohlen memorandum, Hopkins–Stalin conversation, May 26, 1945, *FRUS: The Conference of Berlin (The Potsdam Conference), 1945*, I, pp. 26–27. The published accounts of Hopkins's conversations with Stalin may be complemented by Hopkins own reports of his meetings found in Harry L. Hopkins, Papers, FDRL, Box 338.

[120] Bohlen memorandum, first Hopkins–Stalin conversation, May 26, 1945, *FRUS: The Conference of Berlin (The Potsdam Conference), 1945*, I, p. 27.

[121] Harriman and Abel, *Special Envoy to Churchill and Stalin*, p. 463.

opinion in regard to our relations with the Soviet Union has been centered in our ability to carry into effect the Yalta Agreement on Poland."[122] Finding a compromise solution on this question and removing it as a bone in the throat of U.S.-Soviet relations proved to be Hopkins's main objective in Moscow.

At their second meeting held on the following evening, Hopkins invited Stalin to introduce the issues concerning the United States that worried him. The Soviet leader deftly raised the "impression" that existed within "Soviet governmental circles" that "the American attitude towards the Soviet Union had perceptibly cooled once it became obvious that Germany was defeated, and that it was as though the Americans were saying that the Russians were no longer needed." Stalin then proceeded to specify his complaint and referred to episodes like Argentina's admission to the new world organization, the harsh manner in which Lend–Lease support had been curtailed, and "the attitude of the United States Government towards the Polish question." Hopkins with Harriman's assistance addressed most of the matters raised by Stalin but left the Polish question until last. This, he noted, "had become a symbol of our ability to work out problems with the Soviet Union." He ritually stated the American position "that the Polish people should be given the right to free elections to choose their own government and their own system and that Poland should be genuinely independent." The American envoy then listened to Stalin's defense of his policy on Poland. But Stalin had more on his mind than a simple defense. He indicated a desire to resolve the matter and blithely suggested that the two of them right there in the Kremlin should settle on the composition of a future Polish Government of National Unity. Hopkins requested time to consider this revealing proposal, which overlooked any British role in the matter.[123]

On May 28, Hopkins met Stalin again and directed attention to the war against Japan and the postwar settlement in the Far East. The Marshal indicated that Soviet armies would be in position on the Manchurian border by August 8, 1945. Revealing that he had no difficulty in linking the use of military force with the furthering of his diplomatic objectives, in dramatic contrast to his American interlocutors, Stalin explained that "as to the actual date of operation he felt that would depend on the execution of the agreement made at Yalta concerning Soviet desires." Laughably, he asserted that "it was necessary to have these agreements in order to justify entry into the Pacific War in the eyes of the Soviet people."[124] The Chinese would need to affirm the concessions – especially regarding Soviet influence in Manchuria – which FDR cavalierly had made for them without their knowledge at Yalta. No doubt out of an eagerness to support a Chinese government that would agree to his Far Eastern plans,

---

[122] Bohlen memorandum, first Hopkins–Stalin conversation, May 26, 1945, *FRUS: The Conference of Berlin (The Potsdam Conference), 1945*, I, pp. 24–31.

[123] Bohlen memorandum, second Hopkins–Stalin conversation, May 27, 1945, *FRUS: The Conference of Berlin (The Potsdam Conference), 1945*, I, pp. 31–41.

[124] Bohlen memorandum, third Hopkins–Stalin conversation, May 28, 1945, *FRUS: The Conference of Berlin (The Potsdam Conference), 1945*, I, pp. 41–52. (The rest of the paragraph relies on this source.)

Stalin pledged to support the unification of China under Chiang Kai-shek. He also indicated his support for a policy of unconditional surrender for Japan. All in all, the meeting reinforced the policies put in place by Roosevelt at Yalta. In no way did Truman's emissary seek to restrict the anticipated injection of Soviet power into northeast Asia. Comrade Stalin would reclaim much of what Czar Nicholas II lost in the aftermath of the Russo-Japanese War, and the United States under both Roosevelt and Truman accepted that reality.

Whatever the ultimate geopolitical importance of Soviet participation in the Pacific war and the expansion of Soviet influence in northeast Asia, Poland remained the center of attention in the Hopkins-Stalin discussions. In his report to Truman on his initial meetings, Harry Hopkins told the president that he would try to induce Stalin to further clarify his position on the Polish issue. He did not expect any settlement of the difficult question but looked to explore avenues toward a solution. This he did at his fourth meeting with the Soviet leader on May 30 immediately after obtaining Stalin's agreement for a Big Three meeting in Berlin on July 15.[125] Hopkins's decision to explore the Polish question obviously signified an American willingness to advance the stalled negotiations, and it effectively reversed the British policy of not negotiating over Poland until the noncommunist Poles imprisoned in early May were released.[126] Hopkins obviously felt he needed to make progress on the divisive issue and he adopted a very conciliatory approach. Although he informed Stalin of a "strong feeling among the American people that the Soviet Union wished to dominate Poland," he reassured him that "President Roosevelt and now President Truman had always anticipated that the members of the present Warsaw regime would constitute a majority of the new Polish Provisional government." With this sad continuity established as a backdrop he suggested that a means to break the deadlock might be found through summoning some Poles to work with the Commission (established at Yalta) to form a provisional government. Stalin accepted the idea and Hopkins in turn quickly agreed to his proposal that eight non-Lublin Poles – five from within Poland and three from London – might be called to join representatives of the Soviet-sponsored regime for consultations in Moscow.[127]

Having made this deal, Hopkins had to sell it, but this did not prove particularly troublesome. He quickly cabled Truman with the encouraging news that "it looks as though Stalin is prepared to return to and implement the Crimea decision and permit a representative group of Poles to come to consult with the Commission."[128] Hopkins knew exactly the right entrée to Truman. His

[125] Bohlen memorandum, fourth Hopkins–Stalin conversation, May 30, 1945, *FRUS: The Conference of Berlin (The Potsdam Conference), 1945*, I, pp. 53–54.

[126] On this point, note Sir Llewellyn Woodward, *British Foreign Policy in the Second World War*, 5 vols. (London, 1971), III, p. 546. Hopkins's initiative also represented a reversal of America's own policy as enunciated by Secretary of State Stettinius in San Francisco on May 5, 1945.

[127] On the discussions involving Poland, see Bohlen memorandum, May 30, 1945, *FRUS*, 1945, V, pp. 301–06.

[128] Hopkins to Truman, May 30, 1945, *FRUS*, 1945, V, p. 307.

placement of Stalin's rather minor concessions within the context of returning to the original Crimean decision negotiated by Roosevelt served effectively to persuade FDR's successor. Just the day before, Truman, on reading a speech of Henry Wallace's that praised him for following Roosevelt's policy, declared that "I certainly am. I have conferred with all who knew anything about his policy including the immediate members of his family, and I am doing everything I can to carry it out." According to Wallace, Truman felt that his sending Hopkins to Moscow had cleared up Stalin's misconceptions. The secretary of commerce noted that "Truman feels much more kindly towards the Russians than before."[129] His friendly disposition certainly emerged in his ready support for Hopkins's proposals, which took more specific form after a further meeting with Stalin on May 31 that agreed upon a list of eight carefully vetted Poles to invite to Moscow.[130] Among this group, only Stanislaw Mikolajczyk of the Polish Peasant Party possessed the personal stature and significant political following to give him real weight at any negotiating table. In short, the list highly favored Stalin's minions now ensconced in Warsaw. Sadly, the list was essentially temporary window-dressing to cover the imposition of a communist-dominated regime in Poland.[131]

How clearly Hopkins and other officials recognized that his deal with Stalin meant the end of any prospect of a truly independent Poland remains somewhat unclear. FDR's one-time confidante certainly cabled Truman that "this is a satisfactory list and I urge that you approve it. If you do," he counseled, "then [the] correct time is now." Furthermore, Truman should "press Churchill immediately for his approval and have Schoenfeld [the American chargé to the Polish government-in-exile] see Mikolajczyk at once in order to get his agreement." Hopkins assured Truman of his belief that his arrangement with Stalin "carries out the Yalta agreement in all its essential aspects" and added for good measure that "Harriman and the other officers of our embassy concur."[132] But, contrary to Hopkins's cable, George F. Kennan, counselor in the American embassy in Moscow, refused to give the deal his blessing. When Hopkins summoned him to Spaso House and asked if he thought the United States could do better on a settlement, Kennan told him no. But to Hopkins's further question as to whether "we should accept these terms and come to an agreement on this basis," Kennan again replied in the negative. Wanting to prevent American complicity in the Soviet domination of the Poles, he told Hopkins that the Americans "should accept no share of the responsibility

[129] Blum, ed., *Price of Vision*, pp. 454–55.

[130] Bohlen memorandum, fifth Hopkins–Stalin conversation, May 31, 1945, *FRUS*, 1945, V, pp. 309–13. Also see the memorandum "Summary of preliminary agreement to initiate Polish consultation," in Harry L. Hopkins Papers, FDRL, Box 338.

[131] The sad story of Poland's political subjection can be traced in detail in Jan Ciechanowski, *Defeat in Victory* (Garden City, NY, 1947); Stanislaw Mikolajczyk, *The Rape of Poland: The Pattern of Soviet Aggression* (New York, 1948); and Edward J. Rozek, *Allied Wartime Diplomacy: A Pattern in Poland* (New York, 1958).

[132] Hopkins to Truman, May 31, 1945, *FRUS*, 1945, pp. 307–09.

for what the Russians proposed to do in Poland." In Kennan's recollection, Hopkins then asked him, "[T]hen you think it's just a sin and we should be agin [sic] it." Kennan in essence thought exactly that to which he recalled that Hopkins sadly replied that "I respect your opinion but I am not at liberty to accept it."[133] Hopkins's claim of a restraint on his liberty is understandable only when one appreciates his self-imposed impulse to dirty his hands to the extent sufficient to secure an agreement with Stalin. Kennan might prefer the purity involved in immediately washing American hands of the Polish matter and bluntly acknowledging Soviet domination there. Hopkins by contrast preferred to provide a fig-leaf of continued Big Three cooperation on the matter because this would revivify the prospects for Soviet-American postwar collaboration, which he and his chief had worked so hard throughout the war to facilitate.

If Hopkins held private reservations about the agreement he negotiated with Stalin, he neglected to share them with Truman, and the president certainly displayed no special concern to evaluate the agreement in light of its implications for Polish national independence. There is little evidence that he wrestled with the substantial issues implicit in the Hopkins–Kennan exchange. He appears not to have suffered any pangs of conscience for a Poland that lay in Mikolajczyk's words "exhausted, bewildered and most of all – abandoned."[134] Typically reliant on his advisers, he simply accepted the Hopkins proposal wholeheartedly and sought to implement it. He moved immediately, just as Hopkins suggested, to gain Churchill's agreement, telling the prime minister on June 1 that the Hopkins agreement with Stalin "represents a very encouraging, positive step in the long drawn out Polish negotiations, and I hope that you will approve the list [of names] as agreed to in order that we may get on with this business as soon as possible."[135] The president also had Grew instruct Schoenfeld to urge Mikolajczyk to concur in the proposed list. Clearly, Truman wanted to remove the Polish thorn from the side of Soviet-American relations, and he soon made progress toward this objective.

Churchill and Mikolajczyk eventually endorsed the Hopkins–Stalin arrangement. Both the British and Polish leaders after complimenting Hopkins's efforts raised concerns about the continued imprisonment of the Polish underground leaders.[136] Such concerns raised fears on the American side that the issue might torpedo the agreement. Hopkins warned Truman on June 3 that "it would be a mistake" to make the release of the imprisoned Poles "a condition to agreement on the list of names and the starting of the consultation in Moscow

[133] Kennan, *Memoirs, 1925–1950*, pp. 212–13.
[134] Mikolajczyk, *Rape of Poland*, p. 123. It is still surprising how few American diplomatic historians – a group rarely hesitant to express moral indignation at U.S. actions – have noted this. They seemingly endorse the view that the freedom of the Poles and the East Europeans was "expendable" in the interest of a settlement of a sort with the Soviet Union.
[135] Truman and Churchill, June 1, 1945, *FRUS, 1945*, V, p. 314.
[136] Schoenfeld to secretary of state, June 2, 1945, *FRUS, 1945*, V, pp. 316–17, and Churchill to Truman, June 2, 1945, *FRUS, 1945*, V, p. 317.

promptly."[137] Hopkins even set to work to lobby Churchill directly. "I am doing everything under Heaven to get these people out of the Jug," he assured the prime minister in a cable dispatched through British Ambassador Sir Archibald Clark Kerr, "but the more important thing it seems to me is to get these Poles together in Moscow right away."[138] Meanwhile in Moscow, Truman's representative tried to persuade Stalin to relent on the matter in a private meeting after a Kremlin dinner held in his honor.[139] Despite the effusive toasts made to Hopkins at the dinner and the attempt to shower his wife with gifts of beautiful fur coats and precious stones, the Soviet regard for Hopkins did not extend to conceding any ground to him on this issue.[140] In the end, Churchill succumbed to Hopkins's request. On June 4, he advised Truman of his agreement that the matter of the imprisoned Poles should not interfere with the opening of discussions in Moscow. The powerless Mikolajcyzk also fell in line, hoping against hope to rescue something from the Yalta framework and the Moscow negotiations and acutely aware that he could not simply hold out in London and abandon his compatriots to their fate.[141]

While agreeing to permit consultations of the various Polish representatives in Moscow, Churchill endeavored to alert Truman to the limited nature of the Soviet concessions. All they had was an agreement for a number of "outside Poles to take part in preliminary discussions, out of which some improvements in the Lublin Government may be made." For him this was "a milestone in a long hill we ought never to have been asked to climb." He warned against assumptions that the Polish problem had been solved and cautiously counseled that "renewed hope and not rejoicing is all we can indulge in at the moment." In such circumstances, he took the occasion to argue again for an earlier meeting of the Big Three than July 15 and to repeat his "profound misgivings [at] the retreat of the American Army to our line of occupation in the central sector, thus bringing Soviet power into the heart of Western Europe and the descent of an iron curtain between us and everything to the Eastward."[142] But Churchill's voice no longer carried effectively in American circles. Truman continued to resist the suggestion that the genuine settlement of crucial issues in Europe such as Poland's political future should be a prerequisite for any withdrawal to agreed zonal boundaries. He preferred the accommodating course being charted by Hopkins in Moscow aimed at obtaining a good postwar working relationship with the Soviet Union.

---

[137] Hopkins to Truman, June 3, 1945, *FRUS*, 1945, V, p. 319.

[138] Hopkins to prime minister through Sir A. Clark Kerr, June 3, 1945 (Cable No. 2245), Churchill Papers, Char 20/220.

[139] Hopkins to Truman, June 3, 1945, Harry L. Hopkins Papers, FDRL, Box 338.

[140] On the dinner, see the colorful account by Harriman's daughter, Kathleen, in a letter dated June 4, 1945, in Averell Harriman Papers, Library of Congress, Box 179. On the gifts, see Henry H. Adams, *Harry Hopkins: A Biography* (New York, 1977), p. 392.

[141] Mikolajczyk, *Rape of Poland*, pp. 118–20.

[142] Churchill to Truman, June 4, 1945 (No. 72), Churchill Papers, Churchill Archive Center, Char 20/220.

In their final conversation on June 6, Hopkins and Stalin finalized the list of Polish representatives to be invited to Moscow. Hopkins again attempted to gain the release of the Polish prisoners but did not press the issue when Stalin refused.[143] Instead, Stalin chose this as the occasion to give ground on another matter of less consequence to his ambitions to dominate in Eastern Europe but designed to evoke gratitude from the Americans who witnessed him play "good cop" to Molotov's bad. Stalin "overruled Molotov" and agreed to accept the American position on voting procedures in the proposed Security Council of the new world organization, an issue that had proved a serious stumbling block for the delegates in the San Francisco conference.[144]

This resolution of the veto question, which Robert Sherwood later effusively described as "the real news that the San Francisco Conference had been saved," guaranteed that American policy makers would judge Hopkins's mission a resounding success.[145] Convinced that "Hopkins has done a good job in Moscow," Truman confided to his diary on June 7 his fervent hope that "San Francisco [might] be a success yet" and his optimism regarding postwar peace.[146] This optimism increasingly pervaded lower levels in the administration. Based on Harriman's reports, Assistant Secretary of War John J. McCloy, a close Stimson aide, told Navy Secretary Forrestal that Hopkins's visit "had largely dispelled the growing suspicion [that is felt by] Stalin and Molotov."[147] Admiral Leahy acknowledged that Hopkins "had been very successful in allaying some of the suspicions that the Russians had about our motives and interpretations, notably of agreements made at the Crimea Conference."[148] Even Joseph Grew, who had pushed the State Department's tough line on the Soviet Union, was moved by the achievements of Hopkins's mission to apprise a Cabinet meeting on June 8 that while he didn't believe "in crowing before the sun is really up, . . . I may say that the international scene is a great deal brighter today than it was even two days ago."[149]

Harry Hopkins did nothing to dispel the optimistic evaluation of his mission. Robert Murphy, Eisenhower's political adviser, recalled him "bubbling with enthusiasm about his meetings with Stalin," during his stopover in Frankfurt on his return journey to Washington. His "confidence in Soviet-American co-operation was impressive." He assured his fellow Americans that "we can do business with Stalin! He will cooperate!"[150] Hopkins had departed Moscow

---

[143] Bohlen memorandum, sixth Hopkins–Stalin conversation, June 6, 1945, *FRUS*, 1945, V, pp. 328–29.

[144] Hopkins to Truman, June 6, 1945, Harry L. Hopkins Papers, FDRL, Box 338. The Soviets had wanted to apply the veto power of the permanent members of the UN Security Council even to the discussion of an issue as opposed to action in response to it.

[145] Sherwood, *Roosevelt and Hopkins*, p. 912.

[146] Diary entry, June 7, 1945, Ferrell, ed., *Off the Record*, p. 44.

[147] McCloy quoted in Millis, ed., *Forrestal Diaries*, p. 68.

[148] Leahy, *I Was There*, p. 383.

[149] Joseph C. Grew, *Turbulent Era*, Vol. II, p. 1518.

[150] Murphy, *Diplomat Among Warriors*, p. 260.

on June 7 and with Stalin's permission first had visited Berlin where Marshal Zhukov served as his host. He toured the ruined city with a group of Soviet generals and in a spirit of warm comradeship shared a buffet lunch with them, which Bohlen later described as "light on food and heavy on vodka."[151] The Russian generals allowed him to take some books from Hitler's private library as a souvenir of the victory over Nazi Germany for which he had worked so hard to ensure U.S.-Soviet cooperation. Armed with his souvenirs, he moved on to Eisenhower's headquarters where he and his wife stayed as the general's personal guests. Hopkins made clear to Eisenhower that he thought Churchill's warnings about the Soviet Union were "overwrought and insubstantial."[152] In sharp contrast to the British leader, the two Americans found themselves in complete agreement on the need to withdraw to the assigned occupation zones in Germany so as to allow the Allied Control Council to begin operation. Hopkins cabled his strong recommendation to Truman for prompt action on the matter which he portrayed as "of major import to our future relations with Russia."[153]

The firm rejection of British counsel on dealing with the Soviet Union came into stark clarity in a small episode sparked by Churchill's attempt to persuade Hopkins to visit London on his return home. The prime minister hoped that he could communicate with the American official who had come to the rescue in his nation's darkest hour and convey his concerns regarding the Soviets. But Hopkins begged off meeting Churchill in a phone conversation, so the British leader directly appealed to Truman. Hopkins "has so much to tell that would be helpful," he explained, "and he could then bring on my tale for you to hear." Indicative of what that "tale" might include, Churchill lamented that "I have never been more anxious than I am now about the state of Europe."[154] Truman demonstrated no desire to subject himself via Hopkins to a catalogue of Churchill's anxieties. He replied simply that it was impossible for Hopkins to stop in England.[155] Meanwhile, the American envoy and his wife moved on from Frankfurt to Paris where they spent a pleasant weekend visiting friends before Hopkins flew back across the Atlantic to report to Truman. Once in Washington, he understood better why Truman had vetoed any visit to London. The president desired to prevent even the appearance of Anglo-American collusion against the Soviet Union. With Davies as his guide, Truman now fancied the United States more as the mediator between the USSR and Britain, and he did not want to be "in cahoots with" either of them.[156]

---

[151] On his tour, see Sherwood, *Roosevelt and Hopkins*, p. 912, and Bohlen, *Witness to History*, p. 222.

[152] McJimsey, *Harry Hopkins*, p. 389.

[153] On this matter see Hopkins to Truman, June 8, 1945, *FRUS*, 1945, III, pp. 333–34, and Murphy, *Diplomat Among Warriors*, pp. 260–61.

[154] Churchill to Truman, June 7, 1945 (No. 78), Churchill Papers, Churchill Archive Center, Char 20/220.

[155] Truman to Churchill, June 7, 1945 (No. 64), Churchill Papers, Churchill Archive Center, Char 20/220.

[156] Davies journal, June 14, 1945, Joseph E. Davies Papers, Library of Congress, Box 17.

Hopkins arrived back in Washington on June 12 and the next morning reported to Truman at a breakfast meeting, which Davies and Leahy also attended. Truman thanked his special envoy for his accomplishments in Moscow. Later that day, the president held a press conference and publicly declared the results of the Hopkins and Davies missions as "completely satisfactory and gratifying." He emphasized the importance of continued "unity [and] mutual confidence" among the victorious powers so as to ensure "a just and durable peace." Asked about the Polish situation, he claimed it to be "on the road to a complete settlement," which had been made possible by "a very pleasant yielding on the part of the Russians to some of the things in which we are interested." The president assured the assembled journalists that "if we keep our heads and be patient, we will arrive at a conclusion; because the Russians are just as anxious to get along with us as we are with them." For good measure he added that "they have showed it very conclusively in these last conversations."[157]

The Hopkins mission displayed, as Charles Bohlen later observed, perhaps with some deliberate understatement, "that the United States was prepared to go to considerable lengths to preserve friendship with the Soviet Union."[158] The mission and Truman's positive reaction toward it should lay to rest once and for all suggestions that the president was not genuinely seeking cooperation with Moscow. His eagerness to improve relations with Stalin led him to agree to a significant amelioration of the American stance on Poland as articulated in April. Like his predecessor, he chose not to force the issue of Polish political independence and national sovereignty at a cost to U.S.-Soviet relations. Preferable now was the shunting off of the Polish question to a commission in Moscow. His confrontational meeting with Molotov resided in a seemingly distant past when he had been guided by the advice of more hard-line officials than Davies and Hopkins. Truman's satisfaction with the work of his two special envoys and his respect for their counsel guaranteed that he would request that they continue to work for him and to attend the Big Three conference in July. But Hopkins declined the invitation. The combination of his serious health problems and some recognition of the potential for tension between himself and Byrnes convinced him to bring his governmental service to an end. On July 2, he submitted his resignation. Truman accepted it with true regret and deep gratitude for the service Hopkins had rendered in the prosecution of the war.[159] Hopkins quickly departed the stage, and in fact he would die within the year, but this still left Joe Davies very much in the spotlight.

---

[157] Truman news conference, June 13, 1945, Truman, *Public Papers of the Presidents of the United States: Harry S. Truman, 1945*, pp. 120–23.

[158] Bohlen, *Witness to History*, p. 223.

[159] On Hopkins's resignation, see Adams, *Harry Hopkins*, p. 395. For Truman's letter of July 3, accepting Hopkins's resignation as special assistant to the president, see Truman, *Public Papers of the Presidents of the United States: Harry S. Truman, 1945*, pp. 156–57.

"A Russophile as Most of Us Were"

In the weeks from the conclusion of Hopkins's mission until Truman's departure for the Potsdam conference, the United States approached a series of issues involving the Soviet Union in a business-like and largely conciliatory manner. Those recommending a more forceful and quid pro quo approach to the Soviets largely had lost in the battle to guide and instruct the new president. The effort during June of 1945 centered on settling issues or simply deferring them for later deliberation and decision. Naturally there remained many matters over which the United States differed, but these came to be seen within a framework of continued Soviet-American friendship. Truman himself gave expression to these sentiments in diary reflections on June 7 where he reacted against anti-Soviet remarks of Senator Burton Wheeler by noting that "every time we get things going halfway right with the Soviets some smart aleck has to attack them. If it isn't Willie Hearst, Bertie McCormick or Burt Wheeler it is some other bird who wanted to appease Germany but just can't see any good in Russia." While assuring himself that he was "not afraid of Russia," he tellingly noted that "they've always been our friends and I can't see any reason why they shouldn't always be so."[160]

To foster the development of Soviet-American friendship and to help plot his foreign policy, Truman kept Joseph Davies close at hand. Davies participated in important meetings and at Truman's suggestion worked in the office of the president's naval aide, Commodore James K. Vardaman, reviewing top-secret cables. He became a regular in the White House Map Room, working on dispatches for the president.[161] Davies also deepened his personal connection with Truman by currying favor with the first lady and first daughter. On his return from London, he forwarded an autographed copy of his *Mission to Moscow* to Margaret Truman, then majoring in political science, along with some "English war scarves" for her and her "wonderful mother" in order to commemorate "an incident [his visit to Churchill] which may be one of the most memorable historical situations which the President initiated to try to preserve the fruits of Victory." For good measure, he added his praise "that a college girl from our own middle west, is conducting herself with such admirable and typical American

---

[160] Truman's reflections in this diary entry contain a number of amazingly simplistic observations about the Soviet Union such as: "There's no socialism in Russia. It's a hotbed of special privilege"; and "But I don't care what they do. They evidently like their government or they wouldn't die for it. I like ours so let's get along." Also note his comparison of American missionaries and Soviet propagandists: "We send missionaries and political propagandists to China, Turkey and India and everywhere to tell those people how to live. Most of them know as much or more than we do. Russia won't let 'em in. But when Russia puts out propaganda to help our parlor pinks – well, that's bad – so we think. There is not any difference between the two approaches except one is 'my' approach and the other is 'yours.' Just a 'mote & beam' affair." Diary entry, June 7, 1945, Ferrell, ed., *Off the Record*, pp. 44–45.

[161] See the list of Davies's various meetings and Map Room assignments in diary entries, June 14, 19, 20, 26, 27, 28, and July 2, 1945, Joseph E. Davies Papers, Library of Congress, Box 17.

modesty, good sense, and fine judgment," and, in words that he would have known the president would read, he concluded with the unintentionally patronizing observation that "the country is finding the greatest of satisfaction in the quality of the Trumans." Not surprisingly, the president soon replied telling of his daughter's and his own pleasure at Davies's note. Margaret added her own thanks to the "very great man who was kind enough to help my father as only you were able to do."[162] Davies's desire to continue his assistance remained strong. On June 25, he reassured a worried labor leader, Sidney Hillman, that he was doing what he could "to offset the reactionary influences."[163] His confidence increased as he witnessed the Truman administration's policy decisions.

Progress, if that be the term, now came quickly on the Polish issue. On June 15, representatives from the various Polish camps arrived in Moscow, and by June 21 they advised the Allied commission that they "had reached agreement among themselves." At the final meeting of the commission on June 22, Ambassador Harriman made clear that the Americans would consider any new government as "provisional" until it held free and unfettered elections in Poland as provided for in the original Yalta agreement.[164] But the commission wasted little time obtaining assurances of such elections. Instead, it quickly accepted the agreement reached among the Poles. On June 28, the composition of the new government was announced, and it took office immediately. Mikolajczyk gained the seemingly prestigious but essentially powerless position of deputy prime minister.[165] The Lublin Poles held tight control of the real levers of power. The new government immediately requested recognition from the major powers, and Truman, working on the basis that "no useful purpose would be served by further delay," formally recognized the Polish Provisional Government of National Unity on July 5.[166]

In recognizing the provisional government, Truman, influenced especially by Davies and Hopkins, employed the same mixture of poorly grounded hopefulness and sheer denial that had characterized FDR's policy toward Poland. There certainly existed a true continuity between the two men. The likelihood of Soviet domination of Poland remained high, but one could still optimistically hold out some prospect of an improved political situation if elections were held there – and no one could say with absolute certainty that they would not be permitted. Perhaps Stalin might relax his vise if he felt more secure. It was a weak reed but an acceptable one for Truman to grip on to given the other

---

[162] Davies to Margaret Truman, June 15, 1945; Truman to Davies, June 24, 1945, enclosing Margaret Truman to Davies, Joseph E. Davies Papers, Library of Congress, Box 17.

[163] Diary entry, June 25, 1945, Joseph E. Davies Papers, Library of Congress, Box 17.

[164] Harriman to secretary of state, June 23, 1945, *FRUS*, 1945, V, p. 355.

[165] For Mikolajczyk's comment on the new government, see his *Rape of Poland*, p. 127.

[166] For the formal recognition announcement and Truman's letter to the prime minister of the Polish Provisional Government of National Unity, see Truman, *Public Papers of the Presidents of the United States: Harry S. Truman, 1945*, pp. 166–67. Also see Truman, *Year of Decisions*, pp. 356–57.

demands upon him. Charles Bohlen later alleged that "Truman and Churchill gave up on Poland" by recognizing the new government and there is some truth to his charge.[167] And yet, in football parlance, Truman simply punted. He wanted the issue removed as a major irritant in U.S.-Soviet relations, and he saw this as an acceptable option. In January 1954, when reminiscing for his memoirs, Truman recalled that he wanted Poland "restored as a free country," but rather nonchalantly he commented that "it didn't work out." Referring to the former American ambassador to Poland Arthur Bliss Lane's book *I Saw Poland Betrayed*, which he correctly summarized as arguing "that we had thrown Poland away," the former president observed sarcastically that "I guess he thought we should have had a war to keep Poland free just as Britain had tried to with Hitler."[168] This was a price he never contemplated paying for Polish freedom.

Whether there were other more preferable yet less dangerous courses of action is a question that the historian might pose but cannot answer definitively. What can be said is that the British and the London Poles had great reservations about the course of action followed in 1945 but felt compelled out of weakness to follow the American lead. Mikolajczyk had expressed grave doubts about even accepting the invitation to Moscow but had gone at Churchill's insistence even though the prime minister had told him that "I'm more pessimistic than you are." In fact, he explained to the democratic Polish leader, who would barely escape Warsaw with his life in 1947, "I'm pessimistic about the future of all of Europe, as well as Poland. Poland will be farther away from us than ever before because the Russians will come to the Elbe and perhaps to the Rhine and establish themselves between our two countries."[169] Whatever the possible alternatives, it seems almost irrefutable to argue that the Truman administration accepted a Polish settlement favorable to the Soviets because of its clear desire to improve its relationship with Moscow prior to the Big Three meeting. This goal also guided Truman's actions in other areas such as withdrawal of troops to agreed-upon occupation zones.

Winston Churchill's spirited efforts to persuade Truman to use troop withdrawals to assigned zones of occupation in Germany as a negotiating tool with the Soviets ended in final and complete rejection in June of 1945. On June 9, the prime minister made his last effort to prevent withdrawal by suggesting that it would be "better to refuse to withdraw on the main European front" until an appropriate settlement had been reached for occupation arrangements in Austria.[170] To Churchill's great and lasting dismay, Truman replied two days later that he "was unable to delay the withdrawal of American troops from the

---

[167] Bohlen, *Witness to History*, p. 219.
[168] Interview with Truman, January 22, 1954, Harry S. Truman Papers: Post-Presidential Files, Memoirs, HSTL, Box 643. Also see Arthur Bliss Lane, *I Saw Poland Betrayed* (Indianapolis, 1948).
[169] Mikolajczyk, *Rape of Poland*, p. 117.
[170] Churchill to Truman, June 9, 1945, *FRUS*, 1945, III, p. 132.

Soviet zone in order to use pressure in the settlement of other problems."[171] As Truman noted, these arrangements had been approved previously by President Roosevelt as well as Churchill and Stalin. The task of implementing them fell to him, and he proceeded to do it. On June 14, he cabled Stalin offering June 21 as the date for Allied troops to begin the withdrawals to their designated zones. Much to Truman's surprise, Stalin requested that the withdrawals be delayed until July 1, but the broad process was underway before Truman departed for Potsdam.[172]

The decision to relinquish not only the German territory but the possible negotiating strength that its possession furnished confirms the conciliatory nature of American policy toward the Soviet Union prior to Potsdam. Advised by General Eisenhower and Robert Murphy, Truman knew that the Allied Control Council for Germany could not begin to function until American and British troops vacated the zone assigned to the Russians.[173] Furthermore, Harry Hopkins had outlined for him the importance of settling this matter for improved relations with the Soviet Union and the likely negative consequences of leaving the issue in abeyance prior to the Big Three meeting.[174] Truman found such arguments compelling especially when linked to the related factor that by withdrawing the troops he adhered to the agreements negotiated by FDR.[175] In retrospect, Truman expressed some second thoughts about his action. "If I had

[171] Truman to Churchill, June 11, 1945, *FRUS*, 1945, III, p. 133–34. As to Churchill's great and lasting dismay see the comments in his memoirs: "to give up the whole centre [sic] and heart of Germany – nay, the centre and key-stone of Europe – as an isolated act seemed to me to be a grave and improvident decision. If it were done at all it could only be as part of a general and lasting settlement. We should go to Potsdam with nothing to bargain with, and all the prospects of the future peace of Europe might well go by default." The British prime minister concluded that "in the moment of victory was our best, and what might prove to have been our last, chance of durable world peace allowed composedly to fade away." Churchill, *Triumph and Tragedy*, pp. 602–03.

[172] Truman to Stalin, June 14, 1945, and Stalin to Truman, June 16, 1945, *FRUS*, 1945, III, pp. 135–37.

[173] Eisenhower and his political adviser, Murphy, met with Marshal Zhukov in Berlin on June 5 after the Four Power Declaration regarding the defeat of Germany and the assumption of supreme authority by the Allied powers. As Murphy reported: "Marshal Zhukov [made] it abundantly clear that disposition of the troops into their respective zones is a Soviet *sine qua non* to the operation of the Control Council." Murphy to secretary of state, June 6, 1945, *FRUS*, 1945, III, pp. 327–28. Also see Murphy, *Diplomat Among Warriors*, pp. 257–60.

[174] In a cable sent from Frankfurt on June 8, Hopkins warned that the "present indeterminate status of date for withdrawal of Allied troops from [the] area assigned to the Russians is certain to be misunderstood by Russia as well as at home." Hopkins recommended that "prompt action be taken to dispose of the issue." Hopkins to Truman, June 8, 1945, *FRUS*, 1945, III, pp. 333–34.

[175] Interestingly Winston Churchill captures Truman's position quite well in his memoirs. Speaking of Truman he noted that "the case as presented to him so soon after his accession to power was whether or not to depart from and in a sense repudiate the policy of the American and British Governments agreed under his illustrious predecessor. He was, I have no doubt, supported in his action by his advisers, military and civil. His responsibility at this point was limited to deciding whether circumstances had changed so fundamentally that an entirely different procedure should be adopted, with the likelihood of having to face accusations of breach of

been in touch with the whole situation at the time," he said in a 1959 interview, "I don't think I would have withdrawn the American Army from the eastern boundary in Germany, and then we wouldn't have serious trouble, but I labored under the feeling, as did a great many other people, that the Russians would keep their agreements."[176] Whatever the wisdom of Truman's second-guessing of his own actions it confirms his attitude in June of 1945. He planned to keep his agreements and expected the Soviets to keep theirs.[177]

Truman's refusal to endorse the Churchillian strategy on the troop withdrawals emphatically marked the American policy of marching to the beat of a quite different drummer than the British in dealing with the Soviet Union. In an effort to convey the reality of this policy to the Soviets, the Americans consciously avoided giving any grounds for suspicion that they and the British were "ganging up" on their Slavic ally. This sentiment lay behind Truman's refusal to meet with Churchill prior to the Potsdam meeting.[178] It also caused the American joint chiefs of staff to reject the suggestion of their British counterparts that they meet in London prior to the Big Three heads of state meeting in Germany. The British historian Sir Llewellyn Woodward rightly observed that Truman "maintained and even exaggerated" Roosevelt's efforts "to avoid the impression of an Anglo-American drive against the Soviet Union," and given Davies's influence upon him, it could hardly be otherwise.[179]

Even Churchill, a man veritably possessed by his dreams of Anglo-American amity and unity, eventually got the message. On June 17, he wrote to Sir Alexander Cadogan, the permanent secretary of the Foreign Office, observing that British policy should be to "stave off as much as possible till 'Terminal,'" the code-name assigned to the Potsdam meeting. He explained to Cadogan that where this couldn't be done they must simply wait for the Americans to express their views and fall in line. Then, in a telling comment, he observed that it lay "beyond the power of this country to prevent all sorts of things crashing at the present time. The responsibility lies with the United States and my desire is to give them all the support in our power. If they do not feel able to do anything,

---

faith." And the great memoirist rather generously added: "Those who are only wise after the event should hold their peace." Churchill, *Triumph and Tragedy*, p. 608.

[176] Interview, September 9, 1959, "Mr. Citizen" file, Box 2, Folder 1, quoted in Ferrell, *Harry S. Truman*, p. 421. Not every American involved proved so susceptible to second thoughts. General Eisenhower defended the withdrawals in 1961 by arguing that the "West's leaders were earnestly striving to bring about...a basis for better relations with the Soviet Union: – had they failed to make this attempt we would today be wailing about lost opportunities and 'might-have-beens.'" See his "My View of Berlin," *Saturday Evening Post*, 234 (December 9, 1961), pp. 19–29.

[177] Truman later wrote: "We were about 150 miles east of the border of the occupation zone line agreed to at Yalta. I felt that agreements made in the war to keep Russia fighting should be kept and I kept them to the letter. Perhaps they should not have been adhered to so quickly." Quoted in McCullough, *Truman*, p. 399.

[178] Truman to Churchill, May 11, 1945, *FRUS: The Conference of Berlin (The Potsdam Conference), 1945*, 1945, I, p. 8.

[179] Woodward, *British Foreign Policy in the Second World War*, Vol. III, p. 573.

then we must let matters take their course." Ominously, he concluded, "indeed that is what they are doing."[180]

Truman held a quite different view of the international situation. Rather than matters crashing, as Churchill alleged, he considered that they were being resolved or set on the road to resolution. And this characterized the situation not only in Europe but also in Asia. In the Far East, the compelling need to maintain momentum in the war against the Japanese guided American actions. The desire to gain Soviet participation in the Pacific conflict remained strong and guaranteed that Truman would move to facilitate the implementation of the Yalta Far Eastern Accord once Stalin had confirmed to Hopkins his commitment to enter the war in August. When some word of the Yalta terms reached the Chinese in June, Chiang's foreign minister, T. V. Soong, hurried from the UN meeting in San Francisco to Washington. There, Truman explained the detailed terms of the Yalta accords to him and made very clear his strong commitment to the agreement reached by President Roosevelt.[181] Not surprisingly, Soong feared that Stalin had extracted a very high price at Chinese expense for his commitment to enter the war. The president turned to the seemingly omnipresent Joseph Davies to convey to the Chinese official that the price needed to be paid, and this he coolly did.[182]

When Truman himself held a further meeting with the Chinese foreign minister on June 14, he hardly overflowed with empathy when Soong expressed concern about the Soviet demand for Manchurian concessions contained in the agreement the United States expected his nation to endorse. He promised to "do nothing which would harm the interests of China," but clarified that "his chief interest now was to see the Soviet Union participate in the Far Eastern War in sufficient time to be of help in shortening the war and thus save American and Chinese lives." In a revealing comment that captured well his attitude at this time, Truman added that "the United States desired above all to see these postwar questions settled in a way as to eliminate any tinderboxes both in Europe and in the Far East which might cause future trouble or wars."[183] So briefed in Washington, Soong soon departed for Moscow in a bid to clarify and agree on the details of the accord. The Soong–Stalin talks were still in progress when the American delegation departed for the Big Three conference, but Truman believed he had acted appropriately to fulfill FDR's Yalta pledges designed to gain Soviet participation in the costly war against the ferocious Japanese foe whose tenacity had led to such high casualties on Iwo Jima and Okinawa.

---

[180] Minute from Churchill to Cadogan, June 17, 1945 (M.635/5), Churchill Papers, Char 20/209.

[181] Grew memorandum of Truman–Soong conversation, June 9, 1945, *FRUS*, 1945, VII, p. 896. For Truman's own account of this meeting and the whole question of implementing the Yalta Far Eastern Accord, see his *Year of Decisions*, pp. 298–301.

[182] Davies recorded in his diary that Truman "told me to see Minister Soong and advise him of the necessity of his government and Russia getting together by treaty to fulfill commitments to Roosevelt, so as to have them fulfilled by the time of our meeting with Stalin." This Davies did that same day. Diary entry, June 12, 1945, Joseph E. Davies Papers, Library of Congress, Box 17.

[183] Grew memorandum, June 14, 1945, *FRUS*, 1945, VII, pp. 901–03.

Before departing for Potsdam, the president also played his part in bringing to fruition the endeavors involved in creating the United Nations Organization. Following Hopkins's intervention with Stalin, the major powers – the future permanent members of the Security Council – closed ranks on the matter of the council's procedures and moved the conference to a conclusion. In a concession to the smaller countries, the British and the Americans accepted their proposal that any matter might be discussed in the General Assembly. The Soviet delegates initially refused this seemingly innocuous provision and the time taken to settle the issue delayed the closing ceremony, which initially was scheduled for June 23.[184] Truman had left Washington on June 19 to pay a brief visit to the Pacific Northwest as the guest of Washington Governor Mon Wallgren, a former Truman Committee colleague. He extended his stay and actually had the chance to relax a bit and to try his hand at salmon fishing. On June 25, he flew to San Francisco and enjoyed a ticker-tape reception on his journey downtown to the Fairmont Hotel.

The next day he watched proudly as Secretary Stettinius signed the United Nations Charter for the United States and then addressed the delegates from fifty nations assembled in the Opera House for their final session. "The Charter of the United Nations which you have just signed," he declared, "is a solid structure upon which we can build a better world." As befit his sincere internationalist sentiments, his words were deeply felt, and he hoped that they marked a historic day. The united spirit of the Allies, which had inspired them to defeat fascism, must continue, and the "powerful nations [must] assume the responsibility for leadership towards a world peace." Calling upon the memories of Woodrow Wilson and Franklin Roosevelt, he called on the representatives "to grasp this supreme chance to establish a world-wide rule of reason – to create an enduring peace under the guidance of God."[185] Truman's lofty rhetoric aimed to match the grand occasion and reflected the high hopes and, it also must be said, the inflated and unreal expectations that many Americans held for the United Nations.[186] At the very time that certain nations used raw power and military force to determine the future of Europe, talk of a "world-wide rule of reason" must be labeled as unrealistic – to put it mildly.[187] This disjuncture failed to enter the president's thinking, and he left San Francisco in high spirits.

---

[184] On this dispute over the authority of the General Assembly, see Campbell, *Masquerade Peace*, pp. 188–89; Hoopes and Brinkley, *FDR and the Creation of the U.N.*, p. 202; and Vandenberg, Jr., ed., *Private Papers of Senator Vandenberg*, pp. 188–89.

[185] Address at the closing session of the United Nations Conference, June 26, 1945, Truman, *Public Papers of the Presidents of the United States: Harry S. Truman, 1945*, pp. 138–39.

[186] On the high hopes and inflated expectations, see Schlesinger, *Act of Creation*, pp. 264–67.

[187] William C. Widenor makes a similar point in noting that "it is doubtful that the United Nations ever represented a 'supreme chance to establish a world-wide rule of reason – to create an enduring peace under the guidance of God.' One might call this wisdom in retrospect – a view colored by what has happened in the last thirty-five years, a view influenced by the persistent failure of the United Nations as a collective security organization – but that history was predictable. The United Nations, fatally flawed from the beginning, was never capable of fulfilling Truman's promises." Widenor, "American Planning for the United Nations: Have We Been Asking the Right Questions?" *Diplomatic History*, 6 (Summer 1982), p. 247.

After his speech, he flew to Kansas City to make his first visit to his much-loved midwestern home since becoming America's president. At a reception in the crowded auditorium of the Church of the Reorganized Latter-Day Saints – the largest in Independence – he told the men and women who knew him as "Harry" and had seen him run for county judge and for the Senate that San Francisco was but "the first step" in winning the peace. He asked their continued support as he persisted in his efforts toward this great goal.[188]

Back in Washington, Truman personally delivered the Charter of the United Nations to the Senate of the United States. The chamber and galleries were filled to capacity as the president moved up the central aisle of the legislative body he loved so much. Behind him came his military aide, Brigadier General Harry H. Vaughan, carrying the blue-bound charter. Loud applause erupted when Truman handed it up to Senator Kenneth McKellar, president pro-tempore of the Senate, placing it at the mercy of his one-time colleagues. The president spoke briefly but forcefully and called on the Senate to ratify the treaty quickly. "This Charter points down the only road to enduring peace," he implored. "There is no other."[189] In subsequent hearings of the Foreign Relations Committee, the treaty met with wide approval, and before the month was out, the Senate ratified the UN treaty by a vote of eighty-nine to two. Even a political genius like Franklin Roosevelt could hardly have done better.

During his stopover in Independence on his return journey from San Francisco, Truman held a press conference at which he announced Edward Stettinius's resignation as secretary of state and his nomination as the first American representative to the United Nations. Shortly thereafter he confirmed, what all political insiders already knew, that James F. Byrnes would be nominated to run the State Department. Truman wanted the South Carolinian, whose negotiating skills he so admired, to be at his side at Potsdam. The Byrnes nomination sailed through the Senate by unanimous vote on the same day that Truman delivered the UN charter. Truman's foreign policy now moved to a new stage in which the newly appointed secretary of state would prove the dominant figure.

The months since his accession to the presidency had proved very challenging for Truman, but on the eve of Potsdam, he felt relatively confident of the prospects for genuine peace and for continued cooperation among the wartime allies. He had navigated the American ship away from the dangerous shoals of Soviet-American confrontation and, under the influence of Davies and Hopkins, had rejected the tough approach to the Soviets favored by Winston Churchill and members of the State Department represented by Joseph Grew. Naturally, he expected continued negotiation and hard bargaining with the Russians on a variety of issues, but such transactions were to be expected in dealing with any other major power including Britain.

The sincerity of Truman's hopes and expectations for good relations with the Soviet Union must be well appreciated by all who would gain some true

---

[188] For further details, see Moskin, *Mr. Truman's War*, p. 152.
[189] Moskin, *Mr. Truman's War*, p. 153.

understanding of his foreign policy. Some years after he left the presidency, Truman expressed regret that Dean Acheson had not been with him at Potsdam rather than Byrnes and Davies. In the midst of his musings about what might have been, he described Davies as "a Russophile" and then added notably "as most of us were."[190] Unquestionably, he put himself in this Russophile category and with some good reason. He had pursued the essentials of Roosevelt's policy designed to guarantee the collaboration of the major powers as the bedrock of a stable and peaceful postwar world order. He believed such an order to be possible and was serenely and naïvely unaware that Stalin was reading from a completely different script in terms of his postwar vision. The time has come to drive the stake finally and completely through the heart of the false accusation that Truman quickly reversed Roosevelt's accommodating approach. One might wish that he had, but an alteration in the conciliatory approach came only after further American efforts to do business with Stalin. Truman prepared to undertake them at Potsdam.

[190] Truman to Acheson, March 15, 1957, Harry S. Truman Papers, Post-Presidential Files, HSTL: Box 44.

5

Negotiation

Truman and Byrnes at Potsdam

Byrnes, the Atomic Bomb, and the Pacific War

The Potsdam Conference holds a rather hazy place in American memory. This last of the three wartime conferences of the leaders of the Soviet Union, Great Britain, and the United States took place in the latter half of July 1945 in the Berlin suburb from whence it drew its name. It attracted neither the same contemporary fervor of public interest and hope nor the intense "fire of later criticism" as did the Yalta meeting.[1] Details of the conference agreements are shrouded in a fog of ignorance and equivocation. Historians similarly have been ambivalent about the significance and the success of the gathering at which Truman met Stalin and Churchill for the first time. One sympathetic student of the conference concluded that Potsdam was a partially successful meeting, although he recognized that much of its success was "purchased by deferral" of the more explosive issues.[2] A strong critic of American diplomacy at Potsdam branded the gathering as "a final, half-hearted and largely unsuccessful effort to preserve something of the earlier wartime relationship" among the Allied powers.[3]

Few observers present Potsdam as an especially memorable affair. The greatest drama associated with it rests in its supposedly serving as the venue for atomic diplomacy.[4] Yet, a close examination of the conference deliberations reveals an American effort, spearheaded by the new Secretary of State James F. Byrnes, but bearing Truman's endorsement, to negotiate something

---

[1] George F. Kennan, "An Historian of Potsdam and His Readers," *American Slavic and East European Review*, 20 (April 1961), p. 289.

[2] James L. Gormley, *From Potsdam to the Cold War: Big Three Diplomacy 1945–1947* (Wilmington, DE, 1990), pp. 63–65, 71.

[3] George F. Kennan quoted in George F. Kennan and John Lukacs, "From World War to Cold War," *American Heritage*, 46 (December 1995), p. 60.

[4] This is the view offered most notably and dramatically by Gar Alperovitz in *Atomic Diplomacy: Hiroshima and Potsdam* (rev. ed.).

approaching "a spheres of influence peace." As Marc Trachtenberg astutely emphasized, Potsdam constituted an important step toward the division of Europe "as the basis of the postwar international order."[5] Such a division was not the painful consequence of the failure of negotiations but the very object and culmination of these negotiations. Byrnes led the way at Potsdam in tough bargaining with the Soviets designed to settle some of the major issues that the victorious powers confronted, in particular the future of Germany. Understanding the Byrnes–Truman approach at Potsdam is essential for grasping the real nature of American diplomacy at this crucial time, and it allows for a clear evaluation of the extent to which Truman's policies followed along the paths charted by Franklin Roosevelt.

Harry Truman allowed his new secretary of state great latitude in devising foreign policy. From the moment he took his oath, Byrnes dominated both policy formulation and implementation, and he, much more so than the president he served, directed the American strategy at the Potsdam meeting. The capable South Carolinian possessed tremendous gifts for politics, and his insightful biographer rightly titled his study *Sly and Able*. Comparing FDR and Byrnes, David Robertson asserted with some justification that "Roosevelt publicly outshone Byrnes at making friends; but behind the scenes Jimmy Byrnes was the better politician, and he knew it."[6] By the time he took command at the State Department, he had held a number of positions any one of which might have served others as the culmination of a fine career – Senate majority leader, Supreme Court justice, and director of the Office of War Mobilization and Reconversion (OWMR), where his tremendous work running the home front earned him the sobriquet of "assistant president." Byrnes, of course, desired another prize. He wanted to be president, but Franklin Roosevelt – influenced by the northern political bosses – refused to anoint this particular southerner as his running mate in 1944. So instead Byrnes watched as the nomination went to the junior senator from Missouri who previously had agreed to place his own name in nomination.

Byrnes reacted to what must have been a crushing disappointment with outward calm and true professionalism. His self-confidence and high regard for his own capacities were in no way damaged. He continued his important work at OWMR and even gave a nationally broadcast radio speech in support of the Roosevelt–Truman ticket in October of 1944.[7] Perhaps he hoped that FDR would select him to succeed his friend Cordell Hull at the State Department, but the president judged Byrnes too independent for that task and picked the more malleable Stettinius. Despite being passed over yet again, this

[5] See the chapter, "A Spheres of Influence Peace?" in Marc Trachtenberg, *A Constructed Peace: The Making of the European Settlement, 1945–1963* (Princeton, NJ, 1999), direct quotation from p. 14.

[6] Robertson, *Sly and Able*, p. 6. This is a tremendous biography, and I readily acknowledge my debt to it.

[7] Robertson, *Sly and Able*, p. 363.

ambitious and capable politician accepted Roosevelt's invitation to accompany him to Yalta. Subsequently, he used his considerable talents to sell the Yalta agreements to the Congress and the American public, even going so far as to misrepresent the Polish problem. Byrnes publicly identified himself with Franklin Roosevelt's foreign policy approach. Privately he did the same and was not associated with those administration officials increasingly troubled by Soviet ambitions and behavior. In a letter written to Walter Lippmann soon after FDR's death, he argued that peace "will depend upon what is in the hearts of the people of Russia, Britain and the United States." It would not be fostered "by promoting distrust of the Soviets." Rather, he continued, "we must have confidence in each other. And if we expect them to fulfill promises, we must scrupulously fulfill our pledges to them."[8]

Byrnes's journey with Roosevelt to the Crimea hardly transformed him into a foreign policy expert. Despite his presence in the Yalta conference room, he was not particularly well versed in the details of foreign policy nor did he possess any significant international experience. Foreign policy issues had never been of primary concern for him. Domestic politics and policies always held the central claim on his attention and efforts. As secretary of state, his concern about the domestic political consequences of international initiatives would influence strongly their nature and content. Truman and Byrnes held this in common. An astute British observer at the time rightly commented that Truman, "like Mr. Byrnes, [has] an outlook to some extent limited by concern with the home scene of the United States."[9] Indeed, to understand the policies forged and pursued by the Truman–Byrnes partnership, one must appreciate that these men were at heart politicians rather than international strategists. Truman's selection of Byrnes as his secretary of state owed largely to political concerns and to Truman's confidence in and regard for his former Senate majority leader's abilities. It certainly did not indicate any desire to take foreign policy in a new direction. Neither Truman nor Byrnes had any well-developed notion in April–May of 1945 what such a direction might be. While Byrnes eventually availed himself of opportunities to learn the details of foreign policy developments, he avoided offering any substantive recommendations on such matters.[10] His political savvy guided him to avoid giving cause for accusations that he was interfering with or undercutting Stettinius's efforts and so to bide his time at home in Spartanburg.

[8] Byrnes to Lippmann, April 30, 1945, James F. Byrnes Papers, Cooper Library, Folder 199.

[9] This is the assessment of General Sir Gordon Macready, head of the British Army Mission in Washington. See Annex III to Orme Sargent, "Stocktaking after VE Day," in Prime Minister's Operational File (Premier 4), Public Record Office, File 31, Folder 5.

[10] Byrnes apparently began reviewing Map Room files well before he was named secretary of state. George Elsey, who worked in the Map Room at the time, recalled that he was directed to show Byrnes "any of our Map Room files that he wished to review," but that their meetings were "clandestine, because this was many weeks before there was any announcement that he was going to replace Edward Stettinius as Secretary." George Elsey, "Speech at Dedication of Harry S. Truman Building," *Whistlestop: Harry S. Truman Library Institute Newsletter* (Winter 2000), p. 2.

There was but one major issue from Truman's swearing-in until the eve of Potsdam on which Byrnes exercised real impact on policy. His membership on the Interim Committee allowed him to influence decisively American policy on the use of the atomic bomb. Through his work at OWMR, Byrnes had developed a personal and political investment in the work of the Manhattan Project and a desire to justify the more than two billion dollars expended on it by 1945.[11] He had put this view firmly to Roosevelt in late 1944 and early 1945. He even warned FDR in a memorandum on March 3, 1945, that "if the project proves a failure, it will then be subjected to relentless investigation and criticism" and recommended an impartial review of the project's progress.[12] Now he found himself strategically located to act upon it as the "president's personal representative" on the Interim Committee.

While Henry Stimson chaired this impressive committee, Byrnes exercised significant influence within it. He firstly blocked any moves aimed at a sharing of atomic research with the Soviets or even the British. That smacked of a giveaway and would be "politically untenable in Congress," and his view of the tenability of any measure in Congress proved difficult to dispute.[13] More significantly, at the end of May, he lowered the boom on suggestions that either "the United States not use the atomic bomb on Japan or that it warn Japan before the bomb's use."[14] The distinguished physicist Leo Szilard put such views before Byrnes when he and two colleagues, Harold Urey and Walter Bartky, traveled to Spartanburg on May 28, but they made no headway whatsoever. In discussing the politics of using the atomic bomb, Byrnes's biographer rightly has noted, the scientist and the future secretary of state "had not even spoken the same language." Szilard worried about the impact on relations with the Soviet Union, but as Robertson persuasively argues, for Byrnes "domestic political concerns were primary." Congress would want a return on the national investment in the Manhattan Project to be sure, but more importantly Byrnes believed that "both the public and their representatives would be outraged if the Truman administration later were shown to have displayed any reluctance to win the war with Japan as quickly as possible by forgoing the use of this weapon."[15] Quite possibly, he also hoped that the new weapon might have some beneficial diplomatic dividend in U.S. relations with the Soviet Union, although that could hardly be relied upon.[16]

---

[11] For details see Robertson, *Sly and Able*, pp. 392–93.

[12] Memorandum for the president, March 3, 1945, James F. Byrnes Papers, Cooper Library, Folder 596–2.

[13] Robertson, *Sly and Able*, p. 398. (I rely on Robertson's interpretation here.)

[14] Robertson, *Sly and Able*, p. 399.

[15] Robertson, *Sly and Able*, p. 405.

[16] Leo Szilard remembered of their conversation that "Mr. Byrnes did not argue that it was necessary to use the bombs against the cities of Japan in order to win the war. . . . Mr. Byrnes' view was that our possessing and demonstrating the bomb would make Russia more manageable in Europe." Leo Szilard, "A Personal History of the Atomic Bomb," *University of Chicago Roundtable*, 601 (September 25, 1949), pp. 14–15, quoted in Barton Bernstein, "Commentary," in Richard S. Kirkendall, ed., *The Truman Period as a Research Field: A Reappraisal,*

The use of the atomic bomb at Hiroshima is an event seared into the world's psyche. The mere mention of "Hiroshima" fuels the imagination with images of vast death and destruction on a scale never seen before. Yet it is crucial to recall that members of the Interim Committee never acted with that ghastly vision before them. Their minds were troubled instead by the horrors of the Pacific war as seen through an American lens. The treachery of Pearl Harbor, the reports of Japanese atrocities, the suicidal resistance of the Japanese military at Iwo Jima and Okinawa stoked a deep antipathy to the Japanese empire.[17] Little reserve of either respect or sympathy remained for the Japanese military and people who were viewed increasingly in a stereotyped racialist manner.[18] The task at hand centered on defeating this ferocious foe as quickly as possible. To achieve this end, the Americans pursued a number of strategies – tightening the naval blockade of the Japanese home islands; continuing a massive conventional bombing assault by General Curtis LeMay's B-29s, which rained incendiary napalm bombs on Japanese cities; and preparing for an invasion and subsequent ground war.

The Interim Committee reached its crucial decisions in a meeting on June 1 under Byrnes's forceful guidance. The consensus held that the bomb be used against Japan as soon as possible, that it be used on "a vital war plant employing a large number of workers and closely surrounded by workers' houses," and that it be used without prior warning.[19] At the committee meeting's end Byrnes left the Pentagon and hurried to the White House where he personally briefed Truman on its conclusions. At this meeting, the two men reviewed the estimates of American casualties should an invasion of Japan take place and, as David Robertson put it, "the likelihood that the shock of an unannounced atomic attack would force Japan to surrender unconditionally without the necessity of the two invasions [planned for Kyushu and Honshu]."[20] These two politicians saw the matter clearly. Moral complexities or future diplomatic implications failed to complicate their straightforward thinking. The atomic bomb might possibly save American lives. This remained the essential thinking that guided the decision to use the horrific weapon against Hiroshima and Nagasaki in August of 1945.

1972 (Columbia, MO, 1974), p. 172. Byrnes denied Szilard's recollection of their conversation. See Hewlett and Anderson, *New World*, p. 355.

[17] For a powerfully suggestive essay on the ferocity of the Pacific war, see John Gregory Dunne, "The Hardest War," *New York Review of Books*, 48 (December 20, 2001), pp. 50–56. Note that Dunne makes the valuable point (p. 56) that "almost immediately after Hiroshima, the unremitting horror of the Pacific campaign began to slip even what tenuous claim it had on American attention." But the Interim Committee had this "horror" right before them in May–June of 1945.

[18] On racial stereotypes, see John W. Dower, *War Without Mercy: Race and Power in the Pacific War* (New York, 1986). Also see Ronald Takaki, *Double Victory: A Multicultural History of America in World War II* (Boston, 2000), pp. 168–70.

[19] See the discussion in Hewlett and Andersen, *New World*, pp. 358–59. (These authors rely on the notes of the Interim Committee Meeting, June 1, 1945, Manhattan District Records.)

[20] Robertson, *Sly and Able*, p. 411.

Truman received other briefings on the work of the Interim Committee, but Byrnes proved to be his key adviser.[21] When Secretary of War Stimson saw him on June 6 to brief him on the work of the Interim Committee, Truman admitted "that Byrnes had reported to him already about it and that Byrnes seemed to be highly pleased with what had been done." Stimson attempted to brief Truman on the potential bargaining power of the new weapon, especially as regards the Soviet Union. He explained that "no disclosure of the work should be made to anyone until all promises of control were made and established," and then discussed "further *quid pro quos* which should be established in consideration for our taking them [the Soviets] into the partnership." This hardly constituted a recipe for atomic intimidation but rather saw the potential sharing of the new weapon as a means to foster Soviet cooperation through diplomatic trade-offs. Stimson's increasing obsession with the diplomatic implications of the possible new weapon led to his raising the issue whenever he got near Truman. The president appeared not to share his secretary of war's obsession. He humored Stimson on June 6 by agreeing that he had given some thought to the *quid pro quo* approach, but then redirected the conversation to "the accomplishment which Harry Hopkins had made in Moscow," relating to Stalin's Far Eastern promises.[22] In fact, Truman preferred to keep some distance from the actual discussions on the use of the atomic bomb. He trusted Byrnes and followed his counsel.

Untold gallons of ink have been spilled to facilitate discussion and debate over the decision to use the bomb, but the actual decision proceeded rather smoothly. Reading backward as citizens of the atomic age, historians have given the decision to use this devastating weapon an importance that it didn't obtain at the time. As one astute scholar has noted among the responsible decision makers "there was no debate over *whether* to use the bomb when it became available; the question was *how*."[23] Truman made no profound and wrenching decision to use the atomic weapon. While certain scientists like Szilard were filled with anguish, there is little evidence for the president's agonizing over the matter. This was a "buck" that came to his desk merely so that he could endorse the consensus of his advisers. The president showed no inclination to question in any way the guiding assumption that had prevailed under his predecessor's administration that the bomb was a weapon of war built to be used. His willingness to authorize the dropping of the atomic bomb placed him in a direct continuity with FDR for, as Gerhard Weinberg has argued, "nothing suggests that Roosevelt, had he lived, would have decided differently."[24] Truman's

---

[21] For example, when Budget Director Harold Smith raised questions about the Manhattan Project, Truman told him to contact Byrnes. See Harold D. Smith diary, June 5, 1945, Harold D. Smith Papers, HSTL, Box 1.

[22] Stimson memorandum of conversation with the president, June 6, 1945, Henry Lewis Stimson Papers, Sterling Memorial Library. See also entry for June 6, 1945, Stimson diary.

[23] Robert James Maddox, *The United States and World War II* (Boulder, CO, 1988), p. 305.

[24] Gerhard L. Weinberg, *A World at Arms: A Global History of World War II* (New York, 1994), p. 573.

"decision" ultimately was, as General Leslie Groves of the Manhattan Project later suggested, the negative one of not interfering in a course already charted and powerfully driven. Perhaps Groves went too far in suggesting that so powerful were the forces that they carried Truman forward to the use of the bomb "like a little boy on a taboggan" careening downhill.[25] Yet, one must acknowledge that Truman possessed neither the capacity nor the desire to question the logic of the bomb's use.

Whatever the hopes for the atomic weapon, the prospect of its successful testing in no way delayed the American commitment to proceed forward with the land attack on Japan. In mid-June 1945, Truman approved the unanimous recommendation of the joint chiefs of staff for the invasion. Operation Olympic, a fourteen-division operation, provided for attacks on the southern island of Kyushu beginning November 1. Operation Coronet, which would involve twenty-four divisions, set out plans for a later major assault on the Tokyo Plain of the main island of Honshu tentatively scheduled for March 1, 1946. Casualties from these military exercises were expected to be high. Although Truman's later suggestion that he received advice that the United States might suffer a million casualties has been contested of late, "there is no question that Truman thought casualties would be heavy," as Robert James Maddox noted.[26] Indeed, the president feared "an Okinawa from one end of Japan to the other."[27] Later-day historians disputing just how many thousands of casualties the United States might sustain bear a certain resemblance to medieval theologians debating how many angels could dance on the head of a pin.[28] They neglect the central point that resides in the American desire to reduce the cost in American blood to secure Japan's surrender. The bottom line, so to speak, for Truman and for Byrnes lay in saving American lives – whatever the number.

[25] Leslie R. Groves, *Now It Can Be Told: The Story of the Manhattan Project* (New York, 1962), pp. 264–66. Groves's "boy on a taboggan" reference is quoted from John Newhouse, *War and Peace in the Nuclear Age* (New York, 1989), p. 43.

[26] Maddox, *The United States and World War II*, p. 306. I rely on Maddox for some of the factual details in the preceding sentences.

[27] Minutes of meeting, June 18, 1945, *FRUS: The Conference of Berlin (The Potsdam Conference), 1945*, I, p. 909.

[28] For a representative sampling of opinions on this issue, see Michael Kort, "Casualty Projections for the Invasion of Japan, Phantom Estimates, and the Math of Barton Bernstein," *Passport: The Newsletter of the Society for Historians of American Foreign Relations*, 34 (December 2003), pp. 4–11; Barton J. Bernstein, "Marshall, Leahy, and Casualty Issues – A Reply to Kort's Flawed Critique," *Passport*, 35 (August 2004), pp. 5–14; Barton J. Bernstein, "Truman and the A-Bomb: Targeting Noncombatants, Using the Bomb, and His Defending the 'Decision,'" *Journal of Military History*, 62 (July 1998), pp. 547–70; D. M. Giangreco, "'A Score of Bloody Okinawas and Iwo Jimas': President Truman and Casualty Estimates for the Invasion of Japan," *Pacific Historical Review*, 72 (February 2003), pp. 93–132; and Rufus E. Miles, Jr., "Hiroshima: The Strange Myth of Half a Million American Lives Saved," *International Security*, 10 (Fall 1985), pp. 121–40.

Truman finalized the military planning for the Pacific war at a meeting with his senior military and civilian advisers on June 18. A few days before Admiral Leahy had alerted the joint chiefs of staff of the president's desire for "an estimate of the time required and an estimate of the losses in killed and wounded that will result from an invasion of Japan." Leahy explained that Truman wished to pursue a campaign "with the purpose of economizing to the maximum extent possible in the loss of American lives."[29] Truman's anxiety over the prospect of high American casualties caused some anxiety in turn among American military planners, who worried about the president's commitment to the invasion strategy they had developed.[30] But at the meeting and following a lengthy presentation by General Marshall, Truman accepted the unanimous recommendation of the joint chiefs "after weighing all the possibilities of the situation and considering all possible alternative plans, . . . that the Kyushu operation is the best solution under the circumstances."[31] Operation Olympic got the immediate go-ahead with Operation Coronet reserved for a later final decision. A naval blockade and continued bombing were deemed insufficient to bring about Japanese capitulation. Marshall affirmed the value of gaining Russian participation in the conflict so that the Red Army could "deal with the Japs in Manchuria (and Korea if necessary)," and Truman reassured the group that one of his objectives at Potsdam "would be to get from Russia all the assistance in the war that was possible."[32]

Other issues surfaced at this meeting. Admiral Leahy tried to question the unconditional surrender terms being held out before the Japanese, but Truman evaded the issue by deeming it a topic for Congress to address. He implied, however, that American public opinion would not tolerate any change in such conditions.[33] Truman seemed more open to a suggestion from Assistant Secretary of War John J. McCloy that Japan should be warned of the impending use of a "terrifyingly destructive weapon" and also given some indication that they might be permitted to retain the emperor on the basis of a constitutional monarchy. According to McCloy's later account, Truman agreeably encouraged him to take his suggestions up with Byrnes. The proposal for a warning gained support, but his latter idea regarding the emperor met a less than enthusiastic reception with the South Carolinian. Byrnes thought the proposal might be viewed by the Japanese as weakness on the American part, which might only

[29] Leahy memorandum to joint chiefs of staff, June 14, 1945, quoted in Douglas J. MacEachin, *The Final Months of the War with Japan: Signals Intelligence, U.S. Invasion Planning and the A-Bomb Decision* (Langley, VA, 1998), p. 11.

[30] See MacEachin, *The Final Months of the War with Japan*, pp. 12–13.

[31] Minutes of meeting, June 18, 1945, *FRUS: The Conference of Berlin (The Potsdam Conference), 1945*, I, p. 908.

[32] Minutes of meeting, June 18, 1945, *FRUS: The Conference of Berlin (The Potsdam Conference), 1945*, I, pp. 905, 909.

[33] Minutes of meeting, June 18, 1945, *FRUS: The Conference of Berlin (The Potsdam Conference), 1945*, I, p. 909.

encourage their resistance. He advised McCloy that he "would oppose any 'deal' as a concomitant of a demand for surrender."[34] And that was the end of it because, as June came to an end, Jimmy Byrnes ruled the deck of the Truman administration's foreign policy ship. He had charted the course for Truman on the use of the atomic bomb. His portfolio now expanded rapidly as he assumed the duties of secretary of state.

To Potsdam

Truman left Washington on June 19th to journey west for the closing session of the San Francisco meeting. He announced Stettinius's resignation on June 27 and Byrnes's appointment on June 30. After his lightning and unanimous approval by the Senate, Byrnes enjoyed a rather festive swearing-in ceremony on July 3 in the Rose Garden of the White House. Surrounded by his friends, he swore his oath using his wife's Bible. Upon completing it, the president jokingly encouraged him to kiss the Bible. This he did whereupon he "handed it over to the President and told him to kiss it too." Truman obliged much to the enjoyment of the gathered crowd.[35] Truman relished having Byrnes in charge of foreign policy matters. He held no lengthy session briefing for his new secretary on his hopes and expectations in the foreign policy realm. Rather he expected Byrnes to brief himself on the pressing issues and then to guide the administration's foreign policy.

The new secretary of state took office at a time when numerous issues demanded attention and with his departure for a major international conference less than a week away. A less capable person might have faltered, but Byrnes pushed forward with preparations for the Potsdam meeting.[36] His independence, pragmatism, and tactical skill stood him in good stead. Byrnes now held the office of secretary of state, but he operated without relying heavily on the department he headed. Instead, he depended on a small circle of trusted confidantes, which initially included his secretary Walter Brown, the State Department counselor Ben Cohen, and the Soviet specialist Charles Bohlen, who translated for the American delegations at both Yalta and Potsdam. He came to his new office without any grand strategic vision. Tactics rather than strategy were

---

34 For McCloy's recollections of the June 18 meeting and his subsequent meeting with Byrnes, see "McCloy on the A-Bomb" included as an appendix in James Reston, *Deadline: A Memoir* (New York, 1992), pp. 495–500. Also see John J. McCloy, *The Challenge to American Foreign Policy* (Cambridge, 1953), pp. 41–43; and McCloy's comments to Forrestal in Millis, ed., *Forrestal Diaries*, pp. 70–71.

35 This account and the direct quotation is drawn from the diary entry for July 3 of Byrnes's associate Walter Brown. See "WB's Book" (hereafter Brown Diary), in James F. Byrnes Papers, Cooper Library, Folder 602.

36 Byrnes, however, did express some concerns after his first full day on the job. He told his confidante Walter Brown on July 5 that "as matters stood last night he would gladly have taken Justice Robert's place on the Supreme Court." (Justice Owen Roberts announced his resignation on July 5, 1945.) See entry for July 5, 1945, in Brown Diary, James F. Byrnes Papers, Cooper Library, Folder 602.

PHOTO 7. James F. Byrnes is sworn in as U.S. secretary of state succeeding Edward R. Stettinius, Jr., on July 3, 1945. Left to right are Chief Justice Richard S. Whaley of the U.S. Court of Claims, who administered the oath; Mrs. James F. Byrnes; the new secretary of state; and President Harry S. Truman. (Courtesy National Archives)

his forte, but he brought with him over three decades of experience as a negotiator. He prepared to put that talent to special use at Potsdam.

Byrnes identified with the broad policies set forth by Franklin Roosevelt for the postwar world, and he came to his new office with a genuine desire to maintain good relations with the Soviet Union. He possessed no sympathy for the more hard-line attitude that certain State Department officials aimed toward the Soviet Union. Tellingly, he proved as open as Truman to the advice of Ambassador Joseph Davies. In late May in response to a rising strain of anti-Soviet commentary in the press, Byrnes encouraged Davies to explain to "our Russian friends" that "those in responsible positions are determined to let nothing interfere with the friendly relations existing between our two countries."[37] Byrnes joined Truman and Leahy on June 3 to hear Davies's report on his return from his encounter with Churchill. But with Davies, one briefing rarely proved sufficient. A further briefing specifically for Byrnes followed on June 5 over lunch at the Davies estate, Tregaron, where the wealthy host warned that "Churchill seemed bent on controlling the balance of power in Europe even at the expense of peace, and he intended to use American resources to back him up."[38] Davies received reassurance from Byrnes who declared "that there was only one hope for peace and that was to hold the confidence of the Soviets in our good faith." In a meeting with Davies the following evening, Byrnes clarified more of his stance. He confided that he left Yalta convinced "that Stalin could be relied upon once his word was given." Furthermore, he demonstrated little sympathy for the London Poles and rejected the more stringent interpretation of the Yalta agreement on Poland offered by Harriman. Clearly he wanted to move beyond that troublesome matter.[39]

Davies's capable biographer, Elizabeth Kimball MacLean, suggested that the approach of both Byrnes and Davies "to the art of diplomacy was strikingly similar. Both," she explained, "had long been committed to the resolution of conflict through negotiation and compromise." There is some truth to this observation as of June–July 1945, although Byrnes would prove a much more canny and tough-minded negotiator than Davies in dealing with the Soviets. Byrnes himself admitted his approach in his 1947 memoir, *Speaking Frankly*, where he asserted that "good government lies in seeking the highest common denominator. This is as true in international councils as it is in the county court house."[40] He certainly aimed to achieve the highest common denominator in the councils at Potsdam.

Joseph Davies continued his regular meetings with Byrnes through late June and early July. Clearly there existed a close connection between them. Davies occasionally visited Byrnes at his apartment at the Shoreham Hotel, and they met over meals such as dinner on July 1 where they "discussed Potsdam problems and Russia." Presumably, it was with Byrnes's ready agreement that Truman called Davies aside at the swearing in of the new secretary of state and told him that he was "counting on" his going to Potsdam.[41] The inveterate Soviet sympathizer needed no prompting. He left the next day from New York on the ocean liner *Queen Elizabeth* bound for London, from where he traveled on to Frankfort and then to Potsdam. He would sit beside Truman and Byrnes and Admiral Leahy at the conference table.

[37] Byrnes quoted in MacLean, *Joseph E. Davies*, p. 152.

[38] These words are those of MacLean summarizing Davies's position. See her *Joseph E. Davies*, p. 152.

[39] This account relies directly on MacLean, *Joseph E. Davies*, p. 153.

[40] James F. Byrnes, *Speaking Frankly* (New York, 1947), pp. 91–92. (My reading of MacLean led me to Byrnes's comment.)

[41] The Davies–Byrnes meetings can be tracked in the relevant diary and journal entries in Joseph E. Davies Papers, Library of Congress, Box 17. Davies's account of Truman's invitation for him to attend Potsdam is also included there in his diary entry for July 3, 1945.

While Davies secured an invitation to the Big Three gathering, other senior administration officials still scurried to obtain presidential approval to join his team in Germany. Secretary of War Stimson and Treasury Secretary Morgenthau each angled for the opportunity to exercise influence at the conference, but Truman displayed little enthusiasm for their presence. Poor Stimson, the distinguished elder statesman of the Cabinet no less, tepidly raised the matter with Truman on July 2 by inquiring if the president feared whether he "could not physically stand the trip."[42] He had spent their meeting yet again instructing Truman on the importance of the atomic bomb to his meeting with Stalin and Churchill and implying the value of his presence to offer counsel on this matter, but Truman deflected his inquiry and merely promised to consider his request. Nonetheless, Stimson continued to press his views on Truman. In a further meeting with Truman in the Oval Office on July 3 after Byrnes's swearing-in ceremony and acting with the endorsement of the Interim Committee, he advised Truman as to how to inform Stalin regarding the A-bomb. He then focused on Germany. Continuing his campaign against the residual impact of the Morgenthau Plan, he warned against "vengeance" and a harsh approach to the Germans. Knowing that Byrnes sympathized with his approach, he told Truman to ignore the Treasury secretary and to leave matters in the hands of the new secretary of state. Truman hardly needed the waspish old man, who sprinkled his counsel with negative remarks about the "the problem of our Jewish people here," to reach this conclusion. But presumably upon seeing their accord, he invited Stimson to attend the Potsdam meeting.[43] The secretary of war would not be a full participant in the main negotiating sessions but would be available for consultation.[44]

Stimson at least received an invitation to attend the Big Three meeting. Morgenthau was not so fortunate. The Treasury secretary's anxiety about the direction on German policy, his relationship with Truman, and the appointment of Byrnes came to a climax in a meeting at the White House on July 5. There are competing claims as to what took place at this meeting. Truman recalled with predictable color that "when the trip to Potsdam was being arranged, Morgenthau came to see me and said he had to go along. I said 'I don't need you and it's not your business.'...He said, "If I can't go to Potsdam, what's going to happen to the Morgenthau Plan?' I said they could throw it out the window. He pouted and said he would quit. 'All right,' I said, 'I accept your

---

[42] Stimson diary, July 2, 1945, Henry L. Stimson Papers, Sterling Memorial Library.

[43] Stimson diary, July 3, 1945, Henry L. Stimson Papers, Sterling Memorial Library. Also see Michael Beschloss's account of the Truman–Stimson meeting, which highlights the negative comments toward Jews made by both men. *The Conquerors*, p. 246.

[44] Also note that Secretary of the Navy James V. Forrestal arrived in Potsdam virtually self-invited, while Ambassador to Moscow Averell Harriman underwent the humiliation of requesting permission to attend, only to be ignored by Truman and Byrnes at the conference. See Millis, ed., *Forrestal Diaries*, pp. 88–89; *FRUS: The Conference of Berlin (The Potsdam Conference), 1945*, I, pp. 132, 144; and Harriman and Abel, *Special Envoy to Churchill and Stalin*, p. 488.

resignation right now.' "[45] This account suffers from the usual retrospective Truman embellishment and neglects the fact that Truman already had conveyed to Morgenthau that he would not go to Potsdam.[46] Perhaps it reflects what Truman wished he had said to Morgenthau, but the more reliable description of the meeting comes from Morgenthau. He asked the president to scotch the rumors that he was about to be sacked and requested confirmation that Truman wanted him "to stay until VJ-Day." Truman vacillated and suggested that he might want to appoint a new Treasury secretary. "Staggered and hurt," as Michael Beschloss put it, Morgenthau demanded an affirmation of confidence and a commitment of support. With none forthcoming, he submitted his resignation and insisted that it be announced that very evening.[47]

Truman had hoped that Morgenthau would stay on until after Potsdam when he would replace him with the OWMR director and former congressman, Fred Vinson. Morgenthau's emotion and some concerns about his being next in line in presidential succession to Truman and Byrnes as they left the country prompted Vinson's nomination to be hurried forward. By the time Truman left for Potsdam on July 7, Morgenthau's twelve-year reign at the Treasury had come to an end.[48] His sudden demise no doubt pleased Byrnes who had warned Stimson as late as July 4 that Morgenthau was "on the prowl" again and eager to get to Germany.[49] With Morgenthau out of the picture and Stimson endorsing his authority, Byrnes knew that he would have basic control of the formulation of policy toward Germany. This, he clearly recognized, would be central to the American endeavor to secure a viable postwar peace in Europe and one that would need approval at home.

Byrnes's antennae were well tuned on German matters and their implications for both the United States and European stability. Along with Harry Hopkins, he had alerted Truman in his first week in office as to the importance of the German reparations issue, which in turn had prompted Truman to select Edwin Pauley as his negotiator and to clarify that the United States would not finance German reparations either directly or indirectly. The new secretary shared and strengthened Truman's conviction that the United States should not bear any responsibility to subsidize reparation payments. He also shared Truman's concern at the danger of political, social, and economic upheaval in Europe in the

---

[45] Truman interview with aides, January 22, 1954, Harry S. Truman Papers: Post-Presidential Files, HSTL, Box 643. For a more tempered Truman version, see his *Year of Decisions*, pp. 362–63.

[46] On Truman's prior decision on Morgenthau and Potsdam, see Beschloss, *The Conquerors*, pp. 242–43.

[47] This account of the meeting, which relies heavily on material in Morgenthau's papers, is drawn from Beschloss, *The Conquerors*, pp. 247–48. Also see Blum, ed., *From the Morgenthau Diaries*, Vol. 3, *Years of War*, pp. 465–67.

[48] Beschloss gives more details on all of this including the concerns about Truman and Byrnes being succeeded "by an unelected Jewish President, poised to enact his vindictive plan against Germany." *The Conquerors*, p. 249.

[49] Stimson diary, July 4, 1945, Henry L. Stimson Papers, Sterling Memorial Library.

wake of Hitler's defeat. Truman addressed the issue on May 22 in a public letter to the heads of various war agencies such as the War Production Board and the War Food Administration. Reflecting the influence of Stimson and McCloy, he argued that "the future permanent peace of Europe depends upon the restoration of the economy of these liberated countries including a reasonable standard of living and employment." He warned that "a chaotic and hungry Europe is not a fertile ground in which stable, democratic and friendly governments can be reared."[50]

The prospect of calamity in the part of Europe under Anglo-American control troubled policy makers greatly. Encouraged by the state and war departments, Truman put the matter to Churchill in late June. "From all the reports which reach me," he wrote, "I believe that without immediate concentration on the production of German coal we will have turmoil and unrest in the very areas of Western Europe on which the whole stability of the continent depends."[51] As Melvyn Leffler has clarified well, Truman's letter revealed the "emphasis American officials immediately assigned to Germany as a source of coal for the stabilization and reconstruction of all of western Europe." They soon realized that addressing the coal situation could not be done in isolation. Increasing coal production "depended upon solving transportation problems, alleviating food shortages, and establishing currency stability." Furthermore, as General Lucius Clay, the newly appointed American military governor in Germany quickly discerned, in order to resuscitate coal production "substantial amounts of food, clothing and even machinery would have to be imported into Germany."[52] Such imports would cost money – money that Byrnes quickly concluded should not come from the United States.

Jimmy Byrnes, deft operator as always, determined upon a suitable course of action. Payments to cover German import costs would be the first charge on German exports from current German production. He held this proposal vastly preferable to any program of American payments to cover such costs. But this proposal had major implications for the whole question of reparations, which Pauley attended to in meetings at Moscow at that very time. Byrnes quickly conveyed to his reparations negotiator the need for the Soviets to appreciate that their reparations demands would not take precedence over the necessity of covering the German import costs deemed essential to foster the crucial coal industry's revival.[53] The creative – some might even say devious – mind

[50] Letter to the heads of war agencies, May 22, 1945, Truman, *Public Papers of the Presidents of the United States: Harry S. Truman, 1945*, p. 61.

[51] Truman to Churchill, June 24, 1945, *FRUS: The Conference of Berlin (The Potsdam Conference), 1945*, I, p. 612.

[52] Melvyn P. Leffler, *The Struggle for Germany and the Origins of the Cold War* (Washington, DC, 1996), pp. 18–21. Leffler is especially helpful on this subject.

[53] Byrnes to Pauley, July 3, 1945, *FRUS: The Conference of Berlin (The Potsdam Conference), 1945*, I, p. 623. For helpful details on the significance of the "reparations issue" for American policy makers, see James McAllister, *No Exit*, pp. 78–84.

of Byrnes began to focus on the various ramifications of the German issue and its connection to U.S.-Soviet relations. These related matters would be the dominant topic of discussion and deliberation on his journey to Potsdam with Truman.

After his arrival in Moscow in mid-June, American Reparations Ambassador Pauley resisted the Soviet effort to discuss reparations in terms of the exact dollar amount, twenty billion dollars, mentioned at Yalta. He argued instead for a survey of German ability to pay and the adoption of a reparations formula that would emphasize "percentages rather than dollars."[54] After further instructions from Byrnes and right as the American delegation set out for Potsdam, Pauley proposed a list of principles to govern the preparation and administration of a reparations plan. The final principle stated plainly that "in working out the economic balance of Germany the necessary means must be provided for payment of imports approved by the gov[ernmen]ts concerned before reparation deliveries are made from current production or from stocks of goods."[55] Approved imports must be a "prior charge" on German exports. As Pauley later explained to his Soviet opposite on the Reparation Commission, Ivan Maisky, that if "indispensable imports . . . are not a charge against the exports, then you, or we or some other economy will have to pay for the imports."[56] In the Byrnes–Pauley view, it would not be the United States. Thus, the Americans and Soviets would arrive at Potsdam quite divided over the amount of and procedure for collecting reparations from Germany.

Truman fully approved of the Byrnes–Pauley approach, although he gladly let Byrnes make the running on the subject. He had devoted significant time in May and June to preparation of the budget for fiscal year 1946.[57] He also had made Cabinet changes in a number of domestic portfolios replacing Postmaster General Frank Walker with Robert E. Hannegan, Attorney General Francis Biddle with Tom C. Clark, Secretary of Labor Frances Perkins with Lewis B. Schwellenbach, and Secretary of Agriculture Claude R. Wickard with Clinton P. Anderson. He evidenced greater comfort in this realm. His preference for domestic issues and reticence to engage in international diplomacy became more obvious as the Potsdam departure date approached. Few are the American chief executives who privately whined so much about attending an international meeting. "I am getting ready to go see Stalin and Churchill," he

[54] See Pauley to secretary of state, June 19, 1945, *FRUS: The Conference of Berlin (The Potsdam Conference), 1945*, I, pp. 510–11.

[55] For this list, see Pauley to secretary of state, July 6, 1945, *FRUS: The Conference of Berlin (The Potsdam Conference), 1945*, I, pp. 527–28.

[56] Pauley to Maisky, July 13, 1945, *FRUS: The Conference of Berlin (The Potsdam Conference), 1945*, I, pp. 547–48. Pauley's tough negotiating style was applied against the British as well as the Soviets. See J. E. Farquharson, "Anglo-American Policy on German Reparations from Yalta to Potsdam," pp. 914–26.

[57] See the range of topics he discussed in weekly meetings with Budget Director Harold D. Smith in Smith's diary, Harold D. Smith Papers, HSTL, Box 1.

wrote to his mother and his sister Mary on July 3. "I have to take my tuxedo, tails, Negro preacher coat, high hat, low hat and hard hat as well as sundry other things. I have a briefcase filled up with information on past conferences and suggestions on what I'm to do and say. Wish I didn't have to go, but I do and it can't be stopped now."[58] On the day of his departure for Europe he confided to his diary: "Talked to Bess last night and the night before. She wasn't happy about my going to see Mr. Russia and Mr. Great Britain – neither am I." He summarized his feelings by exclaiming on paper: "How I hate this trip!"[59]

However reluctantly, Truman geared up to undertake this major international mission and his first trip across the Atlantic since his time in uniform during World War I. The general American approach centered on obtaining agreements and settling the "remaining wartime problems so that U.S. military and economic responsibilities in Europe could be terminated."[60] The Americans, it must be stressed, did not set off with an anti-Soviet disposition. Truman, perhaps with some retrospective exaggeration, recalled that he "went to Potsdam with the kindliest feelings in the world toward Russia."[61] Even Joseph Grew at the State Department complained that Churchill's list of proposed topics for the conference "is so drawn as to give the appearance largely of a bill of complaints against the Soviet Government," which he archly noted, "seems hardly the proper approach to the forthcoming meeting."[62] Regardless of their sincere desire for agreements, however, the Truman–Byrnes team went to Potsdam with a different approach to negotiations than the one pursued by Franklin Roosevelt guided by Harry Hopkins. Neither Truman nor Byrnes focused either on winning Stalin's trust or coaxing him into concessions. Instead the new American leaders approached their discussions with the Soviets, and the British as politicians and practical men eager to reach the best deal they could for THEIR country. "I'm not working for any interest but the Republic of the United States," Truman confirmed in his diary on the very day the USS Augusta set out to carry him and his party across the Atlantic.[63] The president and his secretary of state essentially saw the representatives of the nations with whom they must deal as mirror images of themselves – practical men with

[58] Truman, *Year of Decisions*, p. 367. Truman recalled in a television interview with David Susskind on *Open End* (channel 5 TV) September 1961, that "he was uneasy about leaving Washington. He felt the President should remain in the United States and not go traipsing around Europe, but at the same time he felt obliged to go to Potsdam in order to implement the Yalta Agreements." Quoted in Herbert M. Druks, *Harry S. Truman and the Russians, 1945–1953* (New York, 1966), p. 76.

[59] Diary entry, July 7, 1945, Ferrell, ed., *Off the Record*, p. 49.

[60] This is the argument of Randall B. Woods and Howard Jones in their *Dawning of the Cold War*, p. 58.

[61] Interview with Truman, January 22, 1954, Harry S. Truman Papers: Post-Presidential Files, HSTL, Box 643.

[62] Grew to Truman, June 14, 1945, *FRUS: The Conference of Berlin (The Potsdam Conference), 1945*, I, p. 164.

[63] Ferrell, ed., *Off the Record*, p. 49.

whom a deal could be struck, who would be working for the interests of their respective countries.[64]

Truman and Byrnes considered it especially important that the Potsdam settlement be politically palatable in the United States. On July 6, his final day in Washington before the trip, the president received a memorandum signed by his personal advisers and presidential aides, John Snyder, Sam Rosenman, and George Allen, outlining the "consensus" reached at a meeting they held with Truman on July 4 at which they discussed the important issues for and desired outcomes of the conference. Notably they listed "the entry of Russia into the Japanese War," as the first objective for the president with the "economic stabilization of Europe" listed second. They went on to express to Truman their view that "as a well known Missouri horse trader, the American people expect you to bring something home to them."[65] Truman's determination to be a "Missouri horse trader" made him receptive to Pauley's efforts on reparations and to Byrnes's developing approach built around hard negotiations with the Soviets and the British. As he left the United States, he referred approvingly to Byrnes as his "able and conniving Secretary of State," adding that he had "a keen mind" and was an "honest man." Addressing Pauley's efforts in Moscow, Truman complained that "the smart boys in the State Department, as usual, are against the best interests of the U.S. if they can circumvent a straightforward hard hitting trader for the home front. But they are stymied this time. Byrnes [and] I shall expect our interests to come first. Pauley is doing a job for the United States."[66]

The *Augusta* set forth from Newport News bound for Antwerp on July 7. Truman had Byrnes and Leahy as his principal advisers, and Byrnes, in turn, drew advice from Ben Cohen, the New Dealer whom he appointed as counselor in the State Department, and from State Department professionals H. Freeman Matthews and Charles Bohlen. Truman also brought along his press secretary, Charlie Ross; his military aide, Brigadier General Harry Vaughan; his naval aide, Captain James K. Vardaman; and an old Missouri friend, Marshal Fred Canfil. None of these men had any substantive policy role, but, especially in case of Vaughan and Canfil, they served as court jesters and card players with the president. Truman found the trip rather to his liking. Although reticent to leave the United States and nervous about meeting the legendary leaders of Great Britain and the Soviet Union, he enjoyed the ocean cruise and the entertainment provided on board the ship.[67] Every night the president's party gathered in the captain's cabin for a movie or some musical program. Watching

[64] Woods and Jones make this same point in *Dawning of the Cold War*, p. 58.

[65] Snyder, Rosenman, and Allen to Truman, July 6, 1945, *FRUS: The Conference of Berlin (The Potsdam Conference), 1945*, I, p. 228.

[66] Truman diary entry, July 7, 1945, Ferrell, ed., *Off the Record*, p. 49. (It is unclear who exactly Truman had in mind in targeting the State Department officials.)

[67] Charles Bohlen, who traveled with Truman, reported that the president was "understandably somewhat nervous about confronting such awesome figures as Churchill and Stalin." Bohlen, *Witness to History*, p. 226.

Bob Hope in *Princess and the Pirate, Something for the Boys* starring Carmen Miranda, and the Betty Grable showpiece, *Diamond Horseshoe*, apparently helped lift his spirits as did his morning walks on deck, the bracing sea air, and lengthy poker sessions with his cronies.[68]

Of course the trip was hardly a pleasure cruise. During the mornings, Byrnes gathered with Cohen, Matthews, and Bohlen to discuss the issues to be raised at the upcoming meeting. The State Department had prepared a massive book of briefing papers addressing a whole range of issues under the broad topics of general questions, European questions, Far Eastern questions, and Near Eastern and African questions.[69] They honed down the enormous State Department brief into manageable objectives for agreement. Byrnes relayed the substance of their discussions to Truman in conversations each day. They focused primarily on Germany and the implications of its treatment for the stability of Europe. Bohlen remembered that the president took advantage of the conferences on the ship "to absorb information and ask pertinent questions." He also noted that Truman "rarely philosophized about the future of the world."[70] Such philosophizing had no appeal to Truman. He wanted results such as the early entry of the Soviet Union into the war against Japan and, at base, "to come out with a working relationship to prevent another world catastrophe."[71]

By the time Truman's party arrived in Europe, they had settled on four major issues upon which they would seek agreement above and beyond the U.S. interest in obtaining Soviet military support against the Japanese. The first involved developing "procedure and machinery for peace negotiations and territorial settlements." Truman and Byrnes had no expectation that Potsdam would serve as the location for fashioning peace treaties with the defeated foes. Rather, it would be the place where agreement could be reached on the process for preparing such treaties. Here lay the basis for the American proposal to establish a council of foreign ministers. Not surprisingly German matters occupied a crucial place on the American list. The United States would seek to settle on principles to govern the occupation and also would seek a new approach on reparations following on the failure of the Reparations Commission in Moscow to finalize this matter. Lastly, the Americans wanted agreement on "plans for carrying out the Yalta Declaration on Liberated Europe, with the hope," as Byrnes remembered, "of ending the constant friction which had prevailed over Russian policy in eastern Europe since the Crimea Conference."[72] They had other objectives such as Truman's pet proposal to guarantee free navigation of Europe's inland waterways, but these major issues lay at the core of the American diplomatic

---

[68] Byrnes apparently was annoyed at the time Truman devoted to poker over his diplomatic briefings. See Ferrell, *Harry S. Truman*, p. 204.

[69] The various recommendations and papers that constituted the president's brief for the Potsdam meeting are included in *FRUS: The Conference of Berlin (The Potsdam Conference), 1945*, I, pp. 283–1054.

[70] Bohlen, *Witness to History*, p. 226.

[71] Truman, *Year of Decisions*, p. 358.

[72] Byrnes, *Speaking Frankly*, pp. 67–68.

PHOTO 8. President Truman, Secretary Byrnes, and Admiral of the Fleet William D. Leahy, on a tour of Berlin, stop to view the ruins of the Reichstag building, July 16, 1945. (Courtesy National Archives)

purpose at Potsdam. Byrnes eventually would seek to relate them in developing a compromise agreement.

On July 14, the *USS Augusta* and its accompanying cruiser, *USS Philadelphia*, reached British waters off Portsmouth where a British fleet met the American vessels. The ships exchanged honors, and Truman received the salute. The next day, the *Augusta* docked in Antwerp where General Eisenhower met the president and his party. From Belgium, the American team flew to Berlin, the seat of the thousand-year Reich, which now lay in ruins. The president and his party then drove to the Babelsberg district of Potsdam where the Soviets had assigned Truman to a yellow stucco villa by a small lake, which became the "Little White House." Here he settled in and readied himself for the meetings ahead at the conference to which Churchill, with unwitting insight, had given the codename of "Terminal." The symbolic overtones and implications of this codename should not disguise the fact that Truman thought this would be but the first of a series of meetings to secure the peace.

Potsdam Preliminaries

The portrayal of the Potsdam conference usually focuses on the interactions of the principals Truman, Stalin, and Churchill, whose place as prime minister was taken by Clement Attlee midway through the meeting.[73] Their conversations and the formal meetings around the conference table at the Cecilienhof Palace, once the estate of the former Crown Prince Wilhelm, hold their own importance, but they were not central to the ultimate outcome of the meeting. The essential discussions took place one level down, and James F. Byrnes played the crucial role in designing the final settlement at this meeting. He, not Truman, proved to be the principal American negotiator, a role he undertook with Truman's approval. Neither Churchill nor Stalin initially appreciated fully Byrnes's importance. They eagerly sought out the new president wanting to take the measure of the man who now stood in the shoes of FDR.

On July 16, Winston Churchill called upon Harry Truman at the Little White House. The garrulous British leader had been eager to visit his American opposite late the previous evening, but Truman had put him off, thereby indicating that he did not share the prime minister's nocturnal inclinations. They eventually conversed for two hours beginning at the ungodly hour (for Churchill) of 11:00 A.M. The prime minister later wrote of Truman's "gay, precise, sparkling manner and obvious power of decision."[74] He confided to his daughter Mary immediately after the meeting that he "liked the President immensely," and felt sure that he could work with him.[75] There is no transcript of the meeting, but Truman's summary of it gives a reasonable sense of its contents. "He gave me a lot of hooey," Truman wrote of Churchill in his diary, "about how great my country is and how he loved Roosevelt and how he intended to love me etc. etc." Churchill no doubt effusively sought to establish a close relationship with FDR's successor, but he now dealt with a more plain character. After his meeting, Truman expressed his own confidence that they could "get along if he doesn't try to give me too much soft soap." The Allied leaders "struck a blow for liberty," although in scotch rather than bourbon much to Truman's dismay. After photos were taken, each man then took the chance to tour the remnants of Berlin. Observing the damage Truman observed accurately: "Hitler's folly."[76]

---

[73] For an overview of the conference see Charles L. Mee, Jr., *Meeting at Potsdam* (New York, 1975).

[74] Churchill, *Triumph and Tragedy*, p. 630.

[75] Mary Soames letter, July 16, 1945, quoted in Martin Gilbert, *Winston S. Churchill*, VIII, p. 61.

[76] Truman diary entry, July 16, 1945, Ferrell, ed., *Off the Record*, p. 51.

Stalin arrived in Potsdam on July 16. Joseph Davies acted as go-between with the Soviets and relayed that the Soviet leader expressed a desire to visit with Truman that very evening. As with Churchill, and much to the dismay of the anxious Davies, Truman – an unreconstructed "morning person" – declined and deferred their meeting to the next day.[77] Stalin came to the Little White House right before noon on July 17, and after initial pleasantries they "got down to business" according to Truman's account. Truman explained that he was "no diplomat" but wanted to answer "yes or no" on hearing the arguments. He straightforwardly assured Stalin of his friendship. So assured, Stalin, with his usual negotiating skill, set forth a number of items for the conference agenda that might be considered a reach even for a man of his voracious appetite for power and control. Truman referred to them as "dynamite," presumably for their likely explosive impact on Churchill. The Soviet leader mentioned removing Franco's fascist government in Spain, appropriately disposing of Italian colonies in North Africa, and obtaining a share of the German fleet. In a bid to gain American goodwill and perhaps also to clarify the American need for Soviet support against Japan, the Generalissimo maligned Churchill and the British effort in the Pacific war and suggested that now the Russians and the Americans form an alliance to defeat Japan while Great Britain had little to offer.[78] Truman welcomed the assurances of Soviet participation in the Pacific war. He observed in his diary that evening regarding the Soviet commitment to declare war against Japan in mid-August that it would mean "fini Japs [sic] when that comes about."[79] The president prevailed on his Soviet opposite to stay for lunch and after the usual round of toasting at any gathering involving the Russians there followed the inevitable photos.

Truman appreciated his meeting with Stalin. "I can deal with Stalin," he reassured himself, and then offered the flawed assessment that "he is honest – but smart as hell."[80] The Missouri trader seemed to believe that Stalin's "honesty" bore a certain resemblance to that of a tough political boss in the United States like Tom Pendergast, an analogy both astoundingly naïve and ample

[77] On Davies's efforts to arrange the meeting and his dismay when Truman deferred it, see Potsdam journal, July 16, 1945, Joseph E. Davies Papers, Library of Congress, Box 18.

[78] This summary of the first Truman–Stalin meeting relies upon Bohlen's cryptic notes printed in Mee, Jr., *Meeting at Potsdam*, pp. 90–94, and Truman's diary entry, July 17, 1945, Ferrell, ed., *Off the Record*, p. 53.

[79] Diary entry, July 17, 1945, Ferrell, ed., *Off the Record*, p. 53. The exact meaning of this late-night diary entry has been much debated and probably overly so. The remark most likely points to Truman's excitement that Soviet entry would hurry along the defeat of Japan. The suggestion that this comment illustrates a belief that Soviet entry would be sufficient, of itself, to bring about Japan's defeat seems far-fetched. As J. Samuel Walker recently has noted, the military guidance that Truman had received held that "an invasion or 'imminent' invasion, combined with Soviet participation in the war," would be required to bring about Japan's defeat. In that Truman hardly felt capable of challenging the judgment of his military advisers, his diary entry should be interpreted in light of the military advice he received on the matter. J. Samuel Walker, "Recent Literature on Truman's Atomic Bomb Decision: A Search for Middle Ground," *Diplomatic History*, 29 (April 2005), p. 320.

[80] Diary entry, July 17, 1945, Ferrell, ed., *Off the Record*, p. 53.

grounds for poor Boss Tom, whatever his flaws, to pursue legal action for defamation of character were he still alive.[81] Truman's regard and even affection for Stalin was genuine and surfaced on subsequent occasions, most famously during his 1948 campaign when he publicly admitted: "I like old Joe," and went on to brand him "a prisoner of the Politburo."[82] The president certainly maintained a friendly disposition to Stalin at Potsdam. On July 18 at a lunch at Stalin's residence, he asked the Soviet leader to travel to the United States and even promised to send the battleship *Missouri* to bring him on such a friendly visit. One wonders what Stalin's suspicious mind made of the prospect of his being transported to America on a U.S. battleship, but his vocal response instead raised the issue of misunderstandings between the American and Soviet peoples. Truman earnestly responded "that we each could help to remedy that situation in our home countries" and promised to "to try with all I had to do my part at home."[83] Truman hardly approached Stalin warily as a harsh dictator let alone as one of the world's greatest moral monsters. Just like FDR, he wanted to secure Soviet-American friendship in the postwar years and to firm up Soviet participation in the war against Japan.[84]

Joseph Davies represented a constant voice in the ear of Truman and Byrnes, promoting a conciliatory stance toward the Soviet Union. He arrived at Potsdam a day before Truman and engaged in discussion with Ed Pauley, Averell Harriman, and other U.S. officials. Taken aback by Pauley's tough approach on reparations and Harriman's negative attitude to Soviet demands on the Dardanelles and Eastern European issues, Davies worked himself up into a lather of concern and pronounced the general atmosphere to be "not cooperative" but rather "hostile." The intention of some of the American delegation to get "the best of a horse trade" offended him.[85] When Truman and Byrnes

---

[81] On Truman's view of Stalin as a tough political boss, see Deborah Welch Larson, *Origins of Containment: A Psychological Explanation* (Princeton, NJ, 1985), pp. 177–78. Alonzo Hamby noted that "the idea that Stalin could be thought of as a tough political boss analogous to Tom Pendergast, Ed Kelly, or other such American types was widespread in the America of 1945; it was among the most distinctive expressions of the innocence with which the United States began its assumption of world leadership." Hamby, *Man of the People*, p. 314.

[82] For the quote and further discussion of the 1948 episode, see Clark Clifford with Richard Holbrooke, *Counsel to the President*, pp. 200–01. Note that this was not simply a case of Truman's "mis-speaking" on the campaign trail. Asked years later by *Washington Post* White House correspondent Edward T. Folliard why he made the comment in 1948, he replied of Stalin: "Because I did like him." See Oral History Interview with Edward T. Folliard, August 20, 1970, HSTL, transcript p. 48. In a letter drafted for but not sent to Dean Acheson after leaving office, Truman referred to Stalin as "the unconscionable Russian Dictator" but then noted: "And I liked the little son of a bitch." See Truman to Acheson, March 15, 1957, in Monte M. Poen, *Strictly Personal and Confidential: The Letters Harry S. Truman Never Mailed* (Boston, 1982), p. 33.

[83] Diary entry, July 18, 1945, Ferrell, ed., *Off the Record*, p. 54.

[84] On July 18, Truman wrote to his wife that "I've gotten what I came for – Stalin goes to war August 15 with no strings on it....I'll say that we'll end the war a year sooner now, and think of the kids who won't be killed! That is the important thing." Truman letter, July 18, 1945, Ferrell, ed., *Dear Bess*, p. 519.

[85] Davies diary, July 14, 1945, Joseph E. Davies Papers, Library of Congress, Box 17.

PHOTO 9. Triple handshake! President Truman held Churchill's and Stalin's hands in a triple handshake during the opening day of the Potsdam conference. The occasion was a dinner given by Churchill at his residence for Truman and Stalin on July 17, 1945. (Courtesy National Archives)

arrived the next day, Davies had ready access to them. He engaged in a lengthy conference with Byrnes trying to inoculate the secretary from the influence of the more hard-line American advisers. They also addressed the possibility of the conference reaching "an over-all agreement in principle as to the vital matters" so as to prevent "long-drawn-out negotiations and discussions on single countries instead of the world peace problem."[86]

---

[86] Davies diary-journal, July 15, 1945, Joseph E. Davies Papers, Library of Congress, Box 18. Davies wanted to avoid "sparring on isolated and lesser issues, which would arouse suspicions and ill-will."

Byrnes and Davies continued their discussions the following day with the secretary of state raising concerns about Soviet actions in Bulgaria and Rumania. Davies replied vigorously by comparing Soviet behavior to the unilateral British actions in Greece in late 1944 and 1945. Sounding rather like a Soviet representative, he emphasized the need for the Soviets to guarantee their physical security and warned that they could not be either "bluffed" or "dictated to." Then in an exquisite "prima donna" performance Davies offered that it might be best if he returned home, which brought the presumably desired response from Byrnes that he must stay. Byrnes declared Davies's service as "invaluable" and requested that he sit beside him at the conference table.[87] Davies later pulled a similar stunt with Truman and also received from him a request that he stay, along with a heartfelt promise that he was "trying my best to save the Peace and to follow out ROOSEVELT's plans."[88] He still genuinely believed this.

Truman and Byrnes hardly needed the added burden of placating Davies's fears and concerns at this time. They had much else on their minds including events occurring thousands of miles away. Early in the morning of July 16 at "Trinity," the codename for the Manhattan Project test site in Alamogordo, New Mexico, a group of officials and scientists led by General Leslie Groves and J. Robert Oppenheimer witnessed the first explosion of an atomic bomb. They saw the dramatic flash of light and the huge fireball and felt the shockwaves from the explosion almost a minute after the light had flashed. On closer inspection, the observers noted the severe destruction well over a half mile from the bomb's crater. They judged the bomb a success beyond their expectations. Groves quickly conveyed word of the test to Stimson's aide George Harrison, who relayed the news to the secretary of war in cryptic fashion: "Operated on this morning. Diagnosis not yet complete but results seem satisfactory and already exceed expectations."[89] Stimson, filled with excitement, gave Truman a preliminary report in the evening after the president's return from his tour of Berlin. The reality of the bomb in no way altered Truman's decision to use it. It simply, as he reportedly said, took a "great load" off his mind.[90]

Stimson briefed Byrnes at some length on the atomic test the next morning and tried to persuade him that the United States now should alter its plan to utilize the new weapon. Aware of the existence of Japanese peace "feelers" and their efforts to use the Russians as intermediaries, Stimson argued that the combination of a strong warning about the bomb and a firm assurance that the Japanese could retain their emperor might suffice to bring about a Japanese capitulation.[91] Strongly influenced by former Secretary of State

[87] Davies diary-journal, July 16, 1945, Joseph E. Davies Papers, Library of Congress, Box 18.

[88] Davies journal, July 16, 1945, Joseph E. Davies Papers, Library of Congress, Box 18. (Emphasis as in original.)

[89] Harrison to Stimson (War Dept. 32887), July 16, 1945, quoted in Mee, Jr., *Meeting at Potsdam*, p. 86.

[90] Davies diary, July 16, 1945, Joseph E. Davies Papers, Library of Congress, Box 18.

[91] The United States had cracked the Japanese code for diplomatic correspondence and followed the exchanges between Japanese Foreign Minister Togo and Japanese Ambassador in Moscow

Cordell Hull, Byrnes bluntly rejected both ideas.[92] He continued, as David Robertson explained, "to think about the use of the atomic bomb and the end of the war against Japan primarily in terms of U.S. political consequences."[93] Byrnes, the experienced politician, saw twin dangers for himself and for the president he served. On the one hand, retreating from the unconditional surrender terms might be exploited by the Japanese as a sign of American war weariness and cause a political firestorm among a public that held no love for Japan or its ruler. On the other hand, not taking advantage of measures that might bring the war to a speedy end and prevent further American casualties would leave him and Truman vulnerable to harsh later criticism. From Byrnes's perspective, using the atomic bomb addressed both dangers. It allowed the United States to maintain the surrender terms it had set forth and yet promised a quick end to the struggle. Byrnes easily ignored the hand-wringing of Stimson and others, and with Truman's general endorsement proceeded forward with his diplomatic machinations.

Byrnes and Truman now realized that the atomic attacks on Japan might bring about a surrender prior to the Soviet entry into the Pacific war. After talking over matters with Byrnes and others, the president expressed the belief in his diary that "Japs will fold up before Russia comes in. I am sure they will when Manhattan appears over their homeland."[94] Truman took this as positive news, but he made no moves to depreciate or curtail Soviet participation in the war. His attitude seems to have been that the Allies should apply all possible force to compel Japan's surrender. He wrote his wife on July 20 that he wanted "the Jap war won and I want 'em [Great Britain and the Soviet Union] both in it."[95] In some contrast, Byrnes immediately saw the possession of the atomic bomb in diplomatic terms. As further confirmation of the bomb's explosive force arrived over the coming days, he altered his attitude toward Soviet entry into the war against Japan.[96] His biographer portrayed him as an "atomic *diplomat*," pursuing a diplomatic strategy concerning the Far East influenced by the upcoming

Sato regarding using the Russians to explore peace terms. See transcripts of these messages for July 2, July 5, July 11, July 12, July 15, 1945, in James F. Byrnes Papers, Cooper Library, Folder 571. On July 15, Ambassador Sato argued: "In the long run, since Japan sincerely desires the termination of the war, I believe that she has indeed no choice but to accept unconditional surrender or terms closely approximate thereto." Regrettably, the Japanese government refused to act immediately on his advice.

[92] See the Hull–Byrnes exchange, July 16–17, 1945, in *FRUS: The Conference of Berlin (The Potsdam Conference), 1945*, II, pp. 1267–68. For a discussion of the broader debate in the Truman administration over unconditional surrender, see Richard B. Frank, *Downfall: The End of the Imperial Japanese Empire* (New York, 1999), pp. 214–20.

[93] Robertson, *Sly and Able*, p. 415.

[94] Diary entry, July 18, 1945, Ferrell, ed., *Off the Record*, p. 54.

[95] Truman to Bess Truman, July 20, 1945, Ferrell, ed., *Dear Bess*, p. 520.

[96] Byrnes associate Walter Brown recorded in his diary on July 19 that "JFB determined to out maneuver Stalin on China. Hopes Soong will stand firm and then the Russians will not go in war. Then he feels Japan will surrender before Russia goes to war and this will save China." Entry, July 20, 1945, Brown Diary, James F. Byrnes Papers, Cooper Library, Folder 54 (1).

use of atomic weapons against Japan.[97] This occasional atomic diplomacy bears little resemblance to the elaborate scheme posited by Gar Alperovitz and company, yet it testifies to Byrnes's tactical approach and recognition that he might be able to exploit the powerful new weapon for diplomatic purposes. He reacted quickly to new developments and undertook new approaches to further American ends. Ultimately, however, his attempt at atomic diplomacy was not to mean much.

Diplomacy – Atomic and Otherwise

While Truman and Byrnes came to terms with the meaning and implications of having atomic weapons in the American arsenal, the Potsdam conference formally began on the evening of July 17, the first of its thirteen plenary sessions. Soon after 5:00 P.M., the three delegations entered the large and bright conference room with a fine view of the Cecilienhof Palace gardens. Truman had Byrnes, Davies, Admiral Leahy, and translator Bohlen with him at the large oaken round table. Churchill had Foreign Secretary Eden, Clement Attlee, the now opposition leader (and his soon-to-be successor), along with Sir Alexander Cadogan, a senior foreign office official, to support him. Stalin inevitably had Molotov at his side along with Vyshinsky and Gromyko. Behind each group sat a phalanx of other advisers. Pauley, Harriman, Will Clayton, Ben Cohen, and H. Freeman Matthews were some of the American officials in the conference room, although Stimson did not receive an entry ticket. Stalin immediately proposed that Truman chair the gathering. Although somewhat nervous, the president in businesslike fashion began by outlining agenda items.[98] The formal work of the conference had begun.

Relying on the briefing summary prepared for him, Truman placed four agenda items on the table. Two called for the establishment of bodies to handle some of the crucial postwar issues – first, a council of foreign ministers to negotiate peace treaties with the defeated powers, and then, an Allied control council for Germany that would work to oversee a common policy over what remained of the Axis power. His other items held more of a charge. They called for the implementation of the Yalta Declaration on Liberated Europe in Eastern Europe and finally for the rehabilitation of Italy into the community of nations.

---

[97] Robertson, *Sly and Able*, pp. 420–21.

[98] Truman wrote Bess: "I was so scared I didn't know whether things were going according to Holye or not." [Hoyle had written a book governing the rules of the game of bridge, and "according to Hoyle" was a common expression meaning "playing by the rules." My thanks to John Young, C.S.C., for this information.] Letter to Bess Truman, July 18, 1945, in Ferrell, ed., *Dear Bess*, p. 519. Andrei Gromyko later commented on Truman's nervousness. "There is Truman," he wrote in his memoir. "He is nervous but he mobilizes all his self-control so as not to show it. It looks at times as if he is about to smile, but this is a false impression. I have the feeling that the President is somehow huddled into himself. No doubt the fact that he has no experience of meetings at such a high level, and never met Stalin before, plays a part. But to give him his due he is never rude or discourteous." Andrei Gromyko, *Memories*, trans. Harald Shukman (London, 1989), p. 113.

Churchill specifically added the Polish question to the list of agenda items and referred specifically to "the early holding of free elections" in Poland, which "would truly reflect the will of the Polish people."[99] Then Stalin voiced his concerns – eight in all – ranging from reparations to the disposition of the German fleet to the elimination of the Franco regime to trusteeships over the colonies of former Axis powers. The Soviet approach focused on obtaining as much as possible from their former enemies, while the American (and British) approach centered on providing for stability in Europe and establishing procedures to reach settlements there. It hardly constituted grounds for an easy match.

Some haggling occurred the next day regarding the membership of the Council of Foreign Ministers (CFM). The Americans proposed that France and China join the Big Three, but Churchill balked at Chinese participation, and Stalin resisted the involvement of both the Chinese and the French. In the end, they agreed that China might be involved only on Far Eastern matters, while France could participate in the treaty-making process with all the nations with whom she had signed the relevant armistice (which they interpreted to mean both Germany and Italy).[100] The establishment of the CFM became the first approved act of the Berlin conference. The importance of the foreign ministers to the peace-making process was not limited to their future work. The regular meetings of Eden, Molotov, and Byrnes became the key venue for negotiation at Potsdam. The foreign ministers hashed out issues and tried to settle on proposals that could be presented to their principals in the late afternoon meetings in the conference room. The referral of matters to the foreign ministers even prompted Stalin to joke to his opposites that "we will have nothing to do."[101]

The use of the foreign ministers, however, could not prevent the surfacing at the conference table of the major issues that divided the three powers. Most of these related to Germany and to Poland and more broadly to the nature of postwar Europe. On July 18, Churchill asked his colleagues what exactly constituted Germany, and this broke open the dispute over German boundaries. Since the Soviets gouged such a large portion of prewar Poland in the east, they wished to "compensate" Poland in the west at German expense. Prior to Yalta, the Soviets suggested the Oder River as the new Polish-German border. By Yalta, their demands had escalated so that they proposed that the border should run along the Oder–Western Neisse Rivers, thereby providing an additional 8,000 square miles to postwar Poland, an area, so they later clarified, from which no reparations might be drawn. Roosevelt and Churchill balked at this request at

[99] Martin Gilbert, *Winston S. Churchill*, VIII, p. 63.

[100] For final approval of the CFM and arrangements for its first meeting in London, see Cohen notes, July 20, 1945, *FRUS: The Conference of Berlin (The Potsdam Conference), 1945*, II, p. 178. Byrnes gives a good account of the foundation of the CFM in his *Speaking Frankly*, pp. 70–72.

[101] Stalin quoted in Brown Diary on Potsdam, July 17, 1945, James F. Byrnes Papers, Cooper Library, Folder 54 (1).

Yalta, and Churchill and Truman initially did the same at Potsdam.[102] Stalin, in turn, balked at the American proposals on reparations and tried without success to retain the monetary sum of ten billion dollars as the Soviet share. The procedures for governing occupied Germany and especially control arrangements for the industrial Ruhr area also put the Soviets and the Western allies at odds. So too did the issues of recognition of the Soviet-dominated regimes in Bulgaria, Rumania, and Hungary and, inevitably, the application of the Declaration on Liberated Europe to the people of Poland.

By the time Churchill, Attlee, and Eden left Potsdam to return to London to hear the delayed British election results, the conference discussions had bogged down on major issues.[103] Churchill had taken on Stalin on a number of issues with true British bulldog spirit. He negated Stalin's proposal to overthrow Franco's regime, criticized Tito's behavior in Yugoslavia, demanded access from Stalin to the assigned western zones in Austria, sidetracked the Soviet interest in the Italian colonies, clashed with Stalin over his proposal to establish a Russian military base in the Dardanelles, and vigorously opposed the Soviet proposal on the German-Poland border.[104] From the British perspective he had kept "his end up," despite Truman's "not giving him much support."[105] Truman had not tried to play the role of mediator or honest broker between the British and the Russians that some British officials had predicted on the eve of the conference, but he continued to hope and work for viable agreements so he could return home from what he described as "this terrible place."[106] He had his disagreements with Stalin at the conference table, but,

---

[102] Truman wrote Bess on July 25 that "Russia and Poland have gobbled up a big hunk of Germany and want Britain and us to agree. I have flatly refused." Ferrell, ed., *Dear Bess*, p. 521.

[103] Truman's assessment of progress was more positive. See his letter to Bess, July 25, 1945, where he records the establishment of the CFM and the occupation arrangements for Germany as accomplishments as well as the fact that his inland waterways proposal had been discussed. He, of course, also noted that the conference was bogged down on reparations, the Polish-German border issue, and the recognition of satellite governments. Ferrell, ed., *Dear Bess*, p. 521. Joseph Davies had a different and more alarming view. "As Churchill left Potsdam," he wrote, "it has become clear that the chief protagonists in this terrible drama and possible tragedy (unless we secure agreement) were Churchill and Stalin." Davies record on ninth session, July 25, 1945, Joseph E. Davies Papers, Library of Congress, Box 19.

[104] Gilbert provides a good summary in *Winston S. Churchill*, Vol. VIII, pp. 78–91.

[105] This is the judgment of Admiral Sir Andrew Cunningham, quoted in Gilbert, *Winston S. Churchill*, Vol. VIII, p. 89.

[106] Note the warning of the British ambassador to Washington, Lord Halifax, to Churchill on the eve of the conference where he shared his judgment "that American tactics with the Russian will be to display at the outset confidence in Russian willingness to co-operate." He added his expectation that in dealing with the British the Americans will "be more responsive to arguments based upon the danger of economic chaos in European countries than to balder pleas about the risks of extreme Left governments or the spread of communism." Halifax with some prescience suggested that the Americans were "likely to pick their occasions [to stand up with us to the Russians] with care" and he predicted that they were "half expecting to play or at any rate, to represent themselves as playing, a moderating role between ourselves and the Russians." Halifax to Churchill (No. 4747), July 7, 1945, Churchill Papers, Churchill Archive Center, Char 20/222. For Truman's description see Ferrell, ed., *Off the Record*, p. 54.

with Davies as his constant monitor, he continued to assure the Soviet leader of his genuine hopes for peace.[107] He pushed for reorganization of the satellite governments under Soviet control but never with the gusto of Churchill, and he never pressed with the force of the British prime minister for the quick holding of the promised elections in Poland.[108] His main concerns, if one can rely on his diary reflections, remained to secure the quick end to the Pacific war and to make sure that the United States avoided subsidizing the peace settlement.[109]

Soviet behavior at the conference and beyond it troubled Secretary Byrnes much more than it did the president. On July 24, the day before Churchill departed, he confided to Walter Brown that "somebody had made an awful mistake in bringing about a situation where Russia was permitted to come out of a war with the power she will have." Rather ironically, Byrnes did not assign any culpability to the United States and didn't reflect on what might have been done differently at the Yalta conference or earlier by the Americans. No, the culprit in the Byrnes analysis turned out to be England, which he opined "should never have permitted Hitler to rise" because "the German people under a democracy would have been a far superior ally than Russia." Moving beyond Byrnes's excursion into the wisdom of hindsight, it was clear that he recognized that the collapse of German power allowed the Russians to extend their sphere of power far into Europe. Now he worried about how to arrest this Soviet expansion. He feared that maintaining a "long-time program of co-operation" with the Soviets would be difficult given their ideological differences with the United States and the United Kingdom.[110]

Such legitimate and well-grounded fears did not paralyze the pragmatic Byrnes. He played the hand he had been dealt and proceeded forward to gain the best arrangements and settlements he could. Also he had other matters demanding his and the president's attention, especially the matter of forcing Japan's

---

[107] Note that Truman reported to Davies on July 21 that he had assured Stalin "that we are on the level, and interested in Peace for a decent world and had no purposes hostile to them; that we wanted nothing for ourselves but security and peace with friendship and neighborliness in a free world, with no interference by anyone in the internal affairs of other nations. I spread it on thick and I think he believed me. I meant every word of it." Davies diary, July 21, 1945, Joseph E. Davies Papers, Library of Congress, Box 18. On Davies's "monitoring" role, note the incident at a plenary session where Truman "wrote out on a piece of paper: 'Joe, how am I doing?'" to which Davies replied: "You are batting 1000%. You are holding your own with the best at this table." Davies account of second session, July 18, 1945, Joseph E. Davies Papers, Library of Congress, Box 18.

[108] Marc Trachtenberg has pointed out that, at the Potsdam conference in July 1945, "it was the British delegation that carried the ball on Poland. The Americans were passive." Marc Trachtenberg, *Constructed Peace*, p. 13.

[109] See his diary entry of July 20 where he recorded that he told Stalin and Churchill that the "U.S. had ceased to give away its assets without returns." Ferrell, ed., *Off the Record*, p. 55. Also see his letter to Bess Truman, July 20, 1945, where Truman expressed his determination not to "pay reparations, feed the world, and get nothing for it but a nose thumbing." Ferrell, ed., *Dear Bess*, p. 520

[110] Diary entry, July 24, 1945, Brown Diary, James F. Byrnes Papers, Cooper Library, Folder 602.

surrender. With the amazing destructive force of the atomic bomb fully confirmed by subsequent reports after July 17, the United States prepared to issue a final warning to the Japanese. Stimson still sought to amend the surrender terms specifically to allow for a guarantee for the Japanese to retain their emperor, but Truman and Byrnes with Churchill's agreement held to the unconditional surrender demand. Thus on July 26, the very day Churchill resigned his commission as prime minister, the leaders of the United States and the United Kingdom (with the further endorsement of the Chinese) issued the Potsdam Declaration. It warned the Japanese to surrender immediately or to face "prompt and utter destruction." The Declaration denied any intention "that the Japanese shall be enslaved as a race or destroyed as a nation" but promised that "stern justice shall be meted out to all war criminals." It promised that Allied occupation forces eventually would be withdrawn as soon as "there has been established in accordance with the freely expressed will of the Japanese people a peacefully inclined and responsible government." The Potsdam statement did not mention the emperor but called for the unconditional surrender of "all Japanese armed forces."[111]

Two days prior to the issuance of the Potsdam Declaration, Truman idled over to Stalin at the conclusion of the July 24 plenary session and advised him that the United States had developed a "new weapon of unusual destructive force." He gave no specific information on the atomic bomb. According to Truman's account, Stalin responded that "he was glad to hear it and hoped we would make 'good use of it against the Japanese.'"[112] Anthony Eden standing close by thought Stalin merely nodded and said, "thank you."[113] However this may be, Truman made no effort to clarify for Stalin the extent and power of the new weapon.[114] One might have thought that if the president aimed to take advantage of the diplomatic potential of the atomic weapon, then he might have played up the power of the new weapon to the full, allowing the Soviets to understand that the United States held this new force in its arsenal – a weapon that obviated the need for any Soviet support in the Pacific war. Of course, he did no such thing because he had no intention of engaging in such explicit diplomacy. His attention focused on the use of "the most terrible bomb" against Japan. On the eve of the Potsdam Declaration, he noted in his

[111] "Proclamation Defining Terms for Japanese Surrender" (Potsdam Declaration), July 26, 1945, *Department of State Bulletin*, 13 (July 29, 1945), pp. 137–38. Robert Maddox suggests that "the vagueness regarding the emperor was deliberate: If there were to be any deviation from unconditional surrender, it must not appear as a sign of eroded American will but as a generous gesture to the defeated enemy." Maddox, *The United States and World War II*, p. 304.

[112] Truman, *Year of Decisions*, p. 458.

[113] Eden, *The Reckoning*, p. 635.

[114] Stalin hardly needed his briefing from Truman. He had his own sources on the bomb including the spy Klaus Fuchs who was at Alamogordo. See David Holloway, "The Atomic Bomb and the End of the Wartime Alliance," in Ann Lane and Howard Temperley, eds., *The Rise and Fall of the Grand Alliance, 1941–45* (New York, 1995), pp. 211–12. For further details, see Holloway's *Stalin and the Bomb: The Soviet Union and Atomic Energy, 1939–1956* (New Haven, CT, 1994), pp. 115–33.

diary: "I have told Sec. Of War, Mr. Stimson, to use it so that military objectives and soldiers and sailors are the target and not women and children." Indicative of his attitude toward the Japanese, he continued, "even if the Japs are savages, ruthless, merciless and fanatic, we as the leader of the world for the common welfare cannot drop this terrible bomb on the old capital [Kyoto] or the new [Tokyo]."[115]

Byrnes, of course, attempted his own limited exercise in diplomacy influenced by the American possession of the atomic bomb. On July 23, he explained his effort to Churchill. The secretary of state had cabled Chinese Foreign Minister T. V. Soong and encouraged him not to make any further concessions to the Soviets on the Sino-Soviet agreement foreshadowed at Yalta. He encouraged Soong to keep on negotiating, obviously hoping that the Soviet Union would delay its entry into the war until agreements were finalized. Churchill well appreciated the Byrnes tactic and wrote to Eden that "it is quite clear that the United States do not at the present time desire Russian participation in the war against Japan."[116] Byrnes shared his hopes with Navy Secretary James Forrestal on July 26 and told him he "was most anxious to get the Japanese affair over with before the Russians got in, with particular reference to Darien and Port Arthur." As Byrnes understood well: "Once in there, he felt it would not be easy to get them out."[117] In retrospect, Byrnes's attempt to limit and restrict Soviet encroachment in the northeast Asian region is admirable and speaks to his developing grasp of international realities. Sadly, the attempt failed. From the outset, it more resembled wishful thinking than a serious diplomatic initiative. As Byrnes eventually understood, nothing the United States might do could keep the Soviets out of the war. They simply possessed the military force to have their way in Manchuria and northern China. The secretary of state regretfully accepted this reality, and thus, noted David Robertson correctly, "ended Jimmy Byrnes' brief flirtation with atomic diplomacy."[118] Or, at least it did for the time being.

---

[115] Diary entry, July 25, 1945, Ferrell, ed., *Off the Record*, p. 55. Truman continued: "The target will be a purely military one and we will issue a warning statement asking the Japs to surrender and save lives. I'm sure they will not do that, but we will have given them the chance." As Barton Bernstein rightly has noted, this comment reveals "what can only be regarded as self-deception," regarding the number of noncombatants who would be killed by the atomic bomb. See Barton J. Bernstein, "Understanding the Atomic Bomb and the Japanese Surrender: Missed Opportunities, Little-Known Near Disasters, and Modern Memory," *Diplomatic History*, 19 (Spring 1995), pp. 257–58.

[116] Churchill to Eden, July 23, 1945, Churchill Papers, Churchill Archive Center, Char 20/209. Byrnes also explained his thinking to Walter Brown who recorded on July 24 that "JFB still hoping for time, believing after atomic bomb Japan will surrender and Russia will not get in so much on the kill." Entry, July 24, 1945, Brown Diary, James F. Byrnes Papers, Cooper Library, Folder 602.

[117] Millis, ed., *Forrestal Diaries*, p. 78.

[118] Robertson, *Sly and Able*, p. 422.

The Potsdam Deal

Much to the surprise of the American delegation, the British voters sent a new prime minister and a new foreign secretary back to Potsdam on July 27. Churchill had expected victory on the strength of his great wartime leadership, but the British electorate concentrated on domestic concerns and looked forward rather than backward. The political tide ran against the Tories, who seemed to offer a return to the 1930s, in favor of Clement Attlee's Labour Party, which proposed a transformation of Britain including the nationalization of key industries and the development of major components of what would come to be known as the welfare state. Churchill absorbed the bitter blow with as much grace as he could muster, while Truman wrote him of his "shock" on learning of the election result. He told the new leader of His Majesty's opposition that he was missed at Potsdam and rather clumsily he wished him "the happiest possible existence from now until the last call and we shall always remember that you held the barbarians until we could prepare."[119] Truman's final words paid tribute to Churchill's "standing alone" against Hitler and his hordes until 1941. They read as thoughts offered to a man whom the president expected to move forever off the international stage. Little did he realize that political longevity constituted an essential part of Churchill's make-up and that before the next year passed he and the British leader would share a stage in an obscure Midwestern town named Fulton, Missouri.[120]

Churchill feared that his successors might not be up to the task that lay ahead for them. He confided to Sir Alexander Cadogan in early August that "a very formidable event [the change of government] has occurred in Britain, and I fear it will diminish our national stature at a time when we most need unity and strength." He encouraged Cadogan, a permanent civil servant, to continue his good efforts with the new British leaders and took note of his having played "a man's part in this glorious struggle, which we got into one muddle and have come out of in another."[121] Churchill's questioning of the competence of the Labour leaders to navigate Britain out of the current "muddle" with the Soviets proved ill-founded. Attlee and, more notably, his foreign secretary Ernest Bevin eventually emerged as key contributors to the Western response to the Soviet Union. The transition from Churchill and Eden to Attlee and Bevin occurred with remarkable ease, a product no doubt of the Labour ministers having served in Churchill's war cabinet. In marked contrast to Truman's coming to power,

---

[119] Truman to Churchill, July 30, 1945, Churchill Papers, Churchill Archive Center, 2/142.

[120] Perhaps Churchill had more prescience as he responded to Truman: "I am sorry that our work together has been nipped in the bud, but I cherish the hope that our friendship will continue to ripen, and that there may be occasions when it may be of service to both our countries and to the common cause they pursue." Churchill to Truman, July 30, 1945, Churchill Papers, Churchill Archive Center, 2/142.

[121] Churchill to Cadogan, August 5, 1945, Alexander G. Cadogan Papers, Churchill Archives Center, File 2/7.

Attlee and Bevin were well briefed on international developments, and Attlee had fully participated in the Potsdam plenary sessions thus far.[122] Whatever the differing visions of Labour and the Conservatives in the British domestic realm, the emergence of a new government brought about no major departures in British foreign policy. Attlee and Bevin returned to Potsdam working essentially from the same policy briefs. At the end of the conference, Attlee wrote Churchill and assured him that "we have, of course, been building on the foundation laid by you, and there has been no change of policy."[123] The bonds built during the war continued in its aftermath as Attlee and Bevin willingly shared material with their predecessors and even sought their advice on occasion.

An outside observer might have predicted that a British government of a democratic socialist complexion might move toward playing some kind of mediating role between the liberal capitalist United States and the communist Soviet Union. But any person making such an observation would have lacked both an appreciation of the democratic temper that guided Attlee and Bevin and a clear recognition that their own political philosophy stood unalterably opposed to the totalitarianism that characterized Stalin's form of government. Attlee had few illusions about Soviet international goals. According to one careful student, he judged that the Soviets' "European ambitions were imperialistic, whether ideological or territorial," and he believed that Britain "needed to be involved in Europe to balance Soviet influence."[124] Although Attlee and Truman shared a number of experiences and characteristics – both veterans of World War I, both followed "great men," both possessed plain, no-nonsense dispositions – they did not develop a close friendship. Their relationship proceeded largely on a business-like basis without any special personal rapport, a reality that also owed something to their preoccupations with domestic matters after the war while leaving their respective foreign ministers a free hand on diplomatic matters.[125]

Attlee, a man of modest appearance and mild manner, possessed a wonderful complement in the memorable Bevin. Dean Acheson, who treasured his later working relationship with the doughty foreign secretary, described him as "short and stout, with broad nose and thick lips, [who] looked more suited for the roles he had played earlier in life than for diplomacy." An illegitimate child who never knew his father and who possessed just a few years of formal education, Bevin worked in various laborer jobs – "blue-collar" work as the British would say – and then went on to become a trade union leader and the

---

[122] Churchill made a special effort to keep Attlee briefed during the election campaign. See his letters to Attlee of May 31, 1945, and June 2, 1945, Churchill Papers, Churchill Archive Center, Char 20/194A.

[123] Attlee to Churchill, August 1, 1945, Churchill Papers, Churchill Archive Center, 2/3, quoted in Gilbert, *Winston S. Churchill*, VIII, p. 116.

[124] Folly, *Churchill, Whitehall and the Soviet Union*, p. 139.

[125] As Chapter 7 will clarify, Attlee was more engaged in foreign policy matters than Truman in late 1945 and 1946.

general secretary of the huge Transport and General Workers' Union. In his union work, Bevin developed a firm dislike of communism and communists, and he relished his "hatreds." He served as minister for labour in Churchill's war cabinet where his strength and toughness were well harnessed. He hoped to serve as chancellor of the exchequer (treasurer) in Attlee's government, but the prime minister prevailed upon him to lead the foreign office. Looked at in the perspective of over half a century it remains the best of Attlee's appointments.[126] Bevin's gruff manner and his concern to push the Russians and their puppets in Poland on the issues like free elections won him the admiration of Averell Harriman, but Truman and Byrnes never replicated Harriman's regard. Bevin proved too confrontational for their liking at a time when they wanted to reach agreements.[127]

The British leaders, who returned to the Potsdam conference table on July 28, found that negotiations were moving ahead rapidly to try to forge a compromise settlement on the major disputed issues. Byrnes seized the initiative. He already had planted some seeds prior to the departure of Churchill when he proposed to Eden and Molotov on July 24 that "as something like 50% of the goods available for reparation are in the Russian zone and as Russia claims 50% of reparation, Russia should take what it likes from her own zone." Further, he suggested that "the other zone commanders should make what deliveries they decide to make each from their own zones to the other countries entitled to reparations so as to satisfy their shares." Molotov had responded cautiously by offering that he would consider the idea so long as the Soviet Union might obtain additional "deliveries worth $3 billion from the Ruhr," an amount Byrnes would not countenance.[128] The reparations issue, like the Polish-German boundary, remained as seemingly impossible hurdles for the conferees to jump.

Into this stalemate stepped the irrepressible and inevitably fretting Joseph Davies. On July 28, he met with Byrnes and listened as the secretary shared his view that the news of the A-bomb might gain some diplomatic leverage with the Russians. Davies challenged that notion immediately arguing that any "threat

[126] For Acheson's brief portrait of Bevin, see *Present at the Creation*, pp. 270–71. For further detail on Bevin as foreign secretary, see Alan Bullock, *Ernest Bevin: Foreign Secretary, 1945–1951* (New York, 1983). Bevin was hardly a saint. As Geoffrey Warner has noted, even his admirers have conceded that he "was long-winded, vain, vindictive, profoundly suspicious and prejudiced against – among others and in no particular order – Jews, Germans, Roman Catholics, and intellectuals of all kinds." Warner, "Ernest Bevin and British Foreign Policy, 1945–1951," in Craig and Loewenheim, eds., *The Diplomats*, p. 104.

[127] Harriman conveyed to his daughter that Bevin was "the big hero of the meeting." See Kathleen Harriman to Mary and Shirley, August 8, 1945, Averell Harriman Papers, Library of Congress, Box 181. Halifax wrote Churchill on August 3, 1945, that Truman and Byrnes "hadn't taken much to Ernie Bevin who they thought was graceless and rough." Halifax to Churchill, August 3, 1945, Churchill Papers, Churchill Archive Center, Char 2/141. On Bevin's working hard on Polish issues, see Edward J. Rozek, *Allied Wartime Diplomacy*, pp. 410–11.

[128] See Eden's minutes of the meeting, July 24, 1945, Avon Papers, Main Library Special Collections, University of Birmingham, 20/13/236.

PHOTO 10. The conference table at Potsdam with the British delegation now led by Prime Minister Clement Attlee and Foreign Secretary Ernest Bevin. Stalin (in dress uniform!) has his faithful Commissar for Foreign Affairs Vyacheslav Molotov at his side. Truman is flanked on his right by Admiral Leahy and Secretary of State Byrnes and on his left by Charles E. Bohlen and Ambassador Joseph E. Davies. (Courtesy National Archives)

of exclusion from participation in this new war weapon" would only create distrust and cause the Soviets to get their backs up. He offered a different strategy. Rather ironically given his condemnation of the American officials like Pauley who had arrived at Potsdam eager to engage in hard bargaining, he now suggested the time had arrived "to get down to a little 'horseback [sic] trading.'" In his view, nothing more could be gained by "talk." Instead, he posited, "might it not be a good thing to tie up Reparations, the Satellite States, the Polish Border and Italy together in a package proposal and try to get an end to debate and secure an agreement through simultaneous concessions, and dispose of them together?" Byrnes replied, according to Davies's account, "I think you've got something there."[129] He certainly meant what he said and proceeded forward to act on the Davies suggestion.

Byrnes briefed Attlee and Bevin upon their return about his proposal on reparations and gained their approval. Thereafter he began to negotiate with the Soviets. Molotov acted as an intermediary of sorts as Stalin supposedly had succumbed to some illness and remained in his residence. Over a series of meetings from July 29 to July 31, the negotiators forged the outline of a compromise.[130] Byrnes gave ground on the cession of German territory to Poland and gave some limited promise of recognition to the Soviet-sponsored regimes in Rumania, Hungary, and Bulgaria. In turn, he put pressure on Molotov to concede on the reparations issue and to forego any reference to fixed dollar amounts of payments. Furthermore, the Russians would be assigned no involvement in the Ruhr. Molotov objected in one meeting to Byrnes's reneging on the Yalta reparations accord, but Byrnes met his complaint by indicating that circumstances had changed. The level of destruction in Germany was greater than expected and also the Soviets unilaterally had consigned to Poland a much larger portion of Germany than that expected at Yalta. On the morning of July 31, according to Byrnes's account, the secretary of state met with his Soviet counterpart, explicitly linked the three issues, and asked him to present his proposal to Stalin. Byrnes put the issue bluntly. "I told him," he recalled, "we would agree to all three or none and that the President and I would leave for the United States the next day."[131] It represented a "package deal, take it or leave it," as Charles Mee noted.[132]

At the plenary session later in the afternoon of July 31, Stalin, now recovered from his illness, joined Attlee and Truman at the conference table. At Truman's request, Byrnes set forth his proposal, and Stalin tried to chip away at the terms set forth. He especially objected to "the tactics of Mr. Byrnes" in linking the three issues. Truman and Byrnes ignored his objection, although the Western allies gave a slight concession regarding the percentage of capital equipment

---

[129] Davies journal, July 28, 1945, Joseph E. Davies Papers, Library of Congress, Box 19. (One assumes that Davies meant "horse-trading" rather than "horseback-trading"!)

[130] The various meetings are tracked quite well in Mee, Jr., *Meeting at Potsdam*, pp. 255–68.

[131] Byrnes, *Speaking Frankly*, pp. 84–85.

[132] Mee, Jr., *Meeting at Potsdam*, p. 262.

they would trade from their zones in return for food, coal, and other natural resources from the Soviet zones. They refused to budge further, and Stalin faced the reality that he now dealt with a genuine quid pro quo American approach. He decided to accept the deal that Byrnes offered. With Soviet agreement on the compromise, the settlements flowed quickly – reparations, the German-Polish boundary, limited recognition for the East European governments. Other issues such as the treatment of war criminals were settled quickly and incorporated into the Potsdam protocol.[133] A Big Three agreement emerged. Joseph Davies wrote approvingly of the session. He praised Byrnes for his "great skill" in achieving "complete acceptance of his three-cornered proposal." Naturally, he thought Stalin "magnanimous" for his concessions. As he saw it, this compromise "brought the conference to a successful conclusion, where disunity had seriously threatened."[134]

Byrnes led the way for the United States as the conferees wrapped up the Potsdam agreements on August 1, 1945, in afternoon and evening sessions. Truman clearly played more of a supporting role. The president allowed Byrnes to take the initiative on major questions, although he tried at the final afternoon session to have his pet proposal of free waterways in Europe and beyond mentioned in the final communiqué. He asked Stalin for permission to have the communiqué mention that his proposal guaranteeing all nations access to such waterways as the Kiel Canal in Germany and the Rhine–Danube River system had been referred to the Council of Foreign Ministers. Stalin sharply responded "nyet." Clearly he felt he had made sufficient compromises and concessions to the United States and its representatives. Truman's recollections of Stalin's pointed rejection undoubtedly contributed to his later description of himself at Potsdam as "an innocent idealist at one corner of that Round Table who wanted free waterways."[135] At the time, however, he overcame his irritation and resumed discussions to finalize the conference.

Late in the evening of August 1, at an hour when Truman normally would be awake only if playing poker and drinking bourbon, the leaders of the Big Three gathered for the final plenary session. Drafts of the final communiqué and of the Potsdam accords lay before the principals, and they worked their way through them section by section. Stalin, as relentless as ever, tried to secure further approval for the satellite regimes in Eastern Europe. Attlee and Bevin objected. Truman tried to move the meeting to a conclusion. Eventually the president, the generalissimo, and the prime minister signed the accords. Truman, the neophyte diplomat, then abruptly declared the Berlin conference adjourned, observing that he hoped the next meeting would be in Washington. Stalin, a former seminarian unused to invoking the Almighty, replied: "God willing."

---

[133] Protocol of proceedings, August 1, 1945, FRUS: *The Conference of Berlin (The Potsdam Conference), 1945*, II, pp. 1477–98.

[134] Davies diary, July 31, 1945, Joseph E. Davies Papers, Library of Congress, Box 19.

[135] Truman (unsent letter) to Acheson, March 15, 1957, in Poen, ed., *Strictly Personal and Confidential*, p. 33.

PHOTO 11. The Big Three – Prime Minister Clement R. Attlee, President Harry S. Truman, and Generalissimo Josef Stalin – and their foreign ministers (along with Admiral Leahy) gather in the palace garden on the last day of the Potsdam conference, August 1, 1945. (Courtesy National Archives)

Attlee came to Truman's rescue and attended to some of the diplomatic pleasantries such as thanks to Stalin for the accommodations and to Truman for his presiding at the sessions. He also expressed the hope that "this conference will be an important milestone on the road which our three nations are taking together towards a stable peace, and that the friendship among the three of us who have met here will be strong and enduring." Stalin and Truman endorsed his sentiment. Stalin, with a hint of a barb, also thanked "Mr. Byrnes, who has helped our work very much and has promoted the achievement of our decisions." Byrnes, recognizing that Stalin alluded to the deal he fashioned, responded with exaggerated emotion that he felt "deeply touched by the Generalissimo's kind words." The air was getting thick in the conference room. After Stalin declared the conference "a success," Truman for the second time declared the meeting closed. It was already early morning on August 2. Handshakes were exchanged and good wishes extended for safe travel and the conferees dispersed. By 8:00 A.M., Truman's plane departed Berlin to return him back to the United States. His first – and last – major exercise in international summitry had ended. He would never see Stalin again.

A Sphere of Influence Peace?

Potsdam proved a demanding experience for Truman. His frustration at times bubbled over in the remarks he confided to his diary or into the letters he wrote his wife and mother. To the latter he wrote on the eve of the compromise break-through that "you never saw such pig-headed people as the Russians. I hope I never have to hold another conference with them." He then added tellingly, "but of course I will."[136] Despite the frustrations, he worked hard to reach a cooperative settlement with the Soviets. Amazingly, his regard for Stalin was such that he worried on July 30 about the havoc for European peace if "Joe suddenly passed out" and was replaced by "some demagogue on horseback" who controlled "the efficient Russian military machine."[137] In that the Soviet dictator essentially controlled half of Europe by this point, one might consider Truman's concerns a trifle misplaced, but they reflect the belief shared by Truman and Byrnes that they could work with Stalin and settle issues with him.[138] This surely represented continuity with Franklin Roosevelt. Truman never suffered from the Rooseveltian conceit that he could satisfy Stalin's demands and so soothe his insecurities, but he found the Soviet leader a man of his word with whom the United States could do business. And as the American delegation left Potsdam, its leaders, Truman and Byrnes, assumed that there would be much further business to undertake with the Soviets.

Both Truman and Byrnes judged Potsdam a success of sorts. Byrnes recalled that "the conference ended in good spirits," although he admitted that the returning delegation from Berlin "probably was less sanguine than the one that had departed from Yalta." The ill-based optimism of the Yalta gathering had been tempered by the subsequent months of difficulties and disagreements among the Allies. And, the hard bargaining at Potsdam seemed to indicate that there would be no easy resolution to divisive issues. Nonetheless, Byrnes thought that "a basis for maintaining our war-born unity" had been established at the conference. He believed that the Potsdam agreements "would provide a basis for the early restoration of stability in Europe." Writing in 1947 in his memoir *Speaking Frankly*, Byrnes held that "the agreements did make the conference a success but the violation of those agreements has turned success into failure." Potsdam, he maintained, was "the success that failed."[139] Truman shared this outlook. Like Byrnes he saw the difficulty of Potsdam in the failure of the Soviets to abide by the agreements negotiated there. In 1957 he referred to

---

[136] Truman to Mary Ellen Truman, July 31, 1945, quoted in Beschloss, *The Conquerors*, p. 268.

[137] Diary entry, July 30, 1945, Ferrell, ed., *Off the Record*, p. 58.

[138] On August 7, 1945, Truman spoke with members of the White House staff about the Potsdam meeting and his impressions. According to Eben Ayers, "the president seemed to have been favorably impressed" with Stalin "and to like him." He even offered the suggestion that Stalin "could be depended upon." Entry, August 7, 1945, Ferrell, ed., *Truman in the White House*, p. 59.

[139] Byrnes, *Speaking Frankly*, pp. 86–87.

the large number of agreements which were reached there – "only to be broken as soon as the unconscionable Russian Dictator returned to Moscow."[140]

Truman certainly presented the Potsdam results as a success in the report he gave to the American people on his return. He associated his efforts at Berlin with those of his predecessor and assured his listeners that "strong foundations of good-will and cooperation had been laid by President Roosevelt." He reviewed the various elements of the Potsdam accord, paying special attention to the role of the Council of Foreign Ministers as the body that would draft peace treaties with the former enemy countries – Germany, Italy, Rumania, Bulgaria, Hungary, and Finland. He outlined the principles that would guide the occupation of Germany, and he emphasized the details of the reparations settlement. Predictably, he assured his domestic audience that "we do not intend again to make the mistake of exacting reparations in money and then lending Germany the money with which to pay." He acknowledged that the approach agreed to at Potsdam represented a departure from the fixed-dollar sum approach of Yalta, but he justified the "formula of taking reparations by zones" as likely to lead "to less friction among the Allies" than the proposal tentatively offered at Yalta.

On the issue of Poland, Truman gave a Rooseveltian reassurance that agreements had been reached to hold free elections and quickly moved on to address the boundary issue. While noting that the final determination on borders would await the formal peace conferences, he gave an explanation for consigning German territory in the east to the Poles. When discussing Polish matters, he explained that all international agreements involved an "element of compromise." Perhaps wary of possible criticism that he and Byrnes had given up too much in order to obtain an agreement, he argued that "no nation can expect to get everything that it wants. It is a question of give and take – of being willing to meet your neighbor half-way." He went on to mention the reorganization of the Eastern European governments and his beloved free waterways proposal, before turning to make remarks about the war against Japan. The president concluded with a call to use "all our resources and all our skills in the great cause of a just and lasting peace" and with a final assurance that "the three great powers are now more closely than ever bound together in determination to achieve that kind of peace." Linking himself again with FDR, he proclaimed: "From Tehran, and the Crimea, and San Francisco, and Berlin – we shall continue to march together to our objective."[141]

Truman's presentation of the result of the American labors at Potsdam had a certain disingenuous quality about it. For the most part, what he said reasonably reflected the details of the accords, but he failed to make clear that, guided by his new secretary of state, he had moved in the direction of forging

[140] Truman (unsent letter) to Acheson, March 15, 1957, Poen, ed., *Strictly Personal and Confidential*, p. 33.

[141] Report of the president on the Berlin conference, August 9, 1945, *Department of State Bulletin*, 13 (August 12, 1945), pp. 208–13.

a sphere-of-influence peace. Although Truman, in the usual pious American fashion, even included a line in his statement reaffirming that the Eastern European nations were not to be included in the "spheres of influence of any one power," the Potsdam deliberations belie his stance.[142] This whole matter has not always been well appreciated even by some of the most astute of observers including Henry Kissinger, who branded Potsdam "a dialogue of the deaf," which "accomplished little," and Alonzo Hamby, who maintained that Potsdam "reached no significant substantive decisions" aside from the reaffirmation of the Soviet pledge to enter the war against Japan.[143] Such views ignore the underlying rationale and the ramifications of the deal that Byrnes negotiated at Potsdam. Such views disregard that Byrnes and Truman laid the foundations at Potsdam for what they hoped would be a workable postwar settlement with the Soviet Union.[144]

Byrnes had kept Truman fully briefed as he negotiated the outlines of the final settlement with Molotov. The president readily accepted Byrnes's proposal as a way to break the impasse that beset the conference and that kept him trapped in Germany for over two weeks. He did not see the Potsdam deal as constituting a major break with the policies of his predecessor. Even though it clearly marked a retreat from some of the specific terms of the Yalta accord, especially regarding reparations matters and the economic administration of Germany, Truman believed the arrangements forged would secure continued cooperation between the United States and the Soviet Union. Like his predecessor, Truman accepted that the Soviets would dominate in the part of Europe their army occupied. In a conversation with James Forrestal on July 28, he blamed Hitler for the reality that "we shall have a Slav Europe for a long time to come," but then he added rather nonchalantly in words that would have troubled all genuine Eastern European democrats, "I don't think it is so bad."[145] Clearly, he had no idea what lay ahead for those who would contest Soviet (Slav) domination.

Truman and Byrnes explicitly discussed the matter of spheres of influence with Stalin on the final day of the Potsdam meeting. In deliberations on the division of "German gold, shares and other assets abroad," Stalin stated that his delegation "will regard the whole of Western Germany as falling within your sphere, and Eastern Germany, within ours." As Charles Mee notes, "Truman then extended the notion of two spheres and projected the division of Germany onto Europe as a whole by asking whether Stalin meant to establish 'a line

---

[142] Truman's report on Berlin conference, August 9, 1945, *Department of State Bulletin*, 13 (August 12, 1945), p. 211.

[143] See Kissinger, *Diplomacy*, pp. 330–31; and Hamby, *Man of the People*, p. 330.

[144] The insightful work of Marc Trachtenberg has been crucial to guiding my own thinking on this subject. See his *Constructed Peace*, pp. 22–33. Also see the thoughtful discussion of "Byrnes and the Potsdam Settlement," by James McAllister in his *No Exit*, pp. 84–98.

[145] Diary extract for July 28, 1945, Forrestal diaries, Vol. 2, James V. Forrestal Papers, Seeley G. Mudd Manuscript Library. (I am grateful to Marc Trachtenberg for making this full entry available to me.)

running from the Baltic to the Adriatic.'" The generalissimo replied positively and even specified that he considered Finland in his zone. "Yugoslavia was not," he continued, "but the eastern part of Austria was in their zone." He followed up by proposing that German investments should be divided in light of these spheres. "As to the German investments in Eastern Europe, they remain with us, and the rest, with you." Such a division settled the question quickly. Mee rightly observed that "spheres of influence were no longer a naughty secret hidden in Truman's briefing book or in private bargains struck by Stalin and Churchill."[146]

Yet there were some limits to the American commitment to a spheres-of-influence peace. It is crucial to appreciate that the American policy makers virtually backed into this arrangement in order to obtain agreements with the Soviets at Potsdam. This was not the deliberate formulation and execution of a grand strategy, but tactical policy making on the run. Truman and Byrnes had not arrived at Potsdam set upon negotiating a spheres-of-influence peace. However, the firm American resolve not to subsidize German reparations either directly or indirectly, along with a concern to lay some foundation for economic and social stability in postwar Europe, had prompted them to settle on the arrangement whereby each occupying power would take reparations from its own zone. This arrangement, however, had significant strategic ramifications for the broader postwar settlement. Although it evolved out of a sincere desire to forge a settlement with the Soviets and to limit the bases for future disputes, it moved significantly in the direction of dividing Germany. While the political arrangements of the Allied Control Council rather contradictorily still provided for a unified German occupation, the Potsdam agreement arranged "for Germany to be split into two economic units which would exchange goods with each other as though they were separate entities engaged in international trade – or, more precisely, international barter."[147]

The irony in the American approach needs to be emphasized. Byrnes and Truman wanted to reach a genuine settlement with the Soviet Union and to maintain a decent, cooperative relationship with their wartime ally into the postwar years. Yet, in order to do that and to meet their own key objective regarding reparations, they had to limit the extent of their cooperation with

---

[146] Minutes of Twelfth plenary meeting, August 1, 1945, *FRUS: The Conference of Berlin (The Potsdam Conference), 1945*, II, pp. 566–69. Mee, Jr., *Meeting at Potsdam*, pp. 272–73, discusses this well.

[147] Trachtenberg, *Constructed Peace*, p. 26. Charles Mee goes further and argues: "It has often been said that the Potsdam conference failed because it did not resolve Europe's most crucial postwar problem, the fate of Germany. In fact, however, the conference solved that problem most satisfactorily by dividing Germany. Without resorting to the Morgenthau plan or some other drastic measure, the Big Three reduced Germany's power severely." Mee, Jr., *Meeting at Potsdam*, p. 267. Also note the discussion in Lloyd C. Gardner, *Spheres of Influence: The Great Powers Partition Europe, from Munich to Yalta* (Chicago, 1993), pp. 260–61, where he notes that the "Potsdam decisions on German reparations set a pattern for independent action that would be a powerful spur to 'blocism.'"

the Soviets. Marc Trachtenberg captures Byrnes's underlying sentiment well in arguing that for the Western allies and the Soviets, "the way to get along was to pull apart" and to reach an "amicable understanding."[148] Trachtenberg takes his formidable analysis further in suggesting that "the two sides would go their separate ways, but the United States would try to be accommodating: the divorce need not be bitter."[149] Hence, the American concessions to the Soviets on the German-Polish border question might be seen as a sweetener of sorts to make the divorce settlement more palatable for Stalin. Yet the marriage/divorce metaphor rather overstates the depth of both the initial relationship and the subsequent separation. While FDR did some significant courting of Stalin, neither Truman nor Byrnes attempted to play the role of suitor. And whatever FDR's delusions about his relationship with Stalin, he had never reached a point where final commitments were made. Truman and Byrnes arrived on the scene intent on following FDR and so to continuing decent relations with the Soviet Union, but they operated as politicians who would make adjustments to forge a decent settlement, not as a disaffected marriage partner negotiating divorce terms. Byrnes once compared the Soviets to the U.S. Senate: "You build a post office in their state, and they'll build a post office in our state."[150] At Potsdam he operated out of this perspective.

Of course, the Potsdam settlement did not end contact between the Soviets and the Americans. Indeed, the Allied powers through the Potsdam agreements locked themselves into institutional structures to continue their cooperation both through the Council of Foreign Ministers and through the Allied Control Council to oversee the German occupation. Additionally, even though Truman and Byrnes made concessions regarding Soviet influence over the governments of Eastern Europe they had not withdrawn completely from any concern for the region. Byrnes would spend much time in late 1945 and in 1946 negotiating in the CFM on final peace treaties for nations in the area. Nor did Truman or Byrnes clearly articulate their limited commitment to a sphere-of-influence peace to their subordinates. In fact, Byrnes allowed the American military governor in Germany, General Lucius Clay, and his political advisor, Robert Murphy, significant autonomy in late 1945–46 during which time they acted upon their preference for a unified Germany and worked to reach agreements with their Soviet counterparts on a range of matters both political and economic. Some significant future disagreements, including the currency dispute, which led to the Berlin Blockade, might have been avoided had Byrnes fully enforced his new approach at the outset, but he could not publicly support a clear division of Germany at the time. Nor had he decisively concluded that he should work to that end. Such were the limits of American policy making. Germany's future would be debated off and on for another four years.

[148] Trachtenberg, *Constructed Peace*, pp. 27, 28.
[149] Trachtenberg, *Constructed Peace*, p. 29.
[150] Quoted in Larson, *Origins of Containment*, p. 194

Even though the American approach at Potsdam altered some of the Yalta terms for governing postwar Germany, the end result seemed to be in sync with the broad Rooseveltian approach. Joseph Davies, the most sympathetic of the major American participants both to FDR's approach and to the interests of the Soviets, certainly thought so. He believed that "the decisions reached at the conference furthered the goals of Roosevelt's Grand Design."[151] Clearly, he saw the acknowledging of Soviet predominance in its sphere as consistent with what FDR had approved both before and after Yalta. He later observed that "Potsdam repaired Big Three harmony."[152] Truman and Byrnes left Germany hopeful that the compromise reached there would afford good relations with Soviets. Truman gladly deputized Byrnes to continue the deliberations that would wrap up all the details and ready the way for the final peace conference, which he expected to attend with Stalin and Attlee. There had been no reversal on his part of the effort by his predecessor to work cooperatively with Stalin.

Nonetheless, Potsdam provided the location for some movement away from the accommodating approach of Roosevelt. Byrnes led it, and Truman followed him. Byrnes began to appreciate the real danger that the expansion of Soviet power represented in both Europe and in northeast Asia. He tried without success to prevent expansion in the latter region but eventually recognized that Soviet movement into Manchuria and Korea was a fait accompli. Even if the Soviets were not needed to defeat the Japanese, nothing could prevent them from rushing in to grab some share of the spoils of victory. In Europe, Byrnes implicitly drew a limit on further Soviet advances. Perhaps he didn't fully appreciate all the implications himself but by forcing the reparations settlement on Stalin, he limited significantly the opportunity for the Soviet Union to meddle in the western half of Germany. Given that Stalin hoped to impose a "Soviet-style antifascist democracy [sic]" on postwar Germany and that his ambitions certainly extended well beyond the German lands occupied by his brutal army, Byrnes's initiative must be acknowledged as crucial in the postwar effort to secure Western Europe.[153] Byrnes, at least, began at Potsdam to appreciate that "the most likely future threat to the nation's security was the Kremlin's potential to gain preponderance in western Europe through the success of Communist parties or by maneuvering to gain control of all of Germany."[154] The American effort at Potsdam placed some real obstacles in the way of Soviet ambitions beyond their sphere.

Byrnes and Truman also offered Stalin a different face at Potsdam. Neither was a brilliant geopolitical player, but at least they moved beyond the sad

---

[151] MacLean, *Joseph E. Davies*, p. 161. (The following sentence also draws on MacLean's work.)

[152] Davies note, not dated, Joseph E. Davies Papers, Library of Congress, Box 19, "Folder 1–3 August, 1945."

[153] On Soviet ambitions in Germany, see R. C. Raack, *Stalin's Drive to the West, 1938–1945: The Origins of the Cold War* (Stanford, CA, 1995), pp. 112–13.

[154] Leffler, *Struggle for Germany and the Origins of the Cold War*, p. 24.

Rooseveltian effort to offer concessions in hopes of winning Stalin's trust. R. C. Raack, the historian of Stalin's wartime diplomacy, exaggerates somewhat in asserting that "the new Western leaders Stalin met at Potsdam [Truman/Byrnes and Attlee/Bevin] were very much tougher minded and more skeptical than their predecessors had been at Teheran and Yalta."[155] Yet, with the Axis powers defeated, the glue that had bound the Allies together was much diluted and the seeming need for direct collaboration less essential. Both Truman and Byrnes actually liked Stalin, but neither thought that he could establish a personal relationship with him and neither attempted to do so. Their experience told them one did not need a personal friendship in order to do political business. They knew that much, but they did not know enough to think of the Soviet dictator as an adversary filled with suspicion who would seize whatever opportunities presented to enlarge the realm of his power. They still had much to learn.

George F. Kennan has argued that "if at Yalta certain opportunities were missed, certain points yielded, and certain fateful obscurities brought into existence, it was for the most part at Potsdam, five months later, that the final lines were drawn." The one-time diplomat and Soviet specialist suggested that "it could well be argued that there was less excuse, this time, either for illusions with regard to Soviet intentions or for hesitation about carrying forward Western desiderata." As Kennan noted, the war in Europe was over, the danger that the Soviets posed to Germany's future should have been apparent, Stalin's purposes and modus operandi should have been clear from the Polish case. In light of all this he concluded that "here, at Potsdam, one might have thought, was the time for a showdown – perhaps not the best time, but certainly the last."[156] There is much justification for Kennan's forceful criticism, and perhaps if Averell Harriman rather than Joseph Davies had sat with Truman and Byrnes at the Potsdam conference, a more blunt American approach might have been adopted. This would have rejected outright the Soviet land-grab at German expense to compensate the Poles for the Soviet seizure of their territory in the east. The British, of both Tory and Labour persuasions, felt quite uneasy about the final compromise, which essentially gave the land to Poland. In opposing this Soviet measure, the Western powers also might have placed greater pressure on Stalin to allow for genuine democratic regimes in Eastern Europe. At the least, they might have refused to acquiesce in Soviet domination and control and to have named it for what it was. But they did not. In the end, they were still trapped in Roosevelt's assumptions regarding the need for continued cooperation with the Soviets. They left Potsdam wiser about their dealings with the Soviet Union but with those assumptions largely intact.

---

[155] Raack, *Stalin's Drive to the West*, p. 148. This ignores Churchill's earlier efforts to mount some opposition to Stalin's expansion. Churchill later maintained that he would have been tougher with the Soviets than the final Potsdam compromise. He later wrote: "I am not responsible for Potsdam after I left. I would never have agreed to the Western Neisse and was saving it up for a final 'showdown.'" See Gilbert, *Winston S. Churchill*, Vol. VIII, p. 117.

[156] Kennan, "An Historian of Potsdam and His Readers," p. 289.

Truman and Byrnes hurried back across the Atlantic as soon as the Potsdam conference concluded. One might have thought the president would take advantage of his proximity to London to visit the capital of his nation's closest wartime ally and to pay tribute to its courageous citizens. But time was of the essence, so he allowed a quick shipboard visit with Britain's head of state, King George VI, to suffice. Truman wanted to get home. He and Byrnes appeared to spend little time debriefing on the Potsdam meeting and taking the measure of the Soviet leader they dealt with there. Their focus now rested on the future and bringing the war with Japan to a successful end. They received further reports of Japanese peace "feelers" and worried that Japan might seek to surrender through the Soviet Union rather than some neutral country like Sweden. Most of all they waited anxiously for news of the atomic bomb. On August 3, the president and his secretary of state good-naturedly chided Admiral Leahy "not to hold out news on the atomic bomb."[157] The old admiral, trained in another age, still expressed doubts about the military impact of the bomb and his negativity about the weapon was well known. Before the *USS Augusta* reached its American port, however, Admiral Leahy had been shown to be quite wrong. Hiroshima had been bombed.

[157] Entry, August 3, 1945, Brown Diary, James F. Byrnes Papers, Cooper Library, Folder 602.

6

Intimidation

Hiroshima, the Japanese, and the Soviets

The Most Controversial Decision?

The commemoration of the fiftieth anniversary of the dropping of the atomic bombs on Hiroshima and Nagasaki sparked a significant scholarly and popular dispute. A bevy of books appeared; they wrestled in rather familiar fashion with questions concerning the necessity, the wisdom, and the morality of America's use of the new weapon in 1945.[1] A more inflammatory and public controversy centered on the text developed to accompany the planned exhibit at the Air and Space Museum of the Smithsonian Institution of a part of the fuselage of the *Enola Gay*, the American B-29 aircraft that had dropped the atomic weapon on Hiroshima on August 6, 1945. Supposedly reflecting the most recent scholarly findings and self-consciously unafraid to puncture prevailing national "myths," the Smithsonian text gave a privileged voice to an interpretation that held that the atomic bomb was neither necessary to end the Pacific war nor to save American lives. The predictable public outrage apparently caught the Smithsonian curators by surprise, which, incidentally, raised questions about their political and cultural sensitivity. The historian J. Samuel Walker recounted that "veterans' groups led a fusillade of attacks that accused the Smithsonian of making the use of the bomb appear aggressive,

---

[1] A sample of the works published around the fiftieth anniversary includes Gar Alperovitz, *Decision to Use the Atomic Bomb and the Architecture of an American Myth*; Robert James Maddox, *Weapons for Victory: The Hiroshima Decision Fifty Years Later* (Columbia, MO, 1995); Robert Jay Lifton and Greg Mitchell, *Hiroshima in America: Fifty Years of Denial* (New York, 1995); Robert P. Newman, *Truman and the Hiroshima Cult* (East Lansing, MI, 1995); and Stanley Weintraub, *The Last Great Victory: The End of World War II, July–August 1945* (New York, 1995). The more recent sixtieth anniversary passed in more subdued fashion with a mere flurry of op-ed pieces and magazine articles published in early August 2005. For the best of these, see Richard B. Frank, "Why Truman Dropped the Bomb," *Weekly Standard*, 10 (August 8, 2005), pp. 20–25.

immoral, and unjustified."[2] With considerable congressional support, the aging veterans, members of the proverbial greatest generation, forced the Smithsonian to back down, to modify the text considerably, and to alter the thrust of the exhibit. This led in turn to lengthy lamentations that blatant political pressure essentially had censored a well-researched, historical presentation.[3] Yet, viewed through the perspective of the most accurate historical research of the past decade, it is clear that the veterans' groups saved the Smithsonian from the embarrassment of highlighting a deeply flawed interpretation. Irony of ironies, the veterans' historical understanding holds up much better than the initial view offered by the Smithsonian curators and the scholars who advised them.

The commotion surrounding the *Enola Gay* exhibit ultimately generated much more heat than light. It proved to be just another in a series of disputes and debates which has made the use of the atomic bombs Harry Truman's most controversial decision.[4] At base these debates arose out of a rejection of the arguments put forth by policy makers like Truman and Stimson that the atomic bomb "obviated the need for an invasion of Japan, accelerated the conclusion of the war, and saved a vast number of American lives."[5] Especially after the appearance of Gar Alperovitz's *Atomic Diplomacy* in 1965, various writers increasingly challenged the notion that the atomic bombs were needed to defeat a Japan that supposedly balanced on the verge of surrender. Alperovitz has been nothing if not consistent, and in his massive book marking the fiftieth anniversary of the bomb's use, he reiterated his contentious thesis along with its corollary that the Truman administration used the atomic weapons as part of its diplomacy aimed primarily at the Soviet Union and in order to address certain domestic-political concerns.[6] As one close observer of the "atomic debate" noted, Alperovitz's work "redirected the focus of questions that scholars asked about the bomb." Instead of attending to the necessity of the bomb, "the central questions had become: What factors were paramount in the decision to use the bomb and why was its use more attractive to policymakers than

[2] J. Samuel Walker, "The Decision to Use the Bomb: A Historiographical Update," in Michael J. Hogan, ed., *America in the World: The Historiography of American Foreign Relations Since 1941* (Cambridge and New York, 1995), p. 206.

[3] For further details of the Smithsonian controversy told largely from the perspective of those sympathetic to the originally planned exhibition, see Edward T. Linenthal and Tom Englehardt, eds., *History Wars: The* Enola Gay *and Other Battles for the American Past* (New York, 1996).

[4] Samuel Walker surveys the debate that reached especially high "temperatures" in the years immediately after the use of the bombs, then again in the 1960s when Gar Alperovitz strode onto the historiographical stage with his "atomic diplomacy" thesis. See Walker, "Decision to Use the Bomb," pp. 207–19. Walker has updated his work in a recent essay where he discerns a "balanced position" emerging on Truman's use of the bomb. See "Recent Literature on Truman's Atomic Bomb Decision: A Search for Middle Ground," *Diplomatic History*, 29 (April 2005), pp. 311–34.

[5] Walker summarizes this position in his "Decision to Use the Bomb," p. 207.

[6] See Gar Alperovitz, *Decision to Use the Bomb and the Architecture of an American Myth*.

other alternatives."[7] This seemingly subtle change of emphasis in effect put the Truman administration on trial for its use of the powerful new weapons. Why had it done what wasn't really necessary went the reasoning. But Alperovitz built his approach on a quicksand of faulty assumptions, especially as regards the likelihood of an early Japanese surrender, and so contributed handsomely to a generation of confusion and misunderstanding regarding the use of the atomic bomb.[8] The time has come to move beyond him and his distorted "thesis" once and for all.

The questions a historian asks hold great importance and influence significantly how well any explorer of the past can map and understand its difficult terrain. In such contested and controversial territory as the use of the atomic bombs, it seems wise to clarify at the outset the questions that this chapter addresses and seeks to answer. First, it examines why the bombs were used and then goes on to investigate the role they played in Japan's surrender. Answers to such questions shed light upon the crucial issue regarding the necessity of using these new and terrible weapons. These related matters are surely the province of the historian and might reasonably suffice in the effort to understand Truman's foreign policy and to reach conclusions regarding his continuing or reversing the policies of his predecessor. Yet, given the intensity of the conflict surrounding the atomic bomb, it seems essential to also confront the question regarding the morality of the atomic bomb – was it right for the United States to use this weapon against Hiroshima and Nagasaki? I find convincing the observation of John Lewis Gaddis that one "can't escape thinking about history in moral terms," and rather than doing this implicitly or subconsciously, I prefer here to engage the issue explicitly.[9]

Harry Truman spent little time brooding about future historiographical controversies as the *USS Augusta* transported him back across the Atlantic. The seaboard journey gave him time to relax and included a similar complement of movies and musical concerts for evening entertainment as had the journey to Potsdam. Enjoying the calm seas, he continued his regular practice of rising early and getting in a good walk before breakfast. He consulted occasionally with

---

7 Walker, "Decision to Use the Bomb," p. 213.
8 See the devastating on-line review of the most recent Alperovitz book by John Bonnett on the H-Net diplomatic history service (*http://h-net2.msu.edu/~diplo/balp.htm*), which convincingly makes this case. Bonnett's work has influenced my thinking. Also see the insightful essay review by Brian L. Villa and John Bonnett, "Understanding Indignation: Gar Alperovitz, Robert Maddox, and the Decision to Use the Atomic Bomb," *Reviews in American History*, 24 (September 1996), pp. 529–36. Also note the recent conclusion of J. Samuel Walker, a historian noted for his efforts to find common ground between rival interpretations on the use of the atomic bomb, that the "recent literature on the atomic bomb has inflicted even greater damage on key elements of the revisionist interpretation. It has gravely undermined if not totally refuted the fundamental revisionist tenets that Japan was ready to surrender on the sole condition that the emperor remain on the throne and that American leaders were well aware of Japan's desire to quit the war on reasonable terms." Walker, "Recent Literature on Truman's Atomic Bomb Decision," p. 333.
9 John Lewis Gaddis, *The Landscape of History: How Historians Map the Past* (New York, 2002), p. 122.

Secretary Byrnes, Admiral Leahy, and White House Counsel Samuel Rosenman on the report he would offer the American people on the Potsdam meeting. And, of course, with assistance from his naval and military aides, Captain Vardaman and Brigadier General Vaughan, he monitored developments from the Pacific battlefronts. These developments held both positive and tragic news for the American president eager to bring the bloody war to an end. While the American Air Force and Navy continued their relentless efforts to pound the Japanese into submission, the costs in American lives continued to mount. The sinking of the cruiser *USS Indianapolis* by a Japanese submarine on July 29 left just 316 survivors from a ship's crew of 1,200 – "the worst American catastrophe at sea during the entire war."[10] It served as a painful reminder of the Japanese determination to defend their homeland.

Truman's attention gravitated on the prospects for the atomic bomb and its likely consequences for the war against Japan. On August 3, he spoke with the small contingent of White House press corps members onboard the *Augusta* and gave them a scoop they were unable to use before the ship reached port. He told them that the United States had developed a new and powerful weapon that might hasten the end of the war. Naturally, he gave no indication that he possessed any hesitations about using the weapon. Whatever the subsequent controversies over the atomic bomb, Truman hardly was torn up over its use. This decision caused him none of the anxiety that afflicted him at the time he decided to fire Douglas MacArthur in 1951. It constituted an important but hardly a "controversial" decision for him.

Meanwhile, on the Pacific Island of Tinian in the Marianas chain, the flight and ordnance crews under the respective commands of Colonel Paul W. Tibbets, Jr., and Captain William S. ("Deak") Parsons made their final preparations to use that weapon in warfare.[11] During the evening of August 5, the loading crew hoisted the bomb, known as "Little Boy," into the bomb bay of the *Enola Gay*. Early in the morning of August 6, the crews of Tibbets's plane and those of the accompanying weather and observer planes heard their chaplain pray for them to God that "armed with Thy strength may they bring this war to a rapid end." At 2:45 A.M. (Tinian time) Tibbets took off and flew toward Japan. Once the *Enola Gay* reached its steady flying altitude, Parsons entered the bomb bay and made the final adjustments to the bomb to allow for its eventual detonation. Guided by the reports of the weather plane, Tibbets concluded that they should attack their primary target. Around 8:15 A.M. (Japanese time, which was 7:15 P.M., August 5, in Washington, D.C.), the *Enola Gay* dropped its solitary weapon on the city of Hiroshima.[12]

---

[10] For a powerful description of the sinking of the *Indianapolis* and the harrowing ordeal of its survivors see Stanley Weintraub, *Last Great Victory*, pp. 295–98, 307–10, 326–28, 345–47, 366–71, direct quotation p. 369.

[11] On the preparations, see Weintraub, *Last Great Victory*, pp. 396–99, 413–18.

[12] This summary account draws primarily from Weintraub, *Last Great Victory*, pp. 413–18. (For the chaplain's prayer see p. 415.)

In the northwest Atlantic on Sunday evening, August 5, at the actual time the bomb exploded over Hiroshima, Truman may well have been watching the comedy/mystery film *Thin Man Goes Home* starring William Powell and Myrna Loy. Not until the next day as he ate his lunch in the sailors' mess did he receive the first reports about the mission Tibbets and his crew completed. Stimson informed him that the "big bomb" had been used on Hiroshima and that "first reports indicate complete success which was even more conspicuous than earlier test." According to his own later account, Truman "was deeply moved." He passed along the news to Byrnes and then with gushing enthusiasm proclaimed to the sailors gathered with him that "this is the greatest thing in history. It is time for us to get home." A further message arrived that confirmed the initial assessment. With palpable excitement, Truman informed his mess hall compatriots of the powerful new bomb, which he described "as twenty thousand times as powerful as a ton of TNT." Then he raced to the ship's wardroom to share the news with the *Augusta*'s officers. An observant journalist remembers him almost running as he moved about the ship "spreading the news." As the president later put it, he could not keep back his "expectation that the Pacific war might now be brought to a speedy end."[13] Here lay his primary and deepest hope regarding the impact of the atomic bomb.

The real audience for Truman's thoughts on the bomb did not reside onboard the USS *Augusta*, however, but in Japan. Provision had been made for a statement, prepared before he left for Potsdam, to be issued under the president's name as soon as confirmation came through on the success of the first atomic bombing mission. As his ship ploughed its way back to Newport News, this statement was distributed far and wide. It gave basic details of the attack against Hiroshima, and an elemental description both of the power of the new weapon and the scientific effort that allowed the Anglo-Americans to win "the battle of the laboratories" against the Germans to produce it successfully. He described the atomic bomb as harnessing "the basic power of the universe." In words that might have been expected to penetrate through to the purported descendant of the Sun God then sitting on the Japanese throne, the American leader held that "the force from which the sun draws its power has been loosed against those who brought war to the Far East." Clearly intent on shocking and intimidating the Japanese, Truman warned that the United States was "now prepared to obliterate more rapidly and completely every productive enterprise" that lay above ground in any city in Japan. There should be no mistake, he threatened, "we shall completely destroy Japan's power to make war." Piling on the verbal pressure, he explained that the Potsdam ultimatum had been issued "to spare the Japanese people from utter destruction," but that Japanese leaders had rejected it. This time they should act differently. In words that implied the use of further atomic bombs, he uttered a brutal warning to the Japanese leadership: "If they do not now accept our terms they may expect a rain of

---

[13] For Truman's account, which includes the two messages he received, see *Year of Decisions*, pp. 464–65. Also see Weintraub, *Last Great Victory*, pp. 420–21, which includes the observation of the journalist Merriman Smith.

ruin from the air, the like of which has never been seen on this earth. Behind this air attack will follow sea and land forces in such numbers and power as they have not yet seen and with the fighting skill of which they are already well aware."[14] Naturally, Truman hoped that the awesome display of air power over Hiroshima would obviate the need to utilize the sea and land forces.

On board the *Augusta*, Truman and Byrnes drew satisfaction from the successful use of the atomic bomb. Indicative of his domestic political focus, Byrnes recalled how as director of war mobilization he had become "worried about the huge expenditure and feared repercussions because he had doubt of its working." Stimson, however, had reassured him. Truman, who also had dealt with Stimson during the war, spoke to the importance of having men like the secretary of war "who have the respect of people" and whom congress held in such regard as to authorize such "huge expenditures in secrecy."[15] Now, the two politicians hoped, the huge amounts expended on the Manhattan Project would pay such notable political dividends in forcing Japan's defeat so as to disarm even the most severe fiscal critics. The use of the bomb hopefully would validate the enormous scientific and financial endeavor pursued under Roosevelt's administration.

Neither Truman nor Byrnes raised any concerns regarding whether the atomic bomb was a legitimate weapon of war. Nor did either man raise any questions about the plans to use further bombs against the Japanese. Truman continued to act as a sort of "chairman of the board" who validated and confirmed recommendations that came up to him from subordinates.[16] He had stepped into FDR's shoes and also into his assumptions that the weapon should be used to secure victory in the war.[17] Furthermore, his approval of the use of the atomic bomb reflected the Rooseveltian preference to "achieve complete victory at the lowest cost in American lives." The A-bomb proved yet another arrow in the impressive quiver of America's "industrial might and technological prowess," which allowed U.S. casualties to be kept so light relative to the losses of other major participants in the war. Samuel Walker correctly noted that "Truman inherited from Roosevelt the strategy of keeping American losses to a minimum, and he was committed to carrying it out for the remainder of the war."[18]

[14] See Statement by the President Announcing the Use of the A-bomb at Hiroshima, August 6, 1945, Truman, *Public Papers of the Presidents of the United States: Harry S. Truman, 1945*, pp. 197–200.

[15] Diary entry, August 6, 1945, Brown Diary, James F. Byrnes Papers, Cooper Library, Folder 602.

[16] Alonzo Hamby refers to Truman as "chairman of the board" in *Man of the People*, p. 324.

[17] Barton Bernstein in particular emphasized the importance of Roosevelt's legacy on Truman's decisions on the atomic bomb. See Barton J. Bernstein, "Roosevelt, Truman, and the Atomic Bomb, 1941–1945: A Reinterpretation," *Political Science Quarterly*, 90 (Spring 1975), pp. 23–69. Also see his more recent "Understanding the Atomic Bomb and the Japanese Surrender," p. 230, where he concludes that "the combat use of the A-bomb was, unfortunately, virtually inevitable. Truman's commitment to its use was, basically, the implementation of the assumption that he had inherited."

[18] See J. Samuel Walker, *Prompt and Utter Destruction: Truman and the Use of Atomic Bombs Against Japan* (Chapel Hill, NC, 1997), p. 9.

Notably, no action of the Japanese government or military encouraged either Truman or Byrnes to consider any change in strategy. Quite the opposite! Having broken the Japanese codes, the Americans knew of the tentative, back-channel efforts of certain civilian officials in Tokyo to enlist the Soviet Union in negotiating some kind of peace settlement that would *not* require either a surrender or any occupation of the home islands.[19] But such terms were completely unacceptable to the Allies. The American-led alliance intended "unrestricted occupation of Japanese territory, total authority in the governing of Japan, dismantlement of Japan's military and military-industrial complex ('demobilization'), a restructuring of Japanese society ('demilitarization'), and Allied-run war crimes trials."[20] Japan must concede fully as had Germany. No indication of such a surrender occurred, of course, because the influential Japanese decision makers could not countenance it.[21] So the Americans waited in vain for the Japanese to respond positively to the Potsdam Declaration's call for immediate and unconditional surrender. Japan's prime minister Suzuki Kantaro publicly dismissed the Potsdam terms on July 28 and on July 30, when referring to the terms, he confided to a senior cabinet official that "for the enemy to say something like that means circumstances have arisen that force them also to end the war. That is why they are talking about unconditional surrender. Precisely at a time like this, if we hold firm, then they will yield before we do." He did not "think there is any need to stop [the war]."[22]

In the post-Potsdam period, the Tokyo government held back from any official contact with the Allies through the formal channels provided by the Swiss government. Despite the thunderous bombing campaign of General Curtis LeMay's B-29s from March to August, which had left no sizable city untouched, the Japanese planned to continue their war effort.[23] Indeed, members of the Japanese military appeared to relish the opportunity to punish

[19] See the collection of Japanese diplomatic cables from July 2 to August 16 to which Byrnes had access in James F. Byrnes Papers, Cooper Library, Folder 571. On the limits of Japan's negotiating terms as revealed in these diplomatic exchanges, see Frank, *Downfall*, pp. 229–30.

[20] These terms are set forth in Douglas J. MacEachin, *The Final Months of the War with Japan*, p. 36

[21] For brilliant expositions of the Japanese determination throughout 1945 to continue fighting see Richard B. Frank's, *Downfall*, esp. pp. 83–86; and Herbert P. Bix, "Japan's Delayed Surrender: A Reinterpretation," *Diplomatic History*, 19 (Spring 1995), pp. 197–225.

[22] Suzuki quoted in Bix, "Japan's Delayed Surrender," p. 208. Tsuyoshi Hasegawa discusses Suzuki's public statement in his *Racing the Enemy: Stalin, Truman, and the Surrender of Japan* (Cambridge, MA, 2005), pp. 165–68. He presents Suzuki's brief public comment that the Japanese government would ignore [*mokusatsu*] the Potsdam proclamation as resulting from direct pressure from the military. Hasegawa also asks "how Suzuki's vague statement became a justification to drop the atomic bomb" but fails to acknowledge that for the Americans anything short of a full acceptance of the Potsdam terms would be viewed as a rejection of them. Also as Hasegawa's own work makes clear, the Japanese military could not contemplate any acceptance of the Potsdam terms.

[23] For a vivid portrayal of the bombing campaign, see Ronald Schaffer, *Wings of Judgment: American Bombing in World War II* (New York, 1985), pp. 128–42.

American invaders who dared intrude on their home islands.[24] Late in July, American intelligence, utilizing the Ultra code-breaking system, determined that the Japanese troop levels in Kyushu dedicated to repelling any invasion had now reached six divisions and that more soldiers were arriving. General MacArthur's intelligence chief, Major General Charles Willoughby, even expressed the fear that Japanese forces could "grow to [the] point where we attack on a ratio of one (1) to one (1)," which, he helpfully added for even the most obtuse of his readers, "is not the recipe for victory."[25] The prospects for the Olympic invasion now appeared decidedly problematic, and the likelihood of significant American casualties commensurately increased. In such circumstances, none of the American military leaders either in the Pacific theater or in Washington cautioned Truman to reconsider his use of the atomic bomb. The on-the-ground reality of a Japanese military "girding for Armageddon" and convinced "that it could achieve success against an invasion," must be well appreciated by all who genuinely seek to understand why the atomic bombs were used.[26] In short, Japan hardly stood on the verge of surrender. The time has come to explode permanently the myth of a Japan ready to surrender – a notion that received much of its currency from the terribly flawed report of the U.S. Strategic Bombing Survey conducted after the war and publicly issued in July of 1946.[27] This view has done enough damage to proper understanding of the use of the atomic bomb.

Eager to force Japan's defeat before paying any invasion's high cost in American blood, Truman simply allowed the predetermined policy to proceed. Numerous concerned commentators writing from a post-Hiroshima perspective have sought to supply all kinds of alternatives to the A-bomb for the American president's use, but Truman operated in a pre-Hiroshima world. Like Byrnes and Stimson, Truman and his associates didn't seek to avoid using the bomb, and those who focus on "alternatives" distort history by overemphasizing them.[28]

---

[24] Frank details the main elements of the *Ketsu-Go* ("Decisive" operation) designed to crush the American invaders in *Downfall*, pp. 83–86.

[25] This analysis relies upon, and Willoughby's evaluation is quoted in, Richard B. Frank, *Downfall*, pp. 211–12.

[26] These descriptions of the Japanese military are from Frank, *Downfall*, p. 238. Tsuyoshi Hasegawa confirms the likely high costs of any invasion by projecting from the casualties the Soviet Union incurred in its efforts to seize the Kuril Islands. Note his interesting discussion in *Racing the Enemy*, pp. 263–64, where he concludes that "had Olympic been implemented, the result would have been an unprecedented bloodbath."

[27] On the serious flaws of the U.S. Strategic Bombing Survey, see Robert P. Newman, "Ending the War with Japan: Paul Nitze's 'Early Surrender' Counterfactual," *Pacific Historical Review*, 64 (May 1995), pp. 167–94; and Barton J. Bernstein, "Compelling Japan's Surrender Without the A-Bomb, Soviet Entry, or Invasion: Reconsidering the US Bombing Survey's Early Surrender Conclusions," *Journal of Strategic Studies*, 18 (June 1995), pp. 101–48. Bernstein noted that "analysts can no longer trust the Survey's statements of counterfactual probabilities about when the Pacific War would have ended without the A-Bomb or Soviet entry. On such matters, the Survey is an unreliable guide." (p. 105).

[28] The most recent work to focus attention on "alternatives" is Tsuyoshi Hasegawa's *Racing the Enemy*, which argues (p. 299) that "evidence makes clear that there were alternatives to the

As Barton Bernstein persuasively has clarified, the American leaders "easily rejected or never considered most of the so-called alternatives to the bomb."[29] They saw no reason to do so because they viewed the atomic bomb as another weapon in the Allied arsenal along with such complements – *not* alternatives – as the naval blockade, continued conventional bombing, the threat of invasion, and Soviet entry into the war. Together, they hoped, these might secure a Japanese surrender before American troops waded ashore on the southern plains of Kyushu.

Forcing a Japanese surrender formed the prism through which Truman also viewed both the use of a second atomic bomb and the Soviet Union's decision to enter the war. By the time the president arrived safely back on American soil on August 7, preparations had begun to ready the other available A-bomb, known as "Fat Man," for use in accord with established plans. The governing strategy called for the dropping of a second bomb a few days after the first so as to convey to Japanese decision makers that the United States had an unlimited supply of them and to drive home unmistakably the warnings about the "rain of ruin from the air." The initial plan had been to use the second weapon on August 11, but fears of bad weather forced the crews on Tinian to move the date forward to August 9. This didn't upset the ordnance experts readying "Fat Man" because, as one of them recalled, "everyone felt that the sooner we could get off another mission, the more likely it was that the Japanese would feel that we had large quantities of the devices and would surrender sooner."[30] Coincident with these preparations, the United States continued its massive conventional bombing efforts and also dropped leaflets over Japanese cities informing their residents of Hiroshima's destruction and calling upon them to evacuate their cities immediately.[31]

While the Americans readied their next atomic assault, the Soviet Union pounded another nail in the coffin of Japan's war effort on August 8 when it declared war and soon thereafter launched a powerful attack on Japanese forces in Manchuria. The Soviets had some sense of the force of the new weapon and recognized, it would seem, that they must enter the war immediately in case the Hiroshima bombing persuaded the Japanese to surrender.[32] They conveniently put aside their supposed need to reach a satisfactory settlement with the Chinese

---

use of the bomb, alternatives that the Truman administration for reasons of its own declined to pursue." Hasegawa argues, unconvincingly in my view, that the Soviet entry into the war would have been sufficient to force Japan's defeat without the use of the atomic bombs. See his case in *Racing the Enemy*, pp. 295–96.

[29] Bernstein, "Understanding the Atomic Bomb and the Japanese Surrender," p. 235. Bernstein (p. 235) also points to the risk of "distorting history" by "framing a post-Hiroshima analysis in terms of *alternatives* to the use of the A-Bomb."

[30] Ensign Bernard J. O'Keefe, a member of the assembly team, quoted in Weintraub, *Last Great Victory*, p. 446.

[31] For further details, see Weintraub, *Last Great Victory*, pp. 447–49.

[32] On Soviet reactions to the Hiroshima bombing and for the Soviet decision to declare war on Japan, see David Holloway's *Stalin and the Bomb*, pp. 127–29, and Hasegawa, *Racing the Enemy*, pp. 186–91.

regarding postwar arrangements in north Asia so as to establish themselves formally as opponents of Japan. Late in the afternoon of August 8, Molotov called in Japanese ambassador Sato and broke the news to him, thereby ending whatever remaining hopes existed in Tokyo that the Soviets might serve as an intermediary for peace negotiations. Later in the evening, Stalin met with U.S. ambassador Harriman and his embassy counselor, George Kennan. Harriman voiced the official American position and expressed "his gratification at the fact that we were once again allies."[33] They discussed initial reports of Soviet military actions and the likely impact of the atomic bomb on the Japanese in a correct manner, whatever might have been the subtext of their conversation.[34]

The Americans appreciated well that the Soviets had rushed their declaration of war, but the reigning American assumption, as Byrnes had learned at Potsdam, held that the Soviets would have their way in Manchuria whatever happened elsewhere in the Pacific theater.[35] Truman took the Soviet intervention in stride and made a brief announcement to White House reporters that "Russia has declared war on Japan." Nonetheless, he deemed the matter as "so important" as to do it in person with Secretary Byrnes and Admiral Leahy flanking him. Clearly, he wanted to add to the pressure on the Japanese without engaging in any effusive commentary that might exaggerate the extent of the Soviet contribution to Japan's ultimate defeat. In his radio report on the Potsdam conference given during the evening of August 9, Truman referred to Soviet entry into the war in the Pacific and "gladly welcomed into this struggle against the last of the Axis aggressors our gallant and victorious ally against the Nazis."[36]

This radio address contained further pointed warnings to the Japanese. Truman declared to the American people and beyond them to an audience he hoped included Japan's leadership that "the first atomic bomb was dropped on Hiroshima, a military base. That was because we wished," he continued,

[33] Memorandum of conversation, August 8, 1945, Averell Harriman Papers, Library of Congress, Box 181.

[34] David Holloway suggests that the subtext should read: "Stalin: we have entered the war, in spite of your attempt to end it before we did so. Harriman: the atomic bomb will end the war; we have it, and it was very expensive to build; it will have a great impact on postwar international relations. Stalin: Japan was about to surrender anyway, and the secret of the atomic bomb might be hard to keep." Holloway, *Stalin and the Bomb*, p. 129. (Neither Harriman nor Kennan, however, confirmed this subtext either then or later.)

[35] Truman later told his aides, including Eben Ayers, that after Hiroshima "Stalin hastened to get in before Japan could fold up." Notably Truman affirmed in this conversation that he had gone to Potsdam "entirely for the purpose of making sure that Stalin would come in then [August 15] or earlier if possible." He expressed no regret at his efforts. See Ayers's diary entry, August 9, 1945, in Ferrell, ed., *Truman in the White House*, p. 62. There is little evidence to support either the contention of Tsuyoshi Hasegawa that Truman felt a "sense of betrayal" at the Soviet entry into the war or his suggestion that Truman was a "disappointed man" because of the Soviet action. See Hasegawa, *Racing the Enemy*, pp. 193–94.

[36] Radio Report of the President to the Nation, August 9, 1945, *Department of State Bulletin*, 13 (August 12, 1945), p. 209.

"in this first attack to avoid in so far as possible, the killing of civilians." Then
he cautioned that the first attack must be understood as "only a warning of
things to come." Raising the stakes still further in the psychological warfare
effort to intimidate the enemy, Truman apprised all his listeners that "if Japan
does not surrender, bombs will have to be dropped on war industries and, unfortunately, thousands of civilian lives will be lost." He urged "Japanese civilians
to leave industrial cities immediately, and save themselves from destruction."[37]
Unfortunately for the residents of the Japanese city of Nagasaki, before any of
them could learn in translation of Truman's latest warning their city had been
subjected to the second atomic attack.

The primary target for the crew of *Bock's Car*, which delivered the "Fat Man"
bomb, was the Kyushu city of Kokura, but smoke and smog obscured that target, so the Americans flew on to the secondary target, the port of Nagasaki,
home to Mitsubishi shipyards and industrial plants.[38] There the second
A-bomb fell without warning on the city. Yet again a solitary plane delivered a
horrific blow that far exceeded what could have been inflicted by hundreds of
B-29s armed with conventional bombs. The planned message to the Japanese
reverberated one more time – surrender or face utter destruction. Mercifully, it
began to be heard in Tokyo.

The Japanese Surrender

The first of the two nuclear weapons used in war caused a blinding explosion
over the center of Hiroshima. It produced enormous damage and killed approximately eighty thousand people while wounding a similar number. Many of the
maimed died soon thereafter from the effects of their exposure to the radioactiv-
ity let loose by the explosion. Hiroshima contained military targets – a military
headquarters, an assembly area for troops, a communications center, and a
port that served as the main embarkation center for China – yet its civilian
residents suffered greatly from the destructive power of the atomic blast.[39] The
Japanese government emphasized the civilian nature of the target in the protest
it transmitted to the United States through the good offices of the Swiss government on August 9. The statement contested Truman's claim that Hiroshima
counted as a military target noting that the city lacked "military fortifications
or installations." It zeroed in on the indiscriminate nature of the bomb pointing
out that "the zone of damage spread over a wide area and all persons within
this area, without discrimination as to belligerents and non-belligerents and
irrespective of sex or age, were killed or wounded by the blast and radiated

[37] Radio Report of the President to the Nation, August 9, 1945, *Department of State Bulletin*, 13
(August 12, 1945), p. 212.
[38] On the bombing of Nagasaki, see Weintraub, *Last Great Victory*, pp. 481–91. Tsuyoshi
Hasegawa rather strangely asks in his *Racing the Enemy*, p. 194, "why, given the knowledge
that the Soviets had entered the war, didn't Truman order the suspension or postponement of
the Nagasaki bomb?" This question reveals a lack of understanding of the American strategy
to "shock" the Japanese into surrender.
[39] Weintraub notes the military targets in *Last Great Victory*, p. 426.

heat." It presented the enormous and indiscriminate slaughter as contrary to the "basic principles of the international rules of warfare which state that a belligerent does not enjoy an unrestricted right in the choice of methods of attack and that the belligerent shall not make use of any weapon which would cause unnecessary suffering."[40]

Reports of the extensive damage to Hiroshima reached Tokyo beginning on August 7. A cabinet meeting on that day received this information and the associated details of Truman's threatening statement calling for immediate surrender. The knowledge that more bombs might be on their way was certainly understood as of August 8, but the Japanese authorities held back from any decision in reaction to this threat. Instead, the Supreme War Leadership Council agreed to meet on August 9 by which time its members also had the devastating news of the Soviet declaration of war to consider.[41] This body [the Big Six] brought together both the civilian and military leadership of Japan and they eventually divided into war and peace factions. According to one participant "a rather bullish atmosphere" prevailed at the outset of their morning meeting.[42] After some hours of debate and discussion, Prime Minister Suzuki, Foreign Minister Shigenori Togo, and, rather hesitantly, Navy Minister Mitsumasa Yonai favored the acceptance of the Potsdam terms with the important and essential exception of preserving the Imperial system. But War Minister Korechika Anami, Army Chief General Yoshijiro Umezu, and Navy Chief Admiral Soemu Toyoda would not agree to such terms. They preferred to fight on unless the Allies agreed to the additional conditions of "self-disarmament, Japanese control of any war-crimes trials, and, above all, no Allied occupation of Japan." Richard B. Frank has tellingly clarified that "these terms would permit, at some later and better moment, Japan's warriors to inculcate a myth that they were never really defeated and only of their own volition laid down arms to spare the world more ravages of war."[43]

Into the midst of their meeting came the initial news of the atomic bombing of Nagasaki.[44] This report, which shattered any doubts concerning the American capability to use more than one weapon, did not alter the firmly held

---

[40] The cable from Tokyo (Togo) to Bern, August 9, 1945 including the text of the protest is included in the materials gathered in James F. Byrnes Papers, Cooper Library, Folder 571.

[41] Hasegawa provides valuable details on the impact of the Soviet declaration of war on the Japanese leadership. See his *Racing the Enemy*, pp. 198–200. This said, one should also note Hasegawa weaves an argument that elevates the significance of the Soviet entry while diminishing the impact on Japanese leaders of the atomic bombs.

[42] Admiral Toyoda quoted from his memoirs in Frank, *Downfall*, p. 291.

[43] Frank, *Downfall*, p. 291. My summary of the August 9 meeting and the outline of the additional conditions of the Japanese military also are drawn from Frank, pp. 290–91. On the "One Condition vs. Four Conditions," also see Herbert Bix, "Japan's Delayed Surrender," pp. 218–23.

[44] On the impact of the second atomic bomb, see Sadao Asada, "The Shock of the Atomic Bomb and Japan's Decision to Surrender – A Reconsideration," *Pacific Historical Review*, 67 (November 1998), pp. 490–93. Asada notes that "the strategic value of the second bomb was minimal," but he concluded that "from the standpoint of its shock effect, the political impact of the Nagasaki bomb cannot be denied." (p. 492).

positions of the Japanese leaders. No consensus emerged to support the acceptance of the Potsdam terms with the proviso regarding the Imperial system. Indeed, as Frank has shown, it seems likely that Suzuki came to the Imperial Palace early in the afternoon of August 9 and recommended acceptance of the Potsdam terms with the *four* conditions that represented "the lowest common denominator of agreement within the Big Six."[45] These conditions most certainly would have been interpreted by the Truman administration as a clear rejection of the Potsdam terms. Only some intense lobbying by the indefatigable senior statesman Prince Fuminaro Konoe of the emperor's brother Prince Takamatsu and also by former foreign minister Mamoru Sigemitsu of the emperor's key aide Koichi Kido raised questions in the Imperial Palace about this course.[46]

Meanwhile, Suzuki chaired a meeting of his full cabinet during the afternoon of August 9. Again, no consensus emerged despite hours of discussion, which ended at 8:00 P.M. Because the Japanese procedures called for unanimity for any decision to be presented to the emperor, Suzuki left for the palace to explain the situation. Technically, he should have resigned and advised the emperor to appoint another prime minister to form a government, but he did not. Instead, he advised Hirohito to convene an Imperial Conference to allow the emperor to hear the arguments of the members of the Supreme War Leadership Council.[47] And so it was that the Big Six along with Baron Kiichiro Hiranuma, the president of the Privy Council, and a few aides gathered in an underground air-raid shelter a few minutes before midnight on August 9 and bowed low as the emperor entered the room. According to the most measured accounts of this meeting Suzuki again presented the *four* condition terms as the consensus view of the Council.[48] Foreign Minister Togo made the case for surrender with only the insistence on preserving the emperor's prerogatives. Anami, Umezu, and Toyoda still vigorously opposed this position. Anami spoke of resolutely proceeding with the prosecution of the war and declared that "if the people of Japan went into the decisive battle in the homeland determined to display the full measure of patriotism and to fight to the very last, Japan would be able to avert the crisis facing her."[49] Hiranuma and Suzuki lent some indirect support to Togo's position and spoke of the developing unrest within the Japanese population and the prospect of its increasing as bombing continued.

Eventually, Suzuki asked the emperor to decide between the two proposals. This he did. He concluded that "the time has come when we must bear the unbearable." Strangely associating himself with his ancestor, the Emperor Meiji, at the time Japan had been forced to back down from some of its demands

---

45 Frank, *Downfall*, p. 291. I am guided by Frank's impressive work.

46 Frank, *Downfall*, p. 291. Also see Hasegawa, *Racing the Enemy*, pp. 205–09.

47 Sadao Asada argues that Suzuki made his suggestion based on a previous understanding with Emperor Hirohito. See Asada, "The Shock of the Atomic Bomb and Japan's Decision to Surrender," p. 495.

48 See Frank, *Downfall*, pp. 293–96; and the classic account provided in Robert J. C. Butow, *Japan's Decision to Surrender* (Stanford, CA, 1954), pp. 168–76.

49 For Anami's position see Butow, *Japan's Decision to Surrender*, p. 170.

on China at the conclusion of the Sino-Japanese War in 1894–95, Hirohito concluded: "I swallow my own tears and give my sanction to the proposal to accept the Allied proclamation on the basis outlined by the Foreign Minister."[50] He then left the room. Suzuki asked the gathered officials to accept this decision and promptly gathered together the members of his cabinet. "Sometime between 3:00 and 4:00 A.M.," as Richard Frank recounts, "the ministers officially adopted the 'Imperial decision,' therefore swaddling the Emperor's words spoken only an hour before in legal force."[51] Notably, at this meeting, Anami clarified with Suzuki that Japan would fight on if the Allies refused to accede to the Japanese demand regarding the emperor's authority. With the decision made, foreign ministry officials quickly dispatched cables through their official intermediaries in Berne advising the Allies that Japan would accept the Potsdam terms with the crucial proviso that this would "not comprise any demand which prejudices the prerogatives of His Majesty as a Sovereign Ruler." The Japanese note expressed the sincere hope that "this understanding is warranted" and requested that "an explicit indication to that effect will be speedily forthcoming."[52]

The Japanese had made their decision, and now it fell to the United States and its allies to consider Japan's offer. Rather surprisingly, the key American officials were not gathered together in fervent expectation of an immediate Japanese surrender, and there had been little planning for such an eventuality. As Richard Frank ably has demonstrated, there had been no decision on Truman's part to take any measures to begin the shift from a wartime to a peacetime economy. Clearly, he assumed no sudden Japanese concession. Secretary of War Stimson planned to depart Washington on August 10 for some days of vacation, "an eloquent indicator of how far official Washington believed that Japan remained from surrender even after two atomic bombs."[53] Truman had not spent any inordinate amount of time following upon his return to the White House late on August 7 fixated on the A-bomb. Stimson had briefed him on the huge damage done to Hiroshima and the numerous casualties, and the president began to feel some reservations about the destruction.[54] But there

---

[50] See Hirohito's full statement in Butow, *Japan's Decision to Surrender*, pp. 175–76.

[51] Frank, *Downfall*, p. 296.

[52] The Japanese note is included in Swiss Chargé d'Affaires Grassli to Secretary Byrnes, August 10, 1945, printed in *Department of State Bulletin*, 13 (August 12, 1945), p. 205. Through their officials in Berne and Stockholm, the Japanese also communicated their willingness to surrender to the governments of Great Britain, China, and the Soviet Union.

[53] Frank, *Downfall*, p. 300.

[54] On August 9, Truman replied to a letter from Georgia Senator Richard Russell calling for the continued atomic bombing of Japan that "I know that Japan is a terribly cruel and uncivilized nation in warfare but I can't bring myself to believe that, because they are beasts, we should act in the same manner." He continued that "for myself, I certainly regret the necessity of wiping out whole populations because of the 'pigheadedness' of the leaders of a nation and, for your information, I am not going to do it until it is absolutely necessary.... My object is to save as many American lives as possible but I also have a humane feeling for the women and children in Japan." Truman to Russell, August 9, 1945, quoted in Bernstein, "Understanding the Automic Bomb and the Japanese Surrender," pp. 267–68.

had been no elaborate discussion of how the United States might respond to a Japanese surrender containing the proviso regarding the emperor. Once again, policy would be formulated quickly.

The first news of the Japanese offer came courtesy of the Magic code breakers and then from Army radio monitors who gathered reports from Radio Tokyo. By early morning (Washington time), Truman determined that these reports, while not official, warranted discussion, and he asked Admiral Leahy to gather Stimson, Byrnes, and Forrestal together at 9:00 A.M. to review the situation. As is well known, at this meeting Leahy and Stimson encouraged Truman to accept the offer, but Byrnes, not only motivated by his domestic political concerns but also acting on the advice of his Japan experts, held back.[55] According to what he later told his associate Walter Brown, Byrnes pointed to the "unconditional surrender" demands of the Potsdam declaration and then expressed his concern at why "we should go further [in concessions] than we were willing to go at Potsdam when we had no atomic bomb, and Russia was not in the war." Byrnes's intervention proved successful and thus the meeting shelved Leahy's proposed memorandum simply accepting the Japanese offer – a position which, Byrnes remarked later that day, "would have led to [the] crucifixion of [the] President."[56] Instead Truman accepted the suggestion of Navy Secretary Forrestal that "we might in our reply indicate willingness to accept, yet define the terms of surrender in such a manner that the intents and purposes of the Potsdam Declaration would be clearly accomplished."[57] The president charged Byrnes with drafting such a reply.

Byrnes returned to the White House by noon with a draft reply, and he and Truman discussed it over lunch and prepared for a full meeting of the cabinet at 2:00 P.M. They also drafted messages to London, Moscow, and Chungking requesting the approval of the terms that set forth that "from the moment of surrender the authority of the Emperor and the Japanese Government to rule the state shall be subject to the Supreme Commander of the Allied powers who will take such steps as he deems proper to effectuate the surrender terms." The terms placed the burden on the emperor to call on all Japanese forces to cease their operations and to surrender their arms and made specific provisions for prisoners of war. Then, in unmistakable terms, the proposed response made clear that "the ultimate form of government of Japan shall, in accordance with

---

[55] Robertson emphasizes "domestic politics" as Byrnes's "primary motivation" in *Sly and Able*, pp. 435–36. Hasegawa in his *Racing the Enemy*, p. 218, clarifies that "Byrnes, who was initially inclined to accept Japan's condition [for surrender], had to be convinced that preservation of the imperial prerogatives demanded by Japan would be incompatible with America's basic objective in the war. [Joseph] Grew approached him twice, followed by [Eugene] Dooman and [Joseph] Ballantine, before Byrnes agreed that, despite the nation's war-weariness, they could not accept Japan's condition of surrender."

[56] Diary entry, August 10, 1945, Brown Diary, James F. Byrnes Papers, Cooper Library, Folder 602. Byrnes was angry at Leahy's actions and told Brown that "Leahy still thought he was Secretary of State, just as he was under Roosevelt, and he had to show him differently."

[57] Truman, *Year of Decisions*, p. 472.

the Potsdam Declaration, be established by the freely expressed will of the Japanese people." It promised that "the armed forces of the Allied Powers will remain in Japan until the purposes set forth in the Potsdam Declaration are achieved."[58] This hardly constituted any "explicit guarantee that the Imperial institution would continue, much less that Hirohito would remain on the throne."[59]

Eager to end the war without any further American losses the Truman administration asked their allies for a speedy response to the terms that Byrnes drafted. The British and the Chinese soon advised of their essential agreement. Soviet approval came more grudgingly as Ambassador Harriman discovered when he met with Molotov late in the evening of August 10. The Soviet foreign minister initially tried to delay his nation's response. When Harriman insisted on an answer, Molotov met with him and the British ambassador at 2:00 P.M. to provide it. He indicated agreement with the response to the Japanese, but, in the case of an affirmative reply, he asserted that "the Allied Powers should reach an agreement on the candidacy or candidacies for representation of the Allied High Command to which the Japanese Emperor and the Japanese Government are to be subordinated."

Harriman followed up and discerned that the Soviets expected to play a major role in the occupation. Molotov even speculated that "it was conceivable that there might be two Supreme Commanders; [Soviet General] Vasielevski and [General] MacArthur." With barely controlled anger, Harriman branded such an arrangement as "absolutely inadmissible." Molotov told the ambassador bluntly that, regardless of his personal thoughts, the Soviets wanted the message transmitted to Washington. Harriman agreed to do so but with a parting flourish drew to Molotov's attention "that the United States had carried the main burden of the war in the Pacific on its shoulders for four years. It had therefore kept the Japanese off the Soviet's back. The Soviet Government had been at war for two days. It was only just that the Soviet government should place in American hands the choice as to who would be Supreme Commander. The present Soviet position was absolutely impossible." Molotov apparently reported back to Stalin on Harriman's strongly negative reaction against their provocative gambit to muscle in on the occupation. By the time Harriman returned to his embassy office, Stalin's translator Vladimir Pavlov called to retreat somewhat. He clarified that the Soviets sought only "consultation" rather than "agreement" on the occupation arrangements.[60] Harriman quickly conveyed the Soviet response back to Washington.

---

[58] For the early draft of Byrnes's proposed response, see Truman, *Year of Decisions*, p. 473. The slightly modified final version that went to the Japanese is included in Byrnes to Swiss Chargé d'Affaires Grassli, August 11, 1945, *Department of State Bulletin*, 13 (August 12, 1945), pp. 205–06.

[59] Frank, *Downfall*, p. 302.

[60] The account of this meeting and the various texts involved are included in Memorandum of Conversation, August 10, 1945, Averell Harriman Papers, Library of Congress, Box 181.

Once the approvals from the Allies arrived, Byrnes issued the response on behalf of all four governments and placed the onus for a decision back on the policy makers in Tokyo, especially Hirohito. Truman's support for Byrnes's astute tactical move now forced the Japanese leaders to face squarely the reality that they truly must admit defeat and subject themselves to a full occupation. The emperor would need to subject himself to the authority of an American general. In the end, he agreed to this course, but again only after a major division occurred among his advisers.[61] While Foreign Minister Togo recommended immediate acceptance of the allied terms, War Minister Anami now backed by Baron Hiranuma opposed them fearing the fate of the emperor. Inside the War Ministry and among Army and Navy officers in the field, suggestions that Japan should surrender met with disbelief and rejection. In an increasingly tumultuous situation in the Japanese capital, military officers geared up to reverse any decision to accept the Potsdam terms.

Tracing the intrigues and internecine battles among Japanese civilian and military figures is beyond the scope of this study, but it must be said that the harrowing ordeal of the peace faction gives the lie to any notion of a Japan just waiting to surrender. Fortunately, Hirohito backed by his chief aide Kido and the imperial family members decided to accept the terms of the Byrnes note.[62] On August 14, the emperor had to again intervene directly in a meeting of a divided Supreme War Council along with other officials. He listened to Anami, Toyoda, and Umezu repeat their arguments of August 9 but rejected them. "I have surveyed the conditions prevailing in Japan and in the world," he told his officials, "and it is my belief that a continuation of the war promises nothing but additional destruction." He insisted that Japan must accept the allied terms. Furthermore, he agreed to make a broadcast to his people explaining the necessity of ending the war.[63] The emperor and his officials shed tears of sorrow as he finally called upon each man present "to exert himself to the utmost so that we may meet the trying days which lie ahead."[64] The decision made, the aged and exhausted Suzuki convened the cabinet which then ratified the emperor's wishes. Thereupon the foreign ministry transmitted this news to the four allied powers through their intermediaries in Berne and Stockholm.

One might think that action should have ended matters, but hardly so. Gerhard Weinberg has summarized well that "military figures in key positions in the capital tried to kill their opponents, seize and destroy the recording with the Emperor's broadcast to the people of Japan, and take over power with

---

[61] The story of the divisions in Japan over the surrender terms is told with dramatic flair in William Craig, *Fall of Japan* (New York, 1967), pp. 135–201. Also see Richard Frank's incisive account in *Downfall*, pp. 308–21.

[62] Hasegawa, *Racing the Enemy*, pp. 230–33.

[63] On the August 14 meeting, see Frank, *Downfall*, pp. 314–15; and Butow, *Japan's Decision to Surrender*, pp. 206–09.

[64] Hirohito's words are recorded in Butow, *Japan's Decision to Surrender*, pp. 207–08.

the intention of continuing the war."[65] On the evening of August 14, fanatical young officers unsuccessfully targeted Prime Minister Suzuki, Baron Hiranuma, and the emperor's chief aide Marquis Kido. Rebellious troops occupied the Imperial Palace grounds and killed General Takeshi Mori of the Imperial Guards Division in the process.[66] Fortunately for Japan and for peace, Anami and Umezu refused to endorse plans for a full-blown coup, and officers loyal to the emperor put down the rebellion. Suzuki's government stayed in place and readied itself for the burdens of surrender, and only then submitted its resignation. Nonetheless, it was, as Weinberg concluded in his characteristically balanced fashion, "a close call, and in a way shows that the earlier fears of the peace advocates within the government, that any open move to end the war could lead to a coup which would prolong rather than shorten the conflict, was warranted."[67]

On August 15, the Japanese citizenry heard Hirohito speak over the radio and announce that he had accepted the terms set forth by the Allies. The war must end said the man who sat "by the Grace of Heaven" upon "the Throne occupied by the same Dynasty changeless through ages eternal." As Robert Butow pointed out, the emperor never mentioned such words as "defeat," "surrender," and "capitulation," but framed the need for Japan's concession in terms of Japanese interests. Hirohito explained to his people that "the war situation has developed not necessarily to Japan's advantage, while the general trends of the world have all turned against her interest." He also specifically mentioned that "the enemy has begun to develop a new and most cruel bomb, the power of which to do damage is indeed incalculable, taking the toll of many innocent lives." Indicative of the place of the atomic bombs in forcing the Japanese surrender, he continued that "should We continue to fight, it would . . . result in an ultimate collapse and obliteration of the Japanese nation."[68] The next day, an imperial ceasefire order to all the Japanese armed forces was issued and Emperor Hirohito enlisted the support of family members, like his brother Prince Yakamatsu, to ensure that the various Army and Navy commands obeyed. The formal surrender came on the battleship *USS Missouri* on September 2.

Washington probably received some initial news of the Japanese decision to surrender from the Magic code breakers, but the first public notification came to Byrnes at mid-afternoon on August 14, when the U.S. ambassador to Switzerland informed him that Japan's government accepted the terms he had outlined. He rushed to the White House and shared the information with Truman. At 6:00 P.M., the Swiss chargé d'affaires in Washington delivered the formal and official acceptance of the surrender terms to the secretary of state, who immediately took the news to the president. By 7:00 P.M. Truman gathered

---

[65] Weinberg, *World at Arms*, p. 891.

[66] Craig, *Fall of Japan*, pp. 181–201; Hasegawa, *Racing the Enemy*, pp. 241–48.

[67] Weinberg, *World at Arms*, p. 891.

[68] For Butow's comments and Hirohito's address, see *Japan's Decision to Surrender*, pp. 2–3. Villa and Bonnett point to the significance of Hirohito's mentioning the "most cruel bomb" in their "Understanding Indignation," p. 532.

PHOTO 12. Harry Truman gives the news of Japan surrender to the White House press corps on August 14, 1945. Byrnes is at his side while Franklin Roosevelt's portrait is in the background. (Courtesy National Archives)

PHOTO 13. Surrounded by his cabinet, Truman reads the Japanese acceptance of surrender. Seated on his right are Admiral Leahy and Secretary Byrnes. On his left sits former Secretary of State Cordell Hull whom Truman specifically invited to the ceremony. (Courtesy National Archives)

PHOTO 14. Harry and Bess Truman wave to the cheering crowd that gathered in front of the White House after the announcement of the Japanese surrender on August 14, 1945. (Courtesy National Archives)

in his office his wife, the service chiefs, and most cabinet members. He also made a special effort to include the former secretary of state, Cordell Hull, who had received the Japanese declaration of war following the Pearl Harbor attack and who counseled tough surrender terms right to the end. There in the Oval Office before the White House press corps, amidst the flashing of camera bulbs and under the blazing klieg lights for the newsreel cameras, the president advised of the Japanese reply. He deemed it "a full acceptance of the Potsdam Declaration which specifies the unconditional surrender of Japan." He also announced that arrangements were progressing for the formal surrender and General Douglas MacArthur's appointment as Supreme Allied Commander (SCAP) to receive that surrender.[69]

Rumors of the Japanese surrender had been circulating throughout the afternoon, and crowds had gathered in front of the White House. Harry and Bess Truman, hardly the most charismatic occupants of that storied residence,

[69] This account along with the text of Truman's statement is drawn from Truman's *Year of Decisions*, pp. 480–82. Stanley Weintraub notes of Cordell Hull that he "had been there at the beginning and now at the end." See *Last Great Victory*, p. 614.

walked to the north lawn and greeted the gathered throng. Truman even allowed himself to flash "a V sign in the manner of Churchill," which brought cheers from the overjoyed and celebrating assembly. A more flamboyant politician might have played more to this spontaneous audience, but Harry Truman retreated back into the White House to call his elderly mother back in Missouri. Yet, at eight o'clock he appeared on the north portico, and this time shared some words with the crowd that had chanted: "We want Truman." He told his fellow citizens, "This is a great day, the day we've been waiting for. This is the day we've been looking forward for since December 7, 1941." Then, in words that suggest not only a desire to give the crowd what it needed to hear, but also a continuing naiveté, he idealistically proclaimed that "this is the day for free governments in the world. This is the day that fascism and police government ceases in the world."[70] Franklin Roosevelt assuredly would have expressed the same sentiment. Two weeks later in his radio address to the American people on the formal signing of the surrender documents in Tokyo Bay, Truman paid tribute to "our departed gallant leader, Franklin D. Roosevelt," whom he described as the "defender of democracy, [and] architect of world peace and cooperation."[71] Having suddenly been forced to take on FDR's mantle, Harry Truman had led his nation and its allies to victory over nazism and Japanese militarism. He had "won the war," but the task of winning "the peace" would prove even more challenging.

Around the United States from Times Square in New York City to the smallest towns in the west and the south, Americans joined in the victory celebration. Two days of public holidays provided time for the celebration, although neither could be officially termed V-J day because the official surrender had yet to occur. In Washington, as Weintraub noted, "priorities shifted to conversion to peace." Announcements and new orders were issued in rapid succession, and several snafus occurred, including an executive order authorizing time-and-a-half pay for the two-day holiday which Truman had to reverse![72] No wonder he wrote to his mother on August 17 that "things have been in such a dizzy whirl here." Mistakes had been made, and everyone had been "going at a terrific gait," but he hoped that "we are up with the parade now." Indicating his own expectation that his energies needed to shift to the home front and the domestic political arena he confided to his "Mamma" that "it is going to be political maneuvers that I have to watch."[73]

Truman's announcement of Japan's defeat set off deep and heartfelt celebrations among American soldiers, sailors, and airmen in the Pacific theater and among those in Europe preparing to transfer there.[74] They would not have to risk their lives in the feared invasion of Japan. Instead they could return to their

[70] Truman, *Year of Decisions*, p. 482.
[71] Truman's radio address, September 1, 1945, Truman, *Public Papers of the Presidents of the United States: Harry S. Truman, 1945*, p. 256.
[72] Weintraub provides details in *Last Great Victory*, p. 642.
[73] Truman to Mamma and Mary, August 17, 1945, in Ferrell, ed., *Off the Record*, p. 62.
[74] See the classic essay by Paul Fussell, "Hiroshima: A Soldier's View," *New Republic*, 185 (August 22 & 29, 1981), pp. 26–30.

homes and resume their peacetime lives. Rather than fighting the 5,400,000 men who remained in the Japanese army and the 1,800,000 serving in the navy, the allied soldiers prepared to accept their surrender.[75] Furthermore, as Weinberg has noted, "the surrender obviated Japanese plans to slaughter Allied prisoners of war as fighting approached the camps where they were held, a project for which considerable preparations had evidently been made, to the horror of prisoners who had already suffered enormously."[76] Truman justifiably could claim that his actions to end the war had saved American lives.

One nation, however, which showed no desire to quit the fighting was the Soviet Union. On August 15, Truman provided for Stalin a copy of the initial SCAP order, which set forth basic procedures and arrangements for the occupation. Stalin immediately proposed that the Soviets enlarge their realm by occupying northern Hokkaido. On August 18, Truman rejected this out of hand, but this did not stop the Soviet's theater commander, Marshal Vasielevski, from seeking Moscow's permission to seize the island before a surrender could be made to American troops. Fortunately, for the long-term good of the people of Hokkaido, continued Japanese resistance on Sakhalin, which was to be the launching point for a Soviet attack on Hokkaido, slowed any Soviet military operations. On August 22, Stalin ordered Vasilevski to back off. In forcing this action, Richard Frank holds Truman's "firm reply" of August 18 as being "crucial."[77] But this episode, rarely emphasized these days by American historians, suggests the clear intention of the Soviets to occupy as much as possible of the main Japanese islands.[78] Who knows how much they might have procured and at what cost to the Japanese people without the surrender the atomic bombs had forced.

Necessary, But Was It Right?

In the 1950s, General George C. Marshall, Army chief of staff during World War II and the great "organizer of victory," sat for a series of interviews with his biographer Forrest C. Pogue. Asked about the necessity of dropping the

---

[75] I take these numbers from Weinberg, *World at Arms*, p. 892.

[76] Weinberg, *World at Arms*, p. 892. Sadly, the surrender did not prevent all killing of American POWs. On August 15 at Fukuoka, officers of the Japanese Western Army Headquarters brutally executed 16 B-29 crew members. See Craig, *The Fall of Japan*, pp. 214–15, for the ghastly details.

[77] Frank, *Downfall*, p. 323–24. This paragraph relies on Frank's crucial work. Also see the fine work of Tsuyoshi Hasegawa on this subject in *Racing the Enemy*, pp. 252–89. Hasegawa's work leaves one in no doubt of the extent of Stalin's expansionist designs on Japan. He notes that while "historians tend to treat Stalin's demand for the northern half of Hokkaido as a bargaining ploy," there was no doubt that "Stalin was dead serious about the Hokkaido operation" (p. 271).

[78] An early exception was Samuel Eliot Morison who observed in 1960 that if the Soviets had been a full partner in any conventional effort to defeat Japan that "there is a fair chance that Japan would have been divided like Germany and Korea, if not delivered completely to the mercy of the Communists." See Morison, "Why Japan Surrendered," *Atlantic Monthly*, 206 (October 1960), p. 47.

atomic bombs, Marshall replied that "I think it was quite necessary to drop the bombs in order to shorten the war." He explained that "what they [the Japanese] needed was shock action, and they got it. I think it was very wise to use it."[79] Marshall took no pleasure in their use, but the distinguished soldier-statesman understood that the two terrible weapons had forced the Japanese surrender when it occurred. The brief review of Japanese decision making at the war's end included above, which relies directly on the careful research of scholars like Richard B. Frank, Sadao Asada, and the venerable Robert Butow, clarifies that the bombing of *both* Hiroshima and Nagasaki, especially when combined with the Soviet declaration of war, played an indispensable role in persuading the Japanese leadership to surrender. By July of 1945, the Japanese had been subjected to months of devastating attacks by B-29s, their capital and other major cities had suffered extensive damage, and the home islands were subjected to a naval blockade that made food and fuel increasingly scarce. The Japanese military and civilian losses had reached approximately three million, and there seemed no end in sight. Despite all this, however, Japan's leaders and especially its military clung to notions of *Ketsu-Go*, to a plan that involved inflicting such punishment on the invader in defense of the homeland that the invader would sue for terms. Even after Hiroshima, Nagasaki, and the Soviet attack in Manchuria, the military still wanted to pursue that desperate option, but Hirohito broke the impasse in the Japanese government and ordered surrender.[80] He understood that the atomic bomb undermined "the fundamental premise" of *Ketsu-Go* "that the United States would have to invade Japan to secure a decision" in the war.[81] Ultimately, the atomic bombs allowed the emperor and the peace faction in the Japanese government to negotiate an end to the war.[82] George Marshall portrayed the matter correctly. The atomic bombs ended the war in the Pacific.

Writers engaging in wishful thinking and fanciful recreations have sought to fashion circumstances in which the A-bombs might be seen an unnecessary

---

[79] Larry Bland, ed., *George C. Marshall Interviews and Reminiscences for Forrest C. Pogue* (Lexington, VA, 1991), pp. 424–25.

[80] It would seem that the A-bomb even eventually helped the Japanese military accept their defeat. Prime Minister Suzuki and Baron Kido both made this point. As Frank noted: "[T]he atomic bombs served not only as an important cause but as an indispensable excuse for the surrender." He quotes Baron Kido as recalling that "if military leaders could convince themselves that they were defeated by the power of science but not by lack of spiritual power or strategic errors, they could save face to some extent." Frank, *Downfall*, p. 347. On this point, also see Asada, "The Shock of the Atomic Bomb and Japan's Decision to Surrender," pp. 505–07, which suggests that the army "accepted surrender partly because the atomic bomb paradoxically helped them save 'face.'" (p. 506).

[81] Frank, *Downfall*, p. 348.

[82] Sadao Asada discussed this well in his "The Shock of the Atomic Bomb and Japan's Decision to Surrender," pp. 496–97. Asada quotes Baron Kido from a November 1945 interview as noting that he and the emperor felt "that if we took the occasion and utilized the psychological shock of the bomb to follow through, we might perhaps succeed in ending the war." In the same interview, Kido held that "we of the peace party were assisted by the atomic bomb in our endeavor to end the war."

(and then as almost certainly wrong and immoral). Yet the painful reality that fair-minded observers must concede is that Japan most certainly would have fought on considerably longer unless the United States and its allies had accepted major changes to its Potsdam surrender terms. "Those insisting that Japan's surrender could have been procured without recourse to atomic bombs," Richard Frank noted, "cannot point to any credible evidence from the eight men who effectively controlled Japan's destiny."[83] The Japanese scholar Sadao Asada made essentially the same point in concluding that, "given the intransigence of the Japanese military, there were few "missed opportunities" for earlier peace and that the alternatives available to President Truman in the summer of 1945 were limited."[84] Now it is clear that the United States eventually could have defeated Japan without the atomic bomb, but one must appreciate that all the alternate scenarios to secure victory – continued obliteration bombing of Japanese cities and infrastructure, a choking blockade, the terrible invasions – would have meant significantly greater allied casualties and, most likely, much higher Japanese civilian and military casualties.[85]

Those who rush to "judge" Truman's decision to use the atomic bombs must hesitate a little so as to appreciate that had he not authorized the attacks on Hiroshima and Nagasaki, thousands of American soldiers, sailors, marines, and airmen might have been added to the lists of those killed in World War II. And, added to their number would have been the thousands of allied prisoners of war whom the Japanese planned to execute. Could an American president have survived politically and personally knowing that he might have used a weapon that could have saved their slaughter? To further complicate the rush to judgment, one must acknowledge that Truman was likely correct in March 1958, when he told Tsukasa Nitoguri, the chairman of the Hiroshima City Council, that the A-bombs prevented a quarter of a million Japanese deaths in an invasion.[86] Hard as it may be to accept when one sees the visual record of the terrible destruction of Hiroshima and Nagasaki, Japanese losses probably would have been greater without the A-bombs. Furthermore, the atomic attacks changed the whole dynamic of the occupation of Japan. Ironically, they facilitated a quick and easy surrender and a broadly cooperative populace in a way that no other method of military victory could have guaranteed.

If the atomic bombs shortened the war, averted the need for a land invasion, and saved the lives of thousands on both sides of the ghastly conflict,

---

[83] Frank referred to the Big Six, Baron Kido, and Emperor Hirohito. As he continued: "Not only has no relevant document been recovered from the wartime period, but none of them [the Japanese leaders], even as they faced potential death sentences in war-crimes trials, testified that Japan would have surrendered earlier upon an offer of modified terms, coupled to Soviet intervention or some combination of events, excluding the use of atomic bombs." *Downfall*, p. 343.

[84] Asada, "The Shock of the Atomic Bomb and Japan's Decision to Surrender," p. 512.

[85] See the thoughtful consideration of "alternatives" in Barton J. Bernstein, "Understanding the Atomic Bomb and the Japanese Surrender," pp. 236–59.

[86] Truman's letter of March 12, 1958, in response to the critical resolution of the Hiroshima City Council in Harry S. Truman Papers: Post-Presidential Files, HSTL, Box 20.

does this make their use moral? From the outset, many Americans, including some involved in devising military strategy during World War II, have answered unequivocally in the negative. As early as August 9, Samuel McCrea Cavert, the general secretary of the Federal Council of the Churches of Christ of America, protested to Truman about the "indiscriminate" nature of the atomic bombing.[87] Admiral Leahy, a perennial skeptic about the utility of the A-bomb, later blasted the use of what he refused to call a bomb or an explosive but described as "a poisonous thing that kills people by its deadly radioactive reaction, more than by the explosive force it develops." In his memoir, Leahy expressed his sentiment that "in being the first to use it we had adopted an ethical standard common to the barbarians of the Dark Ages." The old admiral noted that he "was not taught to make war in that fashion" and then asserted that "wars cannot be won by destroying women and children." Using these "new and terrible instruments of uncivilized warfare" represented for him "a modern type of barbarism not worthy of Christian man."[88] Such castigations could be replicated many times over.

Harry Truman could not avoid facing such powerful and emotionally charged criticisms of his actions. On August 11, he responded to Samuel Cavert and admitted that "nobody is more disturbed over the use of Atomic bombs than I am." Yet he went further in his own defense and explained, "but I was greatly disturbed by the unwarranted attack by the Japanese on Pearl Harbor and their murder of our prisoners of war." Indicative of his frame of mind as he waited for Japan's surrender, he clarified for Cavert that "the only language they seem to understand is the one we have been using to bombard them. When you have to deal with a beast you have to treat him as a beast. It is most regrettable," he acknowledged, "but nevertheless true."[89] Fire, it seemed to him, needed to be countered with fire. Long after the war ended, Truman regularly reacted to critics of the A-bomb – whom he once referred to as (in a letter to Eleanor Roosevelt of all people) as "sob sisters" – by sneering at their failure to criticize the Japanese attack on Pearl Harbor and "the murders committed there." It revealed to him a "double standard of morality." He regularly reassured himself that even though the critics assailed him, "the men who were on the ground doing their jobs share my opinion that their lives and the lives of a half million other youngsters were saved by dropping the bomb."[90] In April 1962, the former president defended his action with a similar argument in a letter he drafted but never sent to the diplomatic historian Herbert Feis. Describing the inquisitive Feis as "like the usual egghead," he went on to note forcefully that it was "a great thing that you or any other contemplator 'after

[87] Cavert to Truman, August 9, 1945, in Robert H. Ferrell, ed., *Harry S. Truman and the Bomb: A Documentary History* (Worland, WY, 1996), pp. 71–72.

[88] Leahy, *I Was There*, pp. 441–42.

[89] Truman to Cavert, August 11, 1945, in Ferrell, ed., *Harry S. Truman and the Bomb*, p. 72.

[90] Truman to Eleanor Roosevelt, August 7, 1959, Harry S. Truman Papers: Post-Presidential Files, HSTL, Box 509.

the fact' didn't have to make the decision. Our boys would all be dead."[91] The unsent note reflected his true feelings.

Truman's firm conviction that he had done the necessary thing in dropping the bomb and thus ending the war and saving numerous lives in the process did not stave off his moral qualms about the action. On the day after the bombing of Nagasaki, he told his Cabinet of his order that no more atomic bombs be dropped. In words that reveal his personal anguish and his growing recognition that Hiroshima and Nagasaki were much more than "military targets," he explained that "the thought of wiping out another 100,000 people is horrible." As Secretary of Commerce Henry Wallace recorded in his diary, "he [Truman] didn't like the idea of killing, as he said, 'all those kids.'"[92] Truman's experience in August of 1945 deeply colored his whole attitude to nuclear weapons. He never again spoke of them as military weapons to which the United States could make easy resort and indicated some retreat from his pre-Hiroshima view that the A-bomb was "just" another military weapon. At the time of the Berlin blockade crisis in July 1948, when certain advisers sought the transfer of atomic weapons from civilian to military control, he refused their request and explained: "I don't think we ought to use this thing [the atomic bomb] unless we absolutely have to.... You have got to understand that this isn't a military weapon.... It is used to wipe out women and children and unarmed people, and not for military uses. So we have got to treat this differently from rifles and cannon and ordinary things like that."[93] In his farewell address in January 1953, the president held that "starting an atomic war is totally unthinkable for rational men." When questioned on his address by Atomic Energy Commissioner Thomas E. Murray who spoke to the "morality of atomic warfare," Truman responded bluntly that using the atomic bomb was "far worse than gas or biological warfare because it affects the civilian population and murders them by wholesale."[94]

Truman, however, hardly became a nuclear pacifist. He understood that the United States must maintain its nuclear capability and, indeed, must be willing to use it if need be. In May 1948 the president received briefings on atomic tests on Eniwetok Atoll from Atomic Energy Commission (AEC) Chairman David Lilienthal. In the course of their conversation, Truman referred to Hiroshima and Nagasaki and told the AEC chief, "I don't want to have to do that again, ever." And yet, while he encouraged Lilienthal to pursue atomic energy for constructive purposes, he made clear that the weapons must stay. "Until we are

[91] Truman to Feis, late April 1962, in Poen, ed., *Strictly Personal and Confidential*, p. 34.

[92] Blum, ed., *Price of Vision*, p. 474.

[93] Diary entry for July 21, 1948, David E. Lilienthal, *Journals of David Lilienthal*, Vol. II, *The Atomic Energy Years, 1945–1950* (New York, 1964), p. 391.

[94] See the exchange of letters between Murray and Truman, January 1953, in Harry S. Truman Papers: President's Secretary's File, HSTL, Box 112. (I am grateful to Barton Bernstein for making these letters available to me.)

sure about peace, there's nothing else to do," he concluded.[95] The following year he again conversed with Lilienthal and conveyed to him that the A-bomb "isn't just another weapon," but he nonetheless pledged, "we will never use it again if we can possibly help it."[96] And, even during the Berlin blockade crisis when he refused to surrender the bomb into the hands of the military, he told Secretary of Defense James Forrestal that "he prayed he would never have to make such a decision again, but if it became necessary, no one need have a misgiving but [that] he would do so."[97]

A continuing recognition that he might in some future terrible circumstance be called upon to use atomic weapons again never removed Truman's angst about the two bombings he did authorize. In his final weeks in office, Truman attended a dinner in honor of Winston Churchill at the British embassy in Washington, D.C. Reveling in being Britain's prime minister once again, and no doubt eager to stimulate a lively evening, Churchill asked Truman "whether he would have his answer ready when they both stood before Saint Peter to account for their part in dropping atomic bombs on Japan."[98] The question clearly troubled the president and the other dinner companions had to move the conversation quickly in other directions. Truman obviously didn't appreciate discussions of guilt or innocence however much they might be mixed with cigars, port, and Churchill's company. Perhaps they cut this normal man too close to the quick. When Los Alamos Laboratory Director J. Robert Oppenheimer met the president in late 1945 and told him that he believed that he had blood on his hands, Truman reacted angrily. He recalled telling the famous physicist that "the blood is on my hands. Let me worry about that." The president later reportedly told his undersecretary of state, Dean Acheson, that "I don't want to see that son-of-a-bitch in this office ever again."[99] It would seem that Oppenheimer had touched a raw nerve.

If Truman had blood on his hands, which the evidence suggests he thought privately that he did, he hardly stood alone among the participants in the enormous, ghastly struggle that came to be known as World War II. Well over fifty

---

[95] Lilienthal, *Journals of David Lilienthal*, Vol. II, p. 342. David S. Broscious concluded that "Truman viewed the use of nuclear weapons with great solemnity." See Broscious, "Longing for International Control, Banking on American Superiority: Harry S. Truman's Approach to Nuclear Weapons," in Gaddis et al., eds., *Cold War Statesmen Confront the Bomb*, p. 20. Broscious's fine work guided me to Truman's conversations on the use of nuclear weapons.

[96] Lilienthal, *Journals of David Lilienthal*, Vol. II, p. 474.

[97] Millis, ed., *Forrestal Diaries*, p. 487.

[98] See the account in Acheson, *Present at the Creation*, pp. 715–16.

[99] On this episode, see Kai Bird and Martin J. Sherwin, *American Prometheus: The Triumph and Tragedy of J. Robert Oppenheimer* (New York, 2005), p. 332. As Kai Bird and Martin Sherwin note, Truman embellished this story over the years. In the most celebrated version of the encounter, Truman reportedly gave Oppenheimer his handkerchief and asked him if he would like to wipe the blood off. On this, also see Paul S. Boyer, *By the Bomb's Early Light: American Thought and Culture at the Dawn of the Atomic Age* (Chapel Hill, NC, 1994), p. 193; and David McCullough, *Truman*, p. 475.

million people lost their lives in that gigantic conflict, which descended to new lows of barbarism in both European and Pacific theaters. Restraints that previously had directed soldiers to spare noncombatants were thrown off. Barton Bernstein has observed insightfully that "the older morality crumbled in the crucible of what became virtually total war." In this "emerging conception of nearly total war," Bernstein explained further, "the enemy was not simply soldiers but non-combatants. They worked in factories, ran the economy, maintained the civic life, constituted much of the nation, and were the core of national cohesion. Kill them, and soon production would tumble, the national fabric would rip, armies would soon feel homeless, and the government might surrender."[100] Merely listing such cities as Shanghai, Nanking, Leningrad, Rotterdam, Coventry, London, Dresden, Hamburg, and Tokyo makes the point. As a number of writers have noted succinctly, a "moral Rubicon" had been crossed long before Hiroshima and Nagasaki.[101] Indiscriminate bombing had become the norm for the Anglo-American forces by 1945. By that year, Stimson's biographer noted that "the sheer scale of the frightfulness inflicted by the Nazis in Europe and in Russia and by the Japanese in China had hardened military hearts and relaxed military consciences."[102] Churchill and Roosevelt both approved the brutal endeavors to break the morale of their foes, which they hoped ultimately would secure victory and save lives. The Tokyo fire-bombings took place on FDR's watch after all.[103]

Surprisingly, however, in the moral assessments of the war, Churchill and FDR escape the moral condemnation heaped on poor Harry Truman. No doubt, this rests in significant part because Hiroshima and Nagasaki became the focus of so much attention. John Hersey's powerful and emotionally challenging *Hiroshima*, which first appeared in the *New Yorker* in 1946, began the trend, and it hasn't really stopped. The American bombings became the subject of extensive dissection and analysis. But in all of this, as the historian Morton Keller angrily noted around the fiftieth anniversary of Hiroshima, most critics "ignore[d] the character of the Japanese regime that brought war to the Pacific." He deemed this the "equivalent of discussing the end of the European war by dwelling on the bombing of Dresden while saying little about the Nazi regime."[104] While rarely given the attention accorded Hitler's dastardly attempt to exterminate the Jewish people, the Japanese perpetrated vast atrocities throughout Asia, but especially in China from 1937 to 1945. Some estimates place Chinese losses at over ten million, "the vast majority of them noncombatants," as Frank points out, and noncombatant deaths at Japanese

---

[100] Bernstein, "Understanding the Atomic Bomb and the Japanese Surrender," pp. 259–60.

[101] See Frank, *Downfall*, pp. 46–47. Also see on this broad point Ronald Schaffer, *Wings of Judgment*; and Michael Sherry, *The Rise of American Air Power: The Creation of Armageddon* (New Haven, CT, 1987), pp. 256–316.

[102] Hodgson, *The Colonel*, p. 278.

[103] On casualties from this raid, see Frank, *Downfall*, p. 18.

[104] Morton Keller, "Amnesia Day: Forgetting V-J Day," *New Republic*, Nos. 4209 & 4210 (September 18 & 25, 1995), p. 14.

hands in Asia during 1945 totaled upward of 100,000 people per month.[105] Perhaps some of those fixated on Hiroshima might spare a thought for these innocent victims.

Truman's accusers might also refrain from putting him in the dock of history at least until they carefully consider the responsibility of the Japanese leadership for the fate of their own people. Postwar Japanese leaders effectively played up their "victim" role so as to induce a certain guilt among Americans about the war's ending. This helped disguise the important reality explained by Herbert Bix that "it was not so much the Allied policy of unconditional surrender that prolonged the Pacific war, as it was the unrealistic and incompetent actions of Japan's highest leaders. Blinded by their preoccupation with the fate of the imperial house, those leaders let pass every opportunity to end the lost war until it was too late."[106] In moral terms, surely the Japanese leadership had a responsibility to surrender at least by June of 1945, when there existed no reasonable prospect of success and when their civilian population suffered so greatly. Instead, the twisted neo-samurai who led the Japanese military geared up with true banzai spirit to engage the whole population in a kind of national kamikaze campaign. Their stupidity and perfidy in perpetrating and prolonging the war should not be ignored.

After all this, must we still ask was it right? Must we still wrestle with the morality of the atomic bomb? Harry Truman hardly spent much time on the moral aspects of the matter *before* the bombings. The decision to use them required no tortured agonizing for him, a reality aided by his refraining from probing the "military" nature of the targets. He hoped that the bombs would end the war and secure peace with the fewest American casualties, and so they did. Surely he took the action any American president would have undertaken. Perhaps the effort to evaluate his action in moral terms is misplaced. Should there be a distinction between the "moral" aspects of Truman's decision and the "political-military" quality of it? The much maligned and misunderstood political genius Niccolo Machiavelli would certainly have thought so.

In his advice to the magnificent Lorenzo d'Medici, the brilliant Florentine political philosopher pointed to the harshness and evil in the world and observed that "a man who wants to make a profession of good in all regards must come to ruin among so many who are not good." Hence he counseled that "it is necessary to a prince, if he wants to maintain himself [and his state], to learn to be able not to be good, and to use this and not use it according to necessity."[107] At times he must explicitly turn his back on religiously based morality because the prince "cannot observe all those things for which men are held good, since he is often under a necessity, to maintain his state, of acting against faith, against charity, against humanity, against religion." For Machiavelli, the prince,

---

[105] Frank, *Downfall*, pp. 162–63.
[106] Bix, "Japan's Delayed Surrender," p. 223.
[107] Niccolo Machiavelli, *The Prince*, translated and introduced by Harvey C. Mansfield, 2nd ed. (Chicago, 1998), p. 61.

in order to secure his state, "must not depart from good, when possible, but know how to enter into evil, when forced by necessity."[108] Isaiah Berlin in his astute commentary on Machiavelli summed up the argument well: "One can save one's soul, or one can found or maintain or serve a great and glorious state; but not always both at once."[109] In an imperfect world, Berlin interprets Machiavelli as conveying, "force and guile must be met with force and guile."[110]

Harry Truman rarely, if ever, thought of himself in the same category as Lorenzo d'Medici nor did he classify himself with Cesare Borgia and the other case studies of *The Prince*. It's likely he would have described anyone who referred to Machiavelli in discussing his actions as an "egghead" like Herbert Feis. Yet clearly reasons of state motivated Truman and Stimson and Byrnes. In retrospect within the privacy of his own heart and soul, it is likely that Truman understood he had been forced by necessity to enter into evil. And, so he had. He ordered the bombing of cities in which thousands of noncombatants, among them the elderly and the sick, women and children, were annihilated. Evaluated in isolation, each atomic bombing assuredly was an immoral act. The fact that it did the least harm possible of the available options to gain victory, and that it brought an end to destruction, death, and casualties on an even more massive scale cannot obviate this.

And yet from the perspective of six decades, Truman's use of the bomb viewed in the context of the long and terrible war should be seen as his choosing the lesser of the evils available to him. He did not weigh the options in a moral calculus and proceed forward with that understanding, but fair-minded observers will see that he chose what might be termed a necessary evil. Henry L. Stimson had it exactly right when he wrote in 1947 that "the decision to use the atomic bomb was a decision that brought death to over a hundred thousand Japanese. No explanation can change that fact and I do not wish to gloss over it. But this deliberate, premeditated destruction was our least abhorrent choice."[111] "Abhorrent," for sure, but "least abhorrent" must be understood as well if the bloodshed was to be brought to an end. Truman, along with many others, has blood on his hands, but he also stopped the veritable flood of blood on all sides. The reality that he prevented much greater bloodshed must be acknowledged.

As future anniversaries of the dropping of the atomic bombs on Hiroshima and Nagasaki occur, one might hope for less condemnation of Truman's decision and more empathy for the man who felt required to make it and carried the burden of it. Harry Truman of Independence, Missouri, was hardly some moral monster who needs to be placed retrospectively on trial for war crimes. Those

---

[108] Machiavelli, *The Prince*, p. 70. (Note the discussion in Chapter 18 in particular.)

[109] Isaiah Berlin, "The Originality of Machiavelli," in his *Against the Current: Essays in the History of Ideas*, ed. Henry Hardy (New York, 1980), p. 50. (I am grateful to John Lewis Gaddis for this reference.)

[110] Berlin, "The Originality of Machiavelli," p. 51.

[111] Henry L. Stimson, "The Decision to Use the Atomic Bomb," *Harper's Magazine*, 194 (February 1947), pp. 97–107; quotation from p. 107.

who from the safe distance of fifty or sixty years criticize his decision would do well to place themselves in his shoes and ask what they might have done in the circumstances.[112] Perhaps they might also ask if the weapon had been ready say a year before would they have refrained from using it against Hitler's Berlin where they might have wiped out the viperous head of the Nazi regime and possibly saved the lives of millions on the battlefields and in the gas ovens. Or, instead, perhaps they simply might pray, if they be so inclined, that leaders in our own time and in the future are never forced by horrible circumstances to make such decisions.

Byrnes, the Soviets, and "Atomic Diplomacy" Again

Harry S. Truman and James F. Byrnes had little time to catch their breath and to reflect on future directions as World War II ended. Pressures and demands came at them relentlessly. Without any formal decision, Truman gravitated more to domestic politics and policies, while Byrnes saw himself as the main player in the foreign policy domain.[113] Truman hardly seemed perturbed by the division, and had full confidence in his chosen appointee. Byrnes had but a few weeks from the victory over Japan to gear up for the first meeting of the Council of Foreign Ministers body established at Potsdam. Before he departed Washington, he made some changes in the Department of State. To replace Undersecretary Joseph Grew, who retired, Byrnes – despite some mishaps conveying his request – appointed Dean Acheson.[114] Acheson, at this stage, had nothing of the strong anti-Soviet reputation he would later develop. He had aligned with Byrnes in supporting tough surrender terms for Japan and had been involved in negotiating the Dumbarton Oaks agreements, which laid the groundwork for postwar international cooperation, albeit on American terms.[115] His appointment did not shed light on the "direction" in which Byrnes planned to take either the department or the foreign policy it was charged to formulate and execute. Acheson acted as secretary in Byrnes's regular overseas absences, and this appointment proved a crucial one for Acheson's career and ultimately for U.S. foreign policy.

Byrnes sought Acheson's help to administer the State Department, but he requested the assistance of the Republican foreign policy expert John Foster Dulles to join him at the various CFM meetings. With his eyes clearly on the domestic political scene and with prescience concerning "the gradual

---

[112] This observation draws on Gaddis, *Surprise, Security, and the American Experience*, p. 33.

[113] Alonzo Hamby notes that "Truman, increasingly preoccupied with domestic re-conversion, appears to have paid only limited attention to diplomacy after Potsdam." See *Man of the People*, p. 340.

[114] For details of Acheson's appointment, see his *Present at the Creation*, pp. 119–21. Also see James Chace, *Acheson: The Secretary of State Who Created the American World* (New York, 1998), pp. 113–15.

[115] On Acheson and his outlook at this stage, see Robert Beisner, "Patterns of Peril: Dean Acheson Joins the Cold Warriors, 1945–46," *Diplomatic History*, 20 (Summer 1996), pp. 321–55.

re-emergence of Congress as a major influence on the making of foreign policy," Byrnes aimed to ensure that his foreign policy had a bipartisan gloss and that Dulles would assist him in enlisting Republican support for any and all treaties he negotiated.[116] Dulles went through the ritual of clarifying with Byrnes that he was not being asked "for political reasons." Byrnes, always the effective politician, told Dulles that "he did not give a damn about politics" and that he approached him because he believed "he had something to contribute." Laying it on more thickly than necessity demanded, Byrnes cagily pronounced: "I have no political ambitions. I never expect to run for anything else as long as I live. I want to win the peace. I do not know how much help you can be and I do not know whether you will want to work with me, or I will want to work with you. The best thing to do is for you to attend the first conference and then decide what to do in the future when the conference ends."[117] Dulles had been hooked nicely. He agreed to serve.[118]

Byrnes clarified in his conversation with Dulles that he intended to be a secretary of state who took the lead in foreign policy formulation. He told the Republican adviser, who salivated to serve in his position, that he would never be bypassed and ignored in the manner that FDR treated Cordell Hull. Byrnes's ability to make good on this assurance increased as other individuals who had influenced Truman retreated from the policy-making scene. Harry Hopkins, the most influential of Roosevelt's advisers, who had helped Truman conciliate difficult issues with Stalin and opened the way for the Potsdam meeting, now withdrew fully from policy making. Truman greeted him at the White House on September 4 and awarded him the Distinguished Service Medal at a Rose Garden ceremony. Hopkins, still suffering from congenital illness, moved to New York and died in January of 1946, by which time he assuredly recognized that the brave new world of Soviet-American amity envisaged by himself and the man he served so devotedly had not come to pass.

Joseph Davies returned from Potsdam rather dispirited. Although not as sick as Hopkins, he felt exhausted and ailing and decided to step back from the world of official Washington in order to recuperate and regain his health. Byrnes dispatched a note of thanks to him in August, voicing his appreciation for "the very effective assistance and cooperation" he had rendered at Potsdam. But Byrnes didn't follow up with any significant requests for Davies's counsel. Instead, Davies became "an observer rather than a participant in affairs."[119]

---

[116] On the reemergence of Congress as a factor in the making of foreign policy, see Gaddis, *The United States and the Origins of the Cold War*, pp. 254–63.

[117] Diary entry, August 22, 1945, Brown Diary, James F. Byrnes Papers, Cooper Library, Folder 602. For Dulles's account of Byrnes's offer and his consideration of it, see Memo of August 23, 1945, John Foster Dulles Papers, Seeley G. Mudd Manuscript Library, Box 26, Folder: "Byrnes, James F. 1945."

[118] For Dulles's formal appointment as "Consultant on the United States Delegation" see Byrnes to Dulles, August 29, 1945, John Foster Dulles Papers, Seeley G. Mudd Manuscript Library, Box 26, Folder: "Byrnes, James F. 1945."

[119] MacLean, *Joseph E. Davies*, p. 162.

He continued to hold strongly sympathetic views toward the Soviets and to be critical of anything that hinted at a tough line toward them, but his direct and significant influence on policy had ended. Nonetheless, he continued to have access to both Truman and Byrnes, and, rather ironically, the president would use him as an intermediary to his secretary of state later in the year. But Davies's lamentations about the deterioration of U.S.-Soviet relations and his exhortations to continue a conciliatory approach proved peripheral to the actual development of future policy.[120] Nonetheless, Truman maintained a friendship with Davies that lasted until the latter's death in 1957. The former ambassador contributed to the construction of the Truman Library and exchanged occasional friendly letters with the president.[121] But as Byrnes readied himself to meet with Molotov and Bevin in London in September, he knew he would not have Joseph Davies by his side at the conference table. This does not appear to have troubled him. Nor did the retirement of Secretary of War Henry L. Stimson.

After his distinguished public career culminating in his great service in World War II, Stimson prepared for retirement now that victory had been secured. However, the old man did not plan to go quietly into private life but rather to influence the Truman administration's direction on policy regarding the atomic bomb. Stimson had tried to tutor Truman about the "master card," which he thought could give the U.S. important leverage in settling postwar issues. The president in that instance proved an inattentive pupil. Yet Stimson possessed true determination as a teacher, and he also displayed a willingness to revise his lecture notes. After the dropping of the atomic bombs and the Japanese surrender, Stimson withdrew to a hunting club in the Adirondacks for some much deserved rest. There, in the midst of restoring his physical health, Stimson worried about the meaning of the American atomic monopoly for future international relations. He feared that an American attempt to maintain its monopoly and to apply pressure on the Soviet Union would lead to failure and an arms race.[122] With the aid of Assistant Secretary of War John McCloy, Stimson began to formulate a proposal for the international sharing of atomic information. Here his developing ideas began to run up again the hopes and plans of Jimmy Byrnes.

After visiting with Stimson in the Adirondacks, John McCloy raised their ideas for international sharing of atomic technology with the secretary of state upon his return to Washington. Byrnes's thinking had advanced on a quite different track. He quickly conveyed to McCloy his belief that it would be

---

[120] Davies's lamentations can be tracked in the various memorandums and diary entries found in Joseph E. Davies Papers, Library of Congress, Box 22.

[121] See Truman to Davies, October 13, 1953; Davies to Truman ("Boss"), October 21, 1953, Harry S. Truman Papers, Post-Presidential Files, HSTL, Box 64. Also see the letter to Truman from Davies's daughter, Eleanor Davies Tydings (circa 1957), responding to Truman's message of sympathy on the death of her father. She thanked Truman for being an honorary pallbearer and wrote: "I knew how much your friendship meant to Daddy – how he admired and loved you, Mr. President." Harry S. Truman Papers, Post-Presidential Files, HSTL, Box 64.

[122] See Hodgson, *The Colonel*, pp. 356–61.

a long time before the Soviets could catch up with the Americans. With the London CFM on the very near horizon, Byrnes told McCloy that "the Russians were only sensitive to power and all the world, including the Russians, were cognizant of the power of this bomb, and with it in his hip pocket he felt he was in a far better position to come back with tangible accomplishments even if he did not threaten anyone expressly with it."[123] Byrnes put essentially the same view to the secretary of war on the elderly statesman's return to the nation's capital. When Stimson raised "how to handle Russia with the big bomb," he found that Byrnes "was very much against any attempt to cooperate with Stalin." Stimson confided to his diary that Byrnes's "mind is full of the problems with the coming meeting of the foreign ministers and he looks to having the presence of the bomb in his pocket, so to speak, as a great weapon to get through the thing."[124] Stimson met briefly with Truman and tried to convey his reservations about the Byrnes approach but had little impact. Instead he scheduled a longer meeting at which he would present the memorandum on which he and McCloy still worked. By the time of that meeting, Byrnes had left Washington for his London meeting uninhibited by any of Stimson's thinking.

Stimson obviously judged Byrnes's approach regarding the possible diplomatic advantage of the atomic bomb as unseemly and unwise. Yet, given Byrnes's difficult negotiating experience with the Soviets at Potsdam and his long experience as a political operator, it hardly seems surprising that he wanted to enter the London discussions backed by the possible diplomatic weight of the A-bomb. More surprising is how little consideration the Truman administration gave to how its possession of the A-bomb might be exploited diplomatically, especially with regard to the Soviet Union. Byrnes neither commissioned planning documents on this matter nor assigned members of his department to consider potential strategies. In retrospect, the truly astonishing quality about America's atomic monopoly is how little policy makers deliberated about some possible diplomatic advantage. Byrnes engaged in mere wishful thinking that the bomb might assist his negotiating position, while Stimson and McCloy focused from the outset on sharing atomic technology. With all the debate over "atomic diplomacy," this obvious point is rarely stressed.[125] The Truman administration failed to practice atomic diplomacy in a deliberate manner. Of course, whether it could have exploited the diplomatic power of the A-bomb effectively must remain in the realm of speculation. That it didn't try seriously is a matter of historical fact.

---

[123] John McCloy diary, September 2, 1945, quoted in Kai Bird, *The Chairman: John J. McCloy, The Making of the American Establishment* (New York, 1992), pp. 261–62.

[124] Stimson diary, September 4, 1945, Henry Lewis Stimson Papers, Sterling Memorial Library.

[125] An exception is Thomas T. Hammond, "'Atomic Diplomacy' Revisited," *Orbis* 19 (Winter 1976), pp. 1403–28. Writing in 1976, Hammond reflected that "looking back on it today, it seems almost incredible that the United States failed to take fullest advantage of its atomic monopoly in 1945. One would think America's exclusive possession of atomic weapons then would have permitted it to impose its will anywhere in the world" (p. 1428).

Truman largely left Byrnes to his own devices as the secretary set off for his London meetings. The president, "increasingly preoccupied with domestic conversion," as Alonzo Hamby noted, "appears to have paid only limited attention to diplomacy after Potsdam."[126] Matters such as manpower requirements, and the liquidation of war agencies increasingly garnered his interest. Naturally, he maintained his responsibilities as head of state and hosted France's President Charles de Gaulle on his visit to Washington in late August. But his specific remarks on foreign policy bore a very general, almost clichéd quality. In a national address to the American people marking the formal surrender of the Japanese to General Douglas MacArthur on board the *USS Missouri* in Tokyo Bay, Truman platitudinously proclaimed that "with the other United Nations we move towards a new and better world of cooperation, of peace and international good will and cooperation."[127] Once in London, Secretary Byrnes soon discovered that cooperation hardly characterized the approach of his Soviet opposite.

The Potsdam protocols established the Council of Foreign Ministers primarily to oversee the drafting of peace treaties for Germany's defeated European allies such as Italy, Romania, and Bulgaria. The London CFM meeting opened on September 11, the first of six meetings over the next year and a half where the foreign ministers attempted to resolve a variety of issues in hopes of forging a postwar settlement. Byrnes arrived in the British capital intent on making progress on a number of issues.[128] Whatever his optimistic hopes for cooperation, Byrnes along with Ernest Bevin quickly clashed with the obstinacy of Molotov, who appeared resolved to prevent serious negotiations. After initial procedural disagreements and a full day, September 13, during which the foreign ministers failed to even greet each other at the conference table, Byrnes approached Molotov at a reception at the House of Lords. In what Walter Brown described as "typical Senatorial fashion," he asked when they might get "down to business." Indicative of what held the center of his attention, Molotov responded by asking Byrnes if he had "an atomic bomb in his side pocket." Byrnes, continuing in good senatorial form, told Molotov: "You don't know Southerners. We carry our artillery in our hip pocket." He went on in a good-natured fashion to tell Molotov that "if you don't cut out all this stalling

---

[126] Hamby, *Man of the People*, p. 340.

[127] Truman's Radio Address, September 1, 1945, Truman, *Public Papers of the Presidents of the United States: Harry S. Truman, 1945*, p. 257.

[128] On his way to London onboard the *Queen Elizabeth*, Byrnes had explained to members of his delegation that "I know how to deal with the Russians. It's just like the U.S. Senate. You build a post office in their state, and they'll build a post office in our state." As David Robertson astutely concluded: "Indeed, rather than becoming Stimson's bellicose atomic diplomat intent upon intimidating the Soviet Union, Byrnes' diplomacy at his first postwar conference was based upon his willingness to offer the Soviets a quid pro quo of diplomatic recognition of the Soviet regimes in Asia, in Eastern Europe, and in the Balkans in exchange for Soviet cooperation in quickly finalizing the drafts of the preliminary peace treaties." See Robertson, *Sly and Able*, pp. 446–47.

and let us get down to work, I am going to pull an atomic bomb out of my hip pocket and let you have it."[129] His tone contained not the slightest hint of a serious threat. Molotov and his interpreter greeted the comments with laughter and so ended Byrnes's humorous yet most direct effort ever to raise his possession of the atomic bomb to his Soviet colleague. It could hardly have been done more benignly and amusingly even if deliberately planned, and it had all the impact of a feather landing on a cushion.[130]

Later in the meeting Molotov even came close to mocking Byrnes for the American atomic monopoly.[131] In response, Byrnes kept his cool and worked to further genuine negotiations. One might ask why, after Molotov so quickly shattered Byrnes's hopes that the atomic bomb's mere presence in the American arsenal would make the Soviets more amenable to negotiation, the secretary of state did not ratchet up the pressure. Pointing to the effective American atomic monopoly into the 1950s, John Lewis Gaddis framed a related if broader question – "so why did Washington not issue an ultimatum demanding the dismantlement of Soviet authority in eastern Europe, perhaps even of the Soviet dictatorship itself, backed up by the threat...that Moscow would be bombed if it didn't go along?"[132] The reasons for American reticence are complex, but certainly at the time of the London meeting, Byrnes had no intention of trying to intimidate the Soviet Union into concessions. He simply didn't think in these categories. While Japan needed to be intimidated into surrender to stop the ghastly war and the loss of American lives, the immediate postwar circumstance called for no such horrendous measures. No ultimatums would be put before the Soviets. Whatever his frustrations in dealing with Molotov, Byrnes soldiered on in trying to reach agreements to secure the postwar peace. Meanwhile, back in Washington, Truman under the influence of Stimson supported notably by Undersecretary of State Acheson agreed after a lengthy cabinet meeting on September 21 to pursue efforts to place atomic energy under international control so as to avoid a devastating arms race.[133] The hope that motivated this

---

[129] Diary entry, September 13, 1945, Brown Diary, James F. Byrnes Papers, Cooper Library, Folder 602.

[130] One can only endorse the conclusion of McGeorge Bundy that "revisionist historians have accused Byrnes of practicing atomic diplomacy in this [London] session, but the records do not bear them out." See Bundy, *Danger and Survival*, p. 145. Robert Messer's suggestion that Byrnes applied some "coercive atomic diplomacy" simply does not hold up. See Messer, *End of an Alliance*, pp. 130–31.

[131] On September 17 after Byrnes gave a speech at a dinner at St. James's Palace, Molotov offered a "tribute" to Byrnes in which he noted Byrnes's eloquence and then added sarcastically that Byrnes also had an atomic bomb. See the report in Diary entry, September 17, 1945, Brown diary, James. F. Byrnes papers, Cooper Library, Folder 602. For more on Molotov and the atomic bomb, see Holloway, *Stalin and the Bomb*, pp. 156.

[132] Gaddis, *Surprise, Security, and the American Experience*, p. 62. See also pp. 62–63 for Gaddis's discussion of the issue.

[133] Stimson's efforts, the Cabinet discussion, and Truman's subsequent decisions are well outlined in Bundy, *Danger and Survival*, pp. 136–45. For Stimson's memorandum of September 11,

action, which eventually developed into the so-called Acheson–Lilienthal plan, rested in a desire to ensure stable relations among the major powers in a situation where the American atomic monopoly could not be forever guaranteed.[134] It reflected a continued willingness to collaborate with the Soviet Union, which Acting Secretary of State Dean Acheson referred to as the "great Ally upon our cooperation with whom rests the future peace of the world."[135]

In London, Byrnes acquiesced in the cabinet decision on international control of atomic energy whatever his hesitations in that regard. He maintained an admirable focus on working to reach settlements with an obtuse Molotov, who gave no ground on the crucial issue of lessening Soviet domination of nations like Bulgaria and Rumania. Consistent with their compromise arrangement at Potsdam, Byrnes made clear to his Soviet counterpart that he understood the Soviet need for "friendly" governments in Eastern Europe. Nonetheless, he encouraged Molotov to permit some openness such as allowing American news correspondents into these countries. Such measures, he explained, would help facilitate the U.S. Senate's ratification of the treaties they might negotiate.[136] Molotov remained quite unmoved by Byrnes's entreaties. Revealing his strategy that offense proved the best defense the Soviet minister attacked Byrnes's flanks with demands regarding Soviet participation in the occupation of Japan and demands for certain Italian colonies in Africa which only deepened Byrnes's fears about Soviet expansionism. The London Conference crawled to an inglorious end without substantial progress and with "Big Three unity in serious disarray."[137]

The disarray surprised and troubled Byrnes. He had ventured to London determined to make progress on a postwar settlement and ready to engage in

---

1945, outlining his full position for Truman, see Ferrell, ed., *Harry S. Truman and the Bomb*, pp. 77–82. Truman asked participants after the September 21 meeting to submit their views in writing to him. For the counsel of Dean Acheson, who warned in his cover memorandum that "a policy of secrecy is both futile and dangerous," see Acheson to Truman, September 25, 1945, Truman Papers: President's Secretary's File, HSTL, Box 199.

[134] For a good summary of the American international control efforts, see Bundy, *Danger and Survival*, pp. 145–61.

[135] Indicative of the views of Dean Acheson, the future "cold warrior," which indicate sympathetic attitudes to the Soviet Union at the time, note James Forrestal's summary of Acheson's comments at the September 21 meeting where the Navy secretary recorded that the acting secretary of state "[s]aw no alternative except to give full information to the Russians, however for some *quid pro quo* in the way of a mutual exchange of information. [He] could not conceive of a world in which we were hoarders of military secrets from our Allies, particularly this great Ally upon our cooperation with whom rests the future peace of the world." Millis, ed., *Forrestal Diaries*, pp. 94–96.

[136] For Byrnes's discussions with Molotov, see Bohlen minutes, Byrnes–Molotov Conversations, September 16 and 19, 1945, *FRUS*, 1945, II, pp. 194–201, 243–47. Walter Brown suggests that Byrnes approached Molotov in a "pleading manner" appealing to him to "relax his position in the Balkans for the peace of the world." Diary entry, September 16, 1945, Brown Diary, James F. Byrnes Papers, Cooper Library, Folder 602.

[137] Gaddis, *The United States and the Origins of the Cold War*, p. 266.

PHOTO 15. U.S. Secretary of State James F. Byrnes and British Foreign Secretary Ernest Bevin confer during the Council of Foreign Ministers meeting at Lancaster House, London, September 21, 1945. (Courtesy National Archives)

genuine compromise to achieve it. In London, however, he worried about what Soviet obstinacy foreshadowed, and he found Molotov almost impossible to deal with. Byrnes even told Walter Brown on September 21 that "M[olotov] was trying to do in a slick dip [?] way what Hitler had tried to do in domineering smaller countries by force." Yet Byrnes did not quickly give up hope on the possibilities of negotiation and shift to some strategy designed to address an intransigent Soviet Union. He still sought cooperation. Ironically and almost laughably in light of Stalin's domination over and control of Molotov, Byrnes concluded that he would have to appeal over Molotov to Stalin. He thought "Stalin wants peace" and even expressed fear "for the world if Stalin should die."[138] He resolved to continue his efforts to negotiate agreements at another foreign ministers meeting which he wanted held in Moscow, where he would have direct contact with Stalin.

On his return to Washington, Byrnes put the best public face on a bad situation by informing a national radio audience of the "considerable areas of agreement" among the foreign ministers and that the London conference demonstrated "the hard reality that none of us can expect to write the peace in our own way." He looked ahead to a "a second and better chance to get on with the peace."[139] Privately, he criticized the Soviets bluntly. He told his predecessor Edward Stettinius, now U.S. ambassador-designate to the United Nations, that "we were facing a new Russia, totally different than the Russia we dealt with a year ago." In Byrnes's rather naïve analysis: "As long as they needed us in the War and we were giving them supplies we had a satisfactory relationship but now that the War was over they were taking an aggressive attitude and stand on political and territorial questions that was indefensible." John Foster Dulles chimed in with public and private comments to affirm Byrnes's analysis and to praise the secretary's determination to "stand firm for basic principles" at the London meeting.[140] But again it must be emphasized that Byrnes did not rush to abandon his efforts to negotiate a settlement with the Soviets. In fact, his deep, almost instinctual, tendency to seek compromise had led him while in London to raise tentatively to Dulles that "we have pushed these babies [the Russians] as far as they will go and I think we better start thinking about a compromise."[141] Dulles firmly rejected that option. The future Republican secretary of state "equated compromise on the question of the Balkan treaties with the appeasement of Hitler before the war and warned Byrnes that any such violation of 'principle and morality' at the London meeting would cause him to break with the American delegation and publicly denounce its surrender to the Russians."[142]

---

[138] Brown Diary, September 21, 1945, Folder 602. The remarkable regard for Stalin among American officialdom is noted in Leffler, *Preponderance of Power*, pp. 52–53.

[139] Byrnes radio address, October 5, 1945, *Department of State Bulletin*, 13 (October 7, 1945), pp. 507–12.

[140] For Byrnes's comment to Stettinius and Dulles's comment on Byrnes, see Gaddis, *The United States and the Origins of the Cold War*, pp. 266–67. I am guided by Gaddis's careful research here.

[141] Yergin, *Shattered Peace*, pp. 129–30. See also John Foster Dulles, *War or Peace* (New York, 1950), pp. 29–30, where Dulles politely recalls that Byrnes asked "whether I did not feel that there was some basis upon which we could effect a compromise."

[142] Messer, *End of an Alliance*, p. 133. Dulles's intervention appears to have been embellished in the retelling over the years. Theodore Achilles, a State Department official, heard from Mrs. Dulles at a cocktail party that "What Foster didn't say in that book [*War or Peace*] was that he not only followed Secretary Byrnes into his bedroom to tell him that [no compromise], but had followed him on into the bathroom, and told him, if he did not agree, he would telephone Senator Vandenberg who would denounce him on the floor of the Senate the next day." Interview with Theodore Achilles, May 7, 1966, Dulles Oral History Collection, Seeley G. Mudd Manuscript Library, transcript pp. 1–3. According to the account Thomas E. Dewey heard from Dulles, Jimmy Byrnes had "put his arm around his [Dulles's] shoulder

Byrnes quickly backed away from acting on his proposal in London in order to shut Dulles up, but the incident gives an early hint as to his thinking as did his earlier expressed desire to get to Moscow for direct negotiations with Stalin. He would be prepared to give ground in bargaining at some future point. Even before leaving London he indicated American willingness both to recognize the government of Hungary pending free elections and "to consider Moscow's request for establishment of an Allied Control Council in Japan."[143] In his report to the American people on the London meeting, he confessed his belief "that peace and political progress in international affairs as in domestic affairs depend upon intelligent compromise." He promised further that the United States would "continue to act in that spirit at future conferences." He offered that the London meeting had been beneficial for getting out on the table differences that he presented as necessary "before we can intelligently consider means of reconciling them." He publicly laid the groundwork for such reconciliation, and, despite exploring the areas of disagreement over the governments in the Balkans, he gave explicit assurances that "the American Government shares the desire of the Soviet Union to have governments friendly to the Soviet Union in eastern and central Europe." While critical of the Soviets' procedural maneuvers at the London meeting, Byrnes "remained undeterred by temporary setbacks" and promised not to "relax in our efforts to achieve a just and lasting peace for ourselves and all nations."[144]

In private communications with Moscow, Byrnes maintained a similarly conciliatory tone. He arranged to have a message sent to Stalin under Truman's name, which addressed the tensions in London over the recognition of governments in Bulgaria and Rumania. The American message assured the Soviet leader that "our policy in regard to recognition of the Provisional governments of Finland, Poland, Hungary and Austria indicates that we are anxious, and are willing to go far, to concert our policy with the Soviet Union." The American note assured Stalin that the U.S. government sought only to fulfill Roosevelt's policy agreed to at Yalta. It went on to address in moderate tone the procedural difficulties involved in the participation of the French and the Chinese in the CFM sessions, which Molotov had used to sabotage the London gathering.

and said, 'Foster, I think we've got to give them their way on this, or this conference is going to be a failure.' Foster said, 'If you do, I will resign and go home and tell the American people why.'" Interview with Thomas E. Dewey, January 22, 1965, Dulles Oral History Collection.

[143] Gaddis, *The United States and the Origins of the Cold War*, p. 275. See further evidence in Gaddis, pp. 275–76, of Byrnes's actions designed to facilitate productive negotiations with the Soviet Union, including his assurances to Joseph Davies that he would try to compromise on Rumania and Bulgaria and his commitment to respect legitimate Soviet security interests in Eastern Europe.

[144] Byrnes address, October 5, 1945, *Department of State Bulletin*, 13 (1945), pp. 507, 508, 510, 512.

The whole thrust of the message aimed to settle disagreements over procedural matters so that the Allies could get back to the important task of forging peace settlements in an atmosphere of co-operation.[145]

In making his plans in London and for the future, Byrnes faced no restraints from the president he served. As Robert Messer clarified, Truman "gave no indication of any special interest in the details of Byrnes's negotiations" in London. He gave Byrnes "general support and encouragement" and allowed him considerable discretion in determining American tactics and strategy. In light of Truman's later complaint against Byrnes for not providing him with adequate reports on overseas meetings, it is notable that at this stage "he merely endorsed whatever Byrnes had done or proposed to do by saying 'use your best judgment and I am sure thing[s] will come out right' or 'in the final analysis do whatever you think is right.'"[146] Truman's dependence on and trust in Byrnes remained very strong. After determining that he would proceed ahead with plans for international control of atomic energy he made clear that his secretary of state would have the responsibility for supervising all discussions on the topic.[147] He deemed Byrnes as the key person to help him carry forth the plans to secure the postwar peace.

Truman's own thinking at this time is, to be kind, a little hard to pin down. It is frankly rather confusing and reflects his continued uncertainty. Occasional statements suggested he hewed toward a tougher policy toward the Soviet Union, but these were countered by reassurances of his continued hopes for accommodation with Stalin's Russia. Truman included both of these broad approaches, in the Navy Day speech he gave on October 27. Seemingly unperturbed by the contradictions of the two approaches the president spoke of continued American military strength and promised an American foreign policy "based firmly on fundamental principles of righteousness and justice" and on refusing to "compromise with evil." The United States, he assured his listeners, would never recognize governments forced on their peoples. Despite such simplistic assertions, Truman also affirmed the importance of collaboration with wartime allies. In words that he presumably meant to be heard in foreign capitals, the president insisted that "the world cannot afford any letdown in the united determination of the allies in this war to accomplish a lasting peace." He stated that "the cooperative spirit of the allies" could not be allowed to disintegrate, and he pronounced confidently that there were no "hopeless or irreconcilable" differences among them. In support of Byrnes's desire for compromise and negotiation, he asserted that "there are no conflicts of interest among the victorious powers so deeply rooted that they cannot be resolved."[148] One can

---

[145] Truman to Stalin included in Byrnes to Harriman, October 12, 1945, *FRUS*, 1945, II, pp. 562–63.
[146] Messer, *End of an Alliance*, p. 126.
[147] Bundy, *Danger and Survival*, p. 145.
[148] Truman speech, October 27, 1945, Truman, *Public Papers of the Presidents of the United States: Harry S. Truman*, *1945*, pp. 431–38. One should note that in his address Truman paid

easily imagine Franklin Roosevelt offering such a similar assurance in these circumstances.

Whatever their concerns about Soviet behavior, neither Truman nor Byrnes had given up on the goal of securing a cooperative postwar relationship with the Soviet Union. They remained wedded to a Rooseveltian vision of collaborating with Moscow to secure postwar peace. To this end, Truman placed special hopes in the successful working of the United Nations organization.[149] Like Byrnes, he expressed a special confidence in dealing with Stalin whom he deemed to be "a moderating influence in the present Russian government." Truman admitted in late October of 1945 that serious differences existed between the Soviets and the Americans, but he believed "that we could work them out amicably if we gave ourselves time."[150] He planned to offer such time to his secretary of state and to leave him alone in undertaking the necessary work. Constantly under pressure, the president had other matters to occupy him.[151] Indicative of his overall thrust, Truman wanted to take another part of the Rooseveltian legacy and to extend it and put his own stamp upon it. On September 6, 1945, he sent a message to Congress defending central New Deal programs and calling for their enhancement and development. He included in his message the economic "bill of rights" that FDR earlier had outlined with its calls for decent employment, housing, health care, and education for all Americans. The message marked the real beginning of his "Fair Deal" in which he laid out "the details of the program of liberalism and progressivism," which he later presented as "the foundation of my administration."[152] Truman's deep

---

a moving tribute to his predecessor. After paying tribute to the American naval effort in World War II, he continued: "And history will never forget that great leader who, from his first day in office, fought to reestablish a strong American Navy – who watched that Navy and all the other might of this Nation grow into an invincible force for victory – who sought to make that force an instrument for a just and lasting peace – and who gave his life in the effort – Franklin D. Roosevelt" (p. 432).

[149] Truman placed exaggerated confidence in the United Nations organization and didn't foresee that the UN would be largely paralyzed in its peacekeeping role by disagreements among the major powers. In his Navy Day speech, October 27, 1945, he affirmed that "our American policy is a policy of friendly partnership with all peaceful nations, and of full support for the United Nations Organization." Truman, *Public Papers of the Presidents of the United States: Harry S. Truman, 1945*, p. 436.

[150] Truman quoted in Gaddis, *The United States and the Origins of the Cold War*, p. 275. On October 6, Truman assured a fretting Joseph Davies regarding the "Russian situation" that he was "not in the least alarmed about it. We will get it worked out before we get through provided, of course, nothing happens to Stalin." Truman to Davies, October 6, 1945, Harry S. Truman Papers: President's Secretary's File, HSTL, Box 117.

[151] An indication of the pressures on Truman comes in a plaintive letter he wrote to his mother and sister in October 1945 where he explained that "the pressure here is becoming so great I can hardly get my meals in, let alone do what I want to do." Truman to "Mamma & Mary," October 13, 1945, in Ferrell, ed., *Off the Record*, p. 69.

[152] Truman, *Year of Decisions*, p. 532. For Truman's message, September 6, 1945, see Truman, *Public Papers of the Presidents of the United States: Harry S. Truman, 1945*, pp. 263–309. For thoughtful analysis of the content and significance of this address, see Hamby, *Man of the People*, pp. 362–64.

commitment to full employment made clear that he would not retreat from the activist government that characterized FDR's administration. Over the coming weeks and months Truman forwarded legislation to the congress for implementing the goals outlined in his message including plans for a national health program and for expanding the social-security system. This realm of domestic politics and policies was the one he preferred and felt competence in. He gladly would leave foreign policy matters to Byrnes. But foreign policy issues and questions proved too much even for the clever Jimmy Byrnes. Truman would never manage to put them on the back burner. Indeed, they dominated his administration.

7

Indecision

Floundering Between Collaboration and Confrontation

Seeking Compromise

Indecision and even confusion continued to characterize American foreign policy from late 1945 through late 1946.[1] Only slowly and in a rather disorganized manner did the United States object to Soviet policies that it deemed threatening to its interests. Neither Truman nor Byrnes possessed a clear understanding of the nature of Stalin and his regime, and they wobbled and wavered in forming a coherent policy to respond to Soviet actions. Truman remained essentially content to delegate most policy-making responsibility to Byrnes, although he sometimes complained at the results of his secretary of state's efforts. The president provided no firm hand on the tiller of the American ship of state as it navigated into increasingly uncharted waters. As late as September 1946, his ineptitude at overseeing the development of a clear foreign policy approach leapt into public view with the internecine clash between Secretary of Commerce Henry Wallace and Byrnes. Eventually, a dithering Truman fired Wallace, but in a manner that demonstrated both his own lack of clarity about policy direction and the difficulty he had in finally detaching himself from the Rooseveltian paradigm of continued cooperation among the victorious wartime allies.

Secretary Byrnes also proved to be a disciple of sorts of FDR's cooperative approach well into 1946. His character as a classic improviser and compromiser naturally led him to seek to reach agreements with the Soviets. Byrnes aimed to make deals that would settle the various issues troubling relations between the United States and the Soviet Union, and so to assure the vaunted postwar peace that Roosevelt had led Americans to expect. By the fall of 1946, when he gave his famous Stuttgart speech, Byrnes had worked his way to a firmer approach toward the Soviets, but he certainly attempted lengthy negotiation,

[1] For essential accounts of American policy making at this time, see Deborah Welch Larson, *Origins of Containment*; Fraser J. Harbutt, *Iron Curtain*; and John Lewis Gaddis, *The United States and the Origins of the Cold War*, pp. 282–346. These works provide much more detail than this chapter, which is focused more on the issue of continuity or reversal in policy, aims to supply.

mutual concessions, and compromise before that. He continued his efforts to deal amicably with the Soviets well after British Foreign Secretary Bevin had recognized the futility of that endeavor and moved to toughen his approach to Moscow.

Surprisingly, neither Byrnes nor Truman appeared to grasp fully the dramatic impact of World War II on the architecture of the world. The multipolar world of the interwar period had included a number of significant actors, among them Britain, France, Italy, Japan, and Germany as well as the Soviet Union and the United States. The devastation and destruction of the war, however, transformed the international system into a more bipolar structure. Britain lingered on in name as a great power, but it no longer possessed the strength to oversee the world system in which it had worked throughout the nineteenth and the twentieth centuries to prevent the domination of the Eurasian landmass by any one power. But neither Truman nor Byrnes thought primarily in these power reality categories. Truman still hoped in good Wilsonian fashion that the new United Nations might help settle disputes, and Byrnes counted on his own negotiating skills to secure the peace. Both saw the necessity of carrying out the agreements that had already been reached. Neither man saw in 1946 that they confronted a decisive moment in American foreign relations in which the United States would need to decide among grand strategic options framed in light of Britain's decline.

Walter Russell Mead has argued brilliantly that in retrospect we might see the whole period from 1914 to 1947 as a time when America wrestled among three major options. As he put it: "[S]hould the United States supplement British power as it waned, propping up Britain as it [in turn] propped up the global order? Should the United States instead stand back and let the world order look after itself? Or should the United States replace Great Britain as the gyroscope of world order, with all the political, military, and economic costs, benefits, and responsibilities that role would entail?"[2] The United States eventually chose the third option through a series of key decisions and actions from 1947 to 1950, but this choice appeared by no means obvious in late 1945 and 1946. Truman and Byrnes did not see themselves as involved in any effort to construct a new grand strategy for their nation. The hold of Roosevelt's notion of a world guided by great power cooperation still exerted a real check on the capability of American officials to develop new policies in light of the plain reality of both a greatly weakened Britain and of a Soviet Union intent on dominating well beyond its borders. Almost ludicrously, in retrospect, some Americans in late 1945 and 1946 still thought in terms of the United States serving as a mediator between the British and the Soviets. How the United States moved beyond the shackles of the Rooseveltian approach in order to confront the postwar power realities is investigated here. The effort is not to provide a detailed account of all foreign policy issues that arose in these months but rather to track the key

[2] See Walter Russell Mead, *Special Providence: American Foreign Policy and How It Changed the World* (New York, 2002), pp. 81–84, direct quotation from p. 83.

incidents and the major developments as the United States awkwardly moved away from a policy of some accommodation toward a "get tough" approach to the Soviets, away from the perception of the Soviet Union in the American official mind as a difficult ally to its being a potential foe, and, in the end, away from Roosevelt's to the Truman administration's own distinct approach.

The ad hoc and rather confused nature of the Truman administration's policy making revealed itself in early November 1945 after the president announced he would meet Prime Minister Attlee and the Canadian leader William MacKenzie King to discuss international control of atomic energy. When Vannevar Bush, the director of the Office of Scientific Research and Development, approached Byrnes barely a week before the scheduled meeting of the leaders whose nations had cooperated to develop the atomic bomb, he learned that "there was no organization for the meeting, no agenda being prepared, and no American plan in form to present." Byrnes deftly took the chance to task a surprised Bush with formulating such a plan, which he quickly did, and it formed the basis for the Anglo-American-Canadian agreement signed on November 15.[3] Here Truman endorsed an approach of cautious openness regarding the sharing of atomic technology. The policy did not rush to engage the Soviets nor did it signal any desire to exclude them. The declaration observed that no single nation could maintain a monopoly on atomic weapons, and in rather high-minded fashion, it called both for using atomic energy to benefit all mankind and for the prevention of its use for "destructive purposes." To these ends, the signatories declared their willingness to allow for the exchange of basic scientific information. Such exchanges would be overseen by a specially created UN commission, which also would work to control the use of atomic energy to peaceful purposes only and would arrange eventually for the elimination of atomic weapons from national armaments. The commission also would bear responsibility for instituting a system of inspections and compliance procedures to effectively safeguard the application of atomic technology to peaceful ends. The work of the commission, they concluded, "should proceed by separate stages, the successful completion of one of which will develop the necessary confidence of the world before the next stage is undertaken."[4]

The consignment of this challenging issue to the fledgling United Nations no doubt pleased Truman, although his apparent willingness to "share" information on atomic energy stirred up considerable opposition in Congress.[5] Secretary Byrnes, thinking more directly in terms of major power relations and influenced by his advisers Ben Cohen and Leo Pasvolsky, eventually saw that

---

[3] For the direct quotation and more elaborate discussion of this subject see Gaddis, *The United States and the Origins of the Cold War*, pp. 270–71.

[4] For the formal statement, see President's News Conference, November 15, 1945, Truman, *Public Papers of the Presidents of the United States: Harry S. Truman, 1945*, pp. 472–75.

[5] Gaddis is excellent in tracking the congressional reaction. See Gaddis, *The United States and the Origins of the Cold War*, pp. 272–73.

the matter of the proposed UN commission should be discussed with the Soviets before the first meeting of the UN General Assembly scheduled for January in London.[6] This issue provided him with a further motivation to pursue his proposal for a meeting of Soviet, British, and American foreign ministers in Moscow in December, which he had made on November 23.[7] The seeds for Byrnes's proposed Moscow meeting lay in his recognition after the London CFM experience that in order to make real progress in negotiations with the Soviets he would need to be in a position to appeal to Stalin over Molotov's obstinate head. His idea germinated through late October as he directed Ambassador Harriman to travel to see Stalin at the dictator's holiday residence near Sochi on the Black Sea coast. There the ambassador engaged in lengthy discussions designed to break the procedural logjams regarding which nations should participate in conferences to frame peace treaties with the defeated Axis powers.[8] By November, Byrnes decided the time was ripe for him to continue such discussions in person.

The secretary of state proposed the foreign ministers meeting without any detailed discussion with Truman and without any prior consultation with Foreign Secretary Bevin. The president didn't object in the least as he remained glad to have Byrnes carry the burden on foreign policy matters. Ernest Bevin proved less understanding.[9] Surprised and angry that Byrnes made his proposal without notifying the British in advance, Bevin told Byrnes on November 27 in a teletype conversation that he feared a new foreign ministers meeting "without adequate preparation would only lead to another failure." He pointedly asked if there had been any changes in the American attitudes expressed in London and warned of likely stalling tactics by the Soviets in any negotiations. Byrnes responded by pointing to the possible benefits of the three foreign ministers meeting prior to the first meeting of the UN General Assembly in less formal circumstances than the London CFM and in a locale where Stalin might be consulted.[10] Bevin remained skeptical.

Whatever the reservations of his British opposite, however, Byrnes remained determined to meet with the Soviets.[11] His attitude came through clearly in a conversation with the British ambassador to Washington, Edward Halifax,

---

[6] Gaddis, *The United States and the Origins of the Cold War*, pp. 276–77.

[7] Byrnes to Molotov included in Byrnes to Harriman, November 23, 1945, *FRUS*, 1945, II, p. 578.

[8] For memorandums on Harriman's lengthy meetings of October 24 and 25, 1945, see *FRUS*, 1945, II, pp. 567–76.

[9] For Byrnes's proposal to Bevin, see his message to Winant, November 25, 1945, *FRUS*, 1945, II, p. 580.

[10] Record of conversation, November 27, 1945, Bevin Papers – Conferences, 1945–46, Foreign Office Records, FO 800/446, Public Record Office (hereafter Bevin Papers with file designation).

[11] On Byrnes's thinking at this stage, see the thoughtful analysis of Robert Messer in his *End of an Alliance*, pp. 140–50. Messer emphasizes Byrnes's approach on atomic weapons control as central to his preparations.

where he admitted his initiative might cause difficulties with the excluded France and China, but he explained this counted for less than "getting even one or two matters settled with the Russians."[12] FDR could not have expressed it better. Bevin, however, proved much less inclined to attempt again to settle matters. He maintained his reluctance to attend a Moscow meeting despite the entreaty of his own ambassador there that he take up this "opportunity of dissipating, not only with Molotov himself but with Russia in general, the absurd notion that you are a big, bad wolf."[13] Ambassador Clark Kerr's further report of the enthusiasm of Maxim Litvinov, a Soviet official known for his contacts with the West, for the proposed meeting that he thought might lead the former wartime allies "out of the dark valley" also appears to have had little impact on Bevin.[14] Bevin delayed in making a final decision until December 5 when Byrnes met with Ambassador Halifax and made some telling points. He emphasized that unless the foreign ministers met for preliminary discussions in Moscow, they would be "courting another fiasco" like the London CFM when they gathered for the UN meeting. Furthermore, Byrnes explained there was "no specific target" for the Moscow meeting so the question of "failure" was negated. Finally, Byrnes applied his full court press. Noting that ten days had passed since "he had first broached the matter," he requested of Bevin that they "should walk hand in hand in this as in all matters" but explained that if the foreign secretary refused "he would still feel it right to go to Moscow himself and to do his best alone."[15]

In the end, Bevin could not risk a Byrnes–Molotov meeting. His adviser Sir Alexander Cadogan asked rhetorically: "Can we trust Mr. Byrnes to uphold our interests?" Cadogan went further and raised the likelihood of Britain being faced after a separate U.S.-Soviet meeting "with pressure to give way on points on which a separate American-Russian bargain would have been made."[16] Faced with this prospect an annoyed Bevin grudgingly agreed to pack his bags for Moscow.[17] On December 7, the State Department released news of the meeting scheduled for December 15. The meeting, so the department held publicly, would provide "an opportunity to the British, American, and Soviet Governments for informal and exploratory discussions on a number of matters of current concern to the three countries and also for an exchange of views on the subject of control of atomic energy."[18] Privately, Byrnes hoped for real progress in settling divisive issues through negotiation and compromise.

Around the very time that Byrnes arranged for the Moscow meeting of the three foreign ministers, he and Truman gave further evidence of their fidelity to Roosevelt's vision in foreign affairs through their approach on China policy.

---

[12] Halifax to Bevin (reporting on conversation with Byrnes), November 29, 1945, Bevin Papers, FO 800/446.

[13] Clark Kerr to Bevin, November 29, 1945, Bevin Papers, FO 800/446.

[14] Clark Kerr to Bevin, November 30, 1945, Bevin Papers, FO 800/446.

[15] Halifax to Bevin, December 5, 1945, Bevin Papers, FO 800/446.

[16] Cadogan memorandum, Bevin Papers, FO 800/446.

[17] On Bevin at this time, see Alan Bullock, *Ernest Bevin*, pp. 198–200.

[18] Press release, December 7, 1945, *Department of State Bulletin*, 13 (December 9, 1945), p. 935.

FDR had accorded China major power status during the war as symbolized by his meeting with the Chinese leader, Chiang Kai-shek, at Cairo in 1943 and by China's inclusion as a permanent member of the Security Council of the United Nations in 1945. Sadly the accoutrements of big power status failed to alter the reality of Chiang's internal weakness. His Kuomintang (KMT) government's most notable characteristics lay in the fields of intrigue, mismanagement, and corruption. Upon the defeat of the Japanese, the long-simmering conflict between Chiang's Nationalists and the Chinese Communist Party (CCP) led by Mao Tse-tung threatened to explode. Without really understanding the true depth of the problems it confronted, the Truman administration held faithfully to the well-established goal of "the development of a strong, united, democratic China," which might play an important role in the United Nations.[19] The United States hung to the illusion that somehow Chiang and Mao could resolve their fundamental differences and fashion a new China in line with Roosevelt's hopes and American principles.

Even after the American ambassador to China, General Patrick J. Hurley, suddenly resigned and launched a barrage of ranting criticism against the State Department in which he charged that certain American officials supported Mao's side in the looming civil war, Truman and Byrnes held steady on policy – although, rather predictably, Truman blew off steam by describing Hurley to the cabinet as a "son-of-a-bitch."[20] In an appearance before the Senate Foreign Relations Committee on December 7, Byrnes defended his departmental officers against the Hurley charges and called anew for genuine compromise among the competing factions in China. In an effort to bring the major Chinese factions together, Truman appointed General George C. Marshall to travel to China to mediate the conflict among them in what, in retrospect, may be seen as an endeavor guaranteed to fail. Reconciling Chiangs's KMT and Mao's CCP proved beyond the talents of even the "organizer of victory" in World War II.[21] The point here, however, is neither to focus on America's China policy in general nor General Marshall's mission in particular, but simply to note that the thrust of the Truman–Byrnes effort in this important area revealed that they still shared the assumptions on China that Franklin Roosevelt established.

---

[19] See Byrnes's statement, "America's Policy in China," made before the Senate Committee on Foreign Relations, December 7, 1945, *Department of State Bulletin*, 13 (December 9, 1945), p. 930. Also see Truman's statement, "America's Policy in China," released by the White House on December 16, 1945, in *Department of State Bulletin*, 13 (December 16, 1945), pp. 945–46.

[20] For Byrnes's initial response to Hurley's charges, see "Secretary Comments on Criticism by Ex-Ambassador Hurley," *Department of State Bulletin*, 13 (December 2, 1945), pp. 882–83. Henry Wallace recorded Truman's description of Hurley in his diary. See Blum, ed., *Price of Vision*, p. 519.

[21] On the Marshall mission, see John Robinson Beal, *Marshall in China* (Garden City, NY, 1970); and Steven I. Levine, "A New Look at American Mediation in the Chinese Civil War: The Marshall Mission and Manchuria," *Diplomatic History*, 3 (Fall 1979), pp. 349–75. For Marshall's own recollections of his mission, written at Truman's request in May 1954, see his "Memorandum on China," May 18, 1954, Harry S. Truman Papers: President's Secretary's File, HSTL, Box 174.

Further confirmation for broad continuity in policies between the Roosevelt and early Truman administrations came with the American attitude toward a postwar loan to Great Britain. The British delegation led by John Maynard Keynes optimistically hoped for an American commitment of perhaps $8 billion dollars either through an outright grant or as an interest-free loan. The American negotiators led by Treasury Secretary Fred Vinson, his deputy Harry White, and Assistant Secretary of State Will Clayton quickly disabused Lord Keynes and his collaborators of that possibility. In the end and despite considerable reservations in the U.S. Congress, the American government provided Britain with a loan of $3.75 billion at 2 percent interest. This loan, along with essentially the cancellation of Britain's Lend–Lease debt, helped the British through a difficult period, but it came with a high price tag. The loan placed two chief requirements on the British – first, "to make the pound sterling convertible into other currencies" and, second, "not to use import restrictions to discriminate against each other's trade." In this way, as Diane Kunz explained, the United States "intended to unravel the 'imperial preference' system" and to force the "dismantling of the 'sterling area,' the group of nations that used the pound as their main currency."[22] FDR and Cordell Hull could hardly have hoped for such success in breaking down the British Empire's tariff and currency restrictions, which inhibited the free-trade world of their dreams. The Treasury Department officials played especially tough with the British and used the liquidity problems and financial exhaustion of their wartime ally to force it to accept major changes in the British economic system. Byrnes planned to make demands of no such significant consequence in his dealings with the Soviets in Moscow.

The secretary of state prepared for the Moscow meeting in his usual manner by hunkering down with a few key advisers led by Ben Cohen so as to devise his strategy and proposals. Prompted by the Truman–Attlee–King declaration's call to fashion a UN commission to oversee atomic energy matters, Byrnes placed this matter high on his proposed agenda for Moscow. He adopted a plan aimed at facilitating negotiations that emphasized the exchange of scientific information and implied that such exchanges might be authorized before the safeguards called for in the tripartite declaration were in place. Byrnes breezily informed certain key senators of his planned approach at a meeting on December 10 and succeeded only in raising their concerns. Despite some anxious criticism growing out of the belief that safeguards should precede any exchange of information, Byrnes declined to alter his plan.[23] The anxiety of the senators led by Tom Connally, the Texas Democrat, and Arthur Vandenberg, a Michigan Republican, reached such heights that they sought a meeting with Truman. But

---

[22] See Diane Kunz, *Butter and Guns*, pp. 19–21. For a detailed account of the Anglo-American negotiations, see Randall Bennett Woods, *A Changing of the Guard: Anglo-American Relations, 1941–1946* (Chapel Hill, NC, 1990), pp. 332–62. For a British perspective, see David Reynold's thoughtful and concise treatment in *Britannia Overruled: British Policy and World Power in the Twentieth Century* (London, 1991), pp. 159–60.

[23] See Gaddis, *The United States and the Origins of the Cold War*, pp. 277–78.

the president declined to take up their suggestion that no scientific information be supplied unless and until safeguard procedures were in place. Later in the day Truman explained to his cabinet that he thought the senators "were wrong" because "the Russians had just as good scientists as we had; that the scientific information was now available to everybody and that it was important to help create an atmosphere of worldwide confidence."[24] Truman obviously understood and supported Byrnes's conciliatory approach on the issue.

Although willing to go along with the substance of Byrnes's policies, Truman increasingly grew perturbed at the independent manner of his chosen secretary of state. Truman even enlisted Joseph Davies to serve as an intermediary between himself and Byrnes. While visiting with Truman on the presidential yacht, the *USS Williamsburg*, on December 8, Truman asked the confirmed sovietophile "to talk with Byrnes about what he was going to do in Moscow." Truman confessed to being "fond of Byrnes" but described him as a "conniver." Davies concluded that "someone had been needling" the president against Byrnes, and he confided to his journal his fear that "Jim has not kept his lines of communication with the Commander in Chief sufficiently active."[25] The obvious question as to why Truman didn't simply make plain his desire to Byrnes for regular reporting and briefings must be passed over here and left to those who want to wrestle with Truman's psyche at this time, but the fact that Truman selected Davies as his troubleshooter on the matter cannot be ignored.

The former ambassador's selection confirms that Truman's concern with Byrnes was one primarily of style not of substance as the president could never have asked Davies's assistance if he really sought to challenge the quid pro quo approach Byrnes planned for Moscow.[26] Indeed, when Davies met Byrnes for a lengthy session on the day prior to the secretary's departure for Moscow, he spent all his time advising Byrnes to be even more conciliatory to the Soviets and appears not to have emphasized the president's concerns.[27] Even while Byrnes labored away in Moscow, Truman groaned with displeasure to his aides about the secretary of state. Samuel Rosenman, FDR's longtime assistant who now helped Truman with his major speeches, told Davies on December 18 that the president was "sour on Jim," and that he would make "a change there before long." Rosenman identified the source of Truman's resentment as Byrnes's failure to consult him and went on to ask Davies if he would "take on the job," something for which he thought the president would be keen.[28] Whether or not Truman might have ever considered Davies is another question that can be passed over here, but this exchange indicates that Truman's anger at Byrnes's independence and failure to consult had been sown before the Moscow

[24] Truman as recorded by Henry Wallace in Blum, ed., *Price of Vision*, p. 530.
[25] Davies journal, December 8, 1945, Joseph E. Davies Papers, Library of Congress, Box 22.
[26] Alonzo Hamby makes the style/substance distinction in *Man of the People*, p. 342.
[27] Davies journal, December 11, 1945, Joseph E. Davies Papers, Library of Congress, Box 22.
[28] Davies journal, December 18, 1945, Joseph E. Davies Papers, Library of Congress, Box 22.

meeting was well under way.[29] In summary, Truman's attention in December 1945 centered on his getting tough with Byrnes not with Byrnes getting tough with the Soviet Union.

Getting out of Washington must have pleased Byrnes a great deal given the mounting criticism from various quarters against him. Even the prospect of traveling to the Soviet capital in the wintertime did not dampen his desire to get back to the negotiating table. Byrnes's optimism increased when Stalin cut short his vacation at Sochi and returned to Moscow to meet with him. According to the American observers, Stalin's presence proved decisive. At a Kremlin dinner, Molotov reverted to his London conference form and began a kind of "atomic diplomacy" in reverse by highlighting and joking about the weapon. In toasting Dr. James Conant, the Harvard University president and a science administrator intimately involved in the Manhattan Project, Molotov asked if Conant "might have in his waist-coat pocket a piece of fissionable material." Stalin intervened, rebuked Molotov, and declared that nuclear fission "was much too serious a matter to be the subject of jokes." Stalin even went on to praise the American and British scientists for their achievements in a manner that Charles Bohlen thought effectively changed Soviet policy toward greater openness to negotiations.[30]

Whatever the real impact of Stalin's intervention, Byrnes made progress in his search for agreements. At the conclusion of the Moscow conference, he had reached more than just one or two agreements with the Russians. Molotov, undoubtedly with Stalin's approval, undertook to cosponsor a resolution at the initial session of the General Assembly of the UN, which would establish a commission for the international control of atomic energy. On China, Byrnes obtained a recommitment of continued Soviet support for Chiang's government. Also, both the United States and the Soviet Union restated their desire to remove their troops from China, with Molotov pledging that Soviet troops would leave Manchuria by February 1946 and Byrnes less specifically guaranteeing that the American forces in North China would depart as soon as they oversaw the disarming and deportation of remaining Japanese troops. The American politician-diplomat skillfully gained Soviet participation in the Allied Far Eastern Commission, a largely ineffectual body, which would meet in Washington, D.C., while carefully circumscribing the Allied Control Council for Japan, on which a Soviet representative sat, to an advisory role.[31] "In this way," as Robert Messer noted, Brynes "brought the Soviet Union into nominal participation in Japan, without impairing MacArthur's policymaking authority

---

[29] The Truman–Davies relationship appeared solid, however, in late 1945. Truman and Treasury Secretary Fred Vinson dined with Davies at his home on December 19 and discussed a wide range of topics, both foreign and domestic. At this meeting, Davies confirmed to Truman that he had seen Byrnes before he left. See Davies journal, December 19, 1945, Joseph E. Davies Papers, Library of Congress, Box 22.

[30] This account of the dinner is drawn from Bohlen, *Witness to History*, p. 249.

[31] For the Moscow conference communiqué, December 27, 1945, see *FRUS*, 1945, II, pp. 815–24.

as supreme commander."[32] The three foreign ministers also affirmed their commitment to reestablish a free Korea and even provided for the establishment of a joint Soviet-American commission to assist in the formation of a provisional Korean government.

There was another side to the Byrnes ledger as might be expected in quid pro quo negotiations. The secretary of state backed away from his London CFM stance and agreed that the drafting of peace treaties with the former Axis allies such as Italy, Rumania, Bulgaria, and Hungary should be completed only by the powers who signed the armistices with these states. For the most part, this limited the task to the Big Three powers. It reduced France and China, who had participated in the London CFM, to an essentially ceremonial role, just as it did other states that had fought the Axis enemy. In regard to Rumania and Bulgaria, Byrnes accepted a Soviet commitment to broaden the existing governments after which he promised formal diplomatic recognition.[33] The expectations for such "broadening" were very modest, to put it mildly, and amounted to little more than token gestures of adding a few opposition figures to the respective governments. An astute observer on the American embassy staff recalled his "contempt" for the Byrnes "effort to rescue something of the wreckage of the Yalta Declaration on Liberated Europe" by adding "some fig leaves of democratic procedure to hide the nakedness of Stalinist dictatorship."[34]

Byrnes had justified his call for the foreign ministers meeting as a fulfillment of an understanding reached at Yalta that the three officials would meet regularly. Yalta, however, appeared to provide much more than the explanation for the gathering. It also served as a virtual model for Byrnes's effort in Moscow, at least in the eyes of a number of capable historian-observers. Robert Messer observed that Byrnes reverted "to the pragmatism of Roosevelt at Yalta," by attempting, as he noted astutely, "to add a Western democratic 'fig leaf' to Soviet dominance in Eastern Europe."[35] Byrnes, like FDR at Yalta, hoped that the Soviets might make the domination of their East European sphere more palatable to Western observers by allowing a patina of democratic forms. Elizabeth Kimball MacLean described the American effort as "an attempt to put into practice FDR's Grand Design by dealing forthrightly with geopolitical realities while cloaking the decision in the garb of the Atlantic Charter."[36] John Lewis Gaddis suggested that by December 1945, "Byrnes had come to much the same conclusion that Roosevelt had a year earlier: that the only way to reconcile the American interest in self-determination with the Soviet interest in security

---

[32] Messer, *End of an Alliance*, p. 150.

[33] See the sections on "Rumania" and "Bulgaria" in the Moscow conference communiqué, December 27, 1945, *FRUS*, 1945, II, pp. 821–22.

[34] The observer was George F. Kennan, *Memoirs, 1925–1950*, p. 284. See his diary entry for December 19, 1945, included in his *Memoirs, 1925–1950*, pp. 286–88, which gives a flavor of his contemporaneous observations.

[35] Messer, *End of an Alliance*, p. 155.

[36] MacLean, *Joseph E. Davies*, p. 166.

was to negotiate thinly disguised agreements designed to cloak the reality of Moscow's control behind a façade of democratic procedures."[37]

And yet, to focus on the Moscow meeting as simply a reprise of Yalta is to miss the continuity in American policy through Truman's first year in office from the Stalin–Hopkins agreement over Poland in June 1945, through the Potsdam settlement and beyond. The secretary of state had gone to the London CFM intent on maintaining this continuity through serious negotiation with Molotov but met only obstruction. Byrnes, with Truman's agreement, always had been prepared to arrange deals that would allow the United States and the Soviet Union to get along. He continued the practice in Moscow. Although Truman at times seemed uncomfortable with or confused about the arrangement, Byrnes only confirmed in Moscow the essential Yalta/Potsdam concession of Eastern Europe to the Soviets as an area vital to their security.[38] The evolving American concern lay in protecting Western interests elsewhere, such as in Japan and in the Middle East, and in getting the process of cooperation back on track. In the interests of the latter, Byrnes only objected tepidly to the continued Soviet military occupation of northern Iran and, much to Bevin's annoyance, he removed the issue as a formal agenda topic. He hoped to persuade the Soviets in "informal" discussions to give ground on this matter.[39] Byrnes pragmatically accepted that Europe had been divided and aimed to make the best of it. He hoped that a cooperative relationship might be maintained with the Soviets, and to that end he tried to limit the issues over which they might conflict.[40]

The achievements of the Moscow conference pleased Byrnes, and he returned home intent on informing the American people of his success.[41] The secretary requested that his deputy, Dean Acheson, arrange for a national radio

[37] Gaddis, *Strategies of Containment*, pp. 17–18.

[38] On the American willingness to concede the Soviets a sphere of influence in Eastern Europe, see Eduard M. Mark, "American Policy Toward Eastern Europe and the Origins of the Cold War, 1941–1946: An Alternative Interpretation," *Journal of American History*, 68 (September 1981), pp. 313–36. On this, also see Mark's "Charles E. Bohlen and the Acceptable Limits of Soviet Hegemony in Eastern Europe: A Memorandum of 18 October 1945," *Diplomatic History*, 3 (Spring 1979), pp. 201–13.

[39] See Bruce R. Kuniholm, *The Origins of the Cold War in the Near East: Great Power Conflict and Diplomacy in Iran, Turkey and Greece* (Princeton, NJ, 1980), pp. 284–91.

[40] Obviously, I am greatly influenced in my analysis here by the insightful work of Marc Trachtenberg in his *Constructed Peace*, pp. 14–15. However, I think Trachtenberg overstates the definitiveness of Byrnes's approach when he argues that "Byrnes was not trying to buy Soviet goodwill in the hope of propping up a regime of great power cooperation. He had come to the conclusion very early on that Russia and America were too far apart on basics for the two sides to work hand in hand with each other." For Byrnes, according to Trachtenberg: "The division of Europe was a fact, and if both sides accepted it, an end could be put to the quarreling and the allies could go their separate ways in peace." This exaggerates Byrnes intention at this stage of the two powers going in completely separate ways.

[41] Robertson even suggests that Byrnes was "ebullient" because he believed that "he had 'gotten through' to Stalin and that he had successfully continued the Soviet-U.S. entente cordiale into the postwar world." See his *Sly and Able*, p. 452.

broadcast for him. He showed no indication that he would need to brief the president on the results of the conference before addressing his radio audience. His sense that he oversaw foreign policy without need for any close presidential sanction and support had led him in Moscow to reject the well-meaning suggestions of Averell Harriman and Charles Bohlen that he provide written reports to Truman.[42] When the three Moscow principals publicly released the conference communiqué before Truman had the chance to peruse it, the Missourian's temper flared up.[43] Through Acheson, the president arranged that Byrnes report to him directly before he gave his speech over the radio.[44] Hardly making it easy for his exhausted secretary of state, who had to complete the tiring air-journey across the Atlantic, Truman sailed down the Potomac in the *Williamsburg* with some of his aides and cronies before Byrnes's arrival. An exhausted Byrnes caught up with the group at Quantico, Virginia, on December 29.

Truman and Byrnes agreed that they met in the stateroom of the *Williamsburg* but beyond that their recollections of the meeting are at complete odds. According to Jonathan Daniels in his *Man of Independence* published in 1950, Truman claimed that Byrnes "got the real riot act after Moscow." The president remembered telling Byrnes that "our policy was not appeasement and not a one-way street."[45] Acheson recalled in 1955, that Truman maintained that he gave Byrnes "unshaded hell."[46] Truman's own later account has him complaining about being "left in the dark" and particularly upset at the public issuance of the Moscow conference communiqué prior to his receiving it. He supposedly warned Byrnes that he "would not tolerate a repetition of such conduct."[47] Byrnes's account denies the confrontational nature of the meeting. He remembered that Truman "expressed his hearty approval" of the accomplishments of the Moscow conference and agreed that Byrnes should make his radio address. Furthermore, in the Byrnes recollection, Truman insisted that the secretary stay for dinner, which undoubtedly was preceded by the liberal consumption of bourbon, and he endorsed Byrnes's efforts in front of the other dinner companions. He also insisted that Byrnes return to the *Williamsburg* to spend New Year's Eve, which Byrnes did. On this second visit, Truman complimented him

---

[42] See interview with W. Averell Harriman, December 8, 1954, in Harry S. Truman Papers: Post-Presidential Files, HSTL, Box 641, transcript p. 13. Harriman recalled that Byrnes was concerned about leaks from the White House. Also see Bohlen, *Witness to History*, pp. 250–51.

[43] When filing the communiqué some days later, Truman wrote on the cover memorandum: "Received an hour after its release." Harry S. Truman Papers: President's Secretary's File, HSTL, Box 159.

[44] Acheson, *Present at the Creation*, p. 136.

[45] Jonathan Daniels, *The Man of Independence* (Philadelphia, 1950), p. 310. Daniels interviewed Truman for this book in 1949.

[46] See interview with Dean Acheson, February 18, 1955, Harry S. Truman Papers: Post-Presidential Files, HSTL, Box 641, transcript p. 21. Interestingly, Acheson tends to doubt Truman's version of events.

[47] Truman, *Year of Decisions*, p. 604.

on his now-delivered radio address. As Byrnes rightly noted such invitations hardly indicated some severe break in their friendly relations.[48]

It seems likely that Truman may have raised mild concerns about appropriate reporting and the timing of the public issuance of the conference communiqué. Byrnes hardly took them as major matters and rightly explained that the latter resulted from the time it took to decode the communiqué message sent from Moscow hours earlier than its public release. He then proceeded to brief Truman on the substance of the agreements in Moscow. Truman supported his secretary's efforts and the men left their meeting on cordial terms.[49] Perhaps Truman felt the point had been made by having Byrnes journey to Quantico to see him. What seems clear is that Truman's later account of the meeting reflected his retrospective bravado and his tendency to "refashion reality," as Alonzo Hamby put it, so as to fulfill some later need to "demonstrate mastery over Byrnes."[50] Clearly, what Truman didn't do at his December 29 meeting was either raise any objections of substance regarding Byrnes's report or ask him to alter that report. Presumably, he would have had he thought Byrnes's Moscow achievements added up to "appeasement" of the Soviet Union.

Byrnes delivered his radio report on December 30. It reflected his effort to convey to the American people that the process of negotiation and compromise had made real progress in the Moscow discussions in settling some of the issues that had divided the wartime allies. Byrnes admitted that some of the arrangements hardly constituted "ideal solutions," but he persuasively defended the arrangements to give the Rumanian and Bulgarian governments the façade of "broadening." He made it quite plain that he recognized the "real interest" of the Soviet Union in Eastern Europe. He proceeded on to explain positively the settlements reached on Japanese occupation arrangements and in Northeast Asia as well as on the creation of a UN Atomic Energy Commission.[51] In Byrnes's view, the Moscow meeting had laid the groundwork for further constructive deliberations and negotiations at the upcoming first session of the UN General Assembly. After barely a week back in Washington, the secretary of state left again to participate in this session.

Before he left for the London gathering, Byrnes met with Truman in the Oval Office on January 5. There, according to Truman, he read Byrnes a letter that he later included in full in his *Memoirs* first published in 1955. In this missive, which has achieved a certain iconographic status in Cold War literature, Truman supposedly informed Byrnes that "I have the utmost confidence in you and

---

[48] Byrnes, *All in One Lifetime*, p. 345. In 1950, Byrnes prepared a response to the Truman claims as presented in Daniels's book. This is included in James F. Byrnes Papers, Cooper Library, Folder 573. Byrnes's direct quotations are from this memorandum.

[49] The accounts of Robert Messer, *End of an Alliance*, pp. 156–57; Alonzo Hamby, *Man of the People*, p. 345; and Robertson, *Sly and Able*, pp. 454–57, provide more details and support this broad interpretation.

[50] Hamby, "An American Democrat," p. 48.

[51] Report by secretary of state on the meeting of foreign ministers, December 30, 1945, *Department of State Bulletin*, 13 (December 30, 1945), pp. 1033–36, 1047.

your ability" but rehashed earlier concerns about reporting procedures. Then, Truman launched into a litany of complaints about Soviet behavior not only in Eastern Europe but in Iran. He concluded this with a warning that "Russia intends an invasion of Turkey and the seizure of the Black Sea Straits to the Mediterranean." Then, in words that are much quoted by Cold War historians of every stripe, Truman supposedly opined that "unless Russia is faced with an iron fist and strong language another war is in the making. Only one language do they understand – "How many divisions have you?" He advised Byrnes that he did not think "we should play compromise any longer." In classic "give 'em hell, Harry" style he allegedly exclaimed in conclusion: "I'm tired [of] babying the Soviets."[52]

How else should one interpret these remarks but as a clear indication that Truman wanted a quick move to a "get tough" approach to the Soviets away from a policy of compromise and even indulgence pursued throughout 1945? But the document cannot be taken at face value. Truman almost certainly did not read the letter to Byrnes, who claimed with some validity that he would have resigned immediately had it been read to him. Little evidence exists that Byrnes left for London having been upbraided by Truman. But should the document at least be seen as an expression of Truman's private convictions and beliefs on U.S. foreign policy at this time? Here the answer remains more murky and inconclusive. There is no doubt that Admiral Leahy, still ensconced on the White House staff, fed Truman a regular diet of criticisms of both Soviet actions and of Byrnes's supposed weakness in confronting them. It also seems likely that the old admiral, an accomplished Washington operator, also fed the press stories critical of Byrnes and highlighting Truman's supposed dissatisfaction with the policy of his secretary of state.[53] It's possible that Truman in an exercise of private venting did express some genuine concerns.

Yet, the real target of Truman's letter seems to be less American policy and more the particular American policy maker. In this circumstance, my own speculation – and I emphasize it as such – is that after Byrnes's farewell meeting with the president in which he gave a typical, less-than-extensive review of his plans, the embers of anger and even resentment at Byrnes flared again in Truman. Truman, who was nursing some personal anxiety about his capacities to serve in the office that relaxing on the *Williamsburg* had failed to quell, hurriedly scribbled down all the criticisms aimed at Byrnes on both the procedural and policy fronts that he had either felt or heard over the preceding days.[54] The

---

[52] See the letter included in *Year of Decisions*, pp. 604–05. It is also included in Ferrell, ed., *Off the Record*, pp. 79–80. Robert Messer correctly suggested that Truman's final sentence was "among the most-quoted phrases in the history of the early cold war." *End of an Alliance*, p. 158.

[53] Messer suggests Leahy as the likely source for the stories negative to Byrnes in *End of an Alliance*, p. 167. For an illustration of an article highlighting the Byrnes–Leahy clash, which internal evidence suggests had its source with Leahy, see "Washington's Dog Eat Dog," *Newsweek*, January 14, 1946, pp. 25–26.

[54] On Truman's anxiety, see his unsent letter to Bess Truman, December 28, 1945, in Ferrell, ed., *Off the Record*, p. 75, where he referred to the White House as "the great white sepulcher of

result emerged as his diatribe "letter" to Byrnes. After this exercise in letting off "steam," Truman moved beyond the letter and filed it. In the mid-1950s, however, in order to address certain psychological needs of his own, and perhaps also to demonstrate to his then strongly anti-Soviet audience that he grasped the need for "toughness" long before his "appeasing" secretary of state did, he decided to make it public. Knowing full well he hadn't sent the letter directly, he invented, although possibly himself believed, the story of his having read the letter to "dear Jim."[55]

Whatever the true story regarding his "letter" to Byrnes, the historian can ask if Truman sought to implement the new and tough approach he allegedly proposed to his secretary of state. Here the evidence conclusively supports Byrnes for the Truman administration hardly shifted gears to adopt a new approach to the Soviets. Assuredly, Byrnes increased his opposition to the Soviet presence in Iran, although he did this more vigorously *after* Iran lodged a protest against the Soviets at the UN and as the Soviets gave few signs of conceding anything on the issue. But the secretary of state set off to London eager to build on the accomplishments of the Moscow meeting. Furthermore, Truman called for no major policy papers or special meetings to assess the situation and to flesh out his alleged belief that the Soviets needed to face an "iron fist." Notions that Harry Truman led the way in altering the broad direction of American foreign policy at the beginning of 1946 should be shelved. He remained quite dependent on Byrnes, although his regard for his secretary of state had frayed from the communiqué episode and from the anti-Byrnes rumors and comments that circulated in the White House.[56] The major transformation in policy would take time. In the early months of 1946, however, it received a significant boost from the efforts of George F. Kennan and Winston S. Churchill.

A Disposition of Firmness

Ernest Bevin certainly would have welcomed the forceful "iron fist" approach, which Truman later purported to have commended to Byrnes. The former

---

ambitions and reputations," and admitted that he felt "like last year's bird's nest which is on its second year." Bess Truman apparently had criticized the brief time the president spent at home in Independence over Christmas. Her husband explained that he had had to do "at least 100 things I didn't want to do" and admitted to being upset that she viewed him "like something the cat dragged in." He asked that "you [Bess], Margie, and everyone else who may have any influence on my actions must give me help and assistance; because no one ever needed help and assistance as I do now."

[55] I am influenced in this analysis by the careful efforts of Robert Messer to test "the document's credibility and utility as historical evidence." See *End of an Alliance*, pp. 159–66.

[56] On the fraying in the Truman–Byrnes relationship, see the exchange between Joseph Davies and Byrnes's close friend, Justice Dick Whaley of the Court of Claims. Whaley blamed the fraying on "the constant needling and poisoning of the President by Admiral Leahy and others of the 'Palace Guard.'" According to Davies, he responded: "Whoever prompted it, I agreed that he was right. I thought, however, that Jim was partly responsible himself. Jim after all was not President. He was the President's agent and should get his principal's views and directions more often." Diary entry, January 28, 1946, Joseph E. Davies Papers, Library of Congress, Box 2.

trade unionist felt no need to conciliate or accommodate the Soviet Union. He wanted decent relations with Moscow, but Soviet expansionist tendencies worried him greatly. In an off-the-record conversation with British diplomatic correspondents on January 1, 1946, he explained that Russia was "seeking to put around herself for security purposes whole groups of satellites in the south, east and west with the view of controlling every kind of place which is likely to come in contact with her."[57] The increasing communist domination in Eastern Europe bothered him, as did the rising appeal of communist parties in France and Italy. Even more importantly, the threat of Soviet expansion in the Mediterranean and the Middle East troubled the British foreign secretary.[58] Bevin expressed his concerns regarding Soviet intentions toward Greece, Turkey, and Persia (Iran) to Byrnes when the two men met in Moscow, but Byrnes's primary concerns lay elsewhere.[59]

Bevin knew instinctively that the Soviet Union under Stalin held deep-seated enmity for the social democratic parties in Europe such as his own. He already had enough indication of Soviet behavior in Eastern Europe to have a premonition of the dastardly treatment that would be meted out to those of the moderate democratic left by Stalin's puppets over the coming years.[60] He recognized that Soviet expansion represented a major threat to traditional British interests. While Prime Minister Attlee, and even more so those on the left of the British Labour Party, expressed concerns about his approach, Bevin, to his everlasting credit, stood firm.[61] He warrants due recognition as the first major Western statesman of the postwar era to clearly challenge the Soviet Union. While Truman and Byrnes – still in Rooseveltian mold – worked to settle issues with the Soviets, Bevin courageously raised objections and sought to contest threatening Soviet behavior. The Soviets clearly appreciated this reality. Britain became the principal target of Soviet propaganda in late 1945 and 1946, as Alan Bullock and other British and European scholars have pointed out.[62] In fact, as the Norwegian scholar Geir Lundestad argued correctly, "in 1945–46 the main antagonists were Britain and the Soviet Union, not the United States and the Soviet Union."[63] Although it is not always well appreciated by American

---

[57] Bevin, quoted in Bullock, *Ernest Bevin*, p. 214.

[58] A good summary of Bevin's concerns is found in Reynolds, *Britannia Overruled*, p. 157.

[59] Bullock, *Ernest Bevin*, p. 206.

[60] For tragic accounts of the fate of the social democratic parties of Eastern Europe, see Denis Healey, ed., *The Curtain Falls: The Story of the Socialists in Eastern Europe* (London, 1951). This book, which should be required reading for all those of the political left who write on the Cold War, included an introduction by Aneurin Bevan, which shared this powerful warning: "The Communist Party is the sworn inveterate enemy of the Socialist and Democratic Parties. When it associates with them, it does so as a preliminary to destroying them" (p. 6).

[61] On Attlee's reservations, see Raymond Smith and John Zametica, "The Cold Warrior: Clement Attlee Reconsidered, 1945–47," *International Affairs*, 61 (1985), pp. 237–52.

[62] See Bullock, *Ernest Bevin*, pp. 216–17. Bullock explained: "It was British imperialism, not American capitalism, which was made the target of a concerted attack through Communist-controlled radio and press."

[63] Geir Lundestad, *The United States and Western Europe since 1945: From "Empire" by Invitation to Transatlantic Drift* (New York, 2003), p. 48.

historians who prefer to write the history of the Cold War as simply a bipolar confrontation, the British so objected to Soviet behavior that it is right to speak of the "Anglo-Soviet Cold War."[64]

Bevin pursued the good fight through 1946 always unsure of what the American response would be.[65] The fact that deep disagreements developed between Britain and the Truman White House over the Palestine issue hardly helped matters.[66] But Bevin, strongly encouraged by Winston Churchill, knew that Britain could not counter an expansionist Soviet Union on its own.[67] It would need American support. Bevin aimed to build it. During the London UN meeting in January, he dined with the Republican delegates, Senator Arthur Vandenberg and John Foster Dulles, and raised his concerns about the northern tier states. Referring to a map, he explained "how Russian intrigues in Iran were also directed against the Turks and how a Soviet-controlled province of Azerbaijan would enable the Russians to penetrate and put further pressure on Turkey." The tough British socialist encouraged these influential Americans to stand up to the Soviets on Iran. Furthermore, he cogently drew a parallel between the Soviet "technique" of "one at a time" and that of Hitler. The needed path was clear: "If they checked Russia over Iran, they also could save Turkey." Pointedly, he observed, the United States "could not and must not stand aloof."[68]

Bevin's efforts to rouse the United States received unknowing yet valuable assistance from the Soviet Union. Despite the efforts at persuasion of Byrnes and Bevin in Moscow, the Soviets remained determined to occupy northern Iran militarily. In response, the Iranians filed a protest with the UN Security Council, making use of the fledgling institution to highlight their grievance. Tensions developed on this issue through the early months of 1946 and generated anxiety as to the nature of Soviet intentions.[69] Further uncertainty about the real intentions of the Soviets emerged in response to the so-called election

[64] See Fraser Harbutt's chapter entitled "Anglo-Soviet Cold War, United States-Soviet Rapprochement," in his *Iron Curtain*, pp. 117–50.

[65] Reynolds notes Bevin's uncertainty about the United States in his *Britannia Overruled*, p. 161.

[66] For an overview of Truman's policy on Palestine, which touches on his disagreements with the British, see Hamby, *Man of the People*, pp. 405–17.

[67] Bevin and Churchill stayed in touch, and Bevin even shared diplomatic cables with his chief from the wartime cabinet. Not surprisingly, Churchill felt free to share his counsel with his onetime minister for labour. In November 1945, he foreshadowed his "Iron Curtain" address by writing Bevin that "the future of the world depends upon the fraternal association of Great Britain and the Commonwealth with the United States. With that," he continued, "there can be no war. Without it, there can be no peace." For the British elder-statesman, "[t]he fact that strategically the English-speaking world is bound together, will enable us to be all the better friends with Soviet Russia, and will win us the respect of that realistic state." Churchill to Bevin, November 13, 1945, in Avon Papers, Main Library Special Collections, University of Birmingham, 20/42/132A.

[68] Bullock, *Ernest Bevin*, p. 235.

[69] On the issue of Iran and its effects on American policy toward the USSR, see Kuniholm, *Origins of the Cold War in the Near East*, pp. 304–50, 383–99; and Gary R. Hess, "The Iranian Crisis of 1945–46 and the Cold War," *Political Science Quarterly*, 89 (March 1974), pp. 116–46.

speeches that Stalin and his associates delivered in early February 1946. The Soviet dictator used his speech to clarify for his battered people that there would be no easing of the wartime emphasis on heavy industry in favor of production of consumer goods which might ease their difficult lives. In effect, he used the speech, as Eduard Mark has explained, "to reassert Marxist-Leninism at home" and to justify the emphasis on capital goods and armaments production. Utilizing rather crude and orthodox Marxist-Leninist theory which held that "imperialist" rivalries would lead to war, Stalin argued that the Soviets must be prepared for any eventuality should such a war spill over to involve their nation. His speech neither aimed to influence Western opinion nor to signal a change in policies to Western governments.[70] Yet, it caused speculation in the West as to what it meant for the Soviet future. Why would Stalin need to impose upon his war-weary people rearmament demands that Soviet security needs hardly appeared to warrant?

Officials in the State Department certainly wanted greater clarity about Soviet intentions, and they dispatched a request for an explanation of recent Soviet behavior to the chargé d'affaires at the U.S. embassy in Moscow, George F. Kennan.[71] In a dolorous state of mind and laid up in bed with cold, fever, sinus, and tooth troubles, not to mention an attack of the ulcers which bedeviled him, Kennan decided to make the most of this opportunity to get a hearing for his views.[72] His response, dubbed the Long Telegram and dated February 22, traced the basic features, background, and prospects of Soviet foreign policy and their implications for American policy. Examining the Soviet "outlook," he discerned that the "party line is not based on any objective analysis of the situation beyond Russia's borders; that, it arises mainly from basic inter-Russian necessities." For him, the motivation for Soviet policy lay in the need of the Kremlin to justify its rule. Marxist dogma provided for the Kremlin inhabitants "the fig leaf of their moral and intellectual respectability" – a veritable cover for their tyranny – but at the bottom of the Kremlin's "neurotic view of world affairs" resided the "traditional and instinctive Russian sense of insecurity." Stalin needed an enemy to justify his harsh rule. Coexistence, in Kennan's view, was a charade. From such premises, he went on to predict that the Soviet Union would aim to increase in every way the "strength and prestige of the Soviet state" and, whenever considered timely and promising, to "advance the official limits of Soviet power." But Soviet power was "neither schematic nor adventuristic. It does not work by fixed plans. It does not take unnecessary

---

[70] On Stalin's speech, see Eduard Mark's letter of January 25, 1999 on the H-Diplo list (*http://h-net2.msu/~diplo/*) and Mark's brilliantly researched "October or Thermidor: Interpretations of Stalinism and the Perception of Soviet Foreign Policy in the United States, 1927–1947," *American Historical Review*, 94 (October 1989), pp. 937–62.

[71] For the departmental request, see Matthews to Kennnan, February 13, 1946 (861.00/2-1346), State Department Records, Central Decimal Files, National Archives.

[72] Kennan had felt ignored since his return to Moscow in 1944. In his *Memoirs*, he captures his own sentiments well: "They had asked for it. Now, by God, they would have it." See Kennan, *Memoirs, 1925–1950*, p. 293.

risks. Impervious to the logic of reason, it is highly sensitive to the logic of force." Kennan asserted that Soviet power usually withdrew upon strong resistance and, he emphasized, "if the adversary has sufficient force and makes clear his readiness to use it, he rarely has to do so."[73]

The Long Telegram had an impact on senior policy makers in Washington, although it should not be exaggerated. "The timing of Mr. Kennan's communication...was strategic," Louis Halle later claimed. "It came right at a moment when the [State] Department...was floundering about, looking for new intellectual moorings. Now in this communication it was offered a new and realistic conception to which it might attach itself."[74] Kennan's cable certainly exercised a catalytic effect upon State Department thinking especially as regards the possibility of the United States achieving any nonadversarial relationship with the USSR. Even Undersecretary Acheson, never one to excessively praise Kennan in retrospect, noted the value of his "predictions and warnings."[75] Averell Harriman, now back in Washington, sent a copy of his former deputy's cable to Navy Secretary Forrestal describing it as "well worth reading." Forrestal obviously agreed and, beginning his self-appointed role as Kennan's promoter, had the piece mimeographed and distributed to other members of Truman's cabinet and to higher officers throughout the armed services.[76]

Kennan's cable, however, exercised no immediate impact on policy. Truman apparently neither read nor commented on the message that brought Kennan's "official loneliness" to an end and helped make his reputation. Its influence must be assessed in less specific fashion. The Long Telegram contributed to the construction of the intellectual supports for the developing disposition of firmness toward the Soviet Union. It gave added ballast to the efforts of such administration figures as Admiral Leahy to move to a tougher stance toward Stalin's regime. At the same time, it tore at the heart of Roosevelt's notion that a reassured and "domesticated" Soviet Union might be integrated into a new world system, and it raised doubts about whether the Byrnes approach based on bargaining and compromise could truly facilitate a stable settlement with the USSR. Stalin, Kennan rightly judged, proved a figure beyond reassurance. Thus, as John Lewis Gaddis encapsulated the Kennan argument, "there could be...no permanent resolution of differences with such a government, which relied on the fiction of external threat to maintain internal legitimacy."[77] These ideas percolated among American policy makers and seemed confirmed by events.

---

[73] For the Long Telegram, see Kennan to secretary of state, February 22, 1946, *FRUS, 1946*, VI, pp. 696–709. Direct quotations from pp. 699–701, 707. My discussion of the Long Telegram here borrows from my treatment of it in Miscamble, *George F. Kennan and the Making of American Foreign Policy*, pp. 25–28.

[74] Louis J. Halle, *The Cold War as History* (New York, 1967), p. 105.

[75] Acheson, *Present at the Creation*, p. 151.

[76] Harriman and Abel, *Special Envoy to Churchill and Stalin*, p. 548. On Forrestal's reactions, see Millis, ed., *Forrestal Diaries*, pp. 135–36.

[77] Gaddis, *Strategies of Containment*, p. 20. (The preceding sentence also relies on John Gaddis's analysis in *Strategies of Containment*, p. 19.)

Even in London, Jimmy Byrnes began to get the whiff of Soviet intransigence such as to unsettle his compromising assumptions. The American secretary of state arrived in the British capital for the UN General Assembly meeting to face issues including not only the continued Soviet occupation of northern Iran but also the failure to make progress in implementing the cosmetic provisions to "broaden" the Rumanian and Bulgarian governments that he had reached in Moscow.[78] With Vandenberg now along with him as a de facto overseer, Byrnes simply aimed to defer both matters for further discussion.[79] He secured his principal goal of the establishment of the UN Atomic Energy Agency and then returned to Washington, D.C. He had not given up on negotiation and bargaining, but he approached the Soviets more cautiously in 1946 with any optimism that he could reach an enduring settlement with Stalin and Molotov quite tempered.

By late February, Byrnes addressed the Overseas Correspondents Club in New York and pointed to the rise of "suspicion and distrust" on the international scene. He warned, presumably with the Soviet occupation of Iran specifically in mind, that "we have a responsibility to use our influence to see that other powers live up to *their* covenants." He still expressed the conviction that despite the increased tensions and suspicions "satisfactory solutions can be found," but this would require "a stop to this maneuvering for strategic advantage all over the world." The American approach to the Soviets, he argued, must be based on "patience and firmness."[80] The speech might be read as Byrnes both calling upon and warning the Soviets to moderate their aims and work together for peace. The Byrnes speech, dubbed the "Second Vandenberg Concerto," followed by a day a tough Vandenberg speech on the Senate floor in which this key figure in fashioning any bipartisan foreign policy called for the United States to speak plainly to and deal firmly with the Soviets. Together the speeches reveal the developing trend in official Washington away from any accommodationist approach to the Soviet Union.

Winston Churchill aimed to hurry this trend along. He visited the United States from mid-January through to March of 1946 ostensibly as a "private citizen" to take the sun and enjoy the hospitality of a wealthy Canadian, Frank Clarke, at his Florida home. Of course, the indefatigable Churchill, now recovered from the depression bought on by his 1945 election defeat, also seized the opportunity to lobby for his treasured vision of full Anglo-American collaboration to secure the peace of the world. He put the need for such collaboration to Truman in private discussions at the White House on February 10 and received a seemingly positive endorsement from the president.[81] And,

---

[78] Byrnes, *Speaking Frankly*, p. 123.

[79] Byrnes suggested that he brought Vandenberg to all conferences in 1946 so as to avoid misunderstandings. Byrnes, *All in One Lifetime*, p. 348.

[80] Byrnes provides a summary of his speech in *All in One Lifetime*, p. 350.

[81] For the thoughtful discussion of the February 10 meeting at the White House, see Harbutt, *The Iron Curtain*, pp. 161–65. Harbutt presents this meeting as a decisive turning point in American policy making. I think Harbutt overreads the extent to which Truman agreed to Churchill's entreaties.

in what is well known as one of the signature moments of the early Cold War, he expressed this view publicly in his famous speech at Westminster College in Fulton, Missouri, with the American president beside him on the dais.

Restraint must be exercised here in discussing one of the most famous speeches of the twentieth century. The endeavor primarily must be to discern the significance of the speech for Truman and American foreign policy. One must pass over the colorful details of the train ride to Missouri, the developing relationship between "Winston" and "Harry," the card playing, and Churchill's unrelenting consumption of whiskey and soda.[82] Along the way, Truman informed Churchill that he planned to use the battleship, the USS *Missouri*, to return the body of the Turkish ambassador, who had died during the war, back to his homeland. Admiral Leahy added that the powerful warship and an accompanying naval task force would remain in the eastern Mediterranean for an indefinite period as a show of support for the Turks.[83] One might have expected the introduction of this subject to spark a wide-ranging discussion of the pressing international situation, but poker took priority over international politics on this trip. Truman glanced at the final draft of Churchill's speech on the train and received a briefing on it from Byrnes, who had received an advance copy prior to his departure from Washington, but he maintained a public distance from it and later claimed he heard it at Westminster College for the first time. Whatever Truman's supposed concerns about the "babying" of the Soviets and his occasional forays toward a tough approach to them, he refrained from publicly endorsing Churchill's speech.

Clark Clifford, who, while technically acting as naval aide, had assumed some speechwriting duties at the time, captured Truman's disposition well in suggesting that the president "was torn between a growing sense of anger at, and distrust of, the Soviet Union and a residual hope that he could still work with Stalin." Truman instructed Clifford to put into his introduction of Churchill some positive words about Stalin so as "to keep open channels of communication" with the Soviet leader.[84] Thus, when Truman took the podium at Westminister College, he noted that he first had met both Churchill and Stalin at Potsdam. He admitted that he "became very fond of both of them" and

---

[82] For details on the trip to Independence, see Clark Clifford's recollections in *Counsel to the President*, pp. 99–101; and those of Harry H. Vaughan in Oral History Interview, January 14 & 16, 1963, HSTL, transcript pp. 140–42. Vaughan recalled that Churchill on receiving his first whiskey and soda held it up to the light and recalled: "You know, when I was a young subaltern in the South African War, the water was not fit to drink. To make it palatable, we had to put a bit of whiskey in it. By diligent effort I learned to like it."

[83] See Churchill's report on this exchange in his letter to Attlee and Bevin, March 7, 1946, Churchill Papers, Churchill Archive Center, Chur 2/4.

[84] Clifford, *Counsel to the President*, p. 102. The direct quotation is Clifford's summary of Truman's instruction.

PHOTO 16. Winston Churchill gives his famous V for victory sign as he and President Truman leave Union Station in Washington, D.C., on the special Baltimore & Ohio train en route to Fulton, Missouri, March 4, 1946. (Courtesy National Archives)

described them as "men, and they are leaders in this world today when we need leadership."[85] This hardly constituted an indication that a major change in American policy was in progress.

Churchill paid a tribute to the United Nations in his address but warned that in the face of twin dangers of war and tyranny the new organization might be challenged beyond its capacity. To bolster it, a "fraternal association" of the English-speaking peoples – led by the United States and Britain – was needed. Zeroing in on the source of international unease, the British statesman observed that no one knew "what Soviet Russia and its Communist international organization intends to do in the immediate future, or what are the limits, if any, to their expansive and proselytizing tendencies." Professing his admiration for the Russian people and for Stalin and his understanding of legitimate Russian security needs, he nevertheless felt obliged to place before his audience "certain

[85] Truman's introduction of Churchill, March 5, 1946, Harry S. Truman Papers: President's Secretary's File, HSTL, Box 115.

facts about the present position in Europe." There followed his famous *and* accurate assessment:

From Stettin in the Baltic to Trieste in the Adriatic, an iron curtain has descended across the Continent. Behind that line lie all the capitals of the ancient states of Central and Eastern Europe. Warsaw, Berlin, Prague, Vienna, Budapest, Belgrade, Bucharest and Sofia, all these famous cities and the populations around them lie in what I must call the Soviet sphere, and all are subject in one form or another, not only to Soviet influence but to a very high and, in many cases, increasing measure of control from Moscow.

Turning to Soviet intentions, Churchill discerned, again with telling accuracy, that the Soviets did not desire war. Rather, "what they desire is the fruits of war and indefinite expansion of their power and doctrines." In light of this and his belief that the Soviets respected strength rather than weakness, Churchill argued that the Anglo-American association must reach "a good understanding on all points with Russia under the general authority of the United Nations Organization."[86] In brief, the key elements of Churchill's policy were "strength and negotiations."[87]

In effect, Churchill recommended further negotiations with the Soviet Union in order to obtain a "settlement." Both Truman and Byrnes favored that possibility. But two additional points made the "iron curtain" speech controversial in the United States and prompted the American leaders to distance themselves from it. First, Churchill publicly and bluntly named the reality of Soviet control of Eastern Europe and asked where Soviet ambitions stopped. Second, Britain's wartime leader – the very one who opposed appeasement of Hitler and led his nation so courageously against the Nazis – raised the alert about another potential danger to peace, and he called for a unified Anglo-American effort to check it. This latter suggestion of the United States and Great Britain cooperating to confront the Soviet Union drew bitter criticism. "His speech," Klaus Larres summarized, "was condemned both in Britain and in the United States as the pronouncement of a warmonger."[88] The self-appointed doyen of American newspaper columnists, Walter Lippmann, branded the "iron curtain" speech an "almost catastrophic blunder" designed to gain American support for Britain's empire and to foster conflict between the United States and the Soviets.[89] Congressional critics like the liberal senators Claude Pepper and Glenn Taylor bellowed that Churchill aimed to "cut the throat of the United Nations Organization."[90]

---

[86] Churchill's speeches from his U.S. visit in 1946 including the "iron curtain" speech entitled "The Sinews of Peace," March 5, 1946, are included in Churchill Papers, Churchill Archives Center, Chur 5/4. For a detailed explication of it, see Martin Gilbert, *Winston Churchill*, Vol. VIII, pp. 197–203; and Harbutt, *Iron Curtain*, pp. 183–208.

[87] This point is made by Klaus Larres, *Churchill's Cold War*, p. 125.

[88] Larres, *Churchill's Cold War*, p. 106.

[89] Ronald Steel, *Walter Lippmann and the American Century* (Boston, 1980), pp. 428–29.

[90] See the story on the joint statement issued by Senators Pepper and Taylor criticizing Churchill's speech in *New York Times*, March 7, 1946, p. 1.

Truman held no desire to be linked to the "warmonger" calumny. As Clifford recalled, the president made a "distinction between his relationship with Churchill and his reaction to the speech, which he admired but whose message he was not yet ready to embrace."[91] To indicate the differences between himself and Churchill, Truman ordered Undersecretary Acheson not to attend a reception for the British leader in New York the following week because it might be seen as an official endorsement. And the president dispatched a message to Stalin expressing his desire for better relations and inviting the Soviet dictator to come to the United States to make a similar speech, "for exactly the same kind of reception." For good measure he even promised to introduce Stalin personally just as he had Churchill.[92]

Needless to say, Joseph Davies, who stayed in regular contact with Truman, used his influence to contest the main lines of Churchill's arguments. Davies saw Truman a number of times at the end of March and in early April. In a letter of April 3, he aimed to clarify for the president that his administration's policy remained "the preservation of Peace" by working through the UN organization and by maintaining unity among the wartime allies. He warned the president that the Soviet leadership would react negatively if they felt "they are being 'ganged up' on by Britain and ourselves." He congratulated Truman for maintaining "a position of absolute impartiality as between the rival fears and ambitions of Britain and Russia" and beseeched the president to make a reassuring public statement confirming this approach.[93] One might have thought that a president fully converted to a "get tough" approach to the Soviets might have found better uses for his time than regular meetings with one of Stalin's most well-placed American apologists. Yet Truman remained to be fully converted. He replied to Davies on April 4 in a reassuring tone and suggested to Davies that he would be pleased with an upcoming Chicago speech, "which covers the situation thoroughly and in a manner which will clear up any misunderstanding."[94]

Two days later, Truman gave a national broadcast address on Army Day from Chicago. In it, the president paid a tribute to "that gallant warrior in the White House – Franklin D. Roosevelt," and emphasized that the United States would remain strong in its quest for peace. In words that must have

---

91 Clifford, *Counsel to the President*, p. 108. In a personal letter to Churchill on March 12, 1946, Truman thanked Churchill for his visit and reported that "the people of Missouri were highly pleased with your visit and enjoyed what you had to say." Noticeably absent was any supportive reaction of his own to the speech. See Truman to Churchill, March 12, 1946, Harry S. Truman Papers: President's Secretary's File, HSTL, Box 115.

92 The above sentences rely on Clifford, *Counsel to the President*, p. 108.

93 Davies to Truman, April 3, 1946, Harry S. Truman Papers: President's Secretary's File, HSTL, Box 117. Indicative of Davies's continuing regular contact with Truman he visited the White House March 27 and 28 and April 3. See Davies diary, Joseph E. Davies Papers, Library of Congress, Box 23.

94 Truman to Davies, April 4, 1946, Harry S. Truman Papers: President's Secretary's File, HSTL, Box 117.

pleased Davies, he also revealed his "conviction that the Security Council of the United Nations . . . is fully capable of reaching agreements between the peoples of the world – however different their traditions and philosophies, and however divergent their interests." The president proceeded to a brief tour d'horizon of major areas of concern in the world – the Far East, the Middle East, and Europe. In his survey, he refrained from explicitly identifying the Soviets as the source of problems in any area. On the contrary, he optimistically gave such assurances as: "In Korea we are even now working with our Soviet Allies and with the Korean leadership to create a provisional democratic government" and "No country, great or small, has legitimate interests in the Near and Middle East which cannot be reconciled with the interest of other nations through the United Nations."[95] These were not the words of a president now convinced that he must lead the United States forcefully to contest Soviet power and influence.

Churchill had reported to Attlee and Bevin right after his Fulton address that, based on his association with the president and his inner circle over the previous days, he believed they were disturbed by Russian actions and partial to the Churchillian approach that "some show of strength and resisting power is necessary to a good settlement with Russia." He predicted that "this will be the prevailing opinion in the United States in the near future."[96] As it turned out, however, it took rather longer for the Churchill view to prevail than he predicted and, yet again, this must be understood well in order to appreciate how the Cold War evolved. The combination of the Kennan and Churchill efforts certainly helped both to erode the legitimacy of the policy of cooperation with the Soviet Union and to transform the perception of the Soviets in the American official mind from difficult ally to potential foe.[97] But it is striking to gauge how little positive impact on policy this new perception of the Soviets actually exercised. The United States possessed by the end of March 1946 an enhanced disposition to challenge and to confront the Soviets on particular incidents. Byrnes certainly displayed this in standing up vigorously and forcing the Soviets to abandon their occupation of northern Iran that very month.[98] But such a disposition hardly constituted a coherent policy that could be explained to the American congress and people. The Long Telegram and the "iron curtain" address in no sense put an end to the floundering in American policy formulation. After her detailed examination, Deborah Welch Larson astutely concluded that even "at the end of a year [1946] of drift and indecision, of waffling between confrontation

95 "Address in Chicago on Army Day," April 6, 1946, Truman, *Public Papers of the Presidents of the United States: Harry S. Truman, 1946*, pp. 185–90.
96 Churchill to Attlee, March 7, 1946, Churchill Papers, Churchill Archive Center, Chur 2/4.
97 On "policy legitimacy," see Alexander L. George, "Domestic Constraints on Regime Change in U.S. Foreign Policy: the Need for Policy Legitimacy," in Ole R. Holsti, Randolph M. Siverson, and Alexander L. George, eds., *Change in the International System* (Boulder, CO, 1980), pp. 232–62. Also note the argument of John Lewis Gaddis that "from this time on American policymakers regarded the Soviet Union not as an estranged ally, but as a potential enemy, whose vital interests could not be recognized without endangering those of the United States." Gaddis, *The United States and the Origins of the Cold War*, p. 284.
98 For a full account of Byrnes's efforts on Iran, see Robertson, *Sly and Able*, pp. 462–76.

and collaboration, Truman still had no new policy, nor did he perceive any alternatives to the present policies, except the unacceptable prospect of war."[99] Policy, it would seem, could not be created by either a document or a speech. It was much more complicated – a reality which historians wedded to the importance of a certain document or speech sometimes neglect.[100]

A greater disposition of firmness characterized American policy in the spring of 1946, but an even more notable feature of the Truman administration's policy resided in its ad hoc quality. This manifested itself on a number of issues and revealed an administration that largely operated without an over-all strategic framework. The president failed to provide broad guidance. He still waited for policy recommendations to come to him and relied heavily on Byrnes. His engagement with foreign policy remained episodic at best.[101] Certainly he played no important role in the development of policy on Germany in 1946, where General Clay, the head of the American occupation, worked with substantial independence. In the early months of the year, Clay aimed to gain Soviet support to establish a unified economic administration for all of Germany. When in May of 1946 he suspended reparations payments to both the French and Soviet occupation zones, he intended the measure to force coopera-tion from these two states. Senior figures in the State Department, like Acheson and Will Clayton, continued their efforts to fashion a four-power accord on Germany that would attract the Kremlin's interest and support.[102] They gave no indication of giving up on the possibilities of negotiation and compromise with Moscow.

Further confirmation that the combined Kennan/Churchill salvo failed to provoke a major reversal in American policy came with the determination of policy on the international control of atomic weapons. Byrnes tasked Acheson to lead the formulation of an American proposal to submit to the newly established UN Atomic Energy Commission. Acheson built upon his earlier efforts supporting Stimson. With the significant assistance of David Lilienthal of the Tennessee Valley Authority and Robert Oppenheimer, he fashioned the "Acheson–Lilienthal report." This document's proposals called for genuine international control of nuclear research and technology. And, as Robert Beisner explained, "precisely to attract Soviet support, they [Acheson, Lilienthal and

---

[99] Larson, *Origins of Containment*, p. 301.

[100] Clark Clifford appreciated the point and noted of Churchill's speech that "there is a natural tendency to simplify history and give it more coherence than a detailed examination of the facts warrants. The Fulton speech is now treated as revelation and prophecy, a turning point in the evolution of policy and popular understanding of the Soviet threat." He went on to contest that interpretation. Clifford, *Counsel to the President*, p. 107.

[101] Robert Ferrell has it right in noting that "the president's part in diplomatic events of late 1945 and throughout 1946 is not easy to discern, and one has the feeling that it was most formal. In family letters he stressed busyness with domestic politics. On only a few occasions did he undertake personal contributions to foreign policy." Ferrell, *Harry S. Truman: A Life*, p. 234.

[102] On German policy, see Leffler, *The Struggle for Germany, and the Origins of the Cold War*, pp. 28–30. Also see Walt W. Rostow, *The Division of Europe After World War II: 1946* (Austin, 1981).

Oppenheimer] deemphasized inspections, which they saw as resistant to accomplishment, incapable of offering foolproof protection, and profoundly intrusive to Russian leaders."[103]

When Truman and Byrnes, in a bid to ensure congressional support for the American initiative, appointed Bernard Baruch, an elderly, vain, but politically well-connected financier, as a special envoy to present the American proposal at the United Nations, they indicated no dissatisfaction with the Acheson–Lilienthal proposal.[104] Rather, Baruch took the initiative and revised the plan to include inspections, sanctions for violations and a specific ban on using the UN security council veto to escape punishment in this area.[105] In April 1946, Baruch had pressed Oppenheimer on the fundamental point of whether the Acheson–Lilienthal plan was "compatible with the current Soviet system of government." In reply, the brilliant physicist admitted some concerns in that regard but argued that the American position "should be to make an honorable proposal and thus find out whether they have the will to cooperate."[106] Acheson and Lilienthal certainly endorsed this approach to obtain Soviet cooperation through to the middle of the year. Baruch, however, proved unwilling to forego inspections and sanctions and, in June, forced a showdown, which compelled Truman, who appeared to decide more in "sorrow than in anger," to endorse his delegate to the UN. He could hardly afford Baruch's resignation, which assuredly would have prompted a congressional outcry. Furthermore, by July, the president clearly leaned toward Baruch's position. He told the one-time donor to his 1940 reelection campaign, that "we should not under any circumstances throw away our gun until we are sure the rest of the world can't arm against us."[107] He didn't rule out international control, but any arrangements could not gamble with American security by simply relying on Russian good faith. In retrospect, this seems a reasonable position especially given the nature of the Soviet system and the sustained campaign of Soviet espionage to gain information of the atomic bomb. That it took Truman until mid-1946 to reach it, and then only because Baruch brought matters to a head, is truly notable.

---

[103] Beisner, "Patterns of Peril," p. 330. For Oppenheimer's important role in drafting the plan, see Bird and Sherwin, *American Prometheus*, pp. 340–42.

[104] On the reasons for Baruch's appointment, see Truman, *Memoirs*, Vol. II, *Years of Trial and Hope* (New York, 1956), pp. 20–21. On this appointment, also see Byrnes's letter to Baruch of April 19, 1946, in which the secretary of state explained that "I have advised you that I am favorably impressed by the report which has come to be called the State Department report and which was prepared under the direction of Mr. Acheson. I have, however, advised you that I am not of the opinion that it is the last word on the subject and, on the contrary, that I shall give careful consideration to any views that may be presented by you after you consider the problem." Byrnes to Baruch, April 19, 1946, Harry S. Truman Papers: President's Secretary's File, HSTL, Box 113.

[105] On Baruch and his nuclear activities, see Margaret Coit, *Mr. Baruch* (Boston, 1957), pp. 565–85. Also see Hewlett and Anderson, *The New World*, pp. 562–76.

[106] Oppenheimer quote in Bird and Sherwin, *American Prometheus*, p. 343.

[107] Truman to Baruch, July 10, 1946, quoted in Truman, *Years of Trial and Hope*, p. 25.

The American desire to control carefully the sharing of information on atomic weapons and technology was applied concurrently and with much less justification against Britain, the nation that had partnered the United States in the Manhattan Project. Giving the lie to the view that the Truman administration had been persuaded by Churchill's notion of a close association between the two democracies, Truman signed the McMahon bill into law on August 1, 1946. He enthusiastically endorsed the bill's provisions guaranteeing civilian control of atomic energy, but he also supported its provisions that sharply limited any international exchanges of information including with Great Britain.[108] Attlee's government vigorously objected to such arrangements, which it saw as being in direct contradiction to the agreement Truman had signed in November of 1945 with the British and Canadian prime ministers. Undeterred by the November agreement, which promised "full and effective cooperation in the field of atomic energy," Truman shamelessly defended the new arrangement much to Britain's dismay.[109] Clearly, the American strategy, if that be the term, in 1946 involved no effort to work closely with Britain in displaying close Western cooperation to the Soviets. The United States obviously felt no special need to boost British power in the Anglo-Soviet contest.

There must have been moments during 1946 when Secretary Byrnes truly wished the United States had rejected negotiation and had decided simply to meet Soviet attempts at expansion with clear demonstrations of force. This presumably would have saved him from the purgatorial experience of participating in a series of tortuous international conferences designed to secure peace treaties with the former Axis allies. Instead, Byrnes demonstrated his possession of sizable quantities of both patience and firmness as he worked in meetings in Paris and New York right through to the end of 1946 to negotiate treaties with Italy, Finland, Bulgaria, Hungary, and Romania.[110] He still hoped that these would be preliminary to the wartime allies reaching further treaties with Germany and Austria, although Soviet intransigence in cooperating on German matters dimmed his hopes regarding this possibility.[111] The Soviet refusal to cooperate on a unified economic approach in Germany prompted policy initiatives by Byrnes in the latter half of 1946, as we shall see, but these did not end his hopes for an appropriate settlement with the Soviet Union. To this end over the course of 1946, Byrnes held his nose, formally recognized the governments of Bulgaria, Rumania, and Hungary, and negotiated peace treaties with them.

---

[108] Truman gives his perspective on this matter in *Years of Trial and Hope*, pp. 25–30.

[109] For background detail, see Margaret Gowing, *Independence and Deterrence: Britain and Atomic Energy, 1945–1952* (London, 1974), pp. 104–13.

[110] For Byrnes own account of his efforts, see *Speaking Frankly*, pp. 123–55.

[111] Byrnes, *Speaking Frankly*, p. 203. Discussing the German issue in 1947, Byrnes noted: "The United States wants no separate peace. We trod that path once before. We want to make the peace collectively – with all the Allies if possible. But if it is not possible to secure the co-operation of all states, we should seek to enlist the assistance of as many as are willing to join in the task."

Ultimately he refused to end the possibility of cooperation by holding out for more legitimate governments. He essentially held to the Potsdam settlement.[112]

On April 12, Byrnes visited the U.S. Naval Hospital at Bethesda, Maryland, for a medical examination that revealed "added myocardial damage," which was interpreted "as indicating chronic coronary sclerosis." The naval doctor advised his patient "to refrain from excesses of physical exertion and mental strain and to avoid gaining weight."[113] A few days later, the secretary of state submitted a letter of resignation to President Truman reporting that he must "slow down." Certainly this was a genuine desire on Byrnes's part, but he also must have wished to put an end to the constant media criticism of his efforts – some of which was inspired by his critics within the administration like Leahy. Nonetheless, Byrnes graciously thanked Truman for his "wholehearted support" and noted that despite "the controversial character of the problems that have confronted us, it is rather remarkable that we have never failed to agree as to foreign policies."[114] Byrnes volunteered to soldier on until the Paris peace conference to wrap up the peace treaties and Truman accepted the arrangement. Later, the president recalled that "Byrnes became obsessed with a 'bad heart' and quit me at a crucial moment," but his animus to the South Carolinian had mounted by that point after the 1948 election campaign and its aftermath.[115] In 1946, it appears that he and Byrnes continued their cooperation with Byrnes still taking the lead on major matters.

Byrnes's "patience with firmness" approach received the favorable endorsement of Senator Vandenberg who became a regular participant in the international gatherings as a member of the American delegation. Reporting to John Foster Dulles from a Paris meeting of the CFM in May 1946, the Michigan senator confided that "Byrnes has 'stood up' 100%. He only 'almost weakened' once – at which point I put on one of my well-known exhibitions." Indicative however of his view that American policy was still in some flux, Vandenberg observed to Dulles: "I am more than ever convinced that communism is on the march on a world-wide scale which only America can stop. I am equally convinced that we can stop it <u>short of war if we take</u> the moral leadership which a dismayed and disorganized world awaits (with WANING expectancy) and if we clear the track at home."[116] What exactly Vandenberg meant by "clearing the track at home" remains unclear. Perhaps he meant that officials like Undersecretary Acheson, who still worked for cooperative settlements with the Soviets, would need to be converted to his own tough approach. Perhaps

---

[112] For notes on the public release and then the signing of the peace treaties with Bulgaria, Hungary, and Rumania (as well as Italy), see *Department of State Bulletin*, 16 (January 26, 1947), p. 167; and 16 (February 2, 1947), p. 199.

[113] See the medical report in James F. Byrnes Papers, Cooper Library, Folder 617.

[114] Byrnes to Truman, April 16, 1946, James F. Byrnes Papers, Cooper Library, Folder 618.

[115] Truman confided this evaluation of Byrnes in a letter to his cousin Ethel Noland, September 13, 1950, in Ferrell, ed., *Off the Record*, p. 191.

[116] Vandenberg to Dulles, May 13, 1946, John Foster Dulles Papers, Seeley G. Mudd Manuscript Library, Box 30 (underlining and capitals as in original).

he meant further that the American president would have to demonstrate the "moral leadership" to halt the worldwide march of communism. If so, then Vandenberg's hopes were to be realized. In the second half of 1946, Acheson increasingly adopted the policy of toughness and confrontation as his own, and he eventually would guide Truman on how to implement it.

Gauging and Facing the Soviet Threat

Judging the extent of Stalin's expansionist intentions and the nature of the Soviet threat has proved to be a controversial topic among Western historians. Many historians of a revisionist perspective, and even some in the "post-revisionist" camp, tended to emphasize the limited nature of Stalin's ambitions. This allowed them to argue that if only the Truman administration policy makers had been more wise and insightful in 1945–47 and conceded Stalin's supposedly legitimate security needs in Eastern Europe, then the Cold War might have been avoided.[117] In variations of this formulation, the United States overreacted to Stalin's actions and, especially through the Marshall Plan in 1947, forced the Soviet leader to cement his total control of Eastern Europe.[118] American exaggeration of the supposed Soviet threat and excessive response to what was allegedly "a figment of American imaginations" brought on the four-decade conflict, which, one must note, mercifully ended with the collapse of the Soviet Union.[119] The naivete about Stalin that grounded such assertions and the sheer misunderstanding of American policy in 1945–46 can only be described as staggering. Rightly or wrongly, Truman and Byrnes followed FDR in refusing to contest the Soviet domination of Eastern Europe. Ultimately, their concerns about Moscow grew from fears that Soviet designs stretched far beyond their East European sphere. These fears were well grounded, to say the least.

Since the end of the Cold War and the limited opening of Soviet and East European archives, historians have shed important new light on Stalin's motives and actions. While some emphasized that Stalin, although obsessed by his "insatiable craving" for security, possessed no "master plan" for expansion and that he acted opportunistically, it has become increasingly difficult to remove the Soviet dictator from the center of a story of an unappeasable appetite for

---

[117] For a classic revisionist position, note Gabriel Kolko's argument that "the Russians...had no intention of Bolshevizing Eastern Europe if – but only if – they could find alternatives." Kolko, *Politics of War*, p. 619. For a more recent example, see Offner's *Another Such Victory*.

[118] See, for example, Scott Parrish, "The Marshall Plan, Soviet-American Relations, and the Division of Europe," in Norman Naimark and Leonid Gibianskii, eds., *The Establishment of Communist Regimes in Eastern Europe, 1944–1949* (Boulder, CO, 1997), pp. 269–90; and Michael Cox and Caroline Kennedy-Pipe, "The Tragedy of American Diplomacy? Rethinking the Marshall Plan," *Journal of Cold War Studies*, 7 (Winter 2005), pp. 97–134. Also see the withering critique of the Cox–Kennedy-Pipe essay by Laszlo Borhi entitled "Was American Diplomacy Really Tragic?" *Journal of Cold War Studies*, 7 (Winter 2005), pp. 159–67.

[119] The quoted words are those of Walter Laqueur, *The Dream that Failed: Reflections on the Soviet Union* (New York, 1994), p. 122. Laqueur's comments (pp. 121–25) influenced my own thinking.

control.[120] This was a man, after all, who feared and distrusted the very people who expended twenty million lives to defend their homeland. "Instead of relaxing repression after the war," Anne Applebaum has noted, "the Soviet leadership embarked on a new series of arrests, again attacking the army, as well as select ethnic minorities, including Soviet Jews."[121] After the war, Soviet ex-POWs and other citizens who had contacts beyond the realm of Stalin's propaganda machine, especially Ukrainian and Baltic nationals, found themselves placed in "a series of so-called 'filtration camps,' in which experienced NKVD/NKGB and officers of Smersh (Stalin's murderous counterespionage apparatus) separated 'lambs' from 'wolves,' sending the latter to expiate their sins in Siberia and other distant places."[122] Thousands upon thousands were dispatched to the Gulag Archipelago in a vain effort to reassure a twisted and vile man.

In retrospect, it can be seen that Stalin – at least theoretically – faced two broad choices at the war's end. The first, as articulated by Vladimir A. Pozniakov, involved "political and economic cooperation with the Allies and with the west in general." Such an approach "could lessen tensions that had surfaced in interallied relations by the end of the war, lower the level of military expenditures, and thus allow more rapid restoration of the Soviet national economy and higher living standards in the Soviet Union." The second possibility "was to impose tighter control over the Soviet people, crushing hopes for change in the Soviet political and social system" so as to provide the basis for forging a Soviet empire, supposedly needed to guarantee Soviet security. Stalin, of course, chose the latter and so planned for a policy of confrontation with the West which, as Pozniakov explained, "could also help to solve many domestic problems; by creating new images of enemies abroad and at home, Stalin could easily explain and justify the necessity of maintaining strict control over domestic life, suppression of real and imaginary opposition, and inevitable privations for the population." Additionally, he "could also justify maintaining strict military and political control over neighboring states."[123]

In the early years after the war, Stalin gave some show of allowing independence to the states of Eastern and Central Europe. In the euphemisms of the day, he permitted "peoples democracies" where all "friendly" groups might be represented in "national front" governments. This strategy may now be seen

[120] See, for example, Vojtech Mastney, *The Cold War and Soviet Insecurity: The Stalin Years* (New York, 1996); and Vladislav Zubok and Constantine Pleshakov, *Inside the Kremlin's Cold War.* See the critical review of these works in Richard C. Raack, "The Cold War Revisionists Kayoed: New Books Dispel More Historical Darkness," *World Affairs*, 162 (Fall 1999), pp. 43–62. Also see Ilya Gaiduk, "Stalin: Three Approaches to One Phenomenon," *Diplomatic History*, 23 (Winter 1999), pp. 119–25.

[121] Anne Applebaum, *Gulag: A History*, pbk. ed. (New York, 2004), p. 462.

[122] Vladimir V. Pozniakov, "Commoners, Commissars, and Spies: Soviet Policies and Society, 1945," in Arnold A. Offner and Theodore A. Wilson, eds., *Victory in Europe 1945: From World War to Cold War* (Lawrence, KS, 2000), p. 188.

[123] Pozniakov, "Commoners, Commissars, and Spies," p. 197.

as an effort to dupe Western leaders and peoples as Stalin pursued his ambitious agenda. Stalin, at least, apparently had no doubts on the matter. As is well known, he told the Yugoslav communist Milovan Djilas as the war ended that "this war is not as in the past; whoever occupies a territory also imposes on it his own social system. Everyone imposes his own system as far as his army can reach. It cannot be otherwise."[124] As two distinguished scholars of postwar Soviet behavior have concluded, "[F]rom the very beginning of their occupation of Eastern Europe, the Soviets manipulated East European leaders, bullied and deceived the populations, arrested and shot political opponents. They operated cynically and forcefully to accomplish their aims."[125] A Russian specialist in the history of Soviet espionage elucidated that in the second half of 1944 and through 1945 "Soviet intelligence and counterintelligence services secured almost total control over the newborn governments of Poland, Bulgaria, and Romania; heavily penetrated those of Czechoslovakia, Hungary, Finland, and Albania; and operated wide networks in Yugoslavia, Greece, Iran, and Turkey."[126] Such control along with the brutality and violence it engendered is not to be minimized; yet Stalin held back a little.[127] He could tolerate some delay in his ultimate goal of the sovietization of Eastern Europe in order to lay the groundwork for Soviet expansion elsewhere. His strategy is persuasively demonstrated by Eduard Mark who revealed that Stalin aimed to advance socialism by "caution and deception" and that his "national-front strategy" applied to Western Europe – Italy, France, and Germany – as well as to the East.[128]

American observers on the spot told the story of increasing Soviet domination early on.[129] Sadly they received a limited hearing. The region simply did not constitute a vital American interest. Indeed, based on American policies in 1945 and the first half of 1946, Stalin might have been able to pursue his chosen approach of sovietization without much objection from the United States if he

---

[124] Milovan Djilas, *Conversations with Stalin* (New York, 1962), p. 114.

[125] Norman Naimark and Leonid Gibianskii, "Introduction," in Naimark and Gibianskii, eds., *Establishment of Communist Regimes in Eastern Europe*, p. 10. The authors further explained that "for most Central Committee leaders, there is no question that the period of diversity from 1944–45 to the end of 1947 was nothing more than a tactical maneuver to prepare for final communization of the region. Foreign ministry archives in both Russia (AVPRF) and in the countries of Eastern Europe support this conclusion." On this point, also see Vladislav Zubok, "Stalin's Plans and Russian Archives," *Diplomatic History*, 21 (Spring 1997), pp. 298–99.

[126] Pozniakov, "Commoners, Commissars, and Spies," p. 196.

[127] The essays in Naimark and Gibianskii, eds., *Establishment of Communist Regimes in Eastern Europe*, tell the tragic story. See in particular "'Bandits and Reactionaries': The Suppression of the Opposition in Poland, 1944–1946," pp. 93–110.

[128] Eduard Mark, "Revolution by Degrees: Stalin's National Front Strategy for Europe, 1941–47," Working Paper No. 31, Cold War International History Project, Washington, DC, February 2001.

[129] For the recollections of American observers who tried to raise the alarm about Soviet actions in Eastern Europe, see the essays in Thomas T. Hammond, ed., *Witnesses to the Origins of the Cold War* (Seattle, 1982).

had been able to limit his external goals. If Stalin had learned a lesson from the Iran episode in March of 1946 and sat back to enjoy an empire that reached beyond the accomplishment of any of his Czarist forebears, the Cold War might have been averted. But he could not. Stalin overreached and moved beyond cementing his control of Eastern Europe to threaten both in the Mediterranean, particularly in Turkey, and in Western Europe. In this disastrous choice lies the immediate origins of the Cold War.[130] Such was Stalin's paranoid definition of security that he provoked the United States to act, to do what Ernest Bevin had long requested. Turkey and Germany provided the occasions for the initial, major American actions.

As an old man, Viacheslav Molotov recalled that his "task as minister of foreign affairs was to expand the borders of our Fatherland," and he seemed pleased that he and Stalin "coped with this task quite well."[131] But in the matter of Soviet demands on Turkey, including for joint control of the Dardanelles, he recalled that he cautioned Stalin that the Western allies "won't allow it." In response, his master instructed him: "Demand it!"[132] Stalin's desire to impose his will on the Turks reached its climax in August–September of 1946. On August 7, the Soviet Union dispatched a demanding note to Turkey renewing their request for a revision of the Montreaux Treaty, which governed the Turkish Straits. The Soviets enjoined the Turks to accept a joint Soviet-Turkish "defense" of the waterway, which would allow them to establish Soviet military bases on Turkish soil. Official Washington reacted vigorously against these Soviet demands, and it did so, as Eduard Mark has explained, because American officials feared that Soviet troop movements in the Balkans in the summer of 1946 bespoke a major effort to intimidate Turkey and possibly foreshadowed a military attack to force satellite status upon the Turks.[133]

In Washington, the Turkish crisis finally pushed Undersecretary Acheson into the ranks of the cold warriors and he led the charge in fashioning the American response.[134] Acheson in August of 1946 was running the State Department during Byrnes's absence at meetings in Paris, and he guided Truman in the American response on the Turkish crisis. A man of formidable intelligence, Acheson had clerked for Justice Louis Brandeis who "taught him to be both a pragmatist and an empiricist." In his approach to foreign policy – both in 1946 and also later as secretary of state – he "was very much a practical man, one who eschewed

---

[130] John Lewis Gaddis states the matter clearly in his *We Now Know*, p. 25. "Did Stalin therefore seek a Cold War?" Gaddis asked. "The question is a little like asking: 'does a fish seek water?' Suspicion, distrust, and an abiding cynicism were not only his preferred but his necessary environment; he could not function apart from it."

[131] Quoted in Resis, ed., *Molotov Remembers*, p. 8.

[132] Quoted in Resis, ed., *Molotov Remembers*, p. 73.

[133] See Mark's impressively researched article entitled "The War Scare of 1946 and Its Consequences," *Diplomatic History*, 21 (Summer 1997), pp. 383–415.

[134] For further details, see Beisner, "Patterns of Peril," pp. 342–46. I also have had the privilege to see Beisner's discussion of this matter included in his forthcoming and magisterial study of Acheson's service as secretary of state.

visionary schemes." He approached problems directly and was "influenced by solid evidence and concrete situations."[135] Now the evidence on Soviet designs on Turkey seemed incontrovertible to Acheson, and it warranted a strong American response. At a meeting of the State–War–Navy Coordinating Committee (SWNCC) on August 14, he argued that the "only real deterrent to Soviet plans for engulfing Turkey and the Middle East" would "be the conviction that pursuance of such a policy will result in war with the United States."[136] He argued without objection that it should be American policy to support Turkey.

The following day, Acheson, along with Navy Secretary Forrestal and Acting Secretary of War Kenneth C. Royall, put this position to the president they served. Acheson summarized the SWNCC paper. If the Soviets weren't confronted in Turkey, they would proceed to threaten the "whole Near and Middle East." Success in Turkey would confirm them in their expansionist aims. To deter the Soviets, the United States would need to indicate its willingness, "if necessary, to meet aggression with the force of arms." Acheson asked at this stage for authorization to send a firm note of warning to Moscow and also for the Navy to be authorized to strengthen its presence in the eastern Mediterranean significantly. Truman quickly endorsed both measures. But, Acheson wanted to clarify that this might only be the start of a series of escalating steps that could end with outright conflict. In a memorable exchange, he asked Truman if he understood the significance of his decision. Truman, holding that "we might as well find out whether the Russians were bent on world conquest now as in five or ten years," took the occasion to take a map of the Middle East from his desk and to lecture on the region's strategic significance.[137] This was the "Truman" of later public memory, the one ready to take the tough decision and to live with it.

Acheson soon dispatched the U.S. note of protest and warning to the Soviet Union, and Truman ordered the newest American aircraft carrier, the *USS Franklin D. Roosevelt*, and its supporting vessels into the area. Interestingly, as Mark has shown, this brought no quick end to Soviet intimidation of Turkey. Mark's review of intelligence reporting revealed that "what had been in August a steady trickle of reports about Soviet military preparations in the Balkans became in mid-September a torrent." Further reports continued of the Soviets sending infiltrators into Turkey "to fan the flames of separatism and ethnic discord."[138] In such circumstances, the American military began to plan explicitly for war with the Soviet Union and in September 1946 to have discussions

---

[135] These observations on Acheson are drawn from Walter Isaacson and Evan Thomas, *The Wise Men: Six Friends and the World They Made* (New York, 1986), pp. 126, 323–24, 362.

[136] Details of the August 14 meeting are in Mark, "War Scare of 1946 and Its Consequences," pp. 399–400.

[137] On the August 15 meeting, see Mark, "War Scare of 1946 and Its Consequences," pp. 383, 399–400. Also see Forrestal's contemporaneous account in Millis, ed., *Forrestal Diaries*, p. 192.

[138] Mark, "War Scare of 1946 and Its Consequences," pp. 402, 401.

with the British on strategic options.[139] Eventually, alerted to the firmness of American intentions by his British spy in Washington, Donald MacLean, "Stalin back-pedalled," and abruptly adopted a much more conciliatory approach to Turkey.[140] His gambit to gain influence and control in Turkey succeeded in stirring American policy makers into action. "By the end of the year," Eduard Mark noted, these "policymakers had accepted the postulate that war was always possible as long as Moscow pursued expansionist designs, a full set of war plans was nearing completion, and American and British planners had devised a common strategy for fighting the USSR."[141] Looked at through the long view, one must count Stalin's threat against Turkey as a strategic blunder of sizable proportions for it drew the United States directly into an arena where the Soviet dictator had thought he could exploit British weakness. His strategic blunders did not end there.

In June 1946, Maxim Litvinov, onetime People's commissar of foreign affairs and wartime Soviet ambassador in Washington, met the CBS correspondent in Moscow, Richard Hottelet, and warned of "a return in Russia to the outmoded concept of security in terms of territory – the more you've got the safer you are." Litvinov, who wanted U.S.-Soviet collaboration, counseled that accession to Soviet demands "would lead to the West being faced, after a more or less short time, with the next series of demands."[142] This conforms with Molotov's assertion that "our ideology stands for offensive operations, when possible, and if not, we wait."[143] The Turkish episode pushed the United States further along a course where it would become national policy to resist Soviet demands and to create a barrier of sorts to their offensive operations especially in Europe. FDR had not conceived of such a commitment by the United States, but less than two years after his death, Jimmy Byrnes recognized the need to apply a variation of the new approach in Germany.

After the war, the Red Army brutalized the population of its zone in Germany with looting, physical assaults, and the mass rape of German women being the order of the day.[144] Independent of that savagery, Stalin advised the German communist leader, Wilhelm Pieck, in June 1945 to pursue a German version of the national front strategy he recommended to various East European communists. "It was too early, [Stalin] stressed, to impose the Soviet system on Germany."[145] This strategy took particular form in late 1945 and early 1946 through sustained pressure on and harassment of the Socialist party in the

---

[139] Mark discussed these in "War Scare of 1946 and Its Consequences," pp. 403–08.

[140] Mark, "War Scare of 1946 and Its Consequences," p. 408.

[141] Mark, "War Scare of 1946 and Its Consequences," p. 412.

[142] Quoted in David Holloway, *Stalin and the Bomb*, p. 167.

[143] See Resis, ed., *Molotov Remembers*, p. 29.

[144] For details, see Norman N. Naimark, *The Russians in Germany: A History of the Soviet Zone of Occupation, 1945-1949* (Cambridge, MA, 1995).

[145] The quotation is from Eduard Mark summarizing Stalin's instruction that German communists should pursue the national front strategy. See Mark's paper "Revolution by Degrees." On Stalin's efforts in Germany, also see R. C. Raack, *Stalin's Drive to the West*, pp. 112–13.

eastern zone (SPD) which was forced to merge with the Communist party (KPD) to form a new party. This "fusion of the SPD and KPD had tremendous political implications that extended beyond the eastern zone," as James McAllister noted. "If Stalin's only concern was with political control in the eastern zone, he could have forced the SPD to dissolve itself into the KPD and spared himself all of the complications involved in the creation of the Socialist Unity Party (SED)." But, as McAllister observed, "a more plausible interpretation of the fusion decision is that Stalin was hoping to create a political party that could have appeal in both the western and eastern zones."[146] The British saw the political danger of Stalin's move for the western zones, and they quickly shelved any plans to detach the Ruhr from a new German state. Instead, they looked to work with Byrnes to secure the western half of their recently defeated foe.

The economic situation in Germany particularly troubled the American secretary of state. Under his general direction, General Clay had suspended reparations payments from the American zone in an effort to force greater cooperation from the Soviets and the French in the economic stabilization of the country. This produced no immediate results, and Byrnes moved ahead with plans to join the British and American zones into one economic unit so as to arrest the economic deterioration in Germany, which provided fertile ground for a party such as the SED.[147] He had offered to merge the American zone with that of any other power willing to treat Germany as one economy, but the British proved his only taker. Molotov used the forum of the Paris CFM to denounce Byrnes's approach and to play to the Germans by characterizing Western intentions as being to partition Germany and to separate its Ruhr industries from it.[148]

With the Soviet pressure on Turkey as a backdrop, Byrnes took the occasion of a speech at the Stuttgart Opera House to counter Molotov's remarks. Speaking to an audience that included many Germans, the secretary of state sought to quell anxiety that the American forces would leave them to face the Red Army. "We will not shirk our duty. We are not withdrawing," he promised. Obviously clarifying that the Americans would stay as long as the Soviets, he informed his audience that so "long as there is an occupation army in Germany, American armed forces will be part of that occupation army." Furthermore, the American policy maker pledged that his people would "help the German people to win their way back to an honorable place among the free and peace-loving nations of the world." Byrnes also addressed the matter of German unification. "If complete unification cannot be secured," he expounded, "we shall do everything in

---

[146] James McAllister, *No Exit*, p. 108. I rely on McAllister's fine work for subsequent discussion of this matter.

[147] Melvyn Leffler notes that "American and British officials feared that the hardship and deprivation within their areas of control might redound to the benefit of the Kremlin's minions should they be allowed to compete on equal terms and under the guise of a joint partnership with the more moderate Social Democrats." Leffler, *The Struggle for Germany and the Origins of the Cold War*, p. 33.

[148] McAllister, *No Exit*, pp. 114–15.

our power to secure maximum possible unification." He pointedly confirmed that "we do not want Germany to become the satellite of any power."[149]

The Stuttgart declaration that the United States would work for German political and economic rehabilitation prompted Joseph Davies to judge that "Byrnes has 'crossed the Rubicon.'" The untiring advocate for "cooperation" with Stalin realized that the Byrnes speech meant two things: "first, increased tension between the Anglo-Americans and the Russians; second, increased competition among the victorious allies for the good-will of the defeated Germans."[150] It meant much more. Through his speech, Byrnes, as McAllister noted, "went a long way toward distancing the Truman administration from the legacy of the Morgenthau Plan and the popular perception that America would quickly withdraw from Europe."[151] FDR loathed the Germans and wanted the German state reduced in the significance it played in world affairs as part of his larger effort to downgrade the importance of Europe. At Yalta he proffered that American troops would be out of Europe within two years. In contrast, Byrnes came to terms with the reality that Germany and Europe could not be reduced in significance. He accepted that the future of Germany was integral to the future of Europe and that ultimately the United States had vital interests at stake in the matter. Byrnes's successor as secretary of state would act further in light of this fundamental belief the following year.

While the Soviet threat to Turkey pushed Acheson firmly into the confrontation camp and while concern for Germany confirmed Byrnes in measures to arrest the Soviet challenge, President Truman moved at his own pace to cut the cord that still linked him to the Roosevelt approach of conciliation. Obviously, he had approved the strong actions in Turkey, and he endorsed Byrnes's efforts in Germany, but there is evidence that Truman still floundered in an effort to grasp fully Soviet actions and the appropriate measures to resist them. In the summer of 1946, he tasked Clark Clifford to produce "a record of Soviet violations of international agreements." According to Clifford's recollection, the president complained that "the Russians are trying to chisel away a little here, a little there," and then explained that "if the Paris conference busts up, I want to be ready to reveal to the whole world the full truth about the Russian failure to honor agreements."[152] He evidenced some of the very same concern about the honoring of agreements that he demonstrated in his encounters with Molotov in April 1945, and that had led him to abide by the troop withdrawal arrangements in Germany in May–June that year. One might reasonably speculate that he was offended at the Soviet record.

[149] Byrnes address at Stuttgart, September 6, 1946, *Department of State Bulletin*, 15 (September 15, 1946), pp. 496–501. For discussion of the Stuttgart address, see McAllister, *No Exit*, pp. 76–77; and Leffler, *Struggle for Germany and the Origins of the Cold War*, p. 34.

[150] Davies diary, September 7, 1946, Joseph E. Davies Papers, Library of Congress, Box 24.

[151] McAllister, *No Exit*, p. 76.

[152] Clifford, *Counsel to the President*.

Truman's concern about the Soviets manifested itself again on September 10 when he indicated some reluctance to endorse a plan by Joseph Davies to give a speech pleading "for sanity, tolerance, and less heat in an effort to restore the unity of the 'Big Three' who licked Hitler and the Axis." Truman described the international situation as "bad and ticklish" and spoke of his need to ensure the "security of the United States."[153] He by no means denounced poor Davies as naïve and obtuse regarding the Soviet threat, but at long last he gave up on efforts to reassure him. Davies surprisingly lengthy period as an adviser to Truman came to an end. As Davies left the Oval Office, Secretary of Commerce Wallace took his place. Wallace planned to give a speech on Soviet-American relations at a New York election rally at Madison Square Garden two days later. The former vice president, a walking symbol of continuity with FDR, asked Roosevelt's successor to review the speech. Truman, who never felt personally comfortable with Wallace, apparently gave it a less-than-careful read but then announced his approval.[154]

Wallace took the president at his word and during his New York City address he advised his audience that Truman held that his views "represented the policies of his administration." This caused considerable confusion because Wallace launched a frontal assault on the "get tough" foreign policy that had developed in the past months. He explained to his sympathetic left-leaning listeners that "'Get Tough' never brought anything real and lasting – whether for school yard bullies or businessmen or world powers." He warned that "the tougher we get, the tougher the Russians will get." He presented British imperialism as a major source of world problems and cautioned against substantial association with London. He advocated an American stance of impartiality between Britain and the Soviet Union.[155] Troubles for the Truman administration exploded even before Wallace gave his speech. Asked at a press conference on September 12 if he regarded Wallace's upcoming speech as "a departure from Byrnes's policy," the president replied briskly: "I do not."[156] Byrnes took a different view.

Truman handled the matter very poorly. For domestic political reasons, he wanted to keep Wallace in his cabinet, so he tried to halt the avalanche of press

---

[153] Davies diary, September 10, 1946, Joseph E. Davies Papers, Library of Congress, Box 24.

[154] For Truman's defense that he gave the Wallace speech only a cursory read, see his Diary entry, September 17, 1946, in Ferrell, ed., *Off the Record*, p. 94. For further details of this meeting and subsequent details surrounding the eventual firing of Henry Wallace, I rely on the recollections of Clark Clifford in *Counsel to the President*, pp. 116–22, and the careful analysis of Alonzo Hamby in his *Man of the People*, pp. 358–59. Wallace maintained his version of events in a letter he wrote to Truman on April 8, 1949, in which he recalled: "While I was your Secretary of Commerce I did my best to help you to lead the United States to peaceful understanding with Russia. You may remember that you saw eye-to-eye with me on this matter on September 10, 1946, when you read in my presence – and approved – the speech which later led to my resignation." Wallace to Truman, April 8, 1949, Harry S. Truman Papers: President's Secretary's File, HSTL, Box 141.

[155] *New York Times*, September 13, 1946, pp. 1–2.

[156] Truman press conference, September 12, 1946, Truman, *Public Papers of the Presidents of the United States: Harry S. Truman, 1946*, pp. 426–27.

criticism by disassociating himself from the contents of Wallace's remarks while acknowledging his right to make them.[157] This ruse convinced nobody least of all Byrnes, who saw firsthand the damage Wallace's speech and the ensuing imbroglio inflicted on U.S. diplomatic standing. When the best that Truman could arrange after meeting with Wallace was for the commerce secretary to accept a temporary muzzle on foreign policy matters, Byrnes, with the encouragement of Senators Vandenberg and Connally, conveyed home from Paris his request to be relieved of his duties. "When the administration is divided on its own foreign policy, it cannot hope to convince the world that it has a foreign policy," he advised.[158] Forced into a corner by Byrnes's request, Truman faced a choice. Late in the evening of September 19, a full week after Wallace's speech, a weary and anxious president wrote an angry letter to his secretary of commerce demanding his resignation. He repeated the request in a more temperate phone conversation the next day, and Wallace complied.[159] Thus departed from the cabinet the last unreconstructed advocate of the Rooseveltian paradigm of enduring cooperation and friendship with the Soviet Union.

The apparent disarray in the Truman administration's foreign policy and Wallace's direct challenge to Byrnes unfavorably affected the American international position. Byrnes privately admitted early in October that "it affected us not only here at the Conference but in a number of countries where officials had come to believe that we had a policy which would be continued as the American policy."[160] Vandenberg judged the damage to be greater. "Just about all the American prestige which we have painfully built up the last two years has crashed," he reported to John Foster Dulles on September 19. "Europeans are more bewildered than ever. Have we no destiny, they ask, except a Russian one?" Vandenberg agreed with Dulles that talk like Wallace's increased the danger of war by "miscalculation." Rather accurately he held that "Stalin does not want war with us any more than we want war with him," but he astutely argued that "he does want to SHOVE JUST AS FAR as he thinks we'll react like a Chamberlain at Munich." Vandenberg warned that views like Wallace's only encouraged the dictator to shove harder. Working himself up to fever pitch he vividly outlined an awful scenario: "One day he SHOVES TOO FAR. He miscalculates. War! Who's to blame? The men who misled him into his miscalculations!" For good measure he added: "Excuse me – but I hope they fry in

---

[157] With congressional elections coming up, Truman hoped to preserve the unity of the Democratic Party and obviously didn't wish to offend the liberal wing of the party. In 1945, he had told Byrnes that "there were two persons he had to have on his political team, Secretary Wallace and Mrs. Eleanor Roosevelt – Mr. Wallace because of his influence with labor and Mrs. Roosevelt because of her influence with the Negro voters." Byrnes, *All in One Lifetime*, p. 373.

[158] Teletype record, quoted in Byrnes, *All in One Lifetime*, p. 375.

[159] Clifford provided all the details in *Counsel to the President*, pp. 118–22.

[160] Byrnes to Brown, October 4, 1946, James F. Byrnes Papers, Cooper Library, Folder 462.

Hell!"[161] Whatever the accuracy of the Byrnes and Vandenberg assessments of the damage done by the Wallace affair, they attest to the uncertainty that still existed within the American government over its foreign policy approach.

While Byrnes expressed anger and Vandenberg outrage over the Wallace episode, it left Truman feeling depressed. Those who lean toward Truman hagiography always emphasize his decisiveness, but in the later months of 1946 he remained anything but resolved and settled on Soviet policy. Despite occasional bursts of "toughness" he worried about the danger of war and aimed to avoid it. Burdened by a range of domestic problems and subjected to the slogan that "To Err is Truman," one senses a president somewhat torn as to the direction he should proceed. As Alonzo Hamby noted, the president had "told Wallace on two separate occasions in September, that he had not yet fully given up on a general accord with the Soviet Union, especially if he could deal on a man-to-man basis with Stalin." Hamby's conclusion that Truman "did not believe that his move in the direction of a hard line was irrevocable" certainly is confirmed by the president's reception of the memorandum he had asked Clifford to prepare in July.[162]

Clifford largely delegated the task of preparing the paper on Soviet compliance with their agreements to a young naval officer working in the Map Room at the White House, George Elsey, who produced far more than a mere compendium of Soviet infractions. After consulting with Soviet experts like Kennan and Bohlen and certain senior administration figures, the Clifford–Elsey report emerged more as summary assessment of the Soviet threat and a general recommendation for American action in response to it. Clifford submitted it to Truman on September 24 when the president was still licking his wounds from the Wallace firing debacle. It pulled few punches, although it contained little that was especially original. The dual authors informed Truman that "Soviet leaders believe that a conflict is inevitable between the U.S.S.R. and capitalist states, and their duty is to prepare the Soviet Union for this conflict." Responding to Truman's original inquiry, Clifford and Elsey disclosed that "Soviet-American agreements have been adhered to, 'interpreted,' or violated as Soviet officials from time to time have considered it to be in the best interests of the Soviet Union in accordance with the Soviet policy of increasing their own power at the expense of other nations." They warned of Soviet military strength relative to that of the United States and also noted the program of subversion and espionage that the USSR directed against the United States. In their calculation, the United States "must assume that the U.S.S.R. may at any time embark on a course of expansion effected by open

---

[161] Vandenberg to Dulles, September 19, 1946, John Foster Dulles Papers, Seeley G. Mudd Manuscript Library, Box 30. (Perhaps regretting the eternal damnation he wished upon Wallace and company, the sentence expressing his "hope they fry in Hell" is crossed out – although not so that a reader can't easily comprehend it.) [Underlining and capitals as in original.]

[162] Hamby, *Man of the People*, p. 360.

warfare and therefore [it] must maintain sufficient military strength to restrain the Soviet Union." They offered the "hope" that the Soviet leaders "will change their minds and work out with us a fair and equitable settlement when they realize that we are too strong to be beaten and too determined to be frightened."[163]

Truman read the report the very evening it was delivered and immediately called in Clifford to retrieve all the copies. He explained that while the report was "valuable" to him, "if it leaked it would blow the roof off the White House, it would blow the roof off the Kremlin."[164] In the context of tensions resulting from the Wallace affair, Truman's concern about the political damage from leaks is understandable. And, yet, his securing ALL copies of the report such that they were never consulted again seems odd. The recommended policy course, especially the counsel to rebuild the strength of the American military, greatly diminished since the war's end, surely bothered him. Slowing the popular demobilization of the military after the war had not been a task that Truman decided to undertake. Whatever his reason, Truman decided to share the report with no one – neither Byrnes and Acheson in the State Department nor the civilian and military leaders of the Army and Navy. This can hardly be characterized as the action of a president who had worked his way to a coherent strategy and wanted it to guide the actions of his administration.

There exists a seemingly incurable tendency among some American historians to impose more order on the past than existed at the time. This approach has led to the imposition of an artificial coherence on American foreign policy in the Cold War era. In one notable example of this genre, American civilian and military policy makers are portrayed from the end of World War II as choosing deliberately and willingly "to contain and deter the Russians rather than to reassure and placate them." The Americans demonstrated little "tolerance for risk" and determined instead to maintain a preponderant position in the international system. In this view, offered most cogently by Melvyn Leffler, by the fall of 1946, the Truman administration – as revealed by the Clifford–Elsey report – had settled upon a strategy of containment and deterrence, and the Cold War was on in earnest.[165] The task then facing the American policy makers was simply to implement this strategy both in the core area of Germany

---

[163] Clifford–Elsey report, "American Relations with the Soviet Union," September 24, 1946, printed in Arthur Krock, *Memoirs: Sixty Years on the Firing Line* (New York, 1968), pp. 419–82, specific quotations from pp. 422–24, 482. The report also informed the president that the "Soviet Government will never be easy to 'get along with.' The American people must accustom themselves to this thought, not as a cause for despair, but as a fact to be faced objectively and courageously. If we find it impossible to enlist Soviet cooperation in the solution of world problems, we should be prepared to join with the British and other Western countries in an attempt to build up a world of our own which will pursue its own objectives and will recognize the Soviet orbit as a distinct entity with which conflict is not predestined but with whom we cannot pursue common goals."

[164] Clifford, *Counsel to the President*, p. 123.

[165] See Leffler, *Preponderance of Power*, p. 99 for direct quotations and pp. 100–40 for his treatment of 1946.

and Western Europe and in other important areas like the Middle East and East Asia. But this view is too dismissive of the uncertainty and messiness involved in the formulation of American foreign policy at the time. As it turns out, at least until 1950 and the preparation by Acheson and Paul Nitze of National Security Council document 68 (NSC-68), American policy cannot be seen as being a "working-out" of some clearly delineated doctrine or strategy. Although Truman and most of his advisers had concluded by 1946 that certain Soviet actions endangered American security, no explicit course of action was charted for them to respond to this threat. As we shall see, only in a piecemeal and staggered manner did the Truman administration decide upon the major elements of the American response. Administration officials had begun this work in 1946 through the U.S. commitments in the Near East and in Germany. But much more remained to be done, and the course of action was hardly clear – certainly not to Harry Truman![166]

By December of 1946, Byrnes completed the negotiation of the peace treaties with the former German allies and thus fulfilled the commitment he made to Truman to stay on as secretary of state until that work was done. He now determined that the time had come for him to resign before beginning the next stage of treaty negotiations concerning Germany itself. As he explained to Henry Stimson, who wrote to thank and congratulate him on his service, he should not "start work upon the German and Austrian treaties unless I felt sure that I could carry through to the end."[167] He submitted a second letter of resignation to Truman on December 19, and Truman accepted it.[168] In his public letter of reply, he agreed to Byrnes's departure "with great reluctance and heartfelt regret," and he paid tribute to Byrnes as a "steadying hand" who met arduous and complex problems "with rare tact and judgment and – when necessary – firmness and tenacity of purpose."[169] In contemporaneous private comments included in his recently discovered "1947 Diary," the president commented very favorably on Byrnes and paid tribute to his loyalty. In a revealing entry on January 8, Truman opined that "I am very sorry Mr. Byrnes decided to quit. I'm sure that he will regret it – and I know that I do. He is a good negotiator – a very good one. But of course I don't want to be the cause of his death and his Dr. told him in March 1946 that he must slow down. So much for that."[170] Truman also expressed the hope that he could continue to call on Byrnes's

---

[166] Robert Ferrell has it exactly right in noting: "By early 1947 the president was on the verge of making up his mind. The process, however, had been much slower than people then or later believed. It took, in fact, a year and a half after the end of the war before he was willing to move against the USSR." Ferrell, *Harry S. Truman*, p. 251.

[167] Byrnes to Stimson, January 17, 1947, James F. Byrnes Papers, Cooper Library, Folder 540 (2).

[168] Byrnes to Truman, December 19, 1946, Harry S. Truman Papers: President's Secretary's File, HSTL, Box 135.

[169] Truman to Byrnes, January 7, 1947, Truman, *Public Papers of the Presidents of the United States: Harry S. Truman, 1947*, pp. 12–13.

[170] See entries for January 3 and 8 in "Harry S. Truman 1947 Diary," Harry S. Truman Library, posted on the Truman Library website at *http://www.trumanlibrary.org/diary/transcript.html*.

counsel, and, in fact, he did so.[171] Further, he continued a friendly personal relationship with Byrnes in the months after the secretary's resignation. He even tried to persuade Byrnes to accept an honorary degree from Westminster College in Fulton, Missouri, so as to provide the college with a speaker of note – Byrnes had been named *Time* magazine's "Man of the Year" for 1946 – after the attention Churchill's presence had provided the previous year.[172] Private matters of such significance as the president's mother's health and his daughter's concert singing were subjects of their amicable exchanges.[173] Truman gratefully accepted an inscribed copy of *Speaking Frankly*, Byrnes's 1947 account of his secretaryship.[174] It suffices to say that Jimmy Byrnes left the administration on good terms with Harry Truman. The real rupture in their relationship came later when Truman concluded that Byrnes had not supported him sufficiently in the 1948 presidential campaign, and when Byrnes made a speech at Washington and Lee University indirectly critical of Truman's domestic policies.[175]

Byrnes's departure cannot be understood as having any significant policy implications. Truman approached General George C. Marshall to succeed Byrnes not because of any policy views of the great general in World War II, but because he stood in virtual awe of Marshall's strength and personal stature.[176] He might also have hoped that Marshall would administer the State Department more effectively than Byrnes who had largely ignored this responsibility. It must be appreciated that Marshall's unsuccessful efforts to arrange a settlement between the nationalists and the communists in China had not embittered him against negotiations with communists. He probably took office more open to the possibilities of further negotiations than the man whom he replaced. He arrived without any intention to take American policy in any new direction. He, like Truman, maintained good relations with Byrnes and asked

---

[171] See, for example, Truman's request to Byrnes to address John Foster Dulles's comments on foreign policy. Also note that he asked Byrnes's advice on whether Dulles should be a delegate to the Moscow conference scheduled for March 1947. See Truman to Byrnes of January 27, 1947, and February 4, 1947, along with Byrnes's replies of January 31, 1947, and February 8, 1947, in Harry S. Truman Papers: President's Secretary's File, HSTL, Box 159.

[172] Truman to Byrnes, February 4, 1947, Harry S. Truman Papers: President's Secretary's File, HSTL, Box 159. *Time* (January 6, 1947) featured Byrnes on its cover with the photo description: "MAN OF THE YEAR: A nervous nation found a firm and patient voice."

[173] See Truman to Byrnes, February 17, 1947 and March 24, 1947, Harry S. Truman Papers: President's Secretary's File, HSTL, Box 282.

[174] Truman to Byrnes, October 11, 1947, Harry S. Truman Papers: President's Secretary's File, HSTL, Box 282. Byrnes inscription reads in part: "It was easy to speak frankly, but what to discuss, and what not to discuss, required decisions almost as difficult as those *we* had to make during the negotiations about which I have written." (My emphasis.) I am grateful to Elizabeth Safly of the Truman Library for making this inscription available to me.

[175] On the rupture in relations, see Hamby, *Man of the People*, pp. 494–95.

[176] Truman maintains that he used General Eisenhower as an intermediary to ascertain Marshall's willingness to serve as secretary of state after Byrnes introduced his health worries to him, and that when Byrnes firmed up his resignation at year's end, he simply announced Marshall's appointment without consulting him again. Truman, *Year of Decisions*, p. 607. One should note that he had no discussions whatsoever of a policy nature with Marshall.

PHOTO 17. A study in friendship? A smiling President Truman stands between retiring Secretary of State James F. Byrnes who congratulates his successor, George C. Marshall, on the day Marshall was sworn into office, January 21, 1947. (Courtesy National Archives)

his predecessor to serve as the main witness before the Senate Foreign Relations Committee when the Italian and Balkan peace treaties were submitted for ratification in February 1947.[177] As late as August of 1948, in the midst of the Berlin Blockade crisis, he asked if Byrnes would serve on the U.S. delegation to a possible CFM meeting along with himself, Senators Connally and Vanderberg, and John Foster Dulles. Marshall, a man not given to either flattery or exaggeration, explained that he wanted "four men with me who by their very presence would give great emphasis to the American position and American actions."[178] He clearly held Byrnes in high esteem.

Marshall might have been forgiven for taking a slightly more jaundiced view of Byrnes, for his predecessor left office at a time when the United States faced multiple challenges in a grim and menacing international environment. The

[177] Marshall to Byrnes, February 18, 1947, James F. Byrnes Papers, Cooper Library, Folder 593.
[178] Marshall to Byrnes, August 19, 1948, James F. Byrnes Papers, Cooper Library, Folder 615 (1).

Western European economies, plagued by severe shortages of food and coal during a brutal winter, appeared on the verge of collapse. Such a collapse, when joined to evident political weakness and psychological exhaustion, seemed certain to redound to the benefit of local communists, particularly in France and Italy. Further, Great Britain's continuing and grave economic difficulties forced her to acknowledge her military weakness and to reduce her commitments in the world. And, of course, magnifying the threat to America's interest inherent in European military and economic weakness remained the Soviet Union's seeming ambition and capacity to exploit it. What the United States would do to address these circumstances remained largely unclear when General Marshall took the helm at the State Department. But under his leadership and that of his successor Dean Acheson, the State Department led the Truman administration to forge a foreign policy that confronted these difficult international realities and transformed the peacetime role the United States played in the world.

8

Transformation

Truman's Foreign Policy

The Truman Foreign Policy

In 1962 the distinguished Harvard historian Arthur Schlesinger invited seventy-five leading historians to rank the presidents of the United States. The nation's thirty-third president, Harry S. Truman, must have been pleased with the verdict the scholars rendered on him. They labeled him a "near-great" president and placed him in the same company as his hero Andrew Jackson, along with such forceful chief executives as Theodore Roosevelt and James K. Polk. Schlesinger explained why in words that truly reflect the time in which they were written. "Truman," he noted,

discharged impressively the awesome obligations devolving on the United States as the leader of the free world in the cold war with Soviet imperialism. The Truman Doctrine for the protection of Greece and Turkey, the Marshall Plan for the restoration of Western Europe, the Berlin airlift, the Point Four program for backward countries, NATO (our first peacetime military alliance), and the intervention in Korea in support of the United Nations – all these constituted landmarks in an assumption of global responsibilities undreamed of only a few years before.[1]

Clearly, Truman secured his high place – one still confirmed in more recent polls – primarily because of the extraordinary foreign policy developed and implemented during his administration.[2]

Under Truman's leadership, the foreign policy of the United States underwent a major transformation. From restraint and limited engagement in the affairs of the world beyond the western hemisphere during the 1930s, the United

---

[1] Arthur M. Schlesinger, "Our Presidents: A Rating by 75 Historians," *New York Times Magazine* (July 29, 1962), p. 12.

[2] On more recent polls, see Arthur M. Schlesinger, Jr., "The Ultimate Approval Rating," *New York Times Magazine* (December 15, 1996), pp. 46–51; and Donald McCoy, "Chicago Sun-Times Poll," *Presidential Studies Quarterly*, 26 (Winter 1996), pp. 281–83, which reports on the poll conducted by Steve Neal of the *Chicago Sun-Times*.

States assumed sweeping international obligations during the years of Truman's presidency. Roosevelt and Truman together combined to destroy American isolationism, but under Truman's leadership, the United States moved to a level of world engagement and assumed international commitments far beyond anything that Roosevelt had conceived. Motivated in large part by a desire to preserve the security of the noncommunist world from Soviet expansionism, the United States worked to secure the political and economic recovery of the European democracies devastated by a brutal war, and it joined them in forging a military alliance committed to the defense of Western Europe. Furthermore, the United States restored and incorporated into a peacetime alliance structure its defeated foes, Germany and Japan. Franklin Roosevelt would have been staggered to find American troops committed to a military alliance in Europe and American planes supplying the blockaded sections of Berlin – Hitler's capital, no less – within four years of the end of World War II. This didn't match the postwar world he had conceived and for which he planned.

A new conceptual worldview of America's international role surely was framed during Truman's tenure as president. When the Missourian consigned his office to Dwight D. Eisenhower on January 20, 1953, the United States stood unmistakably as a global power with global interests committed to playing a central and abiding role in international affairs. This truly constituted a paradigmatic shift, the exact nature and extent of which were not predicted during the difficult early months of Truman's presidency when he struggled under the enormous weight of responsibilities conveyed to him upon Franklin Roosevelt's death. One must clarify the essential elements of the distinctive foreign policy forged during the Truman administration in order to provide a basis to analyze more fully the areas of continuity and discontinuity between the two administrations.

It must be appreciated, however, that Harry Truman never self-consciously decided to transform the foreign policy content and approach he inherited from FDR. Instead, external circumstances drove the creation of the Truman administration's foreign policy. These circumstances – especially the enmity and expansionist tendencies of the Soviet Union in the face of British weakness, the retraction of British power, and the Central European power vacuum – undermined the validity of the plans and assumptions FDR had developed. Additionally, no well-developed, strategic analysis guided the process of transformation in its initial years. Even though a significant amount of strategic military planning took place within the defense establishment, the major elements of Truman's foreign policy up to 1950 did not emerge from a "process by which ends are related to means, intentions to capabilities, objectives to resources."[3] American policy emerged in a much more haphazard manner.

---

[3] This is John Gaddis's definition of "strategy" in his *Strategies of Containment*, p. viii. Melvyn Leffler referred to some of this military planning regarding overseas bases in his *Preponderance of Power*, pp. 56–59.

Of course, this is not to deny the influence on strategy of specific individuals. John Gaddis notably has emphasized the importance of George Kennan's general notion of containment in clarifying for policy makers that their options need not be drawn from "bipolar extremes: war *or* peace, victory *or* defeat, neither appeasement *nor* annihilation."[4] But the Truman administration policy makers never read from one coherent script, nor did they march to the beat of a single drummer. They disagreed on matters of both policy formulation and implementation. The summary outline provided here of the eventual main features of the Truman foreign policy should not disguise this or dilute the point.[5]

Dean Acheson captured something of the mentality of the American policy makers when he recalled in his memoir that "only slowly did it dawn upon us that the whole world structure and order that we had inherited from the nineteenth century was gone and that the struggle to replace it would be directed from two bitterly opposed and ideologically irreconcilable power centers." Beginning in 1947, the Americans finally recognized with some clarity that the "hoped-for new order" of FDR's and Cordell Hull's soothing, wartime assurances was "an illusion."[6] The American recognition resulted in large part from the forced prompting of the great "balancing" power of the nineteenth and early twentieth centuries – the exhausted Great Britain – which could no longer play its stabilizing role.

The Britain of late 1946 and early 1947 possessed but a shadow of its former greatness. David Reynolds rightly has described it as being "in a desperate predicament." Reynolds explained further that "the growing confrontation with Russia, at a time of limited US help, necessitated military and political commitments that the economy, struggling with a huge post-war balance of payments deficit, could not sustain."[7] Facing major difficulties on the domestic front as well as in both Palestine and India, the British cabinet decided in late February 1947 that it must reduce its financial and military commitments. It determined to hold to an earlier decision and to end British aid to Greece and Turkey as of March 31. The British so advised the Americans and set off a flurry of activity to determine an American response to this new circumstance. Thus, it was a British action, rather than any initiative of an American official, that forced the Truman administration to begin moving seriously beyond the confusion and contradictions of 1946.

In March 1947, the United States framed a program of limited military and economic assistance (four hundred million dollars) to assist the Greeks and the Turks, another action that would have surprised Franklin Roosevelt, who had

---

4 John Lewis Gaddis, "After Containment: The Legacy of George Kennan in the Age of Terrorism," *New Republic*, 232 (April 25, 2005), p. 29.
5 I have tried to illustrate the complexity of policy making from 1947 to 1950 in my own *George F. Kennnan and the Making of American Foreign Policy.*
6 Acheson, *Present at the Creation*, p. 726.
7 David Reynolds, *Britannia Overruled*, p. 163.

resisted Churchill's wartime efforts to draw the United States into commitments in the eastern Mediterranean and southeastern Europe.[8] Primarily to pry funds from a parsimonious Congress, Truman cast his appeal in grandly universalist terms portraying the issue as a conflict between totalitarian repression and democratic freedom. Thus was born the Truman Doctrine with its promise "to support free peoples who are resisting attempted subjugation by armed minorities or outside pressures."[9] Despite this exalted rhetoric the Truman administration, in reality, had no overall plan to respond to the Soviet Union. The aid to Greece and Turkey constituted but a first and restrained element of such a response.[10] Much else was yet to be formulated. This point has not always been well understood by some historians who describe the Truman Doctrine as virtually a prescriptive tract for global containment. But neither the Truman Doctrine nor George Kennan's celebrated article "The Sources of Soviet Conduct," which appeared in the July 1947 issue of *Foreign Affairs* and which called for "long-term, patient but firm and vigilant containment of Russian expansive tendencies," represented a real prescription for policy.[11] Neither outlined in any detail what the United States should do nor charted any explicit course of action. It must be emphasized and understood that only in a gradual manner did the Truman administration decide upon the major elements of the American response to the Soviet Union. This is made most clear by tracking the outlook of the new secretary of state.

By the time that Truman delivered his famous speech to Congress, General Marshall already had left for a Council of Foreign Ministers meeting in Moscow. There he sought to make progress on the reparations issue and German issues more generally in negotiations that extended for almost a month. If anything, Marshall proved more willing to engage in genuine negotiations than his predecessor might have by this stage. The decision to extend aid to Greece and Turkey had not diverted him from an effort to settle issues with the Soviet Union. Guided by Byrnes's key aide, Ben Cohen, the department's counselor, and influenced by the advice of the American Military Governor in Germany, Lucius Clay, Marshall offered real concessions on reparations in return for Soviet cooperation on treating Germany as one economic unit.[12] He made no progress whatsoever. The obstinacy of Stalin and Molotov troubled Marshall,

---

[8] The significance of the Truman Doctrine and the reasons for it are discussed in Bruce Kuniholm's *The Origins of the Cold War in the Near East*; and Howard Jones, *"A New Kind of War": America's Global Strategy and the Truman Doctrine in Greece* (New York, 1989).

[9] For Truman's message of March 12, 1947, see Truman, *Public Papers of the Presidents of the United States: Harry S. Truman, 1947*, pp. 176–80.

[10] On this point see Jones, *"A New Kind of War,"* p. 36.

[11] "X" [George F. Kennan], "The Sources of Soviet Conduct," *Foreign Affairs*, 25 (July 1947), pp. 566–82. For discussion of its significance, see Miscamble, *George F. Kennan and the Making of American Foreign Policy*, pp. 64–67.

[12] Marshall's efforts at the Moscow CFM are well explicated in Philip Zelikow, "George C. Marshall and the Moscow CFM Meeting of 1947," *Diplomacy and Statecraft*, 8 (July 1997), pp. 97–124.

and he drew key conclusions from the failure of the Moscow meeting regarding both Soviet intentions and the requisite American response.

From his firsthand experience, the new secretary of state perceived that the Soviet Union was not content to consolidate its East European empire but hoped to take advantage of the social dislocation and economic desperation of Western Europe. "At the conclusion of the Moscow Conference," Marshall recalled, "it was my feeling that the Soviets were doing everything possible to achieve a complete breakdown in Europe." As he astutely saw it, "the major problem was to counter this negative Soviet policy and to restore the European economy."[13] Marshall began this effort on his return to Washington; under his guidance, the State Department seized the initiative and engaged in a remarkably creative period of foreign policy development. Truman, in sharp contrast to FDR, proved only too willing to let Marshall's State Department make the running. Foggy Bottom rather than the White House emerged as the principal source of policy.[14]

The core group of State Department policy makers shared Marshall's fear that Western Europe's deep economic problems, when combined with its political weakness and its psychological exhaustion, not only would redound to the benefit of local communists – especially in France and Italy – but also leave it vulnerable to exploitation and intimidation by the Soviet Union. Such fears, along with a genuine humanitarian concern for the European populace, drove the United States to generate a program for European economic recovery. Developed in conjunction with the Europeans led by Ernest Bevin, this program, known as the Marshall Plan, eventually provided thirteen billion dollars in economic assistance to aid in the reconstruction and rejuvenation of Western Europe. Furthermore, it prodded the Europeans toward greater economic cooperation and integration, and it concretely revealed the American commitment to this area, which now was deemed vital to American interests and national security.[15]

The Marshall Plan was the decisive step in establishing a political balance in postwar Europe. Fortunately, and at last, the Truman administration conclusively determined that Europe mattered and that its significance in world affairs could not be easily diminished in the manner that FDR had wished. The aid program confirmed the long-term American commitment to the continent, and it stymied the Soviet strategic objective of a weak and fragmented

---

[13] Interviews with George C. Marshall, October 30, 1952, and February 18, 1953, by Harry B. Price, Harry B. Price Papers, HSTL, Box 1. Also see Bohlen, *Witness to History*, p. 263; and James McAllister, *No Exit*, pp. 127–29.

[14] The great exception to this statement proved to be the Palestine/Israel issue. On it, see Michael J. Cohen, *Palestine and the Great Powers, 1945–1948* (Princeton, NJ, 1982).

[15] On the Marshall Plan, see Michael J. Hogan, *The Marshall Plan: America, Britain and the Reconstruction of Western Europe, 1947–1952* (New York, 1987); Gregory A. Fossedal, *Our Finest Hour: Will Clayton, the Marshall Plan, and the Triumph of Democracy* (Stanford, CA, 1993); and Miscamble, *George F. Kennan and the Making of American Foreign Policy*, pp. 44–74.

Europe. It also provoked a more intense response from Stalin, who presumably considered a politically and economically healthy Western Europe a threat to his ambitions and security. In September of 1947, the Soviets and eight other European communist parties, including the French and Italian, established the Cominform – an organization devised by Moscow to control local communist parties – and embarked on a campaign of political warfare. Furthermore, Stalin now discarded any pretense of political tolerance in Eastern Europe. Bevin, Marshall, and their colleagues had risen to meet his "cautious and deceptive" efforts to advance "socialism" through the national front strategy. So blocked, Stalin ordered the establishment of one-party, totalitarian regimes throughout the region where the Red Army held sway, utilizing the savage techniques of arrests, persecution, purges, and liquidations. Surprisingly, a rather peculiar view still exists that the Marshall Plan primarily aimed to challenge the Soviet Union and to contest its hold of *Eastern* Europe, thus forcing Stalin's heavy-handed response and bringing on the division of Europe.[16] The naivete of this stance and the benign portrayal it offers of Stalin and his supposed desire for continued cooperation with the West is hard to match yet very easy to dismiss.[17]

The toppling of the Czech president Eduard Benes by the communist Klement Gottwald in February 1948 gave a stunning confirmation of Stalin's intentions and deepened the fears of Western Europeans who viewed it as a precedent that might be followed in cases like Italy. The Prague Coup and the tragic communization of all of Eastern Europe, however, drew forth a courageous response from the Western Europeans. Again the indomitable Bevin took the initiative and, under his guidance, complemented by the capable assistance of Belgian Prime Minister Paul-Henri Spaak, the British signed a multilateral defense pact with the French and the Benelux countries – the Treaty of Brussels – in March of 1948.[18] This created the Western Union and indicated a Western European collaboration to guard against any future German aggression as well as a refusal to succumb to Soviet intimidation. Bevin recognized from the outset, however, that he would need to draw the United States into a defensive alliance for it to be truly viable, and he worked toward this end throughout 1948. His endeavors would reach fruition in 1949.

During 1948, the evolving contest between the Soviet Union and the Western powers in Europe culminated in a struggle over Germany. The failure of the

---

[16] For a recent voicing of this notion, see Michael Cox and Caroline Kennedy-Pipe, "The Tragedy of American Diplomacy?" pp. 97–134.

[17] For two excellent responses to this argument as offered by Cox and Kennedy-Pipe, see John Bledsoe Bonds, "Looking for Love (or Tragedy) in All the Wrong Places," *Journal of Cold War Studies*, 7 (Winter 2005), pp. 152–58; and Laszlo Borhi, "Was American Diplomacy Really Tragic?" *Journal of Cold War Studies*, 7 (Winter 2005), pp. 159–67. Bonds observes: "I agree that the Marshall Plan divided Europe, but the evidence seems patently clear that it was Stalin who did the dividing, with blatant threats to his reluctant 'friendly allies'" (p. 152).

[18] On Bevin's actions, consult Alan Bullock, *Ernest Bevin*, pp. 513–48: and Martin H. Folly, "Breaking the Vicious Circle: Britain, the United States, and the Genesis of the North Atlantic Treaty," *Diplomatic History*, 12 (Winter 1988), pp. 59–77.

four-power negotiations at the Moscow CFM induced a major redirection in Western policy. Impelled by a desire to develop the western portion of Germany as a contributor to European economic recovery as well as by a need to lower their own occupation costs, the United States and Britain persuaded the French to join them in agreements, known as the London Program, which proposed the creation of a West German government and state. The Soviet Union vehemently opposed this program and aimed to prevent its implementation. To block the London Program's initial step – the introduction of a separate currency for West Germany – and in an attempt to force the Western powers to accept a German settlement more to their liking, the Soviets instituted a blockade of the western sectors of Berlin, which lay wholly within their zone of occupation. The Americans and the British responded imaginatively to this total restriction on surface traffic into Berlin with a dramatic airlift of supplies to the besieged city, which they maintained until the Soviets lifted the blockade in May of 1949. Stalin's risky gambit, intended to inflict a political defeat on the Western powers and to disrupt their plans for Western European economic cooperation, failed disastrously. Ironically, the Soviet maneuver revealed the limits of Stalin's statecraft for it drew forth an even stronger American commitment to Western Europe.

The pressure of events like the Prague Coup and the Berlin Blockade, along with the requests of the British, prompted the Truman administration to consider participation in a mutual defense treaty with Western Europe. Negotiations in 1948 devised the basic framework of a treaty, but the American government marked time while awaiting the result of the 1948 presidential election and the expected change to a Republican administration. When Truman, as always a tough and resilient political campaigner, surprisingly retained office, he appointed Dean Acheson to succeed General Marshall, and the new secretary of state energetically proceeded with negotiations to conclude an Atlantic security pact. The North Atlantic Treaty was signed in Washington, D.C., on April 4, 1949 by the United States, Canada, and ten European countries. Article 5 of the treaty lay at its heart and provided that "an armed attack against one or more [of the signatories] shall be considered an armed attack against them all."[19] The U.S. Senate ratified the treaty with strong bipartisan support and it formed a cornerstone of postwar American foreign policy. Ultimately, fears of Soviet exploitation of Western Europe's weakness drove the United States under Harry Truman to reverse its long practice of refusing to participate in peacetime alliances outside the western hemisphere. A certain ironic quality attaches to the fact that this compelling expansion of American international commitments took place on the White House watch of a one-time Missouri farmer when it was never contemplated by his cosmopolitan predecessor.

Of course at its outset, the North Atlantic Treaty Organization, formed to give substance to the treaty guarantee, possessed little in the way of military

---

[19] For further details on the negotiation of the treaty and its provisions see Miscamble, *George F. Kennan and the Making of American Foreign Policy*, pp. 131–40.

force. Until 1950, it meant little more than a political commitment of support backed by a vague threat of nuclear retaliation. After 1950, some conventional military muscle was added to the skeletal NATO structure. Nonetheless, it served as a caution and a deterrent to the Soviets, and its most crucial immediate benefit lay in the reassurance it provided the citizens of Western Europe. In the end, the principal benefit of NATO lay in its facilitation of European political stability and economic development. Behind the American defensive guarantee, Western Europe subsequently enjoyed a remarkable period of both.

On the German issue in 1949, the United States pursued what appositely has been termed a "two-track" policy.[20] On one level, American officials pursued the implementation of the program to establish a West German state. On another, they gave some consideration to a proposal drafted by George Kennan for an all-German settlement that might involve the withdrawal of both American and Soviet troops from the heart of Europe.[21] The joint chiefs of staff vigorously criticized the American troop regrouping and withdrawals involved in the Kennan plan and ultimately Acheson sided with them.[22] When he traveled to Paris for the CFM meeting in May, he marched as one with his British and French counterparts in supporting the establishment of West Germany. Dealing with the Soviet officials in Paris convinced him that the Soviet Union "sought only to recover the power to block progress in West Germany."[23] He energetically parried their efforts and so assured that by September 1949 the military occupation of West Germany ended. Konrad Adenauer's government took office, and the Federal Republic began a period of gradual advance toward full sovereignty under the mild reign of the civilian High Commission.[24] FDR at a minimum must have turned in his grave.

The creation of the Western military alliance through the North Atlantic Treaty and the formation of the West German state constituted wise measures in response to Stalin's lurking intention to dominate far beyond his nation's boundaries. Inevitably, they also meant the congealment of the division of Europe and the acceptance of the Soviet domination of Eastern Europe. In this region, Stalin pursued his plans to establish total domination of the satellite states within his empire. He even refused to tolerate the independence of the communist leader Josip Broz Tito in Yugoslavia, despite Tito's having proved himself an

---

[20] For discussion of this approach, see Thomas Alan Schwartz, *America's Germany: John J. McCloy and the Federal Republic of Germany* (Cambridge, MA, 1991), pp. 37–39.

[21] For a detailed examination of the formulation of Kennan's proposal, known as Program A, see Miscamble, *George F. Kennan and the Making of American Foreign Policy*, pp. 149–77.

[22] On this, see McAllister, *No Exit*, pp. 166–69; and Melvyn Leffler, *Struggle for Germany and the Origins of the Cold War*, pp. 66–71. Both McAllister and Leffler offer helpful correctives to my own earlier work on this matter, which suggested that Acheson was influenced by the concerns of the British and the French upon the publication of a *New York Times* story on Program A by James Reston. (See Miscamble, *George F. Kennan and the Making of American Foreign Policy*, pp. 169–72.) As both McAllister and Leffler make clear, Acheson had reached his decision to reject Program A prior to the publication of the Reston story and the European reaction.

[23] Acheson, *Present at the Creation*, p. 297.

[24] For details, see Schwartz, *America's Germany*.

eager Stalinist disciple in creating a one-party police state. In June 1948, the Cominform expelled Yugoslavia. Presumably Stalin expected Tito's government to collapse but it did not, thereby presenting an unexpected challenge to policy makers in the West. Indicative of its appreciation that the real enemy in the short term was Soviet power and expansion rather that communism per se, the United States adopted a cautious approach encouraging Yugoslav independence and holding forth the prospect of improved relations.[25] Some American policy makers hoped that Tito might serve as a model for the emergence of other nationalist communist leaderships in the Eastern European countries and saw such possible regimes as a means to limit Soviet power. This very prospect troubled Stalin sufficiently that purges of supposed "nationalist communist" leaders like Gomulka in Poland, Rajk in Hungary, and Clementis in Czechoslovakia were carried out in 1948–50 exemplifying yet again the ferocious intention of the Soviets to maintain their ghastly grip on the satellites. This domination left the Americans after 1949 to pursue only such tactics as trade and credit restrictions, propaganda, support for émigré organizations, and largely ill-conceived covert operations.[26] These did little to force the retraction of Soviet power and control that debased the lives of Eastern Europeans for over forty years. Only the political earthquake in Eastern Europe during the winter of 1989–90, which the indefatigable Solidarity movement in Poland fostered and which Mikhail S. Gorbachev ultimately permitted, mercifully ended the Soviet domination of the region.

The respective relationships of the Soviet Union to Eastern Europe and of the United States to Western Europe in the period from the end of World War II to 1950 contrast sharply and testify eloquently to the nature of the emerging Cold War. The Soviet Union dominated the Eastern Europeans and denied them political freedom and personal liberties. Stalin's definition of security, with all that lay behind it ranging from Russia's bitter history of invasions to communist ideology and his own personal paranoia, led him to rule the Eastern European nations against the will of their populations and to threaten expansion beyond this region. Here lay the principal root and continuing cause of the Cold War. As the preceding summary narrative has clarified, the United States assumed its position of leadership of the West much more reluctantly and haphazardly than the Soviets did in the East. Indeed, the Western Europeans needed to persuade the Americans to commit themselves. Furthermore, through such measures as the North Atlantic Treaty and policy toward Germany, the Western European governments helped shape the nature and structures of the American involvement. Geir Lundestad fittingly has described the American

---

[25] Lorraine M. Lees, "The American Decision to Assist Tito, 1948–1949," *Diplomatic History*, 2 (Fall 1978), pp. 407–22. For further detail, see Lorraine M. Lees, *Keeping Tito Afloat: The United States, Yugoslavia, and the Cold War* (University Park, PA, 1997).

[26] For a provocative review essay, which claims that "propaganda, psychological warfare, and covert operations were critical instruments of U.S. foreign policy in the early Cold War," see Kenneth A. Osgood, "Hearts and Mind," *Journal of Cold War Studies*, 4 (Spring 2002), pp. 85–107, direct quotation from p. 95.

political, economic, and security commitment as an "empire by invitation."[27] The great foreign policy achievements of the Truman administration emerged from this willingness to cooperate with the Western Europeans. Truman and his policy makers moved beyond what Acheson termed the false "postulates" of wartime planning to fashion a new approach that brought the United States to the very heart of European affairs.[28] Regardless of subsequent policy failures and missed opportunities, a certain grandeur characterizes the extraordinary American effort framed during the Truman presidency. It endured for over forty years and provided the umbrella under which the Europeans enjoyed unprecedented prosperity and experienced real security not only from the Soviet Union but also from the fratricide that colors so much of their past and that made "civilized" Europe, in Tony Judt's apt description, "the killing field of the 20th century."[29]

Europe proved to be the primary initial battlefield in the Cold War, but the northeast Asian region also attracted considerable attention from American policy makers during the late 1940s. Again, the Truman administration had to fashion new policies to address changed circumstances. Upon the defeat of the Japanese, a long-simmering conflict broke out in China between the nationalist government of Chiang Kai-shek and the communists led by Mao Tse-tung. Consistent with the Rooseveltian approach to China, the Truman administration extended some postwar assistance to Chiang's government and tried to avert a full-scale civil war in 1946 through the mediatory efforts of General Marshall. When these efforts failed and China became increasingly enveloped in war, the United States pursued a prudent approach. The United States extended further limited assistance in 1948 but refused to become deeply involved. It declined to expend the substantial military and economic resources that would have been necessary to save the incompetent and corrupt nationalist regime.[30] The Truman administration based its decision not only on a clear recognition of the danger and enormity of such a rescue operation but also on a geopolitical assessment that a China controlled by Mao could not threaten the security of the United States. In effect, the American policy makers refused to endorse FDR's wishful notion that China of the 1940s was a "great power." They deemed Japan, not China, as the country in the Far East vital to American security because of its military-industrial potential. The United States, thereupon, stood by in 1949 as nationalist forces on the mainland were defeated. It also refused to grant

---

[27] See Geir Lundestad, "Empire by Invitation? The United States and Western Europe, 1945–1952," *SHAFR Newsletter*, 15 (September 1984), pp. 1–21. See also Lundestad's *The American "Empire" and other Studies of U.S. Foreign Policy in a Comparative Perspective* (Oxford and New York, 1990).

[28] Acheson, *Present at the Creation*, p. 726.

[29] Tony Judt, "Democracy as an Aberration," *New York Times Book Review* (February 7, 1999), p. 11.

[30] There are a number of excellent studies of Sino-American relations prior to the Korean War, but see William Whitney Stueck, Jr., *The Road to Confrontation: American Policy Toward China and Korea, 1947–1950* (Chapel Hill, NC, 1981).

formal recognition to the People's Republic of China (PRC) proclaimed by Mao on October 1, 1949, preferring to wait for "the dust to settle," as Acheson put it.[31]

The strategic assessment according Japan a higher priority to American interests than China guided policy toward the defeated foe in the Pacific war after 1947. Prior to this point, the Allied occupation under General Douglas MacArthur implemented a program emphasizing demilitarization and democratization.[32] Coincident with these efforts, the economic conditions in Japan deteriorated notably. The new international circumstances brought on by Soviet antagonism and expansion in Europe prompted a policy review. Now American policy makers argued the need for Japan to be politically and economically stable to ensure against possible communist penetration and disruption. Further, they planned to prevent the military-industrial potential of Japan falling under the influence or control of the powers in the Kremlin. In 1947–48, Washington charted a "reverse-course" that altered the thrust of the occupation from reform to recovery and advanced the political, social, and economic stability of this strategically crucial nation.[33] The changes helped cement in power the pro-American economic and political forces that have governed Japan ever since. As with West Germany, the Truman administration began to draw Japan – its recently defeated and brutal enemy – into the Western alliance structure and, as Tony Smith has displayed so well, to forge a nation quite different from the militaristic power of the 1930s.[34] The transformations of both Germany and Japan represent two of the most significant accomplishments of American foreign policy in the Truman era. Their respective transformations, however, could not have been accomplished without the major transformation in American foreign policy that ultimately helped to bring them about.

In June of 1950, the northeast Asian region became the focus of international politics when the North Koreans launched an invasion of South Korea.[35] With Stalin's approval, North Korea's Kim Il-Sung sought to destroy the noncommunist regime south of the thirty-eighth parallel. The Truman administration,

---

[31] Nancy Bernkopf Tucker, *Patterns in the Dust: Chinese-American Relations and the Recognition Controversy, 1949–1950* (New York, 1983). Also see Miscamble, *George F. Kennan and the Making of American Foreign Policy*, pp. 212–46.

[32] See Michael Schaller, *The American Occupation of Japan: The Origins of the Cold War in Asia* (New York, 1985); and Howard B. Schonberger, *Aftermath of War: Americans and the Remaking of Japan, 1942–1952* (Kent, OH, 1989).

[33] On the "reverse course," see Miscamble, *George F. Kennan and the Making of American Foreign Policy*, pp. 250–70.

[34] See Tony Smith's chapter, "Democratizing Japan and Germany," in his *America's Mission: The United States and the Worldwide Struggle for Democracy in the Twentieth Century* (Princeton, NJ, 1994), pp. 146–76.

[35] The literature on the Korean War is large and impressive. For a comprehensive account see William Whitney Stueck, Jr., *The Korean War: An International History* (Princeton, NJ, 1995). On the outbreak of the conflict, also see John Lewis Gaddis, *We Now Know: Rethinking Cold War History* (Oxford, 1997), pp. 70–75.

although initially caught off guard, regained its balance quickly and interpreted the aggression in Korea as a part of a broader effort to extend communist influence. It invested the conflict with global implications. Policy makers feared that the Korean War might have been initiated to divert American attention from Europe and to provide a cover for aggressive Soviet actions there. The U.S. government sensibly determined that a communist victory in Korea would severely damage its prestige and would serve only to encourage further aggression. As the South Korean army collapsed and retreated down the peninsula, President Truman, who acted decisively in this crisis situation, authorized the use of American air and ground forces under the auspices of the United Nations. Regrettably, he did this without securing formal congressional approval. Three years passed before this bloody war ended in stalemate. During those three years, the American commitment to contain the Soviet Union took on a decidedly more military cast and U.S.-Soviet relations plunged to a new low.

In Asia, the Korean War dramatically affected American foreign policy. The direct confrontation of Chinese and American troops on the Korean battlefield after December 1950 pushed Sino-American relations into a prolonged period of bitter hostility. Not only did the Korean War destroy any possibility of normal relations, but it also provoked policy reversals on the part of the United States regarding Taiwan and the extension of military aid to Chiang Kai-shek, who had established himself there. It ended the American effort over the previous three years to disengage from the nationalist regime and to hold open the possibility of relations with the Chinese communists.

While the Korean War drove the United States and China even further apart, it brought the United States and Japan much closer together. Japan served as the crucial staging base for the American war effort in Korea, which highlighted its strategic importance. The Korean War confirmed the necessity for American forces to remain in Japan to maintain security in northeast Asia after the occupation ended. John Foster Dulles encapsulated this perception in the arrangements he negotiated terminating the occupation. On September 8, 1951, the United States and its allies in the Pacific war – except the Soviet Union and China – signed a peace treaty with Japan.[36] The United States and Japan then signed a separate security treaty giving the United States the right to station its land, sea, and air forces in and about Japan. Rather than risk the uncertainty of seeing Japan develop as an independent power, the United States chose a strategy of alliance with a militarily dependent Japan. Additionally, and more questionably, the Korean War meant a deepening of American commitments elsewhere in Asia and locked the United States into a more military-oriented approach. The American decisions to recognize the Bao Dai government in Vietnam and to extend substantial military and economic assistance there, which moved the United States down the dangerous slope to its tragic and costly involvement in

---

[36] See the reliable account of Frederick S. Dunn, *Peace-making and the Settlement of Japan* (Princeton, NJ, 1963).

Indochina, testify to this.[37] The logic of containing communism, for good or ill, trumped the anticolonial legacy of FDR.

The significance of the Korean War for American foreign policy has long been noted.[38] It clearly revealed that Truman learned his lessons well from the drama of aggression and appeasement that occurred in the 1930s. The "Munich mentality" would not infect his administration. Looking at the Korean War in the long view, William Stueck astutely noted that "the conflict may be seen as a turning point in which, unlike the 1930s, the political system of the United States and Western Europe rose to the challenge of authoritarianism in a manner that averted the global bloodbath of the previous decade and positioned the West advantageously in the ongoing Cold War."[39] This willingness to react against perceived aggression far from America's shores and the definition of vital U.S. security interests to include northeast Asia constituted notable advances in how the United States operated in the world over the proposed model that Truman inherited in 1945.

The impact of the Korean War resounded far beyond Asia. It largely justified the Truman administration's implementation of the recommendations of National Security Council document 68, which called for a vastly enhanced conception of American national security and a major military build-up. NSC-68 originated in discussions arising in response to the Soviet explosion of an atomic bomb in August–September of 1949. This shattered the implicit sense of security that the American atomic monopoly had engendered among U.S. policy makers.[40] In the years up to 1949, the United States had not met the Soviet challenge by initiating a major rearmament effort to obtain a conventional force capability to counter possible Soviet aggression in Europe or elsewhere. Far from implementing such a measure, Truman successfully limited defense spending for reasons of political popularity and fiscal responsibility. The atomic monopoly served as a deterrent against Soviet utilization of their larger conventional forces. But news that the Soviets now possessed the atomic bomb caused deep disquiet.

In response to the successful Soviet atomic test, President Truman made two key decisions. First, he authorized development of a thermonuclear weapon – the hydrogen bomb. Motivated by both fear and caution, Truman's decision revealed the dynamics that would fuel the arms race through to the 1980s. The Americans feared, correctly it should be added, that the Soviets were engaged already upon developing an H-bomb, and they could not countenance

---

37 George C. Herring provides a balanced discussion of American involvement in Vietnam in his *America's Longest War: The United States and Vietnam, 1950–1975*, 3rd ed. (New York, 1996), pp. 3–19.
38 See John Lewis Gaddis, "Was the Truman Doctrine a Real Turning Point?" *Foreign Affairs*, 52 (January 1974), pp. 386–402; and Robert Jervis, "The Impact of the Korean War on the Cold War," *The Journal of Conflict Resolution*, 24 (December 1980), pp. 563–92.
39 William Whitney Stueck, Jr., *Rethinking the Korean War: A New Diplomatic and Strategic History* (Princeton, NJ, 2002), pp. 215–16.
40 See McGeorge Bundy, *Danger and Survival*, pp. 197–231.

Moscow's grabbing the lead in the nuclear race.[41] Along with the decision to build the H-bomb, Truman requested a full reassement of American foreign and national security policy. Thereupon a small group of officials led by Paul Nitze prepared NSC-68, which has been described as "the first comprehensive statement of national strategy."[42] They presented the results of their intense labors in April 1950.

NSC-68 portrayed the Soviet Union as inherently militant and expansionist "because it possesses and is possessed by a worldwide revolutionary movement, because it is the inheritor of Russian imperialism and because it is a totalitarian dictatorship."[43] Nitze and his colleagues raised the alarm about both Soviet capabilities and Soviet intentions. Nitze, in particular, argued that the Soviets might be tempted to use their superior military forces in a situation of American weakness or a perceived lack of resolve.[44] In this portrayal, the United States needed a major conventional force build-up as well as the development of its nuclear arsenal. NSC-68 provided the budgetary and military guidelines for just this rearmament program. It brought means and ends together in a deliberate way and made clear that greatly enhanced means would be required to implement the general end of containment of Soviet expansion.

The drafters of NSC-68 expected opposition to their recommendations from proponents of fiscal restraint both in Congress and within the Truman administration, including, it must be added, from the president himself.[45] Here is where the Korean War came to the rescue of Nitze and his colleagues. The outbreak of

---

[41] On the Soviet plans, see Andrei Sakharov, *Memoirs*, trans. Richard Lourie (New York, 1990), pp. 98–100; and David Holloway, *The Soviet Union and the Arms Race* (New Haven, CT, 1983), pp. 23–25.

[42] The description of NSC-68 is that of Senator Henry Jackson quoted in Alexander George and Richard Smoke, *Deterrence in American Foreign Policy: Theory and Practice* (New York, 1974), p. 26. On NSC-68, also see John Lewis Gaddis, "NSC 68 and the Problem of Ends and Means," *International Security*, 4 (Spring 1980), pp. 164–70.

[43] NSC-68, "A Report to the President Pursuant to the President's Directive of January 31, 1950," April 7, 1950, *FRUS*, 1950, I, pp. 246–85. For a vigorous critique of the arguments of NSC-68, see Robert P. Newman, "NSC (National Insecurity) 68: Nitze's Second Hallucination," in Martin J. Medland and H. W. Brands, eds., *Critical Reflections on the Cold War* (College Station, TX, 2000), pp. 55–94.

[44] Nitze argued in a February 1950 memorandum that "recent Soviet moves reflect not only a mounting militancy but suggest a boldness that is essentially new – and borders on recklessness." For him, "nothing about the moves indicate that Moscow is preparing to launch in the near future an all-out military attack on the West. They do, however, suggest a greater willingness than in the past to undertake a course of action, including a possible use of force in local areas, which might lead to an accidental outbreak of general military conflict. Thus the chance of war through miscalculation is increased." Nitze memorandum, February 8, 1959, *FRUS*, 1950, I, pp. 142–43. For an analysis, based on a close reading of American intelligence estimates, which suggests that Nitze's argument was solidly based, see Beatrice Heuser, "NSC 68 and the Soviet Threat: A New Perspective on Western Threat Perception and Policy Making," *Review of International Studies*, 17 (1991), pp. 17–40.

[45] On Truman's reticence to authorize enlarged defense spending, see Robert A. Pollard, "The National Security State Reconsidered: Truman and Economic Containment, 1945–1950," in Michael J. Lacey, ed., *The Truman Presidency* (Cambridge, 1989), pp. 230–32.

fighting on the Korean peninsula cut the ground from under potential opponents and seemingly confirmed the analysis of NSC-68. It marked, in Robert A. Pollard's words, "the true watershed in Truman's defense policy."[46] The outlook enshrined in NSC-68 came to dominate the thinking of Truman administration policy makers, and they sold it effectively to Congress and American people.[47] The basic policy of the United States would be to create what Acheson termed "situations of strength." Defense spending received a massive boost. In Europe, the Korean War and the security scare it sparked transformed NATO into a real military alliance with an integrated military structure under American command and with U.S. troops stationed in Europe. It also prompted the decision to rearm West Germany and to set that nation on a path which ended with its inclusion in NATO in 1955.

NSC-68 had described the Soviet assault on free institutions as worldwide in nature and argued that in the "present polarization of power a defeat of free institutions anywhere is a defeat everywhere." This extraordinary security definition, which failed to make proper distinctions between vital and peripheral American interests, transformed international politics into a virtual zero-sum game.[48] The security of the United States apparently meshed with that of all other parts of the world. The implications of this for U.S. foreign policy were enormous. With the lines frozen in Europe, the conflict soon extended into a global contest. American foreign policy makers at times would view developments in the Middle East, Asia, Africa, and Latin America through the sometimes distorting lens of the Cold War. By 1952, relations between the United States and the Soviet Union had reached a total impasse. Each nation strove to build its military strength and distrusted the other deeply. Genuine negotiations between them proved impossible. Even when new leaders assumed power in each country the following year, there was little improvement in relations. As Truman and his advisers understood well, more than mere personalities underlay the profound and costly conflict to which the United States remained committed until it ended in Western triumph.

Truman's presidency encompassed an enormously formative period in American diplomacy. Who would dispute Dean Acheson's finely understated observation that "the postwar years were a period of creation"?[49] Whatever the limitations and mistakes of Truman's foreign policy, they pale in comparison with its genuine accomplishments. On the essential matters, Truman got it right. The American commitment to restore and secure Western Europe and to pursue

---

[46] As Pollard explained further, "the invasion of South Korea appeared to refute the central concept of economic containment, namely that communist political penetration of war-disrupted societies posed a greater danger to Western security than did communist military aggression." Pollard, "The National Security State Reconsidered," p. 232.

[47] See Steven Casey, "Selling NSC-68: The Truman Administration, Public Opinion, and the Politics of Mobilization, 1950–51," *Diplomatic History*, 29 (September 2005), pp. 655–90.

[48] On this subject, see the brilliant chapter on "NSC-68 and the Korean War," in Gaddis, *Strategies of Containment*, pp. 89–126.

[49] Acheson, *Present at the Creation*, p. xviii.

stability in East Asia and to contest Soviet expansion laid impressive foundations for four decades of American foreign policy. Truman's successors with various calibrations and changes in emphasis continued the broad political-military approach established by the Truman administration from 1947 onward. Despite an uncertain start during which the American policy makers worked their way beyond Rooseveltian assumptions, the Truman administration eventually grasped the essential world realities and assumed the demanding responsibilities of genuine international leadership. In circumstances of both uncertainty and crisis, it constructed a foreign policy the main elements of which proved thoroughly apt and lasting. FDR established the foundations by developing American economic and military power, but it was his successor's administration that built the enduring framework for postwar American foreign policy.

In Retrospect – From Roosevelt to Truman

On April 8, 1949, Ernest Bevin sent a note of thanks to Harry Truman on the stationary of the British embassy in Washington, D.C. Four days earlier the British foreign secretary had signed the North Atlantic Treaty in the American capital, and that significant occasion obviously prompted him to reflect on the journey traveled over the previous two years. Bevin expressed gratitude to Truman for his "great efforts on behalf of Europe." He noted that aid to Greece and Turkey had helped secure the "independence of the Middle East," and that a series of measures had helped restore confidence in and secured the independence of the European nations.[50] Truman replied to Bevin soon after and expressed pleasure at the British foreign secretary's survey of the world situation. The president went further and engaged in some retrospective reflection of his own. "Naturally," he wrote Bevin, "we have all been disappointed by the attitude of the Russians. I tried for more than two years to reach an understanding with them but I have at last come to the conclusion that that is an impossibility unless the Russians know they can't run over the rest of the world."[51] Bevin, undoubtedly, would have agreed with Truman's analysis because he expended much energy over the 1945–47 period not only seeking to alert the American administration of the dangers of Soviet expansion but also maneuvering to draw the United States into a more vigorous response to it. Both men understood in retrospect that it took time for the American government to move beyond the assumptions and policies that Truman inherited from Franklin Roosevelt and to address the postwar realities of a weakened Europe and a threatening Soviet Union.

---

[50] Bevin to Truman, April 8, 1949, Harry S. Truman Papers: President's Secretary's File, HSTL, Box 172.

[51] Truman to Bevin, April 16, 1949, Harry S. Truman Papers: President's Secretary's File, HSTL, Box 172. Truman went on to express the view to Bevin that "I believe that we are well on the road of attaining that position, and than I am sure we will have a settlement that will be fair and just to everybody."

What Truman and Bevin clearly understood in 1949 has not always been well comprehended subsequently by American historians who portrayed Truman as overseeing a sharp reversal in FDR's cooperative approach to the Soviets. This study clarifies that such an interpretation is not supported by substantial evidence but rather was built upon a quicksand of faulty assumptions and misused tissues of evidence. The time has surely come for notions of sharp departures or reversals in foreign policy from Roosevelt to Truman to be dispatched to the burial grounds for flawed interpretations so as to join such "classics" as the views of the Dunning school historians on Reconstruction. Claims that Roosevelt's death and Truman's accession to power either caused or contributed significantly to the outbreak of the Cold War need to be pensioned off once and for all from use in accounts of postwar foreign policy. Both general foreign policy surveys and American history textbooks ought to reflect the reality that Truman initially attempted to follow in his predecessor's footsteps. To ensure a well-grounded understanding of American foreign policy from 1944 until 1947, one must comprehend Roosevelt's rather romantic plans and vision for the postwar world, how such plans initially guided Truman, and how it took Truman's administration substantial time to forge a realistic foreign policy including a new approach to the Soviet Union.

Franklin Roosevelt nebulously planned for a postwar world in which continued collaboration between the Big Four of the United States, the Soviet Union, Great Britain, and China would ensure an era of peace and a prosperity powered by free trade among nations. In his visionary scenario, Europe and especially Germany would be greatly reduced in significance in world affairs. FDR expected the United States to be engaged in the world, but he couldn't foresee any extensive and permanent American military or political commitments far beyond the western hemisphere and certainly not in Europe. He thought that Britain and the Soviet Union could oversee European developments. The American leader worked during the war to build a cooperative relationship with his Soviet opposite. Rather naïvely he relied on his hunches and intuitions and held the hope that he could civilize or domesticate the Soviet "beast" and establish a personal connection with Stalin. Operating on this sad delusion, Roosevelt fashioned a strategy toward the Soviets based on personal connections and significant concessions aimed at reassuring them of his bona fides.

Rather than pursuing a hard-headed political-military strategy, which many of his knowledgeable advisers recommended in the aftermath of the Warsaw uprising tragedy of 1944, Roosevelt pursued collaboration with Stalin to the end. Filled with idealistic hopes for the success of a new international body, Roosevelt made concessions to Stalin at Yalta to secure Soviet participation in it.[52] He believed that the UN would serve as a vehicle to prevent American disengagement from world affairs after the war, and, understandably, he vested it with notable importance. But doing so led him to perpetuate an adolescent

---

[52] FDR's commitment to the UN was much on his mind in the final months of his life. See Stephen C. Schlesinger, *Act of Creation*, pp. 57, 71.

idealism among the American people on postwar possibilities and to turn a blind eye to the Soviet establishment of their control over much of Eastern Europe. Better not to confront the real issues that divided the wartime allies. Better to build the UN on foundations of shifting sand rather than honestly face the fundamentally different worldviews and interests of the major powers; these differences inevitably dominated postwar international politics. Franklin Roosevelt, that great conjurer and juggler, left to his successor rather inflated expectations and unrealistic hopes for postwar peace, which influenced and restricted the Truman administration's policy making for almost two years. Indeed, as this study reveals, the Truman administration moved rather slowly and in a halting manner away from Roosevelt's guiding assumptions on cooperation with the Soviet Union and on the importance of the UN.

When Truman came to office, he had neither the interest nor the desire to alter Roosevelt's policies. He sincerely wanted to implement the plans of his revered predecessor and to ensure continuity in policy. His elemental assumptions placed him in the intellectual lineage of FDR. His recognition of the shameful and disastrous consequences of appeasement diplomacy and neutrality led him to fear any return to American isolationism. Like FDR, he wanted the United States to engage the world. Similarly, he held great faith in the benefits of the new international organization, which Roosevelt sponsored and which he vigorously supported and promoted. He hoped to continue cooperative relations with the wartime allies in securing final victory over Hitler and the Japanese militarists and in building a peaceful postwar world. The modest tensions evident in Truman's early dealings with Molotov in late April of 1945 should be understood as part of his effort to secure the implementation of agreements that Roosevelt had negotiated and thus to facilitate a successful meeting in San Francisco to form the United Nations. The dramatic character and political significance of the Truman–Molotov clash of April 23 has been vastly exaggerated and used as an emblem of policy reversal, but the encounter was a mere tactic used in an (unsuccessful) effort to make progress on the Polish issue. Those who focus on this episode, miss the forest while fixating on a single tree.

This study clarifies that the broad sweep of American policy from April 1945 to the Potsdam conference consisted of a genuine effort to maintain cooperative relations with the Soviet Union. Guided by a renowned sovietophile, Joseph Davies, Truman aimed to be evenhanded in his dealings with Churchill's Britain and Stalin's Russia and to avoid any hint of Anglo-American collusion against the Soviet Union. Truman's dispatch of Harry Hopkins to Moscow and his concessions on Poland and on withdrawing American troops from the Soviet zone in Germany testify to his continuity with Franklin Roosevelt. Just like FDR, Truman proved overly concerned about the establishment of the United Nations, and much like the man he succeeded, he squandered negotiating power with the Soviet Union to secure their participation. Regrettably, naivete with regard to Stalin and his intentions hardly ended with Roosevelt's death. Truman's administration worked to obtain the collaboration of the major powers. The alteration of FDR's conciliatory approach came after only further attempts at cooperation.

The appointment of James F. Byrnes as secretary of state brought a different approach to the Truman administration. Byrnes, with Truman's backing, favored the traditional diplomatic tactic of negotiation. He held none of Roosevelt's illusions regarding his abilities to gain Stalin's trust, but he still wanted to maintain decent relations with the Soviet Union by reaching practical settlements of the issues they faced. In light of this, Byrnes largely recognized the division of Europe foreshadowed at Yalta and secured through Soviet military domination of Eastern Europe. He pursued a quid pro quo approach and accepted a spheres of influence peace, hoping that this might secure a workable and stable postwar settlement. Byrnes hoped that America's possession of the atomic bomb might add some weight to his side in the diplomatic bargaining of the post-Potsdam period, but – and this must be clearly understood – Truman authorized the actual use of the atomic bomb to defeat the Japanese and not as part of some anti-Soviet strategy. Fanciful notions of "atomic diplomacy" must be consigned to the historiographical dustbin. Most striking about America's sole possession of the atomic bomb is how little they sought to use it for diplomatic ends and purposes.

The period from the fall of 1945 until the late fall of 1946 constitutes a period of transition. Perceptions of the Soviet Union changed and concerns about its international behavior and ambitions deepened especially as regards Iran and Turkey. And yet, while various general alarms were raised by the likes of Winston Churchill and George Kennan, the American response remained rather episodic. No coherent response emerged, and, much to the distress of Bevin and like-minded Europeans, the United States initially demonstrated no eagerness to step into the breach to balance and to counter Soviet influence on the continent. But in the end, Truman, initially guided by Byrnes and then by Marshall and Acheson, broke free of FDR's "hunches" regarding Stalin. These Americans were less enamored of their own intuition and more willing to draw conclusions from Soviet actions and intentions. They increasingly accepted that U.S. policy must resist Soviet demands and create barriers of sorts to their offensive operations. Byrnes applied the approach in Germany with his Stuttgart proposals and began to clarify that the United States would not abandon Europe. With the Truman Doctrine and the Marshall Plan, the United States finally put to rest Rooseveltian notions that Europe's significance could be reduced and worked instead with a proper understanding of the old continent's true importance in the global balance of power. With those measures came the essential confirmation that the Truman administration had finally abandoned its hopes for cooperation with the Soviet Union and begun to contain Stalin's expansion. Policy shifted from reliance on Roosevelt's assumptions to the construction of the Truman paradigm, which proved so valuable throughout the Cold War.

This examination of Truman's initial foreign policy sheds further light on the development of the Cold War conflict. It certainly raises major questions regarding the criticism that revisionist scholars regularly aimed at the Truman administration for not persisting with the cooperative approach of Roosevelt. As one of the best of this school portrayed it, almost from the end of World War II American policy makers deliberately and willingly "chose to contain and deter the Russians rather than to reassure and placate them."[53] In light of the findings of both this study and those who study Stalin's foreign policy, one might wish that this had been so. Irony of ironies, however, it now seems clear that if the Truman administration warrants criticism for its initial foreign policy measures, then it deserves it not for reversing Roosevelt's policies but for hewing too closely to them. This certainly is the convincing view offered by some of the more astute historians of the Cold War, among them Vojtech Mastny, John Lewis Gaddis, Tony Judt, and John Lukacs. After noting the Soviet "combination of appetite with aversion to risk," John Gaddis wondered "what would have happened had the West tried containment earlier" and went on to note with approval that "to the extent that it bears partial responsibility for the coming of the Cold War, the historian Vojtech Mastny has argued, that responsibility lies in its failure to do just that."[54] Judt agrees. After noting Molotov's dictum that "our ideology stands for offensive operations when possible, and if not, we wait," he concluded that "it probably follows from this that the policy of 'containment' adopted in 1947 might well have worked earlier than it did, had it been attempted."[55] Lukacs allied himself with the 1946 views of Winston Churchill and George Kennan and held that "the American reaction to the Russians was neither too soon nor too drastic but too late."[56]

Regrettably, the Truman administration expended too much energy in 1945 and 1946 negotiating with the Soviets and, in a way, attempting to reassure and placate them and to reach amicable settlements with them. It unfortunately took time for Truman and Byrnes to learn the essential lessons regarding Stalin and his ambitions. For too long, Truman entertained the counsel of Joseph Davies and tried to conform to the expectations established by Roosevelt's public vision. Consequently, the United States largely stood back during the Anglo-Soviet tensions of late 1945 and early 1946, and to a large extent, Truman and Byrnes accepted the "concession" of Eastern Europe to Stalin to try to meet

---

[53] Leffler, *Preponderance of Power*, p. 99.

[54] Gaddis, *We Now Know*, p. 31. Gaddis relies on Mastny's *Russia's Road to the Cold War*, pp. 306–13.

[55] Tony Judt, "Why the Cold War Worked," *New York Review of Books*, 44 (October 9, 1997), p. 41.

[56] John A. Lukacs, "Historians and the Cold War," in Mark F. Wilkinson, ed., *The Cold War: Opening Shots, 1945–1950* (Lexington, VA, 2003), p. 36. One might again note the views of the renowned historian of the Soviet Union, Adam Ulam, who asked rhetorically in 1999: "Could a more vigorous diplomacy by the United States have constrained Moscow to pull in its horns?" He gave a partial answer to his own question by noting that "those who scoff at the idea that anything short of military intervention could have arrested the 'satellization' of Eastern Europe might well ponder the case of Soviet behavior in northern Iran." Adam B. Ulam, "A Few Unresolved Mysteries about Stalin and the Cold War in Europe: A Modest Agenda for Research," *Journal of Cold War Studies*, 1 (Winter 1999), p. 112.

his supposed security needs. But to its eternal credit, the Truman administration drew the line there.

The fact that the United States mounted a defensive effort in 1947 to check Soviet advances and to steady the Western Europeans to resist Soviet pressure and intimidation strangely became in the hands of some Western academics an occasion for lumping on the United States a heavy share of the responsibility for the outbreak of the Cold War. In Melvyn Leffler's portrayal, America's excessive response placed the Soviets on the defensive such that from 1947–48 onward, "Soviet actions were reactive." Consequently, he asserted, there is "reason to assign as much responsibility for the origins of the cold war to the United States as to the Soviet Union."[57] The corollary to this argument is that measures such as the Truman Doctrine, the Marshall Plan, and NATO escalated the Cold War dramatically and inappropriately. Lingering behind this argument lies the assumption that if only American policy makers had been more wise and insightful in 1945–46 by reaching sympathetic agreements with the Soviet Union then the Cold War, as we know it, might have been avoided. Such an assumption is specious and cannot withstand scrutiny as this study makes clear.

Soviet actions from 1944 through 1945 and 1946 occasionally may have exhibited some caution and cunning, but their ultimate purpose remained to extend the Soviet empire and Stalin's vile control as far as possible. It took time for the Truman administration to appreciate this, but it finally did. No action of the Truman administration could have changed or reassured Stalin. No missed opportunity on the American side could have satiated Stalin's appetite for power and control. "All attempts to imagine alternative courses of postwar international relations," David Holloway has observed correctly, "run up against Stalin himself."[58] Otto Von Bismarck reportedly once observed that "no one will ever be rich enough to buy his enemies by concessions." This insight certainly applied to Stalin. Concessions and weakness only encouraged his voracity and urged him on to spread his tyranny.[59]

Looking at Stalin's part in the Cold War from the perspective of half a century, the political scientist Robert Jervis observed perceptively that "while American analysts later came to fear the 'Finlandization' of Western Europe, it is now clear that only if Stalin had been able to 'Finlandize' Eastern Europe – that is, make it strategically harmless without satellizing it – would the USSR have been secure." To a great extent, some variation of a "Finlandized" Eastern

---

57 Leffler, *Preponderance of Power*, pp. 513, 515. The previously cited article by Michael Cox and Caroline Kennedy-Pipe, "The Tragedy of American Diplomacy?" is an even more recent example of this genre.

58 Holloway, *Stalin and the Bomb*, p. 370. See also John Gaddis's discussion of Stalin's centrality in causing the Cold War in his *We Now Know*, pp. 24–25.

59 Stalin's own associates knew the truth about him. Consider Lavrenti Beria's judgment (rendered after his master's death) that "Stalin was a scoundrel, a savage, a tyrant! He held us all in fear, the bloodsucker. And the people too. That's where all his power came from. Fortunately we're now rid of him. Let the snake rot in hell." See William Taubman, *Khrushchev: The Man and His Era* (New York, 2003), p. 246.

Europe is what American policy makers in 1945 and 1946 had hoped might satisfy Stalin, but it never did. As Jervis also noted, for this approach to have worked would have "required communism to be a different system, or at least Stalin to have been a different person." But Stalin remained both the person who "could not be secure as long as there were any enemies around" and the one who "saw enemies everywhere" right to his death.[60] It was simply not within Harry Truman's power as a decent and responsible democratic leader to offer terms that would soothe Stalin's anxieties and insecurities. To have attempted this would have placed the freedom and security of the West at great risk and played into the hands of "the other twentieth-century totalitarian regime."[61] The time has surely come to recognize this and to accept as Tony Judt memorably has put it that " 'Revisionism,' the wishful search for evidence that the US bore primary responsibility for the origin and pursuit of the Cold War, is now a dead duck."[62]

Historians also must acknowledge that after an uncertain start in office the Truman administration worked its way to a deeply responsible and essential counter to the Soviet threat to liberal democracy. Alonzo Hamby is surely right to count Truman's "mobilization of the Western world against the Communist challenge," as an achievement "Churchillian in its significance."[63] The great Englishman used as a reference point by Hamby voiced a similar conclusion. In a well-known assessment offered as Truman came to the end of his presidency, Churchill confessed that initially, "I held you in very low regard. . . . I loathed your taking the place of Franklin Roosevelt." But the great British wartime leader, now returned to office as prime minister, continued: "I misjudged you badly. Since that time, you more than any other man, have saved Western civilization."[64]

Such encomiums to the accomplishments of Truman and his administration are given ballast if one contemplates what might have happened had not Truman led the United States in the immediate postwar years. There was nothing preordained about the Truman foreign policy, and there were other possible directions for the nation. It is fortuitous that they were not taken. For example, Henry Wallace assuredly would have pressed for greater "understanding" of the Soviet position and a more "conciliatory approach," which could have given

---

[60] Robert Jervis, "Stalin, An Incompetent Realist," *The National Interest*, 50 (Winter 1997–98), pp. 84–85. It should also be noted that the critical analysis of Stalin and his part in the Cold War made by Arthur Schlesinger, Jr., three decades ago stands up very well. See Schlesinger, "Origins of the Cold War," pp. 48–50.

[61] This description of the Soviet Union comes from Anne Applebaum in her *Gulag*, p. 576. The general idea presented here is also influenced by her.

[62] Judt, "Why the Cold War Worked," p. 42.

[63] Hamby, *Man of the People*, p. 641. Hamby explained that "however unsophisticated it may have been, Truman's understanding of Soviet totalitarianism and imperialism possessed an elemental comprehension and integrity that were impressive when contrasted with the aimless diplomacy of James Byrnes or the ostrich-like fellow-traveling of Henry Wallace."

[64] Churchill quoted in McCullough, *Truman*, pp. 874–75.

the 1940s its own version of appeasement to rival that of the 1930s. Wallace's ability "to look kindly upon the Soviet Union" knew few bounds.[65] Joseph Persico speculates that Wallace as president would have appointed "Lawrence Duggan as his secretary of state and Harry Dexter White as his secretary of the Treasury."[66] Mercifully this did not occur. Nor did any recourse to the unilateralist-isolationist policies, which had considerable support in the Republican Party and which had their best proponent in Senator Robert Taft. The Marshall Plan and NATO testify eloquently to Truman's capacity to take the country in an internationalist direction. But the fact that Dwight D. Eisenhower entered the Republican presidential race in 1952 to prevent Taft's victory for fear of his reversing "the basic Truman strategy of cooperation with allies and collective security for containing the Soviet Union" suggests the danger Taft represented.[67] One shudders to contemplate the future of Western Europe had Taft's opposition to the Marshall Plan and to NATO proved successful.

All this is not meant to instigate any campaign to canonize Harry Truman. Readers of this work would appreciate that it is hardly an exercise in hagiography. Those favorably disposed to Truman's foreign policy should neither present him as the main architect of it nor exaggerate his capabilities. Obviously, Truman had none of the global visionary qualities of Woodrow Wilson nor the superb domestic political skills of Franklin Roosevelt. He rightly commands no reputation as either a grand strategist or even as a geopolitical thinker. Indeed, he could be naïve and simplistic in his thinking. It took him some considerable time to extract himself from the web spun by Joseph Davies. At times he was uncertain and confused and eager to have others carry the main burden of policy making as in the case of his reliance on James F. Byrnes. But in the end, Truman, aided by some of the most able American policy makers of the twentieth century, moved beyond the foreign policy accomplishments of both Wilson and FDR. He proved capable of tempering his idealism and overseeing a realistic foreign policy that garnered congressional support.[68] His very limitations in the diplomatic arts prevented his deluding himself that he could fashion settlements for the postwar world through personal relations with other

---

[65] For a revealing account of Henry Wallace's visit to Kolyma region of the USSR in May 1944, see Applebaum, *Gulag*, pp. 441–44.

[66] Joseph E. Persico, *Roosevelt's Secret War*, p. 300.

[67] On Eisenhower's decision to enter the Republican race for the presidential nomination, see William B. Pickett, *Eisenhower Decides to Run: Presidential Politics and Cold War Strategy* (Chicago, 2000); and Robert R. Bowie and Richard H. Immerman, *Waging Peace: How Eisenhower Shaped an Enduring Cold War Strategy* (New York, 1998), p. 11. Bowie and Immerman also point out that "Eisenhower's second reason [for running] was his conviction that the Truman policies and programs for carrying out his strategy had to be reshaped to make them more coherent and sustainable for the 'long haul' of the cold war."

[68] Truman was aided immeasurably in maintaining a bipartisan foreign policy by the efforts of Senator Arthur Vandenberg, the leader of the postwar internationalist Republicans. When the Michigan senator left the scene, Truman's bipartisan coalition suffered considerably. On this, see David R. Kepley, *The Collapse of the Middle Way: Senate Republicans and the Bipartisan Foreign Policy, 1948–1952* (New York, 1988).

leaders. In some sense, Truman's genius in office lay in his recognizing he was not a genius and in being able to rely on other capable policy makers.[69]

Harry Truman in a certain sense stands as a representative figure for a postwar generation that emerged from World War II with naïve and idealistic hopes for a postwar peace constructed on FDR's high-sounding principles. Yet, Truman proved capable of learning, revealed that he could face realities, and moved beyond his predecessor's thinking. Like many Americans of his generation, he took a Niebuhrian turn (without reading much of Reinhold Niebuhr) and turned away from excessive idealism and utopian notions of a world where self-determination reigned supreme and where spheres of influence had been eliminated.[70] Instead, Truman navigated a way between appeasement and outright war so as "to restore an international balance of power in which democracies would be secure."[71] It was a more tempered accomplishment than the constructs of the 'visionaries,' but more lasting and well grounded because it acknowledged the persistence of power and conflict in the world and addressed the existence of predatory antidemocratic forces.

Truman clearly recognized the extent of his achievement in the realm of foreign policy. In his farewell address to the American people delivered on January 15, 1953, he focused on the Cold War and admitted that he spent "hardly a day in office that has not been dominated by this all-embracing struggle." He attested confidently that "when history says that my term of office saw the beginning of the cold war, it will also say that in those eight years we have set the course that can win it." He went on to compare favorably the efforts of the United States under his stewardship to those pursued after World War I and during the "years of weakness and indecision" of the 1930s. Truman firmly rejected any atomic preemptive strike against the Soviet Union as a way to "end" the Cold War and offered instead a variation of George Kennan's notion that the Soviet Union would collapse of its own internal weakness, most especially the Soviet "rulers' fear of their own people." Taking the long view, Truman asserted that "the strength of our free society, and our ideals, will prevail over a system that has respect for neither God nor man."[72] Whatever the vicissitudes and travails of American foreign policy in the following four

---

[69] Truman certainly recognized this in the case of Acheson. As he prepared to leave the White House, he wrote his secretary of state: "You have been my good right hand. There is no need for me to go into detail about all you have accomplished. Certainly no man is more responsible than you for pulling together the people of the free world, and strengthening their will and their determination to be strong and free." Truman to Acheson, January 16, 1953, Truman, *Public Papers of the Presidents of the United States: Harry S. Truman, 1952–53*, p. 381.

[70] On Reinhold Niebuhr's influence, see Thomas W. Smith, "The Uses of Tragedy: Reinhold Niebuhr's Theory of History and International Ethics," *Ethics and International Affairs*, 9 (1995), pp. 171–91. Also see Arthur Schlesinger, Jr., "Forgetting Reinhold Niebuhr," *New York Times Book Review* (September 18, 2005), pp. 12–13.

[71] I borrow these words from Gaddis, *Surprise, Security, and the American Experience*, p. 109, who also applies them to FDR's efforts after Pearl Harbor.

[72] Farewell Address to the American People, January 15, 1953, Truman, *Public Papers of the Presidents of the United States: Harry S. Truman, 1952–53*, pp. 1197–201.

decades – and they are substantial – Truman's fundamental point held true. His administration laid the foundation for American triumph in the Cold War.

In his moving eulogy for Neville Chamberlain, his predecessor as prime minister, given in the House of Commons on November 12, 1940, Winston Churchill famously explained that "it is not given to human beings . . . to foresee and predict to any large extent the unfolding course of events. In one phase men seem to have been right, and in another they seem to have been wrong. Then again a few years later, when the perspective of time has lengthened, all stands in a different setting. There is a new proportion: there is another set of values." He further expounded: "History, with its flickering lamp, stumbles along the trail of the past, trying to reconstruct its scenes, to revive the echoes and kindle with pale gleams the passion of former days."[73] The first effort of this study has been to shine new light, however flickering, on the foreign policy pursued in the latter months of Franklin Roosevelt's administration and the early years of Harry Truman's. The scenes portrayed are not always rendered in the sharp and distinctive colors of black and white – confusion, ambiguity, contradictions, and messiness sometimes prevailed.

Yet the historian must surely move beyond a mere reconstruction of past scenes. While Churchill's words are surely a warning to historians, inevitably trapped in the circumstances and assumptions of their own time and place, to curtail their tendency to "moral pontification," the historian cannot divorce himself or herself totally from the responsibility of moral evaluation.[74] Certainly, Churchill as historian did not. He knew that good and evil existed and was unafraid to name them. He took as the theme for *The Gathering Storm*, the initial volume of his history of the Second World War, "how the English-speaking people through their unwisdom, carelessness, and good nature allowed the *wicked* to rearm."[75] Churchill was writing a mere decade after the events that he described in his great work. Writing over half a century after the events described here, surely a proper perspective has been gained to allow the rendering of a judgment of American foreign policy in the early Cold War. Mirroring Churchill's thematic summary, it should be held that after initial attempts at continued cooperation with the Soviet Union, the Truman administration rightly moved – falteringly at first, but then with increasing authority – to meet the aggressive designs of the Soviet Union. Men like Truman, Marshall, and Acheson – men of the political center – and comrades in arms like Clement Attlee and Ernest Bevin – men of the democratic left – deserve praise and gratitude from all those who value democratic ideals today. It is undoubtedly a travesty that Truman and his administration have been subjected to ill-founded criticism by many American academic historians who so easily shrug off the

---

[73] Churchill speech, November 12, 1940, printed in *London Times*, November 13, 1940.

[74] Arthur Schleinger, Jr., makes the point about "moral pontification" in his *A Life in the Twentieth Century*, p. 449. Again my thinking about history in moral terms is influenced by John Gaddis. See his *Landscape of History*, p. 122.

[75] Winston S. Churchill, *The Gathering Storm*, p. ix. (My emphasis.)

danger that Stalin and his system presented.[76] However that may have been, it is essential that historians of today appreciate that Truman's administration navigated through "puzzling and perilous" times to establish eventually a foreign policy whose main elements were appropriate and which protected American security and defended some good measure of democratic freedom in the world.[77]

[76] Arnold Offner's *Another Such Victory* is but the latest exemplar of this genre.
[77] Acheson describes the times as "puzzling and perilous" in *Present at the Creation*, p. 737.

Select Bibliography

I. Primary Sources

A. Manuscript Collections

Alderman Library (Manuscript Division), University of Virginia, Charlottesville, Virginia
Louis J. Halle Papers
Louis A. Johnson Papers
Edward R. Stettinius, Jr., Papers
Bentley Historical Library, The University of Michigan, Ann Arbor, Michigan (microfilm)
Arthur H. Vandenberg Papers
Bodleian Library, Oxford University, Oxford, England
Clement Attlee Papers
William Clark Papers
Paul Gore-Booth Papers
Churchill Archives Center, Churchill College, Cambridge, England
Ernest Bevin Papers
Alexander G. Cadogan Papers
Winston S. Churchill Papers (Chartwell, Churchill, and Premier Collections)
Cooper Library (Special Collections/Strom Thurmond Institute), Clemson University, Clemson, South Carolina.
James F. Byrnes Papers
Franklin D. Roosevelt Library (FDRL), Hyde Park, New York
Anna Roosevelt Halstead Papers
Harry L. Hopkins Papers
Franklin D. Roosevelt Papers: President's Personal File
Franklin D. Roosevelt Papers: President's Secretary's File
Samuel I. Rosenman Papers
Henry A. Wallace Papers
George C. Marshall Library, Lexington, Virginia
Larry I. Bland Collection
W. Walton Butterworth Papers

Marshall S. Carter Papers
Lucius D. Clay Papers
George C. Marshall Papers
Forrest C. Pogue Materials
James W. Riddleberger Papers
U.S. Department of the Army, Plans and Operations Division, Miscellaneous Papers on
    Greece, Japan, and Germany (RG 319)
C. Ben Wright Papers (Kennan Biography Project)
Harry S. Truman Library (HSTL), Independence, Missouri
Dean G. Acheson Papers
George V. Allen Papers
Eben A. Ayers Papers
Ralph Block Papers
William L. Clayton Papers
Clark M. Clifford Papers
Matthew J. Connelly Papers
Jonathan Daniels Papers
George M. Elsey Papers
Thomas K. Finletter Papers
A. Robert Ginsburgh Papers
S. Everett Gleason Papers
Stanton Griffis Papers
Paul G. Hoffman Papers
Joseph M. Jones Papers
Dan A. Kimball Papers
Charles P. Kindleberger Papers
David D. Lloyd Papers
Edward G. Miller Papers
Charles S. Murphy Papers
Frank Pace, Jr., Papers
J. Anthony Panuch Papers
Sumner T. Pike Papers
Harry B. Price Papers
William M. Rigdon Papers
Frank N. Roberts Papers
Samuel I. Rosenman Papers
Charles G. Ross Papers
Harold D. Smith Papers
John W. Snyder Papers
Stephen F. Spingarn Papers
Sidney W. Souers Papers
Charles W. Thayer Papers
Harry S. Truman Papers: Central File
Harry S. Truman Papers: Post-Presidential Files
Harry S. Truman Papers: President's Official File
Harry S. Truman Papers: President's Secretary's File
Harry S. Truman Papers: Senatorial Files and Senatorial and Vice-Presidential Speeches
    File

Harry S. Truman Papers: White House Map Room File
Harry S. Truman Papers: 1947 Diary
James E. Webb Papers
Chaim Weizmann Archives, Rehovoth, Israel (copies)
Houghton Library, Harvard University, Cambridge, Massachusetts
Ruth Fischer Papers
Joseph C. Grew Papers
Library of Congress, Washington, D.C.
Joseph and Stewart Alsop Papers
Charles E. Bohlen Papers
Benjamin V. Cohen Papers
Tom Connally Papers
Joseph E. Davies Papers
James A. Farley Papers
Herbert Feis Papers
Averell Harriman Papers
Loy W. Henderson Papers
Philip C. Jessup Papers
William D. Leahy Papers
J. Robert Oppenheimer Papers
Robert P. Patterson Papers
Laurence A. Steinhardt Papers
Main Library Special Collections, University of Birmingham, Birmingham, England
Anthony Eden, First Earl of Avon Papers
Eden Foreign Secretary Papers (FO 954)
National Archives, Washington, D.C.
Diplomatic Branch:
    Department of State Records: Central Decimal Files
    Department of State Records: Executive Secretariat Files
    Department of State Records: Records of Charles E. Bohlen, 1941–52
    Department of State Records: Records of the Office of European Affairs, 1942–47
        (H. Freeman Matthews and John D. Hickerson Files)
    Department of State Records: Records of the Policy Planning Staff
    Department of State Records: Records of the Inter and Intra Departmental
        Committees (RG 353)
Modern Military Branch:
    National Security Council Documents
    U.S. Joint Chief of Staff Records: RG 218, Central Decimal File, 1948–50
    U.S. Joint Chiefs of Staff Records: William D. Leahy Records
Public Record Office, Kew, England
Cabinet Records
Foreign Office Records
Prime Minister's Operational File (Premier 3 and 4)
Seeley G. Mudd Manuscript Library, Princeton University, Princeton, New Jersey
Bernard M. Baruch Papers
John Foster Dulles Papers
James V. Forrestal Papers
George F. Kennan Papers

Arthur Krock Papers
David E. Lilienthal Papers
Sterling Memorial Library, Yale University, New Haven, Connecticut
Dean G. Acheson Papers
Robert O. Anthony Collection of Walter Lippmann
Hanson Baldwin Papers
Samuel Flagg Bemis Papers
Chester Bowles Papers
Arthur Bliss Lane Papers
Max Lerner Papers
Walter Lippmann Papers
Henry L. Stimson Papers
Arnold Wolfers Papers
University Archives, University of Kentucky, Lexington, Kentucky
Fred M. Vinson Papers
University of Notre Dame Archives, Notre Dame, Indiana
Frank C. Walker Papers

B. Documents

Bundy, Harvey H., and James Grafton Rogers. *The Organization of the Government for the Conduct of Foreign Affairs: A Report with Recommendations Prepared for the Commission on Organization of Executive Branch of the Government.* Washington, DC: U.S. Government Printing Office, 1949.
Etzold, Thomas H., and John Lewis Gaddis, eds. *Containment: Documents on American Foreign Policy and Strategy, 1945–1950.* New York: Oxford University Press, 1978.
Great Britain, Parliament. *Hansard's Parliamentary Debates, 1945–1950.* London: His Majesty's Stationary Office, 1947–50.
Nelson, Anna Kasten, ed. *The State Department Policy Planning Staff Papers, 1947–1949.* New York: Garland, 1983.
Rosenman, Samuel I., ed. *The Public Papers and Addresses of Franklin D. Roosevelt.* Vols. IX–XIII. 1940–1945. New York: Macmillan, 1941–50.
Truman, Harry S. *Public Papers of the Presidents of the United States: Harry S. Truman, 1945–1950.* Washington, DC: U.S. Government Printing Office, 1961–65.
U.S. Congress. *Congressional Record.* Washington, DC: U.S. Government Printing Office, 1934–50.
U.S. Congress. Senate Committee on Foreign Relations. *A Decade of American Foreign Policy: Basic Documents, 1941–1949.* Washington, DC: U.S. Government Printing Office, 1950.
U.S. Department of State. *The Department of State Bulletin, 1941–1950.* Washington, DC: U.S. Government Printing Office, 1941–50.
U.S. Department of State. *Foreign Relations of the United States, 1941–1952.* Washington, DC: U.S. Government Printing Office, 1967–88.
U.S. Department of State. *Foreign Relations of the United States: The Conferences at Cairo and Tehran, 1943.* Washington, DC: U.S. Government Printing Office, 1961.
U.S. Department of State. *Foreign Relations of the United States: The Conference at Quebec, 1944.* Washington, DC: U.S. Government Printing Office, 1972.
U.S. Department of State. *Foreign Relations of the United States: The Conferences at Malta and Yalta, 1945.* Washington, DC: U.S. Government Printing Office, 1955.

U.S. Department of State. *Foreign Relations of the United States: The Conference of Berlin (The Potsdam Conference), 1945.* 2 vols. Washington, DC: U.S. Government Printing Office, 1960.

C. Oral Histories

Columbia University Oral History Project
Charles E. Bohlen
Harvey H. Bundy
W. Averell Harriman
Walter Lippmann
Robert Lovett
Marshall Plan Project
John J. McCloy
Dulles Oral History Collection, Seeley G. Mudd Manuscript Library, Princeton University, Princeton, New Jersy.
Theodore Achilles
John M. Allison
Stewart Alsop
Roswell Barnes
Charles Bohlen
David K. E. Bruce
W. Walton Butterworth
James F. Byrnes
Lucius Clay
John Sherman Cooper
Thomas E. Dewey
Allen W. Dulles
Avery Dulles, S.J.
Dwight D. Eisenhower
Thomas K. Finletter
W. Averell Harriman
John D. Hickerson
George F. Kennan
H. Freeman Matthews
John J. McCloy
Robert D. Murphy
Lauris Norstad
Foreign Affairs Oral History Program, Georgetown University Library, Washington, D.C.
William Attwood
Robert R. Bowie
Marshall Green
Fred M. Vinson Oral History Project, University of Kentucky, Lexington, Kentucky
Benjamin Cohen
Paul Porter
Fred M. Vinson, Jr.
George C. Marshall Library, Lexington, Virginia
George C. Marshall Interviews and Reminiscences for Forrest C. Pogue, 1956–57

Harry S. Truman Library Oral History Collection (HSTL), Independence, Missouri
Theodore Achilles
Konrad Adenauer
George E. Allen
Eben A. Ayers
Robert W. Barnett
David E. Bell
Ralph Block
Henri Lucien Bonnet
Winthrop G. Brown
David K. E. Bruce
Matthew J. Connelly
Jonathan Daniels
Robert L. Dennison
William H. Draper, Jr.
George M. Elsey
Abraham Feinberg
Thomas K. Finletter
Edward T. Folliard
Oliver Franks
Gordon Gray
Loy W. Henderson
John D. Hickerson
Paul G. Hoffman
Benjamin M. Hulley
Walter H. Judd
Marx Leva
Edwin A. Locke, Jr.
Roger Makins
John Maktos
Edward S. Mason
Clifford C. Matlock
Charles S. Murphy
Frank Pace, Jr.
James W. Riddleberger
Samuel I. Rosenman
Francis Russell
Charles E. Saltzman
Durward V. Sandifer
Joseph C. Satterthwaite
Philip D. Sprouse
Isaac N. P. Stokes
John L. Sullivan
Harry H. Vaughan
Edwin M. Wright
John F. Kennedy Library
Dean G. Acheson
Charles E. Bohlen
Roger Hilsman

George F. Kennan
Llewellyn E. Thompson

D. Newspapers and Periodicals

Nation, 1934–47
New Republic, 1934–47
New York Times, 1934–47
Time, 1934–47
U.S. News, 1934–47

E. Published Memoirs, Diaries, and Papers

Acheson, Dean G. *Present at the Creation: My Years in the State Department*. New York: W. W. Norton, 1969.

Acheson, Dean G. *Sketches From Life of Men I Have Known*. New York: Harper, 1961.

Adenauer, Konrad. *Memoirs, 1945–1953*. Chicago: Henry Regnery, 1966.

Allison, John M. *Ambassador from the Prairie or Allison Wonderland*. Boston: Houghton Mifflin, 1973.

Anderson, Clinton P. *Outsider in the Senate*. New York: World, 1970.

Attlee, Clement. *Twilight of Empire: Memoirs of Prime Minister Clement Attlee*. New York: A. S. Barnes, 1962.

Attwood, William. *The Twilight Struggle: Tales of the Cold War*. New York: Harper and Row, 1987.

Balfour, John. *Not Too Correct an Aureole: The Recollections of a Diplomat*. Wilton, Salisbury, Wiltshire: Michael Russell, 1983.

Ball, George W. *The Past Has Another Pattern: Memoirs*. New York: W. W. Norton, 1982.

Barkley, Alben W. *That Reminds Me*. Garden City, NJ: Doubleday, 1954.

Baruch, Bernard. *The Public Years*. New York: Holt, 1960.

Berle, Beatrice Bishop, and Travis Beal Jacobs, eds. *Navigating the Rapids, 1918–1971: From the Papers of Adolf A. Berle*. New York: Harcourt Brace Jovanovich, 1973.

Bidault, Georges. *Resistance: The Political Autobiography of Georges Bidault*. London: Weidenfeld and Nicholson, 1965.

Bland, Larry, ed. *George C. Marshall Interviews and Reminiscences for Forrest C. Pogue*. Lexington, VA: George C. Marshall Research Foundation, 1991.

Blum, John Morton, ed. *From the Morgenthau Diaries*. 3 vols. Boston: Houghton Mifflin, 1959–67. Vol 3. *Years of War, 1941–1945*, 1967.

Blum, John Morton, ed. *The Price of Vision: The Diary of Henry A. Wallace, 1942–1946*. Boston: Houghton Mifflin, 1973.

Blum, John Morton, ed. *Public Philosopher: Selected Letters of Walter Lippmann*. New York: Tickner and Fields, 1985.

Bohlen, Charles E. *Witness to History, 1929–1969*. New York: W. W. Norton, 1973.

Bowles, Chester. *Promises to Keep: My Years in Public Life, 1941–1969*. New York: Harper and Row, 1971.

Braden, Spruille. *Diplomats and Demagogues: The Memoirs of Spruille Braden*. New Rochelle, NY: Arlington House, 1971.

Bradley, Omar N. *A Soldier's Story*. New York: Henry Holt, 1951.

Bradley, Omar N., and Clay Blair. *General's Life: An Autobiography of General of the Army Omar N. Bradley.* New York: Simon and Schuster, 1983.

Brandon, Henry. *Special Relationships: A Foreign Correspondent's Memoirs from Roosevelt to Reagan.* New York: Atheneum, 1988.

Bullitt, Orville H., ed. *For the President: Personal and Secret, Correspondence Between Franklin D. Roosevelt and William C. Bullitt.* Boston: Houghton Mifflin, 1972.

Bullitt, William C. "How We Won the War and Lost the Peace," *Life,* 25 (August 30 and September 6, 1948), 83–97, 86–103.

Bush, Vannevar. *Pieces of the Action.* New York: William Morrow, 1970.

Byrnes, James F. *All in One Lifetime.* New York: Harper and Bros., 1958.

Byrnes, James F. *Speaking Frankly.* New York: Harper and Bros., 1947.

Campbell, Thomas, and George C. Herring, eds. *The Diaries of Edward R. Stettinius, Jr., 1943–1946.* New York: New Viewpoints, 1975.

Chandler, Alfred D., Jr., ed. *The Papers of Dwight David Eisenhower.* Vol. 4. *The War Years.* Baltimore: Johns Hopkins University Press, 1970.

Churchill, Winston S. *The Second World War.* 6 vols. Boston: Houghton Mifflin, 1948–53.

Clark, Mark W. *From the Danube to the Yalu.* New York: Harper and Bros., 1954.

Clay, Lucius D. *Decision in Germany.* New York: Doubleday, 1950.

Clay, Lucius D. *Germany and the Fight for Freedom.* Cambridge, MA: Harvard University Press, 1950.

Clifford, Clark, with Richard Holbrooke. *Counsel to the President: A Memoir.* New York: Random House, 1991.

Conant, James B. *My Several Lives: Memoirs of a Social Inventor.* New York: Harper and Row, 1970.

Connally, Tom. *My Name Is Tom Connally.* New York: T. Y. Crowell, 1954.

Dalton, Hugh. *Memoirs.* Vol. II. *High Tide and After, 1945–1960.* London: Frederick Muller, 1962.

Daniels, Jonathan. *White House Witness, 1942–1945.* New York: Doubleday, 1975.

Davies, Jr., John Paton. *Dragon by the Tail.* New York: W. W. Norton, 1972.

Dilks, David, ed. *The Diaries of Sir Alexander Cadogan, O.M., 1938–1945.* London: Cassell, 1971.

Dixon, Piers. *Double Diploma: The Life of Sir Pierson Dixon, Don and Diplomat.* London: Hutchinson, 1968.

Djilas, Milovan. *Conversations with Stalin.* New York: Harcourt, Brace and World, 1962.

Dobney, Frederick J., ed. *Selected Papers of Will Clayton.* Baltimore: Johns Hopkins University Press, 1971.

Dulles, John Foster. *War or Peace.* New York: Macmillan, 1950.

Eden, Anthony. *Full Circle: The Memoirs of Anthony Eden.* Boston: Houghton Mifflin, 1960.

Eden, Anthony. *The Reckoning: The Eden Memoirs.* Boston: Houghton Mifflin, 1965.

Eichelberger, Clark M. *Organizing for Peace: A Personal History of the Founding of the United Nations.* New York: Harper and Row, 1977.

Ferrell, Robert H., ed. *The Autobiography of Harry S. Truman.* Boulder: Associated Press of Colorado, 1980.

Ferrell, Robert H., ed. *Dear Bess: The Letters From Harry To Bess Truman, 1910–1959.* New York: Norton, 1983.

Ferrell, Robert H., ed. *FDR's Quiet Confidant: The Autobiography of Frank C. Walker.* Niwot, CO: University Press of Colorado, 1997.

Ferrell, Robert H., ed. *Harry S. Truman and the Bomb: A Documentary History.* Worland, WY: High Plains Publishing Company, 1996.

Ferrell, Robert H., ed. *Off the Record: The Private Papers of Harry S. Truman.* New York: Harper & Row, 1980.

Ferrell, Robert H., ed. *Truman in the White House: The Diary of Eben A. Ayers.* Columbia and London: University of Missouri Press, 1991.

Galbraith, John Kenneth. *A Life in Our Times: Memoirs.* Boston: Houghton Mifflin, 1981.

Grew, Joseph C. *Turbulent Era: A Diplomatic Record of Forty Years, 1904–1945.* 2 vols. Boston: Houghton Mifflin, 1952.

Gromyko, Andrei. *Memories.* trans. Harold Shukman. London: Hutchinson, 1989.

Groves, Leslie R. *Now It Can Be Told: The Story of the Manhattan Project.* New York, Harper & Bros., 1962.

Harriman, W. Averell. *America and Russia in a Changing World.* New York: Doubleday, 1971.

Harriman, W. Averell, and Elie Abel. *Special Envoy to Churchill and Stalin, 1941–1946.* New York: Random House, 1975.

Hull, Cordell. *The Memoirs of Cordell Hull.* 2 vols. New York: Macmillan, 1948.

Jackson, Robert H. *That Man: An Insider's Portrait of Franklin D. Roosevelt.* Ed. John Q. Barrett. New York: Oxford University Press, 2003.

Jebb, Gladwyn. *The Memoirs of Lord Gladwyn.* London: Weidenfeld and Nicholson, 1972.

Jessup, Philip C. *The Birth of Nations.* New York: Columbia University Press, 1974.

Johnson, U. Alexis. *The Right Hand of Power.* Englewood Cliffs, NJ: Prentice Hall, 1984.

Jones, Joseph M. *The Fifteen Weeks.* New York: Viking, 1955.

Kennan, George F. *At a Century's Ending: Reflections, 1982–1995.* New York: Norton, 1996.

Kennan, George F. *Memoirs, 1925–1950.* Boston: Little, Brown, 1967.

Kennan, George F. *Memoirs, 1950–1963.* Boston: Little, Brown, 1972.

Kennan, George F. *Sketches from a Life.* New York: Pantheon Books, 1989.

Khrushchev, Nikita S. *Khrushchev Remembers.* Boston: Little, Brown, 1970.

Kimball, Warren, ed. *Churchill and Roosevelt: The Complete Correspondence.* 3 vols. Princeton, NJ: Princeton University Press, 1984.

Kindleberger, Charles P. *Marshall Plan Days.* Boston: Allen & Unwin, 1987.

Kirkpatrick, Ivone. *The Inner Circle.* London: Macmillan, 1959.

Kissinger, Henry. *White House Years.* Boston: Little, Brown, 1979.

Krock, Arthur. *Memoirs: Sixty Years on the Firing Line.* New York: Funk and Wagnalls, 1968.

Lane, Arthur Bliss. *I Saw Poland Betrayed: An American Ambassador Reports to the American People.* Indianapolis: Bobbs-Merrill, 1948.

Langer, William L. *In and Out of the Ivory Tower: The Autobiography of William L. Langer.* New York: N. Watson Academic Publications, 1977.

Lash, Joseph P., ed. *From the Diaries of Felix Frankfurter.* New York: W. W. Norton, 1975.

Leahy, William D. *I Was There.* New York: McGraw-Hill, 1950.

Lilienthal, David E. *The Journals of David E. Lilienthal*, Vol. I. *The TVA Years, 1939–1945*. New York: Harper and Row, 1964.

Lilienthal, David E. *The Journals of David E. Lilienthal*. Vol. II. *The Atomic Energy Years, 1945–1950*. New York: Harper and Row, 1964.

Mikolajczyk, Stanislaw. *The Rape of Poland: The Pattern of Soviet Aggression*. New York: Whittlesey House, 1948.

Millis, Walter, ed. *The Forrestal Diaries*. New York: Viking, 1951.

Moran, Lord. *Winston Churchill: The Struggle for Survival, 1940–1965: Taken from the Diaries of Lord Moran*. London: Constable, 1966.

Murphy, Robert D. *Diplomat Among Warriors*. New York: Doubleday, 1964.

Nitze, Paul H. *From Hiroshima to Glasnost: At the Center of Decision*. New York: George Weidenfeld, 1989.

Pearson, Lester B. *Mike: The Memoirs of the Right Honourable Lester B. Pearson*. Vol. I. *1897–1948*. Vol. II. *1948–1957*. New York: Quadrangle, 1972, 1973.

Perkins, Frances. *The Roosevelt I Knew*. New York: Viking Press, 1946.

Pickersgill, J. W., and D. F. Forster, eds. *The MacKenzie King Record*. 4 vols. Toronto: University of Toronto Press, 1960–70.

Poen, Monte M., ed. *Letters Home by Harry Truman*. New York: Putnam's, 1984.

Poen, Monte M., ed. *Strictly Personal and Confidential: The Letters Harry S. Truman Never Mailed*. Boston: Little, Brown, 1982.

Resis, Albert, ed. *Molotov Remembers: Inside Kremlin Politics*. Chicago: Ivan Dee, 1993.

Reston, James. *Deadline: A Memoir*. New York: Random House, 1992.

Ridgeway, Matthew B. *Soldier: The Memoirs of Matthew B. Ridgeway*. New York: Harper and Bros., 1956.

Roosevelt, Elliott. *As He Saw It*. New York: Duell, Sloan and Pearce, 1946.

Sakharov, Andrei. *Memoirs*, trans. Richard Lourie. New York: Knopf, 1990.

Salisbury, Harrison E. *A Journey for Our Times: A Memoir*. New York: Harper and Row, 1983.

Schlesinger, Arthur M., Jr. *A Life in the Twentieth Century: Innocent Beginnings, 1917–1950*. Boston: Houghton Mifflin, 2000.

Sherwood, Robert E. *Roosevelt and Hopkins: An Intimate History*. New York: Harper, 1948.

Smith, Jean Edward, ed. *The Papers of General Lucius D. Clay: Germany, 1945–1949*. 2 vols. Bloomington: Indiana University Press, 1974.

Smith, Walter Bedell. *My Three Years in Moscow*. Philadelphia: J. B. Lippincott, 1949.

Standley, William H., and Arthur A. Ageton. *Admiral Ambassador to Russia*. Chicago: Henry Regnery, 1955.

Stettinius, Edward R., Jr. *Roosevelt and the Russians: The Yalta Conference*, ed. Walter Johnson. Garden City, NY: Doubleday, 1949.

Stikker, Dirk U. *Men of Responsibility: A Memoir*. New York: Harper and Row, 1966.

Stimson, Henry L. "The Decision to Use the Atomic Bomb," *Harper's Magazine*, 194 (February 1947), 97–107.

Stimson, Henry L., and McGeorge Bundy. *On Active Service in Peace and War*. New York: Harper and Brothers, 1947.

Strang, Lord. *Home and Abroad*. London: Andre Deutch, 1956.

Strauss, Lewis L. *Men and Decisions*. New York: Doubleday, 1962.

Sulzberger, Cyrus L. *A Long Row of Candles: Memoirs and Diaries, 1934–1954*. New York: Macmillan, 1969.

Sulzberger, Cyrus L. *Seven Continents and Forty Years: A Concentration of Memoirs.* New York: Quadrangle, 1977.

Teller, Edward. *The Legacy of Hiroshima.* Garden City, NY: Doubleday, 1962.

Truman, Harry S. *Memoirs.* Vol. I. *Year of Decisions.* New York: Doubleday, 1955.

Truman, Harry S. *Memoirs.* Vol. II. *Years of Trial and Hope.* New York: Doubleday, 1956.

Truman, Margaret, ed. *Where the Buck Stops: The Personal and Private Writings of Harry S. Truman.* New York: Warner Books, 1989.

Vandenberg, Jr., Arthur H., ed. *The Private Papers of Senator Vandenberg.* Boston: Houghton Mifflin, 1952.

Warburg, James P. *The Long Road Home: The Autobiography of a Maverick.* New York: Doubleday, 1964.

White, Theodore H. *In Search of History: A Personal Adventure.* New York: Warner Books, 1978.

Wilson, Evan M. *Decision on Palestine: How the U.S. Came to Recognize Israel.* Stanford, CA: Hoover Institution Press, 1979.

Yost, Charles W. *The Conduct and Misconduct of Foreign Affairs: Reflections of U.S. Foreign Policy Since World War II.* New York: Random House, 1972.

II. Secondary Sources

A. Books

Adams, Henry H. *Harry Hopkins: A Biography.* New York: G. P. Putnam's, 1977.

Adams, Larry L. *Walter Lippmann.* Boston: Twayne, 1977.

Alperovitz, Gar. *Atomic Diplomacy: Hiroshima and Potsdam – The Use of the Atomic Bomb and the American Confrontation with Soviet Power,* rev. ed. New York: Penguin Books, 1985.

Alperovitz, Gar. *The Decision to Use the Atomic Bomb and the Architecture of an American Myth.* New York: Knopf, 1995.

Alsop, Stewart. *The Center: People and Power in Political Washington.* New York: Harper and Row, 1968.

Ambrose, Stephen E. *Eisenhower and Berlin, 1945: The Decision to Halt at the Elbe.* New York: W. W. Norton, 1967.

Ambrose, Stephen E. *Eisenhower: Soldier, General of the Army, President Elect, 1890–1952.* New York: Simon and Schuster, 1983.

Anderson, Terry H. *The United States, Great Britain and the Cold War, 1944–1947.* Columbia: University of Missouri Press, 1981.

Andrew, Christopher. *For the President's Eyes Only: Secret Intelligence and the American Presidency from Washington to Bush.* New York: Harper Collins, 1995.

Andrew, Christopher, and Oleg Gordievsky. *KGB: The Inside Story of its Foreign Operations from Lenin to Gorbachev.* New York: Harper Collins, 1990.

Applebaum, Anne. *Gulag: A History,* pbk. ed. New York: Anchor Books, 2004.

Arkes, Hadley. *Bureaucracy: The Marshall Plan and the National Interest.* Princeton, NJ: Princeton University Press, 1972.

Backer, John H. *Priming the German Economy: American Occupation Policies, 1945–1948.* Durham, NC: Duke University Press, 1971.

Backer, John H. *Winds of History: The German Years of Lucius DuBignon Clay.* New York: Van Nostrand Reinhold, 1983.

Baldwin, Hanson W. *The Price of Power*. New York: Harper & Bros., 1947.

Barnet, Richard. *The Alliance: America-Europe-Japan, Makers of the Postwar World*. New York: Simon and Schuster, 1983.

Beal, John Robinson. *Marshall in China*. Garden City, NY: Doubleday, 1970.

Beichman, Arnold. *The "Other" State Department: The United States Mission to the United Nations*. New York: Basic Books, 1968.

Bell, Coral. *Negotiation from Strength: A Study of the Politics of Power*. London: Chatto and Windus, 1962.

Bellush, Bernard. *He Walked Alone: A Biography of John Gilbert Winant*. The Hague: Mouton, 1968.

Bennett, Edward M. *Franklin D. Roosevelt and the Search for Victory: American–Soviet Relations, 1939–1945*. Wilmington, DE: SR Books, 1990.

Berlin, Isaiah. *Against the Current: Essays in the History of Ideas*, ed. Henry Hardy. New York: Viking Press, 1980.

Bernstein, Barton J., ed. *Politics and Polices of the Truman Administration*. Chicago: Quadrangle, 1970.

Beschloss, Michael. *The Conquerors: Roosevelt, Truman and the Destruction of Hitler's Germany, 1941–1945*. New York: Simon and Schuster, 2002.

Best, Richard A., Jr. *"Co-operation With Like-Minded Peoples": British Influences on American Security Policy, 1945–1949*. Westport, CT: Greenwood Press, 1986.

Betts, Richard E. *Soldiers, Statesmen and Cold War Crises*. Cambridge, MA: Harvard University Press, 1977.

Bingham, June. *Courage to Change: An Introduction to the Life and Thought of Reinhold Niebuhr*. New York: Charles Scribners, 1972.

Bird, Kai. *The Chairman: John J. McCloy, The Making of the American Establishment*. New York: Simon and Schuster, 1992.

Bird, Kai, and Martin J. Sherwin. *American Prometheus: The Triumph and Tragedy of J. Robert Oppenheimer*. New York: Alfred A. Knopf, 2005.

Blum, Robert M. *Drawing the Line: The Origin of the American Containment Policy in East Asia*. New York: W. W. Norton, 1982.

Bohlen, Charles E. *The Transformation of American Foreign Policy*. New York: W. W. Norton, 1969.

Bowie, Robert R. *Shaping the Future: Foreign Policy in an Age of Transition*. New York: Columbia University Press, 1964.

Bowie, Robert R., and Richard H. Immerman. *Waging Peace: How Eisenhower Shaped an Enduring Cold War Strategy*. New York: Oxford University Press, 1998.

Boyer, Paul S. *By the Bomb's Early Light: American Thought and Culture at the Dawn of the Atomic Age*. Chapel Hill: University of North Carolina Press, 1994.

Boyer, Paul S. *Promises to Keep: The United States Since World War II*. Lexington, MA: D. C. Heath, 1995.

Briggs, Philip J. *Making American Foreign Policy: President–Congress Relations from the Second World War to the Post–Cold War Era*, 2nd ed. Lanham, MD: Rowman & Littlefield, 1994.

Buhite, Russell D. *Decisions at Yalta: An Appraisal of Summit Diplomacy*. Wilmington, DE: SR Books, 1986.

Bullock, Alan. *Ernest Bevin: Foreign Secretary, 1945–1951*. New York: W. W. Norton, 1983.

Bundy, McGeorge. *Danger and Survival: Choices about the Bomb in the First Fifty Years*. New York: Random House, 1988.

Burns, James MacGregor. *Roosevelt: The Lion and the Fox*. New York: Harcourt Brace, 1956.

Butow, Robert J. C. *Japan's Decision to Surrender*. Stanford, CA: Stanford University Press, 1954.

Campbell, John C. *Tito's Separate Road: America and Yugoslavia in World Politics*. New York: Harper and Row, 1967.

Campbell, Thomas M. *Masquerade Peace: America's UN Policy, 1944–1945*. Tallahassee: Florida State University Press, 1973.

Carlton, David. *Churchill and the Soviet Union*. Manchester and New York: Manchester University Press, 2000.

Carr, Albert Z. *Truman, Stalin and Peace*. Garden City, NY: Doubleday, 1950.

Casey, Steven. *Cautious Crusade: Franklin D. Roosevelt, American Public Opinion, and the War Against Nazi Germany*. New York: Oxford University Press, 2001.

Chace, James. *Acheson: The Secretary of State Who Created the American World*. New York: Simon and Schuster, 1998.

Chafe, William H. *The Unfinished Journey: America Since World War II*, 3rd ed. New York: Oxford University Press, 1995.

Ciechanowski, Jan. *Defeat in Victory*. Garden City, NY: Doubleday, 1947.

Clemens, Diane Shaver. *Yalta*. New York: Oxford University Press, 1970.

Clements, Kendrick A. *James F. Byrnes and the Origins of the Cold War*. Durham, NC: Carolina Academic Press, 1982.

Cline, Ray S. *Washington Command Post: The Operations Division*. Washington, DC: U.S. Government Printing Office, 1951.

Cohen, Michael J. *Palestine and the Great Powers, 1945–1948*. Princeton, NJ: Princeton University Press, 1982.

Coit, Margaret L. *Mr. Baruch*. Boston: Houghton Mifflin, 1957.

Coleman, Peter. *The Liberal Conspiracy: The Congress for Cultural Freedom and the Struggle for the Mind of Postwar Europe*. New York: The Free Press, 1989.

Craig, Gordon A., and Alexander L. George. *Force and Statecraft: Diplomatic Problems of Our Time*, 3rd ed. New York: Oxford University Press, 1995.

Craig, Gordon A., and Francis L. Loewenheim, eds. *The Diplomats, 1939–1979*. Princeton, NJ: Princeton University Press, 1994.

Craig, William. *The Fall of Japan*. New York: The Dial Press, 1967.

Dallek, Robert. *Franklin D. Roosevelt and American Foreign Policy, 1932–1945*. New York: Oxford University Press, 1995.

Danchev, Alex. *On Specialness: Essays in Anglo-American Relations*. New York: St. Martin's Press, 1998.

Danchev, Alex. *Very Special Relationship: Field Marshall Sir John Dill and the Anglo-American Alliance, 1941–44*. London: Brassey's Defence Publishers, 1986.

Daniels, Jonathan. *The Man of Independence*. Philadelphia: J. B. Lippincott, 1950.

Davis, Lynn Etheridge. *The Cold War Begins: Soviet-American Conflict Over East Europe*. Princeton, NJ: Princeton University Press, 1974.

DeGroot, Gerard J. *The Bomb: A Life*. Cambridge, MA: Harvard University Press, 2005.

Dennett, Raymond, and Joseph E. Johnson, eds. *Negotiating with the Russians*. Boston: World Peace Foundation, 1951.

Destler, I. M. *Presidents, Bureaucrats and Foreign Policy*. Princeton, NJ: Princeton University Press, 1972.

Divine, Robert A. *Roosevelt and World War II*. Baltimore: Johns Hopkins University Press, 1969.

Divine, Robert A. *Second Chance: The Triumph of Internationalism in America During World War II*. New York: Atheneum, 1967.

Donahoe, Bernard, C.S.C. *Private Plans and Public Dangers: The Story of FDR's Third Nomination*. Notre Dame, IN: University of Notre Dame Press, 1965.

Donovan, John C. *The Cold Warriors: A Policy-Making Elite*. Lexington, MA: D. C. Heath, 1974.

Donovan, Robert J. *Conflict and Crisis: The Presidency of Harry S. Truman, 1945–1948*. New York: W. W. Norton, 1977.

Donovan, Robert J. *Tumultuous Years: The Presidency of Harry S. Truman, 1949–1953*. New York: W. W. Norton, 1982.

Dorsett, Lyle W. *The Pendergast Machine*. New York: Oxford University Press, 1968.

Dower, John W. *War Without Mercy: Race and Power in the Pacific War*. New York: Pantheon Books, 1986.

Draper, Theodore. *A Present of Things Past: Selected Essays*. New York: Hill and Wang, 1990.

Driberg, Tom. *The Mystery of Moral Rearmament*. London: Secker and Warburg, 1964.

Druks, Herbert M. *Harry S. Truman and the Russians, 1945–1953*. New York: Robert Speller and Sons, 1966.

Dunn, Dennis J. *Caught Between Roosevelt and Stalin: America's Ambassadors to Moscow*. Lexington: University Press of Kentucky, 1998.

Dunn, Frederick S. *Peace-making and the Settlement with Japan*. Princeton, NJ: Princeton University Press, 1963.

Eckes, Alfred E. *A Search for Solvency: Bretton Woods and the International Monetary System, 1941–1971*. Austin: University of Texas Press, 1975.

Edwards, Lee. *Missionary for Freedom: The Life and Times of Walter Judd*. New York: Paragon House, 1990.

Eisenberg, Carolyn. *Drawing the Line: The American Decision to Divide Germany, 1944–1949*. Cambridge and New York: Cambridge University Press, 1996.

Ellis, Joseph J. *American Sphinx: The Character of Thomas Jefferson*. New York: Alfred A. Knopf, 1996.

Etzold, Thomas H. *The Conduct of American Foreign Relations: The Other Side of Diplomacy*. New York: New Viewpoints, 1977.

Eubank, Keith. *Summit at Teheran: The Untold Story*. New York: Morrow, 1985.

Farnsworth, Beatrice. *William C. Bullitt and the Soviet Union*. Bloomington: Indiana University Press, 1967.

Feis, Herbert. *Churchill Roosevelt Stalin: The War They Waged and the Peace They Sought*, 2nd ed. Princton, NJ: Princeton University Press, 1967.

Feis, Herbert. *From Trust to Terror: The Onset of the Cold War*. New York: W. W. Norton, 1970.

Ferrell, Robert H. *Choosing Truman: The Democratic Convention of 1944*. Columbia: University of Missouri Press, 1994.

Ferrell, Robert H. *The Dying President: Franklin D. Roosevelt, 1944–1945*. Columbia: University of Missouri Press, 1998.

Ferrell, Robert H. *George C. Marshall*. Vol. XV. *The American Secretaries of State and Their Diplomacy*, ed. Robert H. Ferrell. New York: Cooper Square Publishers, 1966.

Ferrell, Robert H. *Harry S. Truman: A Life*. Columbia: University of Missouri Press, 1994.

Ferrell, Robert H. *Harry S. Truman and the Modern Presidency*. Boston: Little, Brown, 1983.

Ferrell, Robert H. *Truman and Pendergast*. Columbia: University of Missouri Press, 1999.

Fitzsimons, M. A. *Foreign Policy of the British Labour Government, 1945–1951*. Notre Dame, IN: University of Notre Dame Press, 1953.

Fleming, Denna Frank. *The Cold War and Its Origins, 1917–1960*. 2 vols. Garden City, NY: Doubleday, 1961.

Folly, Martin H. *Churchill, Whitehall and the Soviet Union, 1940–45*. London: Macmillan, 2000.

Fossedal, Gregory A. *Our Finest Hour: Will Clayton, the Marshall Plan, and the Triumph of Democracy*. Stanford, CA: Hoover Institution Press, 1993.

Frank, Richard B. *Downfall: The End of the Imperial Japanese Empire*. New York: Random House, 1999.

Fromkin, David. *In the Time of the Americans: FDR, Truman, Eisenhower, Marshall, MacArthur – The Generation That Changed America's Role in the World*. New York: Knopf, 1995.

Gaddis, John Lewis. *The Landscape of History: How Historians Map the Past*. New York: Oxford University Press, 2002.

Gaddis, John Lewis. *The Long Peace: Inquiries into the History of the Cold War*. New York: Oxford University Press, 1987.

Gaddis, John Lewis. *Strategies of Containment: A Critical Appraisal of Postwar American National Security Policy*. New York: Oxford University Press, 1982.

Gaddis, John Lewis. *Surprise, Security, and the American Experience*. Cambridge, MA: Harvard University Press, 2004.

Gaddis, John Lewis. *The United States and the End of the Cold War: Implications, Reconsiderations, Provocations*. New York: Oxford University Press, 1992.

Gaddis, John Lewis. *The United States and the Origins of the Cold War, 1941–1947*. New York: Columbia University Press, 1972.

Gaddis, John Lewis. *We Now Know: Rethinking Cold War History*. Oxford: Clarendon Press, 1997.

Gaddis, John Lewis, et al., eds. *Cold War Statesmen Confront the Bomb: Nuclear Diplomacy since 1945*. New York: Oxford University Press, 1999.

Gannon, Robert I., S.J. *The Cardinal Spellman Story*. New York: Doubleday, 1962.

Gardner, Lloyd C. *Architects of Illusion: Men and Ideas in American Foreign Policy, 1941–1949*. Chicago: Quadrangle Books, 1970.

Gardner, Lloyd C. *Spheres of Influence: The Great Powers Partition Europe, from Munich to Yalta*. Chicago: Ivan R. Dee, 1993.

Gardner, Richard N. *Sterling-Dollar Diplomacy: The Origins and the Prospects of Our International Economic Order*, rev. ed. New York: McGraw Hill, 1969.

Garwood, Ellen Clayton. *Will Clayton: A Short Biography*. Austin: University of Texas Press, 1958.

Gellman, Irwin F. *Secret Affairs: Franklin Roosevelt, Cordell Hull, and Sumner Welles*. Baltimore: Johns Hopkins University Press, 1995.

George, Alexander, and Richard Smoke. *Deterrence in American Foreign Policy: Theory and Practice*. New York: Columbia University Press, 1974.

Gerson, Louis L. *John Foster Dulles*. Vol. 17. *The American Secretaries of State and Their Diplomacy*, ed. Robert H. Ferrell. New York: Cooper Square Publishers, 1958.

Gilbert, Martin. *Winston S. Churchill*. Vols. 7–8. Boston: Houghton Mifflin, 1986–88.

Gilpin, Robert. *American Scientists and Nuclear Weapon's Policy*. Princeton, NJ: Princeton University Press, 1962.

Gimbel, John. *The American Occupation of Germany: Politics and the Military, 1945–1949*. Stanford, CA: Stanford University Press, 1968.

Gimbel, John. *The Origins of the Marshall Plan*. Stanford, CA: Stanford University Press, 1976.

Gleason, Philip. *Keeping the Faith: American Catholicism, Past and Present*. Notre Dame, IN: University of Notre Dame Press, 1987.

Glynn, Patrick. *Closing Pandora's Box: Arms Races, Arms Control, and the History of the Cold War*. New York: Basic Books, 1992.

Gormley, James L. *The Collapse of the Grand Alliance, 1945–1948*. Baton Rouge: Louisiana State University Press, 1987.

Gormley, James L. *From Potsdam to the Cold War: Big Three Diplomacy 1945–1947*. Wilmington, DE: SR Books, 1990.

Gowing, Margaret. *Independence and Deterrence: Britain and Atomic Energy, 1946–1952*. London: Macmillan, 1974.

Halle, Louis J. *Civilization and Foreign Policy: An Inquiry for Americans*. New York: Harper and Bros., 1955.

Halle, Louis J. *The Cold War as History*. New York: Harper and Row, 1967.

Hamby, Alonzo. *Beyond the New Deal: Harry S. Truman and American Liberalism*. New York: Columbia University Press, 1973.

Hamby, Alonzo. *Man of the People: A Life of Harry S. Truman*. New York: Oxford University Press, 1995.

Hammond, Thomas T., ed. *Witnesses to the Origins of the Cold War*. Seattle: University of Washington Press, 1982.

Harbutt, Fraser J. *The Iron Curtain: Churchill, America and the Origins of the Cold War*. New York: Oxford University Press, 1986.

Harper, John Lamberton. *America and the Reconstruction of Italy, 1945–1948*. Cambridge: Cambridge University Press, 1986.

Harper, John Lamberton. *American Visions of Europe: Franklin D. Roosevelt, George F. Kennan and Dean G. Acheson*. Cambridge and New York: Cambridge University Press, 1994.

Hartmann, Susan M. *Truman and the 80th Congress*. Columbia: University of Missouri Press, 1971.

Hasegawa, Tsuyoshi. *Racing the Enemy: Stalin, Truman, and the Surrender of Japan*. Cambridge, MA: The Belknap Press of Harvard University Press, 2005.

Hathaway Robert M. *Ambiguous Partnership: Britain and America, 1944–1947*. New York: Columbia University Press, 1981.

Hawley, Ellis. *The New Deal and the Problem of Monopoly: A Study in Economic Ambivalence*. Princeton, NJ: Princeton University Press, 1966.

Haynes, Richard F. *The Awesome Power: Harry Truman as Commander in Chief*. Baton Rouge: Louisiana State University Press, 1973.

Healey, Denis, ed. *The Curtain Falls: The Story of the Socialists in Eastern Europe*. London: Lincolns-Prager, 1951.

Herring, Jr., George C. *Aid to Russia, 1941–1946: Strategy, Diplomacy and the Origins of the Cold War*. New York: Columbia University Press, 1973.

Herring, Jr., George C. *America's Longest War: The United States and Vietnam, 1950–1975*, 3rd ed. New York: McGraw Hill, 1996.

Hewlett, Richard G., and Oscar E. Anderson, Jr., *The New World, 1939–1946*. Vol. I. *A History of the United States Atomic Energy Commission*. University Park: Pennsylvania State University Press, 1962.

Hodgson, Godfrey. *The Colonel: The Life and Wars of Henry L. Stimson, 1867–1950.* New York: Knopf, 1990.

Hogan, Michael J. *A Cross of Iron: Harry S. Truman and the Origins of the National Security State, 1945–1954.* New York: Cambridge University Press, 1998.

Hogan, Michael J., ed. *The End of the Cold War: Its Meaning and Implications.* New York: Cambridge University Press, 1992.

Hogan, Michael J. *The Marshall Plan: America, Britain and the Reconstruction of Western Europe, 1947–1952.* New York: Cambridge University Press, 1987.

Holloway, David. *The Soviet Union and the Arms Race.* New Haven, CT: Yale University Press, 1983.

Holloway, David. *Stalin and the Bomb: The Soviet Union and Atomic Energy, 1939–1956.* New Haven, CT: Yale University Press, 1994.

Hoopes, Townsend. *The Devil and John Foster Dulles.* Boston: Little, Brown, 1973.

Hoopes, Townsend, and Douglas Brinkley. *Driven Patriot: The Life and Times of James Forrestal.* New York: Knopf, 1992.

Hoopes, Townsend, and Douglas Brinkley. *FDR and the Creation of the U.N.* New Haven, CT: Yale University Press, 1997.

Hopkins, Michael. *Oliver Franks and the Truman Administration.* London and Portland: Frank Cass, 2003.

Iatrides, John O., ed. *Greece in the 1940s: A Nation in Crisis.* Hanover: University Press of New England, 1981.

Isaacson, Walter, and Evan Thomas. *The Wise Men: Six Friends and the World They Made.* New York: Simon and Schuster, 1986.

Jones, Howard. *"A New Kind of War": America's Global Strategy and the Truman Doctrine in Greece.* New York: Oxford University Press, 1989.

Kaplan, Lawrence S. *The United States and NATO: The Formative Years.* Lexington: University of Kentucky Press, 1984.

Kennan, George F. *American Diplomacy, 1900–1950.* Chicago: University of Chicago Press, 1951.

Kennan, George F. *Russia and the West Under Lenin and Stalin.* Boston: Little, Brown, 1961.

Kennedy, David M. *The Oxford History of the United States.* Vol. IX. *Freedom from Fear: The American People in Depression and War, 1929–1945.* New York: Oxford University Press, 1999.

Kepley, David R. *The Collapse of the Middle Way: Senate Republicans and the Bipartisan Foreign Policy, 1948–1952.* New York: Greenwood Press, 1988.

Kimball, Warren F. *Forged in War: Roosevelt, Churchill, and the Second World War.* New York: William Morrow, 1997.

Kimball, Warren F. *The Juggler: Franklin Roosevelt as Wartime Statesman.* Princeton, NJ: Princeton University Press, 1991.

Kirkendall, Richard S., ed. *The Truman Period as a Research Field: A Reappraisal, 1972.* Columbia: University of Missouri Press, 1974.

Kissinger, Henry. *Diplomacy.* New York: Simon and Schuster, 1994.

Kohler, Foy D., and Mose L. Harvey, eds. *The Soviet Union, Yesterday, Today, Tomorrow: A Colloquy of American Long Timers in Moscow.* Coral Gables, FL: Center for Advanced International Studies, University of Miami, 1975.

Kolko, Gabriel. *The Politics of War: The World and United States Foreign Policy, 1943–1945.* New York: Harper and Row, 1968.

Kolko, Joyce, and Gabriel Kolko. *The Limits of Power: The World and United States Foreign Policy, 1945–1954.* New York: Harper and Row, 1972.

Kourig, Bennett. *The Myth of Liberation: East-Central Europe in U.S. Diplomacy and Politics Since 1941.* Baltimore: Johns Hopkins University Press, 1973.

Kuklick, Bruce. *American Policy and the Division of Germany: The Clash with Russia over Reparations.* Ithaca, NY: Cornell University Press, 1972.

Kuniholm, Bruce R. *The Origins of the Cold War in the Near East: Great Power Conflict and Diplomacy in Iran, Turkey and Greece.* Princeton, NJ: Princeton University Press, 1980.

Kunz, Diane B. *Butter and Guns: America's Cold War Economic Diplomacy.* New York: The Free Press, 1997.

Lacey, Michael J., ed. *The Truman Presidency.* Cambridge: Cambridge University Press, 1989.

Lane, Ann, and Howard Temperley, eds. *The Rise and Fall of the Grand Alliance, 1941–45.* New York: St. Martin's Press, 1995.

Langer, William L., and S. Everett Gleason. *The Undeclared War, 1940–1941.* London: Oxford University Press, 1953.

Laqueur, Walter. *The Dream That Failed: Reflections on the Soviet Union.* New York: Oxford University Press, 1994.

Larres, Klaus. *Churchill's Cold War: The Politics of Personal Diplomacy.* New Haven, CT: Yale University Press, 2002.

Larson, David L. *United States Foreign Policy Toward Yugoslavia, 1943–1963.* Washington, DC: University Press of America, 1979.

Larson, Deborah Welch. *Origins of Containment: A Psychological Explanation.* Princeton, NJ: Princeton University Press, 1985.

Larson, Lawrence H., and Nancy J. Hulston. *Pendergast!* Columbia: University of Missouri Press, 1997.

Lees, Lorraine M. *Keeping Tito Afloat: The United States, Yugoslavia, and the Cold War.* University Park: Pennsylvania State University Press, 1997.

Leffler, Melvyn P. *A Preponderance of Power: National Security, the Truman Administration and the Cold War.* Stanford, CA: Stanford University Press, 1992.

Leffler, Melvyn P. *The Struggle for Germany and the Origins of the Cold War.* Washington, DC: German Historical Institute, 1996.

Lerner, Max. *Wounded Titans: American Presidents and the Perils of Power,* ed. Robert Schmuhl. New York: Arcade Publishing, 1996.

Leuchtenburg, William. *In the Shadow of FDR: From Harry Truman to Bill Clinton,* rev. ed. Ithaca, NY: Cornell University Press, 1993.

Levering, Ralph B. *American Opinion and the Russian Alliance, 1939–1945.* Chapel Hill: University of North Carolina Press, 1976.

Levering, Ralph B. *The Cold War: A Post-Cold War History.* Arlington Heights, IL: Harlan Davidson, 1994.

Levering, Ralph B. *The Public and American Foreign Policy, 1918–1978.* New York: William Morrow, 1978.

Lieberman, Joseph I. *The Scorpion and the Tarantula: The Struggle to Control Atomic Weapons, 1945–1949.* Boston: Houghton Mifflin, 1970.

Lifton, Robert Jay, and Greg Mitchell. *Hiroshima in America: Fifty Years of Denial.* New York: Putnam's Sons, 1995.

Linethal, Edward T., and Tom Engelhardt, eds. *History Wars: The* Enola Gay *and Other Battles for the American Past.* New York: Metropolitan Books, 1996.

Lippmann, Walter. *The Cold War: A Study in U.S. Foreign Policy*. New York: Harper, 1947.

Lukacs, John. *Churchill: Visionary. Statesman. Historian*. New Haven, CT: Yale University Press, 2002.

Lundestad, Geir. *The American "Empire" and other Studies of U.S. Foreign Policy in Comparative Perspective*. Oxford and New York: Oxford University Press, 1990.

Lundestad, Geir. *The United States and Western Europe Since 1945: From "Empire" by Invitation to Transatlantic Drift*. Oxford and New York: Oxford University Press, 2003.

MacEachin, Douglas J. *The Final Months of the War with Japan: Signals Intelligence, U.S. Invasion Planning, and the A-Bomb Decision*. Langley, VA: Center for the Study of Intelligence, 1998.

Machiavelli, Niccolo. *The Prince*, translated and introduced by Harvey C. Mansfield, 2nd ed. Chicago: University of Chicago Press, 1998.

MacIssac, David. *Strategic Bombing in World War Two: The Story of the United States Strategic Bombing Survey*. New York: Garland, 1976.

MacLean, Elizabeth Kimball. *Joseph E. Davies: Envoy to the Soviets*. Westport, CT: Praeger, 1992.

Maddox, Robert James. *From War to Cold War: The Education of Harry S. Truman*. Boulder: Westview, 1988.

Maddox, Robert James. *The United States and World War II*. Boulder, CO: Westview, 1992.

Maddox, Robert James. *Weapons for Victory: The Hiroshima Decision Fifty Years Later*. Columbia: University of Missouri Press, 1995.

Maney, Patrick. *The Roosevelt Presence: A Biography of Franklin Delano Roosevelt*. New York: Twayne Publishers, 1992.

Marks, Frederick W. *Wind over Sand: The Diplomacy of Franklin Roosevelt*. Athens: University of Georgia Press, 1988.

Mastny, Vojtech. *The Cold War and Soviet Insecurity: The Stalin Years*. New York: Oxford University Press, 1996.

Matloff, Maurice. *Strategic Planning for Coalition Warfare, 1943–1944*. United States Army in World War II: The War Department. Washington, DC: U.S. Government Printing Office, 1959.

May, Ernest R. *"Lessons" of the Past: The Use and Misuse of History in American Foreign Policy*. New York: Oxford University Press, 1973.

Mayers, David. *The Ambassadors and America's Soviet Policy*. New York: Oxford University Press, 1995.

Mayers, David. *George Kennan and the Dilemmas of U.S. Foreign Policy*. New York: Oxford University Press, 1988.

Mazuzan, George T. *Warren R. Austin at the United Nations, 1946–1953*. Kent, OH: Kent State University Press, 1977.

McAllister, James. *No Exit: America and the German Problem, 1943–1954*. Ithaca, NY: Cornell University Press, 2002.

McCloy, John J. *The Atlantic Alliance: Its Origin and Its Future*. New York: Columbia University Press, 1969.

McCloy, John J. *The Challenge to American Foreign Policy*. Cambridge, MA: Harvard University Press, 1953.

McCullough, David. *Truman*. New York: Simon and Schuster, 1992.

McGeehan, Robert. *The German Rearmament Question: American Diplomacy and European Defense After World War II*. Urbana: University of Illinois Press, 1971.

McJimsey, George. *Harry Hopkins: Ally of the Poor and Defender of Democracy*. Cambridge, MA: Harvard University Press, 1987.

McLellan, David S. *Dean Acheson: The State Department Years*. New York: Dodd, Mead, 1976.

McMahon, Robert J. *Colonialism and Cold War: The United States and the Struggle for Indonesian Independence, 1945–49*. Ithaca, NY: Cornell University Press, 1981.

McNeill, William H. *America, Britain, and Russia: Their Cooperation and Conflict, 1941–1946*. London: Oxford University Press for Royal Institute of International Affairs, 1953.

Meacham, Jon. *Franklin and Winston: An Intimate Portrait of an Epic Friendship*. New York: Random House, 2003.

Mead, Walter Russell. *Special Providence: American Foreign Policy and How It Changed the World*. New York: Routledge, 2002.

Mee, Jr., Charles L. *The Marshall Plan*. New York: Simon and Schuster, 1984.

Mee, Jr., Charles L. *Meeting at Potsdam*. New York: M. Evans and Company, 1975.

Merli, Frank J., and Theodore A. Wilson, eds. *Makers of American Diplomacy: From Theodore Roosevelt to Henry Kissinger*. New York: Charles Scribners, 1974.

Messer, Robert L. *The End of an Alliance: James F. Byrnes, Roosevelt, Truman, and the Origins of the Cold War*. Chapel Hill: University of North Carolina Press, 1982.

Mickelson, Sig. *America's Other Voice: The Story of Radio Free Europe and Radio Liberty*. New York: Praeger, 1983.

Miller, James Edward. *The United States and Italy, 1940–1950: The Politics and Diplomacy of Stabilization*. Chapel Hill: University of North Carolina Press, 1986.

Miller, Richard Lawrence. *Truman: The Rise to Power*. New York: McGraw-Hill, 1986.

Milward, Alan S. *The Reconstruction of Western Europe, 1945–1951*. London: Methuen, 1984.

Miscamble, Wilson D. *George F. Kennan and the Making of American Foreign Policy, 1947–1950*. Princeton, NJ: Princeton University Press, 1992.

Morgan, Kenneth O. *Labour in Power, 1945–1951*. Oxford: Clarendon Press, 1984.

Morgan, Roger. *The United States and West Germany, 1945–1973: A Study in Alliance Politics*. London: Oxford University Press, 1974.

Morgan, Ted. *FDR: A Biography*. New York: Simon and Schuster, 1985.

Moskin, J. Robert. *Mr. Truman's War: The Final Victories of World War II and the Birth of the Postwar World*. New York: Random House, 1996.

Moss, Norman. *Men Who Play God: The Story of the H-Bomb and How the World Came to Live with It*. New York: Harper and Row, 1968.

Nadeau, Remi. *Stalin, Churchill, and Roosevelt Divide Europe*. New York: Praeger, 1990.

Nagai, Yonosuke, and Akira Iriye, eds. *The Origins of the Cold War in Asia*. New York: Columbia University Press, 1977.

Naimark, Norman. *The Russians in Germany: A History of the Soviet Zone of Occupation, 1945–1949*. Cambridge, MA: The Belknap Press of Harvard University Press, 1995.

Naimark, Norman, and Leonid Gibianskii, eds. *The Establishment of Communist Regimes in Eastern Europe, 1944–1949*. Boulder, CO: Westview Press, 1997.

Neustadt, Richard E. *Presidential Power and the Modern Presidents: The Politics of Leadership from Roosevelt to Reagan*. New York: The Free Press, 1990.

Newhouse, John. *War and Peace in the Nuclear Age.* New York: Knopf, 1989.

Newman, Robert P. *Truman and the Hiroshima Cult.* East Lansing: Michigan State University Press, 1995.

Ninkovich, Frank. *Modernity and Power: A History of the Domino Theory in the Twentieth Century.* Chicago: University of Chicago Press, 1994.

Nitze, Paul H. *United States Foreign Policy, 1945–1955.* New York: Foreign Policy Association, 1956.

Notter, Harley A. *Postwar Foreign Policy Preparation, 1939–1945.* Washington, DC: U.S. Government Printing Office, 1949.

Offner, Arnold A. *Another Such Victory: President Truman and the Cold War, 1945–1953.* Stanford, CA: Stanford University Press, 2002.

Offner, Arnold A., and Theodore A. Wilson, eds. *Victory in Europe 1945: From World War to Cold War.* Lawrence: University Press of Kansas, 2000.

Ovendale, Ritchie. *The English-Speaking Alliance: Britain, the United States, the Dominions and the Cold War, 1945–1951.* London: George Allen & Unwin, 1985.

Ovendale, Ritchie, ed. *The Foreign Policy of the British Labour Governments, 1945–1951.* Leicester: Leicester University Press, 1984.

Paterson, Thomas G., ed. *Cold War Critics: Alternatives to American Foreign Policy in the Truman Years.* Chicago: Quadrangle Books, 1971.

Paterson, Thomas G., ed. *Containment and the Cold War: American Foreign Policy Since 1945.* Reading, MA: Addison-Wesley, 1973.

Paterson, Thomas G. *Meeting the Communist Threat: Truman to Reagan.* New York: Oxford University Press, 1988.

Paterson, Thomas G. *On Every Front: the Making of the Cold War.* New York: W. W. Norton, 1979, 1992.

Paterson, Thomas G. *Soviet–American Confrontation: Postwar Reconstruction and the Origins of the Cold War.* Baltimore: Johns Hopkins University Press, 1973.

Patterson, James T. *Grand Expectations: The United States, 1945–1974.* New York: Oxford University Press, 1996.

Patterson, James T. *Mr. Republican: A Biography of Robert A. Taft.* Boston: Houghton Mifflin, 1972.

Paul, Allen. *Katyn: The Untold Story of Stalin's Polish Massacre.* New York: Charles Scribner's Sons, 1991.

Payne, Robert. *The Marshall Story: A Biography of General George C. Marshall.* New York: Prentice Hall, 1951.

Pelling, Henry. *Britain and the Marshall Plan.* Houndmills, Basingstoke: Macmillan, 1988.

Perlmutter, Amos. *FDR & Stalin: A Not So Grand Alliance, 1943–1945.* Columbia: University of Missouri Press, 1993.

Persico, Joseph E. *Roosevelt's Secret War: FDR and World War II Espionage.* New York: Random House, 2001.

Peterson, Edward N. *The American Occupation of Germany: Retreat to Victory.* Detroit: Wayne State University Press, 1978.

Phillips, Cabell B. *The Truman Presidency: History of a Triumphant Succession.* New York: Macmillan, 1966.

Pickett, William B. *Eisenhower Decides to Run: Presidential Politics and Cold War Strategy.* Chicago: Ivan R. Dee, 2000.

Pogue, Forrest C. *George C. Marshall: Statesman, 1945–1959.* New York: Viking, 1987.

Powers, Richard Gid. *Not Without Honor: The History of American Anticommunism.* New York: Free Press, 1995.

Price, Harry B. *The Marshall Plan and Its Meaning.* Ithaca, NY: Cornell University Press, 1955.

Pruessen, Ronald W. *John Foster Dulles: The Road to Power.* New York: The Free Press, 1982.

Quester, George H. *Nuclear Diplomacy: The First Twenty-five Years.* New York: Dunellen, 1970.

Raack, R. C. *Stalin's Drive to the West, 1938–1945: The Origins of the Cold War.* Stanford, CA: Stanford University Press, 1995.

Rabel, Roberto G. *Between East and West: Trieste, the United States, and the Cold War, 1941–1954.* Durham, NC: Duke University Press, 1988.

Reynolds, David. *Britannia Overruled: British Policy and World Power in the Twentieth Century.* London: Longman, 1991.

Robertson, David. *Sly and Able: A Political Biography of James F. Byrnes.* New York: W. W. Norton, 1994.

Rogow, Arnold. *James Forrestal: A Study of Personality, Politics and Policy.* New York: Macmillan, 1963.

Rose, Lisle A. *After Yalta: America and the Origins of the Cold War.* New York: Charles Scribners, 1973.

Rose, Lisle A. *Dubious Victory.* Kent, OH: Kent State University Press, 1973.

Rostow, Walt. *The Division of Europe After World War II: 1946.* Austin: University of Texas Press, 1981.

Rozek, Edward J. *Allied Wartime Diplomacy: A Pattern in Poland.* New York: Wiley, 1958.

Rubin, Barry. *Secrets of State: The State Department and the Struggle Over U.S. Foreign Policy.* New York: Oxford University Press, 1985.

Ruddy, T. Michael. *The Cautious Diplomat: Charles E. Bohlen and the Soviet Union, 1929–1969.* Kent, OH: Kent State University Press, 1986.

Russell, Ruth B. *The United Nations and United States Security Policy.* Washington, DC: The Brookings Institution, 1968.

Sainsbury, Keith. *Churchill and Roosevelt at War: The War They Fought and the Peace They Hoped to Make.* New York: New York University Press, 1994.

Sainsbury, Keith. *The Turning Point: Roosevelt, Stalin, Churchill and Chiang Kai-shek, 1943: The Moscow, Cairo and Teheran Conferences.* New York: Oxford University Press, 1985.

Schaffer, Ronald. *Wings of Judgment: American Bombing in World War II.* New York: Oxford University Press, 1985.

Schaller, Michael. *The American Occupation of Japan: The Origins of the Cold War in Asia.* New York: Oxford University Press, 1985.

Schild, Georg. *Bretton Woods and Dumbarton Oaks: American Economic and Political Postwar Planning in the Summer of 1944.* New York: St. Martin's Press, 1995.

Schilling, Warner, Paul Hammond, and Glenn Snyder. *Strategy, Politics and Defense Budgets.* New York: Columbia University Press, 1962.

Schlesinger, Jr., Arthur M. *The Vital Center: The Politics of Freedom.* Boston: Houghton Mifflin, 1949.

Schlesinger, Stephen. *Act of Creation: The Founding of the United Nations: A Story of Superpowers, Secret Agents, Wartime Allies and Enemies, and Their Quest for a Peaceful World.* Boulder, CO: Westview Press, 2003.

Schmitt, Hans A., ed. *U.S. Occupation in Europe After World War II.* Lawrence: Regents Press of Kansas, 1978.

Schoenbaum, Thomas J. *Waging Peace and War: Dean Rusk in the Truman, Kennedy and Johnson Years.* New York: Simon and Schuster, 1988.

Schonberger, Howard B. *Aftermath of War: Americans and the Remaking of Japan, 1945–1952.* Kent, OH: Kent State University Press, 1989.

Schulzinger, Robert D. *The Wise Men of Foreign Affairs: The History of the Council on Foreign Relations.* New York: Columbia University Press, 1984.

Schwartz, Thomas A. *America's Germany: John J. McCloy and the Federal Republic of Germany.* Cambridge, MA: Harvard University Press, 1991.

Sharp, Tony. *The Wartime Alliance and the Zonal Division of Germany.* Oxford: Clarendon Press, 1975.

Sherry, Michael. *The Rise of American Air Power: The Creation of Armageddon.* New Haven, CT: Yale University Press, 1987.

Sherwin, Martin J. *A World Destroyed: The Atomic Bomb and the Grand Alliance.* New York: Knopf, 1975.

Siracusa, Joseph M., ed. *The American Diplomatic Revolution: A Documentary History of the Cold War, 1941–1947.* Port Washington, NY: Kennikat Press, 1977.

Siracusa, Joseph M., ed. *Into the Dark House: American Diplomacy and the Ideological Origins of the Cold War.* Claremont, CA: Regina Books, 1998.

Siracusa, Joseph M. *New Left Diplomatic Histories and Historians.* Port Washington, NY: Kennikat Press, 1973.

Smith, Gaddis. *American Diplomacy During the Second World War, 1941–1945,* 2nd ed. New York: Knopf, 1885.

Smith, Gaddis. *The American Secretaries of State and Their Diplomacy.* Vol. XVI. *Dean Acheson,* ed. Robert H. Ferrell. New York: Cooper Square Publishers, 1972.

Smith, Gaddis. *The Last Years of the Monroe Doctrine, 1945–1993.* New York: Hill and Wang, 1994.

Smith, Michael Joseph. *Realist Thought from Weber to Kissinger.* Baton Rouge: Louisiana State University Press, 1986.

Smith, Tony. *America's Mission: The United States and the Worldwide Struggle for Democracy in the Twentieth Century.* Princeton, NJ: Princeton University Press, 1994.

Snell, John L. ed. *The Meaning of Yalta: Big Three Diplomacy and the New Balance of Power.* Baton Rouge: Louisiana State University Press, 1956.

Spiegel, Steven L. *The Other Arab-Israeli Conflict: Making America's Middle East Policy From Truman to Reagan.* Chicago: University of Chicago Press, 1985.

Stafford, David. *Roosevelt and Churchill: Men of Secrets.* Woodstock, NY: The Overlook Press, 2000.

Steel, Ronald. *Imperialists and Other Heroes: A Chronicle of the American Empire.* New York: Random House, 1971.

Steel, Ronald. *Walter Lippmann and the American Century.* Boston: Little, Brown and Company, 1980.

Stephanson, Anders. *Kennan and the Art of Foreign Policy.* Cambridge, MA: Harvard University Press, 1989.

Stern, Philip M. *The Oppenheimer Case: Security on Trial.* New York: Harper and Row, 1969.

Stiller, Jesse H. *George S. Messersmith: Diplomat of Democracy.* Chapel Hill: University of North Carolina Press, 1988.

Strange, Susan. *Sterling and British Policy: A Political Study of an International Currency in Decline*. London: Oxford University Press, 1971.

Stromberg, Roland N. *Collective Security and American Foreign Policy: From the League of Nations to NATO*. New York: Praeger, 1963.

Stueck, Jr., William Whitney. *The Korean War: An International History*. Princeton, NJ: Princeton University Press, 1995.

Stueck, Jr., William Whitney. *Rethinking the Korean War: A New Diplomatic and Strategic History*. Princeton, NJ: Princeton University Press, 2002.

Stueck, Jr., William Whitney. *The Road to Confrontation: America Policy Toward China and Korea, 1947–1950*. Chapel Hill: University of North Carolina Press, 1981.

Takaki, Ronald. *Double Victory: A Multicultural History of America in World War II*. Boston: Little, Brown and Company, 2000.

Talbott, Strobe. *The Master of the Game: Paul Nitze and the Nuclear Peace*. New York: Knopf, 1988.

Taubman, William. *Khrushchev: The Man and His Era*. New York: W. W. Norton, 2003.

Taubman, William. *Stalin's American Policy: From Entente to Detente to Cold War*. New York: W. W. Norton, 1982.

Taylor, A. J. P. *English History, 1914–1945*. New York and Oxford: Oxford University Press, 1965.

Theoharis, Athan G. *The Yalta Myths: An Issue in U.S. Politics, 1945–1955*. Columbia: University of Missouri Press, 1970.

Thomas, Hugh. *Armed Truce: The Beginnings of the Cold War, 1945–46*. New York: Hamish Hamilton, 1987.

Thompson, John A. *Woodrow Wilson*. London: Longman, 2002.

Thompson, Kenneth W. *Interpreters and Critics of the Cold War*. Washington, DC: University Press of America, 1978.

Thompson, Kenneth W. *Political Realism and the Crisis of World Politics*. Princeton, NJ: Princeton University Press, 1960.

Tint, Herbert. *French Foreign Policy Since the Second World War*. London: Weidenfeld and Nicholson, 1972.

Tompkins, C. David. *Senator Arthur Vandenberg: The Evolution of a Modern Republican, 1884–1945*. East Lansing: Michigan State University Press, 1970.

Tractenberg, Marc. *A Constructed Peace: The Making of the European Settlement, 1945–1963*. Princeton, NJ: Princeton University Press, 1999.

Truman, Margaret. *Harry S. Truman*. New York: William Morrow, 1973.

Tuchman, Barbara. *Practicing History*. New York: Ballantine Books, 1981.

Tucker, Nancy Bernkopf. *Patterns in the Dust: Chinese-American Relations and the Recognition Controversy, 1949–1950*. New York: Columbia University Press, 1983.

Tucker, Robert C. *Stalin in Power: The Revolution from Above, 1928–1941*. New York: Norton, 1990.

Ulam, Adam. *Expansion and Coexistence: The History of Soviet Foreign Policy, 1917–1967*. New York: Praeger, 1968.

Ulam, Adam. *The Rivals: America and Russia Since World War II*. New York: Viking, 1971.

Walker, J. Samuel. *Henry A. Wallace and American Foreign Policy*. Westport, CT: Greenwood, 1976.

Walker, J. Samuel. *Prompt and Utter Destruction: Truman and the Use of Atomic Bombs Against Japan*. Chapel Hill, NC: University of North Carolina Press, 1997.

Walker, Martin. *The Cold War: A History*. New York: Henry Holt, 1994.

Walker, Martin. *The Cold War and the Making of the Modern World*. London: Fourth Estate, 1993.

Walker, Richard L., and George Curry. *The American Secretaries of State and Their Diplomacy*. Vol. XIV. *E. R. Stettinius, Jr. and James F. Byrnes*, ed. Robert H. Ferrell. New York: Cooper Square Publishers, 1965.

Walton, Richard J. *Henry Wallace, Harry Truman and the Cold War*. New York: Viking, 1976.

Warburg, James P. *Germany – Bridge or Battleground*. New York: Harcourt, Brace, 1947.

Watt, D. Cameron. *Succeeding John Bull: America in Britain's Place, 1900–1975*. Cambridge: Cambridge University Press, 1984.

Wedgwood, C. V. *William the Silent*. New York: Norton, 1967.

Weigel, George. Tranquillitas Ordinis: *The Present Failure and Future Promise of American Catholic Thought on War and Peace*. New York: Oxford University Press, 1987.

Weil, Martin. *A Pretty Good Club: The Founding Fathers of the U.S. Foreign Service*. New York: W. W. Norton, 1978.

Weiler, Peter. *British Labour and the Cold War*. Stanford, CA: Stanford University Press, 1988.

Weinberg, Gerhard L. *A World at Arms: A Global History of World War II*. New York: Cambridge University Press, 1994.

Weinstein, Allen, and Alexander Vassiliev. *The Haunted Wood: Soviet Espionage in America – the Stalin Era*. New York: Random House, 1999.

Weintraub, Stanley. *The Last Great Victory: The End of World War II, July–August 1945*. New York: Dutton, 1995.

Weiss, Stuart L. *The President's Man: Leo Crowley and Franklin Roosevelt in Peace and War*. Carbondale: Southern Illinois University Press, 1996.

Wheeler-Bennett, Sir John, and Anthony Nicholls. *The Semblance of Peace: The Political Settlement after the Second World War*. London: Macmillan, 1972.

Wilkinson, Mark F., ed. *The Cold War: Opening Shots, 1945–1950*. Lexington: Virginia Military Institute, 2003.

Williams, Francis. *Ernest Bevin: Portrait of a Great Englishman*. London: Hutchinson, 1952.

Wilson, Theodore A. *The Marshall Plan: An Atlantic Venture of 1947–1951*. New York: Foreign Policy Association, 1977.

Winks, Robin W. *Cloak and Gown: Scholars in the Secret War, 1939–1961*. New York: William Morrow, 1987.

Wittner, Lawrence S. *American Intervention in Greece, 1943–1949*. New York: Columbia University Press, 1982.

Woods, Randall Bennett. *A Changing of the Guard: Anglo-American Relations, 1941–46*. Chapel Hill: University of North Carolina Press, 1990.

Woods, Randall Bennett. *Fulbright: A Biography*. Cambridge and New York: Cambridge University Press, 1995.

Woods, Randall Bennett, and Howard Jones. *Dawning of the Cold War: The United States' Quest for Order*. Athens: University of Georgia Press, 1991.

Woodward, Sir Llewellyn. *British Foreign Policy in the Second World War*. 5 vols. London: Her Majesty's Stationery Office, 1970–71.

Xydis, Stephen. *Greece and the Great Powers, 1944–1947: Prelude to the Truman Doctrine*. Thessaloniki: Institute for Balkan Studies, 1963.

Yergin, Daniel. *Shattered Peace: The Origins of the Cold War and the National Security State*. Boston: Houghton Mifflin, 1977.

York, Herbert F. *The Advisors: Oppenheimer, Teller and the Superbomb*. San Francisco: W. H. Freeman, 1976.

Zubok, Vladislav, and Constantine Pleshakov. *Inside the Kremlin's Cold War: From Stalin to Khrushchev*. Cambridge, MA: Harvard University Press, 1996.

B. Articles

Adler, Les K., and G. Thomas Paterson. "Red Fascism: The Merger of Nazi Germany and Soviet Russia in the American Image of Totalitarianism, 1930s–1950s," *American Historical Review*, 75 (April 1970), 1046–64.

Alperovitz, Gar. "Was Harry Truman a Revisionist on Hiroshima?" *SHAFR Newsletter*, 29 (June 1998), 1–9.

Asada, Sadao. "The Shock of the Atomic Bomb and Japan's Decision to Surrender – A Reconsideration," *Pacific Historical Review*, 67 (November 1998), 475–512.

Barnes, Trevor. "The Secret Cold War: The C.I.A. and American Foreign Policy in Europe, 1946–1956. Part I," *Historical Journal*, 24 (June 1981), 399–415.

Barnes, Trevor. "The Secret Cold War: The C.I.A. and American Foreign Policy in Europe, 1946–1956. Part II," *Historical Journal*, 25 (September 1982), 649–71.

Beisner, Robert. "Patterns of Peril: Dean Acheson Joins the Cold Warriors, 1945–1946," *Diplomatic History*, 20 (Summer 1996), 321–55.

Bennett, Todd. "Culture, Power, and *Mission to Moscow*: Film and Soviet–American Relations during World War II," *Journal of American History*, 88 (September 2001), 489–518.

Berger, Henry W. "Bipartisanship, Senator Taft, and the Truman Administration," *Political Science Quarterly*, 90 (Summer 1975), 221–37.

Bernstein, Barton J. "Compelling Japan's Surrender Without the A-Bomb, Soviet Entry, or Invasion: Reconsidering the US Bombing Survey's Early-Surrender Conclusions," *Journal of Strategic Studies*, 18 (June 1995), 101–48.

Bernstein, Barton J. "Marshall, Leahy, and Casualty Issues – A Reply to Kort's Flawed Critique," *Passport: The Newsletter of the Society for Historians of American Foreign Relations*, 35 (August 2004), 5–14.

Bernstein, Barton J. "Roosevelt, Truman, and the Atomic Bomb, 1941–1945: A Reinterpretation," *Political Science Quarterly*, 90 (Spring 1975), 23–69.

Bernstein, Barton J. "Seizing the Contested Terrain of Early Nuclear History: Stimson, Conant, and their Allies Explain the Decision to Use the Atomic Bomb," *Diplomatic History*, 17 (Winter 1993), 35–72.

Bernstein, Barton J. "Truman and the A-Bomb: Targeting Noncombatants, Using the Bomb, and His Defending the 'Decision,' " *Journal of Military History*, 62 (July 1998), 547–70.

Bernstein, Barton J. "Understanding the Atomic Bomb and the Japanese Surrender: Missed Opportunities, Little-Known Near Disasters, and Modern Memory," *Diplomatic History*, 19 (Spring 1995), 227–73.

Bernstein, Barton J. "Writing, Righting, or Wronging the Historical Record: President Truman's Letter on His Atomic-Bomb Decision," *Diplomatic History*, 16 (Winter 1992), 163–73.

Bischof, Gunter. "The Advent of Neo-Revisionism?" *Journal of Cold War Studies*, 7 (Winter 2005), 141–51.

Bix, Herbert P. "Japan's Delayed Surrender: A Reinterpretation," *Diplomatic History*, 19 (Spring 1995), 197–225.

Bolles, Blair. "Senators and the Peace," *Nation*, 157 (October 16, 1943), 426–28.

Bonds, John Bledsoe. "Looking for Love (or Tragedy) in All the Wrong Places," *Journal of Cold War Studies*, 7 (Winter 2005), 152–58.

Borhi, Laszlo. "Was American Diplomacy Really Tragic?" *Journal of Cold War Studies*, 7 (Winter 2005), 159–67.

Boyle, Peter G. "Britain, America and the Transition from Economic to Military Assistance, 1948–1951," *Journal of Contemporary History*, 22 (July 1987), 521–38.

Boyle, Peter G. "The British Foreign Office and American Foreign Policy, 1947–1948," *Journal of American Studies*, 16 (December 1982), 373–89.

Bradley, Lenore. "When the Lightning Struck," *Whistlestop: Harry S. Truman Library Institute Newsletter*, 23 (1995), 2.

Breindel, Eric. "Hiss's Guilt," *New Republic* (April 15, 1996), pp. 18–20.

Brinkley, Alan. "For America, It Truly Was a Great War," *New York Times Magazine* (May 7, 1995), pp. 54–57.

Brzezinski, Zbigniew. "How the Cold War Was Played," *Foreign Affairs*, 51 (October 1972), 181–209.

Buckley, Gary J. "American Public Opinion and the Origins of the Cold War: A Speculative Reassessment," *Mid-America*, 60 (January 1978), 35–42.

Buhite, Russell D. "'Major Interests': American Policy toward China, Taiwan and Korea, 1945–1950," *Pacific Historical Review*, 47 (August 1978), 425–51.

Buhite, Russell D. "Soviet–American Relations and the Repatriation of Prisoners of War, 1945," *Historian*, 35 (May 1973), 384–97.

Casey, Steven. "Selling NSC-68: The Truman Administration, Public Opinion, and the Politics of Mobilization, 1950–51," *Diplomatic History*, 29 (September 2005), 655–90.

Cashman, Greg, and Arthur N. Gilbert. "Some Analytic Approaches to the Cold War Debate," *History Teacher*, 10 (February 1977), 263–80.

Clayton, William L. "GATT, The Marshall Plan and OECD," *Political Science Quarterly*, 78 (December 1963), 493–503.

Clemens, Diane Shaver. "Averell Harriman, John Deane, the Joint Chiefs of Staff, and the 'Reversal of Co-operation' with the Soviet Union in 1945," *International History Review*, 14 (May 1992), 277–306.

Clifford, J. Garry. "Juggling Balls of Dynamite," *Diplomatic History*, 17 (Fall 1993), 633–36.

Cox, Michael, and Caroline Kennedy-Pipe. "The Tragedy of American Diplomacy? Rethinking the Marshall Plan," *Journal of Cold War Studies*, 7 (Winter 2005), 97–134.

Davis, Forrest. "Roosevelt's World Blueprint," *Saturday Evening Post*, 115 (April 10, 1943), pp. 20–21, 109–11.

De Santis, Vincent P. "Until the Bombs Came," *Notre Dame Magazine*, 24 (Spring 1995), 16–20.

Dinardo, Richard S. "Glimpse of an Old World Order? Reconsidering the Trieste Crisis of 1945," *Diplomatic History*, 21 (Summer 1997), 365–81.

Dulles, John Foster. "A Policy of Boldness," *Life*, 32 (May 1952), pp. 146–60.

Duncan, Francis. "Atomic Energy and Anglo-American Relations, 1946–1954," *Orbis*, 12 (Winter 1969), 1188–1203.

Dunn, Keith A. "A Conflict of World Views: The Origins of the Cold War," *Military Review*, 57 (February 1977), 14–25.

Dunne, John Gregory. "The Hardest War," *New York Review of Books*, 48 (December 20, 2001), pp. 50–56.

Eckes, Alfred A. "Open Door Expansionism Reconsidered: The World War II Experience," *Journal of American History*, 59 (March 1973), 902–24.

Eisenhower, Dwight D. "My View of Berlin," *Saturday Evening Post*, 234 (December 9, 1961), pp. 19–29.

Elsey, George. "Speech at Dedication of Harry S. Truman Building," *Whistlestop: Harry S. Truman Library Institute Newsletter* (Winter 2000), 2–3.

Farquharson, J. E. "Anglo-American Policy on German Reparations from Yalta to Potsdam," *English Historical Review*, 112 (September 1997), 904–26.

Feldman, Ellen. "FDR and His Women," *American Heritage*, 54 (February/March 2003), pp. 53–59.

Fenton, Ben. "Churchill's Plan for Third World War against Soviet Union," *Daily Telegraph* (electronic edition), October 1, 1998.

Fleming, Thomas. "Eight Days With Harry Truman," *American Heritage*, 43 (July–August 1992), pp. 54–59.

Folly, Martin H. "Breaking the Vicious Circle: Britain, the United States, and the Genesis of the North Atlantic Treaty," *Diplomatic History*, 12 (Winter 1988), 59–77.

Frank, Richard B. "Why Truman Dropped the Bomb," *Weekly Standard*, 10 (August 8, 2005), pp. 20–25.

Frazier, Robert. "Did Britain Start the Cold War? Bevin and the Truman Doctrine," *Historical Journal*, 27 (September 1984), 715–27.

Fromkin, David. "Churchill's Way: The Great Convergence of Britain and the United States," *World Policy Journal*, 15 (Spring 1998), 1–9.

Fussell, Paul. "Hiroshima: A Soldier's View," *New Republic*, 185 (August 22 & 29, 1981), pp. 26–30.

Gaddis, John Lewis. "After Containment: The Legacy of George Kennan in the Age of Terrorism," *New Republic*, 232 (April 25, 2005), pp. 27–31.

Gaddis, John Lewis. "Containment: A Reassessment," *Foreign Affairs*, 55 (July 1977), 874–87.

Gaddis, John Lewis. "The Corporatist Synthesis: A Skeptical View," *Diplomatic History*, 10 (Fall 1986), 357–62.

Gaddis, John Lewis. "Intelligence, Espionage, and Cold War Origins," *Diplomatic History*, 13 (Spring 1989), 191–212.

Gaddis, John Lewis. "NSC 68 and the Problem of Ends and Means," *International Security*, 4 (Spring 1980), 164–70.

Gaddis, John Lewis. "The Tragedy of Cold War History: Reflections on Revisionism," *Foreign Affairs*, 73 (January/February 1994), 142–54.

Gaddis, John Lewis. "Was the Truman Doctrine a Real Turning Point?" *Foreign Affairs*, 52 (January 1974), 386–402.

Gaiduk, Ilya. "Stalin: Three Approaches to One Phenomenon," *Diplomatic History*, 23 (Winter 1999), 115–25.

Garson, Robert. "The Role of Eastern Europe in America's Containment Policy, 1945–1948," *Journal of American Studies*, 13 (April 1979), 73–92.

Gati, Charles. "What Containment Meant," *Foreign Policy*, 7 (Summer 1972), 22–40.

George, Alexander L. "Domestic Constraints on Regime Change in U.S. Foreign Policy: The Need for Policy Legitimacy," in Ole R. Holsti, Randolph M. Siverson, and

Alexander L. George, eds., *Change in the International System*. Boulder, CO: Westview Press, 1980, 233–62.

Geselbracht, Raymond H. "Harry S. Truman and the Creation of the 'Atomic Shield,'" *Whistle Stop: Harry S. Truman Library Institute Newsletter* (Summer 2004), 1–4.

Geselbracht, Raymond H., compiler. "Harry Truman Speaks," *Whistlestop: Harry S. Truman Library Institute Newsletter* (Fall 2002), 2.

Giangreco, D. M. "'A Score of Bloody Okinawas and Iwo Jimas': President Truman and Casualty Estimates for the Invasion of Japan," *Pacific Historical Review*, 72 (February 2003), 93–132.

Gimbel, John. "On the Implementation of the Potsdam Agreement: An Essay on U.S. Postwar Policy," *Political Science Quarterly*, 87 (June 1972), 242–69.

Hamby, Alonzo L. "An American Democrat: A Reevaluation of the Personality of Harry S. Truman," *Political Science Quarterly*, 106 (Spring 1991), 33–55.

Hammond, Thomas T. "'Atomic Diplomacy' Revisited," *Orbis*, 19 (Winter 1976), 1403–28.

Harries, Owen. "The Day of the Fox," *National Interest*, 29 (Fall 1992), 107–13.

Harrington, Daniel. "Kennan, Bohlen and the Riga Axioms," *Diplomatic History*, 2 (Fall 1978), 423–37.

Haynes, John Earl. "The Cold War Debate Continues: A Traditionalist View of Historical Writing on Domestic Communism and Anti-Communism," *Journal of Cold War Studies*, 2 (Winter 2000), 76–115.

Hess, Gary R. "Franklin Roosevelt and Indochina," *Journal of American History*, 59 (September 1982), 359–68.

Hess, Gary R. "The Iranian Crisis of 1945–46 and the Cold War," *Political Science Quarterly*, 89 (March 1974), 117–46.

Heuser, Beatrice. "NSC 68 and the Soviet Threat: A New Perspective on Western Threat Perception and Policy Making," *Review of International Studies*, 17 (1991), 17–40.

Hitchens, Christopher. "The Medals of His Defeats," *Atlantic Monthly*, 289 (April 2002), pp. 118–37.

Hodgson, Godfrey. "The Establishment," *Foreign Policy*, 10 (Spring 1973), 3–40.

Hoffman, Stanley. "After the Creation, or the Watch and the Arrow," *International Journal*, 28 (Spring 1973), 175–84.

Hogan, Michael J. "Paths to Plenty: Marshall Planners and the Debate over European Integration, 1947–1948," *Pacific Historical Review*, 53 (August 1984), 337–66.

Hogan, Michael J. "The Vice Men of Foreign Policy," *Reviews in American History*, 21 (June 1993), 320–28.

Hudson, Daryl J. "Vandenberg Reconsidered: Senate Resolution 239 and American Foreign Policy," *Diplomatic History*, 1 (Winter 1977), 46–63.

Jackson, Scott. "Prologue to the Marshall Plan: The Origins of the American Commitment for a European Recovery Program," *Journal of American History*, 65 (March 1979), 1043–68.

Jervis, Robert. "The End of the Cold War on the Cold War?" *Diplomatic History*, 17 (Fall 1993), 651–60.

Jervis, Robert. "The Impact of the Korean War on the Cold War," *Journal of Conflict Resolution*, 24 (December 1980), 563–92.

Jervis, Robert. "Stalin, An Incompetent Realist," *The National Interest*, 50 (Winter 1997–98), 82–86.

Judt, Tony. "Democracy as an Aberration," *New York Times Book Review* (February 7, 1999), pp. 11–12.

Judt, Tony. "Why the Cold War Worked," *New York Review of Books*, 44 (October 9, 1997), pp. 39–44.

Kaplan, Lawrence S. "The Korean War and U.S. Foreign Relations: The Case of NATO," in Francis H. Hellers, ed., *The Korean War: A 25 Year Perspective*. Lawrence: The Regents Press of Kansas, 1977.

Kaplan, Lawrence S. "Toward the Brussels Pact," *Prologue*, 12 (Summer 1980), pp. 73–86.

Kaplan, Lawrence S. "The United States and the Origins of NATO, 1946–1949," *Review of Politics*, 31 (April 1969), 210–22.

Keegan, John. "The West Had to Protect Itself," *Daily Telegraph* (electronic edition), October 1, 1998.

Keller, Morton. "Amnesia Day: Forgetting V-J Day," *New Republic*, Nos. 4209 & 4210 (September 18 & 25, 1995), p. 14.

Kennan, George F. Comment in symposium, "Allied Leadership during World War II," *Survey*, 21 (Winter–Spring 1975), 29–36.

Kennan, George F. "Flashbacks," *New Yorker*, 61 (February 25, 1985), pp. 52–69.

Kennan, George F. "An Historian of Potsdam and His Readers," *American Slavic and East European Review*, 20 (April 1961), 289–94.

Kennan, George F. "History and Diplomacy as Viewed by a Diplomatist," *Review of Politics*, 18 (April 1956), 170–77.

"X" [George F. Kennan]. "The Sources of Soviet Conduct," *Foreign Affairs*, 25 (July 1947), 566–82.

"X" [George F. Kennan]. "Tribute to General Marshall," *New York Times* (October 18, 1959), p. E8.

Kennan, George F., and John Lukacs. "From World War to Cold War," *American Heritage*, 46 (December 1995), pp. 42–67.

Kimball, Warren F. "The Incredible Shrinking War: The Second World War, Not (Just) the Origins of the Cold War," *Diplomatic History*, 25 (Summer 2001), 347–65.

Kimball, Warren F. "Not Unwilling to Act," *Times Literary Supplement* (February 20, 1998), p. 24.

Kindleberger, Charles. "The Marshall Plan and the Cold War," *International Journal*, 23 (Summer 1968), 369–82.

Knight, Wayne. "Labourite Britain: America's 'Sure Friend'? The Anglo-Soviet Treaty Issue, 1947," *Diplomatic History*, 7 (Fall 1983), 267–82.

Kort, Michael. "Casualty Projections for the Invasion of Japan, Phantom Estimates, and the Math of Barton Bernstein," *Passport: The Newsletter of the Society for Historians of American Foreign Relations*, 34 (December 2003), 4–12.

Koshiro, Yukiko. "Eurasian Eclipse: Japan's End Game in World War II," *American Historical Review*, 109 (April 2004), 417–44.

Kreiger, Wolfgang. "Was General Clay a Revisionist? Strategic Aspects of the United States Occupation of Germany," *Journal of Contemporary History*, 18 (April 1983), 165–84.

Kuklick, Bruce. "A Historian's Perspective: American Appeasement of Germany, 1941–1951," *Prologue*, 7 (Winter 1976), 237–40.

Kuklick, Bruce. "The Origins of the Marshall Plan" [Review Essay], *Reviews in American History*, 5 (June 1977), 292–98.

LaFeber, Walter. "Kissinger and Acheson: The Secretary of State and the Cold War," *Political Science Quarterly*, 92 (Summer 1977), 189–97.

Lees, Lorraine M. "The American Decision to Assist Tito, 1948–1949," *Diplomatic History*, 2 (Fall 1978), 407–22.

Leffler, Melvyn P. "The American Conception of National Security and the Beginnings of the Cold War, 1945–48," *American Historical Review*, 89 (April 1984), 346–81.

Leffler, Melvyn P. "The Cold War: What Do 'We Now Know'?" *American Historical Review*, 104 (April 1999), 501–24.

Leffler, Melvyn P. "From the Truman Doctrine to the Carter Doctrine: Lessons and Dilemmas of the Cold War," *Diplomatic History*, 7 (Fall 1983), 245–66.

Leffler, Melvyn P. "Inside Enemy Archives: The Cold War Reopened," *Foreign Affairs*, 75 (July/August 1996), 120–35.

Leffler, Melvyn P. "The United States and the Strategic Dimensions of the Marshall Plan," *Diplomatic History*, 12 (Summer 1988), 277–306.

Levine, Steven I. "A New Look at American Mediation in the Chinese Civil War: The Marshall Mission and Manchuria," *Diplomatic History*, 3 (Fall 1979), 349–75.

Logevall, Fredrik. "A Critique of Containment," *Diplomatic History*, 28 (September 2004), 473–99.

Lundestad, Geir. "Empire by Invitation? The United Sates and Western Europe, 1945–1952," *SHAFR Newsletter*, 15 (September 1984), 1–21.

Maddox, Robert J. "Roosevelt and Stalin: The Final Days," *Continuity: A Journal of History*, 6 (Spring 1983), 113–22.

Maddox, Robert J. "A Visit to Cloudland: Cold War Revisionism in College Texts," *Continuity: A Journal of History*, 20 (Spring 1996), 1–11.

Maier, Charles S. "The Two Postwar Eras and the Conditions for Stability in Twentieth-Century Western Europe," *American Historical Review*, 86 (April 1981), 327–52.

Mark, Eduard M. "Allied Relations in Iran, 1941–1947: The Origins of a Cold War Crisis," *Wisconsin Magazine of History*, 59 (Autumn 1975), 51–63.

Mark, Eduard M. "American Policy Toward Eastern Europe and the Origins of the Cold War, 1941–1946: An Alternative Interpretation," *Journal of American History*, 68 (September 1981), 313–36.

Mark, Eduard M. "Charles E. Bohlen and the Acceptable Limits of Soviet Hegemony in Eastern Europe: A Memorandum of 18 October 1945," *Diplomatic History*, 3 (Spring 1979), 201–13.

Mark, Eduard M. "October or Thermidor: Interpretations of Stalinism and the Perception of Soviet Foreign Policy in the United States, 1927–1947," *American Historical Review*, 94 (October 1989), 937–62.

Mark, Eduard M. "The Question of Containment: A Reply to John Lewis Gaddis," *Foreign Affairs*, 56 (January 1978), 430–40.

Mark, Eduard M. "Venona's Source 19 and the 'Trident' Conference of May 1943: Diplomacy or Espionage?" *Intelligence and National Security*, 13 (Summer 1998), 1–31.

Mark, Eduard M. "The War Scare of 1946 and Its Consequences," *Diplomatic History*, 21 (Summer 1997), 383–415.

McCoy, Donald. "Chicago Sun-Times Poll," *Presidential Studies Quarterly*, 26 (Winter 1996), 281–83.

McLellan, David S. "Who Fathered Containment?" *International Studies Quarterly*, 17 (June 1973), 205–26.

Merrick, Ray. "The Russia Committee of the British Foreign Office and the Cold War, 1946–47," *Journal of Contemporary History*, 20 (July 1985), 453–68.

Messer, Robert L. "New Evidence on Truman's Decision," *Bulletin of Atomic Scientists*, 41 (August 1985), 50–56.

Messer, Robert L. "Paths Not Taken: The United States Department of State and Alternatives to Containment, 1945–1946," *Diplomatic History*, 1 (Fall 1977), 297–319.

Miles, Rufus E., Jr. "Hiroshima: The Strange Myth of Half a Million American Lives Saved," *International Security*, 10 (Fall 1985), 121–40.

Miller, William Lee. "Two Moralities," *Miller Center Journal*, 2 (Spring 1995), 19–39.

Milward, Alan S. "Was the Marshall Plan Necessary?" *Diplomatic History*, 13 (Spring 1989), 231–53.

Miscamble, Wilson D. "Anthony Eden and the Truman-Molotov Conversations, April, 1945," *Diplomatic History*, 2 (Spring 1978), 167–80.

Miscamble, Wilson D. "The Evolution of an Internationalist: Harry S. Truman and American Foreign Policy," *Australian Journal of Politics and History*, 23 (August 1977), 268–83.

Miscamble, Wilson D. "George F. Kennan, The Policy Planning Staff and the Origins of the Marshall Plan," *Mid-America: An Historical Review*, 62 (April–July 1980), 75–89.

Miscamble, Wilson D. "Harry S. Truman, The Berlin Blockade and the 1948 Election," *Presidential Studies Quarterly*, 8 (Summer 1980), 306–16.

Miscamble, Wilson D. "The Origins of the North Atlantic Treaty: Policy Formulation in the Department of State," in Roger J. Bell and Ian J. Bickerton, eds., *American Studies: New Essays from Australia and New Zealand.* Sydney: ANZASA, 1981, 236–56.

Miscamble, Wilson D. "Thurman Arnold Goes to Washington: A Look at Antitrust Policy in the Later New Deal," *Business History Review*, 56 (Spring 1982), 1–15.

Miscamble, Wilson D. "Was the United States Responsible for the Cold War?" *Review of Politics*, 55 (Spring 1993), 363–67.

Mitgang, Herbert. "Of Three Unlikely Allies and Their Conflicts," *New York Times*, July 23, 1991, p. C16.

Moore, Ray A. "The Occupation of Japan as History: Some Recent Research," *Monumenta Nipponica*, 36 (Autumn 1981), 317–28.

Morgenthau, Henry, 3rd. "The Last Night at Warm Springs," *New York Times* (April 12, 1945), p. 25.

Morison, Samuel Eliot. "Why Japan Surrendered," *Atlantic Monthly*, 206 (October 1960), pp. 41–47.

Morton, Louis. "Soviet Intervention in the War with Japan," *Foreign Affairs*, 40 (July 1962), 653–62.

Nelson, Anna Kasten. "President Truman and the Evolution of the National Security Council," *Journal of American History*, 72 (September 1985), 360–78.

Newman, Robert P. "Ending the War with Japan: Paul Nitze's 'Early Surrender' Counterfactual," *Pacific Historical Review*, 64 (May 1995), 167–94.

Newman, Robert P. "NSC (National Insecurity) 68: Nitze's Second Hallucination," in Martin J. Medland and H.W. Brands, eds., *Critical Reflections on the Cold War.* College Station: Texas A&M University Press, 2000, 55–94.

Offner, Arnold A. "'Another Such Victory': President Truman, American Foreign Policy, and the Cold War," *Diplomatic History*, 23 (Spring 1999), 126–55.

Osgood, Kenneth A. "Hearts and Minds," *Journal of Cold War Studies*, 4 (Spring 2002), 85–107.

Ovendale, R. "Britain, The United States, and the Recognition of Communist China," *Historical Journal*, 26 (March 1983), 139–58.

Paczkowski, Andrzej. "The Storm over *The Black Book*," *Wilson Quarterly*, 25 (Spring 2001), 28–34.

Pfau, Richard. "Containment in Iran, 1946: The Shift to an Active Policy," *Diplomatic History*, 1 (Fall 1977), 359–72.

Pickett, William B. "The Eisenhower Solarium Notes," *SHAFR Newsletter*, 16 (June 1985), 1–10.

Pollard, Robert A. "Economic Security and the Origins of the Cold War: Bretton Woods, the Marshall Plan, and American Rearmament, 1944–50," *Diplomatic History*, 9 (Summer 1985), 271–89.

Poole, Walter S. "From Conciliation to Containment: The Joint Chiefs of Staff and the Coming of the Cold War, 1945–1946," *Military Affairs*, 42 (February 1978), 12–16.

Powers, Richard. "Who Fathered Containment?" *International Studies Quarterly*, 15 (December 1971), 526–43.

Propas, Frederic L. "Creating a Hard Line Toward Russia: The Training of State Department Soviet Experts, 1927–1937," *Diplomatic History*, 8 (Summer 1984), 206–26.

Raack, Richard C. "The Cold War Revisionists Kayoed: New Books Dispel More Historical Darkness," *World Affairs*, 162 (Fall 1999), 43–62.

Reynolds, David. "The Origins of the Cold War: The European Dimension, 1944–1951," *Historical Journal*, 28 (June 1985), 497–515.

Roberts, Frank K. "Soviet Policies Under Stalin and Khrushchev: A Comparison Based on Personal Experiences between 1939 and 1962," *South Atlantic Quarterly*, 72 (Summer 1973), 440–50.

Roberts, Geoffrey. "Sexing up the Cold War: New Evidence on the Molotov–Truman Talks of April 1945," *Cold War History*, 4 (April 2004), 105–25.

Roosevelt, Elliott. "FDR vs. Churchill – The Inside Story," *Look*, 10 (September 3, 1946), pp. 21–26.

Rose, Lisle A. "The Trenches and the Towers: Differing Perspectives on the Writing and Making of American Diplomatic History," *Pacific Historical Review*, 55 (February 1986), 97–101.

Rosenberg, David Alan. "American Atomic Strategy and the Hydrogen Bomb Decision," *Journal of American History*, 66 (June 1979), 62–87.

Roskin, Michael. "From Pearl Harbor to Vietnam: Shifting Generational Paradigms and Foreign Policy," *Political Science Quarterly*, 89 (Fall 1974), 563–88.

Rostow, Eugene V. "The Apotheosis of Harry," *Times Literary Supplement* (November 27, 1992), pp. 3–4.

Ruddy, T. Michael. "Realist Versus Realist: Bohlen, Kennan and the Inception of the Cold War," *Midwest Quarterly*, 17 (January 1976), 122–41.

Schaller, Michael. "Securing the Great Crescent: Occupied Japan and the Origins of Containment in Southeast Asia," *Journal of American History*, 69 (September 1982), 392–414.

Schama, Simon. "Rescuing Churchill," *New York Review of Books*, 49 (February 28, 2002), pp. 15–17.

Schild, Georg. "The Roosevelt Administration and the United Nations: Recreation or Rejection of the League Experiment?" *World Affairs*, 158 (Summer 1995), 26–34.

Schlesinger, Jr., Arthur M. "Back to the Womb? Isolationism's Renewed Threat," *Foreign Affairs*, 74 (July/August 1995), 2–8.

Schlesinger, Jr., Arthur M. "Forgetting Reinhold Niebuhr," *New York Times Book Review* (September 18, 2005), pp. 12–13.

Schlesinger, Jr., Arthur M. "Origins of the Cold War," *Foreign Affairs*, 46 (October 1967), 22–52.

Schlesinger, Jr., Arthur M. "The Ultimate Approval Rating," *New York Times Magazine* (December 15, 1996), pp. 46–51.

Schlesinger, Sr., Arthur M. "Our Presidents: A Rating by 75 Historians," *New York Times Magazine* (July 29, 1962), p. 12.

Smith, Gaddis. "Forty Months: Franklin D. Roosevelt as War Leader, 1941–1945," *Prologue*, 26 (Fall 1994), 131–39.

Smith, Raymond, and John Zametica. "The Cold Warrior: Clement Attlee Reconsidered, 1945–47," *International Affairs*, 61 (1985), 237–52.

Smith, Thomas W. "The Uses of Tragedy: Reinhold Niebuhr's Theory of History and International Ethics," *Ethics and International Affairs*, 9 (1995), 171–91.

Steel, Ronald. "Harry of Sunnybrook Farm," *New Republic*, 207 (August 10, 1992), pp. 34–38.

Stefan, Charles G. "Yalta Revisited: An Update on the Diplomacy of FDR and His Wartime Summit Partners," *Presidential Studies Quarterly*, 23 (Fall 1993), 755–70.

Stoler, Mark A. "A Half Century of Conflict: Interpretations of U.S. World War II Diplomacy," *Diplomatic History*, 18 (Summer 1994), 375–403.

Stone, I. F. "Farewell to FDR," *Nation*, 160 (April 21, 1945), pp. 436–37.

Trachtenberg, Marc. "The Marshall Plan as Tragedy," *Journal of Cold War Studies*, 7 (Winter 2005), 135–40.

Tucker, Robert C. "The Cold War in Stalin's Time: What the New Sources Reveal," *Diplomatic History*, 21 (Spring 1997), 273–81.

Ulam, Adam B. "The Cold War According to Kennan," *Commentary*, 55 (January 1973), 66–69.

Ulam, Adam B. "A Few Unresolved Mysteries about Stalin and the Cold War in Europe: A Modest Agenda for Research," *Journal of Cold War Studies*, 1 (Winter 1999), 110–16.

Ulam, Adam B. "Forty Years after Yalta," *New Republic*, 192 (February 11, 1985), pp. 18–21.

Ullman, Richard H. "The 'Realities' of George F. Kennan," *Foreign Policy*, 20 (Fall 1977), 139–55.

Villa, Brian L., and John Bonnett. "Understanding Indignation: Gar Alperovitz, Robert Maddox, and the Decision to Use the Atomic Bomb," *Reviews in American History*, 24 (September 1996), 529–36.

Wagner, R. Harrison. "The Decision to Divide Germany and the Origins of the Cold War," *International Studies Quarterly*, 24 (June 1980), 155–90.

Walker, J. Samuel. "The Confessions of a Cold Warrior: Clinton P. Anderson and American Foreign Policy, 1945–1972," *New Mexico Historical Review*, 52 (April 1977), 117–34.

Walker, J. Samuel. "The Decision to Use the Bomb: A Historiographical Update," *Diplomatic History*, 14 (Winter 1990), 97–114.

Walker, J. Samuel. "The Decision to Use the Bomb: A Historiographical Update," in Michael J. Hogan, ed., *America in the World: The Historiography of American Foreign Relations Since 1941*. Cambridge and New York: Cambridge University Press, 1995, 206–33.

Walker, J. Samuel. "Historians and Cold War Origins: The New Consensus," in Gerald K. Haines and J. Samuel Walker, eds., *American Foreign Relations: A Historiographical Review*. Westport, CT: Greenwood Press, 1981.

Walker, J. Samuel. "Recent Literature on Truman's Atomic Bomb Decision: A Search for Middle Ground," *Diplomatic History*, 29 (April 2005), 311–34.

Warner, Geoffrey. "The Truman Doctrine and the Marshall Plan," *International Affairs*, 50 (January 1974), 82–92.

Weigel, George. "In Remembrance of Things Past: V–E Day, V–J Day, and All That," *American Purpose*, 9 (Autumn 1995), 1–8.

White, Mark J. "Harry Truman, the Polish Question, and the Significance of FDR's Death for American Diplomacy," *Maryland Historian*, 23 (Fall/Winter 1992), 29–48.

Widenor, William C. "American Planning for the United Nations: Have We Been Asking the Right Questions?" *Diplomatic History*, 6 (Summer 1982), 245–65.

Wiebes, Cees, and Bert Zeeman. "The Pentagon Negotiations March 1948: The Launching of the North Atlantic Treaty," *International Affairs*, 59 (Summer 1983), 351–63.

Wright, C. Ben. "Mr. 'X' and Containment," *Slavic Review*, 35 (March 1976), 1–31.

Zeeman, Bert. "Britain and the Cold War: An Alternative Approach. The Treaty of Dunkirk Example," *European History Quarterly*, 14 (July 1986), 343–67.

Zelikow, Philip. "George C. Marshall and the Moscow CFM Meeting of 1947," *Diplomacy and Statecraft*, 8 (July 1997), 97–124.

Zubok, Vladislav. "Stalin's Plans and Russian Archives," *Diplomatic History*, 21 (Spring 1997), 295–305.

C. Unpublished Materials

Bonnett, John. Essay Review of Gar Alperovitz's *The Decision to Use the Atomic Bomb* for H-Diplo (H-Newt Diplomatic History List), – *http://h-net2.msu.edu/diplo/balp.htm*

Mark, Eduard. "Revolution by Degrees: Stalin's National Front Strategy for Europe, 1941–1947," Working Paper No. 31, Cold War International History Project, Woodrow Wilson Center, Washington, DC, February 2001.

Pechatnov, Vladimir O. "The Big Three After World War II: New Documents on Soviet Thinking about Post War Relations with the United States and Great Britain," Working Paper No. 13, Cold War International History Project, Woodrow Wilson Center, Washington, DC.

Schmidtlein, Eugene F. "Truman the Senator," Unpublished Doctoral Dissertation. University of Missouri, 1962.

Index